Pragmatic Strategy

Pra
soc
the
enc
But what ... pragmatism ... us about strategy? H...
matic strategies help businesses to succeed? This innovative book
presents a pragmatic framework for shaping and solving strategic
problems in a practical, creative, ethical and finely balanced manner.
To achieve this, the authors draw from Confucian teaching, American pragmatism and Aristotelian practical wisdom, as well as business cases across industries and nations, particularly from emerging
economies. With significant theoretical depth, direct practical implication and profound cultural sensitivity, the book is useful for
executive managers, public administrators, strategy researchers and
advanced students in the search for pragmatic strategies in an interconnected, fast-moving world.

IKUJIRO NONAKA is Professor Emeritus of the Graduate School of
International Corporate Strategy, Hitotsubashi University. He is also
Xerox Distinguished Faculty Scholar at the University of California,
Berkeley and First Distinguished Drucker Scholar in Residence at the
Drucker School and Institute, Claremont Graduate University. The
Wall Street Journal has identified him as one of the world's most in-
fluential business thinkers and his contributions to strategy have been
recognised by the Emperor of Japan and the Japanese government.

ZHICHANG ZHU is Reader in Strategy and Management, teaching
strategy for the MBA programme at the University of Hull Business
School. His formal education stopped when he was 16 due to China's 'Cultural Revolution'. Zhichang was a Maoist Red Guard, then
worked as a farm labourer, a shop assistant, a lorry driver, an enterprise manager and an IS/IT/business consultant in several countries. Without a high school certificate or a university first degree,
Zhichang earned a British Masters and a Ph.D. and holds visiting/
consultancy positions in China, Germany, Japan and the USA.

Pragmatic Strategy

Eastern Wisdom, Global Success

IKUJIRO NONAKA

ZHICHANG ZHU

CAMBRIDGE
UNIVERSITY PRESS

CAMBRIDGE UNIVERSITY PRESS
Cambridge, New York, Melbourne, Madrid, Cape Town,
Singapore, São Paulo, Delhi, Mexico City

Cambridge University Press
The Edinburgh Building, Cambridge CB2 8RU, UK

Published in the United States of America by Cambridge University Press,
New York

www.cambridge.org
Information on this title: www.cambridge.org/9780521173148

First published 2012

Printed in the United Kingdom at the University Press, Cambridge

A catalogue record for this publication is available from the British Library

Library of Congress Cataloguing in Publication data
Nonaka, Ikujiro, 1935–
  Pragmatic strategy : Eastern wisdom, global success / Ikujiro Nonaka,
  Zhichang Zhu.
    p. cm.
  Includes bibliographical references and index.
  ISBN 978-1-107-00184-8 (hbk) – ISBN 978-0-521-17314-8 (pbk.)
  1. Strategic planning. 2. Pragmatism. 3. Confucianism.
  4. Management. 5. Comparative management. I. Zhu, Zhichang.
  II. Title.
  HD30.28.N66 2012
  658.4′012–dc23
  2012007356

ISBN 978-1-107-00184-8 Hardback
ISBN 978-0-521-17314-8 Paperback

Contents

Figures

Tables

Cited classics

Daodejing (道德经), also known as *Laozi* (老子). In 81 chapters, just over 5,000 words, compiled during the Zhou Dynasty (周, 1111–249 BC), probably in the sixth century BC. A classic attributed to the Taoist sage Li Er (李耳, believed to be a contemporary of Confucius), it is not a philosophy for the hermit who withdraws from social affairs but for the sage-ruler who engages in the world wisely without forced interference. The subtlety of this classic is that, while it advocates 'non-action', it supplies practical advice for making one's way in the world. The ideal is not doing nothing, but doing things naturally. An English translation we recommend is Roger Ames and David Hall's *Daodejing: Making This Life Significant – A Philosophical Translation* (Ballantine Books, 2003).

Daxue (大学, *Great Learning*). In ten chapters, part of a classic *Liji* (礼记, *Record of Rites*) and one of the *Sishu* (四书, *Four Confucian Canons: Analects, Daxue, Zhongyong, Mencius*). It is a collection of treatises written by Confucian scholars in the third and second centuries BC, with later commentaries by Zhu Xi (朱熹, 1130–1200), the leading neo-Confucianist in the Southern Song Dynasty (1127–1279). With a social, political and moral orientation, this classic has as its core the 'eight wires' that translate humanity into the actual experience of achieving harmony between persons and society. We recommend the full translation and commentary by Chan Wing-Tsit in his *A Source Book in Chinese Philosophy* (Princeton University Press, 1963).

Guoyu (国语, *Conversations of the States*). A classic compiled in the fourth to third centuries BC. The version now available is believed to be the work of Zuo Qiuming (左丘明, 556–451 BC), a disciple of Confucius. It is accepted as an authentic record of conversations in various states during the Spring and Autumn Period (春秋, 722–481 BC).

Huainanzi (淮南子). In 21 chapters, written by Liu An (刘安, ?–122 BC), Prince of the Huainan Domain of the Han Dynasty (汉, 202 BC–AD 220) and the guest scholars attached to his court during the second century BC. It is a Chinese philosophical classic that integrates Confucianism, Taoism, the *Yin–yang* School and Legalist teachings, and had a great influence on the later Neo-Confucianism, Neo-Taoism and East-Asian Buddhism. An English translation is available in John Major *et al.*, *The Huainanzi: A Giude to the Theory and Practice of Government in Early Han China* (Columbia University Press, 2010).

Liji (礼记, *Record of Rites*). In 46 chapters, this classic describes the social forms, governmental systems and ceremonial rites of the Zhou Dynasty (周, 1111–249 BC). It was believed to have been written by Confucius himself, but is more likely to have been compiled by Confucian scholars from memory during the Han Dynasty, after Qin Chi Huangdi's (秦始皇帝, China's first emperor) 'burning of books and burying alive Confucian scholars' in the short-lived Qin Dynasty (221–202 BC). An English translation is available in James Legge's *The Sacred Books of the East*, vols. XXVII and XXVIII (Oxford University Press, 1879–1910).

Lunyu (论语, *Analects*). In 20 books, a collection of sayings by Kong Qiu (孔丘, Confucius 551–479 BC) and some of his disciples, recorded by Confucian scholars during the Spring and Autumn (春秋, 722–481 BC) and the Warring States Periods (战国, 403–221 BC), a time of continuous political struggle, moral chaos and intellectual conflict. Generally accepted as the most reliable record of Confucius' teaching, *Lunyu* looks to ideal humans rather than a supernatural being for inspiration, with a profound belief in good society based on good government and harmonious human relations. For an English translation and commentary, we recommend Roger Ames and Henry Rosemont's *The Analects of Confucius: A Philosophical Translation* (Ballantine Books, 1998).

Mengzi (孟子, *The Work of Mencius*). In six books, a collection of sayings of Meng Ke (孟轲, Mencius 371?–289? BC), an 'idealist wing' disciple of Confucius. Usually regarded as the greatest Confucianist only after Confucius, Mengzi advanced beyond the Master and believed that human nature is originally good, that love is an inborn moral quality. As such, everyone can become a sage, and governments become humane governments guided by ideals of humanity and righteousness as long as we fully develop our good nature through learning and socialising. We found a good English translation in Lau Din Cheuk's *Mencius* (Penguin Classics, 2004).

Mozi (墨子). In 71 chapters, a collection of writings of the Moist School, produced almost immediately after Confucius' death. Founded by Mozi (墨子, 479?–438? BC), who was popular among the craftsman class, the school was, from the fifth to at least the third century BC, the greatest critic of traditional institutions and practices and the strongest rival to Confucius' teaching on human relations. The school lost influence after the Han emperor granted Confucianism official domination. An English translation of the key teachings of Mozi is available in Chan Wing-Tsit's *A Source Book in Chinese Philosophy* (Princeton University Press, 1963).

Shijing (诗经, *Book of Odes*, or *Classic of Poetry*). A collection of 305 poems and songs, official as well as folk, collected from the various states during the early Zhou Dynasty (周, 1111–249 BC). Confucius is believed to have selected and edited the poems from a much larger body of material. Confucius held *Shijing* in the highest esteem, regarding it as an important source of good human character and social-political governance. An English translation is available in James Legge's *The Sacred Books of China* (Oxford University Press, 1879–1910).

Xunzi (荀子). In 32 chapters, believed to be the work of Xun Qing (荀卿, 298–238 BC), a 'naturalist wing' disciple of Confucius. While both stressed the vital importance of education and human character, in contrast to Mengzi who emphasised humanity, Xunzi praised wisdom, realism, logic, progress, discipline and the rule of law. Two of Xunzi's pupils, Han Fei (韩非, ?–231 BC) and Li Si (李斯, ?–208 BC), when serving as key ministers in the Qin State and Dynasty, played decisive roles in the grand unification of China. We found an English translation in John Knoblock's *Xunzi: Translation and Study of the Complete Works*, three volumes (Stanford University Press, 1988).

Yijing (易经), also known as *Zhouyi* (周易). One of the basic Confucian classics, divided into texts and commentaries. The texts, which emerged from the ancient practice of divination, are cryptic. The commentaries, usually ascribed to Confucius himself but more likely to have been compiled by unknown Confucian scholars in the early Han Dynasty (汉, 206 BC–AD 220), outline a humanised, rational approach to an experienced universe full of perpetual activity. The cosmology may be naive and crude, but the philosophical spirit is engaging and inspiring. There are numerous English translations available, among which we read Richard Lynn's *The Classic of Changes: A New Translation of the 'I Ching' as Interpreted by Wang Bi* (Columbia University Press, 2004).

Zhongyong (中庸, *Focusing the Familiar*). In 33 chapters, usually translated as *Doctrine of the Mean*. This work, incorporated as part of *Liji* (礼记, *Record of Rites*), was attributed to Zi Si (子思, ?–402? BC), grandson of Confucius. *Zhongyong* achieved truly canonical pre-eminence when it became one of the Confucian *Sishu* (四书, *Four Confucian Canons*). It is a Confucian discourse of psychology and metaphysics, with a profound appeal to both Taoism and Buddhism. An English edition we recommend is Roger Ames and David Hall's *Focusing the Familiar: A Translation and Philosophical Interpretation of Zhongyong* (University of Hawaii Press, 2001).

Zhuangzi (庄子). In 33 chapters. Usually attributed to Zhuang Zhou (庄周, 369?–286? BC), this Taoist classic must, however, have been written after his death. What differentiates Zhuangzi from Confucius, even from Laozi, are probably the manifestations in his work of the transcendental spirit, intellectual freedom, subtle individualism, emphasis on dynamic transformation, dismantling of artificial categories, appreciation of situated particulars and profound interest in how to interact beneficially with all things in the experienced world. An English translation is available in Brook Ziporyn's *Zhuangzi: The Essential Text with Translations from Traditional Commentaries* (Hackett Publishing, 2008).

Zhuangzi Zhu (庄子注, *Commentary on Zhuangzi*). A Neo-Taoist classic compiled after the Han Dynasty by Guo Xiang (郭象, ?–312) and Xiang Xiu (向秀, 221–300). Interestingly, this work, while inclined to Laozi and Zhuangzi in metaphysics, adheres to Confucianism in social and political philosophy and contributed greatly to the later emergence of Neo-Confucianism and East-Asian Buddhism.

Zuozhuan (左传). Probably written or compiled during the third century BC, it is a general history of the China of that time. It is considered to be a commentary on another classic, *Chunqiu* (春秋, *Spring and Autumn Annals*). The latter is a year-by-year chronicle of the state of Lu (鲁, Confucius' native country), from 722 to 481 BC. An English translation is available in James Legge's *The Chinese Classics*, vol. V (Oxford University Press, 1879–1910).

Preface

This book is the outcome of an unexpected cooperation. It began on a sunny winter afternoon in 2007, at Jiro's Hitotsubashi University office overlooking the Imperial Palace in downtown Tokyo. It was the first time Jiro and Zhu sat down together. Two days earlier, Jiro delivered a keynote speech at a conference in Ishikawa. After the speech, as Jiro's students struggled to create a path for him to escape from the enthusiastic audience, Zhu managed to present him with a business card, saying 'Professor, it was I who wrote that article.' The article, just published in a knowledge management journal, was titled 'Nonaka meets Giddens: a critique'. When the conference ended, Jiro invited Zhu to Tokyo.

Zhu expected a barrage of questions, corrections and instructions. Instead, after being served the first round of green tea, the conversation was about the worries and joys of being a father, calligraphy and sushi, Confucius and Dewey, Mao Zedong and T. E. Lawrence, IBM and Lenovo, changes in Japan and the rise of China. Before the second round of green tea, Jiro suggested co-authoring a book on corporate strategy.

Jiro and Zhu talked to each other in English. The differences between them, however, go beyond native languages. Jiro received rigorous training at Waseda University, obtained a degree in political science, worked in a Japanese corporation for ten years and wrote several books on military and business strategies before writing the award-winning *The Knowledge-Creating Company*. At the time of our meeting, Jiro was being bombarded by competing invitations from the worldwide business and academic communities.

In stark contrast, Zhu's formal education stopped when he was 16, due to China's 'Cultural Revolution'. Zhu has been a Maoist

Red Guard, farm labourer, shop assistant, lorry driver, enterprise manager, college teacher, assistant to the dean of a business school, software engineer, system analyst and IS/IT/business consultant. Even today, Zhu does not have a high school certificate, let alone a university first degree.

What brings and binds us – Jiro and Zhu – together, we believe, is our Confucian roots and, perhaps counter-intuitively, our Western educations (Jiro received his masters and doctoral degrees from the US and Zhu from Britain), as well as humble industry experiences, curiosity in knowledge and a keen desire to explore how managers can make the world a better place via business and strategy.

Careful readers will recognise the intellectual continuity of this book. Where *The Knowledge-Creating Company* (Nonaka and Takeuchi 1995) laid down a knowledge foundation and *Managing Flow* (Nonaka *et al.* 2008) forged a theory of the firm, this book focuses on exploring a pragmatic approach to strategy. While many of the ideas in this book can be traced back to the 1995 knowledge foundation and the 2008 theory of the firm, Jiro insists that each book must have unique, interesting things to say. What we dislike most is intellectual laziness – producing a 'new' book every few years, only to repackage old ideas in it, for example. Great scholars continuously push the knowledge frontier forward. The sea of learning has no end (学海无涯), as a Confucian teaching goes. The late C. K. Prahalad set us an example: he never wrote a second paper on the same topic with the same idea; he is still ranked top of the world's most influential business thinkers. We create, therefore we are.

Most of the topics and cases in this book have been written about by many people. In writing this book, our motto is: 'Don't insult the reader's intelligence.' What we have to say must be interesting, offer a distinctive perspective and provide managers with useful ideas to work out. This is not a textbook in the conventional sense of bringing together everything ever said, written and proven on a subject. Our aim is to urge, challenge and facilitate managers to think about and do strategy differently, wisely, beneficially.

In this book we call for a pragmatic turn. While we humans have been pragmatic at our wise moments, pragmatic strategies are not natural or God-given, but the result of managers' purposeful, effortful accomplishments against all odds. If strategy is evolutionary, it is evolution with design; if pragmatism is opportunistic, it is purposeful opportunism. 'It is Man who makes *Tao* great, not *Tao* that makes Man great (人能宏道, 非道宏人)', Confucius famously taught us. In a pragmatic world, strategy is about how firms, in fact, managers, orchestrate material-technical assets, mental-cognitive capabilities and social-normative relationships in a timely, appropriate manner so as to create and capture value. We make our way in a world full of complexity, ambiguity and uncertainty; strategy is purposeful action to get fundamentals right, promote situated creativity and realise common goodness. The numerous business cases cited in this book show us that, by acting pragmatically, we can bridge the practice gap, bring ethics back in and overcome specialised deafness. Understood and practised as such, pragmatism is our best hope for reinventing strategy as a positive force for bettering the material, spiritual and ecological conditions of persons, communities and society.

We decided to use Confucian pragmatism as an overarching narrative. This shapes not only the ideas presented, but also the way in which they are presented. Because of this, we have had to decline many kind suggestions from colleagues. Some suggested that we target the market more precisely – is the book for managers, researchers or students? We turned down this suggestion because, according to Confucius, doing and thinking are one: managers need to be theoretically informed, while researchers and students should be practice-oriented. Others recommended providing a glossary so that readers could grasp the precise and consistent meaning of key concepts. We were not able to do this because, like Confucius, we had difficulty supplying context-free, all-purpose definitions. Still others were concerned with the tangling of rational analysis, judgemental descriptions and emotional comments in many of the case studies. We refused the quest for separation because, in our tradition, logic, beauty and ethics are a reciprocal oneness. Making our way in the world, Newton, Picasso and Confucius are good friends, not rivals or strangers.

We recognise that this may seem inconvenient to some readers in 'the West'. Nevertheless, even for these readers, it is perhaps a good time to note, make sense of and live with different styles of human experience. The world needs to face not only the economic (re-)rise of 'the East', but also its mindscapes. Culture is not just in lion dancing, sushi eating or Hollywood films; it is in the ways we think, interpret and interact. We are aware of the price we may have to pay for the style of this book. By spreading case studies throughout every chapter instead of putting them together into a separate section, for example, we depart from the norm of Western strategy textbooks and make our chapters look lengthy. We notice this, make the choice and are prepared for the consequences. We make this clear to readers, up front.

While recognising uniqueness, we strive to avoid making Confucian teaching and pragmatic strategy a mysterious enterprise. Managers with different cultural roots will search for practically wise strategy in heterogeneous, locally meaningful ways. This is naturally and rightly so. That said, we would consider it our great failure if, after reading this book, managers outside East Asia conclude: 'Excellent. But, this is for them, not us.' There is no universal 'best practice', there can be no provincial wisdom either. In an increasingly diverse and interconnected world, helpful is cultural confidence and sensitivity, not cultural arrogance, fatalism or indifference. Yes, we have passed well beyond the age when 'What is good for America is good for the world' or 'Japan does everything best'; we do not need a new mystique of 'Chinese strategy masters' or 'Indian management gurus'. If Confucianism and pragmatic strategy are wise and good, they must be meaningful, doable and beneficial to people all over the world. Without 'Great Harmony under Heaven [天下大同]', 'the East' cannot have lasting prosperity, and neither can 'the West'.

We started writing this book in 2008. Jiro had to satisfy almost non-stop demands from around the globe and Zhu to fulfil his teaching load in the UK as well as overseas. Despite this, we decided not to rely on any research assistance or funding. As a result, it took us some years to complete the book. What has happened on the world stage since that winter afternoon, not least the near-collapse of Wall Street and the City of London, has only heightened our sense of urgency. Managers and citizens have learned the hard way that, in their own interest and that of their children, it is imperative to engage strategy consciously, purposefully, collectively. At this historical juncture, we present this book to managers, researchers and MBA students; it is our effort to join the ongoing collective search for an alternative strategy paradigm. In the end, it is you, the readers, to judge whether the book is interesting, useful, worthwhile.

We thank our manager friends, academic colleagues and MBA students for their input over the years. We thank Paula Parish of Cambridge University Press for her encouragement, patience, professionalism and warm smile.

Thank you to Sachiko and Xiaoping, for your quiet companionship during those long, peaceful, productive mornings, seven days a week, 365 days a year.

IN and ZZ
Hawaii

PART I   Why pragmatism, why now?

天道远，人道近。
《左传》

The *Tao* of Heaven is far away;
the *Tao* of Man is near.
– *Zhuozhuan*

I Introduction

This is a strategy book. It is about how to strategise creatively, ethically, effectively. Our message is: we humans are pragmatic in our wise moments, and pragmatic strategy is apt for bettering firms, communities, society and Mother Nature. If you want to walk in the world wisely, this book is for you.

But why should we bother with another strategy book, one wonders, at a time when typing 'strategic management' and 'business policy' pops up more than 76,000 results from Amazon and 3,380,000 from Google Scholar?[1] To answer this question, in this introductory chapter let us have a brief look at how strategy has been doing, what is at stake and what pragmatism means to strategy.

STRATEGY IN A CHANGING WORLD

Strategy is one of the oldest practices of humankind. Remember *The Art of War* of Sunzi (孙子), the ancient Chinese general? Yet as a systematic corporate undertaking, a scholarly field of study and a multibillion-dollar consultancy industry, the search for modern strategy did not emerge until the 1950s–1960s when Kenneth Andrews at the Harvard Business School delivered a course called *Business Policy*, Igor Ansoff published his seminal book *Corporate Strategy* in the US, Alfred Sloan illustrated the M-form corporate structure in *My Years with General Motors* and Alfred Chandler laid down the founding blocks of *Structure and Strategy*, *The Visible Hand* and *Scale and Scope*.[2] That was the time of America's undisputed industrial might, economic success and acclaimed business education. For decades, all this served companies well. Subsequently, as McDonaldisation spread around the world, so did strategy based

3

on Western, or more precisely Anglo-Saxon, mindsets and experiences – the world was flat.[3]

But the world is turning upside down. The business landscape facing managers now is a strange one, featuring the collapse of shareholder capitalism, shifting economic gravity, an ambivalent attitude towards globalisation and increasing concern for the ecological environment.

Crisis of shareholder capitalism

Triggered by a credit crunch associated with imploded subprime mortgages in the US, the bankruptcy of leading investment banks such as Lehman Brothers in 2008 threatened to collapse the whole financial system. The danger was real and immediate: people might wake up next morning to find ATMs no longer working. To keep capitalism afloat, governments used taxpayers' money to bail out the banks, but the damage had already been done.[4] Banks refused to lend to each other, let alone to other businesses. Factories were closed, workers laid off and families forced to tighten their belts. Countries, in particular those most exposed to the shareholder model, are now in deep deficit and debt. Advanced economies entered the 2008 crisis with an average budget deficit of 1.1 per cent of national income; by 2010 the figure had risen to 8.4 per cent, and government gross debt is set to rise from around 70 per cent of national income to nearly 120 per cent by 2015.[5] At the time of writing, the US national debt exceeded $14 trillion, $121,000 for each family.[6] At present, annual interest on the federal debt is running at more than $200 billion; at this rate, America will be paying its creditors $928 billion annually in ten years' time.[7] In the hot summer of 2011, the US managed to avoid a default of its national debt at the eleventh hour – by borrowing more. It subsequently lost its top credit rating for the first time in history.[8] In Europe, Greece, Ireland and Portugal were forced to seek EU–IMF rescue packages that imposed deep cuts to public services, high increases in taxes and a huge decrease in living standards.[9] Some other larger economies may follow.[10] We have witnessed an unprecedented boom and bust. Bailing out the banks escalated into bailing out national economies.[11] We have simply transferred liabilities and risk from the private sector to the state.[12] Protesters in the streets are angry: why should the whole world pay for the mistakes of a few greedy bankers who are still filling their pockets with scandalous bonuses? What social model are we living by? Some recall Marx.[13]

But it is not just the bankers who are to blame; we are all in this together.[14] Central banks and rating agencies failed to do their job, governments and politicians pleased voters with frantic spending, companies borrowed money to buy other firms and football clubs, while consumers, i.e. the rest of us, happily lived beyond our means.[15] Our good life was a fake one, built on a few plastic cards. In 'the West', we borrowed cheap money and bought cheap goods from China, India and poorer countries.[16] We managed to believe this could continue forever. Our strategies were plainly flawed: one does not need to be a rocket scientist to be able to anticipate the dangers of investment banks 'leveraging' 42 times their assets to gamble on 'the market'.[17] Some saw the calamity coming and blew the whistle; we did not want to listen and called them 'Doctor Doom'.[18] Ours is a democratic debt. But reality does not allow us to continue; it is payback time. The current crisis, the worst in 60 years, may turn out to be more significant than the collapse of communism. Capitalism is changing in fundamental ways.[19]

At this critical moment, we need to take a long and hard look at our business, corporate, industrial and national strategies. What went wrong?

Shift of economic power

What will emerge from the debris of shareholder capitalism is uncertain. Nevertheless, one consequence is becoming clear: a shift of economic power.[20] Economies in 'the West' were weakened by the crisis.[21] If the toxic mortgage securities and opaque credit swaps were 'Made in the US', European banks were eager buyers. Subsequently, the US paid $700 billion for its hubris, and European governments from Ireland to Germany were forced to shore up their banks.[22] The result was global recession and bankruptcy of nations. In contrast, although compelled to follow 'the West' in cutting interest rates and launching stimulation packages, China, India and a host of emerging economies have continued to grow: China at an annual rate of more than 10 per cent and India 8 per cent during the last five years.[23] Financial crises of the past were things inherent to Latin America, Asia, and Russia, while Washington, London and Zurich watched from a distance and lectured the developing world on how to get out of its mess. No longer. For the first time, the epicentre has been in 'the West', with 'the East' acting as a pillar of stability, recovery and prosperity.[24]

Even before the current crisis, the economic gravity was shifting. As early as 1981, Antoine van Agtmael of Emerging Market Management coined the phrase 'emerging markets', and in 2001, Jim O'Neill of Goldman Sachs the term 'BRICs'.[25] It is customary nowadays to talk about the pace of China's rise, India's emergence as a geopolitical player and the growing potential of Brazil, South Africa, Turkey and Indonesia. It is widely recognised that a new world order is in the making, and this time it will not be on the terms of Western, rich nations.[26] Some in 'the West' begin to challenge the assumption that industrialised countries have 'graduated permanently' into the developed world,[27] while others warn that those things which give 'the West' the edge, e.g. competition and work ethic, are no longer the monopolised property of 'the West'.[28]

What are the implications of all this for corporate practice? As 'fear is in "the West" and hope in "the East"',[29] businesses vote with their feet. IBM relocated its procurement headquarters to the southern Chinese city of Shenzhen,[30] and HSBC moved its chief executive to Hong Kong.[31] As *The Economist* reported in April 2010, *Fortune* 500 companies from developed nations have 98 R&D facilities in China and 63 in India, in addition to manufacturing and software operations.[32] Significantly, emerging countries are no longer content to be sources of cheap hands and low-cost brains, or a marketplace for products designed in rich nations. They are climbing up the value chain, becoming hotbeds of innovation and making breakthroughs in everything from car-making to health care. In 2008, the Chinese telecom equipment supplier Huawei applied for more international patents than any other firm. Companies from emerging economies compete at home, in each other's markets and in advanced economies, on creativity as well as on low cost, with new concepts, models, rules and practices. In the *Financial Times* 500, companies from emerging economies increased from 26 in 2000 to 119 in 2010. In 2009, for the first time, takeovers by emerging world companies of developed world groups exceeded takeovers going the other way.[33] At a time when 'the West' is reluctantly preparing for austerity,[34] India and China are creating one billion bourgeoisie.[35] At the top of multinationals' agendas, Made-in-China is quickly replaced by Made-for-China.[36] 'Go East, young man' looks set to become the rallying cry of the twenty-first century.[37]

Yet the challenges are for everyone. As to 'the East', let us look at just one issue: while there is no doubt that most of its economies will continue to develop in the coming decades, what remains unclear is how the benefits will be distributed – China is today perhaps the most unequal society in Asia in terms of wealth distribution.[38]

How should firms, industries and nations strategise in the face of all of this?

Ambivalence towards globalisation

When the Berlin Wall fell, we proclaimed 'the end of history', celebrated Western-style liberal democracy as 'the final, universal form of human government'.[39] Associated with this was the 'Washington Consensus' that promoted market economy, macroeconomic discipline and openness to the world. Gradually, the Consensus was interpreted in narrower terms: deregulation plus privatisation.[40] State intervention was dead; long live the self-regulating market. Reforms in China, India, Russia and Eastern European countries were taken as evidence.[41]

But history refuses to lie down. It is reborn. The reforming countries apparently created different versions of capitalism. The near-collapse of the shareholder model and a weakened 'West' have reinforced the confidence of rising economies who are no longer willing to be lectured about the virtues of liberal markets. 'The market', which once could do nothing wrong, not only faces setbacks in emerging economies but is put to rest at home, in practice if not in rhetoric. Survival of the fittest is giving way to bail-out politics; the state decides which sectors should live or die.[42] A large chunk of the US and UK financial sectors are now practically nationalised, and the total gross value of state intervention has reached $14,000 billion.[43] Martin Wolf, a distinguished economist, wrote in the *Financial Times*, 'This is state capitalism', while Gao Xiqing, president of the China Investment Corporation, called it 'socialism with American characteristics'.[44] On the other hand, as Western trade and foreign direct investment fall while those of the BRICs soar, poorer countries increasingly conclude, rightly or wrongly, that the BRIC models are more suitable for their development.[45] While some writers passionately defend the supremacy of 'the West' over 'the Rest',[46] the harsh bottom line appears to us that, as long as 'the West' fails to reverse the relative decline in wealth generation, its democratic values and supposed supremacy will come to naught.[47]

While the threat of the Cold War fades, new confrontations between members of the G8, G20 and G2 emerge on other fronts. On the monetary front, for example, while the US insistently accuses the Chinese of unfairly manipulating currencies, the Chinese condemn America's irresponsible 'quantitative easing', now in its 2.0 phase (or 'QE2'), for destabilising the world economy. When the big guys point fingers at each other, smaller economies suffer.[48]

Equally troubling is what some economists call 'deglobalisation'. According to IMF and UNCTAD data, the global movement of goods, capital and jobs is retreating on all fronts.[49] While critics have long been condemning the failure of globalisation to deliver promised benefits to the poor,[50] two-thirds of EU citizens now see globalisation as beneficial only for large firms, not for society.[51] In 2010, China displaced America as the largest manufacturer in the world – the first time the US has lost this top slot in 110 years. Consequently, the majority of Americans consider trade a threat, not an opportunity.[52] Protectionism dies hard, particularly in economic downturns and election times. The US Congress attempted to attach a 'Buy American' provision to the stimulus bill and Gordon Brown, then UK prime minister, pledged 'British jobs for British workers'.[53] Where is their moral authority? Is this not another troubling 'consensus' in the making?

What does all this mean for firms that are seeking global markets, optimising global supply chains and competing the world over for local talents?

Concerns for the environment

The public's perception of a deteriorating biosphere has been heightened in past decades by high-profile industrial accidents. People were horrified by the Chernobyl and Bhopal accidents. As we write, the battle to contain the Fukushima nuclear plant crisis is still ongoing. BP's Deepwater Horizon rig deep in the Gulf of Mexico leaked some 60,000 barrels of oil per day into the ocean after an explosion that killed 11 workers. The oil spill reached the coastline of four US states, threatening an ecological and economic catastrophe.[54] However, these high-profile cases are widely considered merely the tip of an iceberg of industrial pollution, which includes toxic smog, black rivers, hazardous-waste sites, acid rain and ozone depletion. Experts warn that we are living with constant 'technoenvironmental risks'.[55]

Industrial pollution is not the only problem. The world's population has doubled during the past 40 years and is likely to double again in the next 40. As surveys and reports show, this has widespread impacts on the environment: shortage of water, disappearing rainforests, damage to fishery and wildlife, soil degradation, desertification on a massive scale and, arguably, global warming.

Worldwide, there is an awareness of the worsening state of the bio-environment, and the pressure to tackle it is mounting. Solutions from international bodies have so far been elusive. From Kyoto to Bali to Copenhagen, despite sound bites, finger-pointing and tears, collective commitments are hard to come by. 'Meaningful agreements' in Copenhagen, for instance, are merely 'noted', not approved, let alone legally binding. What the crowded summits have so far produced are their own carbon footprints, deepened suspicions and promises of future talks. The *Sunday Times* calls this 'Hot air in our time'.[56] Citizens express their anger outside the summit halls with stones and bricks; they want no more 'Brokenhagens'.

Under pressure, national governments resort to legislation: acts, laws, enactments, amendments. When real decisions are made, however, environmental concerns are quickly undermined by perceived 'benefits to economy and jobs'. While putting on paper a target of reducing carbon emissions by 80 per cent by 2050, for instance, the former UK Labour government decided to build a new runway and terminal at Heathrow. Heathrow, one of the busiest airports in the world, currently has two runways and five terminals. The project would increase the number of flights from 473,000 in 2009 to more than 700,000 by 2030 and raise passenger numbers from 67 million to 120 million and carbon emissions from 17.1 million tonnes to 23.6 million tonnes.[57] The public is wary: 'How dare the government tell us to change all our light bulbs and then do something like this?'[58]

The hidden problem, however, is more fundamental. When we – governments, businesses, unions – urge the Chinese to buy more so as to balance the mammoth deficits run up in boom times by Western economies, does anyone care about the consequential impacts on the planet?[59] Is it not that our whole way of thinking, and of living, is in trouble?

A PRAGMATIC TURN

A changing world demands novel strategies, and strategies are derived from 'paradigms'. Thomas Kuhn's *The Structure of Scientific*

Revolution, regarded as one of the most important books published in the second half of the last century, posits that we live by paradigms – frameworks of how things work.[60] We use paradigms, usually without being conscious of it, to interpret what we see and decide what to do. We use paradigms to think about and do strategies: what the important issues are, what we should value, what customers need, how to serve them and so on.

Amid the unprecedented, continuing crisis, we need to question the paradigm we have been using in the past. We must assess its social, political and intellectual as well as economic consequences, and ask how we could strategise differently. While the conventional paradigm has been shaken by recent events, as we shall detail in later chapters, it lingers, nevertheless, like a 'normal science'.[61] Bankers still manufacture fat bonuses, governments battle for a 1 per cent debt cut, consumers fly more often for overseas holidays and companies promote more, not less, consumption. 'Business has not yet found its Copernicus.'[62]

Let us make our position clear. As we shall propose throughout this book, business can be a positive force and strategy a useful tool for making the world a better place. With proper strategy, nations, industries and firms have made tremendous differences, which we should be proud of. Just look at how the reforms of China, India and Brazil are changing the world, how the Bangladeshi Grameen Bank's microloans and micro-deposits enable millions of the poorest to stand on their own feet, how Nintendo's Wii machine lifts the young and the old, male and female, joyfully into exercise; there are many more success stories. Crucially, all this is achieved despite, rather than because of, the conventional paradigm. The paradigm is chiefly responsible for the crises, calamities and deteriorations we still live with, so much so that many, not least many of those in 'the West', conclude that strategy is 'at a crossroads', 'in a state of crisis'.[63]

Damning evidence and critical analysis, however overwhelming, do not, as Kuhn pointed out, dislodge a dominant paradigm unless a more attractive alternative is presented.[64] Walking in a fast-moving world amid crisis, facing the dangerous return of business-as-usual, we urgently need an alternative. We need to strategise differently, wisely. While sharing the concerns of our Western colleagues who believe that strategy is in crisis (危机), we suggest that in crises there are both dangers (危) and opportunities (机). To neutralise danger and seize upon opportunity, we need a paradigm shift. Strategy needs a workable alternative. This book will explore an alternative useful for strategising differently, wisely, beneficially.

Where will the alternative come from; is an alternative ever possible? Look around, there are confusions. On one side, we have Gary Hamel, a strategy guru, urging us to press the 'reset button': to reinvent strategy in a 'make-or-break' fashion.[65] On the other side, Tom Peters, another guru, warns us about the arrogance of believing that we face unprecedented challenges – what we say now about the Internet we said before about the railway and electricity.[66] Robert Eccles and Nitin Nohria of Harvard Business School, too, remind us of the danger of 'the desperate search for quick solutions to eternal management challenges'.[67] As with many strategy issues, we receive seemingly conflicting advice: to change or not to change? And, if we are to change, how and into what?

Out of the confusion we propose a third way: learning from enduring wisdom so as to strategise here-and-now wisely. Beyond the 'hype of newness', we appreciate enduring wisdom; in the place of 'eternal challenges', we see emerging particulars. It is the responsibility of managers to innovate novel solutions based on enduring wisdom for coping with unfolding problems.

In their shocking 1980 paper 'Managing our way to economic decline', Robert Hayes and William Abernathy called for 'getting back to basics'.[68] At that time, they meant managers should re-embrace the 'traditional basics': getting involved in details, being at the forefront of technology, focusing on core business and so on. Almost 30 years later, after a couple of rounds of boom and bust, when *Harvard Business Review* republished the paper in 2007, Hayes renewed the call, but stressed that 'a mastery of the old basics no longer suffices' because 'changes in the world economy have added more items to the list'. In his view, it is imperative to create and implement 'a new set of essentials': involving multiple parties, better incentive systems and implicit contracts.[69] We acknowledge the call of Hayes and Abernathy, but consider our appeal for 'enduring wisdom' to be different from their 'basics' or 'essentials'. Their basics and essentials appear to concern matters of operation that need to be updated as the world changes.

Our 'enduring wisdom', in contrast, is closer to James Collins and Jerry Porras' 'core values' or 'philosophy'. In their 1994 best-selling *Built to Last*, Collins and Porras, citing John Young, the former CEO of Hewlett-Packard, write: 'We distinguish between core values and practices; the core values don't change, but the practices might.'[70] In this terminology, Hayes and Abernathy's 'old basics' and 'new essentials' are changeable practices, not core values or philosophy that last a company's whole life. With Collins and Porras' 'core values', we feel very much at home.

But, still, our 'enduring wisdom' differs in one important aspect. 'Core values' in *Built to Last* are firm-specific: each visionary company establishes and maintains a unique philosophy. This philosophy is a company's property, not to be shared by other firms. In contrast, the 'enduring wisdom' we explore in this book is meant to be meaningful, doable and workable for managers across the globe as long as they intend to strategise creatively, ethically, effectively. It is a treasure for all; we can all benefit from and contribute to it.

Like Collins and Porras' core values, enduring wisdom is a never-ending, rich spring for doing strategy wisely. But enduring wisdom does not offer ready formulas or quick solutions that can be picked off a shelf. Managers need to translate enduring wisdom skilfully so as to make it work in specific circumstances.

The enduring wisdom we shall share with readers is pragmatism. Why pragmatism? Because the real world appears to reward what works and to penalise what doesn't, and we humans are pragmatic in our wise moments.[71] We see many examples of pragmatism in action, underlying numerous successful strategies. Consider the following:

- What was the strategy that fuelled China's miraculous economic reform in the early years? According to Beijing's official version, it was the Party's 'Four Cardinal Principles', while to Deng Xiaoping, with whom the Chinese people overwhelmingly agree, it was 'crossing the river by touching stones' and 'white cat or black cat, the one that catches the mouse is a good cat'.[72]

- Hank Paulson, the former boss of Goldman Sachs who became Secretary of the US Treasury, is a market-can-do-no-wrong guy; but he intervened in 'the market' in 2008 with a heavy and visible hand in order to prevent financial institutions from immediate total collapse. 'I hate the fact that we have to do this. But it is better than the alternative.'[73]

- In the 1960s, as the story goes, Honda planned to explore the US market with its 500 cc jumbo motorcycle, but switched to marketing the 50 cc Super Cup when the sales team accidentally discovered that local consumers preferred the small machine, which kicked off Honda's sustained success story.[74]

- When Bill Gates started his business, he laid down a principle: in Microsoft no employee should work for a boss who wrote worse computer code than she/he did. As the company grew and business got complicated, Gates quickly abandoned his principle and put experienced managers in place, regardless of whether they were good at programming.[75]

- To Michael Dell, 'the Direct Model is a revolution not a religion'. Since 2007, customers could purchase Dell machines in Wal-Mart and Staples in the US, Carphone Warehouse in the UK, Guomei in China and Bic Camera stores in Japan. Dell also restructured its value chain by acquiring IT distribution and service companies.[76]

Behind all these and many other real-world stories is sheer down-to-earth vigilance and flexibility. In this sense, pragmatism is deeply ingrained common sense and has always been part of strategy. But pragmatism goes beyond mere common sense or flexibility. Our experiences in China, Japan, Europe and the US, and many conversations with managers around the world, tell us that pragmatic strategy is the purposeful accomplishment of idealistic, informed, disciplined experimentations. Pragmatism is not anything-goes or opportunism-without-purpose, despite what many strategy professors would have us believe. Pragmatic, that is, innovative, ethical and effective, strategy is about moral standing, sound judgement, implementation skill and learning capability. Pragmatic strategy grows out of profound intellectual traditions and subtle life experiences.[77]

It is this kind of idealistic and realistic, creative and disciplined, instrumental and ethical pragmatism that we intend to share with readers. It is our best hope for practically wise strategy. Taking pragmatism as a marginal part of strategy is not good enough. Unless we embrace pragmatism as an overarching orientation, the conventional paradigm will linger on, continuing to litter the world with bigger collapses, deeper crises and more painful cuts.

As a legacy of the current crisis, we are waking up to the inadequacy of hyper-rational, overly simplistic views of the complex, ambiguous, uncertain world. We have learnt the hard way that governments and markets can both go wrong and be corrupted. We are all fallible. The economist Anatole Kaletsky suggests in his 2010 book *Capitalism 4.0* that 'experimentation and pragmatism will become watchwords in public policy, economics and business strategy'.[78] It is time to act upon pragmatism consciously and proudly, rather than packaging it with Reason, Truth, Theory or Science. We call for a pragmatic turn.[79]

We choose to base our inquiry on Confucian-samurai pragmatism. This is a considered choice. Confucianism is a tradition that has served a huge population of humankind for around two thousand five hundred years. At its core is a pragmatist orientation: how to engage wisely in this-worldly affairs with all our rational faculties, creative imagination and moral sensibilities so as to achieve harmony between communities and with Nature. Our task is to explore how to make Confucian pragmatism relevant and actionable to managers.[80]

Confucianism is an open, evolving tradition. During its long history, thanks to a profound intellectual and moral confidence, it has been enriched by learning from Taoism, Buddhism and, more recently, Western thought. This enables Confucianism to incorporate useful insights from other pragmatic traditions, e.g. American pragmatism and Aristotelian practical wisdom,[81] which allows us to understand strategy experiences all over the world in a new light, and embrace them into a useful resource pool.

Consider the bulk of research and findings available to date on modern strategy. All of the key studies, such as Andrews' SWOT model, Chandler's scale–scope–speed triad, Porter's industrial analysis, Barney's resource-based view, Hamel and Prahalad's competence thesis, Teece's dynamic capability treaty, Ansoff's planning approach, Mintzberg's crafting school, Collins and Porras' *Built to Last*, Kim and Mauborgne's *Blue Ocean Strategy*, Barnard's *The Functions of the Executive* and Walton's *Made in America: My Story*, are based on Western experience and underpinned by Western thinking.[82] The enormous value of these stories is in no doubt; they are a treasure for the whole of humankind. Meanwhile, Akio Morita's *Made in Japan* and Ikujiro Nonaka's *Knowledge-Creating Company* remain lonely exceptions,[83] while modern Chinese business strategies are almost unknown, let alone lessons from other emerging economies.[84] This does no good to anyone. If the economic powerhouse is indeed moving eastward and the world is on course for an 'Asian century', as many suggest, what unique contributions will Eastern experiences make to strategy? How should people all over the world learn from each other and together make the world better and happier? Seen this way, an inquiry based on Confucian pragmatism might not be a bad idea.

In our view, pragmatism is not the private property of the descendants of Confucius. Rather, it is a treasure shared by the global community. Many other cultures can also contribute to pragmatic strategy. Throughout this book, we use Confucianism as an umbrella to embrace ideas, experiences and findings from many places around the world, from the US to India, from Bangladesh to Japan, from the UK to China. Although rooted in our particular culture, we design for the pragmatic turn a global outlook. We hope that readers will connect this broad church with their local experiences. Inviting contributions from diverse cultures, we shall conclude this book with a chapter titled 'Pragmatism East and West'. Indeed, the whole book can be read as such an invitation.

THE JOURNEY AHEAD

Our journey will take us through four stages (see Figure 1.1). In Part I 'Why pragmatism, why now?', Chapter 2 explores the spirits of pragmatism. This is intended to lay an intellectual platform for the pragmatic turn. We emphasise these spirits: practical, processual, creative, holist, ethical and communal. Individually, these spirits may appear in various forms in many traditions. However, it is the network effect, the working together of the spirits that makes pragmatism an enduring and timely wisdom, that enables us to achieve the urgently needed paradigm shift. Examples discussed in this chapter include the Bangladeshi Grameen Bank, the Toyota Production System, Yamaha's piano innovation, China's Hisap computer retailing business, the Mazda turnaround and the Third Italy community building.

In Part II, 'What do pragmatic strategies look like?', we continue the journey by looking at how the spirits of pragmatism shed new light on our understanding of strategy. Chapter 3 posits that strategy is a form of life experience, it is in what we say, believe, have, do and live through. Strategy is a tool in managers' hands that fulfils various tasks, including prompting action, imposing discipline, gaining legitimacy and consolidating power. As such, strategies in a pragmatic world display rich features: contingent, consequential, continuous, courageous, collective, co-creative; we call these the '6Cs' of strategy.[85] In Chapter 4, we consider strategy formation as multi-path system emergence, a purposeful evolutionary process in which the environment selects strategies while managers' actions change the world. Following this, pragmatic strategy as purposefully opportunistic action is contrasted with the ad hoc image of 'strategy

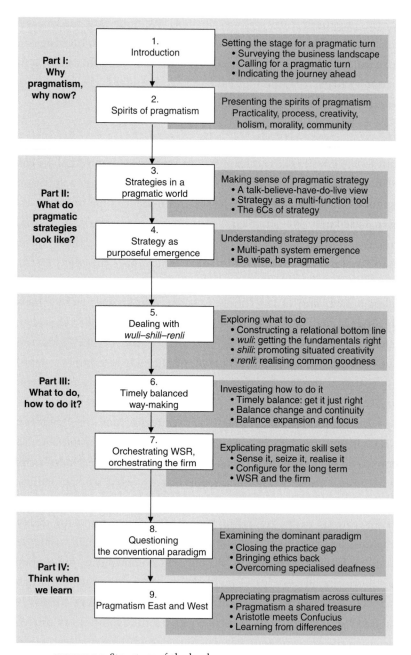

FIGURE 1.1 Structure of the book

without intent'.[86] We shall illustrate pragmatic strategy with cases such as China's economic reform, the cochlear implant industry, Alibaba.com, Master Kong Noodles, Intel Corporation's microprocessor strategy, 3M's iconic Post-it Notes innovation, Lenovo's manoeuvre over China's production licence, and more.

If Part II presents a descriptive view of what pragmatic strategies look like, then Part III probes the all-important normative question 'what to do, how to do it?' In Chapter 5, we begin with a corporate executive's reflection on what managers do on the messy business front line in their efforts to rescue a failing company. We then, based on this reflection, introduce a Confucian worldview that conceives life experience and strategy as ongoing engagements with problems and opportunities emerging from dynamic relationships between *wuli* (物理) the material-technical, *shili* (事理) the mental-cognitive, and *renli* (人理) the social-normative. This relational worldview enables us to discern a triple bottom line that underpins business success: getting fundamentals right, envisioning a valued future, realising common goodness.

A discussion of the Confucian teaching *shizhong* (时中, timely balance) in Chapter 6 then suggests how to make one's way in the world. The art of strategy is pragmatism-upon-time. We shall take strategic options such as change–continuity and expansion–focus as pairs of constructive companions rather than antagonistic contradictions. Questioning the popular 'golden mean', we suggest that practically wise strategy lies not in 'sticking to the middle', 'retaining two extremes' or 'synthesising into a higher whole', but in getting business just right, appropriate, fitting with ever-changing circumstances. Winning strategies may be in the middle, at either end, or somewhere between – it depends on unfolding particulars. It is timely judgement, collective justification and situated experimentation that make the difference.

Following this, Chapter 7 presents a broad 'sensing–seizing–realising' skill set useful for creating and capturing value amid complexity, ambiguity and uncertainty. While one size does not fit all, a broad skill set will enable managers to put in place configurations that allow beneficial strategies and valued outcomes to emerge. Useful configurations include generating a population of initiatives, exercising real options, setting up selection mechanisms and investing in diversity. Part III concludes with a Confucian imagery that conceives the modern firm as a path-dependent constellation of unique *wuli* assets, *shili* capabilities and *renli* relationships evolving in the wider WSR space. Running business and doing strategy, the manager's job is to orchestrate asset complementarities, facilitate co-specialisation, renew capability and heighten ethical sensibility.

Together, the *relational* WSR bottom line and the *temporal* timely balance constitute a mode of thinking that engages managers to generate value efficiently, creatively, ethically. Again, we use practical cases to illustrate the normative implications. These include China Merchants Bank, Xerox, Airbus, Seven-Eleven Japan, Komatsu, Nintendo, Lenovo, Swatch, General Electric, Lego, Li & Fung, Intel, Mayekawa, Hewlett-Packard, IBM, Microsoft, Google, Philips, YKK, Rolls-Royce, Huawei, Tencent, Alibaba, Edison, Honda, as well as the collapse of Polaroid and Marconi, the run on Northern Rock, Toyota's recall and Madoff's Wall Street fraud.

Part IV, 'Think when we learn', reflects on learning from our past and from others. Chapter 8 is a critical examination of the past – the conventional paradigm behind the current crisis. The paradigm is found to be disabling because it diminishes practical orientation, ethical sensibility and holistic thinking. These damaging effects reinforce each other in a vicious spiral. The quest for a scientific status diverts strategy from front-line business; managing-by-numbers marginalises moral sensibility; amoral strategy needs a 'scientific' cover to look good; and specialised deafness is both the cause and effect of all this – it brings comfort to strategies that lack collective purpose, domain experience and practical relevance. In the conventional paradigm, the whole is larger than the sum of its parts, just in value-destroying ways. The damage caused by the conventional paradigm is illustrated by the UK Channel 4's *Big Brother* race row, BP's Gulf of Mexico disaster and China's tainted-milk scandal. Our examination is critical but constructive, aiming at a richer understanding of strategy and ways for strategising differently, wisely.

Chapter 9, 'Pragmatism East and West', is intended to expand the reader's vision by putting pragmatic strategy into a global context. Our message is that pragmatism is a treasure for the whole of mankind, and pragmatic strategy is meaningful and doable to people with different cultural roots. We shall present affinities between Confucian and American pragmatisms along the six spirits we outlined in Chapter 2. We will then compare Confucian and Aristotelian teachings along five dimensions: 'what is' vs 'how to act'; articulative reasoning vs suggestive exemplars; hierarchical vs circular knowledge; polarising-and-choosing vs associating-and-complementing; and brain-driven vs heart-inspired thinking styles. By appreciating these differences we aim at better learning from 'other' and knowing 'the self' in order to pursue pragmatic strategies that are workable in heterogeneous localities.

Throughout the book, we draw enthusiastically from available findings and hard-learnt lessons generated in many places of the world. A pragmatic turn is not to abandon or replace past experiences and insights. We do not strategise with complete doubt or empty hands; we are always already resourced.[87] Pragmatism engages us to enrich our resource pool and to use it for generating timely, workable solutions. The richer our resource pool, the more effective our *bricolage*, and the more successfully we get jobs done. By interpreting past experiences and business cases in a new light, we show how a pragmatic turn can help managers to learn, think and act differently.

This book does not have a separate section for case studies. Instead, plenty of cases are dispersed throughout the chapters. They illustrate pragmatic strategy in action, in real companies, in the

dreams and efforts of real managers framing and solving life problems. It is unwise, from a pragmatic point of view, to separate inquiries and cases, theory and practice, what is on paper and what is at the
front line. We have intentionally selected cases from different industries and sectors, various societal-organisational levels and diverse
cultural-institutional contexts.[88] The world is complex and rich, so
should be our mode of thinking, learning and acting.

Strategies are dead things unless we put them into action. In the
end, it is our ideals, values, purpose, judgement, political will, social
skill, technical competence and experimental action that make the
difference. We believe that business and strategy can be a positive
force for making our world better and happier, not just for the few,
but for all, including Mother Nature. The following business case
convinces us that our optimism is well-founded. The case is small,
yet it gives us a taste of what is to come: the power of technical competence, creative imagination and moral purpose in action.

Strategy for a better world[89]

In 2006, a vaccine to prevent rotavirus was licensed by the US Food
and Drug Administration. Rotavirus is a disease of young children
that causes vomiting, high fever, diarrhoea and dehydration. It killed
2,000 children in the developing world every day and caused a great
deal of suffering in the developed world. Penny Heaton of Merck
was the pharmaceutical company executive who headed the vaccine
programme.

At the end of a pre-licensure study that took four years to
complete, involved 70,000 children and cost about $350 million,
Dr Heaton called together 200 people at her company. She started
with a series of slides. 'This is what the world looks like now', she
said, pointing to a map that contained hundreds of small black dots
concentrated in Asia, Africa and Latin America. 'Each of these dots
represents 1,000 deaths a year from rotavirus.' Then Dr Heaton
showed a map without any black dots. 'Now', she said, 'we have the
technology in hand to eliminate deaths from this disease.'

Then she wept. She stood in front of 200 people with her head down and her shoulders shaking. This is no one's image of a typical pharmaceutical company executive. The rotavirus vaccine is now available in Mali, Ghana, Vietnam, Bangladesh and Nicaragua.

Tomorrow can be better, and the future is in our hands. With hope and aspiration, let us begin our journey.

2   Spirits of pragmatism

Pragmatism is king in our vague new world.[1]
Pragmatism is replacing the old 'Washington Consensus'.[2]
Pragmatism will become the watchword in business strategy.[3]
Corporate pragmatism will get us out of the mess.[4]
Why Rorty's search for what works has lessons for business.[5]

These are the headlines that have, since the recent economic crisis
exploded, featured in the business media and the speeches of world
leaders. Suddenly, everyone appears to be rediscovering pragmatism.
But is this merely a short-lived fashion? Is pragmatism, like austerity, just a short-term measure for sorting out the mess? Will it be
kicked back into the long grass as soon as the world returns to 'normal', and picked up again only when we face another bust? If history
tells us anything, then our caution is not entirely unjustified.

Pragmatism has its roots in many cultures. It is an intellectual and moral sensibility in Confucian traditions.[6] Pragmatism is
also the most distinctive way of American life.[7] A unique pragmatist
spirit is manifested throughout European thought, from Aristotle's
phronesis thesis[8] to Heidegger and Wittgenstein's later works,[9] and
the theories of Nietzsche, Foucault and Habermas.[10] Pragmatism is
the heritage of all humankind. It shows us what to do and how to do
it in our world of shifting experiences. Pragmatism informs our life
in many ways, with or without our being aware of it.

Pragmatism has, however, had a humble history, no less
humble than Galileo Galilei facing the Inquisition. In the name of
Science, it has been caricatured as anything-goes, utilitarian thinking, amoral and opposed to Reason, Truth, Progress. The American
pragmatist thought of Charles Sanders Peirce and William James
was condemned by the whole 'intellectual community' in Europe a

century ago.[11] In Japan, the pragmatist samurai spirit was put aside when the nation embraced Western logic to become modern.[12] Once the communists took power in China, Confucius and John Dewey were sentenced to sudden death.[13] Today, pragmatism continues to be criticised, not least in academic circles, for being 'distasteful of theory' and 'restricting learning'. In business, pragmatism is allegedly responsible for corner-cutting opportunism and corruption. China's recent tainted-milk saga, for example, has been attributed to a get-rich-quickly-by-any-means 'pragmatism'.[14]

Despite all this, pragmatism survives. It is currently going through a renaissance in management studies and the social sciences, regaining influence on business strategy, public policy, international relations and the actions and lives of people around the globe.[15] Why? The reason is plain and simple: pragmatism engages people to act upon what works, and the real world appears to reward what works and penalise what doesn't.[16]

Let us go academic for a moment: pragmatism is a bias for action with focus and energy, a willingness to make-do without knowing how things might unfold, a habit that looks at situated particulars rather than generalised principles, an orientation that seeks knowledge based on the consequences of acting upon it, a mindscape that embraces plural perspectives and methods, an attitude that appreciates novelty and surprises, a conviction that collectively we can make a positive difference, a belief that practical consensus is often achieved at social-cultural-aesthetic levels instead of grounded on Truth or Reason.[17] As such, pragmatism is theoretically engaging rather than soft-heading, instrumentally delivering not empty-talking, morally inspiring instead of anything-goes or paralysing.

Sounds abstract? Then consider Deng Xiaoping, Bill Gates, Chester Barnard, Akio Morita, Honda and Grameen Bank. These, among many others, are real people and real companies delivering real benefits to real people. Their experiences show us that pragmatism is useful, doable, helping us accomplish what we want to achieve. Of course, we are not talking about 'pragmatism' of the

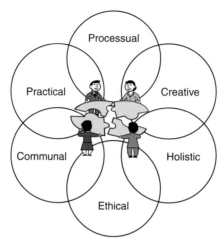

FIGURE 2.1 Spirits of pragmatism

anti-theory or corner-cutting sort. As managers facing pressing problems, what we should explore is the pragmatism that engages us to generate value efficiently, creatively, legitimately. Such pragmatism works when we act upon a set of differentiated yet interconnected spirits. In this chapter we introduce readers to the spirits of pragmatism. Figure 2.1 presents an overview of the forest. Let us have a brief look at each of the trees.[18]

A PRACTICAL FACE

At the core of Confucianism is an 'action orientation': being human is to act in the world. The purpose of mastering way-making (道, *Tao*) is to cope wisely with life problems.[19] If there is truth, it is made through human experience. Detached from experience or abstracted from action, *Tao* is valueless, meaningless.

This 'primacy of practice', as it is called in contemporary Western terminology,[20] has its roots deep in all major East Asian traditions.[21] The purpose of *The Analects* (论语) is not to investigate the essence of the universe, but to recount how the Master made his way in social affairs. The *Daodejing* (道德经) does not purport to supply a mirror of the world, but to advise us to interact wisely with life contexts. The *Yijing* (易经) is not meant to describe every scenario we

might encounter; rather, it offers guidance for responding appropriately to shifting life conditions. Hence we read in the classics:

> It is Man who makes *Tao* great, not *Tao* that makes Man
> great.[22]
>
> *Tao* is not far from men. When men try to pursue a course,
> which is abstracted from men, this course cannot be considered
> *Tao*.[23]
>
> The *Tao* of heaven is far away, while that of humans is
> near ... It is from humans themselves, that good and bad fortunes
> are produced.[24]
>
> *Tao* is made in the walking of it.[25]

Peter Drucker, Russell Ackoff and Sumantra Ghoshal, perhaps the
best minds in contemporary strategy, with their 'bias for action',
would feel at home with Confucius.[26] To the Chinese mandarin, the
sages are great because they engage in here-and-now affairs; to the
Japanese samurai, being a 'man of action' 'on the spot' is far more
important than prudent intellectual abstraction.[27] In contrast with
Descartes' 'I think therefore I am', Confucian pragmatism is characterised by what Kitaro Nishida (西田 幾多郎, 1870–1945) called 'acting intuition': 'the human being-in-the-world as originally having
the character of action; the essential mode is to act on the world,
not to cognise it.'[28] As Roger Ames and Henry Rosemont comment,
Confucius is less a philosopher than a *philosophe*:

> His vision was not simply one to be understood, and then
> accepted, modified, or rejected on the basis of its congruence
> with the world 'objectively' perceived ... On the contrary, his
> vision was one that had to be felt, experienced, practiced, and
> lived. He was interested in how to make one's way in life, not in
> discovering the 'truth'.[29]

What is knowledge, and what is it for? In Confucianism, the prac-
tical-performative dimension is paramount. The Chinese *kanji*
character 知 (know) is composed of an 矢 (arrow) which means to

direct and command, and a 口 (mouth) which means to express and communicate. Hence, 'know' does not simply mean, as usually translated into English, to discover or comprehend a pre-given reality; it denotes coming to realise, make present, actualise a world.[30] Knowledge is the process of experiencing and changing life conditions. The 'product' of this process is less about the nature of things – 'what is it?' than about appropriate action – 'what is to be done?'[31]

To Wang Yangming (王阳明), an eleventh-century Confucian, knowledge and action are one: to know is to authenticate in action (知行合一). Knowing *what* contingent particulars are is, although important, not the purpose; knowing *how* to envision a valued future and make it real by acting upon those particulars is.[32] Faithful to Wang Yangming's spirit, Ikujiro Nonaka suggests: 'knowing is a bodily action with a will to bring about changes in the state of affairs rather than with a detached stance toward the world.'[33] Donald Munro, a 'Westerner', observes: 'in Confucianism there was no thought of knowing that did not entail some consequence for action.'[34] Knowledge is our capacity to act; it is not representational, but performative. We act, therefore we are.

Not all actions, however; only actions with a compelling purpose. The late Indian-born strategy professor Sumantra Ghoshal stressed, in his wonderful 2004 book *A Bias for Action*, the difference between 'purposeful action-taking' and 'active non-action'. While the former gets what matters done against all odds, the latter keeps busy all the time but fails to make a difference. A purposeful action-taker solves pressing life problems with a clear focus and persistent energy.[35] Confucius is a good example. In his time, people were suffering from betrayal, cruelty, wars and natural disasters, and the Middle Kingdom was in pieces. Confucius devoted his whole life to a single mission: engaging people to restore harmony in and between communities, as well as between man and Nature.

Not all knowledge either; managing-by-numbers will not do. Sam Steinberg, the founder-manager of Steinberg Inc., a supermarket chain headquartered in Montreal, told the Canadian strategy professor Henry Mintzberg the secret behind the company's success:

'Nobody knew the grocery business like we did. Everything has to do with your knowledge. I knew merchandise, I knew cost, I knew selling, I knew customers. I knew everything, and I passed on all my knowledge; I kept teaching my people. That's the advantage we had. Our competitors couldn't touch us.'[36] In the twenty-first century, the practical spirit that focuses on coping with pressing problems continues to underpin strategic successes. Given the plentiful suffering and limited resources around, the spirit is urgently needed, as the case below illustrates.

Muhammad Yunus: a scholar who changed the world[37]

After completing his Ph.D. on a Fulbright scholarship in the US, Muhammad Yunus became the head of the Economics Department at the Chittagong University in his birth-country Bangladesh. That was 1974. That year, Bangladesh had a severe famine and Yunus saw, day after day, people dying on the university's doorstep. This shook him to the core of his being:

> I used to get excited teaching my students how economics theories provided answers to economic problems of all types. I got carried away by the beauty and elegance of these theories. Now all of sudden I started having an empty feeling. What good were all these elegant theories when people died of starvation on pavements and on doorsteps?
>
> My classroom now seemed to me like a cinema where you could relax because you knew that the good guy in the film would ultimately win. In the classroom I knew, right from the beginning, that each economic problem would have an elegant ending. But when I came out of the classroom I was faced with the real world. Here, good guys were mercilessly beaten and trampled. I saw daily life getting worse, and the poor getting ever poorer. For them death through starvation looked to be their only destiny.
>
> Where was the economic theory which reflected their real life? How could I go on telling my students make-believe stories in the name of economics?

> I wanted to run away from these theories, from my
> textbooks. I felt I had to escape from academic life. I wanted
> to understand the reality around a poor person's existence and
> discover the real-life economics that were played out every day
> in the neighboring village – Jobra.[38]

So Yunus abandoned the bird's-eye view and adopted a worm's-eye view. What he saw in Jobra shook him further. In the village, he found poor women borrowing from money-lenders to purchase materials in order to make bamboo furniture and sell it in the market. On a good day, these women earned 50 *paisa* – 2 US cents – for a whole day's work. The money-lenders charged them 10 per cent in interest per week or even per day. Borrowers would have to borrow again just to repay the first loan, and the only way out was death. Watching one villager, Sufia Begum, busy making bamboo furniture with her hungry children around her, Yunus began to understand the real world. Sufia was poor not because she was stupid or lazy. She had useful skills and worked all day long, doing complex physical tasks. She suffered because the bamboo cost 5 *taka* and she didn't have that cash to start with. Her life was miserable because she could not find that 5 *taka*. She did not have credit: banks served only the rich, not the poor. She survived in that tight cycle by borrowing from the trader and selling back to him. She could not break free; when she died, she would pass the tight cycle on to her children. With all this unfolding before his eyes, Yunus got angry:

> She earned the equivalent of 2 US cents a day and it was this
> knowledge which paralysed me. In my university courses, I
> dealt in millions and billions of dollars, but here before my eyes,
> the problems of life and death were posed in terms of pennies.
> Something was wrong. Why did the university course I taught
> not mirror the reality of her life? I was angry at myself, angry at
> the world which was so uncaring.[39]

Within a week, Yunus and his students made a list of how many of the poorest Jobra villagers were borrowing from traders and losing the fruit of their labour. The list named 42 women who had borrowed a total of 856 *taka*, less than US$27. Yunus handed his student Maimuna that sum of money and told her, 'Lend this money out to the forty-two on our list. They can repay the traders what they owe and sell their products wherever they can get a good price.'[40] Yunus knew, however, this would not be sufficient because it was an ad hoc, personal, emotional solution. Handing out a pittance is a way of making ourselves feel good while leaving the fundamental problem unsolved. We have merely thrown money at it and walked away. What the poor needed was an institutional solution.

In 1976, overcoming many difficulties, Yunus secured a loan from the governmental Janata Bank to lend to the poor. This was based on his faith in human nature – both its ingenuity and desire to do good, given the opportunity. The microfinance project was designed to provide those opportunities to the poorest.

However, doing good was not easy. When Yunus tried to convince the villagers to accept loans, these were the usual replies:

> Your words frighten us, Sir.
>
> I wouldn't know what to do with money.
>
> No, no, not me. We have no use for money.
>
> No, no, we cannot take your money.
>
> No, when my mother died the last advice she gave me was never to borrow from anybody.
>
> Give the loan to my husband, he handles the money, I've never touched any. And I don't want to.
>
> We have all had enough trouble with dowry payments that we don't want another fight with our husbands. Professor, we don't want to get into more trouble.[41]

The villagers sent Yunus away, day after day, telling him not to come again. According to local custom, Yunus could not enter the women's houses, so he brought a female student with him. While Yunus stood in the courtyard between houses, the student introduced him, spoke on his behalf and brought back any questions the women had.

The student shuttled back and forth for over an hour without any result. One day, during the monsoon, both Yunus and the student were caught in a downpour. One of the women said, 'Let the professor take shelter next door, there is no one there. And that way the girl won't get wet anymore.' Then, the conversation continued, with Yunus and the women shouting questions and answers directly back and forth across the bamboo wall. Through the monsoon, Yunus and his students tramped around the village; during the dry season, they visited the same houses under the hot sun.

There were other obstacles. Money-lenders and mullahs threatened to hurt Yunus and his students, and told the villagers that anyone who accepted a microloan would be tortured, sold into prostitution, dropped at the bottom of the sea, denied a Muslim burial or sent to hell. In the end, it was usually the most desperate women – abandoned by their husbands, trying to feed their children by begging – who took the lead in accepting microloans. Whatever the mullahs threatened, these desperately poor women had no other choice: get help through microfinance or watch their children die. Other women then followed when they recognised that what the mullahs said were merely lies.

In 1983, the Jobra pilot project began operation as a fully fledged institution and was renamed the Grameen Bank (*Village Bank*). On 13 October 2006, Yunus and the Grameen Bank jointly received the Nobel Prize for Peace – the first time it was ever awarded to a business. By that time, microfinance had spread to more than 100 countries, from Uganda to the US, benefiting more than 100 million people through loans of often less than $100. As of March 2011, Grameen Bank had $955 million in outstanding loans to 8.3 million borrowers, of whom 97 per cent were women, with a 99 per cent repayment rate. Borrowers owned 94 per cent of the bank, with the remaining 6 per cent owned by the government. The bank also provided a micro-deposit service and helped villagers build houses and send their children to school. It lent to beggars free of interest, diversified into textiles, fisheries, irrigation and mobile phone operations: 260,000 'phone ladies' provided a phone service for more than 80 million people in some 28,000 villages all over the country. In the 1970s, 80 per cent of Bangladeshis lived below the poverty line; today the number is 38 per cent, with more than half of borrowers raised out of acute poverty. In its prize announcement, the Norwegian Nobel Committee said:

> Muhammad Yunus has shown himself to be a leader who has managed to translate visions into practical action for the benefit of millions of people, not only in Bangladesh, but also in many other countries. Loans to poor people without any financial security had appeared to be an impossible idea. From modest beginnings three decades ago, Yunus has, first and foremost through Grameen Bank, developed microcredit into an ever more important instrument in the struggle against poverty.[42]

For a young nation usually known for its massive poverty, natural disasters and political violence, the Nobel Prize was a source of national pride. Thousands of Bangladeshis poured onto the streets of Dhaka, with a big banner that read 'Professor Yunus, we are proud of you'.[43]

A PROCESSUAL FACE

The root metaphors of life in Confucianism are change (易), movement (动) and activity (行). It has been, and still is, a widely shared concept that whatever we experience in life is transitory, undetermined.[44] This is expressed beautifully in *The Analects*: 'The Master was standing on the riverbank, and observed, "Isn't life's passing just like this, never ceasing day or night!"'[45] Becoming, even from life to death, is to be celebrated. When his beloved wife died, the Chinese Taoist Zhuangzi (庄子 396?–286? BC) danced and sang with passionate gratitude. The Japanese Buddhist, Yoshida Kenkō (吉田兼好, 1293–1350), praised perishability in poetic language:

> If man were never to fade away like the dews of Adashino, never to vanish like the smoke over Toribeyama, but lingered on

forever in this world, how things would lose their power to move us![46]

The world does not just change, it changes in unrepeated, unpredictable ways:

> Since events are never repeated, their production is unfathomable. The *Tao* of heaven and earth is broad, is thick, is high, is brilliant, is far-reaching, is enduring.[47]
>
> The *Tao* of heaven operates mysteriously and secretly (天道玄默); it has no fixed shape (无容), and it follows no definite rules (无则); it is so great that you can never come to the end of it, it is so deep that you can never fathom it.[48]

Confucius, Zhuangzi and Kenkō are not alone in this view. On the other side of the globe, Heraclitus famously said that no one could step into the same river twice, while strategy scholars in 'the West' today are busy promoting 'process philosophy'.[49] But there are differences. Confucianism has no interest in replacing 'a universe of things' with 'a universe of events'. The 'ontology of process' is, from a pragmatic point of view, no better than the 'ontology of substance'. It is just another 'misplaced concreteness', as Alfred North Whitehead might say. Mistaking process metaphysics for process thinking is unfortunate, as it distracts managers from the front-line practical problems. What is the point lecturing the grieving mothers that the toxic Chinese milk that killed their babies was *process* not *substance*?[50]

Whereas in 'the West' uncertainty is usually considered a source of grief to be contained,[51] in Confucianism uncertainty is a desirable quality. 'The most precious thing in life is its uncertainty', said Yoshida Kenkō.[52] In China, traditional ink drawings are valued for their fuzziness; in Japan, people love the asymmetrical features of traditional pottery. It is such aesthetic appreciation that frees humans to think 'outside the box', perform unmediated practices, fulfil their potentials. This is in contrast with the rationalist tendency that uses modern physics to affirm 'the process nature of the universe' that fits uncertainty into familiar rules and logic. Does it matter to Muhammad Yunus what the sub-atomic world 'really' is when he persuades the poor villagers to benefit from microcredit?

In a pragmatic mindscape, uncertainty is beautiful, inviting, fulfilling. To live in the no-fixed-shape, no-definite-rules world, sensibility and responsiveness are indispensable virtues:

> The Master was entirely free from four things (子绝四): he had no preconceptions, no predeterminations, no obstinacy and no egoism.[53]
>
> The wise embrace all knowledge, but they should deal with what is of the greatest urgency.[54]
>
> The system of change is that by which the sage … examines their subtle emergence.[55]

Coping with urgency and emergence, there can be no proved principles. Confucius never pretended otherwise. While fully committed to the virtue of authoritative conduct (仁), for example, he refused to supply a context-free definition for this key ethical concept.[56] To Confucius, there were no immortal formulas; all depended on circumstances, always in-the-making.[57]

What, then, is the value of knowledge amid flows of uncertainty? Knowledge can be taken metaphorically as a walking stick. A walking stick generates hope, prompts action, embarks us on unknown paths. It implies no certainty or comfort, only the distance from the present to future alternatives. In a pragmatic world, the future is not determined but made, and depends on how we actually beat the path ahead. Remember 'Tao is made in the walking of it'? A walking stick always reminds us that our theories and past successes are merely a starting-point, they can be typically affected by the unknown path that we advance along. Knowledge as a walking stick allows us to experience what is not present,[58] and the leader's job is not to fix a destination but to engage people on a journey, encouraging everyone to help in shaping its course.[59]

The critical question in strategy becomes this: how are we to correlate emerging particulars so as to realise their productive effects in the service of common goodness?[60] This demands a shift beyond the mentality of predicting and controlling, towards a practice of sensitising and improvising. Always look at unfolding contingencies; be ready to change the rules and reinvent ourselves. These qualities underline the accomplishments of Deng Xiaoping, Bill Gates, Michael Dell and Honda, as we indicated in the last chapter. But process thinking is more than mere flexibility, important as that is. A subtle challenge to managers is how to move beyond ad hoc adjustment, incorporating process thinking into systems and operations so that companies can benefit from uncertainty in a disciplined way. Sounds paradoxical? This brings us to Toyota's production system at its best moments.

Toyota at its best: process integration[61]

To those interested in process thinking, how Toyota organises its production is far more significant than how many cars it sells. The Toyota Production System (TPS) as a set of philosophies and practices was developed to continuously ease the workflow by eliminating *muda* (無駄, non-value-adding work), *muri* (無理, excessive workload) and *mura* (ムラ, uneven pace of production).

The 'principle of flow' is not a Toyota invention; it underpinned both Frederick Taylor's scientific management and Henry Ford's assembly line. Indeed, Shigeo Shingo cited Taylor's *Principles of Scientific Management* as his inspiration. When asked in the 1980s by US delegations what inspired his thinking, Taiichi Ohno laughed and said he learned it all from Ford. But Shingo and Ohno took the idea of flow in a different way.

Taylor was most famous for breaking down the workflow into a series of small, repetitive tasks. He was in no doubt who was responsible for this 'time and motion' study: 'The work of every workman is fully planned out by the management at least one day in advance, and each man receives in most cases complete written instructions

... This task specifies not only what is to be done but how it is to be done and the exact time allowed for doing it.'[62] Managers alone would do the 'thinking', planning every detail *ex ante*, while workers did the 'doing', executing instructions. Behind this was a fear of dependence on skilled workers with high turnover rates. Jobs were designed so that workers would need only minimum training and be interchangeable. By separating thinking from doing, 'managing flow' broke up production.

Henry Ford shared Taylor's tenet, and pushed the division of labour to its ultimate extreme by dividing the workflow into ever smaller tasks so that unskilled workers could be slotted into any role in the 'process'. According to a highly influential book, *The Machine That Changed the World*:

> the assembler on Ford's mass-production line had only one task – to put two nuts on two bolts or perhaps to attach one wheel to each car. He didn't order parts, procure his tools, repair his equipment, inspect for quality, or even understand what the workers either side of him were doing. Rather, he kept his head down and thought about other things. The fact that he might not even speak the same language as his fellow assemblers or the foreman was irrelevant to the success of Ford's system.[63]

The 'thinkers', on the other side of the divide, rarely touched a product or entered a factory. Their job was to design tasks, parts and tools that could be handed down to the 'doers'.[64] At General Motors (GM), designers under Alfred Sloan were 'freed of the daily distractions' of actual production so that they could concentrate on preproduction design. Sloan housed them in GM's technical centre outside Detroit.[65]

'Divide and separate' was applied to 'thinkers', too. So much so that a *design* engineer who spent his whole career designing doorlocks only needed to determine how the locks should work, without ever considering how to make one – that was the job of the *manufacturing* engineers.[66] The designer and the manufacturer of the same lock might never talk to each other! At Chrysler, the manufacturing department was not represented on the product design committee until 1981.[67]

Ford's approach was powerful, able to reduce manufacturing effort by 60–90 per cent. It shortened the time for assembling a Model T, for example, from 13 hours in 1913 to an hour-and-a-half in 1914. A triumph. As one of its chief architects put it, 'if there is such a thing as a master principle, it is probably the principle of flow.'[68] This worked well for the mass production of a single model serving a stable market. But efficiency was achieved at the cost of flexibility and creativity. In the face of changing demands from uncertain markets, breaking up flows was no longer a solution, but a problem: Ford found it tremendously difficult to introduce a successor to the Model T. In his excellent book, *The New Competition*, Michael Best attributes the thinking–doing gap as 'the Achilles heel' of 'American capitalism'.[69]

In TPS, by contrast, managing flow means getting the right thing to the right place at the right time in the right quantity. The process must be understood, executed and improved by those who actually build the real thing. It is the production-line workers who own the process and make it work. In TPS, 'just in time' is about more than supply management. The aim is not waste reduction per se but 'smoothing the workflow'. During the actual process of making things, problems of design, production and quality are exposed and solved, with waste reduction as a side effect. The ideal is not a brilliant engineer inventing a big-bang design that drives down cost and improves quality, but an ongoing social practice in which problems are continuously identified and solved.

Hence, in TPS, workers are problem-solvers, not just machine-minders. They think when they work. Their task shifts from following instructions to refining the process. For this to work, first, the workflow must be easy for all to observe and operate. 'Mr Ohno said if a production line could not be understood with one's own eye, then it was not a good production line.'[70]

Then, breakdowns are viewed as opportunities for improvement, rather than causes of chaos. Every worker who detects a problem can stop the assembly line by pulling a cord above his work station so that fellow workers come together to work on the problem, on the spot. In this 'worldview', complete reliability cannot be designed into systems; it can only be achieved in the process of actual operations. Workers ask 'five whys' to trace each error to its cause and fix it, so that it will not occur again.[71] This is known as *genchi genbutsu* (現地現物, go and see for yourself to thoroughly understand the situation), during which the doers become learners and innovators through *hansei* (反省, relentless reflection) and *kaizen* (改善, continuous improvement).

Third, in contrast to the 'relay model' that links design, engineering, manufacturing and selling in sequence, in TPS people work as a 'rugby team' where 'every member of the team runs, tosses the ball left or right, and dashes toward the goal'.[72] Unlike the GM door-lock designer, TPS design engineers pay endless attention to 'manufacturability'. The 'thinkers' are, too, responsible for 'doing': even the most advanced engineers spend a month each year working in other functional areas. This allows dispersive knowledge to be brought to bear on design at each stage. As a result, Toyota in the 1980s was able to develop new models twice as fast and at half the cost, compared to its Detroit competitors.[73]

Finally, TPS integrates suppliers and customers into the system. Toyota organises suppliers into tiers and deals directly with a selected few. These suppliers receive functional, not physical, specifications, and submit prototypes for testing. If a prototype works, the supplier will get an order. This is the so-called 'Black Box Parts' system: Toyota does not design the 'inside' of auto parts, leaving that to suppliers. Instead, Toyota sends engineers to help the suppliers improve design, engineering, operation and quality control. Similar mechanisms are in place between first-tier and lower-tier suppliers.

On the demand side, Toyota builds up a network of dealers who develop a lifelong relationship with individual customers. As dealers visit the same customers frequently, Toyota does not have to build cars for unknown demands, but can convert to build-on-order production. Actual consumers thus become the first step in the extended *kanban* system.[74] *Kanban* (看板) was originally an internal system that linked upstream and downstream stations along the assembly line through returnable containers and slips signalling requests for part supplies. With the extension of *kanban*, dealers now send up-to-the-minute concrete orders to Toyota factories for specific deliveries with a short lead time.[75]

Over time, TPS integrates processes along both dimensions. Vertically, it is centred on 'shop-floor sovereignty' (*genba-shugi*, 現場主義), based on which engineers have to sell their ideas or equipments to the shop floor. As representatives of the 'customer', shop-floor workers make the final decision on whether or not to accept. Meanwhile, workers themselves are downstream-oriented, as a result of the continuous efforts of corporate educators; this is further extended to suppliers and dealers. Horizontally, once innovations are proven workable, they are quickly disseminated across factories via special projects and personnel rotations. Toyota calls this 'horizontal deployment' (*yoko-tenkai*, 横展開).

In the view of Edward Deming, a quality expert, TPS is an exemplar of integrated thinking and doing, systems and processes. Ironically, Toyota's recent worldwide car recalls can be seen as the consequence of breakdowns of such integration. What matters is thus not whether you're a GM or a Toyota, an American or a Japanese company, but which approach you adopt. When Toyota drifted away from TPS, the company failed; when others take TPS seriously, they catch up.[76]

Almost 25 years ago, Konosuke Matsushita, founder of the Matsushita Electric Industrial Company, had this to say:

> We will win and you will lose … Your companies are based on Taylor's principles. Worse, your heads are Taylorised too. You firmly believe that sound management means executives on

the one side and workers on the other, on the one side men who think and on the other side men who can only work.

We have passed the Taylor stage. We are aware that business has become terribly complex ... We know that the intelligence of a few technocrats – even very bright ones – has become totally inadequate to face these challenges. Only the intellects of all employees can permit a company to live with the ups and downs and the requirements of the new environment. Yes, we will win and you will lose. For you are not able to rid your minds of the obsolete Taylorisms that we never had.[77]

Harsh words, which one might dismiss as Japanese hubris of the pre-bubble 1980s. In view of pragmatism, however, Matsushita's comment is as fresh today as it was a quarter-century ago. It captures the two contrasting approaches to 'managing flow': breaking up flows by separating thinking from doing vs integrating flows by making thinking and doing a coherent process. How should we respond to Matsushita's criticism? How to understand process thinking and make it work in practice? The implications for business strategy could be enormous.

A CREATIVE FACE

Creativity is a great virtue in Confucianism. David Hall and Roger Ames comment on Confucius thus:

The signature of the qualitatively achieved person is found in the creativity, imagination, and influence to make community not only different, but better. Throughout the classical corpus, the *Shengren* (聖人 sage) is frequently associated with *zuo* (作 innovative activity). When Confucius says of himself, 'Following the proper way, I do not forge new paths (述而不作),' he is in fact with modesty saying, 'I am not a sage.'[78]

In *Zhonyong* (中庸), another Confucian classic, the praise of creativity is straightforward:

> Cheng (诚 creativity) is the way of *tian* (自然 nature); *cheng* is the proper way of becoming human ... It is thus that, for *junzi* (君子 exemplary persons), it is creativity that is prized.[79]

To Confucius, virtuous action is geared towards a future inventively imagined and actualised. 'Having this kind of spirit', the contemporary neo-Confucian Fung Youlan suggested, 'it is at one and the same time both extremely idealistic and extremely realistic, and very practical, though not in a superficial way.'[80] This underlines Nonaka's uncompromising insistence that it is knowledge *creation*, not knowledge per se, that fuels winning strategy.[81] To know is not to stockpile knowledge, but to continuously renew it through experimental activities. To strategise is to create: to design a new product, provide a new service, configure a new business model, build a new market, establish new relationships and live a new life. Confucian pragmatism is not just any pragmatism, it is idealistic pragmatism. We create, therefore we are.

This goes directly to a persistent puzzle: why do firms envision different futures and end up with different strategies, even at the same time, in the same industry? Environment-analysis models suggest that industry structure matters; for example, there are entry barriers to exploit for seeking monopoly rents.[82] Alternatively, according to the resource-based view, it is the bundle of particular resources that enables a firm to generate Ricardian rents.[83] Both, in our view, have an element of truth and should be part of strategic thinking. But, given that industry structures are supposedly transparent to everyone while firms that benchmark each other for decades can develop similar resources, why are there still good and bad performances, winners and losers?

In light of pragmatism, the differences are rooted in 作 and 诚 (creativity).[84] Effective strategies and above-normal performances are the result of idealist imagination and unconventional envisioning, not just industrial analysis or resource audits. Such idealistic pragmatism underlies Akio Morita's enduring mission: 'Sony does not serve markets; Sony creates markets.' To Sony, strategy is designed to envision a valued future and make it real. In the 1960s, popular

TV programmes caused people to change their daily schedules so as to avoid missing favourite shows. 'It was that control of people's lives that I felt was unfair.' How to bring forth a fairer world? Morita and his colleagues envisioned a future where people could watch a programme whenever they chose to. And they realised it with passion, curiosity, imagination and a sense of adventure, invented the video machine and brought freedom back to people. Via creativity, Sony asked the right question and found novel answers for it.[85]

Not just the future, but also the present is creatively 'brought forth'. This moves the pragmatist concern with context beyond a given 'environment' of Porter's five-forces sort. To know is to create: we must 'realise' the world, for example an industry or a market, in order to 'know' it.[86]

In *Zhonyong*, we read: 'Where there is creativity, there is understanding; where understanding, creativity.'[87] Why is it so? To the extent that knowledge is the capacity to act, our perceptions of a situation already incorporate concepts of certain actions that could be taken. In other words, the actions we are able to take are part of the situation we are in.[88] Given different capacities to act, people see different structures in the same industry and different opportunities or threats in the same environment. While there might be a same one reality, it means different things to different people. To Michael Dell, the 1980s PC industry 'clearly demanded a Direct model'; 'I still don't know why other people did not see it.'[89]

In their 2005 best-selling book *Blue Ocean Strategy*, Chan Kim and Renée Mauborgne posit that firms can generate growth by creating new value in an uncontested market space. With 'red ocean' strategy, companies compete head-on for known markets, struggling to outperform rivals in order to grab a greater share of existing demands. It is a zero-sum game. As products become commodities, cut-throat competition turns the crowded ocean red. In 'blue ocean' strategy, demand is created rather than fought for. In blue oceans, the wider, deeper potential of the marketplace is untapped, not yet known. Market boundaries and industrial structures exist only in people's minds, Kim and Mauborgne suggest, so managers should not let these 'constructs' limit their thinking. To blue-ocean-inspired managers, ample opportunities are always available; the crux is to unlock them. In blue oceans, competition becomes irrelevant; by expanding demand, new wealth is created.[90]

Look deeper and ask yourself: is extra demand 'out there', waiting to be discovered? Or does it not yet exist, to be envisioned and made real? To entrepreneur-managers, this is not a minor issue. Jay Barney, a key proponent of the 'resource-based' view, uses the metaphors 'mountain climbing' and 'mountain building' to illustrate the difference. A 'discovery' mountain-climbing perspective assumes that, due to market imperfection, opportunities arise exogenously, objectively out there, available to everyone. Different managers perform differently due to their different abilities to scan the environment, and to the levels of 'alertness' in recognising those opportunities.

A 'creation' mountain-building perspective, in contrast, sees opportunities as dependent on the action taken to create them. New demands are endogenously 'enacted' by entrepreneur-managers. Managerial action is the essential source of opportunities. Thoughtful managers take action, and in doing so form opportunities. Opportunities cannot be seen until they are created; they exist only because they are created when entrepreneur-managers generate, test, modify and act upon their perceptions of yet-to-exist markets.

For mountain-climbers, winning strategy lies in secrecy, speed to market and barriers that stop relevant information becoming publicly available and block others doing the same thing. For mountain-builders, on the other hand, competitive advantages come from path-dependent tacit learning, knowledge creation and dynamic capability, which is, even if publicly known, costly to imitate.[91]

In view of pragmatism, to know is to envision and realise, not just to discover or tap.[92] Those who create markets know better, which we can learn from Genichi Kawakami's experience.

Others researched the market; Kawakami created one[93]

Yamaha Corporation is famous for musical equipment, despite its later diversification into other product lines such as motorbikes and tennis rackets. The company became a classic case in strategic innovation because it successfully revitalised the piano market, not once but twice, led by Genichi Kawakami, the 'Piano Man'. Kawakami joined the company in 1937 after graduating from college, and succeeded his father as its president in 1950.

By that time, Yamaha had a high reputation for its instruments, but faced a dismal domestic market as the Japanese were busy rebuilding their ruined economy after the Second World War. Market research concluded that 'the market' was not there. The average Japanese house was too small for a piano, which was seen as an unaffordable luxury that few people could play. No pianists, no market. Outside Japan, the situation seemed equally unpromising. In 1953, Kawakami toured the US and Western Europe. Yes, the victorious countries were prospering and consumers were spending happily. There was a booming market for recreational products, but not for pianos. 'In the [post-war] culture of the jukebox, the piano seemed old-fashioned. Playing the piano was something that parents might do, but not their children.'[94] Solid data and field observations all indicated that the piano market was, to put it mildly, not ready.

Yet Kawakami envisioned a marketplace that the army of market researchers could not see. Morita proudly proclaims: 'Sony does not serve markets; Sony creates markets.' So did Kawakami of Yamaha. How did he do it? He invented the electronic piano and ran music schools. Built with digital technology, electronic pianos occupy little space and fit conveniently into the average Japanese home. They also have various functions that would be unimaginable in a traditional piano. These functions allow consumers to choose pre-set programmes, follow tuition, perform entertainments or just play for fun. Through its music schools, Yamaha taught the rudiments of music to children. Launched in 1954 in Hamamatsu, where the Yamaha factory was located, the music schools evolved into a worldwide franchise chain. More than five million children passed through the schools; later, many adults joined in. With technology, product and marketing innovations, Yamaha created a new market – customers who had never thought of owning a piano before. The company helped to fuel a music boom, making the piano a household necessity around the world.

Henry Ford is believed to have said: 'Ask the customers, they'll tell you they need a faster horse.' Steve Jobs told an interviewer: 'We do no market research. We just want to make great products.' Akio Morita wrote: 'Our plan is to lead the market with new products, rather than ask them what kind of products they want. The public does not know what is possible, but we do.'[95] And Peter Drucker reasoned: 'The first sign of fundamental change rarely appears among one's customers' because existing customers can answer questionnaires or interviewers only in terms of what they already know.[96] Indeed, when Kawakami talked to pianists, they simply asked for a 'better' piano, just as customers told Henry Ford they wanted a faster horse. These great thinker-businessmen remind us of the limit of researching 'the market': it tends to refer you back to red oceans.

By the mid 1980s, Yamaha was already the industry leader, producing high-quality pianos. In the traditional grand piano sector, Yamaha overtook Steinway and became the piano of choice, with 40 per cent of the global market. Not a minor achievement. Yet, by that time, demand was dropping at a rate of 10 per cent each year. In his *Harvard Business Review* article 'Getting back to strategy', the chief of McKinsey's Tokyo office, Kenichi Ohmae, describes the situation thus:

> [Around the world] most of these 40 million pianos sit around idle and neglected – and out of tune – most of the time. Not many people play them anymore. No one seems to have a lot of time anymore – and one thing learning to play the piano takes

is lots of time. What sits in the homes of these busy people is a large piece of furniture that collects dust. Instead of music, it may even produce guilt. Certainly it is not a functioning musical instrument. No matter how good you are at strategy, you won't be able to sell that many pianos – no matter how good they are – in such an environment.[97]

That was the 1980s; the booming 2000s piano market in the BRIC countries was yet to emerge. If you were Kawakami, what would you do, what could you do? Cut costs, proliferate models, invest more in your brand name, grab a bigger share of the shrinking pie? Kawakami did none of these. Nor did he label the piano business a 'dog', or divest it from the corporate portfolio, withdrawing from that 'unattractive' sector, as the conventional analysis models would have suggested. Rather, Kawakami determined to create a new market out of the millions of pianos already there. He achieved this by adding value to the existing pianos.

Based on a sophisticated combination of digital and optical technology, Yamaha developed a system that can record and reproduce each keystroke of piano performance with great accuracy. The record, using the same kind of 3.5" disks, can be processed in a personal computer, or sent back and forth over the phone line, in a way that is similar to uploading/downloading film clips from YouTube today. By retrofitting an idle piano with the Yamaha system at a cost of $2,500, customers could enjoy the piano in many different ways. You could record, or buy a disc of, the live performance of your favourite pianist; then, 'in effect, invite the artists into your home to play the same compositions on your piano.' You can do it in private, or use it to entertain your friends at home. If you play the violin, you can invite someone over to accompany you on the piano and record the performance. 'Then, even when your friend is not there, you can practice the piece with full piano accompaniment,' at the time of your choice. There are all kinds of possibilities.[98]

Think about the prospect of a market worth a $2,500 sale to each of the 40 million existing customers with pianos. In fact, the market is much bigger if you include software recordings, piano fine-tunes, revitalising the popularity of piano and associated services. A market in decline? A market reborn? A market created? However you see it, the reality is that the company, consumers and society all benefit.

Genichi Kawakami passed away in 2002, but his legacy lives on. In 2005, when Yamaha Music Schools opened in Beijing and Shanghai, they were fully subscribed within three days. Frequently, when we, during our academic visits, walk through the narrow streets of Bangkok or pass by apartment buildings in Mumbai, we hear the electronic piano, then the laughter of children, and then of the parents. Every time, we are deeply moved. 'Thank you Genichi', from our hearts. 'You bring so much happiness to ordinary families.'

A HOLISTIC FACE

It is almost redundant to stress holism, or the relational spirit, in Confucianism. As in other Eastern philosophies, there is a tacit emphasis on the relatedness of everything. The Chinese *kanji* 仁 (authoritative conduct) is made up of the elements 人 (person) and 二 (two). This etymological composition signifies the belief that 'unless there are at least two human beings, there can be no human beings'.[99] A Buddhist monk pressing his hands together whenever he meets a stranger is another symbolic appreciation: one's existence is related to, and depends upon, others.[100] The relatedness is further extended from man-to-man-ness to man-and-all-happenings: 天人合一 (Nature and Human are one). Zhuangzi famously taught us: 'We are one with all things.'

This tacitly shared worldview is not simply another model of 'metaphysical essence' because it immediately stresses how to act in this all-related world:

Between human beings:

> Authoritative persons establish others in seeking to establish
> themselves and promote others in seeking to get there
> themselves. Correlating one's conduct with those near at hand
> can be said to be the method of becoming an authoritative
> person.[101]
>
> Everything is here in me. There is no joy greater than to
> discover creativity in one's person and nothing easier in striving
> to be authoritative in one's conduct that committing oneself to
> treating others as one oneself would be treated.[102]

Towards Mother Nature:

> To fell a single tree, or kill a single animal, not at the proper
> season, is contrary to filial piety.[103]

The relational spirit nurtures an emotional attitude: deference
(恭), respect (敬), propensity (畏).[104] We share a moral existence with
Nature; our well-being and hers are one.

What does all this mean to strategy? To begin with, the holistic spirit inspires us to see that strategic issues tend to be multifaceted, reciprocal and mutually determined. Consider the hole in the
ozone layer over the Antarctic. As Bruno Latour, the French socio-
philosopher, supposes:

> The ozone hole is too social and too narrated to be truly natural;
> the strategy of industrial firms and heads of state is too full
> of chemical reactions to be reduced to power and interest; the
> discourse of the ecosphere is too real and too social to boil
> down to meaning effects. *Is it our fault if the networks are
> simultaneously real, like nature, narrated, like discourse, and
> collective, like society?*[105]

The moral of Latour's scenario, to quote Robert Hayes and William
Abernathy, is that in strategy there can be no 'simple and pure'

problem.[106] This we can also learn from the *Challenger* disaster. On a cold 1986 morning, the NASA space shuttle was prepared to take off. Behind the scenes, there were lengthy, intensive, emotional arguments over a possible technical deficit on the shuttle. In the end, the *Challenger* took off and, after 73 seconds, exploded in the sky, killing all seven astronauts on board. The technical deficit was no doubt a problem, but it alone did not lead to the explosion. Commercial pressure and political calculation pushed the technical deficit into, instead of preventing it from, disaster.[107] Managing-by-numbers blocks us from seeing such relatedness. In an interconnected world, reductionist thinking is dangerous. While professors can hide behind single-issue models, managers cannot. If they do, they will be punished by real-world complexities.[108] We will examine this in more detail in Chapter 8 through business cases that include the UK reality TV show *Big Brother*'s race row, BP's Gulf of Mexico oil spill, Made-in-China tainted milk and the LSE economists' blindmen confession.

That Confucianism has been able to enrich itself and remain alive is not for nothing. Confucius is quoted saying:

> Exemplary persons seek harmony not sameness (和而不同); petty persons do the opposite.[109]
>
> Exemplary persons associating openly with others are not partisan (周而不比); petty persons are the opposite.[110]
>
> The Master had no foregone conclusions, no arbitrary predeterminations, no obstinacy, and no egoism (子绝四).[111]

Preparing his disciples to become statesmen, Confucius urged them to respect 'the hundred schools' and instructed them to master 'the six arts': 'The *Book of Song* (诗) describes purposes; the *Book of History* (书) describes events; the *Book of Rite* (礼) directs conduct; the *Book of Music* (乐) secures harmony. The *Book of Changes* (易) shows the principles of the *Yin* and *Yang*. The *Spring–Autumn* (春秋) shows distinctions and duties.'[112] In the same spirit, when he reflects on Sony's history, Morita submitted: 'seeing things from many view-points is important for business.'[113] No wonder that firms are eager to seek outside-the-box ideas. GLG, a $19 billion London-based hedge fund, recently hired Niall Ferguson, an Oxford–Harvard history pro-fessor, because 'he doesn't think like everyone else'.[114]

Listening to others, we shall judge their voices not by how they fit with unchanged principles, but on their ability to help us cope with unfolding contingencies.[115] Competing theories are problem-atic only for those seeking theoretical elegance, not for those solving practical problems. Managers do not need to take up scholars' philo-sophical disputes; they must not translate competing theories into conflicting strategies. Remember: the hallmark of strategy is 'the pragmatic use of an available stock of ideas rather than disciplinary purity'.[116]

Theories do not and need not represent the world all in one. This is why 'fundamental choices' are harmful. Coherent strategy is not about once-and-forever integration of competing theories either; that goal is hopeless. Instead of 'which discipline is more basic: economics or sociology?', 'which approach will lead us to success: planning or learning?' or 'which tells us the truth: industry ana-lysis or resource-based view?', we shall ask 'what can we learn from Grameen Bank and Lehman Brothers?', 'why does a Direct model benefit Dell but not IBM?', 'how does Nintendo create new mar-kets by combining technology, product, marketing innovations?' and 'how can we learn from them and do better?' Then, we can be hopeful.

In searching for winning strategy, at the beginning, anything goes: 'don't restrict your imagination'.[117] We are not obliged to accept any single principle or model.[118] It is arrogant to consider any single theory universally and timelessly more true than others. 'In prin-ciple', Einstein had proved Newton 'wrong'; in solving practical prob-lems, Newton's 'wrong' theory time and again works well for us. In the end, something works better: some theories, judged by the

consequences of acting upon them, enable us to cope more effectively with here-and-now problems.[119]

Which theory works better? That is an empirical matter; it can
be investigated only when theories are put into use to get specific
jobs done. As pragmatic managers we know of no guide to principle
except successful performance. 'Theories are more or less useful,
that is all, dependent on the circumstance', Henry Mintzberg suggests.[120] We agree.

Harmonise Wal-Mart, Dell, McDonald's and win[121]

IT retailing is a crowded industry in China, very crowded. It is populated by almost all the big names: Toshiba, Sony, Fujitsu, Samsung,
HP, Dell, Apple, Acer, Lenovo and many more. Apart from their
own stores, these big players use local distribution channels, such
as Guomei and Suling. The huge local IT and consumer electronics
retailers are monopoly giants; in the struggle with smaller retailers, their economies of scale and ruthless tactics always win – well,
almost always.

Since 2001, a small start-up has managed to achieve yearly
growth at a three-digit rate, emerging as the number one IT
retailer in the east China area. In Jiangsu province, where the firm
is headquartered, its market share is near 70 per cent. Since 2003,
the firm has year by year been ranked 'No. 1 computer retailer in
China' by IDG and one of 'China's Top Ten consumer electronics
retailers' by *Twice China*. By the end of 2007, the firm had opened
over 200 stores in dozens of cities over the east China provinces,
selling 32 categories of 10,000 products under 1,000 brand names,
with a turnover of over ¥10 billion. In the thick red ocean, this
firm is an alien: unlike the exclusive big-name producers, it sells
IT goods of all brands; unlike the local 'pure' retailing giants, it
also sells products under its own ISO9001-2000 certified Hiteker
brand.

The firm is Hisap, or 宏图三胞 (Hongtu Shanbao) in Chinese.
How did it survive and grow?

Table 2.1 *Hisap's performance: start-up years*

Year	Number of chain stores	Revenue (billion *yuan*)
2001	5	0.5
2002	10	1
2003	20	2.5

Source: Weng 2004.

After graduating from college in 1988, Yuan Yafei, the Hisap founder, got a government job in a district audit bureau in the city of Nanjing. He felt the job boring, demeaning. In 1993, after Deng Xiaoping's 1992 'southern tour' pushed for wider, deeper, faster reform, the city of Nanjing tried an 'intercalation' policy that allowed government employees to leave their posts, without pay, for a period. Yuan was the first in the district to take this opportunity, to 'jump into the sea'. In the next few years, Yuan was one of the millions of petty pedlars in the street, buying and selling rice, cloth and anything else, with several ups and downs. In the mid 1990s, Yuan settled down to trading computers and related goods, not because he knew much about these things (he still does not know how to use email today), but because of the high margin. He purchased IT products from the southern city of Shenzhen and transported them to Nanjing for resale, sometimes on his back, literally. Yuan managed to earn some money, chiefly by aggressive advertising and competing on price. He knew very well that technology and product innovation were not his 'competence'; so where was his future? At that time, Guomei, Suling and a few retail giants were already growing rapidly.

In 1999, during a normal purchase trip to Shenzhen, Yuan visited a newly opened Wal-Mart store. He was impressed. All superstores sold the same things: vegetables, seafood, toilet paper and so on, but why did Wal-Mart do exceptionally well, with customers queuing behind all 40 check-outs? Yuan was curious. He bought a copy of the Chinese version of Sam Walton's *Made in America: My*

Story, and found so many useful ideas in it: the chain-store advantage, logistics systems, distribution centres, direct procurement from factories, global outsourcing, rapid reaction mechanism, customer one-stop shopping, all goods on display for customer to choose, comfortable shopping environment and on and on. Yuan read all night. He decided the petty pedlar experience was over for him. He imagined a new direction: adopt the Wal-Mart model and become a specialised IT chain store so as to benefit from economy of scale and superior customer service.

If this was the end of Yuan's learning process and the limit of his imagination, Hisap would have been no different from many other ambitious retailers, quickly destroyed by the giants in the red ocean. Were you bigger than Guomei or Suling? Why should the giants give you breathing space? What made Hisap tick was Yuan's open mind and inclusive attitude. He consciously combined Wal-Mart's retail chain store with Dell's direct model and McDonald's standardised service. More significantly, when he learnt, Yuan innovated.

It took only seconds for Yuan to appreciate the merits of the Dell model of direct sales – during his years of buying and selling computers, he had suffered a lot from various kinds of middlemen. Combining Wal-Mart with the Dell model, Yuan envisioned that economy of scale would enable him to bypass the middlemen, directly purchasing from producers and selling to the end consumer. Hisap would be the only middleman; for its own-brand products, there would be no middleman at all. The benefit to consumers could be huge.

During the learning process, Yuan transformed the Dell model so that it fit China's circumstances. Dell 'directs' to the customer via the Internet. In the US, this is Dell's winning formula. In China, it is its Achilles heel. China's consumers might be comfortable buying a few books or CDs on the Internet, but not anything as expensive as a computer. So Yuan 'directs' to the customer differently: with a human touch. In every Hisap store, next to the area for displaying and selling ready-made computers, there is a 'DIY

Point', more formally called 'Customised Computer Production and Maintenance Workshop', where professional sales representatives guide, in fact educate, shoppers, discussing their needs and recommending the right specifications. Yuan could afford this because there were plenty of well-trained, inexpensive engineers in China at that time.[122]

This was one of Yuan's dreams and now he was to realise it: putting the assembly line into the store. After the customer settles the order, she can watch her computer taking shape through the wide glass window that separates her from the on-site manufacturing process. For children, it is an exciting experience; for the family, it is a happy day out; for Hisap, it is the sale of one more own-brand computer. Hisap extended this tailored, integrated, complete solution to small and medium-sized businesses, too, at the 'Business Users' Purchasing Station', also located in the stores. All this is part of the standardised service that customers can expect from every Hisap store: the same quality, price, after-sale service call number and 'Nine Service Promises'. What you see is what you get across all Hisap stores, a practice modelled on McDonald's.

Proudly, Yuan calls his business model WDM (Wal-Mart+Dell+McDonald's), or 王大妈 (Grandma Wang) in Chinese. He founded Hisap in 2000 and launched the model in 2001 in the first Hisap store. Since then, the model has borne fruit, as evidenced by Hisap's three-digit yearly growth. Consolidated data shows that direct, large-scale purchasing enables the company to sell goods at prices 10–40 per cent lower than its competitors. To China's price-sensitive consumers, this is no small thing.

While Schumpeter promoted innovation through new combinations of technology, product, process and organisation,[123] Yuan dared to seek creative combination of business models.[124] Yuan knows where he wants to go, and is confident that his integrated business model will enable him to realise his ultimate dream.

AN ETHICAL FACE

What distinguishes Confucian pragmatism from relativism is the emphasis on moral conduct: 'Exemplary persons understand righteousness (义); petty persons are driven by personal gain (利).' Ethics is in everything we do: 'Becoming authoritative is in one's conduct'; 'How could authoritative conduct (仁) be at all remote?'[125] Confucius set a tough standard for his disciples: 'When a scholar stands in a prince's court and the *Tao* is not carried into practice, it is a shame to him.'[126] He praised those 'giving up life to achieve authoritative conduct', and, reflecting on his own life just before dying aged 73, said 'How dare I claim to be a benevolent man?'[127] From wise kings to the masses in the street, one's fortune or misfortune is shaped by one's conduct, not heavenly mandate.[128] Humans differ from animals because of the values we share and the purposes we pursue.[129] Doing strategy, as walking in the world, one needs to 'know the heavenly way [知天命]' – how to act ethically.[130]

From a holistic perspective, human conduct is contextual; according to process thinking, contexts are always changing. Accordingly, ethical conduct cannot be captured in fixed, universal codes. Although Confucianism offers substantive ethical values – shared by the mandarins and samurai, they included harmony (和), benevolence (仁), sincerity (诚), intellect (智), courage (勇), justice (义), loyalty (忠) and sympathy for the weak (善)[131] – the meanings of values depend on circumstances. To Confucius, ethics 'is specific and cannot be deduced from abstract general principles', 'general standards have no utility.'[132] Although fully committed to authoritative modes of conduct (仁), Confucius was unable to articulate a context-free code, as he himself made clear:

> I do not have fixed rights and wrongs.[133]
>
> The exemplary person in making his way in the world is neither bent on nor against anything; what is appropriate he will follow.[134]

The code-based approach is not workable because most business situations involve 'moral uncertainty', in which ethical issues cannot be starkly defined.[135] There are usually conflicting obligations and expectations. Is it right to grow bio-fuel instead of food crops on limited land when much of humankind is starving? Should Nike terminate its contract with a supplier that uses child labour in a country that cannot provide the poor with any sort of welfare net? Should a worker go out at 5:00 p.m. to serve a customer, or go home to care for her disabled kid?[136] As different ethical principles often yield conflicting implications for action, managers find themselves 'damned if you do, damned if you don't'.[137] Ethical codes are helpful for heightening sensibility, but useless and even confusing when making here-and-now decisions.

Rejecting code-based ethics does not mean we have to accept relativism. The Confucian solution is aesthetic consensus. In Confucianism, ethical consensus is achieved at aesthetic-practical levels rather than referring to 'reason' or 'method'. Hall and Ames call this 'the aesthetic orientation of Confucianism'.[138] It contrasts with, and complements, 'procedural ethics' (pace Habermas) or 'political resistance' (pace Foucault); the limits of the last two are on display in the conference halls of Copenhagen and the streets of Athens.[139] Hence, in a spirit shared by the Buddhists and the Taoists: 'The Master said, "In hearing litigation, I am like any other body. What is necessary, however, is to cause the people to have no litigation."'[140]

How to achieve 'no litigation'? Believing that character is the platform of action, Confucius promoted character cultivation, not just any character but 'whole character'.[141] In some traditions, a person can be viewed as immoral or amoral but smart.[142] In Confucianism there is a much closer link between intelligence and morality.[143] To be ethical requires one to act in accordance with one's knowledge of appropriateness. Knowledge is thus our ability to make situated right judgements. A wise, i.e. 'full', person is not just intellectually clever, but morally capable too: 'The Master said, "If a person with talents more admirable than those of the Duke of Zhou is arrogant and nig-gardly, the rest of his qualities are not worthy of notice.'"[144] Are the 'masters of the universe' at Bear Stearns, Lehman Brothers, Merrill Lynch and Royal Bank of Scotland smart? Interestingly, and perhaps not surprisingly, the new dean of the Harvard Business School, Nitin Nohria, makes it his priority to improve 'the character as well as the intellect' of his MBA students.[145]

To cultivate whole character, ritual practice (礼) is important because it forges people's action patterns (性). *The Book of Rites* (礼记) describes ritual practice as 'the actualisation of rightness'.[146] Confucius praised the exemplary person as one who 'has a sense of appropriateness as his basic disposition, and develops it in ritual practice'.[147] Through ongoing ritual practice, people cultivate and share aesthetic qualities. This enables them to avoid privileging any one perspective, and to appreciate each perspective on its own terms, in relation to unique circumstances. While the aesthetic-beautiful and the ethical-good are synonymous in Confucianism,[148] ritual practice promotes communication at a level that precludes the need for debates.[149] It is not a quick fix, not glamorous or spec-tacular, but broad, unhurried, subtle, forceful, enduring. It is 'soft power' at its best.[150]

One does not own a character, one practises it with joy beyond utilitarian purpose. The very first sentence in *The Analects* reads: 'Is it not pleasant to learn with a constant perseverance and appli-cation?'[151] Added to this was a ritual practice that cultivated deep deference towards ancestors, cultural heroes and historical leg-ends who supplied unwritten guidance for action. We read in *The Analects*: 'The *Tao* of Kings Wen (文王) and Wu (武王) has not col-lapsed utterly – it lives in the people. Those of superior character (贤) have grasped the greater part, while those of lesser parts have grasped a bit of it. Everyone has something of Wen and Wu's *Tao* in them.'[152] From this, Hall and Ames foresee a peculiar form of democracy in the future of Confucian societies: 'democracy of the dead.'[153] In the same spirit, we promote 'ethics of the dead': the dead heroes, legends and sages in our culture, tradition and history tell us how to act ethically. Real wisdom is enduring, even in a (post-) modern world.

Situated ethics: the Mazda turnaround[154]

In 1975, two years after the Arab oil embargo, Toyo Kogyo, the manufacturer of Mazda automobiles, was on the brink of bankruptcy: total losses of ¥17.3 billion, 31 per cent drop in car sales and 140,000 unsold cars in parking lots, with 37,000 employees on the payroll plus another 23,000 employed by dependent suppliers.[155] Faced with similar situations, GM and Chrysler closed factories, laid off workers and downsized benefits, which was followed by strikes, walk-outs, media criticism, bankruptcy proceedings, frantic lobbying and government guarantees at the eleventh hour. Mazda took none of these options, yet the company's turnaround was dramatic: 'By 1980, debt had been reduced considerably. Cash and deposits had grown by 100 billion yen. Revenues from sales had more than doubled and, most critically, production per employee had gone from 19 to 43 vehicles per year. Profits as a result of these improvements doubled in relation to their pre-oilshock levels.'[156]

No wonder the Mazda turnaround has become a classic strategy case study. Many factors and lessons have been suggested: implicit guarantee from the government, categorical support from the main bank, continuing loans from financiers, commitments from local city councils and companies to buy Mazda vehicles, efficiency improvements on the shop floor and changes in management. In the context of ethics, we focus on the dynamics of management–union relations – how Mazda used its workers intelligently while the workers made sacrifices for the common good – and the role played by national culture.

At the end of 1975, when the crisis deepened, Mazda's management called an emergency meeting with the union, asking workers to accept a postponement of 60 per cent of their end-of-year bonus payments and to approve a plan to send employees to dealers to boost sales. The yearly bonus, equivalent to 4.8 months' salary, was normally paid in two instalments. Due to the crisis, Mazda had no money to pay the December 1974 instalment. Postponing this payment would alleviate a critical cash-flow problem. This measure was later extended to the three following instalments over 18 months, resulting in an increase in annual cash flow of around ¥4 billion.

In addition, several thousand 'volunteer' employees were sent to the dealers around the country. They received two weeks of training, then visited potential customers door-to-door selling Mazda cars. The dealers would pay each worker-salesman ¥150,000 per month and cover local housing costs, while Mazda paid the remaining salary and benefits. This reduced the annual labour cost of ¥1.8 million per dispatched worker. Initially, dispatched workers, leaving their families behind, served for six- to twelve-month intervals. Later, workers were sent out, with their families, for two years with an optional third year. Some 8,000 workers participated in the first phase, while the average annual number of dispatched workers grew to about 2,900 during the second phase. Altogether, this scheme saved Mazda ¥30.1 billion in labour costs over the seven-year turnaround period, and brought in an additional 400,800 auto sales, three times the excess inventory on hand at the start of 1975. Surprisingly, the dispatched workers sold more cars than ordinary salesmen: customers were impressed by their professional knowledge. After all, who knew the car better than the people who built it? Furthermore, when workers returned to the factory, they had lots of fresh ideas about the market, and made numerous improvements on the shop floor.

Together, in cost-cutting terms, the two measures generated over half of Mazda's total savings in 1975, and a quarter in 1976, at critical moments in the crisis. Although much more was involved in turning Mazda around, the union's cooperation and the workers'

SPIRITS OF PRAGMATISM 61

sacrifices were a key factor in reducing cash-flow pressure and unsold inventory and hence surviving the crisis.[157]

After the fact, the two measures seem all the smarter. Mazda was not a charity – as a company it had to get value out of its workers when sales were down and payrolls up, particularly given the impossibility of lay-offs due to lifelong employment commitments. The case fits well with the popular image of Japan: workers' company loyalty; management's cosy paternalism; and warm corporatism linking management, workers and unions. It is tempting to reach the quick conclusion that Mazda was just one more 'typical Japanese' case illustrating the role that culture can play at the micro level in determining business success. Compare Chrysler or GM with Mazda, look at how they managed turnarounds differently. The implication might be that Japan is unique. However enviable the Mazda case, there is nothing the Americans, the British or even the Chinese can do to emulate it.

Yet the story was more complicated than stereotypes would suggest. Before the 1974 emergency meeting, 'management were not fully open with the union when the company's problems became serious. The two sides sat down on a regular basis to talk about the company's results, but the excess of inventory and the financial difficulties were not seriously examined'.[158] On the other side, according to the Mazda union president Hayato Ichihara, 'our union had always negotiated with strong member support. We would take a strike vote and go in with a threatening posture. The members supported a union that fought hard with management for the gains it achieved.'[159]

When the two rescue measures were suddenly put on the table, the atmosphere became extremely tense and the union was under enormous pressure. The situation was nonetheless clear: if the company went under there would be no other jobs for the workers; Hiroshima was virtually 'Mazda city'. 'We are all in this together': sacrifices must be made. The union president recalled:

> Toyo Kogyo is a crucial part of the Hiroshima economy. If it
> fails we lose our jobs and so do many of our neighbours. We had
> no choice but to do our part in the effort to help Toyo Kogyo.
> There would have been immediate public disapproval and
> great dissension in the union if we had resisted management's
> proposals even though the company's problems were primarily
> management's responsibility.[160]

Still, there was much hard bargaining. The company agreed to arrange a bridge loan for union members who could not meet personal payments as a result of the bonus postponement. The company also promised that: (1) the dispatch programme would be voluntary; (2) appropriate living standards and working conditions would be guaranteed; and (3) no career would be penalised if a worker did not perform well as a salesman. The union was granted the right to monitor the programme, visit dispatched workers and check personal files in order to protect workers' interests. The union explained this to the workers and managed to get their agreement within three weeks.

Although the dispatch programme was 'voluntary', there was no flood of volunteers. Instead, managers were allocated targets, and nearly every section was expected to supply 'volunteers'. Middle-aged family men generally took the lead: section heads, work-group leaders, senior workers and white-collar employees who had the greatest obligation to set an example. Then, however reluctantly, the 'rest' had to step forward and take a turn; there was great peer pressure once the programme was rolling. Changes in management personnel, philosophy and style also made a difference. The arrival of the taskforce led by Tsutomu Murai from the main bank office in Tokyo, the diminishing power of the then president K Matsuda of the founding family, and the leadership of the new president Yamasaki, who had worked his way up through the ranks inside Mazda, all helped to unlock the strength of thousands of Mazda employees. They pulled together, contributing hard work, sacrifices and creativity for the common good. Richard Pascale and Thomas Rohlen, who studied and published the case, comment:

> While it is clear that this sacrifice was far from a spontaneous outpouring of company loyalty, it was the product of the strong sense of common interest and collegial responsibility (especially in the older workers). Japanese culture and the Japanese orientation toward company organisation provided the foundation of obligation that resulted in acquiescence to the plan. The results, however, were not simple to achieve or just a product of Japanese values. A great deal of management effort and union cooperation were required ... Western values, unionism, management assumptions, and employment systems do not favour acceptance of such an approach. While cultural and other Japanese factors help 'explain' success, they did not cause such a program. But they do provide a positive context ... From the union's standpoint, Murai's arrival was the turning point. And following in this course Yamasaki as president actively pursued a philosophy of cooperation with the union. States the union president: 'K Matsuda never appeared in collective bargaining; it was done by the director of industrial relations. In contrast, Mr Yamasaki always attends collective bargaining personally.'[161]

Is it ethical to ask workers to leave their families for a year or to postpone their personal financial commitments in order to improve the company's cash flow, given that we now know many workers made sacrifices under pressure from peers and targets? Taking the case off from that specific time, place and circumstances, we do not have a meaningful answer; applying universal principles might have driven Mazda to the wall, bringing everyone down with it. That is the problem of code-based ethics. Standing in the workers' shoes, recognising that your job and future were tied inextricably with the fate of the company, knowing that Mazda executives were taking deep salary cuts while workers took none, knowing also that even Mr Murai, the executive vice president, was working 18 hours a day and seeing his wife only once a week during those turnaround years, you'll understand why the workers decided to participate.

Interestingly, and perhaps not surprisingly, the turnaround also relied on the 'whole character' of employees. The new president, Yamasaki, initiated job rotations between section heads and ordinary workers, introduced Zen meditation and organised competitions between assembly teams, a 50-km mountain climb up Mt Oro and a 'walking rally' – a night-time contest in which teams learned to navigate through the city without watches. The Director of Training explained: 'the underlying purpose is to train intensively in order to build each employee's character. Character provides the basis for individual day-to-day capability.'[162] Ah, Confucius is alive not only in schools, but also in companies. With this, let us turn to the last of the six spirits.

A COMMUNAL FACE

That a communal spirit is paramount in Confucianism is not in question.[163] Nor is the spirit alien to contemporary strategy thinking. Today, we read and hear with growing frequency that the firm is a 'wealth-creating community, with members rather than employees' (Handy),[164] that 'a company is not a machine-with-people. It is actually the inverse: a self-perpetuating work community of people-with-machines' (de Geus)[165], that we should 'treat the enterprise as a community of engaged members, not a collection of free agents' (Mintzberg),[166] and on and on. Given this, the interesting questions are rather: what makes a community a community, how do relationships function inside and between communities, and what does all this mean to strategy?

To answer the first question, one might suggest 'belongingness', 'identity', 'shared destiny', and so on. But these concepts are not indigenously Confucian. Furthermore, these 'things' are outcomes, not causes. We do not belong to a community; a community is not to be found or joined. Instead, a community has life and effect only in our collective experience. This is clearly manifested from the very beginning of the Confucian civilisation.

The Chinese *kanji* 聖 (sage) is composed of an 耳 (ear, to listen) and a 口 (mouth, to speak), which indicates that the legitimacy and power of a sage are not God-given but achieved via talking and listening to people, sharing his vision with others and taking their views into account.[167] Another character 君子 (exemplary person) is similarly defined by the etymonic elements 尹 (to oversee, manage, order, regulate) and 口 (to talk, express, persuade). 君子 is then associated with 群 (to gather, be together), which combines an exemplary person (君) and an adumbrated picture of sheep (羊). The implication is that 君子 is the person gathering people, acting together with and leading them. The authority of the sages and exemplary persons is therefore measured by their success in drawing the hands and hearts of people together to realise common goodness.[168] No talking, listening or acting together, no community; no community, no authoritative conduct and we cease to be human. Ralph Stacey, a researcher in complexity and organisation studies, posits that strategy is about people talking to each other in localities;[169] and Akio Morita attributes Sony's success to its founders' ability to mould a group of 'young and cocky engineers' into a community where 'everyone was encouraged to speak out'.[170] We are not born into communities; we create and maintain communities.[171]

The Confucian ideal of community is harmony and Confucian harmony is, in contrast to mistaken stereotypes, generated from diversity not uniformity. Confucius said, 'exemplary persons seek harmony (和), not sameness (同)'.[172] A contemporary neo-Confucian Fung Yulan elaborated:

> *Tong* (同) means uniformity or identity, which is incompatible
> with difference. *He* (和) means harmony, which is not
> incompatible with difference; on the contrary, it results when

> differences are brought together to form a unity. But in order
> to achieve harmony, the differences must each be present in
> precisely their proper proportion, which is *zhong* (中, balance).
> Thus the function of *zhong* is to achieve harmony.[173]

Hence, Confucian harmony is not equivalent to 'equilibrium' or 'stability'. Instead, it incorporates specific personal goods, in the plural, in the making. Strategy is about adjusting and coordinating such personal goods into a shared common good appropriate to particular situations. Since situations are ever-changing in unrepeated and unpredictable ways, the more diverse a community's capacities to act, the more chances it will have to sense, seize and realise emerging opportunities. Economists, including the Nobel Prize-winner Douglas North, call this 'adaptive efficiency'.[174] A Confucian community is therefore not intolerant of diversity; it needs diversity to flourish. One division manager told the Harvard-trained professor Takahiro Fujimoto that, during the formation of the TPS, the firm worked like an 'open tournament of new ideas' in which anyone, regardless of rank, might jump in.[175]

Promoting diversity is not easy. Amid the 2008–2009 banking crisis, Chuck Prince, the then Citigroup chief, remarked, 'as long as the music is playing, you've got to get up and dance'.[176] This was not healthy diversity; it was dream-walking, group-think. This happened in the supposedly freest market and most democratic society in the world, and it harmed us all in a big way. It is a challenge to everyone, ancient and modern, East and West.

Looking outward, the Confucian communal spirit nurtures mutual respect between communities. A Confucian community is not simply a group: 'The Master said, "Exemplary persons are self-possessed but not contentious; they gather together with others, but do not form cliques (群而不党)." '[177] And what differentiates a community from a gang? Tan Sor-hoon explained:

> A group is not a community in the ideal sense unless it
> contributes to the growth of other groups, of individuals outside

it but affected by its actions. A community is a group that interacts flexibly and fully in connection with other groups to form a greater community ... When it fails to do so, it limits the possibilities for growth of its own members and therefore of itself.[178]

Russell Ackoff wrote in a similar spirit: 'ethics necessarily requires the preservation and increase of legitimate options available to others as well as to oneself. Legitimate options are those that do not reduce the options available to others.'[179] Sounds simple, but it is a tough call. During the mid 1920s, GM, in conjunction with oil and tyre companies, acquired the electric rail network and then uprooted the tracks. The purpose was 'strategic': 'to enlarge the market for cars, oil and tires by blocking other modes of transportation.' As a consequence, consumers today have plenty of options, as long as they involve a car.[180] In the 2010s, our problem with Facebook is not its intention to make a profit, but the way it goes about making it: Facebook turns user data into 'publicly available information' without giving users a clear choice.[181]

In promoting the communal spirit, Confucius was not a soft-headed idealist who ignored power and conflict; his teaching is explicitly sociological and political. When asked about governance, Confucius replied: 'What is necessary is to rectify names ... If names be not correct, language is not appropriate to actuality. If language is not appropriate to actuality, affairs cannot be carried on to success.'[182] This is Confucius' famous teaching of 'rectifying names' (正名): the actual must be made to match the name. Living in a period of chaos, war and suffering, Confucius promoted this teaching in order to restore righteousness and harmony. Because he insisted that rectifying names must begin from the top, his teaching has usually been interpreted as a call for obedience below. What is lost in such a translation, however, is the communal ideal that rectification of names serves the many, not the few. This is the Confucian hierarchy: 'the people are the most important element; the spirits of the land and grain are secondary; and the sovereign is the least.'[183] Hence, when a community came to rectify names, it was not just the 'rebellious ministers and villainous sons who were struck with terror', but also the 'disordered, distorting sovereigns'.[184] In modern times, with rectification of names starting at the top, there will be no hiding place for badly behaved politicians, greedy CEOs or community-destroying 'strategies', of the Lehman Brothers and Chinese toxic milk sort. In this spirit, we must keep asking at each here-and-now moment: how shall we live, what should we do, in the name of what, for whose benefit, do our strategies serve communal goodness?

The Third Italy: 'collective entrepreneurs'[185]

Distinct from the northern industrial heartland of Milan–Turin–Genoa (the First Italy) and the agricultural south (the Second Italy), the Third Italy covers the 'industrial districts' of the north-central part of the country, including Prato, Como and Biella. Each district specialises in a range of loosely related products, such as clothing, furniture and machinery, and consists of associations of thousands of small craft firms employing no more than ten, with an average five, workers. Each firm concentrates on a specific stage of the technical process leading to final products. Collectively, these firms pursue a design-led, high-quality, high-skill, high-income, continuous innovation strategy. With independent ownership, autonomous decision-making and cooperative production, these mutually adjusting firms act as a 'collective entrepreneur'. Each firm depends on the existence of others; together they lead rather than react to markets.[186] The internal interdependence of these firms generates externally specialised capabilities and regional advantage, which enable the Third Italy to compete successfully in global markets. Italian furniture produced in the districts, for example, collapsed the entire furniture industry of north London in the 1980s. At its peak, the districts' small-firm-based economy enjoyed the highest rates of investment, new firm creation, per capita income and export in the country, when, as a whole, Italy was experiencing the fastest rate of growth of the big four European economies.[187]

The Third Italy supplies much food for thought for strategy. In many ways, these small firms anticipated the innovative start-ups of the Silicon Valley although they were not in high-tech sectors and did not rely on venture capitalist funding nor end up becoming large corporations. On the other hand, unlike many Chinese-Taiwanese small original equipment contractors that adopt 短-平-快 (short-term objectives, general-purpose equipment, quick returns) strategy moving in and out of geographical areas for low costs, the Third Italy small firms enjoyed high margins and good brands while being rooted in stable localities.

Significantly, the Third Italy embodies a unique way of competing on community advantages. In Japan, as the Toyota and Mazda cases illustrate, exemplar 'business communities' take the form of exclusive, hierarchical networks of businesses, configured around a leading firm, sustained by a main bank, relying on tiers of suppliers. The Third Italy, on the other hand, excels in partnering small, specialised firms without a family head at the top or a big brother at the centre. The question is how they did it.

A working community relies on mutual trust, and the Third Italy is no exception. Without such a social medium, no entrepreneur would invest in specialised capability useful only for a specific stage along a dispersed production line.[188] Studying the Third Italy, the economist Masahiko Aoki stressed that 'inherited' social capital is inadequate, workable social capital must be 'invested'.[189] For Michael Best, similarly, the communal spirit should not be regarded as an 'exogenous parameter': 'For community is subject to erosion unless the norms, shared understandings, and mutual obligations that reinforce it are sustained by a collective memory and reinforced by shared activities.'[190] In our terminology, community is not received, but made and remade. There is no fatalism here; different people can build community in their own ways that suit local histories and circumstances.

The Third Italy achieved this innovatively. Helped by national craftsmen's associations and local governments, local small firms established sectoral business associations and service centres. In the province of Modena, for example, there are 14,000 member firms, representing 39,000 artisans and dependent workers, grouped into 11 sector federations such as metalwork, clothing and woodworking. For a membership fee, the service centres provide targeted services including accounting, finance, real estate, export marketing, bulk purchasing and computer-aided design. As woodworking firms require sawdust extraction, for example, the collective provision of such a service from the service centre reduces the cost for each firm. The service centres permit small firms to achieve a 'minimum efficient scale of production'. There is no need to have expensive in-house accountants, marketers, general staff or general-purpose equipment, nor to purchase these from the market. The bigger, the better, always? Think again.

Perhaps most telling are the financial consortia that facilitate favourable bank loans for member firms. Banks lending to small firms rely on the judgement of entrepreneurs' potential. This is hard to do because data is not economically available. Even if you can buy data, you cannot buy honesty, and without honesty information is suspect. Facing numerous specialised markets and thousands of small firms, the best source of honest information is communal peer review. Hence the birth of the Loan Guarantee Consortia. In Modena, the consortium has 3,500 member firms and 18 board members drawn from the ranks of the craftsmen and association officials. The consortia, relying on the craftsmen's knowledge, evaluate each entrepreneurial proposal, assess incentive and the ability to pay back a loan, as well as means for recovering funds in case of default. If the proposal is accepted, the application is then sent to the banks with a loan guarantee from the consortia. With this guarantee, the banks are more willing to lend. As a result, the consortia are able to reduce the interest on loans to member firms below that of non-members. By joining the consortia, member firms thus receive a substantial financial benefit on the basis of their innovative ideas and communal standing. The banks receive benefits, too. Out of a total of over $40 million in loan guarantees during a ten-year period, only $70,000 was unrecovered – a rate of 0.175 per cent. Mutual trust and obligation is the key: 'the person who receives a loan from the cooperative will stay up at night thinking of ways of repaying his loan; whereas the person who receives a bank loan will stay up at night thinking of ways of not repaying his loan.'[191] A consortium is neither a private business nor a public agency. It is rather a purpose-built communal institution. Its success lies in the benefits of collective action that go beyond the reach of individual small firms. Individuals honour the principle of reciprocity because it is enforced by other members. They recognise that cooperation with other members today will be repaid tomorrow. This does not mean that people 'naturally' care about the common good, but that building a community can lead to a supply of common goods as long as the social medium is safeguarded by the community's ability to exclude individuals. Purpose-built communal institutions are an effective solution to the 'tragedy of the commons'.[192]

Why don't we see such successful industrial districts duplicated around the world? According to Aoki and Best, the Third Italy succeeds not in a vacuum but in certain historical conditions. First, since the end of the Second World War, the Third Italy region has been governed by the Italian Communist Party and its associates, which during the anti-fascist underground period developed a democratic consensus and alliances with small businesses. They were 'more a political party of the community than a party based upon doctrinaire principles of communist political theory'.[193] Nowhere was small business more ably supported by local government than these areas, where private interests were deliberately channelled in pursuit of common goodness. Second, the small, specialised firms were an unintended consequence of the collapse of integrated companies in the 1960s due to the failed national industry policy and labour disputes. Skilled workers released from closed companies were encouraged to purchase specialist equipment at discounts and to establish their own enterprises. Finally, geographical proximity is an important factor. The owners of those small firms were not strangers, they had already 'invested a significant amount of social capital as the members of the civic community and/or labour organisations which confronted the old integrated companies'.[194] The sectoral associations, service centres and industrial districts they built together allowed them to 'interact socially and politically as well as economically'.[195]

Hence the most useful question is not whether to duplicate the Third Italy, but how to understand the significance of communal practice in business strategy, to challenge the ill-conceived 'contradictions' between market and plan, private and public, the economic and the political. We see Toyota and Mazda doing it one way, the Third Italy another. In addition, we have the Silicon Valley and the Singaporean, Malaysian and, more recently, Indian and Chinese experiments. The communal spirit is alive and communal strategy evolving. There is no one universal best way. Managers and policy-makers must build communities that are appropriate to their unique circumstances, and this is the essence of pragmatism.

SUMMARY

We want the six 'faces' we bring forth – practical, processual, creative, holistic, ethical and communal – to move us beyond common-sense pragmatism and shed new light on the understanding of knowledge and strategy. After looking at each of the trees, it is now time for a brief overview of the forest.

Confucian pragmatism views action and knowledge as one; actions are theory-latent and hence theory matters. We appreciate Kurt Lewin's famous epigram that there is nothing so practical as a good theory. Yet we move a step further, asking: what is a good theory and what is it for? In the spirit of pragmatism, good theory is actionable. It begins with understanding situated emergencies, and focuses on shaping and solving problems in order to make favoured differences. What is true depends on who we are (values), where and when we look at it (context) and what we bring forth with it (consequences). Not 'ideal-type', 'generic' values, contexts or consequences, but situated, particular, here-and-now *whos, whats, wheres, whens* and *hows*. If knowledge is 'justified true brief', this is how it is justified.[196]

What is strategy in such a view, then? Strategy is a 'science of the specific': there can be no universal, timeless 'laws of business',[197] no 'one best truth' for strategy,[198] no 'rule for riches',[199] no 'foundation for being ethical'.[200] Strategic opportunities and successes are rooted in situated particulars,[201] local knowledge,[202] entrepreneurial envisioning,[203] alertness,[204] communal judgement[205] and political manoeuvring,[206] which can rarely be generalised or formalised. If there are laws of competitive advantage, competitors will all follow them, resulting in the advantage being quickly competed away.[207] So much so that, posits Michael Porter, strategy is about deliberately choosing to be different, about doing different things and doing things differently.[208] Creativity is at the heart of strategy. In this view, benchmarking is a useful tool, but with limits. It may bring short-term gain by benefiting from other people's experiences, but it is unlikely to enhance the innovative capabilities critical for long-term success. With benchmarking alone, you cannot create something unique, novel or outstanding; the best you can hope for is me-too strategy. The same can be said of 'best practice'. Me-too strategies and 'best practice' amount, in the long run, to strategic suicide: you struggle in the red ocean, or die in it. 'Strategy is what is right for you', not for 'average companies', John Kay, the former head of Oxford's Business School, reminds us.[209]

To pragmatism, a practically wise strategy is based on technical competence, situated judgement, moral sensibility, communal justification, openness to diversity and on-the-spot experimentation. In Part II, we will take a more detailed look at what Drucker called 'specifications' of pragmatic strategy, and investigate what strategies look like in a pragmatic world.[210]

PART II What do pragmatic strategies look like?

人能宏道，非道宏人。
《论语》

*It is Man who makes Tao great,
not Tao that makes Man great.*
– Analects

3 Strategies in a pragmatic world

What would strategies look like in light of pragmatism? In this second part of the book, we invite readers to investigate the 'specifications' of pragmatic strategy. We shall conduct our investigation in the context of the purposes, contents, functionalities and processes of strategy. This chapter outlines the major features of pragmatic strategy, while the next focuses on strategy formation. Our aim is to explore how a pragmatic turn will enable us to see strategy differently, wisely. We shall draw from cases such as China's economic reform; Intel Corporation; Sony's Akio Morita; *USAToday*; cochlear implants; the e-commerce company Alibaba.com; Lenovo, the Chinese PC-maker; 3M Corporation's Post-it Notes; and Huawei, the world's fastest-growing telecom equipment provider. This is mainly a descriptive and explanative investigation, to prepare readers to proceed to the next part of the book where we shall explore normatively what to do and how to do it in the search for pragmatic strategies.

BEYOND TALKING AND WALKING

Henry Mintzberg famously stated: 'it is important to remember that no one has ever seen a strategy or touched one.' We can hold a mobile phone in our hands, take pictures of the clouds in the sky or enjoy an opera at the theatre. None of these things can be said about strategy. What and where is it? Mintzberg further suggests that strategy is merely a figment, an abstraction, perhaps even an illusion, in one's mind.[1] If we don't imagine that we have a strategy, it simply won't exist. Has anyone seen God or touched his hand?

In the spirit of pragmatism, we have a different view: strategy is a life experience, always with us, almost everywhere, in different ways and many forms. We invite managers to look around our experienced world. What shall we find?

Theories: what we *talk* about. Theories help, or mislead, managers to make sense of pressing concerns, situated problems and possible solutions. According to Ralph Stacey, talking is walking and strategy is conversation, i.e. what and how we communicate with each other.[2] Historically, strategy began when we started systematising and codifying it, generating prescriptions on how to strategise better:[3] from Sunzi's *The Art of War* on bamboo slips to *Strategy for Dummies* at modern airport bookshops. We are no longer able to forget Drucker, Chandler, Porter, Prahalad and Nonaka. Theories inform actions in one way or another, with or without our awareness. Theory matters, for better or for worse. This is why we write books (including this one), publish papers, attend seminars, study for an MBA and create a huge business media industry. And this is why, despite damning criticism, strategic theories proliferate and business education is booming.[4] We cannot turn ourselves back into apes; we grow up in a theorised world. What we can do is create and act upon better theories.

Exemplars: what we *believe*. These are widely accepted, tacitly shared narratives of what strategy is and how it should be done, in forms of 'best practices', '*Fortune* Businessman of the Year', etc. Managers may be sceptical of theories, but seldom question exemplars. Exemplars are the 'shapers' and 'movers' of strategy. Exemplars can be general and grand, such as Total Quality Management and Business Process Re-engineering, or detailed and handy, such as 'portfolio planning matrix' or 'balanced scorecard'.[5] Exemplars also reflect legendary companies and heroes, such as the legends of Honda conquering the US motorcycle market and Dell inventing the Direct model. Over time, they become icons and metaphors. There are life cycles, too: new exemplars quickly eclipse old ones, and business schools and consulting houses are eager and skilful in this. General Motors in America and Lord Browne of BP lost their shine, but we now have Google and Huawei, plus Steve Jobs, Ratan Tata and many more. The details don't matter, the inspiration does. And this is the point of exemplars: they inspire millions of entrepreneur-managers to make our world a different place.

Contents: what we *have*. Firms have visions, missions, objectives and so on, articulated or otherwise. These are the 'carriers' of a firm's projected identity: who we are, what we are for, what we do, how we do it. To Peter Drucker, strategy is the 'theory of the business'. Every firm has one, and the manager's job is to make sure it works.[6] David Collis and Michael Rukstad suggest that 'companies that don't have a simple and clear statement of strategy are likely to fall into the sorry category'.[7] Put positively, clear strategy helps managers to focus energy and take purposeful action. Companies also need to be seen as serious: investors will not give you money without seeing a convincing strategy. Rightly or wrongly, as John Kay observes, no self-respecting business today would be without 'these things'.[8] This is true not just for businesses, but also for the public sector, non-for-profit organisations and charities. In some organisations, renewing strategy at all levels is now a compulsory, routine undertaking. Be mindful, though: in 1999, Enron declared, 'We work with customers and prospects openly, honestly and sincerely. When we say we will do something, we will do it; when we say we cannot or will not do something, then we won't do it.'[9] What you see is what you get? Not necessarily.

Activities: what we *do*. Strategy is the art of accomplishing what we want to achieve.[10] It is about situated judgement and collective justification, skilful persuasion and timely manoeuvre, decisive decision-making and muddling-through, amid complexity, ambiguity and uncertainty. Not standard 'strategic activities', but specific ones. It is about how things actually play out in the boardroom as well as on the shop floor, at critical moments as well as through incremental adjustments. Until recently, strategic studies has focused mainly on 'generic patterns' retrieved from databases and 'knowledge warehouses', ignoring strategy as situated creativity.[11] Not surprisingly, for some, these 'macro findings' are the road to hell and 'focus on the details' is the rallying cry.[12] But 'details' are meaningful only when they serve a compelling purpose. Be aware of what Sumantra Ghoshal called 'active non-action': running all the time, extremely busy, but getting nowhere, perhaps even not knowing what one is doing.

Consequences: what we *live*. We may choose to condemn theories, joke about exemplars, burn strategic plans and withdraw from any activity deemed strategic. So, strategy has nothing to do with you? Strategy doesn't matter? Think again. We cannot escape the consequences of strategy. Consequences may be beneficial or harmful; they are here to stay and we all live with them. 'While practitioners do not have to justify their decisions intellectually, they must be able to survive the consequences', Taieb Hafsi and Howard Thomas remind us.[13] We enjoy the iPhone – an intended outcome of Apple's bold strategy; we love the Internet – the unintended consequence of a Cold War invention; and we are still suffering from the banking crisis that no one intended – even the few bankers who 'strategised' subprime mortgages did not intentionally create mayhem.[14] Russell Ackoff wisely advised us: plan, or be planned for.[15] It is in our own interest to engage in strategy. We humans are a learning species; we learn from consequences. We can generate something positive out of even the worst consequences.

This is our pragmatic view: strategy is the network effect of theories, exemplars, contents, activities and consequences. All these involve in strategy, in making a difference. Every strategy can be seen as such an interactive process and contingent accomplishment. One aspect of strategy – talking, believing, having, doing or living – cannot be understood or coped with properly without being linked to other aspects. Remember the holistic spirit? Activity without informed justification is a nightmare, micro activity cut off from macro happenings goes nowhere, process is trivial if it is non-consequential, knowledge is meaningless if not put to work and strategy is worthless if it is not practical. Who translates theories and

Industries, markets, society, eco-environment

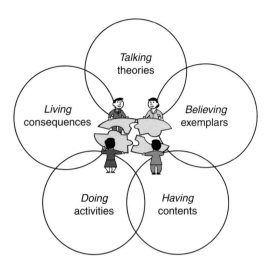

FIGURE 3.1 No one touches a strategy but it is always with us

exemplars into contents and activities that produce consequences? Who talks, believes, has, does and lives with strategies? First and foremost, you – managers.

Such a holistic view, we believe, is useful for achieving effectively wise strategy. Too often, issues important to strategy have been framed in either/or terms: contents vs process, substance vs style, deliberate planning vs emergent crafting, macro analysis vs micro sense-making, and so on. These, we are told, are 'incommensurable' things. Worse, according to gurus, we must make a 'fundamental choice' in each dichotomy. In contrast, the pragmatic talk–believe–have–do–live view encourages managers to appreciate multiplicity, connectivity and reciprocity. An open, embracing view of strategy is useful for coping with life problems in a connected, fast-moving world.

So, while to Mintzberg strategy is nowhere except in one's mind, to us strategy is everywhere in our experienced world. These are obviously different views and, to borrow Mintzberg's words, 'both sides are right – and wrong'.[16] Our pragmatic view is right in that it engages managers to approach every aspect of their jobs with a sense of strategic responsibility; it is wrong if it is used to justify the claim 'we have a strategy – look, in this company booklet'. Mintzberg's view, also a pragmatic one, is right in reminding managers that there are no general principles for strategy, that imagination and creativity make the difference; it is wrong if taken to mean 'strategy is all that I think'. Used properly, the two different views enrich understanding; which is more meaningful depends on situated tasks.

Reform without a theory? The China experience[17]

That China's economic reform has achieved nothing less than a miracle is nowadays seldom disputed; what remains a question is the strategy behind the miracle. Some regard China's strategy as incremental, in comparison with Eastern Europe and the former Soviet Union's (EEFSU) 'big bangs'. Others suggest the reform succeeded not because of, but despite, gradualism. To the Chinese, such a dichotomy is ill-founded and misleading.

Indeed, no theoretical model of how the market worked in China could be found, even after years of reform. China just survived, at that critical moment, from the devastating 'Cultural Revolution' chaos. The grand socialist blueprint collapsed and once-sacred theories lost credibility. There was merely a painful awareness of the strategic vulnerability beneath a powerful northern neighbour, the economic backwardness in comparison with Japan and some smaller 'Asian Tigers', and a subsequent acceptance that anything to raise national economic output had a valid place. The reform was triggered by mundane survival, not codified principles, whatever the official rhetoric might claim.

The rationale of the day was Deng Xiaoping's 'crossing the river by feeling for stones' and 'white cat or black cat, the one that catches the mouse is a good cat'. To Deng, plan and market were two convenient 'methods', not systemic 'paradigms'. The reform process was either ad hoc responses to particular constraints in the old system or took advantage of the loopholes in it, 'more like the extension of the market by stealth'.[18] The party did issue 'policies', usually in the form of 'Document No. 1 of Year 19xx'. Often, policies were little more than *ex post* approval of what had already happened in many parts of the country and consisted mainly of vague statements, offering little indication of where would undergo reform or how it would be carried out. If 'policies' had been taken seriously, no reform could have occurred. For example, the document of the famous 1978 Third Plenum of the Eleventh Central Committee of the Communist Party of China, a meeting commonly regarded as the foundation of the reform, did not mention institutional reform at all. Rather, it reaffirmed that the commune system 'should remain unchanged', only to see communes dismantled all over the country immediately afterwards. Like other reform 'strategies', the document was as remarkable for what it did not say as for what it did; it was conveniently open to interpretations, negotiations and reversals.

To the Chinese, gradualism and radicalism are *ex post* descriptions that are of interest only to onlookers, not *ex ante* strategy choices for hands-on change agents. Outside China, some are sympathetic: 'that China's economy has succeeded while more sophisticated ones have failed has something to do with the Chinese refused to take theory seriously. While Eastern Europe theorists wrestled with the uneven task of integrating market and plan into a workable system, Chinese farmers and entrepreneurs were allowed to go off and do what came naturally.'[19] Others are critical: 'The mixture of half-plan, half-market; neither-plan, nor market; pretend-socialism, pretend-capitalism ... or "socialism with Chinese characteristics", is an unstable condition – economically and ethically.'[20] Such comments, sympathetic or critical, in effect confirm that China's reform followed no available theory.

Without a reasoned model or clear destination, or even any 'road map', how did China's reform proceed? We investigate this based on a *wuli–shili–renli* dimensionality, which is summarised in Table 3.1.[21]

Table 3.1 *Key factors that shape China's reform*

Wuli (物理)	*Shili* (事理)	*Renli* (人理)
Regulative-material resources	Psycho-cognitive mentalities	Moral-normative orientations
Fiscal federalism	Anti-abstraction/ codification	Low trust
Hard budget constraint		Differentiated pecking order
Imbalanced economic structure	Dislike articulation/ argumentation	Achievement-orientation
Shortage in consumer goods	Ambiguity tolerance	Utilitarian familism
Low commercialisation		Commercial virtue
Low urbanisation	Uncertainty acceptance	Utilitarian reciprocality
Lack of welfare protection	Virtue over truth	Commodified personal connection
Commune-brigade enterprises	Pragmatic culture	Bureaucracy–business alliance
	Confucius' 'No four devils'	
	Shizhong (timely balance)	
Exemplar manifestation: huge opportunities and strong incentives for growth	Exemplar manifestation: 'red-hat enterprises' as best entrepreneurial innovation	Exemplar manifestation: family businesses booming despite state discrimination

Source: Zhu 2007a, p. 1512; the copyright of the publisher Sage is acknowledged.

First, *wuli* regulatory-material conditions. Before the reform, China's was neither a market nor plan economy; it was a 'command' one. Tiered governments were given greater autonomy, less subsidies and harder budget constraints, in comparison with EEFSU. During 1971–1975, even in the strategic iron-steel industry, for example, local investment accounted for 52 per cent of the total; the share of tax revenue accruing to the central government amounted to 34 per cent of GDP, less than in most market economies. Such 'regional decentralisation and fiscal federalism, Chinese style' provided incentives for local governments to promote economic growth.[22]

Hostile to central planning, Mao Zedong advocated a *xiao tu quan* (小土全, small, local, full-range) policy, encouraging rural authorities to run non-agricultural commune-brigade enterprises (CBEs). By the time of the reform, 1.5 million CBEs already employed over 29 million farmers, produced 15 per cent of national industrial output and 30 per cent of gross rural output, with an average annual growth rate of 25.7 per cent. Investment in CBEs accounted for 13 to 60.5 per cent of rural earnings. Out of plan, Mao's CBEs provided useful infrastructure and entrepreneurial talent for the reform.[23]

Less planned than the EEFSU though, China's economy was no less imbalanced. The percentage of industry in national income increased from 12.6 per cent in 1949 (the year the communists came to power) to 46.8 per cent in 1978 (the year the reform began), while agriculture declined from 57.72 to 32.76 per cent and other sectors from 22.75 to 17.84 per cent. The result was a severe shortage of consumer goods and agricultural products. This created a huge seller's market, a situation exploited by non-state sectors as soon as entry permits were available.[24]

In pre-reform China, farmers lived at subsistence level, outside the state welfare net. Once economic liberalisation began, non-state sectors grew rapidly, relying on the flow of labour from agriculture. Farmers were virtually beating at the gates of government to dismantle the restraints and let them work. When the gates were opened, they rushed in and produced that remarkable surge of output. The reform was thus basically to transform a poor agricultural society into a balanced industrial one, a 'Pareto-improving process' during which, particularly in the early stages, nearly every sector in society gained without great loss.[25]

The reform was less costly also because of 'abandonability'. Unlike abandoning plans in a planned economy, which produces disruption at least for a short period, abandoning 'commands' leads only to positive effects, regardless of whether market mechanism or planned control was subsequently adopted. Like its farmers, China had nothing to lose in abandoning the command economy.[26]

Then, in the *shili* psycho-cognitive sphere, the Chinese are 'biased' against abstraction and codification. Laozi famously proclaimed: 'The *tao* that can be articulated is not the eternal *Tao*', 'Those who articulate do not know, those who know do not articulate.'[27] Disliking detached rationality, impersonal order and universal rules, the Chinese generated a highly entrepreneurial, informal 'network capitalism' whereby:

> The key skills required here are not those of codification but those of negotiation; the name of this game is not to economise on bounded rationality or to exorcise opportunism but to capitalise on them in a linked network of hierarchical face-to-face relationships in which personal power is traded, using loyalty, compliance, and protection as the medium of exchange.[28]

Closely related is tolerance of ambiguity. A Chinese proverb goes: *nan de hutu* (难得糊涂, ambiguity is gold). The highest virtue is not to reveal the concrete or detail, but to nurture fuzziness, emptiness and chaos from which imagination and creativity can emerge.[29] A government think tank posits: 'ambiguity is the imperatively important feature of the Chinese traditional mentality.'[30] The property rights of the Township-Village Enterprises (TVEs) was an exemplar: as the powerhouse of China's phenomenal growth for around two decades, the structure of TVE property rights was anything but clear, transparent or stable. The official position was to allow 'the coexistence of multiple forms of ownership based mainly on public ownership'. Nominally, TVEs were publicly owned; in reality TVEs did not, in the terms of Western property rights theory, have any legitimate owner. But they worked, and worked effectively.[31]

Presenting the 'science of muddling through', the American political scientist Charles Lindblom posits that policy-making 'requires no theory' since no theory can accommodate the huge uncertainty involved.[32] This brings us to the Chinese temperament of uncertainty-acceptance. The British economist Mark Casson distinguishes 'theoretical' and 'pragmatic' cultures thus:

> Some cultures emphasise the importance of theory; it is important
> to understand the situation before acting, they maintain, and
> such understanding can only be provided by a theory of some
> kind. Other cultures are more pragmatic; they suggest that it
> is sufficient to know that, on the basis of experience, a certain
> course of action produces good results in certain circumstances
> without knowing exactly why this is the case.[33]

In China, as we mentioned in Chapter 2, Confucius is respected as the ultimate sage because he rejected the 'four devils'. In the *Yijing* (易经, *Book of Changes*), *shizhong* (时中, time-balance) is regarded as a great virtue: one should respond positively to changes and opportunities in accordance with unfolding particulars, not previously held theories. In such a mindscape, rules are made to be broken, not obeyed. The following observation is telling:

> toward the end of 1978, a small number of production teams,
> first secretly and later with the blessing of local authorities,
> began to try out the system of contracting land, other resources,
> and output quotas to individual households. A year later, these
> teams brought in yields far larger than those of other teams.
> The central authorities later conceded the existence of this new
> form of farming but required that it be restricted to poor regions.
> However, most teams ignored this restriction. Full official
> acceptance of HRS [Household Responsibility System] was
> eventually given in late 1981, when 45 per cent of the production
> teams in China had already been dismantled. By the end of 1983,
> 98 per cent of production teams had adopted HRS.[34]

So much so that Daniel Kelliher summarises thus:

> Policy and politics in the reform period came to follow a
> distinctive pattern: One year the state would discover peasants
> pursuing some deviation and issue a proclamation to ban
> it. Then a year later the same practice would be pronounced
> tolerable under 'special circumstances'. By the time another year
> passed, the very same activity would be declared official policy
> to be followed uniformly throughout the nation.[35]

It is not that the party-state was irrelevant, rather, the state had the
ultimate, total, absolute power to decide which innovations to sanction; but that the state did not initiate those innovations and its
sanctions were anything but theory-guided.

Finally, how about *renli* human relations? The state had been
insistently discriminating against private and other non-state sectors
via ideological and operational instruments. To shield themselves
from discrimination from 'above', entrepreneurs 'below' invented
many tactical manoeuvres. One was the famous 'red hat': private
enterprises paid an 'administration fee' of up to 30 per cent of profits to register as 'public'. The 'red hat' supplied political protection.
By the mid 1980s, over 90 per cent of private firms wore a 'red hat'.
Crucially, this was officially praised as 'emancipating the mind':
'emancipating the mind' was good because Deng said so.

According to Francis Fukuyama, the Chinese are low-trust.[36]
They distrusted state policies: *zhongyang de zhengce xiang yueliang,
chuyi shiwu bu yiyang* (中央的政策象月亮, 初一十五不一样, Like the
moon, the Centre's policies change within a fortnight). Public institutions were not only unstable, they were not creditable at the first
instance: governments were at once the rule-maker, referee, enforcer
and player. During the 1980s–1990s, 60–90 per cent of governmental
bodies ran 'administrative companies' while controlling the allocation and pricing of resources. In such an environment, grass roots
had to play creatively: *shan gao huangdi yuan* (山高皇帝远, The mountains are high and the Emperor is far away), *shang you zhengce, xia*

you duice (上有政策, 下有对策, Regulations from above, manoeuvres from below). Critically, both 'above' and 'below' saw this as a normal, indeed moral, way of life.

The Chinese distrusted anyone outside their families, which rendered the society highly family-centred and individualistic. Fukuyama comments:

> In its contest with the traditional family, communism has clearly lost ... [O]ut of the wreckage of twentieth-century Chinese history, the one institution that has emerged stronger than all the others is the patrilineal Chinese family. The latter has always been a refuge against the capriciousness of political life, and Chinese peasants have understood that in the end, the only people they could really trust were members of their immediate family.[37]

This, combined with an 'achievement-orientation',[38] a 'commercial virtue' form of materialism[39] and a preference for personal owner-ship,[40] had forged a 'utilitarian familism',[41] which was channelled during the reform era to enable family businesses to thrive through a 'societal marketisation' process: massive establishment of private firms and extensive hidden privatisation of collectives. Familism also brought in vast foreign direct investment (FDI) when China was in desperate need of advanced technology, managerial expertise and international markets. Most FDI came from overseas Chinese through family ties, despite occasional media headlines about big investments from Western or Japanese multinationals.[42] In socio-logical terms, the reform was 'simply the restoration of older Chinese social relationships'[43] and 'social structural features'[44] and 'the revival of a dynamic commercial culture that pre-dates communism'.[45]

In light of pragmatism, it is the combined effect of actual *wuli* conditions, virtual *shili* mentalities and social *renli* orienta-tions at a unique historical moment that favoured China's no-theory reform. With the presence of one or two *li* in isolation, the 'miracle' would probably not have happened. Think about it. 'Actual' business opportunities, brought forth by a distorted economic structure and weak central control, would not have been exploited or even seen as such in the absence of a strong achievement orientation; a 'theoretical culture' would not have allowed vague economic policies or property rights to work; entrepreneurs, however highly motivated, would have found it difficult to generate innovation in a society where everything was under plan (as in the EEFSU) or every move was subject to elaborate rules and procedures (as in 'the West').

Rather, *wuli–shili–renli* complemented each other to allow China's reform 'strategy' to succeed. When China embarked on the reform, utilitarian familism survived despite Mao's continuous 'collective movements', only to be strengthened by a painful sense of insecurity and distrust (*renli*). The reform began with no clear destination or fixed path; in Lindblom's terms, the ends, means and processes were anything but systematic or theoretically defensible (*shili*). Nevertheless, 'benign neglect' from the state permitted wealth-seeking entrepreneurs outside the state sector to creatively exploit numerous empty niches in the shortage economy (*renli* plus *wuli*). High profitability from the provision of basic consumer goods induced a rapid, massive entry of new firms, despite insistent state discrimination (*wuli* plus *renli*). Gradually, these new firms entered the product domain of the state sector, created competition pressure on state-owned enterprises (SOEs) to increase productivity, quality, technological level and competitiveness, which resulted in the rapid growth of the whole economy (*wuli*). The government, lacking clear objectives and administrative capabilities – as these terms are usually defined in the developed, mainly Western world – allowed workable solutions from below, legitimised the outcomes of grass-roots manoeuvres and took credit for whatever looked good, under no pressure to supply systematic justifications (*shili*). In contrast to the EEFSU's 'political capitalism' 'from above', China's 'jumble of ad hoc reforms' 'muddled through' effectively.

So much for why China's reform succeeded. But is it really without a theory? Zhu Zhichang, who was born, educated and worked as a Red Guard, farm labourer, worker and manager in China, suggests:

> China's reform is without a Theory, if Theory means being
> articulated, formal, universal, geared toward mirroring and
> mastering the world. Nevertheless, ... the reform is underlain
> by a holistic and suggestive understanding of how the world can
> be respected and accommodated, by a pragmatic mindscape that
> tolerates paradox, uncertainty and local experimentation, and
> by a culturally and intellectually founded confidence. All these
> may not constitute a conventional Theory. However, given its
> scale, complexity, stake and effect, who can deny that China's
> reform is informed by an intriguing *theory*? Who can reject that
> China's *theory* has made a substantial and practical difference?
> Who can seriously suggest that China's *theory* is less profound,
> subtle, robust, powerful and enlightening than received Western
> Theories, Paradigms, or Consensuses?[46]

Do you agree? What does theory mean to you? How does it work
in your circumstances? How to strategise with, or without, a
theory?

WHAT IS STRATEGY FOR?

Why do we do strategy? What are we to achieve with strategy? At
face value, these questions are almost redundant. Pick up any strategy textbook and the answer is there, clear and simple:

> In the business context, it [strategy] pertains to a process
> by which a firm searches and analyses its environment and
> resources in order to (1) select opportunities defined in terms of
> markets to be served and products to serve them, and (2) make
> discrete decisions to invest resources in order to achieve
> identified objectives.[47]

After painting such an image, textbooks quickly move to introduce
an array of models and techniques, and use case studies to show
how each should work. Listen to managers who engage in the real
world, however, and you may find the answers more complicated,

and exciting. The following is a story about Intel Corporation, a classic case of corporate exit strategy.[48]

Intel was the first company able to manufacture and market Dynamic Random Access Memory (DRAM) successfully – it introduced the world's first DRAM in 1970. By 1972, Intel's DRAM was the world's largest-selling semiconductor product, accounting for over 90 per cent of the company's revenue. As the market leader, Intel's distinctive competence was in combining circuit design, process development and manufacturing activities necessary to make rapid incremental changes and stay ahead of competitors. DRAMs were viewed as the 'technology driver' on which Intel's learning curve depended, and the company routinely allocated resources to this fast-growing business. Throughout the 1970s, DRAM was the business that made Intel successful. Justifiably, Intel saw itself as a 'memory company': 'In a way, DRAMs created Intel.'

As the market matured, DRAMs became a commodity, and production capacity was the new factor determining profitability. The basis for competitive advantage then shifted towards large-scale manufacturing, which was necessary to achieve high yields for each new DRAM generation. This shift favoured highly integrated players such as Samsung, Mitsubishi, Toshiba and Hitachi due to their aggressive capacity expansion and price competitiveness. Over time, Intel's distinctive competence lost its magic, and the company its lead position in the industry. By 1980, Intel's market share in DRAMs dropped below 3 per cent; in 1985, it was ranked ninth. By 1984, the memory business accounted for only about 3 per cent of the company's total sales revenues. The two 3-per-cents – if data tells anything – showed plainly that Intel was no longer a leading player in the memory sector.

Despite this, even in 1984, top management was still thinking of DRAMs as the core business, and being a 'memory company' remained the official strategy. How did Intel survive and, amazingly, outperform? Fortunately, the company's resource-allocation mechanism allowed investment in products that maximised margin-per-manufacturing-activity. One such product was the microprocessor. An unplanned initiative, microprocessors were developed because Busicom, a Japanese calculator firm, contracted Intel to produce a general-logic chip that could be programmed to carry out different calculating instructions. This product was given financial support, as the then Vice President of Sales, Ed Gelbach, remembered: 'Originally, I think, we saw it as a way to sell more memories and we were willing to make the investment on that base.' Thanks to the subsequent high demand for this device, particularly after IBM decided to use it for PCs, Intel's microprocessor business became highly profitable, grew rapidly and attracted more internal investment.

Meanwhile, the fast-growing microprocessor sector triggered another competence shift: fast upgrade of design architectures and education for customers about its benefits. This was a competence Intel quickly developed from what the company had been distinctively good at. So, even though most managers continued to believe that Intel was a memory company, the actual effect of their investment decisions had made Intel a microprocessor company in all but name. By 1982, microprocessors were the largest component in sales revenue for the company. On the other hand, with continuing decline in both market share and revenue, the DRAM business gradually lost legitimacy. In December 1984, top management finally decided not to produce the 1 Meg DRAM and officially withdrew from the 'memory company' strategy.

The articulation of Intel's microprocessor strategy came almost five years after that strategy had been working effectively in reality. The transformation was an emotional one: so many managers had grown up with DRAMs. As one manager put it, 'it was kind of like Ford deciding to get out of cars'. Fortunately, humans are a species both emotional and rational; the Intel management was capable of recognising the strategy once it had occurred, seizing on it, benefiting from it. As Andrew Grove, the Intel CEO, observed:

> Don't ask managers, 'What is your strategy?' Look at what they do! ... The fact is that we had become a non-factor in DRAM's,

with 2–3 per cent market share. The DRAM business just passed us by! Yet, in 1985, many people were still holding to the 'self-evident truth' that Intel was a memory company. One of the toughest challenges is to make people see that these self-evident truths are no longer true ... I recall going to see Gordon [Moore] and asking him what a new management would do if we were replaced. The answer was clear: Get out of DRAMs. So, I suggested to Gordon that we go through the revolving door, come back in, and just do it ourselves.[49]

Go through the revolving door they did, and come back in as 'new' management with a 'new' strategy! How to square the circle: how to fit Intel's experience into the typical textbook image of what strategy should do and how models and tools should work? In this case, Grove and Moore used strategy to articulate, codify, justify and elaborate on what the company had already been doing. Intel's exit strategy is an example of after-the-fact rationalisation, of *ex post* synthesis. This would hardly be surprising to Confucius, as we read: 'Zigong (子贡) asked about exemplary persons. The Master replied: "They first accomplish what they are going to say, and only then say it." '[50]

STRATEGY: A MULTI-FUNCTION TOOL

In pragmatism, strategy is a tool in our hands. It is up to us how to use it. We use it to cope with life problems, and life problems are massively different, ranging far beyond analysing markets, positioning businesses and designing products. The textbook image is not wrong, just limited, and hence misleading. Put down textbooks and we see more: strategies can be used in many other ways, for different purposes. Let us briefly touch on a few of them.

Prompting action. Strategy is the art of getting jobs done. Engaging people in strategy so that they are alert, look for opportunities and take initiatives. However problematic the original strategy, we can shape it for the better once we embark on the journey. We need to think in order to act; we also need to act in order to

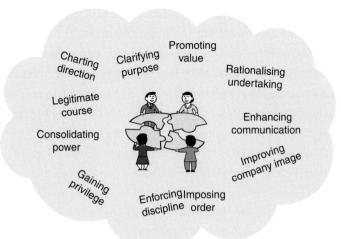

FIGURE 3.2 Strategy: a multi-function tool in our hands

think. You learn only when you do. If Deng had waited for a correct reform model, China would today remain an economic backwater. Deng is great not because he was an all-knowing 'chief architect', but because he allowed over one billion people to jump into experimentation without knowing how things would play out. We try things, and things that work converge gradually into viable patterns that we call strategy. Honda's original strategy for conquering the US motorcycle market got everything wrong. But it landed the Honda people there at the first instance, so that they could learn, firsthand, fast, 'stumbling into enormous success'.[51] Without that deliberate landing, nothing could have emerged.

Informing decision. Engaging in strategy process allows people to share a sense of purpose, attaches meaning to their actions, pulls everyone's efforts in the chosen direction against all odds. In the early days of Sony, its founders introduced the 'Sony spirit': Sony wants to serve the world as a pioneer and will never follow others. In 1955, Akio Morita was desperately looking for retailers in New York to sell an invention, a little $29.95 radio. Many were unimpressed. Finally, the purchasing officer at Bulova said, 'We definitely want some of these. We will take one hundred thousand units.' An incredible order, worth several times the total capital of the young Sony! Just one condition: put the Bulova name on the radios. Morita rejected the order without a second thought, and he was considered crazy. But Morita was proud of that decision, and regarded it as the best he had ever made in his whole life. Sony wanted to be a pioneer, not an equipment supplier for other companies. Should Morita have decided differently, we would not have today's Sony.[52]

Orchestrating effort. As organisations grow, strategic initiatives are likely to emerge at levels below top management.[53] Then, involving people in strategy exercises can pull things together for organisational success. Andrew Grove reflected on his experience in Intel: 'The Strategic Long Range Planning process turned into an embarrassment. Top management didn't really have the guts to call the shots, so we were trying to get middle management to come up with strategies and then taking pot shots at them.'[54] Embarrassing it might be, but decisions from below enabled the company to focus capital investments on its 'profit pools', bypassing the official rhetoric.[55] Similarly, Nonaka depicts strategy-making as a middle-up-down process.[56] Strategy works well only when dispersed efforts meet, compete and converge under a compelling vision. 'It is like building a pyramid or watching a colony of ants; thousands of "little people" doing "little things", all with the same basic purpose, can move mountains.'[57]

Programming agenda. This is to make strategic decisions operational, formalising the strategies that have already been developed. Mintzberg calls this 'strategic planning' and draws our attention to a familiar scenario:

> An appropriate image for the planner might be that person left behind in a meeting, together with the chief executive, after everyone else has departed. All of the strategic decisions that were made are symbolically strewn about the table. The CEO turns to the planner and says, 'There they all are; clean them up. Package them neatly so that we can tell everyone about them and get things going.'[58]

Nowadays, it is fashionable for academics to joke about strategic planning; for example, 'The number crunchers at headquarters produce plans, and then hand them to the staff to implement.'[59] As insiders, however, we note a new irony: fewer and fewer MBA graduates can handle numbers adequately. Students eagerly avoid 'hard subjects', and MBA programmes phase out analytic components from their curricula to please 'the customer'. Sadly, these bSchools are McSchools: they feed students with fast-thought bullet-points.[60] The challenge is to keep the balance: not managing-by-numbers but informed-by-numbers, not allowing planning to dictate strategy but using planning for clarification, operationalisation and communication.

Enhancing discipline. We humans appreciate change but also seek order. Order enslaves us, yet fulfils a deep need for security.[61] No organisation can survive in continuous chaos.[62] Organisations need discipline to get jobs done, particularly complex jobs. One way to enhance discipline is to engage people in strategy exercises. Require your staff up and down the ranks to submit yearly strategy plans, negotiate objectives, settle targets, agree on schedules and ensure everyone knows their duties. The resultant documents are not important; the process is. People may quickly forget the details; it doesn't matter. Strategy fulfils its function as long as people behave in a disciplined manner and the organisation is in order. In a world of limited resources, efficiency is a virtue. Sounds bureaucratic? Have a reality check, then: bureaucracy is as old as civilisation and it's here to stay. The loosely coupled, networked, federalised or virtual organisations in our 'new economy' merely add new features to a basic blueprint, as Professor Harold Leavitt of Stanford University suggested.[63] Where command and control are not viable, discipline or, ideally, internalised self-discipline achieved via strategy exercises will do the trick.

Enabling socialisation. Increasingly, organisations are holding 'strategic away-days', or 'off-site retreats'. This is certainly the case in the business schools where we work. Every year or so, the whole staff enjoys a day out in a luxury hotel or out-of-season ski resort, with mobile phones disabled, student inquiries far away and wonderful food on the table. The procedure is formal but the atmosphere is not. Don't expect new strategy to emerge by the end of the day, because the questions and hints for answers are already printed on an A4 sheet available at the reception desk. Everyone is happy and agrees that the money has been well-spent. We seldom see staff members together, and some we have never met. It is a good time to share ideas with colleagues just next-door to your office; we are all too busy even to say hello in normal times. The away-day is a condensed version of the Japanese practice of drinking together after office hours. It is good for friendship, trust, teamwork, *ba*, you name it. It is also good for reading unwritten rules, getting familiar with informal systems, knowing who-is-who in case it is useful some day, and internalising 'how business is done around here'.[64]

Gaining legitimacy. Companies are open systems, relying for survival on the supply of materials, information, capital and expertise from the business environment. Most crucially, companies need perceived legitimacy from financiers, suppliers, customers, partners, government agencies and the general public, so that these groups have the good will to support companies in achieving what they want to accomplish. Organisation study professors Jeffrey Pfeffer and Gerald Salancik call this 'resource dependence'.[65] No company owns legitimacy; it exists in the minds of outsiders. The image of what you do is as important as what you actually do. It is thus critically important to be seen as having a strategy and taking strategy seriously. Again, the substance is not important, the appearance is. And not just to lure outsiders: within organisations legitimacy is equally critical. Therefore, undertake the exercise even if you already have a strategy. Better yet, if you can afford to, hire consultants to add more weight to your strategy. According to Richard Pascale, who is himself a consultant, 'most consultants will confirm that they have been called in to solve a client's problem only to discover ... the client organisation already had the solution'.[66]

Consolidating power. After the 1989 Tiananmen tragedy, China's reform was in the balance. The conservatives gained political, ideological and military power for a reversal. On the economic front, they launched a 'retrenchment' programme, granting further power to the state sector. 'The market' was in retreat; millions of non-state enterprises went bankrupt. Feeling that there was nothing he could do in Beijing, in 1992 Deng toured the southern cities and visited the iconic *jingji tequ* (经济特区, Economic Special Zones). Reformers from all over the country quickly gathered around him, leaving the conservatives isolated and exposed in Beijing. It was a breath-taking showdown. The outcome was out with the conservatives and in with a wider, deeper, faster reform. Power enables strategy, and strategy consolidates power.[67] When *USAToday* reinvented itself from a newspaper to a thriving multi-media business, this was what Tom Curley, the president and publisher, did:

> So in 2000, he replaced the leader of USAToday.com with another internal executive who was a strong supporter of the network strategy, and he brought in an outsider to create a television operation, USAToday Direct ... He let go a number of senior executives who did not share his commitment to the network strategy, ensuring that his team would present a united front and deliver consistent messages to the staff. He also changed the incentive program for executives, replacing unit-specific goals with a common bonus program tied to growth targets across all three media.[68]

In light of pragmatism, none of these functions is in itself good or bad, core or peripheral. Furthermore, multiple functionalities can be deployed in the same exercise; for example, managers can use a strategy exercise to gain legitimacy, impose discipline and promote socialisation simultaneously. One stone, many birds. The world is multifaceted and shifting, our minds should be equally complicated and accommodating. Substance is critically important, packaging makes a difference too. The means and the ends inform, invite, impact and transform each other. Constrained by a single lens, we will greatly reduce the power of strategy and risk strategising into dead ends. Only variety can handle variety, as the science of cybernetics reveals.[69] Besides technical rationality, we need instrumental and ethical rationality. Strategy is a tool. How to use it, for what purposes, how will it work? It all depends on circumstances, shaped by our ethical ideals, political views, social skills and technical competence. This is the accent of pragmatic strategy.

Cochlear implants: technology as political game[70]

A cochlear implant is a surgically implanted electronic device that allows deaf people to experience the sensation of sound. Until the 1980s, implantation research using human subjects was considered morally and scientifically unacceptable, mainly because the mechanism by which the human ear functioned was poorly understood. Another factor was the lack of testing and evaluating standards, which made it all the more difficult to select the best designs. Cochlear implant design should be based on sound science and technology, to be sure. But, before the 1980s, our knowledge about it was simply too underdeveloped to do the job. This situation occurs time and time again in new product development, particularly when designs involve 'paradigmatic' or 'architecture' technological innovations.[71]

Cochlear implant technology (CIT) later gained legitimacy through certain serendipitous events. In particular, regulatory agencies in the US, such as the National Institutes of Health (NIH) and the Food and Drug Administration (FDA) responsible for ensuring the safety and efficacy of medical devices, decided to support cochlear implantation in response to unrelated European research on neural cortex simulation. Consequently, CIT obtained considerable momentum, and developed rapidly within a few short years.

Multiple players were involved in CIT development: research institutes, commercial companies, regulative agencies and university laboratories. Competition was not waged between professional groups, i.e. research institutes against companies, but between coalitions of those groups, for example, a coalition of pioneering researcher William House and the 3M Corporation against another coalition of researcher Graeme Clark and the Nucleus Corporation. By 1980, there were approximately seven such coalitions. At this early stage of technology-in-the-making, nothing existed but divergent beliefs about what was feasible or worth attempting. All participants were qualified and dedicated, yet each coalition relied on distinctive past experiences, starting assumptions and future expectations, resulting in competing approaches, or 'paradigms'. Everyone shared a belief in science, yet they were at war.

Based on its clinical experiments, the House–3M coalition believed that implants should begin with a simple device, as it presented the least potential harm to patients while providing researchers with essential knowledge for improvement. The belief led House–3M to develop a single-channel technology that used a single electrode implanted at a relatively shallow depth in the cochlea. The device was designed to provide deaf patients with some perception of environmental cues rather than an ability to discriminate between spoken sounds. Consequently, those who pursued this approach firmly held that the ability to perceive environmental cues should be the measure of efficacy.

Other researchers adhered to contrasting assumptions. They believed that normal hearing could only be replicated with multiple electrodes, each inserted deep into the cochlea so that different frequency signals could be delivered to different areas. The deeper insertion of multiple electrodes might eventually provide patients with the ability to understand speech. For multi-channel advocates, such as the Clark–Nucleus coalition, the ability to recognise speech was the primary function of CIT and the most appropriate measure of efficacy. They rejected the argument that multi-channel devices might cause cochlear damage. Instead, they saw more risk in single-channel technology, and considered damage more likely to occur when single-channel patients eventually replaced their implants with multi-channel versions.

Table 3.2 *Competing cochlear implant logics*

	House–3M coalition	Clark–Nucleus coalition
Technological design	Shallow-implanted single-channel device	Deep-implanted multiple-channel device
Functional objective	Perceiving environmental cues	Recognising normal speech
Concern of risk	Deep-implanted multiple device	Future upgrade from single to multiple device
Proposed efficacy measure	Ability to understand environmental cues	Ability to recognise speech
Proposed test sample	Minimum of 100 patients	Based on claims made on device and performance

The emerging technology was thus an 'institutional battle-field' where competing theories fought for domination. Because of the uncertainty inherently associated with revolutionary technologies, it is impossible *ex ante* to determine the success or failure of any particular logic, single- or multi-channel design in this case. Furthermore, several possible evaluation routines existed, each tautological to the specific approaches pursued by competing players.

To settle for a dominant logic, political action came into play so that a set of particular evaluation routines and criteria were adopted and the others selected away. The battle for technology settlement was political because, no matter how formalised or neutral-minded, the NIH/FDA evaluation could not escape from the fact that these regulative bodies, like everybody else, did not have the prerequisite knowledge to judge competing logics. The resolution depended largely on a congruence of beliefs among the researcher–company coalitions and the NIH/FDA administrators. It was, in the end, a subjective matter.

In searching for a favoured settlement, House–3M proposed measuring a patient's ability to understand environmental sounds and the resultant improvement in quality of life. On the other side, the Clark–Nucleus coalition promoted tests that measured a patient's ability to perceive speech and tracked improvements in speech-recognition over time. Consequently, each approach led to the development of an evaluation routine based on and reinforcing its own design logic.

House–3M proposed as a guideline for pre-market approval application (PMAA) that a minimum of 100 patients should be required for establishing efficacy – this was the number of clinical experiences the coalition had already undertaken. To support this, 3M organised seminars on safety issues for FDA staff. If the 3M proposal was accepted, Nucleus would be at a disadvantage because it had so far collected clinical data on only 43 patients. To prevent this, Nucleus audiologists visited the FDA, arguing that sample size should be a function of the actual performance of each device and the claims each manufacturer made for it. During the deliberations, the two coalitions were able to obtain endorsements from other evaluation bodies, such as the American Association of Otolaryngology (AAO) on one side and the University of Iowa on the other. Both were evaluation authorities recognised by the NIH/FDA and were considered to be objective and neutral.

From the vantage point of 3M, multi-channel proponents had overstated the benefits while minimising the risks of their device. In return, multi-channel proponents alleged that 3M exaggerated the performance of single-channel devices. It was not clear who was exaggerating more. Here we observe a perpetual process where 'the struggle to define safety and efficacy, and then measure it, illustrates how researchers projected their own beliefs onto cochlear implants and attempted to influence each other, including regulators. The evaluation routines adopted by researchers were congruent with their beliefs about cochlear implants. These routines, in turn, further reinforced researchers' beliefs'.[72] The FDA eventually accepted the Clark–Nucleus argument that the number of patients for a

PMAA should not be specified, on the ground that requiring a large sample size could put more patients at risk. Instead, the FDA would leave the minimum sample size flexible so that clinical investigators could tailor their studies to collect sufficient data for the purpose of achieving statistically valid results. In hindsight, this was a reasonable yet debatable decision because there were no hard data or objective facts to support or falsify it.

Initially, the FDA had felt comfortable with single-channel technology because its simplicity facilitated the evaluation process, and also because it seemed the safest option. Accordingly, in the early 1980s, single-channel CIT dominated clinical practice. However, once single-channel devices had demonstrated the safety of cochlear implants as a class of products, the FDA shifted its focus to efficacy, emphasising the ability to provide speech discrimination. In 1988, a milestone NIH/FDA consensus-development conference established funding and regulatory guidelines that favoured multi-channel technology. This was a double blow to the single-channel coalitions, since the 'consensus' practically institutionalised the multi-channel design as the dominant logic. Since then, the number of multi-channel implants has steadily increased, while single-channel implants has continuously declined.

A battle was ended, but the war was far from over. Despite failing to become the dominant logic, House–3M researchers continued to advocate the single-channel path. They were given a boost as new data emerged that appeared to refute the claim that single-channel devices were too simple for speech recognition. It is thus too early to rule out a new round of competition that could unseat the current dominant logic and establish a new one. The future of CIT is still uncertain; it depends, once again, at least partly on the political skills of all the players concerned. We all want to assist patients with the best scientific knowledge and technology, but knowledge and technology are settled, time and time again, by politics and relationships as much as by data and logic.

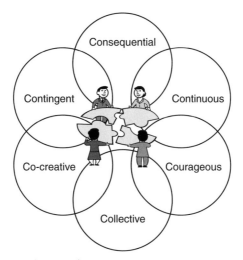

FIGURE 3.3 The 6Cs of strategy

THE 6CS OF STRATEGY

So far in this chapter, we have constructed a pragmatic image of strategy: what and where it is (forms and locus) and what we can use it for (functionalities). For a fuller understanding, we now invite readers to investigate what makes pragmatic strategy particularly useful for assisting us to walk wisely in the world (features and qualities). Figure 3.3 is an overview of the forest.[73] Let us examine the trees.

Contingent

One day in 1943, Edwin Land's three-year-old daughter cried and asked why she could not immediately see the picture he had just taken of her. 'Within an hour, this scientist conceived a camera that would transform his company' – the birth of the Polaroid camera.[74] Early in 1995, Jack Ma took his first trip to the US and was shown the Internet, but when he tried to find Tsingtao beer, he got only American, European, Japanese and South African brands. Back in China, Ma started the country's first online yellow pages in April that year. Having taught English for years at a college in Hangzhou, and knowing nothing about computers, Ma founded Alibaba.com, now the world's biggest online B-to-B service company, with Goldman Sachs and Softbank among its backers.[75]

To Land and Ma, one at a big corporation in 'the West' and the other in a humble apartment in 'the East', winning strategy was not the outcome of cold industry analysis or lengthy resource audit, but about quickly seizing upon unexpected chances. Don't look for textbook principles or x-dimension-y-box methodologies, don't wait for the yearly strategy exercise due in three months. Act now, if you know why your business should exist at all.

Polaroid and Alibaba embody the pragmatic spirit that underpins what James Collins and Jerry Porras call 'visionary companies':

> In examining the history of the visionary companies, we were struck by how often they made some of their best moves not by detailed strategic planning, but rather by experimentation, trial and error, opportunism, and – quite literally – accident. What looks in hindsight like a brilliant strategy was often the residual result of opportunistic experimentation and 'purposeful accidents'.[76]

If contexts are contingent and opportunities unexpected, how can strategies not be? Confucius famously taught us: 'The exemplary person, in walking his way in the world, is neither bent on nor against anything; what is right he will follow';[77] the contemporary German social theorist Hans Joas suggests: 'Pragmatism is, put succinctly, a theory of situated creativity';[78] and Collins and Porras summarise their empirical findings thus: 'the last thing a visionary company would ever do is follow a cookbook recipe for success.'[79]

Be cautious about gurus' one-size-fits-all 'best practice' or 'proved solutions'. Strategy researcher Constantinos Markides has this to say: 'no advice – however sound and practical – will apply to all firms all the time. What a firm should do depends on its own particular circumstances, which are, in turn, determined by its stage of evolution. Strategic advice that fails to put the company in

its historical context runs the risk of being dangerous.'[80] Looking
at the issue from another angle, David Collis and Michael Rukstad
wrote in the *Harvard Business Review*: 'if your firm's strategy can
be applied to any other firm, you don't have a very good one.'[81] What
if you already, God willing, have a good strategy? Congratulations.
Just treat it as a walking stick, prepare for emerging surprises, flexible adjustments and opportunistic learning. As Timothy Luehrman,
who writes about strategic 'real options', puts it:

> When executives create strategy, they project themselves and
> their organisations into the future, creating a path from where
> they are now to where they want to be some year down the road.
> In competitive markets, though, no one expects to formulate
> a detailed long-term plan and follow it mindlessly. As soon
> as we start down the path, we begin learning-about business
> conditions, competitors' actions, the quality of our preparations,
> and so forth – and we need to respond flexibly to what we learn.[82]

Consequential

At the beginning of this chapter, we posited that we all live with the
consequences of strategies. Here, let us present another meaning of
'consequence': strategies are contingent upon what we have done in
the past.

Similar demands for an instant picture might have been made
to many parents, but only Land had the know-how and experience
to make his daughter happy. Many Chinese visiting the US, before
as well as after Ma, were amazed by the Internet, but only Ma envisioned and made real a Chinese online yellow pages. Ma's was not
an empty mind. Business people attending his English classes had
long been complaining about how difficult it was to find buyers and
suppliers in Hangzhou, let alone internationally. And, like many
Chinese professors in those days, Ma was already half in the sea,
having founded a small translation firm handling business documents for clients. God is not blind, he favours the prepared mind.[83]

Where you are depends on where you have been; what you did in the past determines, at least in part, what you can see and choose at the present. This is why Genichi Kawakami saw a market for his piano while others could not. People conceive industries and markets differently, and opportunities for some can be threats to others. This is why, given the same set of strategic options, people select differently. There can be no formula or procedure, however reasoned or proved, to ensure 'rational choice'. People are rational according to their histories. Our experiences, not gurus' models, steer us in making selections. Put in formal language: strategic moves taken at one point in time have ongoing implications for an organisation's fate;[84] constraints and opportunities are often the result of the firm's previous adaptive efforts.[85] History matters, and economists, for example the Nobel Prize-winner Douglas North, call this 'path-dependence'.[86]

The past can be the source of today's advantage as well as undoing, depending on our ability to learn.[87] We do not have a god's-eye view. We humans are fallible beings. The best we can say about our knowledge is that, based on the evidence at hand, it works in the circumstances to which we apply it. We make mistakes. Worse, time and again, past successful strategies become recipes for failure as situations change. Our knowledge is always subject to revisions. Capable managers learn from mistakes and failures. 'Cybernetic explanation is always negative', Gregory Bateson, a system scientist, told us.[88] 'To have proved a hypothesis false is indeed the peak of knowledge', Warren McCulloch, another system scientist, agreed.[89] And, if Jürgen Habermas is right, we know the world only through our mistakes: learning is impossible without 'experience of performative failure in the face of reality'.[90] We fail, therefore we learn.

Closer to business, former Johnson & Johnson CEO R.W. Johnson Jr proudly announced: 'Failure is our most important product.'[91] A Wal-Mart executive explained the secret of the company's success thus: '"Do it. Fix it. Try it." If you try something and it works, you keep it. If it doesn't work, you fix it or try something else.'[92] In

3M Corporation, people are encouraged to make 'fast mistakes'. In Intel, management 'threw a big dinner – not for the group that had been most successful, but for "the failure of the month."'[93] Capable managers 'celebrate failure'.[94] They make the most of experience: 'Let's just try a lot of stuff and keep what works.'[95]

Continuous

To Drucker, strategy is a firm's 'theory of the business', to be constantly worked out. 'It is not graven on tablets of stone. It is a hypothesis. And it is a hypothesis about things that are in constant flux – society, markets, customers, technology.'[96] He further suggested:

> Every three years, an organisation should challenge every product, every service, every policy, every distribution channel with the question, If we were not in it already, would we be going into it now? By questioning accepted policies and routines, the organisation forces itself to think about its theory. It forces itself to test assumptions. It forces itself to ask: Why didn't this work, even though it looked so promising when we went into it five years ago? Is it because we made a mistake? Is it because we did the wrong things? Or is it because the right things didn't work?[97]

To Nonaka, strategy, propelled by knowledge creation, is a process of managing flow.[98] We are always in the flow of life experiences. Strategy is to keep us thinking, questioning and searching for novel answers. Just as the Red Queen tells Alice in Lewis Carroll's *Through the Looking Glass*, in a fast world one must run just to stand still. Not that one strategy follows another, but that strategies infuse into each other, in a flow. Although a beginning and an end might be ascribed to *a* strategy, that is rather arbitrary, for the convenience of onlookers.[99] We do not engage in 'another', 'the next' strategy as a stranger. Each of us already has a history of experience that informs us what to do and how to do it. This is 'path-dependence': strategies do not come from nowhere; each and every strategy has roots in the past, has a pre-history.[100] It is futile to chop off 'a strategy' from the flow in order to analyse why it has succeeded or failed. Without understanding how Toyota's past strategies contributed to its success, we cannot understand its '2010 Vision' prior to the recent recalls, nor can we make sense of the company's handling of the crisis. Toyota's strategies are a flow. Intel's microprocessor strategy illustrates the same point: it did not suddenly come out of the blue at the November 1984 1-Meg-DRAM board meeting.[101]

It is crucial to differentiate process thinking from procedure mentality. Open any popular strategy book, and you will be surprised if there is no 'process model' telling you how to do strategy. One of such textbooks that we happened to pick up, for example, claims to be sympathetic to 'process approaches'; nevertheless in the end it delivers a seven-step model that 'serves as a basis for strategy analysis'. The steps are:

1. defining vision and mission,
2. situation analysis (SWOT),
3. scenario planning,
4. creating a portfolio of plans,
5. decision-making,
6. implementation, and
7. evaluation.

If Confucius is right that life experiences have no fixed shapes (无容), no definite rules (无则), then we do not know how to fit flowing emergencies into these neatly ordered, self-contained steps. With these 'process models' we cannot make sense of Deng Xiaoping, Genichi Kawakami, Intel, Polaroid and Alibaba. Apparently, in mainstream textbooks, x-step procedures and process thinking are one and the same thing: so long as you follow the steps, you are acting upon 'process thinking'. We are all believers in process thinking now, but what does it mean?

Of course, gurus are all quick to claim that their models should not be taken seriously, that steps can be skipped and procedures repeated as many times as you want. Then, what is the point? Why formalise processes into sequential steps in the first place? As the late John Kotter, professor of organisation change, summarised, 'skipping steps creates only the illusion of speed and never produces a satisfying result'.[102] In the end, procedural models bring in through the back door the command-and-control mindset: the world is uncertain, let's use procedures to contain it. Mintzberg mindfully warns us: 'Formal procedures will never be able to forecast discontinuities … or create novel strategies.'[103] Procedural models are good for dummies, not for innovative managers.

Courageous

In the darkest days in China's history, just at the end of the 'Cultural Revolution' and before the reform, 21 farmers in Xiaogang village, Anhui province, decided to divide their farm work among themselves. Putting their blood thumbprints to a secret paper for household farming, they were under no illusions, and were prepared for being put into prison, or worse. There had been previous attempts by farmers to farm under their own will, only to be crushed ruthlessly by the mighty state. The farmers in Xiaogang knew they were taking a life-or-death risk.[104] This was, now officially acknowledged by Beijing, how China's reform started.

On the other side of the globe, Boeing, an American corporation, took a risk of another kind. In 1965, Boeing made the boldest move in business history: to build the 747 jumbo jet. The project nearly killed off the company. In developing the 'big bird', Boeing encountered great difficulties, had to lay off 86,000 workers, roughly 60 per cent of its workforce, in order to fund the project. And, what was in Boeing chairman William Allen's mind? Here it is:

> Boeing became irreversibly committed to the 747 – financially, psychologically, publicly. During the 747 development, a Boeing visitor commented, 'You know, Mr. Allen, [Boeing has] a lot riding on that plane. What would you do if the first airplane crashed on takeoff?' After a long pause, Allen replied, 'I'll rather talk about something pleasant – like a nuclear war.'[105]

As the first 747 took off on the bitterly cold winter morning of 9 February 1969, the engineers and their families wept. Since then, Boeing has sold more than 1,400 jumbos, worth, at today's prices, more than \$350 billion. It is perhaps the best, and commercially most successful, aircraft ever built.[106]

Granted, not all cases are so dramatic. We use the word 'courageous' to stress intent and commitment in strategies. Intent can be vague or articulated, modest or outstanding, and commitments can be graduate or decisive, gut-wrenching or calculated. Yet, without intent and commitment, what makes a strategy a strategy? What distinguishes strategy from simply corporate behaviour, from everyday goings-on?

That strategy largely emerges from multiple paths and gets retrospectively rationalised does not preclude prospectively intended, committed efforts on the part of managers.[107] Making the world a better place is a courageous act. We see all this from Deng Xiaoping and Muhammad Yunus, from the Chinese farmers and the Boeing chairman. Behind any entrepreneurial initiative and anything we call strategy, there is risk; it is with intent and commitment that we cope with risks. We do not have a God's-eye view, we do not have complete knowledge, we cannot foresee the future, but we must take action, here and now.[108] We humble managers are close to 'muddling in the dark'.[109] The American economist Kenneth Arrow, a joint winner of the Nobel Prize for Economics in 1972, observes: 'We simply must act, fully knowing our ignorance of possible consequences ... We must sustain the burden of action without certitude, and we must always keep open the possibility of recognising past errors and changing course.'[110] Intent and commitment enable us to act meaningfully, to take what Sumantra Ghoshal called 'purposeful action' against all odds. Hence we have Akio Morita rejecting Bulovo's order despite the young Sony's desperate need of cash; Jack Ma starting Alibaba without knowing how to build a website; Toyoda deciding to compete with Ford when the Japanese auto industry barely existed. Yet 'against all odds' is not equivalent to 'doing it my way regardless'.

Pragmatism is idealistically reaching towards heaven while being realistically grounded on earth. The other side of the courage coin is fulfilling purpose with opportunistic manoeuvre.

Lenovo, now a top player in the global computer industry, was in the 1980s a start-up belonging to the Institute of Computing Technology at China's Academy of Science. Lenovo set out to make PCs but failed to get a licence. Licences were controlled by another ministry and that ministry had no incentive to give opportunities to 'outsiders'. Against the odds, Liu Quanzhi, the founder of Lenovo, led his colleagues to Hong Kong and developed PCs at the institute's Hong Kong office; there, licensing was not an issue. After Lenovo outperformed all other Chinese PC-makers, it was finally granted a licence, that piece of paper.[111] Liu skilfully exploited Deng's 'one country, two systems' policy to realise Lenovo's bold intent.

Les Kohn, an engineer in Intel, invented the RISC processor (Reduced Instruction Set Computing) that was superior to the company's then 'strategic' x86 series. Knowing that 'an approach which supported rather than challenged the *status quo* would be more likely successful', Kohn sold the design to the Intel management as a co-processor for the x86, rather than a stand-alone chip. 'By the time top management realised what their "co-processor" was, Kohn, with the help of two other champions, had already lined up a customer base for the stand-alone processor.' A lot of those customers were new to Intel. Given its great success, Intel management was happy to amend its strategy to incorporate the RISC business.[112] Lenovo and Intel, at their best moments, showed us that strategies could be courageous and bold and yet creative and opportunistic, like Confucius, who was stubborn in ideals but open-minded in making his ideals real.

Collective

The field of strategy has come a long way in changing our understanding of leadership. The traditional view of the CEO generating a full-blown strategy after analysing situations, charting out opportunities and evaluating options is now balanced by an image of the 'little brain strategy' that mobilises 'little contributions' from 'little people'.[113] Leadership is transformed from the miraculous executive with a magic wand who turns an organisation around to 'one of the guys' whose role is no longer to 'command and control' but to 'facilitate and mentor'.[114] Accordingly, firms strive to capture the hearts and minds of their troops, inviting low-rank staff to board meetings and involving workers in the planning process. To engage people with a sense of urgency, 'one CEO deliberately engineered the largest accounting loss in the history of the company'.[115]

All this should be welcomed, but it is not enough. We need a better-rounded understanding of the dynamic collectiveness of strategy.

Look at Post-it Notes. How were they invented, becoming such an iconic success for the 3M Corporation?[116] A researcher by the name of Spence Silver stumbled during his experiments upon a glue that did not glue. Most people, even within 3M, considered it a failure. 'What can you do with a glue that doesn't glue?' Yet Silver was stubborn enough to believe that he had a solution, just didn't know the problem yet. He continued to show the strange material to his colleagues, despite their indifference. Then, one day, at a church, another 3M employee, Art Fry, suddenly remembered the weak glue as he struggled to mark the pages in his book of hymns. At that moment, far away from laboratory, boardroom, brainstorming or Zen sessions, the concept of Post-it Notes was born. Fry later noted:

> There are so many hoops that a product idea has to jump through. It really takes a bunch of individuals to carry it through the processes. It's not just a Spence Silver or an Art Fry. It's a whole host of people. It's a classic 3M tale. I couldn't have done what I did without Silver. And without me, his adhesive might have come to nothing.[117]

Also involved were two marketing people, Geoffrey Nicholson and Joe Ramey, who hit upon the idea of offering free samples for people to play with. This caught the notice of Lehr, the 3M CEO. Lehr and his top management team sent samples of Post-it Notes to fellow *Fortune* 500 company executives. The rest is history.

What can we learn from the story? We see the locus of strategic action, or what social theorists call 'agency', shifting from one actor to another as a product goes back and forth being formed and transformed. During this process, agency is distributed across the organisation. Individual actors' efforts within the 'action net' are called upon, or 'activated', to make unique contributions, not all at once, but at different times and places, at different levels of involvement, as interactive emergences play out. Think of the 'distributed agency' of Silver, Fry, Nicholson, Ramey and Lehr: is the process bottom-up, top-down, middle-up-down? Or is it circulating, passing, pushing, pulling around? Raghu Garud and Peter Karnøe recommend Nonaka's metaphor of a rugby game: team members take turns to move the ball forward, with an end-in-view but in unpredictable trajectories.[118]

The notion of 'distributed agency' broadens our understanding of strategy. In the next chapter, we consider strategy as multi-path system emergence. Here, it suffices to note that pragmatic emergence is not just any emergence, but interactive emergence. And strategic leadership is no longer the elitist 'facilitating and mentoring', but an invitation to other members to take the lead as 'leadership opportunities' unfold along the way, like members of a rugby team. Leadership, too, is distributed, emerging. This is what Nonaka calls 'distributed *phronesis*'.[119]

Co-creative

In Confucian pragmatism, everything under heaven is related to everything else. The implications for strategy are enormous. As early as the 1980s, a study of production innovation in the tool machinery industries reported that 80 per cent of all product innovations were initiated by customers. The majority of novel ideas didn't flow from R&D labs downwards but from customers upwards.

Increased competition and globalisation only make this more critical. Huawei, the Chinese telecom equipment supplier, originally an 'original equipment manufacturer' selling products via third-party agents, is now a 'solution company' that co-creates value with clients. 'Growing into each other', clients improve strategic performance while Huawei benefits from stable, growing businesses.[120] In this, Huawei is not alone. Apple's iPhone market is co-created by thousands of app suppliers; Audi, the German car-maker, starts co-configuring luxury cars with customers by allowing them to 'activate' initial options; not to mention Wikipedia, YouTube and online games. Not just between customers and suppliers, companies 'tie up' with competitors: Nissan–Renault with Daimler, Yahoo! with Alibaba, Thai Airways with the Singaporean Tiger Airways, to give just a few examples.[121]

Value co-creation happens in other ways, too. Imagine a world where there is only one telephone. The utilisation value of the device will be zero since you can talk to nobody with it. As the number of telephones grows, its value increases. The economist Brian Arthur calls this 'increasing returns', or 'self-reinforcing mechanism'.[122] No wonder telephone companies give their customers handsets for free: you cannot live without it and will continue subscribing to the service as more and more of your bosses, clients, colleagues, friends and family members get locked in. No wonder Tencent, a Chinese online service company with 600 million-plus active customers, competes well on all fronts: instant messaging, e-commerce, online games, social networking and web-searching, with its market value ranked just under Google and Amazon and above all other online companies.[123]

Interestingly, your product need not be 'the best'. As long as you get the customer hooked, you'll win – customers co-create the market for you. The QWERTY keyboard, the piston car engine, the heavy-water nuclear power generator: all still dominate 'the market'. They are 'industry standards', even though we now know there are better options. By seizing a historical window, you acquire resources to refine your 'sub-optimal' or 'second-class' design and to define the market, leaving your competitors' better designs no chance. Remember how, according to some accounts, General Motors in the 1920s dismantled the electric trolley and transit systems in 16 states so as to dominate 'the market'? Remember the battle for the dominant logic of cochlear implant technology? Was JVC's winning video format technologically superior to Sony's? Are IBM's PC and the clones functionally better than Apple's Mac? Does it matter? There is a growing field of research called 'social construction of technological systems' that focuses on these phenomena; companies have no hesitation in exploiting such knowledge for corporate success.[124]

Along this line of investigation, agency is not just distributed among humans, but extended to 'things', for example, materials, artefacts, tools and routines. This 'multiplicity of actors', both human and non-human, work as 'actor-networks', each over time makes its own contribution to strategy. Actor-networks take part in a strategy's success or failure, making us do what we do in the way we do.[125] Napoleon's strategy was not stupid; he was defeated at Waterloo by the weather as much as by the Coalition. Edison had to compromise on a central station model so that his electricity invention could be commercialised. 'The market' simply could not accept any method for distributing lighting apart from the central station model. Gas lighting for houses had always been distributed via central stations, and what was good for gas must be good for electricity, or so the public believed. The gas pipelines underneath New York City amounted to an 'actor' taking part in selecting a strategic option, and we are still living with the legacy.[126]

When it comes to ready-made products, such as CT scanners for hospitals or a computer-aided-software-engineering (CASE) tool for software firms, many issues, for example, how-it-should-work, how-to-use-it and what-benefit-will-be-generated-from-it, are not fixed by producers but configured by users.[127] Viagra was designed to treat heart disease, but it became extremely popular and profitable for an entirely different and surprising reason. It is the customer who dictates the purpose, functionality and consumption of the drug. Value is therefore generated through a 'robust fit' among multiple 'actors'.[128] Rules, routines, systems, structures and products have an impact only when we make use of them. Then, our actions, informed by these 'things' though, result in transforming them. Applying the theory of 'structuration' proposed by the sociologist Anthony Giddens, reflective managers understand this and incorporate it into their strategies.[129]

At a subtler level, even knowledge is co-created, not just among humans through teamwork but between humans and Nature through co-evolution. The French psychologist Jean Piaget saw knowledge as a higher form of evolution.[130] Knowledge is constructed by humans, but we are not free to construct it in whatever way we want. The world is hardly ever what we would like it to be. Like bio-species struggling for survival in the ecosystem, knowledge survives 'if it fits within the constraints of experiential reality and does not collide with them'.[131] Jürgen Habermas called this the 'revisionary power of experience': the frustrations we experience in coping with brute reality force us to change our beliefs.[132] At the same time, strategies, informed by our knowledge, produce world-changing consequences. Hence, the world selects strategies, and strategies change the world. It is a co-creative, co-evolutionary process of which the outcome is the joint product of managerial adaptation and environmental selection.[133] Those who have more experience, keep minds open and learn more effectively will have better chances to survive and outperform.

The more we look around, the more we find things connected. The lines are blurring between producer and consumer, creator and created, business and environment. Using the term 'collective', we stress distributed agency among humans; under the heading 'co-creative' we extend agency to non-human actors and, ultimately, to Nature. This is highly compatible with the Confucian attitude towards Nature: deference (恭), respect (敬) and propensity (畏). We owe Nature our lives, we must strategise accordingly.

Bricolage: a French spirit Confucius would have loved

What do China's Deng Xiaoping and Grameen Bank's Muhammad Yunus have in common? They are both masters of *bricolage*.

Bricolage is a French word that denotes purposeful making-do by applying inventive combinations of the resources at hand to emerging problems and opportunities. *Bricolage*, with its associated forms *bricoler* (verb: to engage in *bricolage*) and *bricoleur* (noun: someone engaged in *bricolage*), were made famous by the French anthropologist Claude Lévi-Strauss in his effort to appreciate a way of acting that is different from the rational, analytic, theoretic style typical in 'the West'.[134] Since then, *bricolage* has been applied to many disciplines and practical domains: art, science, culture, politics and business. In the spirits of pragmatism, we shall draw managers' attention to four aspects of *bricolage*: action-oriented, resourceful, opportunistic, purposeful.

Underpinned by a 'bias for action', *bricolage* places priority on getting jobs done. *Bricoleurs* actively try something to solve situated problems and seize emerging opportunities even without a clear sense of how things will unfold. They do not endlessly analyse a situation to find a systematic, optimal course forward. *Bricoleurs*, like everyone else, are path-dependent. Yet, unlike others, they create and shape paths: they are path-makers. Unlike spectators sitting on the safe dry land, they are, as sociologists would call them, 'change agents', flowing in the sea of challenges and opportunities.[135]

Resourcefulness does not mean acting with infinite resources or waiting for the successful acquisition of well-defined tools before jumping into 'the sea'. Instead, it denotes making-do with whatever is at hand. *Bricoleurs* refuse to enact limitations. Rather, they strive to construct something from nothing, bringing value to resources judged by others as substandard, inferior, backward, cheap, useless or even a liability. *Bricolage* enables change agents to seek workable solutions in constrained environments. *Bricoleurs* are the enemies of perfectionism and optimisation. They are the champions of 'good enough' pragmatism.[136]

Bricoleurs use resources opportunistically, in inventive ways, trying endless new configurations to suit their ends-in-view. In getting jobs done, they do not worry about how the resources in hand might have previously been defined, nor about their 'proper' or 'improper' uses. They discover the properties of resources in the course of action. Indeed, *bricoleurs* create those properties when using resources. They reject 'ideal-type' solutions and constantly change 'the right way' of doing things. As each initiative is informed by past experience but imperfectly understood, *bricolage* begins in uncertainty, and often ends there, too. *Bricoleurs* are the fittest in uncertain worlds.[137]

Bricolering ahead, *bricoleurs* constantly refine resources, at the same time redefining tasks and objectives. While tasks and objectives inform the use of resources, resources redefine tasks and objectives. *Bricolage* is about piecing all this together so as to make a job doable. 'This doesn't mean that *bricoleurs* don't care about results, but that they are willing to experiment to get there.'[138] Lanzara puts it beautifully:

> In a broadly diffused engineering ideology *bricolage* is
> usually associated with second-best solutions, maladaptation,
> imperfection, inefficiency, incompleteness, slowness, but as
> a matter of fact in many design situations it is the only thing
> that we can reasonably do when we are engaged in action. The
> outcomes of it are hybrid, imperfect, transient artifacts, which
> perhaps do not look very elegant, have lots of bugs and gaps,
> frictions and unusable components, but they do their job and can
> be improved.[139]

Bricoleurs have a compelling sense of purpose, always working with what John Dewey called 'ends-in-view'.[140] *Bricolage* amounts to what Sumantra Ghoshal called 'purposeful action-taking'. The opposite is active non-action: spontaneous, extremely busy, willing to accept anything and go anywhere, easily slipping into harmful conduct. To active non-actors, doing something, anything, is the game. In contrast, *bricoleurs* are passionately firm about their vision – knowing what they want to achieve – yet opportunistic and innovative in making their vision real.

In our view, the spirit of *bricolage* and Confucian pragmatism invite each other, despite their different cultural roots. Lévi-Strauss' *bricoleurs* and Confucius' exemplary persons are the natural allies of reflective managers in search of pragmatic strategy. This gives us confidence that people everywhere, regardless of their geographical, racial and historical differences, all have the potential to strategise pragmatically. Let's have a look at Deng Xiaoping and Muhammad Yunus.

Deng and Yunus: the bricolage masters

During China's ten-year-long 'Cultural Revolution', Deng was packed off by Mao to labour in the remote countryside of Jiangxi province, where he obtained on-the-spot understanding of the real China. As a *bricoleur*, Deng knew when to keep his head down and when to take decisive action. In order to survive, he promised Mao three times that he would never betray the 'party line'. Within two months of Mao's death, however, he crushed the 'gang of four' and put Mao's wife into prison. Deng embraced opportunities and challenges; he wasted no time in jumping into 'the sea'. It is 'bias for action' at its best.

What resources did Deng have at hand? First and foremost, he had no official legitimacy. He was not Mao's appointed successor. Before his death, Mao fast-tracked the promotion of a like-minded person to become head of the party, the armed forces and the country. Of course Deng had *guanxi* (personal connections) to the old guard. Yet this 'resource' was far from perfect. Few of the old guard understood Deng's 'Four Modernisations' vision; what united them around Deng was their hatred of the 'gang of four' – for ten years they had all suffered at the gang's hands. With comrades like these, Deng put aside Mao's 'fundamental policy' and embarked the country on unprecedented reform. Without knowing what the outcome would look like, Deng engaged 1.3 billion people in experimentation. If you do not want to get your feet wet searching for stones, you have to remain on the riverside, never crossing the river, Deng told his people. He was one of them, and the people *bricolered* together with him.

In 1992, Deng, touring to the south, won the milestone battle over the conservatives. Crucially, the battle was won not through clarification, but through continued ambiguity. 'Is this Socialism or Capitalism?', the conservatives challenged; 'No debate for one hundred years', Deng replied. And the people lined up with him, striking deeper into 'the sea'.

Previously, we presented some factors that made China's reform work: the imbalanced industrial structure, vague party policy, personalised social order, low trust, weak rule of law and problematic property rights. Retrospectively, we have learned to appreciate the pragmatic value of these 'resources'. Make no mistake: in any paradigm or consensus, whether capitalism or socialism, market economy or plan economy, those factors would be liabilities instead of 'resources'. Many theorists, politicians, leaders and managers would simply want to get rid of them. This is why *bricoleurs* are the fittest species: Deng had the will and skill to make something from less than nothing, inventively turning liabilities into useful resources to get the job done. He was a master of purposeful opportunism.

Deng's reform was not optimal, perhaps even not the 'second best' (who knows?); the Tiananmen tragedy that happened under his watch constitutes some of the evidence. Deng led and was led by flows. Sometimes he was happy to support radical reformers; at other times he placated the conservatives. He even had to leave Beijing to make his voice heard. Deng, like his project, was not perfect. He made mistakes, and his reform experienced ups and downs, frustrations and setbacks. Nevertheless, he never lost his purpose, ideal, vision, spirit or his touch with people. Deng's legacy is still with us. China has dramatically changed the world, but within there are still problems, difficulties, tensions, limitations, bugs and dangers. Deng began the reform with huge uncertainty; even today it is uncertain where China will end up. But perhaps there is never certainty, nor an end, and this is why *bricolage* is particularly useful for making the world better and happier. You can criticise Deng for his betrayal of socialism, half-baked capitalism, bizarre mix of party dictatorship and market economy, but you cannot easily deny that Deng had made a substantial, practical, positive difference.

As to another *bricoleur* par excellence, Muhammad Yunus, we analyse here only one micro episode, based on the Nobel Prize-winner's own account.[141] In 1977, Yunus was still running the Grameen project on the university's small research budget. His hardworking student-workers received no pay, only had their expenses reimbursed. Yunus had to personally sign and guarantee each and every microloan application before submitting it to the Janata Bank for approval. Every time a question arose, it took months to travel up and down the chain of command between the bank headquarters in Dhaka and the university at Chittagong. Even when Yunus travelled abroad, applications were sent to him for processing. Doing good could be extremely frustrating.

One day in October, Yunus happened to meet an acquaintance, Mr Anisuzzaman, the managing director of the Bangladesh Krishi (Agricultural) Bank (BKB). After listening to Yunus' story, as a banker Anisuzzaman found it interesting:

> 'You cannot go on like this. That is absurd. Now tell me what would you want from me?'
>
> 'Well,' my mind was racing and I smiled. 'I guess I would like the Agricultural Bank to set up a branch in Jobra and leave it at my disposal. I'll frame its rules and procedures. And you'll allow me to grant loans up to a total of 1 million *taka*. I'll recruit my own staff.'
>
> 'It is done,' said Mr Anisuzzaman. 'Now what else?'
>
> 'Well, if you give me all that I want, I have nothing more to ask. You have already made me "managing director" of a branch. What else can I ask for?'

'Are you certain?'

'Yes, this gives me all the support I need. How can I ever repay you?'[142]

However, when Mr Anisuzzaman put the proposal to the board of directors of BKB, he was told he could not delegate authority to Yunus, an academic outsider who was not an employee of the bank. Several months later, Yunus met Anisuzzaman again.

'Yunus, you really want to open a new branch of our bank, do you?'

'No, not at all. I just want to lend money to the poor.'

'Do you want to remain a professor?'

'Well, teaching is the only thing I know how to do. It's what I love.'

'I am not pressuring you, I was only thinking out loud.' He blew smoke up to the ceiling. 'Otherwise, you could give up your job at the university and simply become an employee of our bank. Then it would be easy for me to make you my deputy. I could delegate any of my powers to you without anyone complaining.'[143]

After a while:

'I will find a way, don't you worry ... What if on paper I do not make you responsible for the branch. So officially the district manager oversees the branch, but unofficially he does everything you tell him?'

'It's up to you Mr Anisuzzaman, you know best.'

'I will tell him to take his orders from you. You would instruct him on everything you want. And if there is anything out of the ordinary, then he can come to headquarters, to me here and I will approve it.'

'That sounds fine to me. Will the board accept it?'

'I will handle that. But you should submit a list of your students who are currently working for you in Jobra. One of them can become the branch manager, others can become formal employees of the bank.'

'Thank you. Those are good jobs.'

'Yes, and no competitive civil service exam for them.'

'I would call it the Grameen Branch.'[144]

Hence the significant milestone, the precursor of the now globally famous Grameen Bank. Life is full of uncertainty, and full of chances. Yunus embraced them skilfully for his purpose. Given Grameen's success and Yunus' international standing today, the episode looks all the more clever, 'naturally so'. But put the clock back 35 years, would you have been so sure?

Was the deal a brilliant innovation, or just one more example of rule-breaking behaviours common in 'the Third World', repeatedly criticised by Washington, London, Geneva? Is such activity good for development and modernisation? Is it perfect, second-best or simply cheating the system? Should Mr Anisuzzaman receive an award or disciplinary action? What would have happened if Anisuzzaman had backed down, given the board's ruling on one hand and Yunus' refusal to become a bank employee on the other? Would the Grameen Bank have developed without this episode? How many villagers would still be in desperately poor conditions? Then, does the end justify the means? If yes, what are rules for, and what about corporate governance? If no, should such activities be cleared away? What resource did Yunus deploy in this case? Did he use it properly, legitimately? Finally, could this happen, would it be acceptable, in your community, your country, your culture? With friends like Mr Anisuzzaman, in those smoking rooms, what would you do? In the spirit of pragmatism, we invite managers to seek their own answers.

SUMMARY

In this chapter, we introduce readers to what Peter Drucker called the 'specifications'[145] of pragmatic strategy. We posit that pragmatic strategy, in what we say, believe, have, do and live with, is about envisioning a valued future for the common good and creatively realising it, often with non-ideal resources, imperfect solutions and unproved manoeuvres, which is based on historically informed understanding of situated particulars, and thus has better chances of surviving evolutionary selection. In the ambiguous, fast-moving business world, strategy is a messy, risky enterprise. As managers know well, carefully thought-through plans do not always work, winning formulas quickly become recipes for disaster and successful strategies can emerge from unexpected undertakings, locations and events. Around strategy we can expect surprises, setbacks and frustrations as well as accomplishments, triumphs and joy. Good strategists are those who learn best from all this. In the next chapter, we turn to a related question: how are pragmatic strategies formulated, taking shape and producing consequences?

4 Strategy as purposeful emergence

To thoughtful managers, there is hardly another question more concerning than this: how do firms generate winning strategies? The question can be phrased in many ways: how is strategy formed; what lies behind successful strategies: cool analysis, entrepreneurial genius or pure luck? No wonder 'strategy process' has become such a ubiquitous topic that generates so many controversies, so much heat, occasional truces, then more controversies, more heat.[1] What is the pragmatic view of strategy formation? Can the pragmatic spirits bring in some light, not more heat?

In this chapter, continuing our inquiry on what pragmatic strategies look like, we focus on the strategy-formation process. We first present a humanised evolutionary view that conceives of strategy as multi-path system emergence in which the environment selects strategies while strategic actions change the world. We then discuss what pragmatic strategy is and is not, stressing the important role of managers' ideals, values, purposes and capabilities. Cases examined in this chapter include the Toyota Production System, the Chinese reformers and farmers who created household farming and Township-Village Enterprises, Wall Street and the Grameen Bank, Honda's motorcycle and Master Kong Noodles, T. E. Lawrence and Mao Zedong. Together, this and the previous chapter are intended to create a descriptive platform for readers to proceed to Part III, where we will explore the normative question 'what to do, how to do it?' in the search for pragmatic strategies.

So, how are strategies formed and what role do managers play in the process?

MULTI-PATH EMERGENCE

Adopting an evolutionary perspective, we invite managers to view strategy as a social system and strategy formation as a historical process generating outcomes through the interplay of multiple factors. Such factors may include historical imperatives, environmental constraints, human actions, significant events and so on.[2] In the 'ecology of strategies', some strategies survive, others do not. Strategies are selected by the functional criterion of generating competitive performance. In the business world, optimising forces do not always function smoothly or rapidly. That is, selection is 'lenient': weak performers are not immediately eliminated, but allowed some time to learn and improve. In the long run, a firm's capacity to learn, both through planning and opportunistically, is critical for its survival and performance. Such an evolutionary view, inherent in both Confucian and American pragmatism, contrasts with the assumption of the five-forces sort that cause–effect relations will play themselves out quickly, smoothly, independent of the strategy process, firm history or managerial efforts.[3]

To people involved in the emergence process, strategic outcome is a combination of intended and unintended consequences, of managerial actions and environmental factors. System emergence need not, indeed cannot, be explained solely as the product of human foresight or deliberate planning, nor can it be reduced to mindless behaviours or random chances. Systems can emerge on various paths, and a combination of paths is usually required to explain the formation of any particular strategy. The important nuance here is not that different strategies take different paths in a one-to-one manner, but that each surviving strategy emerges from a particular, complex combination of multiple paths. Good performers have the dynamic capability to pursue effective strategies through evolutionary learning, even without prior knowledge of their potential effects.[4] This process Takahiro Fujimoto calls 'multi-path system emergence', and Robert Burgelman 'multiple strategy-making process'.[5]

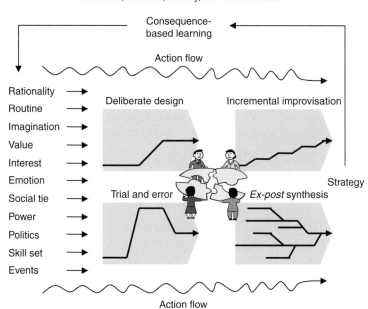

Industries, markets, society, eco-environment

FIGURE 4.1 Strategies as multi-path system emergence (based on and extended from Fujimoto 1991)

Such a view is evolutionary and at the same time pragmatic. It is a humanised one, in contrast with the human-absent tendency.

In the usual new-Darwinian conception which directly applies biological analogies to social phenomena, the focus is almost always at the 'population' level; for example, industries and sectors. What happens beneath that level does not, it is assumed, have any significance. System variations are seen as entirely random happenings, and environmental forces as the dominant selection-retention mechanisms. In all variation, selection and retention processes, the agency of managers is largely absent.[6] So much so that Ronald Coase, a Nobel Prize-winning economist, felt compelled to remind us of the critical difference between natural and social evolutionary processes: 'The IQ of Natural Selection is zero. The IQ of businessmen and politicians may not be too high but it is not zero.'[7] Coase's moral: in contrast to natural evolution, in social-system evolution human decisions make a difference.

Twenty years ago, at the peak of the trend for transplanting insights from the 'science of complexity' into strategy, a similar tendency developed to apply patterns in natural ecology (e.g. the 'butterfly effect' on the world weather; the 'simple rules' governing the movement of large groups of birds) directly onto human affairs. There have subsequently been debates about the unique impact of human organisational capability in comparison with animals and computer 'agents'.[8] Critical of the direct, simplistic analogy, John Seely Brown and Paul Duguid comment:

> Humans and insects show many intriguing similarities, but these should not mask their important differences. In particular, most champions of complicated adaptive systems, particularly those of artificial life, say relatively little about the importance to human behaviour of *deliberate social organisation*. To pursue the analogies from entomology or artificial life much further, we would need to know what might happen if insects decided to form a committee, bats to pass a law or artificial agents to organise a strike or join a firm.[9]

Concurring with Coase, Brown and Duguid, we take strategic initiatives generated by managers as the unit of analysis, emphasise what managers do during the strategy-formation process and stress the significance of learning capacity and entrepreneurial leadership. This humanised evolutionary perspective, informed by the pragmatic spirits, is intended to avoid falling into the ill-conceived dichotomy between free-will 'strategic choice' on one side and 'environmental determinism' on the other.[10] Ours is compatible with David Teece's 'evolution with design' and Sumantra Ghoshal's 'guided evolution' theses. Teece and Ghoshal posit that, while it is evolutionary by nature, shaped by environmental imperatives and the firm's past decisions, strategy formation involves, on the part of managers, intentional design and orchestration efforts, such as envisioning the future, setting goals, evaluating opportunities, making investments, nurturing culture, building trust, coordinating *ba*, configuring assets and renewing capabilities.[11] To Ghoshal, as to Teece, an organisation is 'an ecological system purposefully designed to guide the evolution of strategy'.[12]

'The *Tao* of Heaven is far away; the *Tao* of Man is near (天道远, 人道近).'[13] Confucius' teaching serves to remind us of the human dimension of social-system evolution, including strategy formation. A humanised evolutionary framework takes account of managerial agency and entrepreneurial leadership amid environmental constraints. It can be used as an intellectual umbrella for managers to understand strategy process, an umbrella that embraces the rich insights generated by a wide range of available theories: efficiency, positioning, transaction cost, resource dependency, power, culture, dynamic capability, organisational learning, knowledge creation, human agency, social structure, path-dependence, risk and uncertainty, creative destruction and so on.

The formation of the Toyota Production System

In his excellent book, *The Evolution of a Manufacturing System at Toyota*, Takahiro Fujimoto traces empirically how the main components of the Toyota Production System emerged from combinations of a variety of evolutionary paths. In the following we present one component, the Just-in-Time system.[14]

In 1931, when Kiichiro Toyoda started his automobile business, he set up an ambitious, even reckless, vision: to compete with Ford. From day one, Kiichiro deliberately posted the phrase 'just-in-time' (*jasuto-in-taimu*) on the wall. He insisted that if 20 engine blocks a day were what was needed, workers should receive just 20 in the morning and not more. Kiichiro walked around the factory, throwing away extra materials. The founder's foresight was formidable. As Fujimoto comments:

> Firm-specific entrepreneurial visions sometimes played an
> important role in building distinctive manufacturing capability.
> This was particularly the case when an apparently unrealistic
> vision triggered self-fulfilling efforts to achieve bold objectives.

Kiichiro Toyoda, in the 1930s and '40s, played a pivotal role in advocating cost reduction without economy of scale, catchup with Ford, and the just-in-time philosophy.[15]

When Taiichi Ohno moved in from Toyoda Spinning and Weaving in 1943, he brought in the idea of 'doing things right the first time' (tsukurikomi) and associated practices such as product-focused layout and small-lot production. These he deliberately incorporated into the Toyota assembly line. In 1950 Eiji Toyoda and Shoichi Saito visited the US for benchmarking Ford, but their moment of inspiration was an accident. The delegation noticed that the Piggly Wiggly supermarket only reordered items that had been purchased by customers. The Japanese visitors suddenly found a handy metaphor, the 'supermarket system', to capture Kiichiro's vision.

While 'Learning from Ford' was intentional, planned, the 'supermarket enlightenment' was opportunistic, seized upon. Nevertheless, the 'supermarket system' as a formal instrument for realising Kiichiro's vision did not take shape until Ohno articulated and installed it during the 1950s. The system linked upstream and downstream work stations by returnable containers and reusable slips called kanban (看板). In 1962, kanban were finally adopted across Toyota, transformed from informal experimentation into a company-wide practice. However brilliant Kiichiro's foresight and decisive his leadership, Just-in-Time took various efforts and paths to develop into a competitive practice.

With Just-in-Time on the shop floor, Toyota achieved what it had long intended: productivity increased rapidly. Then, during the 1948–1949 recession, an unintended consequence intruded: finished automobiles piled up quickly in inventory, due to high productivity, and threatened to bankrupt the company. Toyota found itself Just-in-Time for production, but not for sales. Managers were forced to learn once again. Ohno reflected:

> We got a lesson from the crisis that productivity increase and cost reduction had to be accompanied by 'limited volume

production (*genryo seisan*),' which meant that we had to produce just enough to sell and just when we could sell. We learned that productivity increase for the sake of itself was no good, and that we should not simply imitate the American style mass production.[16]

Not all unintended consequences were upsetting. In the 1960s, Toyota extended *kanban* to its suppliers. At that time Toyota managers believed that increasing the engineering activities of suppliers would alleviate the in-house workload problem. This specific solution to the workload problem became a major competitive weapon by the 1980s when it enabled the company to cut costs and hours significantly. Today, Toyota's official documents, as well as many outsider books and case studies, attribute this practice to deliberate strategising. Once the beneficial effects began to bite, Toyota's decisions looked all the more rational, logical and clever. Evidence at hand nevertheless shows us the role of unintended, surprising consequences and the virtue of taking advantage of whatever had already happened.

In the bio-evolutionary world, species are selected by environmental forces; in a pragmatic-evolutionary world, that is only part of the story. Strategy is not any evolution. To capable managers, it is 'guided', 'purposeful' evolution, with a human touch, with deliberate design.[17] Selection processes can take place inside firms as well as outside. Firms can select–deselect and retain–abandon strategic initiatives before they themselves are selected or weeded out by the market.[18] As Robert Burgelman suggests, firms whose internal selection criteria accurately reflect external selection pressures are more likely to make effective choices than other firms.[19] In the last chapter, we saw an example of this in the case of Intel, where internal investment rules directed the firm to seize the vital microprocessor opportunity.

Select, before being selected. Pragmatic leadership in an evolutionary world is about creating 'mechanisms of internal selection' or 'intraorganisational ecological processes'.[20] A competent leader is one who has the ability to realise emergent strategy better than others.[21] Such a leader is able to act as a 'vicarious selector', recognising and retaining viable initiatives on behalf of external forces,[22] by means of shared strategic intent, resource-allocation rules, administrative systems and cultural mechanisms.[23] Of course, to have options to select, you must first create a proper climate in which a variety of initiatives can grow.[24]

Furthermore, for better chances to outperform, with vision and capability managers can purposefully 'strategise the market'. Researchers, chiefly Alfred Chandler, William Lazonick and David Teece, have argued for decades that 'firms shape markets'.[25] At the 'micro level', this can be done in many ways. For example:

- innovating new markets, e.g. Yamaha's electronic piano, Nintendo's Wii machine, Alibaba's electronic China yellow pages and Grameen Bank's lending to millions of poor villagers;
- revising the rules of the game, e.g. Dell's Direct business model, Tencent's mass-customer-based competition and Huawei's co-creating value with clients;
- conducting relationship schemes, e.g. airlines and supermarkets' loyal customer clubs, alliances between firms, share-swap between organisational buyers and suppliers;
- launching advertising programmes: are companies' advertising efforts not ultimately designed to influence 'the market' for their own advantage?

There are, and will continue to be, many more market-strategising, environment-shaping activities. Teece posits that 'capturing values' via 'creating, recreating and co-creating markets' is the reason why firms exist.[26]

At the 'macro level', governments and interest groups frequently manipulate 'the market' for purposes, and there are many markets: financial markets, labour markets, input factor markets, product markets, domestic and international markets, 'mature' as well as 'emerging' markets. Below is just a sample of the evidence.

- Time and again, auto-maker associations lobby for a 'favourable market' against 'unrealistic' environmental legislations.[27]
- In the 1920s, General Motors (GM) bought public transportation firms and then destroyed the tracks and associated facilities so as to consolidate and expand the car market.[28]
- In the 2000s, Honda declared that it would halt investment in Britain if the country remained outside the euro. Honda was talking not primarily to individual consumers, but to 'the market' and the government behind it.[29]
- Not long after the worldwide textile and cloth export quota system was lifted in 2005, the EU forced China to the negotiating table for urgent trading arrangements – to make 'the market' 'fairer'.[30]
- Central banks pumped hundreds of billions' worth of taxpayers' money into 'the market', hoping to save the banking system from a total collapse triggered by American subprime mortgage 'innovations'.[31]
- Before that, Hank Paulson, the architect of the massive bail-out, was among five bank chiefs who persuaded the Securities and Exchange Commission not to extend prudential reserve requirements to banks – he was then the boss of Goldman Sachs.[32]
- 'The market' is not just evolving, it can be built from scratch: just look at how the European Common Market and the Shanghai Stock Market were 'made' at will.[33]
- Citizens in Ireland were forced to vote on the Lisbon Treaty again and again until it was passed, while citizens in other EU countries were denied a vote.[34] Where there is a will, there is a way, and the elites call this 'democracy'; this is certainly true in strategising markets.

Crucially, in all this, at both 'micro' and 'macro' levels, firms and managers are not passively adapting to or selected by 'the market'. They actively strategise 'the market'. Some of these efforts benefit communities and society, others do not. Nevertheless, all are intended to tame 'the market'. The market might or might not be free, it is we who make it so. This has been with us since the 'invisible hand' came into being. Those who play the game successfully get advantages, those who do not, well, become prey.

In a pragmatic-evolutionary world, selection can be a two-way, interactive process. The business environment selects strategies, while managers' efforts change the world. In all this, what matters most is managers' ability to make good judgements, implement decisions, learn from mistakes and grasp benefits that arise from unintended consequences and surprising happenings. We call this 'purposeful opportunism'.

Hence, successful companies outperform others not because they make a 'fundamental choice' between emerging paths, but because they continuously renew their capabilities to capitalise on mixed opportunities generated from both emergent and deliberate formation. Fujimoto summarises this beautifully:

> The evolutionary process is neither totally deterministic nor stochastic. People struggle to make good decisions in the midst of multi-path system emergence. Their foresight and actions almost always influence the system change process, although they may neither fully control nor predict the processes.
> And even if the process is essentially emergent, there are certain firms … that still outperform others in the long-range competition of capability building.[35]

We strategise, therefore we are.

Who created the China miracle: Deng or the farmers?[36]

Household farms (HF) and Township-Village Enterprises (TVE) were the powerhouses of China's phenomenal growth in the 1980s–1990s, the critical early stage of the market-oriented reform. Without the creation of these two novel organisation forms, there would have been no 'China Miracle'. The questions are who created HF and TVE, and how?

Not surprisingly, in the Western media as well as in Chinese state propaganda, an elite image is obsessively erected, for example, 'In the beginning there was Deng, who personally … created a market economy … by favour[ing] … family farms'.[37] However, this image of a mastermind or elite coterie manipulating farmers is questionable.[38]

For the elites, it all began in 1978 when the Third Plenary Session of the Eleventh Party Congress jettisoned the grand socialist countryside project and concentrated on increasing agricultural production. The purpose was to change labour-management methods, not institutions. The Third Plenum resolution insisted that HF was illegal and that collective farming should be consolidated. Deng Xiaoping opposed HF until 1982 when 80 per cent of production teams had already yielded to HF and tremendous agricultural growth been demonstrated. Chen Yun, Deng's long-time comrade and chief of economic affairs, fiercely fought against HF: 'We cannot allow farmers to choose the path which only serves their narrow interests ... Otherwise, the so-called freedom of 800 million farmers will result in the collapse of the state plan.'[39]

While the elites in Beijing were irresolute, farmers far away in the vast countryside manipulated the state's programme in the direction of HF, mainly by illegitimate improvisations.

Secret experimenting. Even before the Third Plenary document reached the countryside, 21 households in Xiaogang (reduced from 34 due to years of collective farming and starvation) secretly started HF. They agreed that HF was not to be mentioned to outsiders; after rendering a harvest to the state, the rest would be divided among households; if anyone was punished because of HF, the other farmers would raise his children. The farmers knew that HF was illegal. HF or starving to death, they had no other choice.

Misconstruing policies. Although it permitted dividing farming tasks among small work groups, the Third Plenum resolution explicitly banned HF. The farmers used the policy as an excuse: 'The smaller the team, the better the production. Dividing the team into work groups is therefore not as good as straightforward disbandment.' 'As long as you're letting us divide into work groups, why not just leave everything to us?'

Voting with feet. In 1979, six weddings took place in Liu Chen village, Anhui province, with five brides coming from the adjacent Jiangsu province. The reason: Anhui tolerated HF, Jiangsu did not.

The flight of women (men were not allowed) was the last chance for farmers to make their preference known. Farmers did not 'voice', they did not 'exit' either; they engaged silently. Soon, HF spread to Jiangsu and beyond.

Appearing as collectives. Farmers packaged illegal family and lineage farms as legal work groups. All over China's country-side there emerged father-and-son, husband-and-wife, Wang-family, Zhang-clan work groups. Farmers did not fight for legitimacy, they cheated for it.

Corrupting the cadres. Households would promise to fulfil a production quota and give the local cadres a bit over. One family took control of a pigsty by promising high payments to the collect-ive; another was allowed to plant a small hillside by paying the bri-gade secretary. Such quiet deals worked best in poor areas where cadres found it hard to turn deals down. Soon, illegal deals, because of their productivity effect, spread to richer areas.

Aggressive productivity. Throwing their energies into illegal undertakings, farmers aggressively boosted production to the point where state elites could no longer resist. With HF, total agricultural output across China grew by 67.6 per cent in merely five years. This the farmers did in conjunction with inflating the cost of state pref-erences by passivity, sabotage and deliberate lethargy, making it unproductive to keep the communes afloat.

Cheating on a massive scale. Farmers in one village would declare they had had a bad year and were unable to meet procure-ment quotas. They then sold the actual good harvest at above-quota price with the help of farmers from other villages, and split the bonus with them. Each year the state reduced quotas, but the farmers kept failing to fulfil them, while the total procurement went up year by year. 'Nationwide, on a massive scale, peasants were cheating.'[40]

Via these illegitimate means, farmers effectively created a new institution within just a few years. The state elites were alarmed and ambivalent. Crucially, before the policy confusion settled down, farmers were able to demonstrate the effects of HF. The elites came to accept the farmers' innovation since in the end they found they themselves could not do without it.

And what about TVE? On 12 June 1987, Deng spoke with great honesty to a guest delegation:

> Generally speaking, our reforms have proceeded very fast,
> and farmers have been enthusiastic. What took us by surprise
> completely was the development of township and village
> industries. The diversity of production, commodity economy,
> and all sorts of small enterprises boomed in the countryside,
> as if a strange army appeared suddenly from nowhere. This is
> not the achievement of our central government ... This was not
> something I had thought about. Nor had the other comrades. This
> surprised us.[41]

TVE was a direct consequence of HF. First, the rapid increase in agricultural productivity released huge surplus labour to be absorbed. Second, the booming markets put funds in the hands of farmers to start businesses. Third, HF enabled farmers to control labour allocation. Fourth, as farmers were not allowed to work in state-owned factories, they were left to their own devices for non-agricultural employment. Hence TVE.

Since the very beginning, the state elites' attitude towards TVE had been ambivalent. For years the government invested almost nothing in rural industry; instead it always criticised TVE and tried to prevent them obtaining raw materials and markets. In his 1989 government report, the premier Li Peng called for a reduction in rural industrial development. Indeed, immediately after the Tiananmen tragedy, about three million TVE went under in 1989 alone. As seasoned observers commented:

> The TVE development so far is not an outcome of any carefully
> designed policy or plan. The government policy changed
> from tolerance to encouragement during the 1980s, only after
> recognizing that the TVE was a vehicle to increase rural income,

and more importantly, to absorb a large amount of rural labor surplus without much need for state investment – a serious problem which had been confronting the Chinese governments at all levels.[42]

Apparently, the state elites did not initiate TVE. Once again, the institutional entrepreneurs were the farmers. The question is how they did it.

Growing out of the plan. TVE were built partly on Mao's commune-brigade enterprises (CBE) set up to serve rural areas and restricted to a narrow range of *wu xiao* (五小, five smalls): iron and steel, cement, chemical fertiliser, hydroelectric power and farm implements. Soon after illegally leasing land to individuals, the farmers did the same to CBE. Meanwhile, private enterprises began to emerge, such as handicrafts in farm households and simple workshops run by individual farmers. 'To a large extent the rural and township enterprises succeeded because they were outside the reach of central planners.'[43]

Manipulating factor markets. There was a *shuanggui zhi* (双轨制, dual-track mechanism) to protect the elites' interest: state-owned enterprises (SOE) received input factors from the state at a low 'plan price', while TVE had to purchase the same factors at a high 'market price'. Farmers got around the system by colluding with SOE. SOE were happy to obtain production factors from the state and sell them to farmers; they used the price difference to give bonuses to city workers. In 1985 alone, SOE made a profit of ¥10.7 billion from such deals.[44]

Bribing product markets. State distribution channels refused to sell TVE products. To cope with this, TVE employed a huge sales army, generally 20 per cent of the total workforce. Outside state control, they offered clients corrupting benefits for sales opportunities. They relied on *guanxi* (personal connections); those who had no *guanxi* created it with tremendous efforts. The story below is typical:

> When the director of a state railway company in Harbin City, Heilongjiang [province], became known locally as a 'greedy

cat', many rural sales people began to knock at his door. One Shandong [province] man found the director's home and told his wife: 'I am from a light fixture factory in Zhaoyuan County, Shandong. I would like the director to help us by buying our factory products. I am from far away and did not bring anything with me. Please accept the 1,000 *yuan* and buy some cigarettes and wine for the director.[45]

Hiding true status. This we have already mentioned in a previous case. To protect themselves from discrimination from 'above', farmers down 'below' invented tactical manoeuvres such as the 'red hat' enterprise: private enterprises paid a fee for registering as 'public' so as to guard against unpredictable risks and improve the operating climate. Nobody knows how many TVE were actually privately owned. According to the *China Daily*, in a county in Hebei province, while the official figure of private enterprises was eight, in fact there were over 1,000 wearing red hats.[46]

In creating TVE, the farmers repeated what they did in building HF: taking risks and initiatives, taking the centre's programme into their own hands. It was quick, messy, dirty, far away from Beijing and spread across the numerous localities over China's vast countryside: localities with diverse histories of commerce, geographical proximities to Hong Kong and Taiwan, levels of development, ambitions and leadership styles of local officials.

There was diversity in the centre, too. Like the countryside localities, 'the centre' was peopled and people were not all the same. HF and TVE might not have survived without the tolerance of some pragmatic leaders. In 1978, for example, party secretary Zhao Ziyang in Sichuan province permitted three local initiatives: specialised contracts, task rates and contract production to work groups. Also in 1978, Wan Li in Anhui province allowed farmers to farm uncultivated land and keep the harvest for survival during a deadly drought. Famous were Zhao's *sibu* (四不, four *don'ts*) and Wan's *shanbu* (三不, three *shouldn'ts*) towards farmers' initiatives: '*Don't* publicize, *don't* oppose, *don't* support and *don't* stop them'; 'It *should not* be publicized, promoted or appear in newspapers'.[47] All this in effect helped to hide the farmers' experimentation, buying them time to demonstrate HF–TVE superiority. This demanded foresight, courage and skill on the part of the leaders.

Who created HF and TVE, then? We find the American sociologist George Herbert Mead's 'conversation of gestures' metaphor enlightening.[48] In Mead's view, strategy is an interactive process of gestures and responses. During the process, leaders (read 'Deng and his colleagues') make gestures in the forms of reform policies, vision statements, campaign programmes and so on. To have meaning and effect, these must be picked up, interpreted and acted upon by local agents on the ground (read '800 million Chinese farmers'). Local responses (read 'farmers' *bricolage*') are usually diverse and surprising. These diverse and surprising local responses will then be picked up as gestures from 'below', and leaders respond in turn, issuing further gestures (read 'Yearly Document No. 1'). The responding gestures from 'above' are seldom homogeneous or consistent either, owing to differences and tensions among leaders as well as unexpected contingencies (read 'Zhao and Wan's tolerance vs the conservatives' hostility'). As such, the strategy process is a series of experimental gestures and responses by all those involved.

Why are there usually differences and inconsistencies within localities 'below' as well as the centre 'above'? In Mead's view, which is in many ways compatible with Confucius' teaching, we humans live in relationships. We cannot do just as we please because we are constrained by relationships and have to draw on the same relationships as resources in order to act effectively. Patterns of actions and interactions emerge because of what everyone is doing, and not doing, in ways our relationships allow. This generates order and continuity. But humans are not blind rule-abiders. We must continuously negotiate local rules for joint action since no rule can ever cover every unforeseeable contingency. Hence, in the face of unfolding particulars, agents participating in the social game must 'particularise the generalised', 'functionalise the idealised' and 'operationalise the abstract' in order to make rules actionable at action moments. Factors involved in such continuous, contingent negotiations include diversity in experiences, interests and power, which produce derivatives, novelty, surprises and unexpected patterns. This results in disorder and change, for better or for worse.

Seen from such an interactive perspective, while no one can design detailed outcomes at a stroke, the micro, flowing interactions of change agents generate macro, consequential patterns. During the gesture–response process, leaders' strategy can be purposeful, deliberate and powerful. There is no historic inevitability.[49] China's reform was not God-given; there was every chance things might go wrong. Hence, no one can take away Deng's decisive, historic contributions. Leaders' strategies generate outcomes – not alone, but in combination with many, many diverse local experiments, which the leaders may or may not have intended. In such a pragmatic view, HF and TVE are the emergent outcome of grand-scale experimentations by hundreds of millions of farmers in China's vastly diverse localities. These farmers took Deng's vague reform agenda into their own hands to advance their own interests, in ways that Deng could never have imagined, as he honestly told his guests, but had the moral capital, courage and skill to endorse.

BE WISE, BE PRAGMATIC

We argue throughout this book that we humans are pragmatic at our wise moments and that pragmatic strategies are achievable. Like China's reform, however, pragmatism is not God-given; it is purposeful, effortful accomplishment against all odds. Letting the chips fall is not strategy, surely not pragmatic strategy. If China's reform, Grameen Bank's microcredit, Nintendo's Wii machine and Boeing's 747 jumbo jet exemplify the power and achievability of pragmatic strategy, then the recent banking crisis is a stark reminder of the painful consequences of ideologically principled strategies. Alan Greenspan, chairman of the Federal Reserve from

1987 to 2006, (in)famously said: 'If the market is letting it happen, it must be good.'[50] With enormous power, he let ideology trump reality, and the outcome was very bad for all. Too often, too easily, we fall into non-pragmatic ways of doing strategy.

It is, therefore, unwise to leave strategy to chance. We managers have a moral responsibility to strategise pragmatically, i.e. innovatively, ethically, effectively. For this, it is useful to understand not only what pragmatism is, but also what it is not. This is the focus of this section. A useful starting point is, again, how strategy is formed and the managers' role in it.

Since Henry Mintzberg posited 'strategy as crafting'[51] and Arie de Geus 'strategy as learning'[52] a quarter-century ago, it is now common sense that adhering to pre-fixed designs regardless of uncertainty often leads to failure, that strategy can emerge from a stream of actions without formal planning, that actions significant for strategic success can occur in 'insignificant' locations and events, and that long-term success derives more from an organisation's learning capability than from one single magic stroke.

Yet the consensus appears to end there. Dan Schendel, the editor-in-chief of the *Strategic Management Journal*, suggests: 'the emergent view is essentially an *ex post* view. For managers as well as researchers, needed is some *ex ante* expectations upon, say, what to do and how it works, to be tested against *ex post* results. Without such a theory, without such an expectation (prediction), there is no role for management of strategy.'[53] It is in responding to the question '*ex ante* what to do' that divergent alternatives emerge.[54,55] In the following pages, we engage with one.

Strategy without intent?

Amid the backlash against spectacular corporate failures and hyper-rationalistic approaches, our field has become populated with comparisons of factors that are 'good' and 'bad' for strategy. With the risk of being simplistic, Table 4.1 captures the accent of this development.

Table 4.1 *'Bad guys' and 'good guys': a 'strategy without intent' view*

'Bad'	'Good'
Purposeful design	Everyday goings-on
Reflective foresight	Thoughtless activity
Deliberate intervention	Indirect action
Conscious choice	Non-deliberate
Goal-directed logic	Non-intentional
Clear goals	Non-purposeful
Bold commitment	Effortless
Instrumental rationality	Mindless
Consequentialist reasoning	Unthinkingly
Building mode	Dwelling mode

The comparisons compel everyone concerned with strategy to ask: what lessons should be learned and what is the way forward? Answers are diverse.

It is suggested, for example, that purposeful actions are harmful, goal-direct interventions are dangerous, conscious judgements are illusive and deliberate investments are wasteful. Managers are persuaded to abandon positions, withdraw from justifications and shy away from commitments. To allow beneficial strategic priorities to emerge, we are told, there is no need for thinking about eventual outcomes, coordinated initiatives or intentional efforts. What managers need to do, the story goes, is to reverse strategic intent by attending indirectly to seemingly insignificant aspects of situations that could lead to surprising ramifications. Managers should just rely on mindless, thoughtless, effortless everyday goings-on. If Wall Street bankers stop strategising, the world will be safe. Let us call this 'strategy without intent'.

Don't get it? You are not alone. Going down that road, there would be no Deng's reform foresight and manoeuvring, no Chinese farmers' life-or-death HF ventures, no Muhammad Yunus' conscious efforts to assist the poor, no Merck scientists' persistent pursuit of a rotavirus vaccine that saves millions of lives, no Akio Morita's bold rejection of the Bulova original-equipment-maker deal, no Boeing's risk-taking 747 project, because all these are purposeful, thoughtful, effortful, instrumental, goal-directed undertakings. To the extent that success, however defined, is purely emergent and unintended, strategy is pointless.

'Strategy without intent', while intended as a corrective to hyper-rationalistic strategy, appears to have confused *ex post* sense-making of 'how things might emerge' with *ex ante* normative suggestions of 'what to do, how to do it'. We do not have a problem with the view that humans are fallible, that planning can let us down, that activities can be unconscious, opportunities unexpected and outcomes unintended. The question is rather: if strategy is all non-intentional, non-purposeful, mindless and effortless, then what is *not* strategy?

Almost ten years ago, Haridimos Tsoukas and Christian Knudsen, asking this same question, reminded us:

> strategy implies coherent action over time, and any theoretical
> framework which does not engage with (or assume) it cannot
> properly be said to be about strategy *per se*. It may well be about
> the evolution of corporate behaviour but, in order to qualify
> as an account of strategy, it needs to make provisions for
> human agency unfolding in time ... This is not to belittle the
> contribution of the configuration school, only to point out that it
> is not a theory of strategy.[56]

Almost 20 years ago, John Kay commented:

> As a description of how real organisations operate, this critique
> [of the rationalist school] is so obviously compelling that at first
> it is hard to see why the rationalist school of strategy remains
> influential. But the reasons why it does are clear enough. Apart
> from a few disinterested scholars, people study and analyse
> strategy because they want to know what to do. To observe that

organisations are complex, that change is inevitably incremental, and that strategy is necessarily adaptive, however true, helps very little in deciding what to do.[57]

Indeed. Are intentless, thoughtless, effortless everyday goings-on the answer to the manager's question 'what to do'?

Learning from Heidegger

In the search for practically wise strategy, many, not least in 'the West', are drawn to Martin Heidegger's notions of 'thrownness', 'readiness-to-hand' and 'dwelling'. We appreciate and have learned much from these.

With the notion of 'thrownness' Heidegger reminds us that we are not alone when making strategy. History matters, culture matters, relationship matters, who and where we are matter. China and Russia choose different paths for their respective reforms; Mazda and GM responded to crises in dramatically different ways. Yet the choices were not managers' alone. There are many 'actors' – human and non-human, now-and-then, in-here and out-there – that combine to make us do certain things in certain ways. Strategy and those who do it are network effects of continuous interactions. Together with Mintzberg's process model and a humanised evolutionary view, Heidegger's notion of 'thrownness' enables us to understand and conduct strategy as a communally informed co-creating process. During the process, our present links to past and future, and 'micro' here-and-now actions flow into 'macro' experimental patterns. Heidegger was a pragmatist at heart. It is one thing to recognise that we are thrown into situations; it is quite another whether, and how, we do something about it. Heidegger does not suggest that strategy is mindless undertaking, or non-taking. We agree with Stephen Cummings who points out that Heidegger challenged us to be mindful, thoughtful, reflexive, to ask strategic questions about who we are, where we come from, where we want to go, as well as how to get there and why.[58]

Communities, histories and cultures are 'made'. Since they are made, suggests Michel Foucault, 'they can be unmade, as long as we know how it was that they were made'.[59] For Foucault, 'thought is the ability to think differently in order to act differently'; and ethical action involves 'thinking differently' with a view to creating new social practices.[60] As long as we recognise and question our 'thrown-ness', we can step back from and do something about it. We need not simply accept thrownness, but should reflect and act upon it. Deng Xiaoping was thrown into a command economy, but he decided to do something about it by engaging his people in 'the sea'. Genichi Kawakami was thrown into a non-market, but he refused to accept it. Instead, he ran music schools, created new demands and brought happiness to ordinary families. Andrew Grove was thrown into a deep-ingrained 'memory strategy', yet he questioned it. He went through 'the revolving door' and came back in with a new 'microprocessor strategy'. This is the power of Heidegger's notion of 'thrownness'.

The point is how to read Heidegger. There are many Heideggers: some read a mindless, thoughtless, effortless Heidegger, while we read a pragmatic, reflexive, engaging Heidegger. Managers must make their own judgements in situated contexts: which Heidegger is helpful for the task at hand?

The same applies to Heidegger's notion of 'readiness-to-hand'. Our reading of Heidegger indicates that this great German thinker cared about all ready-to-hand, unready-to-hand and present-at-hand modes of practice. Together, the three modes supply us with a rich understanding of what strategy is about and how it is done. It is unwise to praise one mode while downplaying others. Amid the backlash of hyper-rationalist strategy, there is a tempting, reductionist tendency to pick up merely 'readiness-to-hand'. Such a selective appropriation of Heidegger appears instantly at odds with the very premise of strategy, innovation and entrepreneurship, i.e. intentionally searching for that which is unready-to-hand, unconventional, out-of-*habitus*, outstanding. Deng did not have a ready-to-hand reform model, nor did Yunus a ready-to-hand microfinance paradigm. Boeing's 747 project was a mission almost impossible, to call it unready-to-hand is an understatement. If Kawakami had cared only about ready-to-hand markets, there would today be no electronic pianos for millions of children.

As Walter Powell and Paul DiMaggio posit, a winning strategy uses deliberate deviation to break from dominant logics and invent new ones.[61] Strategy matters because human beings have intentionalities. Intentionalities make a difference, and innovative strategies are seldom ready-to-hand. Innovative strategies are almost always 'painstakingly developed to suit a firm's unique profile and circumstance'.[62] 'It is not genius; it is hard work. It is not being clever; it is being conscientious', said Peter Drucker.[63]

With Heidegger's notions of 'building' and 'dwelling', then, we can nurture a richer understanding of the relationship between strategy content and style. Content and style, building and dwelling modes are mutually dependent, reciprocal companions. Emphasis and priority is an empirical matter that can only be ascertained in situated circumstances. While it is naive to think that style doesn't matter, it is not much wiser to suggest that style matters above all else. While it may be silly to suppose that process makes no difference, it is mistaken to believe that process makes all the difference. Let us refer again to Dan Schendel:

> But can strategy process research stand alone? The answer to
> the question seems to hinge on whether it is possible to propose
> and recognise winning strategy position *ex ante*. Here is where
> strategy content research enters the strategy process research
> domain. Surely it is possible to describe strategy processes, even
> to suggest *ex post* whether those processes are linked to good
> or bad performance outcomes. The challenge of course is to do
> it *ex ante* and be in a position to prescribe to practitioners, to at
> least be able to predict outcomes, if not causally link them for
> the practitioner. In the matter of application at least, content and
> process would appear inseparable.[64]

There is a moral issue here, too. In Western systems of morality, we only charge those who we think voluntarily do wrong.[65] But if strategy is all mindless, effortless unfolding, then any and every good or wicked act is a matter of 'spontaneous dwelling', not 'intentional building'. If this is the case, none of us could ever be said to be responsible for our strategy, whatever the consequences. Why, then, should someone, anyone, be accountable for the collapse of Lehman Brothers, the Gulf of Mexico oil spill, tainted milk in China, bloodshed in Iraq or our huge national debts?

As Sumantra Ghoshal reminds us, 'morality, or ethics, is inseparable from human intentionality'.[66] Denying intentionality in strategy will only strip managers of their moral sensitivity. It is dangerous to strategy. To understand this one need only to recall the everyday goings-on in Wall Street and the City of London just before the banking crisis: 'As long as the music is playing', you got up, danced, dwelt in the ready-to-hand, unthinkingly, mindlessly ...

To put it normatively, managers have a moral obligation to build strategic intents, and most managers are rightly doing so. As Bart Victor posits, 'failing to make strategy, and to do so with great care and effort, is simply to choose amorality and to do nothing to limit immorality'.[67] Given the poverty, hunger, suffering and injustice around us, there is no excuse for mindlessness or effortlessness. We must not hide behind 'unthinking modes'. Building purposeful, ethical strategies should be firmly on our corporate agenda. We humans are intentional beings;[68] to deny it can only lead to dehumanised, amoral strategy.[69] As Barnard, Ghoshal, Drucker, Ackoff and many others have argued, purpose is vital for shaping strategies. It is purpose that provides the ultimate source of 'organisation advantage' over markets.[70] Muhammad Yunus, Akio Morita and the Merck executives have all illustrated this with their courageous, effective deeds.

Against the hyper-rationalist approach, we need to balance emergence with intentionality, evolution with design. Between building and dwelling modes, we do not need hierarchies or either/

or choices. No mode is 'in principle' more basic or fundamental than others. Promoting crafting and learning, Mintzberg and de Geus stress that effective process is 'deliberately emergent in that the process is consciously managed to allow strategies to emerge en route',[71] that 'all viable strategies have emergent and deliberate qualities'.[72] Theirs is a pragmatic, both/and attitude, good for practically wise actions.

Was Laozi a passive non-doer?

It is increasingly popular to use ancient Eastern thinking, particularly that of the Taoists Laozi (老子) and Zhuangzi (庄子), to justify no-intent, no-design, no-interference 'strategies', and to argue in favour of passivity, ad hoc responses and even withdrawal from everyday life. From Laozi and Zhuangzi, some infer the ideal of 'letting things alone', of allowing situations 'to ripen' and only then 'to channel internal forces' to 'fulfil their natural potential'. People can indeed read Eastern thinking in many ways. But let us begin with reality.

Steve Jobs of Apple would not have found the passive image of Laozi and Zhuangzi very helpful. Engineers in Apple were bright and energetic; they came up with plenty of spontaneous initiatives. The Apple leadership under Jobs never withdrew from interference or let ad hoc things alone. The selection process in Apple was purposeful, forceful, as focused as a laser. Jobs' primary role in the company was to turn emergence down. Every day, the CEO was presented with spontaneous initiatives. His default answer was 'No'. 'I'm as proud of the products we haven't made as I am of the ones we have', Jobs told an interviewer in 2004.[73] How then to make sense of Apple in light of the Lao–Zhuang 'tradition'? First, we must dissolve the myth of the 'passive, withdrawing psyche' of the Eastern people.

To Laozi and Zhuangzi, as to Confucius, making one's way in the world, not withdrawing from it, is a virtue. The sage engages in this-worldly affairs, doing so wisely, without coercion. In chapter 17 of Laozi's *Daodejing* (道德经), we read:

> With the most excellent rulers, their subjects only know
> that they are there,
> The next best are the rulers they love and praise,
> Next are the rulers they hold in awe,
> And the worst are the rulers they disparage.
> Where there is a lack of credibility,
> There is a lack of trust.
> Vigilant, they are careful in what they say.
> With all things accomplished and the work completed
> The common people say, 'We are naturally so.'

Through such teaching, one comes to understand that a ruler's occupation is *wuwei* (无为): to bring together the concerted efforts of the people and to synchronise them with situated particulars, creating maximum benefit in non-coercive ways.[74] It is a tough call. Hard power, push power, planning or re-engineering alone will not do. You need to bring all the pragmatic spirits together and put them into action.[75] This is what makes a sage a sage, and what a manager gets paid for. Your job is to strive for 'all things accomplished and the work completed', not withdraw from them.

What is *wuwei*? *Wu* (无) was a notion common in all Eastern traditions, Confucianism, Taoism, Buddhism and others; so much so that Roger Ames and David Hall call it the '*wu*-forms'.[76] *Wu* has usually been translated, misleadingly, as 'absent', 'without', 'non' or 'no'. Such a translation forces the unique and rich meaning in another's culture into the default categories of one's own. Insofar as strategy is concerned, the *wu*-forms in Table 4.2 are significant.

These *wu*-forms, albeit only a very brief introduction to a deep, rich tradition, signify the bottom line: far from withdrawing from life experience, dismissing deliberate intention or avoiding effort at any cost, Lao–Zhuang encouraged engaging the world with proper intention, contextual knowledge, subtle competence and, above all, consequential experimentation appropriate to situated particulars. Lao–Zhuang are a million miles away from thoughtless, mindless, intentless 'strategies'.

Table 4.2 *A sample of* wu-*forms significant to strategy*

wu-forms	Word-by-word translation	Meaning in context
wuwei 无为	No action	Non-coercive doing
wuzhi 无知	No knowledge	Unprincipled knowing
wuyu 无欲	No intention	Deferential intending
wuzheng 无争	No competition	Non-contentious striving

Although differing in many respects, Confucius and Lao–Zhuang converged on a point critically important to strategy:

> Exemplar persons have no competition ... Even in competition, then, they are still non-contentious (君子无所争, ... 其争也君子).[77]
>
> Is it not because they strive without contentiousness that no one in the world is able to contend with them (非以其无争与, 故天下莫能与之争)?[78]

Translated into modern business language, the sages encourage proper competition, win–win strategy, making a beneficial difference for all and sustainable development in a world where 'we are one with all things'. Managers, like the sages, need to engage in this-worldly affairs with a shared purpose, getting jobs done in appropriate, fitting ways.

In light of pragmatism, 'letting things alone', 'attending to seemingly insignificant things' or 'ad hoc adaptive responses' are found to be:

- too thin. In John Hagel and John Seely Brown's words: 'we risk spreading our resources too thinly as we react to whatever crosses our paths along the way. Desperately diversifying our bets across an uncertain landscape, we may discover that our growing range of under-resourced experiments is tripping us up rather than moving us forward.'[79] *Ex ante*, which 'seemingly insignificant' going-on should we attend to, given that all of them *can* end up significant for strategic success?
- too late. It is all well and good to allow situations to ripen naturally and only then channel internal forces to fulfil their natural potential. However, as Richard Rumelt points out, when an initiative or

phenomenon is understood well enough to be picked up, it is already too late to get much advantage from it.[80] If you are Google, are you waiting for the situation to 'ripen naturally' while Apple launches its iPhone/iPad and sets out to dominate the market?

- too reactive. While ad hoc adaptation is sometimes unavoidable, the question is whether managers should base the prosperity of their firms on ad hoc things alone. In market-oriented economies, Michael Best suggests, 'strategic' refers to market-shaping activities in contrast to market-reacting responses.[81] Henry Ford, Akio Morita, Genichi Kawakami and Steve Jobs would tell you that strategy is about purposefully creating, shaping and leading markets, not reacting to them ad hoc.

It has become a popular caricature that intentional 'macro' coordination is harmful to innovation because, we are told, creativity requires spontaneous initiatives freely emerging in 'micro' localities. Leave 'communities' alone, it is suggested, innovation will ripen naturally. In the real business world, however, an innovative idea is useful only when an organisation has the discipline and infrastructure to realise it. Sony's Akio Morita reflected on his experience thus: 'only if we have a clear goal can we concentrate our efforts.'[82] Chris Bilton and Stephen Cummings agree: 'diversity, naivety and curiosity need to be directed. They must be given a point or purpose for them to lead to strategic innovation.'[83] To pragmatic managers, purpose, goal and discipline are not ad hoc things.

Xerox Corporation is a classic example. Xerox engineers were very bright; they invented many breakthrough technologies and devices, for example, the PC, mouse and graphical user interface (GUI). But the 'local' engineering community failed to connect with the 'local' marketing and sales community at Xerox. 'Macro' coordination broke down and 'micro' mentality prevailed. Consumers benefited only when Xerox inventions flowed outward to Apple, Microsoft and Adobe Systems. Spontaneity and ad hoc activity without goal-directed coordination ended up very costly for Xerox. In a *Sloan Management Review* article, Brown and Duguid commented:

Once separate, groups develop their own vocabularies; organisational discourse sounds like the Tower of Babel. At Xerox, for example, when managers tried to extend the knowledge created at PARC to the rest of the company, what had been intuitive among scientists working on the GUI proved almost unintelligible to the engineers who had to turn the ideas into marketable products. Insurmountable barriers of misunderstanding and then distrust developed between the communities. The scientists dismissed the engineers as copier-obsessed 'toner heads', whereas the engineers found the scientists arrogant and unrealistic. Thus one of the greatest challenges that innovative companies face is the step from initial innovation to sustainable growth.

When an organisation reaches a certain stage in its development, instead of developing like a self-organising string quartet, it becomes more like an orchestra whose disparate sections now need a conductor.[84]

How about Steve Jobs saying 'No' by default to spontaneous initiatives? He was exactly such a great conductor. What ticked behind was his competence cultivated during decades in the industry, and the trust other people placed in him. This came 'naturally' to Jobs. To Apple under Jobs, withdrawing from purposeful judgement was a non-option, letting ad hoc things alone was not leadership and attending to 'seemingly insignificant' goings-on was a myth. We have just pulled down a tyranny of strategy-as-planning; we do not need another tyranny of strategy-as-ad-hoc-responses.

After all, as Lao–Zhuang taught us:

The sages like the rivers and seas perform a synchronizing function that, perceived from a particular perspective, has a nobility to it. Both sages and seas do what they do naturally and well.

Far from being merely passive players buffered about in the emerging order, both sages and seas actively coordinate the massive quantum of energy that flows into them from their constituents, and maximise its circulation to the advantage of all.[85]

In probing 'what pragmatic strategies look like' in this section, we investigate what pragmatism is and is not. To practical managers, what is important is whether and how the ideas are helpful for solving situated problems. This can be known only when managers put ideas into practice and judge them based on the consequences. To facilitate the learning process, we present below different explanations of some well-known business cases and historical events.

Wall Street, Grameen Bank, Honda, Master Kong Noodles, Mao Zedong and T. E. Lawrence

It is not surprising that the Grameen Bank and Wall Street have become popular case studies for business strategy, given the former's achievement in financial inclusion of the poor and the latter's recent value-destroying conduct. The question is how to explain the two cases and what lessons can be learned.

Some suggest that the Wall Street crisis originated in deliberate intents because bankers, industries and governments all had grand strategies but failed to, i.e. did not, allow strategic priorities to emerge spontaneously. That is to say, strategic intent and intervention per se are to be blamed for the crisis. Had there been no deliberate strategy, beneficial priorities would have emerged naturally and there would have been no crisis. Thus the lesson appears to be: next time, just let ad hoc things alone, shy away from any intervention, then everything will be fine. As to the Grameen Bank, it was praised as a model of spontaneous, indirect, everyday coping without intent or effort. The lesson? Sustainable strategic accomplishments are the outcome of attending to seemingly insignificant local happenings. This brings us back to the strategy bad guys and good guys listed in Table 4.1.

Can we explain differently and learn different lessons? Yes we can. Just ask: can't we consider the banking crisis a consequence of the popular but ill-conceived 'end of history' ideology, of the bankers' unthinking immersion in 'the market', of politicians' paralysing 'light-touch' regulation, of consumers' 'spontaneously' living beyond their means, of a prevailing hostility towards collective purpose, of a lack of strategic foresight, courage and capability? In contrast to 'strategy without intent', an alternative moral can be: the banking crisis was due to bad strategy, weak intent, unwillingness and inability to intervene, not strategy, intent or intervention per se. If, when the music was playing, someone had had the courage and ability to call a halt and demand a change, the outcome could have been different.[86] The crisis occurred because we did not take strategic action seriously – we put our faith and fate in 'the market', believing the market would take care of itself and us. We passed our responsibility on to the market. Doing so, we shied away from hard choices; consequently, we had to accept whatever outcomes thrown to us.

We can tell a different Grameen Bank story, too. Muhammad Yunus' own account, in his autobiography *Banker to the Poor*, vividly presents the conscious soul-searching, reflective foresight, bold commitment and deliberate risk-taking that took him from Jobra to worldwide success. Indeed, Yunus had an unshakeable grand vision – 'to eliminate poverty'; he intentionally created a new paradigm – 'credit is a human right'; he refused to accept what is ready-to-hand 'lending on collateral'; he took design seriously – when he *built* the bank he worked through the draft constitution many times, word by word, sentence by sentence, for days and nights with expert friends, leaving nothing to chance. We just find it difficult to separate dwelling and building, immersing and envisioning, coping and designing, everyday hard work and a compelling sense of purpose.

While appreciating spontaneous, local, indirect actions, we still need to ask: how many such actions go nowhere, fail to make a difference? In a world with plenty of suffering but limited resources, is it ethical or wise to shy away from collective purpose, conscious envisioning, bold commitment and deliberate action? We do not deny the significance of spontaneous initiatives; we have already praised the Chinese farmers, 3M's Post-it Notes and Intel's micro-processor business. We are pointing out the limits of indirect action, the immorality of simply following ad hoc things, and the danger of betting our future entirely on thoughtless, effortless goings-on. Again the question is: what is, and is not, strategy?

Let us turn to Honda's motorcycle success in America and Master Kong Noodles in China. The two cases are together brought to us by Robert Chia and Robin Holt, which we consider a great service to the field. Let us quote at length Chia and Holt's story:

> Here, the very 50 cc 'Supercubs' that Honda motorcycle sales staff used for their own transport to visit local distributors unexpectedly became the successful sales product. Rather than their intended export of larger machines, because it unintentionally caught the eye of local dealers, who saw their immediate practical appeal. Moreover, it was not the motorcycle dealers who wanted to sell these smaller machines but sports goods stores. This idea that mundane everyday practical coping action can produce unexpected strategically important outcomes can also be used to explain a similar, more recent incident that helped the Chinese food giant Ting Hsin to become the leading food group in China today ...
>
> Ting Hsin was started by four Taiwanese brothers in 1988, to produce superior cooking oil for the mainland Chinese market. Because it was higher priced and because there was a lack of infrastructure in China, the venture failed. Not deterred, the brothers began producing and selling egg rolls again distinguished by their high quality. Yet again, the cost of advertising and high product cost led to failure. It was then that opportunity knocked unexpectedly to save their ailing business. To save money, the youngest brother travelled by train on an 18-hour trip to Beijing and packed his own food. During the journey, he opened a package of instant noodles that he had brought from Taiwan, and the aroma attracted the attention of

other passengers in the carriage. He then shared the noodles with his fellow travellers, who devoured them with some relish. This rather serendipitous event led him to realise that potential market opportunity for affordable, quality, instant noodles in China. Today, Ting Hsin's Master Kong brand is one of the most recognised brands in China, a success attributable to a seemingly innocuous event that took place on a train in late 1991.

These two examples, one well known another lesser known, show the importance of recognising how much of strategy formation takes place 'on the hoof', so to speak, and it rooted in non-deliberate practical coping that eschews the logic of planned, intentional action.[87]

We enjoy these two cases very much. We would suggest readers to consider: if Honda did not have deliberate intent, plan or effort to explore the US motorcycle market, however 'wrong' the intent, plan and effort turned out to be, why were the Honda people 'coping' there in the first place? Did the then still-very-poor Japanese go to the US for holidays? Did they have a purpose, intent, strategy, or did they not? If not, what would have happened, or not happened?

Also consider: if the Taiwanese brothers had not been desperately seeking winning products to avoid looming bankruptcy, why was the young brother 'dwelling' on board the Beijing-bound train where he 'happened' to note the popularity of instant noodles? Why did this man, not anybody else, sense the opportunity? One might argue that, in strategy, the 'building mode' is derived from the 'dwelling mode'. But, is it not equally meaningful to suggest, based on the same Honda and Master Kong stories, that it is the 'deliberate building mode' that sets the 'thoughtless dwelling mode' into motion in the first place? Furthermore, why should we assume that 'dwelling' and 'building' are an either/or contradiction?

No doubt, many deliberately built strategies go horribly wrong; for sure, no strategy can succeed if it is cut off from everyday coping actions; agreed, strategically important initiatives often emerge at the periphery not the centre; granted, strategy formation displays surprises, unexpectedness and incremental adjustments. A pragmatic approach appreciates all this. Nevertheless, and this is practically crucial: it is one thing to take note of all this, it is quite another to attribute effective strategies as all 'natural outcomes' of unintended, effortless, ad hoc behaviours.

Between appreciating the significance of spontaneity on the one hand and regarding all strategy as mindless behaviour on the other, there is a big jump. In theory, the jump is confusing. In practice, the jump can be dangerous. Join the CEOs, managers and workers, tie the well-being of our families with theirs, cope with booming and busting markets, get our hands dirty with winning and losing products, close down GM and Chrysler factories with painful lay-offs, open new Geely and Tata ventures in the US and Europe, then we would know how much painstaking weighing, conscious soul-searching, calculated risk-taking, intentional sacrificing and deliberate undertaking are involved. Get out of the Wall Street office decorated with $2,000 rubbish bins, accompany the Grameen workers in monsoon rains and the summer sun, and we shall know the difference between mindless behaviour and purposeful action. What makes the difference? Our ideals, values, purpose, intent and commitment. Rather than resorting to mindless, effortless, ad hoc behaviours, we should ask the questions that matter to practical managers. For example: how did it occur to Honda to follow the strategy it did? Why did they do it at that particular time and place? Why this strategy and not something else? What can we learn from it?[88]

Mao Zedong and T.E. Lawrence's guerrilla warfare have also been studied intensively by corporate managers and strategy students. Some have used Mao and Lawrence to justify 'the silent efficacy of indirect action'. In the spirits of pragmatism, we supply a different appreciation. Let's face it: Mao succeeded and Lawrence failed, strategically. Yes, both Mao and Lawrence were masters of guerrilla tactics. However, when the moment of truth came, Mao accomplished what he wanted to achieve, while Lawrence ended in tragedy.

Why was it so? There were many factors. Let us stress one. Mao had clear strategic foresight along the way; guerrilla warfare was merely the tactical means for realising his strategic vision. In every-day goings-on during the eight-year Second World War in China, there were no doubt plenty of 'indirect actions'. At the strategic level, however, there was to Mao nothing ad hoc, mindless or effortless. Before, during and after the war, Mao painstakingly explored, generated, deliberated, tested, justified and reflected on his strategy; the numerous books and articles Mao wrote during this period, a sample of which are listed below, are merely the tip of an iceberg of recorded evidence.[89] Insofar as the Second World War is concerned, Mao was a master of purposeful action with a clear strategic intent; he explicitly dismissed active non-action, be it indirect or not.

1936   Strategic problems of China's revolutionary war
1937   Struggle to mobilise all forces to achieve victory
        by armed resistance
1938   On protracted war
1938   The role of the Chinese Communist Party
        in the national war
1938   Problem of war and strategy
1940   Solidarity to the very end
1940   On policy
1942   The turning-point in World War II
1943   Let us get organised
1945   China's two possible destinies
1945   On coalition government

Lawrence's case, on the other hand, is more complicated. Despite fighting a brilliant guerrilla war at the tactical level, the end game to him was, sadly, a grand strategic failure. 'Arriving at Damascus with the Arabs, who had been promised their freedom if they threw in their lot with the British, Lawrence realised they were themselves going to be tricked. Unable to bear the ruin of this betrayal, Lawrence resigned, and withdrew from the political subterfuge.' When asked about the desert campaign, Lawrence replied: 'I did something'; 'It was a failure.'[90] Indeed. We are still living with the consequences: the suspicion of the Arabs towards the British, 'the West', even towards Lawrence himself, still lingers. Were history to allow Lawrence the Mao-style strategic foresight, could he have acted differently, would the outcome have been different? We do not want to speculate. Based on historical evidence, we can nevertheless appreciate the significance of (Mao's) strategic foresight and the limits of (Lawrence's) indirect action.[91]

SUMMARY

In this chapter, we continue exploring what Drucker called the 'specifications' of pragmatic strategy, with a particular focus on strategy formation.[92] Looking back and looking around, strategies appear as much emergent as planned, as much playful as disciplined; underpinned by styles and substances, chances and commitments; shaped by incremental adjustments as well as decisive foresights; involving culture and politics as well as technical fundamentals and business logic.[93] Taking note of all this, we still believe that no practically wise, effective strategy comes effortlessly. We are of the view that strategy is a painstaking experimental process for making a substantial, practical, valued difference. As Mintzberg insightfully reminds us, strategy is the creative outcome of managerial experience, judgement and introspection.[94] It is purpose, judgement and experimentation that distinguish strategy from everyday behaviour.

So much for description and explanation. Now the normative questions are: how to get the fundamentals right, promote situated creativity and realise communal goodness? That is, during pragmatic way-making, what should we do and how should we do it? With these all-important questions, let us move to Part III.

PART III What to do, how to do it?

道成之于行。
«庄子»

Tao is made in the walking of it.
– *Zhuangzi*

5 Dealing with *wuli–shili–renli*

In previous chapters we questioned the conventional wisdom, called for a pragmatic turn, presented the spirits of pragmatism and investigated what pragmatic strategies look like. Based on this groundwork, we now invite readers to explore the normative question: what to do, how to do it?

We begin with front-line experience: how managers think and act strategically to turn companies around. We then link the experiences of managers with enduring Confucian wisdom. From this we construct a triple-strategy bottom line (WSR): *wuli* (物理), the material-technical; *shili* (事理), the cognitive-mental; and *renli* (人理), the social-relational. Pragmatic strategies based on WSR generate value efficiently, creatively and legitimately by getting fundamentals right, envisioning a valued future and realising common goodness. We illustrate *wuli*, *shili* and *renli* with business cases: Grameen Bank, Northern Rock, China Merchants Bank, Xerox, Airbus, Seven-Eleven Japan, Komatsu, Huawei, Lenovo, Polaroid, Swatch and many more. This *relational* WSR bottom line, addressing the question *what to do*, will be complemented in the next chapter with a *temporal* timely balance guidance on *how to do it*. Now, let our journey continue.

VOICES FROM THE MESSY WORLD

What do managers do in coping with strategic matters, and how do they account for their actions? The following is an account:

> To make a profit. To make a consistent profit. To make a profit in the long run. To make a living. To make things. To make things in the most economical way. To make the greatest number of things. To make things that last the longest. To make things for

the longest possible time. To make things that people need. To make things that people desire. To make people desire things. To give meaningful employment. To give reliable employment. To give people something to do. To do something. To provide the greatest food for the greatest number. To promote the general welfare. To provide for the common defence. To increase the value of the common stock. To pay a regular dividend. To maximise the net worth of the firm. To advance the lot for all the stakeholders. To grow. To progress. To expand. To increase know-how. To increase revenues and to decrease costs. To get the job done more cheaply. To compete efficiently. To buy low and sell high. To improve the hand that humankind has been dealt. To produce the next round of technological innovations. To rationalise nature. To improve the landscape. To shatter space and arrest time. To see what the human race can do. To amass the country's retirement pension. To amass the capital required to do anything we want to do. To discover what we want to do. To vacate the premises before the sun dies out. To make life a little easier. To make people a little wealthier. To make people a little happier. To build a better tomorrow. To kick something back into the kitty. To facilitate the flow of capital. To preserve the corporation. To do business. To stay in business. To figure out the purpose of business.[1]

The account is first-hand, 'un-translated'. But how much does it help us to learn from experience or decide what to do? It is clear that, if we are to make substantial, practical, valued differences, simply accepting such 'native accounts' is not good enough. We need theory, or 'conceptual constructs' as social scientists call it. In a pragmatic world, practice comes first and last, but in between there has to be theory.[2] Without theory, it is all too easy to get lost in active non-action, which is not strategy.

Let's turn to another story, a story supplied by the corporate executive, David Hurst.[3] The story, about turning around Hugh

Russel Inc., a company undergoing profound change, is told from the viewpoint of a group of managers who took strategic actions and then reflected on their managerial roles.[4]

A Montreal-based medium-sized distributor of industrial goods, Hugh Russel was founded in 1936 and went public in 1962. In its early days, the firm was run like a community, consisting of the founding brothers, two managers and a controller. 'There was no hierarchy, and if anyone tried to pull rank, the office had multiple subtle and not-so-subtle ways of signalling its displeasure and taking revenge.' 'Everyone lived in everyone else's pocket, and no secrets, personal or corporate, could be kept so for long.'[5] Until the 1970s, the firm outperformed larger competitors.

Then, in the heyday of conglomerates, Hugh Russel diversified its businesses via aggressive acquisitions, grew in size and reorganised into layered divisions headed by professionals. To maintain efficiency, the firm adopted the 'best practice' of the day, putting in place job descriptions, operation procedures and data-processing systems. The head office annually conducted rigorous budgeting, prioritised growth opportunities and pursued scale economy. So far, so good, until the firm was acquired in a hostile takeover by a private company after a fierce bidding war. The market is a fair game: predators can be preyed on by others.

The 'raider' had taken out a $300 million loan to do the deal. Within six weeks of the takeover, accountants and lawyers discovered that Hugh Russel had been overly evaluated and the transaction vastly overleveraged. The financiers were horrified by the numbers, and immediately demanded their money back. 'Almost overnight, the corporation went from a growth-oriented, acquisitive, earnings-driven operation to a cash-starved cripple, desperate to survive.'[6] The company was in crisis.

The new president hastily called an emergency meeting, with participants from all over the firm regardless of their positions in the old hierarchy. 'Few of them had ever been summoned to the head office for anything but a haranguing over their budgets', 'now they were being told the complete gory details of the company's situation and, for the first time, being treated as if they had something to contribute.'[7] This meeting, the first of many, ended at 2:00 a.m., when the employees went home to tell their families what had happened.

As bankruptcy loomed, 'there emerged a deep sense of shared purpose among everyone involved': 'to rescue the good businesses and refinance them.'[8] People became members of a community again, not just 'human resources'. The change in attitude was noticeable. After an open meeting at the firm's Winnipeg operation, a warehouse manager approached the president, 'Look, I've been talking with the boys and we wondered whether it would help if we took a 10 per cent reduction in pay?' As Hurst later recalled: 'The offer made no logical sense: the savings were minuscule compared with the sums of money we needed, but it spoke volumes about the commitment that the group felt to the company.'[9]

What to do, then? As the situation evolved, members organised themselves into task forces. Some emerged as 'facilitator-networker-framemaker', framed rescue processes, developed team agendas, prepared presentations to financiers and dealt with the press. Others acted as 'organiser-operator-executor', defined priorities and responsibilities, set deadlines and contingency plans, ensured that the rescue processes worked smoothly. Still others took on the role of 'entrepreneur-negotiator-inspirer', made sure that everyone felt the firm was on her/his side, whether financiers, suppliers, buyers, unions or governmental agencies, nurtured a sense of shared fate, navigated the company through a political minefield – they had to report quarterly results when the firm was losing nearly $2 million per week!

It was serious stuff, but the atmosphere was light and open. 'We laughed at ourselves and at the desperate situation. We laughed at the foolishness of the bankers in having financed such a mess, and we laughed at the antics of the feuding shareholders, whose outrageous manners and language we learned to mimic to perfection.'[10] The firm was under tremendous pressure; nevertheless, recalled

Hurst, 'There was a shared recognition that this was an extraordinary time and that we were learning both as individuals and as an organisation.' 'Although we were powerless in a formal sense, our networks, together with our own internal coherence, gave us an ability to get things done invisibly.'[11] This supplied a new context, and new relationships, for effective action. Muddling along but with a strong sense of purpose, members of Hugh Russel created 'new ways of thinking about the world'; and within a year the company managed to refinance the debt, 'just in time to benefit from the general business recovery'.[12]

Trying to make sense of what happened, Hurst generated a model showing 'what managers *actually do* as well as what they *ought to do*'.[13] The model presents three heuristic perspectives:[14]

Rational action. Action is deliberately rational, following calculated thought and directed to achieve well-defined objectives. Unlike trees, plants or other biological organisms, humans are self-conscious, capable of rational action.[15] The focus is on technical efficiency, economic performance and getting fundamentals right. Through rational action, knowledge about cause and effect is acquired, applied, tested and absorbed. The underlying rationality is associated with science, engineering and regularities in the world. The conventional 'rational actor' model may work well here.[16] Examples of rational action in the automobile industry, for example, include dealing with economies of scale, specialising work tasks, controlling cash flow and inventory. Based on front-line experiences, Hurst concludes: 'the rational model isn't wrong: it just isn't enough.'[17]

Constrained action. Managerial action is moulded by social pressures. Hurst emphasises both internal and external 'institutionalisation'. Inside the firm, 'a process of legitimization is required to explain and justify "what we are doing and why".' Externally, 'the corporation is now part of a market economy and must compete for funds with everyone else. Appearances matter when wooing investors: "It's not for us, you understand; it's for them." '[18] Satisfying investor expectations is not optional.[19] For the Big Three auto-makers – Ford, General Motors and Chrysler – operating in a particular business culture, 'the first questions about any project were likely to be "what will the [Wall] Street think?" and "what will this do to our triple-A bond rating?"'[20] Inside as well as outside the firm, social legitimacy is paramount. Seen this way, managers cannot really do very much; strategies are shaped by socio-organisational obligations and expectations.[21]

Emergent action. Social constraints are not sufficient to predict strategy, nor is technical efficiency. This is because of the complexity, ambiguity and uncertainty involved in the formation and selection of strategic options.[22] Hurst draws our attention to emergent action, which is linked with 'experience', 'managerial freedom' and 'entrepreneurial strategy'. Emergent actions break out of prevailing 'cognitive frameworks', generate 'new patterns of meaning', allow 'novelty to emerge'.[23] When coping with emergence, there is little time to think: often, managers must act without referring to established categories, two-by-two matrices or seven-step procedures. Nevertheless, reflective managers are not unthinking or powerless, but inventive and effortful. Amid uncertainty and confusion, they strive 'to live their social visions of the future'.[24,25]

Hurst's reflection is pragmatic: 'the key question is not which of these three models of action is right, or even which is better, but when and under what circumstances they are useful to understand what managers should do.'[26] This outlook allows Hurst and his colleagues to learn not only from their own experiences, but also from the US automobile industry, Nike, GE, Compaq and many others.

The overarching message is, when it comes to 'what to do', strategy is about taking timely rational-efficient, emergent-creative, constrained-normative actions.

WSR, A CONFUCIAN WORLDVIEW

We found a compelling affinity between Hurst the executive's experience in 'the West' and Confucius' pragmatic teaching in 'the East'.

Both suggest that, while situated emergences vary, it is heuristically useful to see strategy as a flow of rational, creative, constrained actions.

In the Confucian tradition, life experience is seen as a dynamic web of relations: relations with the world, relations with the mind, relations with others. This relational imagination provides the Confucians with a common-sense 'order of chaos' for intelligently thinking, talking about and walking in a world where 'everything is here in me'. The triadic relations are called *wuli* (物理), *shili* (事理) and *renli* (人理) respectively, abbreviated here to WSR.

Since the time of Confucius, mastering *Tao* (道, way-making) and achieving *nei sheng wai wang* (内圣外王, sageliness-within and kingliness-without) in the Far East has been informed by the *ba tiaomu* (八条目, Eight Wires), i.e. *eight exemplary doings*, which are elaborated in *Daxue* (大学, *The Great Learning*), a chapter in a 3,000-year-old classic, *Liji* (礼记, *Book of Rites*). The *eight exemplary doings* are usually grouped into three clusters: (1) 格物, 致知 (investigating things, extending knowledge); (2) 诚意, 正心, 修身 (being sincere, rectifying minds, cultivating character); (3) 齐家, 治国, 平天下 (regulating families, governing states, pacifying the world).[27]

These three clusters of *exemplary doings* correspond with *wuli*, *shili*, *renli* respectively: to study the 'objective' world, to reflect on our 'subjective' mind, to care for 'intersubjective' human relations. This has over time become a tacitly shared worldview across intellectual and political divides.[28] Zhang Dongshun, who held senior positions first in the nationalist and then the communist governments in China, for example, suggests that humans should, and indeed do, engage in natural existence, learned knowledge and social affairs.[29]

Li (理) is a key concept common to Confucianism, Taoism and Buddhism, the three main traditions in East Asia. As a noun, it denotes texture, pattern, reason, justice and so forth, which can be actual as well as virtual, for example, patterns in jade, methods of inquiry, norms of giving and receiving. As a verb, it means to engage, cope, serve, care, organise, order, manage and so on. *Li* also

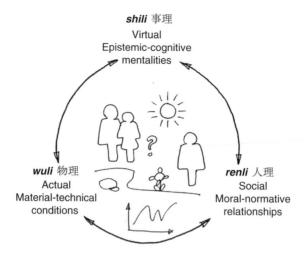

FIGURE 5.1 WSR, a Confucian worldview

covers knowledge of these properties and patterns, including those about human cognitions, value orientations and purposive actions. In Chinese *kanji*, there is no differentiation between the singular and the plural, of *li* and of everything else.[30] *Wuli–shili–renli* is thus a differentiated-interconnected oneness.

Wu (物) in Confucianism means things, objects, contents, 'the world' as differentiated from, and interacting with, humans. *Wu* are 'objective' in the sense of being 'actual', helping or hurting us, facilitating or frustrating strategies, irrespective of our conceptions and interpretations about them. *Wu* manifests in various forms: natural, man-made, material, technological. Accordingly, *wuli* are mechanisms and regularities that form and govern the working and effects of *wu*. *Wuli* is thus confined to the actual, material-technical domain of human experience. Dealing with *wuli*, we rely on technical rationality.

Shi (事) denotes patterns of interaction between 'the mind' and 'the world', i.e. the habits, tendencies, styles and 'paradigms' we are taught and use to see, think, talk and act. *Shili* concerns sense-making, context-interpreting, situation-framing, meaning-giving, fact-projecting, problem-shaping, opportunity-exploring, future-envisioning and so on. It is about the working and effect of structured mentalities and innovative capabilities. *Shili* therefore points to the virtual, mental-cognitive aspects of human life. In dealing with *shili*, we act upon instrumental creativity.

Ren (人) is about human relations. *Renli* concerns how humans should live together, i.e. the ideals and values of social life; the position, role and responsibility one holds; how one is expected to behave; and what one can expect, based on one's conduct, from others. *Renli* is about care and trust, cooperating and competing, personal interest and collective goodness, differentiated loyalty and expanding love, etc. At the core of Confucianism is how to act properly in the prevailing web of expectations, obligations and reciprocities. *Renli* highlights the moral, normative-evaluative sphere of human life. Given that 'everything is here in me', *renli* includes attitudes towards Nature. Dealing with *renli*, we care about social legitimacy.

WSR suggests that *li* shape the conditions, conceptions, processes and consequences of human experience. *Li* are analytically differentiated, logically irreducible while empirically reciprocal, co-dependent on one another.[31] WSR does not form a conceptual hierarchy whereby a particular *li* is always central, higher or more basic. Rather, WSR sees *wuli–shili–renli* as interwoven into a dynamic web within which differentiated *li* invite, inform and transform each other in emerging ways via human action. The relationships between *wuli*, *shili* and *renli* are, metaphorically, flat.

The relevance of WSR to strategy appears to us immediate and apparent. Many strategies, while looking good in isolation, fail to generate valued outcomes due to insensitivity towards differentiated-reciprocal *li*.[32] Just consider how BP concentrated on cost-cutting while ignoring human life and Nature; Channel 4, the British TV broadcaster, focused on viewer ratings while turning a blind eye to bullying and racism; and China's milk producers pursued quick profits with products that harmed society.[33] Not just painful lessons, WSR generates positive insights. In Chapter 3 we used WSR to explain what made China's reform work: the economic-fiscal *wuli* conditions, the ambiguity-embracing *shili* mindscapes and the family-based *renli* achievement orientations. Not just historical, macro transformations, but also mundane, micro experimentations. Remember the three strategic roles of managers in Hurst's story: 'organiser-operator-executor' (*wuli*), 'entrepreneur-facilitator-framemaker' (*shili*), 'networker-negotiator-inspirer' (*renli*)?[34] Let us further look briefly at a small business case, the *Eureka* knowledge-management project at Xerox Corporation.[35]

The Xerox Eureka *project: a WSR view*

Customer service representatives (reps) fixing Xerox machines improved performance chiefly by departing from official guidelines. What did they do? They told stories. The reps posed questions, sought solutions, discussed changes – about the machines, their jobs and customer relations. They generated ideas while eating, playing, chatting, joking and gossiping. In this 'everyday goings-on' process, reps used one another as resources, developing a collective pool of working knowledge.

This locally generated knowledge pool would not benefit other reps unless it spread beyond group boundaries. To enable knowledge-sharing with colleagues worldwide, the reps built a database called *Eureka*. *Eureka* stored their working knowledge in the form of tips. Tips were entered into *Eureka* only after passing a rigorous relevance-and-reliability vetting process conducted jointly by the reps and engineers.

To encourage participation, Xerox management once tried to intervene by proposing a financial reward for each tip. The reps rejected the offer. Instead, they wanted their names attached to the tips in order to earn reputation and bargain for promotion.

Recently, a rep in Brazil fixed a high-end colour machine by replacing a defective 50-cent fuse instead of replacing the problematic machine, which would have cost $40,000. He found the tip online, originally supplied by a Montreal technician, from among about 3,000 tips available through *Eureka*. The 'Eureka Solution', developed in France, connects 24,000 members and receives around 100 new tips and is accessed 2,000 times each month. It has achieved a 5 per cent saving in changed parts and labour without producing obvious losers. Without glamour, *Eureka* delivers real benefits to the workers, the company and customers.

What can we learn from the *Eureka* project? Seen through WSR, the *wuli*-technical database and Internet provide Xerox reps with a useful means for managing job-specific knowledge that has been rigorously tested by scientific-engineering methods. The *shili*-cognitive knowing process is spontaneous, interactive, problem-solving-oriented and full of fun. The reps as knowers insist that they own the solutions and are rewarded in the *renli*-social way that they prefer. *Eureka* delivers because of the network effect of innovations on all knowledge, knowing and knower fronts, and because it combines technical, instrumental and ethical rationality. Focusing on *wuli*, *shili* or *renli* alone, we might have missed many rich insights from *Eureka* and, as experiences have shown, led many one-dimensional imitations into dead ends.

To the paramount leader Deng Xiaoping, the 800 million Chinese farmers, David Hurst the corporate executive and the 24,000 Xerox reps, the world is full of *wuli*, *shili* and *renli*. WSR projects an image of the world we live in, the contexts we strategise in, the flows we cope with and the consequences we produce. The Confucians, like people of other cultures, share an intuitive metaphysical outlook. Following Richard Nisbett, we regard WSR as a Confucian 'folk metaphysics'.[36] When they talk about 'what is', however, pragmatic managers are already thinking about 'what to do'. As Akio Morita commented, Sony's reaction to any idea or phenomenon was invariably 'How can I use this? What can I make with it? How can it be used to produce a useful product?' The spirit of WSR is not so much 'what is the essence of the world?' but 'how to cope with life's problems?'[37]

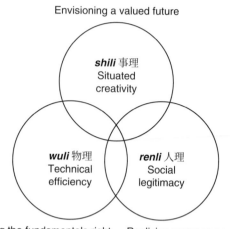

Envisioning a valued future

Getting the fundamentals right   Realising common goodness

FIGURE 5.2 WSR, the strategy bottom line: generating value efficiently, creatively, legitimately

What then is the normative implication of WSR for strategy? We posit that strategy is about getting fundamentals right, envisioning a valued future and realising common goodness. Figure 5.2 visually expresses the WSR strategy bottom line. Let us have a brief look at its implications.

GETTING FUNDAMENTALS RIGHT

Along the *wuli* dimension, strategy is about getting fundamentals right in search of technical efficiency. We interpret the terms 'fundamentals', 'technical' and 'efficiency' broadly.

To begin with, managers need to get the numbers right. Seven-Eleven Japan (SEJ), the convenience-store chain, is an exemplar. The average SEJ store is merely 1,200 square feet and carries only 3,000 units of stock at any one time. Given the limited shelf space, identifying each and every 'dead' or 'hot' item quickly is crucial to customer satisfaction and company profit. A sophisticated point-of-sale data system can reveal change patterns from yesterday to today, but determining what will sell well tomorrow depends on continuing cycles of reading, hypothesising, testing and verifying the specific customer demands made at each store. Ice cream sold well today; does that mean we should order more for tomorrow? Not necessarily. Today, it is sunny, with an outdoor temperature of 25°C. Customers are buying more ice cream because they feel warm after yesterday's 20°C. As the local weather forecast for tomorrow is 23°C with rain, the demand for ice cream is expected to decline. The store should therefore order less ice cream and save shelf space for more timely items such as warm soup. With each of the 12,000-plus stores regularly getting such small, local fundamentals right, the cumulative effect on SEJ is huge. Chairman and CEO Toshifumi Suzuki summarises SEJ's philosophy thus: 'Adaptation to change and getting the basics [read 'fundamentals'] right.'[38]

Then, managers have to deal with technology fundamentals. On 15 October 2007, Airbus finally handed over its first A380 super-jumbo jet to Singapore Airlines. As the delivery was 19 months late, it pushed development costs from an estimated $10.7 billion to $23–24 billion, plunging the holding company EADS into at least two years of big losses. The root of the problem? A 530-km wiring instal-lation on each jet. The problem was traced back to incompatible soft-ware systems at the Airbus operations in Germany and France. In the end, to speed up delivery, Airbus engineers had to do the wiring with handmade products as 'artistic' work.[39] Get the fundamentals wrong, you will be punished.[40] We've seen Toyota recall cars and Sony recall laptop batteries.[41] On 13 July 2010, Apple's iPhone 4 sig-nal-reception problem sent the company's shares down 3 per cent in just a few hours.[42] This is true for all companies, not just those in high-tech industries. Simon Carter, eponymous founder of the world's largest cufflink business, recently explained to the *Financial Times* at its flagship Mayfair shop why he moved production off-shore: 'The reason we make this in China is really due to the quality of manufacturers over there. We used to make stuff in Birmingham, but eight years ago I moved away, with great reluctance. The guy we used to use would stop for a half-day on Fridays; everything was late and all the bits fell off the back.' 'It's the little fundamental things that matter', he said.[43]

Beyond technology and products, there are economic fundamentals. Economy of scale is an obvious example. Made famous by Alfred Chandler's studies on manufacturing companies such as General Motors and DuPont, economies of scale continue to underline corporate strategy in the 'knowledge economy', or 'wikinomics'.[44] During the summer of 2010, HP and Dell competed to acquire the data-storage company 3Par. Through this acquisition, both HP and Dell intended to shift from hardware manufacturing towards 'cloud computing' services. HP triumphed because of an underlining fundamental: 'HP was thought to have an advantage in the takeover battle because, at double Dell's size, its bigger sales force would more quickly be able to extract a return from the acquisition, enabling HP to pay more.'[45] The same fundamental enables Tencent, China's online service company with a massive 600 million-plus active customer base, to compete on all fronts against smaller, specialised rivals.[46] Many of the 'mainstream' strategy models and tools, such as the five-forces model and portfolio matrix sort, are designed to get the economic fundamentals right, as is 'Three Cs' (costs, customers, competitors) analysis, which consultant houses such as Boston Consultant Group and Bain & Company are good at.[47]

In corporate strategy, we include regulative regimes and business practices as fundamentals. Institutions are man-made creatures that serve human purposes. Once settled, however, institutions have 'thing'-like qualities that are not up for negotiation until we have the capability and chance to change them. Laurence Barron, president of Airbus China, commented: 'An aircraft purchase has to be approved by the state authority so we have to sell the aircraft twice – to the airlines and to the government authorities'; 'You just have to deal with it.'[48] In the US, the Congressional Committee on Foreign Investment consistently blocks Huawei's business in-roads, on the ground of a believed link between Huawei and the Chinese military, although the company, unlike Lenovo, was never owned by the state.

Ren Zhengfei, founder and part-owner of Huawei, was not allowed to join the Communist Party when he served in the army because his father had worked briefly, half a century ago, in a nationalist military factory. China's communist regime did not trust Ren because his father once worked for the nationalists; now the US authorities don't trust Huawei because Ren once worked as an engineer in the Chinese army. Setting ideology aside, one can count the US block as protectionist politics: despite product/service superiority and tremendous efforts, the world's second-largest telecom equipment supplier with revenue in 2010 of $28 billion has yet, at the time of our writing, to obtain a big contract or significant acquisition in the US.[49]

The list can go on and on. The above preliminary exploration, we hope, indicates that *wuli* fundamentals critical to business success can be material, technological, economic, institutional, natural as well as man-made. Once normalised and objectified, *wu* become factual and produce consequential impacts. 'Nature cannot be fooled', the Nobel Prize-winning physicist Richard Feily famously told the US Congress hearing on the *Challenger* disaster. The same applies to *wuli*. The more deference (恭), respect (敬) and propensity (畏) we pay to *wuli*, the more accurate our assessment and disciplined our strategy, the more likely we are able to achieve expected outcomes. Given the objectivity of *wuli*, 'to act otherwise' is suicidal. If you aren't prepared to sell an aircraft twice, you had better forget the Chinese market: it is big, growing, just not for you. Without knowing, respecting and acting upon *wuli*, we can't send people to the moon, nor can we reform the banking sector properly.

But just how objective are *wuli*? Doesn't 'getting fundamentals right' conflict with 'particularism' – our emphasis on situated particulars? Isn't there friction between disciplined strategy and *bricolage*? Probing these questions, it is useful to distinguish between objectivity and universality. We agree with Nancy Cartwright of the London School of Economics who posits that, while knowledge can be objective in contexts, contexts are just not universal. We can have truths, not universal but 'nomological' ones. Truths are true under the right circumstances, and enable us to get jobs done in specified conditions. Models of the world can be reliable, but only nomologically. They produce expected outcomes when the required conditions are met. We can repeat the gravity experiment illustrating Newton's laws by cloning required set-ups to allow those laws to work. Without the right conditions, models no longer work and truths no longer hold. In the social world, it is almost impossible to set up 'social laboratories' for 'science of strategy'.[50] This is because, for one thing, in business no two companies are identical.[51] For another, humans tend to produce surprising 'unintended consequences'.[52] 'Theories are successful where they are successful, and that's that', Cartwright concludes.[53] Nomological truths and pragmatism complement each other: *bricolage* demands that we turn away from universal models and acts opportunistically upon particular fundamentals. Pragmatism works precisely because unfolding fundamentals tend to defy generalised principles – the world we experience has no fixed shape (无容), nor definite rules (无则).

Hence, successful companies are successful because they get the firm-specific, purpose-specific, context-specific fundamentals right. To Huawei, a company with a mission to become a world-class technology pioneer, one of the fundamentals is that it should never become a network operator. Why? According to Ren, as long as you are your own customer (supposing Huawei as a telephony operator using its own telecom equipment), you tend to tolerate your own supply, compromise your standards and lose the harsh demands from outside customers as the continual pressure for technology, manufacturing and service excellence. To be excellent, you need the customer's kicking. So much so that 'never enter the telecom service sector' was incorporated into Huawei's constitution, at a time when China's telephony market had just taken off and rivals were weak. However, when Mazda faced looming bankruptcy with tens of thousands of unsold cars, buy your own product, i.e. 'buy Mazda', became a life-and-death fundamental for all who had a stake in the company.

These are fundamentals, hence, objective, law-like, not for negotiation. Get it right, you succeed; get it wrong, you fail. But, and this is crucial, fundamentals are not the same for everyone. Huawei and Mazda were both right, although they adopted opposite strategies. SWOT and five-forces models might be universal, situated fundamentals usually are not. A focusing strategy that enabled Nokia to become an industry leader brought Marconi to its knees.[54] In 1997, the heyday of refocusing, Tarun Khanna and Krishna Palepu of Harvard Business School underscored the particularity of *wuli* fundamentals with their provocative article 'Why focused strategies may be wrong for emerging markets'.[55] Are they right, or wrong, for you? While General Motors and DuPont, as Chandler has shown, benefited from economies of scale, the Third Italy small firms performed well thanks to 'de-economy of scale'.[56] Which, then, works for you: 'economy' or 'de-economy' of scale? Where, when, how and why?

Critically important as they are, fundamentals are not rocket science. Key fundamentals are usually common sense. The reason Simon Carter moved its production to China, for example, is plainly simple and straightforward. Often we know the fundamentals, just fail to act upon them. Does it require a Nobel Prize in economics to see the danger of leveraging a company's asset 42 times to game the market? Does it take rocket science to realise that housing markets can go down as well as up? Do we need a Ph.D. to discover that no household, company or nation can live beyond its means forever? Do we need the loss of human lives and environmental disasters to tell us that safety measures ought to be in place when drilling deeper and deeper into the seabed? Commenting on former Federal Reserve chairman Alan Greenspan's reaction to the banks' risk-management failure, Joseph Stiglitz, an economist at Columbia University, writes: 'The real surprise is his surprise: even a cursory look at the perverse incentives confronting banks and their managers would have predicted short-sighted behaviour with excessive risk-taking.'[57] 'Heads I win (bonus), tails you lose (bail-outs)': no wonder bankers behave like gamblers.

To paraphrase Bill Clinton: it's common sense, stupid. Just before his untimely death in 2005, the Indian-born Harvard, INSEAD and London Business School professor Sumantra Ghoshal urged his academic colleagues to return to 'scholarship of common sense'. He regarded strategy as 'disciplined common sense': 'Business could not be treated as a science, and we would have to fall back on the wisdom of common sense that combines information on "what is" with the imagination of "what ought to be" to develop both a practical understanding of and some pragmatic prescriptions for "phenomena of organised complexity".'[58] We agree. Getting fundamentals right is a common-sense practice which every manager should, and can, do.

Common-sense fundamentals: Northern Rock vs China Merchants Bank

Friday, 14 September 2007. Anxious customers, most of them silver-haired grandparents, queued for hours and hours outside the branches of the British bank Northern Rock, hoping to withdraw their savings. The bank was forced to extend opening hours; its website crashed, overwhelmed by customers attempting to withdraw their money online. This ugly scene was the first run on a British bank in more than 140 years.[59] Make no mistake, customers behaved entirely rationally. George Payan, aged 72, queueing at the Houndsditch branch in East London to withdraw £83,000, said: 'When you have large savings in an account that is unreliable, you want to get it out.'[60] At that time, the UK government guaranteed only £35,000 per depositor.

Northern Rock, Britain's fifth-largest mortgage lender and eighth-largest bank, had just reported a startling increase in lending: 55 per cent in the first eight months of the year. One month earlier, Adam Applegarth, the chief executive, had spoken about the bank's 'robust' credit book, claiming 'the medium-term outlook for the company is very positive'.[61] So, what happened during that short period? The following are the key events that led directly to the bank run:

9 August	Northern Rock's funding problems grew as the international wholesale financial market dried up.
13 August	Northern Rock informed the Financial Services Authority, began seeking cash elsewhere.
16 August	Northern Rock discussed emergency loan with the Bank of England, put itself up for sale.
10 September	Lloyds TSB, the London-based bank, pulled out of secret talks to buy Northern Rock.
13 September	News of the Bank of England loan was leaked to the public by BBC business editor Robert Peston.
14 September	A run on the bank began; emergency funding was approved.
17 September	The UK government promised to guarantee all Northern Rock savers' deposits in full.

Northern Rock subsequently received a £28 billion loan from the Bank of England – taxpayers' money. The European Commission expressed serious doubt about the rescue plan. Almost six months later, on 17 February 2008, after several failed attempts to find a buyer, the British government was forced to put Northern Rock into public ownership – the first nationalisation of a sizeable British bank in a quarter of a century. The immediate consequences were the losses of 2,400 jobs, most of Northern Rock's share value and the dashed reputation of British financial institutions.[62]

By global standards, Northern Rock is a pretty modest bank; the run on it was less spectacular than the collapse of Lehman Brothers. Yet the lesson we can learn from the saga is no less significant.

Northern Rock dates back to the 1860s with the creation of the Northern Counties Permanent Building Society and the Rock Building Society. The two merged in 1965 to form Northern Rock. The building society went on to absorb more than 50 other mutual societies. Based in Newcastle, in the north-east of England, Northern

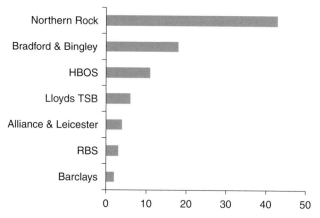

FIGURE 5.3 Securitisation as a % of total funding: British banks
Source: Financial Times 15/16 September 2007, 'The Lex column: Rock bottom'

Rock had a special tradition of serving local communities. It even challenged the Thatcher government by offering flexible mortgages to striking miners in the 1980s. Yet all this changed when the building society listed as a bank in the stock market on 1 October 1997. 'Market is king': Northern Rock was now answerable to shareholders, and they demanded growth and return, fast.[63]

In the transformation from a small building society to a fast-growing high-street bank, Northern Rock created a unique business model, moving from funding by retail deposits to wholesale markets for cash. Compared with the UK banking average of 7 per cent, Northern Rock used wholesale finance for 43 per cent of its funding (see Figure 5.3).

Eschewing retail customer deposits kept operational costs magically low: the bank had just 72 branches in total – how many branches does HSBC have in London alone? Northern Rock packaged up home loans, securitised and sold them on to investors through global markets. To attract more customers, the bank offered loans of 125 per cent of the value of properties to first-time buyers. Such unconventional techniques helped Northern Rock rapidly grow its loan book, market share and profits. Based on its fast growth and low-cost lending, Northern Rock was, until the run on it, regarded as 'the leanest bank in Europe'.[64] Like BP in oil and Enron in energy, Northern Rock in banking became a star, an exemplar of finance innovation.

Yet Nature cannot be fooled, nor can business fundamentals. And it is no good being lean, efficient or innovative if it kills you.[65] Northern Rock's wholesale model, which enabled it to outperform rivals, made it extremely vulnerable to market upsets.[66] When the wholesale finance market dried up in August 2007 due to the sub-prime mortgage collapse thousands of miles away, Northern Rock had to rely almost entirely on the expensive overnight money market to finance its obligations. The mortgage lender was then forced to go to the central bank for an emergency loan; when news of this was leaked, a run on the bank was a logical conclusion.[67]

During the bank run, on 15 September, Applegarth refused to accept responsibility: 'Is the model flawed looking forward? Of course it is. Is it flawed looking back? I think the answer is no because of the markets that we were operating in prior to August 9.'[68] 'It's an astonishing thing to see the sterling three-month interbank market effectively not exist', he said. One month later, facing the UK Parliamentary Treasury Select Committee, Applegarth insisted 'it was a good business model that couldn't cope with unforeseen events in the global markets.'[69] Northern Rock chairman Matt Ridley agreed: 'the Northern Rock business model was a good one', it just suffered from 'unprecedented and unpredictable events'.[70]

Put in plain language, the Northern Rock model was based on short-term borrowing in the wholesale market to fund long-term retail lending, which requires infinitely plentiful liquidity to work. It is not especially complicated.[71] Is it a 'good' one? To Applegarth and Ridley, it is. To many others, however, it is too risky. 'With hindsight, Northern Rock's strategy of relying on the wholesale money markets for the bulk of its funding was flawed. Professional investors have proved less reliable and more prone to funk than the armies of retail depositors on whom more traditional lenders rely.'[72] *The Economist* commented: 'the very innovations on which Northern Rock thrived have savaged its business.'[73] Mervyn King, governor of the Bank of England, acknowledged common sense: 'those outside the financial service industry must have watched recent events unfold with utter bemusement.'[74] Indeed.

> If it is so obvious now, the lay person might ask, why was it not so earlier in the year when Northern Rock was boasting of its success as Britain's fastest-growing mortgage lender? Did anyone tell depositors that a couple of months choppy conditions in global credit markets might sweep it away? Nor could anyone be expected to draw comfort from protestations that this was a crisis made elsewhere.[75]

There was a further bemusement. On 14 September, exactly when the silver-haired customers were queuing, the Northern Rock board decided to pay a £60 million dividend.[76] What is common sense to some is, apparently, not so to others. Remember how BP was still considering a billion-dollar dividend while its Gulf of Mexico oil spill was lapping the American coastline?[77]

On the other side of the globe, the China Merchants Bank (CMB) generates value by acting upon fundamentals, not playing with them. CMB was born in 1984, in the early days of China's reform, in the southern city of Shenzhen, a former fishing village that happened to become one of Deng's *jingji tequ* (经济特区, Economic Special Zones). Within the zone, there was an industrial district consisting of a dozen or so enterprises. Like other businesses, each enterprise had its own accounts, borrowed (at high interest rates) from and deposited (at low interest rates) in the few state-owned banks. District leaders came up with an idea: to establish an internal 'clearing house' so as to deal with the banks via a single account which serves subordinate enterprises. The district could then lend the deposit from one enterprise to another that needed the money, avoiding losing the interest-rate difference to the banks. Was such a clearing house a socialist or capitalist entity, a white cat or black cat? Well, the beauty of the Economic Special Zones was that every cat deserved a try to see whether it caught mouse. The cat was born anyway, and transformed first into a 'finance company' in 1985 and then into the China Merchants Bank in 1986, with the district as the sole owner, ¥100 million in capital, one office and 36 staff. Thanks to China's booming economy, in those days there was plenty of room for many cats. By 1999, CMB found itself with a network of 166 branches across 19 cities, 5,000 staff, ¥150 billion assets and ¥2 billion profit. Impressive.

Yet the competition ahead was formidable. China was then, and is still now, a 'market economy with socialist characteristics', where all cats are equal but some are more equal than others. The 'market' was dominated by the 'big five' state-controlled banks – ICBC, CCB, BOC, BoCom, ABC. The 'big five' grabbed tens of thousands of branches, state-backed borrowers and mega-project transactions such as financing dams, railways and steel mills. The non-state banks were left with individual depositors, small–medium-sized enterprises and tiny networks of branches. This was the fundamentals that CMB had to deal with. You might have room to breathe, but how would you compete with the 'big five', let alone become a *Fortune* 500 company?

The good news is that fundamentals are not merely threats or constraints. For thoughtful managers, fundamentals can be opportunities and enablers. In 1999, around the time China entered the World Trade Organization, CMB got a new president, Ma Weihua. Previously a high-level administrator in the state bureaucracy and the central bank, Ma knew the state banks inside-out. The 'big five' were good at dealing with mega transactions, but had no interest in serving private customers. These 'uniform' players operated (and still do) under the same business model, with similar customers, styles, products and results: three of the 'big five', for example, reported an identical net profit increase of 27 per cent in the first half of year 2010, the other two a slightly higher 30 per cent. Competing with these giants on their terms would be suicidal.

But where were the 'enabling fundamentals'? With a booming economy and an emerging bourgeois class, China's banking sector was facing new demands, Ma and his colleagues reckoned. Consider the following:

- China's new riches called for wealth management; this would become the most lucrative segment.
- Credit would become an acceptable means for the Chinese to finance education, housing and other consumption.
- On top of borrowing and deposit, small–medium enterprises need other financial services, such as managing cash flow, raising capital and avoiding risks.
- The Internet and ICT opened up opportunities to change the resources composition and power balance between banks.

Once these were on the table, everyone agreed: 'Obviously, these are the fundamentals.' The question was then how to act upon them so as to overcome state-bank domination and generate value for consumers. No longer aiming to be a 'cloned' version of the 'big five', CMB's new vision was to become 'a pioneer retail bank with a technology edge'. The CMB model would focus on retail banking and finance management, emphasising product differentiation and personalised services, to be achieved through a *high*-technology platform, *high*-market clients, *high* entry barrier and *high* development potential – the '4 Highs'.

While the 'big five' relied on their huge networks of branches (ICBC alone had over ten thousand branches), CMB built a high-quality IT platform. This platform enabled the bank to launch, in 1996, China's first debit card (一卡通, the All-in-One card). It was an instant success. By 2009, CMB had issued over 45 million All-in-One cards, with an average ¥8,300 deposit. This alone supplied CMB with ¥370 billion in low-cost capital. The 'first-mover advantage' also brought 'economy of scale' – a vast customer base for the bank to launch other services. Importantly, the All-in-One card shaped the public image: 'Online banking is Merchants Bank, and Merchants Bank is online banking.'

In China, a bank transaction costs ¥1.07 at a branch, ¥0.45 by telephone, ¥0.27 via an ATM and ¥0.01 on the Internet. Simply put, online transactions cost less than 1 per cent of bank transactions. This fundamental made online banking a 'profit pool'. In 1999, CMB launched China's first all-in-one online service (一网通, All-in-One Net), allowing customers to conduct transactions – including shopping, deposits, investment, insurance, fund-transfer, utility and other payments – through the Internet and mobile phones. By 2007, China's online bank transactions reached ¥97.6 billion, of which CMB accounted for one-third. Today, 15 per cent of CMB's business transactions are online, and the figure for private customers is 80 per cent. The 'big five's' massive branch networks were not so formidable any more. Rather, the 'big five' stumbled after CMB, just like the giant PC-makers imitated Dell in the 1980s–1990s.

After providing general consumers with retail services, CMB explored the high-end market. The potential would be huge: in 2008 over 300,000 individuals held an average of ¥30 million investable capital, by 2010 there were 100 million middle-class families in China. The fundamental was clear: in CMB's book, clients with an average of ¥0.5 million assets accounted for 0.1 per cent of customer base, while contributing 30 per cent of total business. To attract and retain these clients, the bank had to create value for them. In 2002 CMB launched its 'Gold Sunflower' programme – not a single product but a wide range of wealth-management services. In 2007, CMB launched China's first 'private bank' service for clients who invested over ¥10 million. By 2009, there were 7,000 CMB 'private banks', contributing ¥140 billion to the bank's book. The return was high profitability: CMB issued fewer credit cards than ICBC, yet CMB's high-end card-holders spent an average of ¥70,000 a month, far more than ICBC customers. The high-end segment generated benefits in many other ways. Recently, for example, BMW chose CMB as its sole finance partner in China; the German car-maker saw CMB's clients as potential buyers for luxury cars.

This illustrates how far CMB has travelled. Remember: CMB was established in 1984 to handle 'internal' enterprise transactions; by 1993, enterprises still accounted for 93 per cent of the bank's business. That was, however, a dead end. Because of their huge branch networks and state-backed borrowers, the 'big five' dominate traditional banking, with interest-rate difference accounting for 80–90 per cent of their income. CMB was not the 'big five' and had no such 'advantage'. In 2004, based on rigorous analysis of fundamentals and several years of 'touching the stones', Ma and his colleagues focused CMB's strategy on retail banking. They extended the sector beyond deposit-and-lending to cover customer account settlement, debit/credit business, currency trading, bank-draft processing and wealth and risk management. Ma calls these services 'middle business'; such business does not require substantial capital. The future for CMB is to excel in low-capital-cost, retail, middle business.

So far, the strategy has worked well. In one generation's time, CMB has grown from nothing to an industry leader, China's first shareholding commercial bank. It is the sixth-biggest retail bank in the country, just under the 'big five'. It is ranked within the world's top 30 banks on market value and the world's No. 1 in terms of price/book ratio, and is listed at 121 on the *Financial Times* Global 500. When CMB opened its New York branch in November 2007, the mayor of New York called it 'the spring wind in the winter'. In the summer of 2008, CMB took over Wing Lung, a Hong Kong bank with 35 local branches and one in California. In March 2009, CMB chief executive Ma Weihua was named Retail Banker of the Year by the Asian Banker Excellence in Retail Financial Services Awards Program, which cited CMB's 'impressive retail expansion, upmarket client inroads, and consistently strong franchise performance'.[78] In modern banking, China is a latecomer. Ma and CMB have so far got the fundamentals right. Can they continue managing risk well while selling risk-management to clients?[79] We wish them the very best. After all, as Ma Weihua said, 'China needs good banks'. So does the world.[80]

ENVISIONING A VALUED FUTURE

Polaroid, the photography company, is famous not just for the invention that allowed Edwin Land's daughter and millions of consumers to enjoy what they valued: an instant picture from the camera.[81] The company, like Huawei, was inspired to be a pioneer that led industry via technology innovation, which can be achieved only by committed, long-term investment. As senior Polaroid managers put it, 'What we were good at was major inventions – large-scale, lengthy projects that other firms would hesitate to tackle. We compared ourselves to Bell Labs. Our orientation was: "technical challenge – we can do it."'[82] Polaroid had a glorious history, and was a household name in the developed world. Land himself held over 500 patents. The one-step, waste-free SX-70 instant camera, which consumed eight years' and half-a-billion dollars' research, was a huge commercial success. By 1989, the company had spent 42 per cent of its R&D money on digital technologies and was well-positioned to develop a leading-edge digital camera. Polaroid sensors, for example, could generate a resolution of 1.9 million pixels when rivals generated only 480,000.[83]

Yet Polaroid managed to lose the edge and fall apart; by 2008, Edwin Land was filing for bankruptcy. How did this happen? The huge success of its instant camera locked the company into three 'ontological truths': (1) the PIF (Printer in the Field) market – consumers valued physical instant pictures; (2) razor/blade model – 'You had to be in the hardware business to make money ... where's the film?'; and (3) the advantages of distributing products through mass retailers such as Wal-Mart – this was the way to beat traditional non-instant cameras sold through specialist stores.[84] These 'truths' fed into Polaroid's strategy; the company believed that a digital image as an 'electronic front end' must be converted into an 'immediate physical print'. Polaroid could see no alternatives. The company did not announce its PDC-2000 digital camera until 1996, when over 40 other firms were already busy selling their own brands.[85]

Where Polaroid failed by constraining digital technology at 'the front end', Canon succeeded in designing and selling the digital camera as 'a computer with a lens'.[86] Canon and Polaroid worked under different 'mental models' and envisioned different futures. Given the same technology 'at hand' and the same environment 'out there', how a company sees things can make it a winner or a loser.

Let us have a look at another classic case, the Swatch.[87] During the 1970s, the Swiss struggled to reorient their watch industry in the face of competition from Japan, the US and Hong Kong. Swiss watchmakers, world leaders in mechanical watches for 200 years, developed the initial quartz technology but failed to commercialise it because the market associated with the new technology did not fit the Swiss preconceptions of how a watch (a timekeeping device or luxury item of jewellery bought for life) should be produced and consumed. The consequences were grave. In 1974, Swiss watches made up 40 per cent of the world market; ten years later that figure had fallen to 10 per cent. Many expected the Swiss watch industry to perish in the face of the electronic onslaught.

The Swiss breakthrough came in 1983 when Nicolas Hayek redefined the watch as a high fashion, mood-oriented, mass-market accessory. This new conception, a unique 'way of seeing things', made the crucial difference. Changes in design, production, marketing, pricing, distribution and corporate structure quickly followed. The result was the successful launch of the low-cost, high-tech, artistic, emotional Swatch. Within five years, the Swatch Group had become the most valuable watchmaker in the world. In the summer of 2010, when Nicolas Hayek suddenly died working in the office at the age of 82, sales under Swatch's 19 brands were expected to exceed SFr6 billion (£3.7 billion).[88] Seeing things – in this case watches –differently enabled the whole Swiss watch industry to survive, recover and prosper. In his 1985 *Harvard Business Review* paper 'The discipline of innovation', Peter Drucker wrote: 'A change in perception does not alter facts. It changes their meaning ... opens up big innovation opportunities.'[89]

This brings us to the *shili* mental-cognitive bottom line: strategy is about envisioning, and realising, a valued future. In ancient times, the pragmatic Confucius promoted creativity (作, 诚) as a great virtue; in the last century, Joseph Schumpeter, the Austrian-born economist, famously posited 'creative destruction' as the engine of the capitalist economy.[90] More recently, Chan Kim and Renée Mauborgne's metaphor 'blue oceans' captures the critical significance of *shili* creativity. The opposite of creativity is 'group-think', 'competence trap' or 'core rigidities'.[91]

Managers, consultants and researchers emphasise *shili* at all levels: individual, group, organisational, industrial and societal. For example, individual managers are found to have different 'knowledge structures' or 'frames of reference'; top management teams act upon 'shared narratives' and 'strategic beliefs'; firms possess 'organisational memories' and 'interpretation systems'; industries, sectors and strategic groups share 'industry recipes' and 'dominant logic'; national cultures supply tacit ways of thinking, seeing and acting; and we all live with 'paradigms'. Alongside mental models and managerial cognitions are capabilities, competences and skill sets. All these *shili* shape how strategic matters are perceived, analysed, formulated and tackled. March and Simon, Nelson and Winter, Mintzberg and Spender, Weick and Daft, Prahalad and Bettis, DiMaggio and Powell, Porac and Thomas, among many others, are big names in this *shili* area.[92] Innovation, product development, technology management, organisational learning and knowledge creation, symbolised by the works of Tushman and Anderson, Henderson and Clark, Senge and Nonaka, are the most visible practices through which companies envision and realise valued futures, escape zero-sum red oceans and explore value-generating blue ones.[93]

From the Polaroid and Swatch cases we learn that *wuli* fundamentals alone do not guarantee business success. Fundamentals must generate value for customers. Customers continue to value instant pictures in the digital era, but they no longer demand on-site physical prints. The value of instant print as a consumable had passed. Polaroid's strategic difficulty lies in its failure, even with cutting-edge technology at hand, to envision a future valued by consumers. Companies might get the fundamentals right, as both Polaroid and Canon did; it is their visions of the 'future' that make the difference. Swiss watchmakers developed quartz technology ahead of the Japanese, but failed to profit from it until Nicolas Hayek envisioned a future in which the technology generated artistic, emotional, economic values for consumers. Examples are rife: Sony envisioned a world where people regained their freedom by watching TV programmes whenever they wanted, and invented the video machine to realise it. Muhammad Yunus envisioned a world without poverty, and invented microfinance to help millions of the poorest stand on their own feet. Polaroid's great 'instant' success, before its 'digital' failure, grew out of Edwin Land's vision of a wonderful future his daughter dreamed of. Envisioning a valued future, managers don't just solve problems, they define problems, resulting in 'products that rivals can't touch'.[94]

Firms envision different futures. They must differentiate themselves on their visions and abilities to deliver superior values.[95] But why do so many once-successful companies fail to do it, even with leading-edge technology at hand? The difficulty for incumbents lies exactly in the reliability of their past successes. Remember why it was so difficult for Intel to shift officially to a microprocessor strategy? Intel had locked itself in the memory of its past success. As to the Swiss watchmakers, 'to say that precision metal machining no longer ruled the sacred domain of timekeeping accuracy was simply too much for the centuries-old Swiss tradition to endure'.[96] Strikingly, even after the PDC-2000 mega-pixel camera launch in 1996, the ghost of the razor/blade model still lingered at Polaroid. CEO Gary DiCamillo told a reporter in 1997:

> What are we? What are we good at? We're pretty good at creating image instantly. Not very many companies can do that ... there's both a time and a skill required to take conventional film and make it look good ... In the digital world we believe that hard copy is required ... Unless there is a consumable component, the business model falls apart. So we have to focus on what's consumable and what value-added we can provide that's unique.[97]

Core capabilities or core rigidities? Competence-based strategy or competence trap? Seen through *shili*, these are the two sides of the same coin: coping with cognitive constraints, promoting creativity.

The critical importance of innovation has been widely accepted in strategy, thanks to powerful metaphors such as 'creative destruction' and 'blue oceans'. But what does innovation mean? To many, it is largely confined to technology. Schumpeter's innovation theory of economics is, for example, interpreted by well-known researchers to mean 'the prime driver of economic progress is technological innovation'.[98] Other innovations, if mentioned at all, are framed in terms of technological innovation. In our view, this narrow interpretation is unfortunate. Schumpeter's insight is much broader. In 1943, he wrote that innovations can create 'the new commodity, the new technology, the new source of supply, the new type of organisation'.[99] What distinguishes Schumpeter's from the narrow view is his belief that supply, organisation and other innovations can generate value with or without technology. Technology is important, but it is not the only means of generating value. Closer to practice, Drucker illustrated in his 1985 paper that 'a shift in viewpoint, not in technology, totally changed the economics of ocean shipping and turned it into one of the major growth industries of the last 20 to 30 years'.[100] Similarly, Kim and Mauborgne's 'blue ocean' studies reveal that value creation can be achieved without technology breakthroughs.[101]

Schumpeter and Drucker's broader vision is significant for strategy because it posits wider opportunities and bigger responsibilities to managers. In the spirit of Schumpeter and Drucker, we can consider the following innovations – the list below should be seen as suggestive, not exhaustive:

- *Technology* innovation: the Internet, biotechnology, nanotechnology;
- *Product/service* innovation: Sony Walkman, Tata Nano, Apple iPhone, Grameen microcredit, Starbuck's friendly atmosphere, Hisap's in-shop computer assembly;
- *Standard* innovation: Microsoft Windows operating system, JVC video cassette format, Sony Blue Ray high-definition DVD;
- *Process* innovation: Ford assembly line, Toyota Just-in-Time, Canon cell-production;
- *Organisation* innovation: M-form, project-based, ambidextrous organisations;

- *Market* innovation: ordinary children as Yamaha piano consumers, poorest villagers as Grameen Bank borrowers, women and the elderly as Nintendo gamers;
- *Business model* innovation: Dell Direct, Li & Fung global supply chain, Hisap WDM (Wal-Mart+Dell+McDonald's), Alibaba.com revenue from elite membership schemes not from online transactions;
- *Institution* innovation: The Third Italy Financial Consortia, China's Township-Village Enterprise, Linux's open-source community, online social networks;
- *Concept* innovation: SWOT, experience curve, value chain, five forces, blue ocean, *ba*, managing flow.

The above unfinished list shows that there is no end, no boundary, no limit to innovation. In *shili* terms, then, what is strategy? 'Strategy today is nothing without passion and vision from people creating and implementing it. Indeed, dreams need to be at front and centre of the strategy-making process.'[102] But why *situated* creativity? With the term *situated*, we emphasise practicality. Drucker defined innovation as a conscious effort to create purposeful, focused changes.[103] In the same spirit, Theodore Levitt warned: 'What is often lacking is not creativity in the idea-creating sense but innovation in the action-producing sense, i.e., putting ideas to work.'[104] Not just to work in labs, but also in markets. Xerox's bright engineers invented the graphical user interface (GUI), only to put it on the shelf. It took Apple and Microsoft, years later, to exploit its value in the market. Such is the price of non-purposeful, non-focused, non-situated creativity, paid for by Xerox the inventor. This reminds us of Sumantra Ghoshal and David Teece's pragmatic theme: strategy is getting jobs done and making a real difference, not busy-going-nowhere.[105]

Situated then links creativity to unfolding fundamentals. The razor/blade model once worked well for Polaroid; it also built a strong foundation for the young Sony. Akio Morita recalled the design of the company's tape recorder: 'Our strategy from the beginning was not only to build a machine, but also to make and sell the recording tapes for our customers who bought recorders. If we sold tape recorders and not tape, we would be handing good business to our eventual competitors.'[106] For Polaroid's instant film and Sony's recording tape, the razor/blade model captured the fundamentals of the time. Polaroid's later digital disaster was due to the firm's 'competence trap' when fundamentals changed. Sony profited from recording tape because in the early 1950s a conventional vinyl LP could hold only one album. Today a chip in an iPod or MP3 player stores 20,000; does anyone sell merely 'consumables'? Global supply chain is another example. 'Designed in California, assembled in China' was, once upon a time, the winning formula. No more. According to a report, *Look East: The Changing Face of World Business*, published by HSBC Holdings PLC in 2010: 'The old paradigm, where the West owned the brand, the design and the intellectual property, then outsourced the manufacturing and production to the East, is shifting.'[107]

Creativity must therefore be situated, fitting with circumstances. In the next chapter we call this timely balance. For now, let us engage in an excellent case of promoting situated creativity that benefits consumers, the firm and society.

Nintendo the game changer

Queen Elizabeth II enjoys it; pensioners as old as 103 play it; the American Heart Association endorses it to sedentary people to take the first step towards fitness.[108] What is it? Surprisingly: a videogame machine, the $249.99 Nintendo Wii. It is a wonder in the hands of toddlers and grandmas, husbands and wives, their sons and daughters, hard-core gamers as well as busy professionals. Since its launch on 19 November 2006, the Wii has brought golf swings and tennis serves into living rooms, lifting millions off the sofa to run, stretch and ski. By 2010, Nintendo had sold 70 million Wii, twice the sales of PlayStation 3 and 30 million more than Xbox 360.[109] By 2011, one-third of Japanese households and 30 per cent of US families owned a Wii.[110] Significantly, almost half of those who bought the Wii had never owned a videogame before. While Microsoft and Sony made a loss selling consoles in the hope of making a profit on software sales, Nintendo made a direct profit of $13 per Wii sold in Japan, $49 in the US and $79 in Europe.[111] With the Wii, Nintendo made more profit per worker than Goldman Sachs in 2007, the heyday of investment banking.[112] Compared with Microsoft's $177,000 and Google's $288,000, Nintendo generated $442,000 per worker.[113] Industry observers praise the way in which Nintendo's 'quiet but profound innovation has revolutionised the video games industry'; 'changed how we play, how we talk and how we interact with technology'.[114] Yet just in the mid 2000s, some in the industry thought Nintendo 'was finished'.[115]

In the 40 years since the first videogame was launched, the game industry has grown into a $60-billion-a-year business.[116] Entering the 2000s, the industry was locked in a vicious three-way fight between Sony, Microsoft and Nintendo. In the summer of 2002, *The Economist* reported:

> Nothing illustrates the battle's ferocity better than the eye-watering price cuts of the past few weeks. Sony, whose PlayStation2 console has sold 30m units since its launch in March 2000, cut its price from $299 to $199 in America, and made similar cuts elsewhere. The move was intended to head off competition from Microsoft's Xbox and Nintendo's GameCube, both of which were launched in November and have sold around 4.5m units each. Microsoft followed suit, cutting the price of the Xbox from $299 to $199. Nintendo responded by cutting the GameCube's price from $199 to $149.[117]

Not just the price war. Technologically, the ruling paradigm was 'the more functionality and faster the speed, the better'. Players competed on killer processing power, higher-definition graphics, massive storage capacity and fast Wi-Fi connectivity. This single-minded search for technological supremacy produced an 'unintended consequence': videogames were becoming more expensive, complex and difficult to play and, worst of all, less fun. This in turn led to a stagnated, if not shrinking, market: occasional gamers with busy lives stopped playing, while novices were put off by the humiliating skill-level required. Morally, the industry was regarded as an enemy of society for encouraging violence and anti-social behaviour, and for turning a generation into emotionally stunted couch potatoes. The environment for the game-makers was difficult, unpleasant, technically demanding, spiritually demoralising. 'Creativity was being stifled, and the range of games was narrowing', in the words of Nintendo's legendary designer Shigeru Miyamoto. 'It's like having only ferocious dinosaurs. They might fight and hasten their own extinction.'[118] Well, a typical life in red oceans.

Among the 'vicious three', Nintendo was particularly vulnerable. While Sony might survive through its electronics business and Microsoft through PC software, Nintendo was a dismal toy company, making its living exclusively from games. Launched in 1889, the Kyoto-based company started by making playing cards, old, traditional, low-tech. In 1958, it struck a deal to feature Disney cartoon characters on its cards. There were ups and downs, trials and failures. The company briefly sold instant rice and toy vacuum cleaners, ran a taxi service and a pay-by-the-hour 'love hotel', without success.[119] In the 1970s, Nintendo began to focus on electronic toys and videogames. The truth is, while Sony and Microsoft were technology pioneers from day one, Nintendo was not. In textbook jargon, the company had no defendable positioning, nor obvious competence.

The Japanese name 'Nintendo' is made up of three characters: 任 (nin, leave to), 天 (ten, heaven) and 堂 (do, company). It can be interpreted in many ways: 'The company that leaves everything to heaven'; 'The company's fate is in heaven's hands'; and 'Take care of every detail and heaven will take care of the company.'[120] As the company grew up and learned from experience, the latter meaning gradually became more apt. Nintendo managed to develop the coin-operated Donkey Kong arcade game in 1982, Super Mario Brothers on the Nintendo Entertainment System in 1985 and Game Boy, the world's first handheld videogame with changeable cartridges, in 1989. Not bad for a toy-maker. However, when the wealthy, technologically competent and aggressive giants Sony and Microsoft joined the game, they immediately set high-power rules. Nintendo found itself becoming a second-class player. The company had to learn fast, faster, reinvent itself into a new game boy.

And reinvent it did. In 2002, the company got a new president, Satoru Iwata, who had started as a developer for a firm Nintendo bought in 2000. Watching the PlayStation–Xbox arms race, Iwata was convinced that the competitors were fighting the wrong battle, a battle Nintendo could not win and should not be in. But where was Nintendo's future? What was its strategy? The Nintendo people decided not to fight for a bigger slice of the existing market pie, but to make the pie bigger. In Iwata's words: 'the customers we're approaching aren't just those interested in videogames but also those who have never had an interest or who have never played games for any reason.'[121] 'We are not competing against Sony or Microsoft. We are battling the indifference of people who have no interest in video-games', he said. 'The thing we're thinking about most is not portable systems, consoles, and so forth, but that we want to get new people playing games.'[122] Miyamoto agreed: 'there are only so many teen-age geeks in the market and if we go on only appealing to them, we're going to have a very hard time.'[123] Like Yamaha in pianos and Grameen in banking, Nintendo was to create a new marketplace. To do this, you must generate unique value for customers, even if those customers don't exist yet.

Why should non-gamers come to us? 'People say videogames are a waste of time and are bad for your brain and for your health', Miyamoto recalled. 'We wanted to create something to answer that. We want to broaden the definition of what a videogame is, to cre-ate games for people whether they are five or 95 ... I want to show that computer games can be good for you, can enrich your life.'[124] Needless to say, this could not be achieved by 'Street Fighters' or 'Warcraft'. To realise their dream, Nintendo envisioned 'a machine that makes people smile'. What is more important than improv-ing players' health? What can be more fun than mixing fitness and gaming? What would make mothers happier than playing together with their kids, relatives and friends? And finally, what could be more appealing than fitting a 15-minute tennis game into busy professional lives? Thus was born the concept of sport games on a console. Not conventional videogames played by fingers manipulating buttons, but sport games played with a player's whole body.

Still, you have to make it happen. What should the machine look like, how should it work, how much should it cost? For this, the development team turned to mothers. As Miyamoto recalled:

> It was 2003. We got game designers and engineers together to discuss the future of video games. We talked about what specs and features a console should have. But we knew we would get nowhere if we didn't get moms' approval. So we thought about what might convince moms to buy this for their kids. When that happened, we talked about basic concepts and goals, not about the technical specifications of the console. This was the Wii's first major step.[125]

And this was what the 'moms' told them:

- Games should make people healthier, happier and bring the whole family together; moms did not like their kids staring at a screen alone all day.
- Moms wanted the games based on real-life scenarios; they hated bloody punches, addictive fantasies or playing football with two fingers.
- Power wasn't everything, the machine should be easy to set up and play; moms said graphics didn't matter if the games weren't fun to play.
- The controller should be wireless; moms hated to have wires trailing around their rooms.
- The machine should play every Nintendo game ever made; moms would get annoyed if the kids had to have several consoles lying around.
- And, of course, the games should be inexpensive; moms wanted to get more from less and you must come up with a low-cost machine and titles that would make them happy.[126]

In searching for 'a machine that moms would want', the much-sought-after 'concepts and goals' gradually took shape: the meaning of videogames changed from passive immersion in a complicated, fantasy world targeting young addicts to simple, active workouts in the real world for everyone. And the machine should be affordable, easy to use, fun to play, simple, lean, quiet, with low energy consumption. 'Rather than just picking new technology, we thought seriously about what a game console should be', said Miyamoto. 'We thought that changing the interface would broaden game design and loosen creative constraints.'[127] To achieve this, you need to combine radical concepts with radical designs.

The core of Wii's success is its innovative interface, the Wii Remote controller, or simply Wiimote. Miyamoto wondered: 'we were losing out to the TV remote. So we thought, what kind of controller can we create that won't make people afraid to touch it?'[128] It took three years for Miyamoto and his team to test various kinds of technology and come up with dozens of prototypes, including one that resembled a cellphone and another with an analog stick on top. The development team invited family members to test the prototypes, in different conditions, such as various room sizes.[129] In the end, the magic product was a wireless, wand-shaped, motion-sensitive controller powered by a $2.50 chip based on MEMS (micro electro mechanical system). The MEMS technology was not new; car-makers used it in air bags to detect whether a vehicle was experiencing a collision, and the PC industry used it to detect when a laptop was falling down. Nintendo's innovation was to generate new value from the existing technology, guided by their new concept, meaning and strategy. The white plastic Wiimote not only does the usual remote-control stuff but serves as a virtual baseball bat, tennis racket and skateboard. For the first time, the physical gestures of players become an essential part of the game. And, because the Wii isn't high-definition, a game can cost as little as $5 million to develop, compared with up to $20 million for the PS3. Thanks to this, third-party titles sold well, and Nintendo became the top console-maker to work with.[130]

In addition to creating new customers, new products and new partners, Nintendo revolutionised the industry's marketing. 'Wii', with two lower-case 'i', is meant to resemble two people playing together. 'Wii sounded like "we", emphasising that the console was for everyone. Wii was easy to remember in every language. No confusion. No need to abbreviate. Just Wii', the Nintendo website suggested.[131] TV commercials reinforced the revolutionised meaning. Instead of showing fantasy monsters, aliens or gang masters, the camera turned around 180 degrees to focus on people who were playing, moving, chatting, laughing, enjoying themselves – folks like you and me, just healthier, happier.

The Wii platform, with associated products such as Wii Fit and Wii Music, plus training titles on Nintendo's DS, has created a massive market of first-time players from a completely different demographic. 'Most analysts agree that Wii's success revolutionised the video game industry'; 'Nintendo is setting the trend.'[132] Altogether, Nintendo sold 200 million Wii and DS machines.[133] Four years later, Sony and Microsoft were playing catch-up, trying to launch their own motion controllers by the end of 2010.[134] 'You have to give Nintendo credit for what they've accomplished', says Jack Tretton, president of Sony Computer Entertainment America; Peter Moore, who runs Microsoft's Xbox business, has this to say: 'Nintendo has created a unique and innovative experience. I love the experience, the price point and Nintendo content.'[135]

'With the launch of Wii we began to expand the definition of the videogame', president Iwata tells reporters. 'The reason why Wii has been given so much appreciation is not because of technological superiority; rather, it must be due to the fact that we have been able to provide unexpected and unprecedented entertainment value.'[136] Human-centred, envisioning a future valued by customers and making it happen – this is Nintendo's winning formula. 'Even before someone invented the term blue-ocean strategy, we were exercising it', Iwata smiles. 'It is an unwritten company credo, something that runs deep in our DNA.' 'We are successfully moving up the blue ocean. But once the blue ocean has become big enough for so many people to notice, it is going to change its colour to red.'[137] The company's new vision? To use thoughts to control games and devices – even the Wiimote should go.[138] That is Nintendo's next blue ocean.

'Nintendo will remain small, innovative, and reliant on a culture in which copying what has worked for other companies is a mark of shame.'[139]

REALISING COMMON GOODNESS

Wuli fundamentals and *shili* creativity, if they are to better the well-being of consumers, firms and society, must be matched with collective purpose. Nonaka puts it this way: creativity without purpose is lethal, and innovation should be judged based on common goodness.[140] What do you think of the 'blue ocean' illustrated below?

> Consider Enron, the Houston-based energy company. Enron's roots are traceable to one of the oldest, capital-intensive commodity industries in the world – gas and utilities. Yet, for three consecutive years, *Fortune* has ranked Enron the most innovative company in the United States. During the past fifteen years, Enron has struck upon repeated value innovations, lowering the cost of gas and electricity to customers by as much as 40 per cent to 50 per cent. Enron did so while dramatically reducing its own cost structure by, for example, creating the first national spot market for gas in which commodity swaps, future contracts, and other complex derivatives effectively stripped the risk and volatility out of gas prices. Today, Enron has as many traders, analysts, and scientists – including a rocket scientist from the former Soviet Union – employed by Enron's headquarters as gas and pipeline personnel. Enron exemplifies the transition from the production to the knowledge economy.[141]

Today, we have better ideas of what Enron's innovation was about, how it was achieved and with what consequences. Our purpose in citing this 'blue ocean exemplar' is to stress that creativity without a head on it, or, you may say, without a heart in it, is dangerous. It brings short-term profit to the few while destroying long-term value to many; in the end it hurts everyone. Such oceans, blue or red, are poisonous. We wish this were an issue of the past, but its relevance is increasing by the day. Compared with the bigger, deeper and deadlier oceans of Wall Street and the City of London, Enron appears now as just a water-drop. Look around: governments are watering down financial sector reforms, banks are manufacturing fat bonuses for their 'good people', the public sector is paying 'executive talent' higher salaries than prime ministers, and we are surrounded by drugs sold on the Internet, unhealthy foods sold to kids and fake Ph.D.s purportedly from Beijing University. Dealing with this reality demands a further, inherent strategy bottom line: realising *renli* common goodness.

Calling for a pragmatic turn, in previous chapters we made the case for bringing ethics back in. For too long, in the corporate world, values other than economic efficiency and stock price have been treated as nice-to-have add-ons, while in business schools social responsibility is taught as hard trade-off against corporate profit. To overcome this, we incorporate *renli* the moral-relational into our triple-strategy bottom line – it is the bottom line. It is time to take Tolstoy's question seriously: 'What shall we do and how shall we live?' We invite managers to take purpose and value as an inherent part of strategy. Informed by the spirits of Confucian ethics and community, *renli* denotes a mixture of social norms and values, expectations and obligations, emotion and affection, compassion and commitment, power relations and organisational politics – what is, and is not, proper, appropriate, right, in business.[142] Dealing with *renli*, strategy is about legitimacy, about realising common goodness.

The critical importance of the human dimension has long been recognised by managers. Today, social ties, differentiated networks, communities of practice, within and across organisations, top corporate agendas. The benefits are obvious. Without his good friend Anisuzzaman, the managing director of the Bangladesh Agricultural

Bank, Muhammad Yunus' microfinance might today cover no wider area than the village of Jobra. It is no secret that Deng Xiaoping's reform success relied less on official legitimacy than on his personal connections with the communist old guard. Not just the cosy, murky 'East'; here is a small fairy tale set in the 'West':

> For example, before Microsoft was a household name, Bill Gates had a singular distinction in his network – his mother, Mary Gates, who sat on the board of United Way with John Akers, a high-level IBM executive. At the time, Akers was helping to lead IBM into the desktop computer business. Mary Gates talked to Akers about the new breed of small companies in the computer industry, which she felt were underappreciated competitors of the larger firms with which IBM traditionally partnered. Maybe she changed Akers's vision of who to go to for the new IBM PC's DOS, or maybe her comments confirmed what he already knew. In either case, after their conversation, Akers took proposals from small companies, one of which was Microsoft. The rest is history.[143]

Turning the coin over, we see Enron the energy company and Andersen its consultant-auditor nurturing strong ties, only to sink together. Bernard Madoff harmed investors via his 'social network' with the Austria-based Bank Medici, New York-based JPMorgan Chase and Hong Kong–London-based HSBC, just to name a few. At least 11 global banks and dozens of other financial institutions profited from the fraud.[144] 'Social capital' can do as much harm as good if it is devoid of moral value and collective purpose. As the bottom line, *renli* is more than social ties, networks, *guanxi* and the like.

Promoting value and purpose, we differ from James Collins and Jerry Porras. In *Built to Last*, they suggest that as long as you have a 'core ideology', you are a 'visionary company' and you will last; there is no difference between Philip Morris outperforming rivals selling cigarettes and Merck developing a rotavirus vaccine that saves lives.[145] In contrast, seen through *renli*, there are good and bad 'core values' and 'lasting' per se is too limited a corporate purpose. We are with Confucius that a gang is not a community. While we do not consider Philip Morris a 'gang', we want to stress that not all 'core values' or 'ideologies' are worthwhile. A quarter-century ago, greed was good; today, 'Greed is legal'. Have we really grown up?

Beyond social ties and networks, there are vested interests and political manoeuvring: from the Boeing–Airbus WTO disputes to allegations that Chinese companies violate intellectual property rights, from GM destroying electric rail tracks[146] to the British backlash against Kraft's takeover of Cadbury,[147] from Hewlett-Packard boardroom dramas[148] to Foxconn factory worker suicides.[149] The world is not always as pleasant as the conversation between Mrs Gates and Mr Akers. Failure to deal wisely with *renli* can easily derail smart, well-meaning strategies.

At the heart of *renli* is moral sensibility. Former Canon chairman Ryuzaburo Kaku's ideal of *kyosei* (共生) underlines the *renli* bottom line:

> But how, many have asked, can global corporations promote
> peace and prosperity and at the same time remain true to their
> obligation to secure a profit? The answer, in my experience, is
> *kyosei*, which can best be defined as a 'spirit of cooperation,'
> in which individuals and organisations live and work together
> for the common good. A company that is practicing *kyosei*
> establishes harmonious relations with its customers, its
> suppliers, its competitors, the governments with which it deals,
> and the natural environment. When practiced by a group of
> corporations, *kyosei* can become a powerful force for social,
> political, and economic transformation.[150]

In *renli*, legitimacy is more than law-obeying. Some *renli* are codified, others are not and some will never be. A paradox in *renli* is that codified laws, even those with 'teeth', don't always lead to expected practice. After Enron, we tightened corporate laws and governance regimes, only to see Lehman's spectacular collapse and Goldman's dodgy advice to clients.[151] Legislation is necessary, but has limits. It is useful, to some extent, for fencing off bad behaviour, but lacks the inspiring power to promote common goodness. And, usually, that 'extent' is too, too limited. Gillian Tett of the *Financial Times* wrote in 2011:

> 'Innovation', as it developed in the financial system, was thus about dancing on the very edge of laws, regulations and ratings – but not actually breaking those rules. Indeed, the biggest banks typically hired armies of lawyers to ensure that the letter of the laws was respected, even as the spirit was perverted in increasingly creative, amoral ways ... Right now that is precisely what is happening, poisoning the wider political landscape.[152]

Vision, purpose and value, on the other hand, once shared, are powerfully inspiring, effectively informing, telling managers what is good to do. No law or company constitution required Mazda workers to accept delayed payments or sell cars away from home; yet *renli* told them this was the right thing to do, and the practical outcome was beneficial for all. *Renli* is about being socially and politically wise, about valued ends, appropriate means, proper conduct and desirable outcomes. It is what Robert Bellah called 'habits of the heart'.[153]

As 'habit of the heart', ethics in strategy is not at the glamorous moment you open the cheque book to make a donation. Sharing profit with others is the easy bit; and that bit can be murky. In Hong Kong, there lives a rich man. The number plate on his car reads 'HK 1'. He donates buildings, with his name engraved on each, to hospitals and universities across Hong Kong and mainland China; he even funded a Centre for Chinese Studies at Oxford University. He is knighted by the Queen of England. Where does the money come from? He runs casinos; he is Macao's gambling king. The world looks nicer when you hand out a bit of profit. But on your way to becoming rich, how many people lost out, how many families were destroyed, how many businesses bankrupted? Do the shining buildings symbolise ethics? He is not the only one; we have all played that game. After our farm products bankrupt farmers in developing countries, thanks to American and European agricultural subsidies, we feel good when a beautiful princess or pop star gives handouts to the poor in Congo or Bangladesh – they are unfortunate, unable, suffering, in need.[154]

Ethics is not about giving handouts. It is about generating value in the way businesses pursue profit and growth. It is in each of the small steps Genichi Kawakami took to envision the electronic piano and make it real, in his tireless efforts running music schools. Did he donate money to anyone? We do not know, we have not checked, it is not important. Even if Kawakami kept all his profits, he is to us still a great, ethical businessman – he made profit by bringing so much happiness to so many children and ordinary families. In a pragmatic world, it is legitimate and ethical for businesses to make profits. Profit and ethics, personal interest and the common good, are not either/or trade-offs. Grameen Bank makes a profit but it is still an ethical business. Not because Muhammad Yunus handed $27 to the 42 poor villagers, but because of his daily walks around the tiny village of Jobra under the summer sun and in monsoon rains. Yunus is an ethical businessman because of his manoeuvring in the bureaucratic banking system to procure loans for the poor, his tireless debates with politicians on development programmes and his everyday running of the demanding and time-consuming Grameen. Yunus is great because he envisioned a world with no poverty and made every effort to realise it.

God is in the details; so is business ethics. What strategy needs is ethics in our minute products, services, production processes, promotion programmes, corporate relationships and business models. 'Corporations operate with a licence from society, and we owe society a duty of care', says Indra Nooyi, the Indian-born PepsiCo chief executive. To fulfil that duty, Pepsi embeds in its managers' contracts the goal of creating healthier products, providing nutritional education and encouraging children to pursue an active lifestyle.[155] PepsiCo can do it, why not other companies?

As habits of the heart, *renli* display patterned tendencies. When the Internet became available in the 1990s, Toyota and Honda seized the technology to further improve collaboration with suppliers and dealers; they shared product information with these partners on a larger scale, at faster speed and in more detail. Around the same time, the US auto industry created an electronic network called Automotive Network Exchange (ANX) that linked together automakers and thousands of parts suppliers. The purpose was to reduce information asymmetry and switching cost, to intensify competition and improve efficiency, with estimated savings of $1 billion a year.[156] In *wuli* and *shili* terms, ANX was clever. Did it do harm or good to the Detroit giants? What value did it generate? Marketing professor Philip Kotler was concerned: 'But this represents an abrupt reversal of the industry's recent moves toward close, single-source relationships.'[157] During the 1997 Asian financial meltdown, Toyota's Thailand operation weathered four straight years of losses. Despite this, the order from the then president Hiroshi Okuda was: 'Cut all costs, don't touch any people.' For this Toyota paid a price: in 1998, Moody's downgraded the company's credit rating from AAA to AA1, citing lifetime employment as the reason.[158] In a similar crisis, Alcoa, a top-30 American company, strengthened its balance sheet, doubled cash in hand and sent its stock price soaring – by cutting 28,000 workers, 32 per cent of its workforce.[159] Different *renli*, different Wall Street ratings. Which way would you go? Which is the habit of your heart?

With these examples, two about using technology and two about 'human resources', we want to stress the point that, even with the same *wuli* fundamentals and similar *shili* efforts, *renli* makes a difference in big ways. Ethics in strategy is not abstract up-there, it is real down-here, producing material consequences. It is the duty of every manager to ask: 'Is this the right thing to do, and if so, for what purpose? How to implement it?'

The two pairs of contrasting cases above happen to involve Japanese and American companies. While we do not deny that 'habits of the heart' have much to do with national culture, we warn against fatalism: 'that is cultural, stupid; nothing we can do about it'. Culture does not determine strategies; managers' value judgements make the difference. Like Alcoa, Intel is a US-based company. Yet the two have different 'habits of the heart'. Have a look at Intel:

> During the memory-products blood bath in the early 1980s, when every other semiconductor company in the United States immediately laid off many people, Grove adopted the 90 per cent rule, with everyone, from the chairman down, accepting a 10 per cent pay cut, to avoid layoffs. Then to tide the company over the bad period without losing people he had nurtured for years, Grove sold 20 per cent of the company to IBM for $250 million in cash. When cost pressures continued to mount, he implemented the 125 per cent rule by asking everyone to work an extra ten hours a week with no pay increase, again to avoid cutbacks. Only after all these efforts proved insufficient did he finally close some operations, with the attending job losses.[160]

People look to companies for community as well as for economic well-being.[161] They want to know what the company stands for, not just what it aims for. Accordingly, 'as opposed to being the designers of strategy, managers take on the role of establishing a sense of purpose'.[162] Sounds abstract? How does purpose make a difference? Is it worthwhile? Does it improve performance? Consider Komatsu, the construction equipment company.

For years, Komatsu has been cited as the exemplar of 'strategic intent' – what a company aims to be.[163] In 1964, when Ryoichi Kawai succeeded his father as president, he articulated the aim of 'Maru-C' (encircle Caterpillar). Each year, Komatsu used Caterpillar as the competitive target, translating benchmarking into action plans for improving quality, reducing costs and expanding exports. For two decades, the clear objective of Maru-C worked well: Komatsu achieved a 50 per cent labour productivity advantage over Caterpillar and, in turn, underpriced Caterpillar's products by as much as

30 per cent.[164] Komatsu grew from a tiny local player to Caterpillar's most serious challenger. In the 1990s, as China and other emerging economies changed the business landscape, Maru-C lost its way. The company's profit was in steady decline. In Komatsu, objectives and targets had overshadowed corporate purpose.

To new president Tetsuya Katada, Komatsu's management had become so obsessed with beating competitors that it had stopped thinking about what the company was for and how to generate value for customers. By focusing on Maru-C, for example, Komatsu continued to bias its efforts to outperform Caterpillar on high-end bulldozers when the main source of growth, i.e. the China market, demanded a different category of machines. What was the company's reason for existing? To beat Caterpillar, or to create value for customers? To establish an inspiring sense of purpose, Katada proposed a 'Three Gs' company philosophy: growth, global, group-wide. 'I want everyone to stop concentrating simply on catching up with Caterpillar', Katada said. 'Compared with our old objective, the Three Gs slogan may seem abstract, but it was this abstract nature that stimulated people to ask what they can do and to respond creatively.' The Three Gs pushed managers to look beyond Caterpillar products, to investigate the needs of customers and to envision new ways to satisfy them. Within three years, Komatsu gained new customers in emerging markets by supplying smaller, more efficient, low-price machines. Today, to generate fresh value for customers, Komatsu equips each machine with a GPS for free. The GPS enables the company to locate all Komatsu machines worldwide, which supplies real-time operation information to customers, including fuel efficiency and service schedules.[165]

Komatsu was not alone. In 1970, Honda engineers were working frenetically on the CVCC engine. When America's 1970 Muskie Act tightened fuel-emission control, US auto-makers strongly opposed it. President Soichiro Honda realised that the engine, which would comply with the new standards, would be a powerful weapon against the Big Three. However, Honda engineers told Soichiro that they built the engine not for beating the Big Three, but for the future of their children. It was this encounter, Soichiro recounted years later, that made him realise he was perhaps too old and it was time to retire.[166] This does not apply only to Japanese companies. When executive Penny Heaton and the Merck scientists worked day and night to develop the rotavirus vaccine in 2006, what propelled them was emotion, passion and a sense of moral purpose: 'we have the technology in hand to eliminate deaths from this disease'.[167] Targets or money rewards, even if such existed, were no match for the power of a sense of purpose, passion and morality.[168]

That Komatsu, Honda and Merck perform well is not accidental, and it cannot be attributed just to sound *wuli* fundamentals or smart *shili* innovations. Consider Harvard professor Kenneth Andrews' basic question 'What business the company is in or is to be in and the kind of company it is or is to be?' To tackle this question, Andrews taught us, managers should relate strategy to the needs of society, conducting business to accomplish a purpose.[169] The question is: what value, what purpose?

In the heyday of financial innovation, 'value-based strategy' was popular, with private equity (PE) as the exemplar. In 2007, $700 billion was invested in PE deals. What business were PE firms in? They raised pools of capital from investors, leveraged debt with this capital and then used the fund to buy businesses, whole companies or 'carve-outs' from big corporations. The purpose? To sell these portfolio businesses quickly, in whole or in part, to another buyer, usually within three to five years, for a fast return, regardless of the consequences for the underlying business. 'Because it's all about creating value', 'at every step, the PE firm will typically be thinking: ... should we sell it now, and if so, to whom?'[170] It is legal; as long as you pay tax the authorities are happy. But is it good, for whom, in what terms? After losing the court battle with Citigroup in December 2010 over his PE firm's 2007 loss-making acquisition of EMI, Guy Hands, once the darling of PE, spoke of the need for the PE industry to return to its 'roots of changing and building businesses'.[171] We welcome this. The questions are: what had the industry been doing before his moment of reflection? How will it return to its roots and change its 'habit of the heart'? It is our responsibility to seek good answers, in our business conduct, not in company statements.

Jack Welch, the former boss of GE, declared amid the recent financial turmoil that 'shareholder value is the dumbest idea in the world'.[172] Surprised? A few months before that, we witnessed another reflection:

> When Michael Hammer died in the fall of 2008, the *New York Times* ended his obituary with a surprising quotation, coming from one of the fathers of reengineering: 'I'm saddened and offended by the idea that companies exist to enrich their owners. That is the very least of their roles; they are far more worthy, more honourable, and more important than that.'[173]

Hammer's reflection is touching. What is the worthy, honourable and important role of business? We do not need to look far. Grameen microfinance and Yamaha pianos, Honda engineers and Merck scientists, Nicolas Hayek and Akio Morita are exemplars. They show us that business and strategy can be a positive force for the betterment of humanity and Nature. Ethics is not remote principles, it is the strategy bottom line. It is in everything we do, in getting fundamentals right, envisioning a valued future and realising common goodness.

Lenovo: 'you must know who you are!'[174]

When Liu Chuanzhi put up the signboard 'New Technology Development Company – Institute of Computing Technology – Chinese Academy of Science' on the door of a gatekeeper's shack on the outskirts of Beijing in 1984, no one expected that the venture would, in a generation's time, become the world's third-largest and fastest-growing PC-maker, with 8 per cent of the global market share and 30 per cent in China. The company is known as Legend (联想, *Lianxiang*) in China and Lenovo in the rest of world. It was listed on the Hong Kong Stock Exchange in 1994 and took over IBM's PC division in 2005. Liu was named one of the '25 Most Powerful Business People' by *Time* magazine, 'Star of Asia' by *BusinessWeek* and 'Asian Businessman of the Year' by *Forbes*. 'What I'm especially grateful for is that I still got the opportunity late in life to be an entrepreneur. I was 40 years old. People who were a little older than me didn't have the chance,' Liu told the *Financial Times* in the summer of 2010. 'We grew up in China's era of reform and opening. We knew nothing and just had to learn by ourselves.'[175]

Much has been written in the global media and business schools about Lenovo the brand, Legend the company and Liu the entrepreneur, the product, the industry, the market, the hard work, the sacrifice and the strategy. Less known is how Liu and his comrades coped with *renli* in a society undergoing profound transformation, a market economy with Chinese characteristics. 'Petty companies manage *shi* (事 operational matters), great companies manage *ren* (人 human affairs),' Liu famously said.[176] And he explained to *McKinsey Quarterly*:

> We look at management at two levels. On one level, there
> are the nuts and bolts – marketing and promotions, channel
> management, product marketing, ordering, and logistics
> management – and we built these into the company. Then
> there is a deeper level that deals with what we call culture but
> might also be described as motivation and ethics, and this is
> more problematic than developing the nuts-and-bolts areas of
> management.[177]

Liu and Legend certainly excelled at the 'deeper level'. Let us look at how he coped with company ownership, dealt with rights and wrongs in human relations and danced on the edge between legal and illegal, moral and evil.

In 1984 Deng Xiaoping extended China's reform from the countryside to the cities. For years, neither an outstanding scientist nor a dedicated administrator (he had tried both), Liu was frustrated that the Chinese Academy of Sciences (CAS) seldom made a real contribution to the economy. Gifted scientists spent public money, received award certificates, got regular promotions, put their innovations on the shelf and then started the next cycle. The Institute of Computing Technology had developed over 20 computers, but sold none. Liu hated this. Rumour was in the air that the state was to classify computing as an applied science, that government funding would be reduced by 25 per cent in 1985 and then to zero within five years. 'It's time'; Liu decided to jump into the sea. Together with him were ten CAS colleagues.

From day one, Liu had a bottom line: 'We will not become the reform's sacrificial cow.' Liu was 40 years old and had experienced a lot. He wanted to do something, yet also wanted to protect himself. He determined to have it both ways: opportunities supplied by the reform and protection from the old system. He was to open a new window in the old building, using the material within. However entrepreneurial he was, Liu always tried to keep a place in the old camp. He was a reformer, not a rebel. CAS would be the sole owner of the new company and, in return, Liu gained full decision rights on finance, business and human resources, together with a ¥200,000 loan (approximately $25,000) and the gatekeeper's shack as the company office. With full decision rights in hand, Liu was the boss; with CAS as the owner, the company was the government's baby, enjoying all the political and commercial advantages of a state-owned entity. There were off-contract benefits, too: Liu's staff remained on CAS's payroll and eligible for promotion, moving between the Institute and the company at will. The company used CAS facilities, resources and research outcomes for free. Liu called this 'with your feet in two boats'. Liu was an exemplary idealist, and at the same time a superior realist.

To bypass production licensing and import middlemen, in 1988 Liu registered Legend in Hong Kong, while the Beijing-based parent company became Legend Group Holdings, still wholly owned by CAS. Hong Kong Legend, later renamed Lenovo, had three equal parties: (1) the Beijing parent company, (2) a group of Hong Kong partners and (3) another Hong Kong-registered Chinese state company. Guess who was the head of that third party? Liu's father, a loyal communist. As the father and son always worked closely together, the ownership structure of Hong Kong Legend ensured Liu's absolute control. Liu made no secret that his father had helped Legend secure substantial, desperately needed loans. Years later, the Hong Kong partners became billionaires and left the company; however, it was their initial investment that enabled Legend to gain a foothold outside mainland China, their knowledge and links with the international market also paved the way for Legend's globalisation. Again, Liu had it both ways.

'Great companies manage *ren*.' But how? 'One of our company's missions is to integrate the needs of our employees with those of the company', Liu explained to *McKinsey Quarterly*. 'To make them true masters, from a materialistic standpoint, options play an important role.' To maintain state ownership for strategic advantage on one hand, and to motivate employees with share options on the other, Liu needed tremendous patience and skill. On the eve of Legend's 1994 Hong Kong public listing, Liu convinced CAS, owner of the parent company, to accept his dividend allocation proposal: 65 per cent to CAS and 35 per cent to Legend employees. Liu further divided the 35 per cent dividend into three parts: 35 per cent for the 1984 founders, 25 per cent for those who joined the company before 1986 and 40 per cent for those who came after. At that time, dividends were merely numbers on paper and few people cared. In 2000, however, when China's reform deepend, Liu finally converted the 35 per cent dividend into shares. Overnight, Liu made himself and his comrades into billionaires. He had realised his dream: reformers need not be sacrificial cows; good employees deserve material rewards.

Yet even this was not the end of the ownership story. In September 2009, Liu arranged for the privately held China Oceanwide Holding Group to pay ¥2.7 billion for a 29 per cent stake in Lenovo's parent Legend Holding. In an interview with China's *Caijing* (财经,

Finance & Economy) magazine, titled 'Liu Chuanzhi on Legend's new ownership', Liu revealed his calculation:

> *Caijing*: Why did you choose a private, Chinese enterprise? Why not foreign or something else?
>
> *Liu*: Foreign investors (in China) are not allowed to invest in many areas, which would certainly have made doing business inconvenient.
>
> *Caijing*: It seems clear you didn't want a state-owned enterprise.
>
> *Liu*: I personally did not.
>
> *Caijing*: How does Legend plan to develop going forward? How can incentives be arranged for managers at subsidiaries so that everyone is satisfied?
>
> *Liu*: This issue is related to property rights. I'm always considering the long-term incentives issue, and I've sought approval from the Academy of Sciences and other shareholders.
>
> *Caijing*: The Academy of Sciences' 29 per cent sale portion – how was the structure designed? Will there be further adjustments?
>
> *Liu*: The academy sold 29 per cent, leaving them 36 per cent. This is still higher than the Legend shareholders committee's portion of 35 per cent, making it a relatively large shareholder. I haven't asked for a further reduction in their holdings. This structure is quite good for Legend as we still have a lot of business to do with the government and need this sort of partnership.[178]

Obviously, even today, Liu still has his feet in two boats. However, there is one thing about which Liu had never been ambiguous: 'Putting corporate interests first.' Nothing illustrates this more clearly than the events surrounding the Legend Chinese Card (联想汉卡). In those 1984 early days, Liu and his comrades bought and sold electronic watches, sports clothes, skiing kits and colour TV sets, whatever they could to get their hands on a profit. They then distributed PC hardware and software for the big names: IBM, HP, Toshiba, Cisco and Microsoft. After all, they were computer scientists. Yet even within China, Legend was a latecomer. Like many other small potatoes, it could well have come and gone. The breakthrough came from a revolutionary memory card that translated between English software and Chinese characters. Since its birth, for years, even today, the magic card has been, and is still, attributed to Liu's comrade Ni Nanguang. The company got its name, its market, its foundation and its future from the card. At that critical juncture, the company was the card and the card was the company. 'The company should publicise only one person: Ni Nanguang', Liu ordered. Legend mobilised every means to promote Ni: 'father of the Chinese Card', chief engineer, deputy director, fellow of the Chinese Academy of Science, member of the National People's Congress. The more famous Ni Nanguang was, the better known the Legend Card and the faster-growing the company. Both inside and outside China, the media got busy.

This caught the notice of a quiet person far away at Stanford University. He was Zhu Naigang, a Chinese scientist who had previously worked in CAS, visiting Stanford in 1979 and settling there in 1985. Zhu did not care about financial rewards or public fame, but as a scientist he could not accept distorted history. In 1988 he wrote to a senior *People's Daily* reporter, indicating that he himself was the initiator and organiser of the innovation, and Ni was, as a matter of fact, only one of the inventors. The reporter passed Zhu's letter to Liu: 'what is going on?' After creating the hype himself, with so much hope, energy, interest and emotion attached to the card, for the first time Liu really wanted to know the details. He talked to many people who knew the project, including Legend's founding comrades. There was sufficient evidence that Zhu got it right. He was the group leader, officially as well as intellectually, since 1974, initiating the 'Chinese character recognition system' (汉字识别系统). On the 1979 CAS award certificate for the invention, Zhu's name was listed first, Ni's and others' names followed. When Zhu left for Stanford in 1979, he left behind the unfinished 'Chinese memory card'. Ni finished the card and made it to the market. Now Liu understood Zhu's feeling and recognised that the media hype around Ni was shaky. What should Liu do?

Liu kept Zhu's letter in his pocket, allowing the media hype to continue. At that critical moment, his main concern was not historical details but the bigger picture. Legend needed Ni the symbol as well as his technical competence. Ni was then working day and night with his team to finish the 'Legend 286' PC prototype, which would enable the company to get a foothold in the global computer industry. On the scale of company interest, the detail of property rights-and-wrongs were no longer important. That Zhu had chosen to stay in the US while Ni returned to China to complete the card also made Liu emotionally close to the latter. On Legend's part, they have never applied for a patent for the card. Today, the Chinese Card has fulfilled its function in China's computer history, and the rights-and-wrongs around it dissolved. The dissolution was not based on principle but on common sense, not on personal gain-or-loss but on corporate interest. Liu's pragmatism was as subtle as his ideal, foresight and determination.

Liu could be criticised for such muddling if he had treated himself differently. For corporate interest, Liu bent himself, swallowed his pride and his tears, let alone working so hard that he was hospitalised several times. The company's first distribution deal was to sell 12 IBM PCs to the governmental National Commission of Sport. The company had machines to sell, the commission had money to buy, but neither had a quota. They needed the approval of a third party, and this is what happened in the third party's office:

> *Liu:* We want to sell 12 PCs to the Commission of Sport ...
> A twenty-something officer stopped him: Are you foreign
>   company or Chinese? Or you are an agent?
> Liu put on a smile: Yes we are a distributor ...
> The officer shouted: Distributors are just foreigners. Get out! My
>   building will not have foreign businessmen. Do what I say and
>   get out!
> Liu bit his lip, bowed to the young man, stepped back, and out of
>   the door.[179]

Many years later, Liu recalled: 'It was really too much for me. I was already over 40 ... and it happened in front of so many people ... We in CAS had never experienced this.'[180] Yes, intellectuals were poor in those days, but at least they wanted to keep their integrity. In that office, Liu's integrity was broken into pieces. 'Corporate interest above all', that was the last straw sustaining him. After tremendous effort, Liu befriended the young man, via his classmates (scientists were not good at this). Liu took him out sightseeing and entertained him in restaurants. When the young man mentioned that he wanted to visit Hong Kong, Liu immediately helped him change RMB into foreign currency. When they said goodbye after a banquet, of course paid for by Liu, the young officer finally said: 'perhaps your deal can be considered.'

In 1987, thanks to the Chinese Card, the company managed to achieve a ¥70.3 million turnover, ¥5.5 million cash flow, ¥4 million fixed capital and ¥700,000 after-tax profit. When you are successful, problems follow. One day, Price Bureau officials visited Legend, checked the books, concluded that the company had violated price regulations and should be fined ¥1 million. The whole company was boiling; staff suggested holding a press conference asking for rights-and-wrongs.

'What are you doing?!' The authoritative, short-tempered Liu shouted at his comrades. 'For the good of the company, you all shut up!' 'You must know who you are', Liu repeated many times, to his staff, and perhaps to himself.[181] He knew the officials well – saving face was to them more important than detailed rights-and-wrongs. To get a chance, you had to bend yourself. Liu mobilised all his connections. He went to the office of the tax chief, who claimed to be busy. Liu visited the chief's home on a Sunday, but the target was having dinner with his family. At last, the tax chief gave Liu face and went to his banquet. He then agreed to reduce the fine to ¥400,000.

In April 1989, Liu faced his biggest crisis ever: Legend was caught doing business with smugglers. In the early days of reform, the government still used tariffs to deter imports of computers, as well as many other things. As an unintended consequence, smuggling became a collective activity all through society: in factories, department stores, schools, administrative bodies, in some places the police. Even the military was found smuggling goods on warships. It is a real question where the initial capital for development would have come from for many localities if they had not been involved in smuggling. Legend imported PCs, and the Chinese Card and Legend-brand computers were all built with foreign chips. At that time, the customs duty for PCs was 200 per cent, and 30 per cent for components. No company could have survived without illegal goods, and every business, including 'government babies', played the game. It was a dangerous game and Legend was not in heaven. Although Liu had never dealt directly with smugglers, he turned a blind eye when his import managers did. In that heart-breaking spring of 1989, Legend was caught. The company purchased ¥10 million in components from a gang of smugglers in Guangdong. The evidence was black and white, the police would knock at Liu's door at any moment.

Over the years, Liu's record was full of bad conduct: giving gifts to government clients to get business deals, issuing cash bonuses to employees to avoid bonus tax, changing RMB for foreign currency on the black market to purchase processors and memory. These were not the things Liu wanted to do; he called this 'eating corpses'. Liu hated himself at that time.[182] He wanted to build China's computer, he wanted to compete with IBM. Perhaps in that environment you had to do wrong in order to do good, Liu comforted himself. Corporate interest was above all. In a company speech, Liu talked about 'keeping one-inch distance from the edge'.[183] This time, he was too close to the edge. He had parents, a wife and two children. He felt angry and wronged. 'If we do nothing, the nation has no hope; we do something, then who take care of us?' He wanted to say something. He was afraid that if he didn't say it now he might never have the chance to say it at all. He got out of bed and wrote an 11-page letter to the leaders of the CAS; first the draft, then a clean copy. He wrote:

> For years, we did not want to become capitalists … We had a
> clear vision, we forced ourselves to fulfil our goals every minute
> … What was our motivation, what was our objective? To tell
> the truth, our motivation and objective are changing. At the
> beginning we struggled for survival; when that was achieved we
> wanted to become a bridge that would transform research outcome
> into marketable products. Is this right, is it worth trying, is it
> possible to succeed? … 'Exemplary persons would die for those
> who understand them,' this ancient saying expresses how we
> intellectuals value emotion. Based on which I write this letter.[184]

We do not see Liu explaining the life-and-death smuggling accident
or debating on the rights-and-wrongs of it, perhaps that was redundant since it was already a black-and-white well-known fact. Yet, the
head and deputy head of CAS wrote back to Liu promptly, both were
more emotional than Liu. One wrote:

> Chuanzhi: I shed tears when I read your letter. What is more
> valuable than the loyalty to our nation, people and party? As
> morality collapses around us, I wish there will still be a lively
> oasis in our hearts … In today's society, are we too idealistic,
> have too naïve a vision, too far from reality? … Don't give up,
> don't be dejected, don't look back. The Chinese nation no longer
> has a way back now.[185]

And the other:

> Please pass this to Chuanzhi: I trust them entirely and support
> them with my whole heart. I trust them to devote their whole
> life for the interest of the Chinese nation at this critical moment
> in China's history. I hope that you will be able to conquer the
> global market, and make a great contribution for the prestige and
> power of the Chinese people.[186]

Obviously, neither of the leaders considered Liu had done anything
seriously wrong; at least they did not treat him like someone going

to prison. Perhaps the matter was not so serious after all, or perhaps the law decided to be lenient to him given the reality of the time. If Liu had got anything from this saga, we gather, it must be that the way ahead would be very, very long for Liu and his comrades to learn to cope with *renli* properly. Around the world, managers do business in different institutional contexts. Perhaps all of us need to learn our way to do it ethically, effectively, wisely.

WSR: A WALKING-STICK

With WSR we intend to heighten managers' sensitivity towards the efficiency, creativity and legitimacy aspects of business. Strategic challenges in the twenty-first century are seldom just technical, intellectual or social.[187] Companies produce not merely things but also ideas and relationships.[188] We do not want more *Big Brother* race rows, BP deep-water oil spills, Chinese tainted milk, innovations of the Lehman sort, Toyota recalls or A380 delays. Rather, the world will be a better place when strategies bring us more Grameen microfinance, Yamaha pianos, Merck vaccines and Chinese economic reforms. For this, it is useful to take *wuli–shili–renli* as a bottom line based on which managers initiate, justify and conduct strategies.

At this historical moment, amid the aftershocks of the banking crisis, breaking away from the conventional wisdom of competition and shareholder value, WSR is intended to remind us of the foresight of our great thinkers: in his *Theory of Moral Sentiments*, Adam Smith taught us that economics is a dimension of ethics, and John Maynard Keynes suggested 'it needs no proof that neither economic activities nor any other class of human activities can rightly be made independent of moral laws.'[189] In a pragmatic world, strategy is far more than seeking technical solutions to technical problems. Reflective managers take this to heart. In telling the Hugh Russel story, the executive David Hurst refers again and again to 'value-based rationality', 'value-based ends' and 'value-based behaviour'.[190]

Meanwhile, we warn against throwing five-forces or value-chain models out of the window. Not because they present the truth, but because they can be useful. Put it another way: they are not wrong, they just have limits. Calling for a pragmatic turn, with WSR we are challenging the fallacy of one explanation for everything, be it SWOT analyses, blue oceans, the learning school or social responsibility. The world would benefit from robust strategies based on multiple perspectives. 'The single dominant paradigm is a comfort blanket, and we are better off without it.'[191]

Knowledge useful to strategy takes many forms: science and engineering for investigating *wuli*, epistemic-cognitive inquiries for understanding *shili* and socio-political studies for coordinating *renli*. At the societal level, important decisions – such as whether and how to construct the Three Gorges Dam on China's Yangzi River, build nuclear power plants across Europe, reform Japan's postal system, sort out Britain's pension black hole, reduce America's national debt, rebuild Wall Street, tackle WTO disputes, eliminate world poverty – all demand disciplined data-gathering, rigorous model-building, creative solution-seeking, informed public discourse and legitimate political action, for which diverse sources and forms of knowledge are indispensable.

At the firm level, take the job of a marketing executive as an example. She needs to consider how to deliver products/services in the most efficient way, for which she employs management science. The firm also needs to understand customer preferences and to satisfy them with tailored offerings, for which the executive turns to humanities and cultural studies. Companies need further to know how human relations and social trends shape people's views on the firm's activities that will ultimately determine its survival and growth, for which the executive studies ethics and politics.

Hence, John Law posits that science, politics and aesthetics interweave with each other.[192] In the same spirit, Nonaka suggests that knowledge has to do with truth, goodness and beauty.[193] Metaphorically, we take *wuli*, *shili* and *renli* as Newton's eye

Table 5.1 *Robust strategy based on the WSR bottom line*

Wu 物 Material-technical	Shi 事 Mental-cognitive	Ren 人 Social-relational
Objective particulars, resources, constraints	Subjective mentalities, schemas, mindscapes	Intersubjective orientations, expectations, obligations
Wuli 物理 Analytical rationality Newton's eye	Shili 事理 Instrumental rationality Picasso's eye	Renli 人理 Ethical rationality Confucius' eye
Associating with the world, patterns of connecting, accommodating, transforming	Associating with the mind, ways of seeing, imaging, projecting, communicating	Associating with others, rules of involving, engaging, sharing, bonding, organising

What is ...?	How to ...?	Shall we ...?
Getting fundamentals right	Envisioning a valued future	Realising common goodness

(pursuing efficiency with technical rationality), Picasso's eye (appreciating the beauty of life and enhancing it creatively) and Confucius' eye (considering how people can walk together towards Great Harmony (大同)). Thinking and acting strategically, we should invite Newton (logic), Picasso (aesthetics) and Confucius (ethics) into our projects. We need to invite them as equals. They enrich our life and make our strategy robust, in different yet complementary ways. It is unwise to fit them into hierarchies: which is more basic, Newton, Picasso or Confucius' eye? Strategy works better with multiple perspectives, not paradigm wars or knowledge hierarchies. Table 5.1 summarises the WSR bottom line.

How to prove WSR a truer model, fitting with reality better than, say, the five forces? To pragmatists, this is not an interesting question. WSR is not meant to capture the 'nature' of the world, but to be a heuristic tool to enrich managers' understanding of what they and others are doing, what they need to do and how to do better. WSR translates the pragmatic spirits into a suggestive language for managers to think, talk and act disciplinarily, imaginarily, ethically. With WSR we are not closer to the 'essence' of things. In WSR, as in Hurst the executive's story, robust action, not representational truth, is the 'point'. As long as managers are prompted to think of, talk about and act inclusively upon rationality, creativity and morality, WSR fulfils its purpose. WSR is a walking stick for beating an unknown path; it is for way-makers, not truth-seekers.

In this imperfect world, we do not have a perfect theory, nor do we need one. China's economic reform was set in motion by Deng Xiaoping's seemingly foolish motto 'crossing the river by feeling for stones'. The more humble, open-minded and eager-to-learn we are, the greater the chances our strategy will succeed. To some, this is inconvenient, unsettling. To experienced managers, it is good enough. It is wise to cross the strategy river by touching stones; WSR can be taken as one of the stones. During a workshop, an executive came to us: you see, professor, in China we need to improve the rule of law, why not include *fali* (*fa* 法: law, legislation, regulation, rule, code)? We were moved by the comment and encouraged the executives: please do if this is useful in your situation. It is this kind of creativity that makes strategies practically wise. WSR is not a principle to be accepted and followed, but a metaphor for stimulating questioning, improvising and learning.

We began with Hurst the executive's experience, and referred to real business cases throughout, so as to construct the WSR bottom line. The WSR terminology we derive from Confucian classics, the spirit of which appears enduring to us. We understand that the words *wuli–shili–renli* would be unfamiliar to managers outside the Confucian traditions, perhaps even just pronouncing them could be a burdensome exercise. However, the pragmatic spirit of WSR appears relevant around the globe.

We note a story told by the American pragmatist Hilary Putnam. West Churchman was a disciple of Edgar Arthur Singer, who was in turn an assistant of William James. In his class, the first 'thing' Churchman wrote down on the blackboard was:

Table 5.2 *WSR: common concerns, local narratives*

	Material-technical	Cognitive-mental	Social-relational
Confucius *Eight exemplary doings*	*wuli* Technical efficiency	*shili* Situated creativity	*renli* Social legitimacy
Aristotle *Intellectual virtues*	*Episteme* Analytical	*Techne* Instrumental	*Phronesis* Ethical
Immanuel Kant *Practical action*	Technical Cause–effective	Pragmatic* Means–end	Ethical Judgement–justification
Jean-Paul Sartre *Phenomenological modes of being*	Being in itself	Being for itself	Being for others
Telcott Parsons *Functioning of formal organisations*	Technical subsystem	Managerial subsystem	Institutional subsystem
Jürgen Habermas *Three worlds, cognitive interests, knowledge claims*	Objective world Technical interest Factual representation	Internal realm Emancipatory interest Sincerity	Social world Practical interest Moral rightness
Michel Foucault *Technologies for understanding and action*	Technology for production Between one's thought and reality	Technology for self-transformation With one's own hidden thought	Technology for signs and power Between one's thoughts and conduct

	The material world Physiological agency	The personal world Psychological agency	The social world Sociological agency
Roy Bhaskar *Structure/agency*			
Antonio Gramsci *Strategic coordination/ contestation*	Economics	Ideology	Politics
John Dewey *Elements of generic freedom*	Efficiency in action Carrying out plans and chosen ends	Capacity to vary plans Changing action course and experiencing novelty	Power to frame purpose Judging desires and evaluating choices
George Herbert Mead *Communication of the self*	With physical objects	With oneself	With other selves
Hans Joas *Human action*	Rational	Creative	Normative
Chester Barnard *Factors of corporative systems*	Physical	Psychological	Social
Richard Scott *Pillars of institution*	Regulative	Cognitive	Normative
Jeffrey Pfeffer *Managerial actions*	Rational	Emergent	Constrained

* Kant used the word 'pragmatic' in a narrower sense in comparison with our usage of the word in this book.

1. Knowledge of facts presupposes knowledge of theories.
2. Knowledge of theories presupposes knowledge of facts.
3. Knowledge of facts presupposes knowledge of values.
4. Knowledge of values presupposes knowledge of facts.[194]

At the risk of oversimplifying, isn't it interesting to read Churchman's 'facts' as *wuli*, 'theories' as *shili* and 'value' as *renli*? From our limited contact with 'Western' thought and practice, we have found it widely appreciated across many cultures that practically wise strategy needs to embrace the material-technical, the cognitive-mental and the social-relational. While investigating this in detail is the topic of another book, indeed many books, Table 5.2 tentatively summarises our findings and indicates useful pointers.

Clearly, there are enormous differences between these great thinker-managers. For one thing, the time has long passed since 'what is good for America is good for the world' or 'Japan does it all better', and we do not need another fantasy of 'Chinese strategy masters' or 'Indian management gurus'. For another, some of the schemas in Table 5.2 pertain to 'structure', others to 'agency' or 'action' – to social scientists, these differences are dearly important. For the purpose of reinventing strategy, however, the similarities appear to us overwhelmingly interesting, stimulating, inspiring. Not just the thought schemas, but, more importantly, the business practices across cultures. And this is important: getting fundamentals right, envisioning a valued future and realising common goodness are, after all, meaningful and actionable for managers with different cultural roots. To be pragmatic you do not need to have been born in the birthplace of Confucius.

If dealing with *wuli–shili–renli* makes sense, how to do it? With this question, we invite readers to the next chapter.

6   Timely balanced way-making

If dealing with *wuli–shili–renli* is what pragmatic managers do, how to do it? Readers familiar with the literature would say this question is about strategy process. We agree, but with an immediate qualification: pragmatically speaking, process cannot be properly understood if separated from contexts or contents – who you are, where you come from, what you want to achieve.

In previous chapters, we posited that pragmatic strategies usually emerge from purposefully guided, multi-path evolutionary processes and tend to be contingent, consequential, continuous, courageous, collective and co-creative. While such a view is useful in describing what practically wise strategies look like, the normative question for managers on-the-spot, confronted with an urgent mess, remains: *how to do it, here-and-now*?

Rather than supplying a proven methodology, x-step procedure or y-dimension grid, we shall present a pragmatic mode of strategising: timely balance. We shall begin by making a distinction between timely balance and the 'golden mean'. Popular interpretations of the 'golden mean' will be shown to be theoretically problematic and unhelpful in practice. In contrast, timely balance, which embodies the Confucian ideal of pragmatism-upon-time, emphasises getting business right in unfolding circumstances. Instead of seeing strategies as determined by antagonistic opposites, pragmatism takes human experience as consisting of interdependent, reciprocal, generative companions.

We shall then examine two pairs of generic companions: change–continuity, expansion–focus. These companions are 'generic' in that they underpin a wide range of strategic issues across industries, organisational levels and company life cycles. To illustrate timely balance, we shall use real-world business cases, including General Electric (GE), Lego, Lenovo, Li & Fung, Alibaba, Intel, Mayekawa, Toyota's recall and many more. Let us begin with what timely balance means.

JUST RIGHT, NOT GOLDEN MEAN

Presenting process thinking, in Chapter 2 we cited Confucius and Yoshida Kenkō's poetic appreciations:

> The Master was standing on the riverbank, and observed, 'Isn't life's passing just like this, never ceasing day or night!'[1]
>
> If man were never to fade away like the dews of Adashino, never to vanish like the smoke over Toribeyama, but lingered on forever in this world, how things would lose their power to move us![2]

The world is not just changing, it changes in unrepeated, unpredictable ways:

> The *Tao* of heaven operates mysteriously and secretly; it has no fixed shape, and it follows no definite rules.[3]

Walking in such an uncertain world, sensibility, vigilance and flexibility are indispensable virtues:

> Exemplary persons, in making their way in the world, are neither bent on nor against anything; what is right they will follow.[4]

Hence, the Confucian ideal of way-making is *shizhong* (时中, timely balance). 'Timely' in the context of strategy means more than the temporal dimension. It is an 'umbrella concept' that covers a variety of dimensions: time, space, circumstances. It is a metaphor we use to heighten sensitivity towards unfolding *wuli–shili–renli* particulars. As a persistent theme at the heart of Confucian wisdom, timely balance emphasises emergence, specificity, actuality and adaptability. What is right, appropriate, fitting with circumstances, we shall follow.

Unfortunately, timely balance is usually translated into English as 'golden mean', as an eclectic attitude that suggests 'sticking to the middle' or 'keeping both extremes'.[5] This 'most unfortunate rendering', as Roger Ames and David Hall explain,[6] is a mis-reconstruction of Confucianism via a hidden, particular cultural lens, a lens that can be traced to some ancient 'mean-extreme' teachings, for example:

Socrates: [Man] must know to choose the mean and avoid the extremes on either side, as far as possible.

Plato: If we disregard due proportion by giving anything what is too much for it, too much canvas to a boat, too much nutriment to a body, too much authority to a soul, the consequence is always shipwreck.

Phocylides: In many things the middle has the best. Be mine middle station.[7]

Ironically, attempting to liberate strategy from the mechanistic 'one best way', an increasing number of writers, particularly in 'the West', resort to 'the golden mean', and they call it dialectical thinking. To make a long story short, it began with two McKinsey consultants: Thomas Peters and Robert Waterman. At the end of their 1982 best-seller *In Search of Excellence*, Peters and Waterman suggest: 'Organisations that live by the loose–tight principle are on the one hand rigidly controlled, yet at the same time allow (indeed, insist on) autonomy, entrepreneurship, and innovation.' They apply this 'principle' to many other 'contradictions', quality and cost, efficiency and effectiveness, and so on, and regard it as a 'synthesis' of 'the basics of excellent management practice'. The 'principle', Peters and Waterman promise, allows managers to 'have their cake and eat it too'.[8]

While no manager would reject such a good thing, the question is how to get it. Some writers advise managers to find 'a happy medium', stick to 'the middle way' and avoid 'deficit and excess'.[9] Other writers flatly disagree. James Collins and Jerry Porras, for example, argue in their 1994 best-seller *Built to Last* that, instead of seeking 'the midpoint', visionary companies should pursue the 'Genius of AND': 'the ability to embrace both extremes', 'at the same time, all the time'. And their book attributes the 'both extremes' approach to 'Chinese dualistic philosophy'.[10] Ouch.

To Confucian pragmatism, the 'middle way' and 'both extremes' panaceas are just the same old 'one best way' packaged in new rhetoric. Their logic: regardless of circumstances, no matter where you come from and what problems you face, the solution is already there, simple and easy: stick to the middle, keep both extremes. 'One best way', old or new, is seductive because it suits quick-fit mindsets. Doing this, however, turns process thinking into a 'magico-mythical' enterprise.[11] If the solution is always at the midpoint between extremes, robots could do a better job than managers.

Here lie some fundamental assumptions of a civilisation. According to Aristotle, 'things' in the world have permanent essences which are by definition unchanged, while to Hegel, changes are caused by conflicts between antagonistic opposites. Putting Aristotle and Hegel together, quality and low cost, efficiency and effectiveness, even personhood and community, labour and management, cannot be otherwise but always in 'conflicts'.[12] Given this, the only imaginable alternative to excess and deficit is either 'stick to the middle' or 'keep both extremes'. Other options are logically unviable since change is seen primarily as the rearrangement of that which is unchanging.[13] Hence the whole strategy discourse is confined to the seductive yet mythical 'golden mean': 'just enough of this, just enough of that ...'[14]

As pragmatists, our trouble with the 'middle way' and 'both extremes' is not merely that they are problematic in theory, but more importantly that they don't work in practice. Experienced managers do not dissolve 'paradoxes' in that way. Andrew Grove of Intel Corporation successfully balanced unplanned experimentation and focused projects; did he stick to the 'middle way' or maintain 'both extremes'? Far from it. Grove reflected on his experience:

'a pendulum-like swing between the two types of actions is the best way to work your way through a strategic transformation.'[15] That is the message from the front line: go for either end, or anywhere in between, if this fits the circumstances. Grove is not alone. We see Michael Dell, the king of the direct model, selling PCs in Wal-Mart and buying in IT service companies, and Hank Paulson, the market-can-do-nothing-wrong guy, engineering the biggest state bail-outs. Label them 'sticking to the middle' or 'keeping both extremes' if you like. In view of pragmatism, they are striving to get business right.

GE and Lego: getting it just right

In the autumn of 2010, GE's appliance unit planned to invest $432 million in four US centres that would design and make refrigerators, and pledged to spend more than $1 billion to support 1,300 jobs in the US by 2014. It was a notable reversal of a long-time policy of global outsourcing. Was GE finding the middle way between the 'extremes' of globalisation and localisation? Not quite.

'Twenty years ago we were in the process of moving every appliance manufacturing job to China or Mexico', Jeff Immelt, GE's chief executive, said. '[But] ... when I open up the safe under my desk I can't find the pennies that we've saved ... So the next generation of products are going to be made in the US.' Behind the moves were hard-headed calculations. GE argued that a combination of US production quality, the ability to market goods as US-made and rising transport, currency and labour costs in formerly cheap manufacturing countries had made the relocations practical.[16] The wider background was that China, the largest and fast-growing emerging economy, had shifted its macroeconomic priorities: 'policymakers appear to feel that the country no longer needs so much new foreign capital investment, and would prefer its pillars of industry to be controlled by domestic enterprises instead of multinationals headquartered elsewhere.'[17]

Times changed, GE adapted. And GE was not the only one: companies ranging from Caterpillar, the earth-moving equipment producer, to Wham-O, the manufacturer of Frisbees and Hula-Hoops, made similar adjustments.[18] In the business world, getting-it-just-right pragmatism prevails.

Lego's turnaround is equally telling.[19] For years, 'just-in-time delivery', 'increasing customer choices' and the like had been unquestioned business truths. Companies including Lego struggled to out-play each other in pushing these truths to the limit. In the course of increasing delivery speed and enlarging product range, Lego had created a huge operational complexity: a total of 12,500 stock-keeping units, over 11,000 suppliers and more than 100 different colours for its toy products. All of this cost a great deal of money, and customers were unimpressed. In 1998, the company began to lose money. By 2003, sales had dropped by 26 per cent and in 2004 by a further 20 per cent.

What went wrong? Did Lego fail to deliver up-to-the-minute, or did consumers want more colours? After a series of discussions about product development, sourcing, manufacturing and logistics with its key customer base – the top 20 retail clients that accounted for 70 per cent of its total business – Lego was surprised to learn that its single-minded strategy had got it wrong. Customers demanded better services, not speedier delivery or more colour choices. Toy retailers did not require daily delivery, for example.

Lego determined to get it right. Based on a new strategy approved by the board in October 2004, the company cut the number of colours by half, reduced stock-keeping units to 6,500, delivered to customers just once a week and asked for orders to be placed in advance. As a result, Lego was able to improve services. On-time delivery rose, for example, from 62 per cent in 2005 to 92 per cent in 2008.

Customers valued this, rating Lego as a 'best-in-class' supplier; the company won a European supply-chain excellence award. Lego's sales increased by 35 per cent between 2005 and 2008, its fixed-cost base was reduced by more than half and profitability reached an all-time high. There is no universal business truth or one best strategy;

business success lies in managers' ability to 'get it just right': mind who you are, what business you are in and what your customers value.

PRAGMATISM-UPON-TIME

While *zhong* (中) in Chinese *kanzi* can indeed mean 'centre' or 'middle', the philosophical, aesthetical and practical implications are, primarily and persistently, 'get it just right'. In a third-century BC poem, Sung Yü described a beautiful girl thus: 'If she were one inch taller, she would be too tall. If she were one inch shorter, she would be too short. If she used powder, her face would be too white. If she used rouge, her face would be too red.'[20] In contemplating that beautiful girl, those who search for 'extremes' or 'midpoint' will search in vain. Fung Youlan, a twentieth-century Chinese scholar, posited: '"Just right" is what the Confucians call *zhong*.'[21]

What has been lost in translation is that, in Confucianism *zhong* (中, balancing) is usually used in a pair with *shi* (时, timely). Viewing the endless flux of life, the *Yijing* (易经, *Book of Changes*) makes frequent references to *shi*: in Appendix I, 24 times, in Appendix II, six times. Timely is used in the *Yijing* in many ways: timely standard, timely movement, timely change, timely development, timely release, timely completion, timely stop, timely return, timely coping, timely conduct and so on. 'Eventually, in the *Yijing*, *shi* and *zhong* are united in one phrase: *shizhong*.'[22] Confucius, on top of his other virtues, is ultimately regarded as the 'timely sage' (时中圣人).[23] According to the classics,

> Po I among the sages was the pure one; Yi Yin was the responsible one; Hui of Liu-hsia was the accommodating one; and Confucius was the timely one.[24]
>
> Confucius said, 'Exemplary persons balance familiar affairs; petty persons distort them. Exemplary persons exemplify harmony, because they master timely balance. Petty persons are a source of distortion, being petty persons they lack requisite caution and concern.'[25]

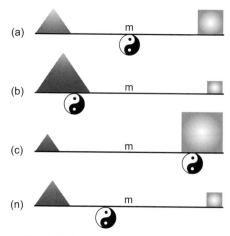

FIGURE 6.1 Timely balance: get it just right

> The notion of balance is the great root of the world;
> harmony then is the advancing of the appropriate way in the
> world. When balance and harmony are achieved, heaven and
> earth maintain their proper places and all things flourish.[26]

What is right, we shall follow. Timely balance promotes appropriate, fitting conduct, appropriate to and fitting with specific circumstances. The Master said, 'balancing for harmony is a task of the highest order',[27] 'whatever he pursues is fitting with time'.[28]

Graphically, timely balance can be illustrated as in Figure 6.1. In some circumstances, 'just right' happens to be at the middle (scenario (a)), while in others, it can be at either end, and you had better go for it, as Andrew Grove did (scenarios (b) and (c)). In Confucian traditions, there is a well-known saying: *jiaowang guozheng* (矫枉过正, exceeding the normal limits is necessary to right a wrong). Well, excess can be good, even necessary. Further, in other times, perhaps most of the time, 'just right' lies somewhere between the ends but not quite in the middle (scenario (n)). Instead of promising quick-fit solutions, timely balance demands profound understanding and disciplined assessment of emerging particulars.[29]

It is the persistent emphasis on appropriate, fitting, just-right conduct that differentiates Confucian process thinking from mechanistic interpretations of the 'golden mean'. Suppose he met Socrates, Plato and Phocylides, Confucius would surely protest that 'sticking to the middle way' or 'keeping both extremes' 'at the same time, all the time' was unwise. He would, however, applaud Aristotle wholeheartedly. Fung Youlan, a neo-Confucianist, read Confucius into Aristotle thus:

> This mean of Aristotle is one that is taken as a guide for
> human emotions and actions, and that differs according to the
> time, place and person which are encountered, thus making
> it impossible to have any fixed rules that will serve as a mean
> under every circumstance. The timely balance spoken of by
> *Zhongyong* [中庸, *Focusing the Familiar*] is precisely like this.[30]

Please note that in elaborating timely balance, we do not refer to 'mean' or 'extremes'; these terms hold no significance in the Confucian vocabulary. Even when the words 'end' and 'middle' are adopted, we do so for the convenience of Western readers. The Confucian civilisation has its own distinctive assumptions about relationships. It emphasises interdependence over contradiction, reciprocity over synthesis. The metaphor 'lips and teeth' in a third-century classic is telling here:

> both the 'self' and the 'other' equally desire to act for themselves,
> thus being as opposed to each other as east and west. On the
> other hand, the 'self' and the 'other' at the same time hold a
> relationship to one another as that of the lips and teeth. The
> lips and teeth never act for one another, yet 'when the lips are
> gone, the teeth feel cold' (唇亡齿寒). Therefore the action of the
> 'other' on its own behalf at the same time plays a great function
> in helping the 'self'. Thus, though mutually opposed, they at the
> same time are mutually indispensable.[31]

We do not treat lips and teeth as extremes, we do not see the self and the other as contradictions. We do not struggle to stay in the middle, nor do we 'transcend', 'integrate' or 'resolve' extremes into a 'higher synthesis'. Ours is a logic of correlations.[32]

The interdependent, reciprocal, generative qualities of relation-ships have been illustrated in another root metaphor *yin–yang*. As a metaphor, *yin–yang* covers differences, plurality, complexity, dyna-mism, with meanings far richer than mere 'duality'. Neither *yin* nor *yang* is self-contained, nor are they in contradiction. Far from being antagonistic extremes, the true *yang* is the *yang* that is in the *yin*, and vice versa. Without one, the other is incomplete and meaning-less. The two are a pair of complementary companions; one exists only because of the other. Remember Canon's company philosophy *kyosei* (共生, co-existing, co-growing)? It is important to understand the infinite possibilities in which new values emerge from *yin–yang* correspondences.[33] Significant are harmonious dialogue, mutual determination and reciprocal transformation in which one compan-ion complements the other and has its own necessary function, like lips and teeth.[34] As Ikujiro Nonaka puts it: what appear to be oppo-sites interact with each other to create something new, beneficial, harmonious. Pragmatic strategy harnesses this process in an appro-priate, fitting, just-right manner.[35]

Making our way in the fast-moving world, we need to liberate timely balance from the default vocabulary of 'mean' and 'extremes'.[36] Timely balanced strategy is not easy. It is not McDonaldised fast thought, it promises no quick fix. In contrast, it challenges managers to look beyond the 'middle way' and 'extremes', to get it just right in no-fixed-shape, no-definite-rule business circumstances. It is an enormous challenge; it is nevertheless a realistic approach. Timely balance helps us to cope with the uncertain world, to appreciate its relatedness, richness and dynamism while benefiting from its gen-erative power.[37] There are many exemplars: Intel, Lenovo, Komatsu, Michael Dell, GE, Lego, and even Hank Paulson. None of them sticks to the middle or synthesises extremes, they act just right under spe-cific circumstances.

Does the world consist of dualist extremes and antagonis-tic contradictions, or of interdependences and complementarities? Well, 'is the glass half full or half empty?' It is a cultural thing;

FIGURE 6.2 Pragmatism-upon-time: the Confucian way-making

it is about tradition, worldview, aesthetics, taste.[38] Yet, it is not a trivial matter. In the world of human experience, subjective perceptions produce material consequences. The more you treat people and things as conflicting and antagonistic, the more they, and you, become so. The more you appreciate, and act accordingly, that people and things depend on and support each other, the more you and they become *kyosei*.[39] Social scientists call this 'self-fulfilling prophesy'.[40] China is well-known for business banquets and Japan for after-office drinks, the UK for back-street deals and the US for lawsuits. Which is more efficient, or wasteful, for business? The choices are not entirely ours, 'decisions' were partly made by our ancestors hundreds or even thousands of years ago. The longer your history and the deeper your cultural roots, the more persistent your strategy patterns.

Lenovo: a global company returning to its roots

After stunning the world by its acquisition of IBM's PC division in 2005, Lenovo moved its headquarters to New York, kept the IBM logo on Think products for five years, adopted English as the company's official language and retained the whole former IBM PC sales team. It also filled half of its top management positions with former IBM managers, appointed as CEO first Steve Ward, a former IBM executive, and then William Amelio from Dell. Liu Chuanzhi, Lenovo's founder, retreated to Legend Holdings, allowing his protégé Yang Yunquing to become the Lenovo chairman. All of these moves were driven by the firm's carefully formulated globalisation strategy. In a presentation to the 2006 Academy of International Business plenary session, Liu revealed Lenovo's strategy:

> The reason to go global was straightforward: with a 30 per cent share of the Chinese PC market, Lenovo realised that its opportunity for further domestic expansion was limited. Since the global PC market was estimated at about $200 billion, it could pose huge potential for us. To expand abroad, we realised that we were lacking several things, including a brand name that had worldwide recognition, a strong presence in the world market, and human talent to run and manage a global company. We recognised that there were two primary ways to globalise. One was to grow organically. We were aware, however, that this approach would involve a very long process. Another way was to expand through mergers and acquisition ... With the help of external advisers and consultants, we decided to adopt the second approach.[41]

Five years on, the strategy was turned upside-down. In 2009, the foreigners bowed out, Liu returned as Lenovo chairman and Yang as CEO. No culture clash or nationalism was involved here. In 2008, Lenovo's global shipments dropped 5 per cent and sales 17 per cent and its global market share fell from 7.9 to 7.3 per cent, making a $361 million loss in the first half of 2009.[42] Time had changed and the balance was shifting. As recession deepened in 'the West', 'Lenovo is now paying a heavy price for failing to address its ... reliance on Western companies', commented *The Economist*.[43] Furthermore, as technology changed, the 'Big Blue' brand proved a burden rather than an advantage. 'The PC industry is no longer an IBM-style business. Anyone who wants to be successful needs to be very nimble, very fast', reckoned J. P. Morgan.[44] Lenovo estimated that the entry-level segment such as notebooks would account for 66 per cent of the world PC market by 2012, up from 31 per cent in 2007.[45] At that point, the iPad was yet to burst onto the scene.

In business, you do not search for the 'middle way' or 'extremes'. You search for what is good for you, here-and-now. You go where the customers are. Ironically, the biggest chunk of the market turned out to be Lenovo's home, China. In 2009, Lenovo shipped 15 per cent more PCs to mainland China than it had the year before. In this context, 'emerging market' had a special meaning: the mass of Chinese consumers outside big cities. Lenovo had built a network of 12,000 shops in more than 2,000 cities and 30,000 townships. 'In 2009, 45 per cent of our desktop computers were sold to consumers in China in what we call "emerging markets". Now [2010] it's 70 per cent. For notebooks, emerging markets accounted for 30 per cent of our customers a year ago, and now it's half', said Tang Jie, general manager of Lenovo's China consumer and channel business.[46] Thanks to the 'emerging markets' at home, by the end of 2009, Lenovo was reporting net profit of $80 million.[47]

Liu believed that the difficult years had been a valuable learning experience. The company would now have to rely on China, the fastest-growing and soon-to-be-largest market in the world.[48] 'Once we left China', Liu said, 'we were good for nothing … just a Chinese company.'[49] Yang agreed: 'in regions [outside China], we could not build a complete and efficient business model.'[50] Lenovo still has plans for expansion. The company started selling its videogame console, the eBox, in November 2010, broadening its product portfolio beyond PCs, exclusively in China. 'China has 120 million urban families. We are focusing on the 20 million users among them', said Jack Luo, Lenovo's videogame chief.[51] China's biggest and most successful computer-maker, once eager to take on the world, is now recognising that the world and home are not opposite extremes, and that corporate success lies in getting business just right, in a timely fashion.

BALANCING CHANGE–CONTINUITY

Let us now explore two pairs of generic companions that businesses have to balance in a timely manner. The first pair is change–continuity.

Change is perhaps the most popular term in the contemporary political and business vocabulary. President Obama won the key to the White House thanks to the popular slogan 'Change – yes we can!' Yet, within just two short years, he was punished by voters in the 2010 midterm election in the name of, guess what, 'change!'[52] In business, continuous change is said to be the only viable strategy. As early as 1979, a *Harvard Business Review* article argued managers '*must* undertake moderate organisational changes at least once a year and major changes every four or five'.[53] The c-word has become an ideology, promoted as always beneficial, a good thing on its own, with stability, continuity and persistence reduced to, at best, secondary qualities.[54]

Does the hype work in the real world? The evidence is that it doesn't. Business surveys persistently report that as many as 70 per cent of change initiatives fail. 'Where the change is an acquisition, synergies are not often realised; where the change involves re-engineering, both time and costs can escalate; where the change entails downsizing, financial performance may be weaker; and where it involves quality programmes, the expected results are not always produced.'[55] Indeed, the business landscape is littered with expensive 'strategic changes': Coca Cola's 'New Coke' formula, British Airways' dropping of the Union Flag, the UK Royal Mail's 'new' brand Consignia, Ford's purchase of Volvo, Jaguar and Land Rover, and the American clothing retailer Gap's 2010 logo fiasco, to name only a few.[56]

Even worse, the hype is a self-fulfilling prophesy: the more you change, the more you want to do it, regardless of the impact, at any cost. Take restructuring as an example. William McKinley and Andreas Scherer found that corporate restructuring has produced two unanticipated consequences: (1) frequent restructuring inside and outside the company generates a cognitive bias among executives to perceive the need for additional restructuring, and (2) restructuring programmes drive companies into further restructuring just in order to cope with the environmental disorder, which is of the companies' own making.[57] You see, it is a vicious circle. Recently, the dark side of frantic change has been for all to see: bankers pressed each other for continuous changes in the form of 'financial innovations' until the changes got out of everyone's hands.

Experienced managers do not buy the ideology. Mike Eskew, chairman and CEO of United Parcel Service, an Atlanta-based provider of global logistics services, for example, encourages managers 'stick with your vision'. According to Eskew, companies in thrall to constant change are the ones most likely to fail. Even in the age of globalisation and outsourcing, Eskew posits, you must have the mettle to stick with your vision, planning and research. 'Our fastest-growing and most profitable business today, international small packages, took more than 20 years to produce consistent profit.'[58]

Intel, Lenovo, Lego, GE and Dell all made changes, but not for change's sake. Indeed, once a strategy decision is made (or, in our terms, once a valued future is envisioned), capable managers make it happen with iron persistence and a laser-like focus, against all odds. Reviewing the evolution of the Toyota Production System, Tokyo University professor Takahiro Fujimoto discerns remarkable continuity in practices that date back to the founding of the company, such as Kiichiro Toyoda's Just-in-Time philosophy.[59] Similarly, legend has it that Konosuke Matsushita, founder of Panasonic, drafted a 1,000-year corporate plan based on his unshakeable vision, while Masayonshi Son's plan for his technology investment giant Softbank was a little short-sighted – a mere 300 years![60] While we don't suggest managers go this far, we do consider Henry Mintzberg's reminder insightful: 'Managing strategy is mostly managing stability, not change ... [The] obsession with change is dysfunctional. Organisations that reassess their strategies continuously are like individuals who reassess their jobs or their marriages continuously – in both cases, people will drive themselves crazy or else reduce themselves to inaction.'[61] In a similar tone, David Teece warns us of the danger of change for

FIGURE 6.3 Balancing change–continuity

change's sake: 'Change is costly and so firms must develop processes to minimise low pay-off change.'[62]

Don't get us wrong. Process thinking and change practice are at the heart of Confucian pragmatism.[63] *Shili*, with which we promote creativity and innovation, for example, is about initiating and realising valued changes. Exemplars of beneficial change, thanks to managers' imagination and hard work, are plentiful: Muhammad Yunus changed the banking industry by introducing the new paradigm 'credit is a human right', Nicolas Hayek changed the Swiss watch industry by redefining the value and functionality of watches, Nintendo changed the videogame industry by inventing the Wii machine, Intel reinvented itself from a memory to a processor company and Thomas Edison changed the world with his electric light innovation that restructured physical artefacts, public understanding and a whole set of institutions.[64] Change is at the heart of pragmatic strategy; not for change's sake but sensible, workable, viable changes. The key, and the challenge, is timely balance, balance between change and continuity, change and stability, change and stop.

In Confucianism as in Taoism, *dong* (动, action) and *jing* (静, stillness) are seen as mutually attractive companions that constitute this-worldly process. As complementary forms of the process oneness, like *yin* and *yang*, one is differentiable from, irreducible to and complementing the other. This applies to many other process-related companions (Table 6.1).

Table 6.1 *The* yin–yang *of this-worldly process*

Dong (动)	Jing (静)
action	stillness
change	persistence
transformation	continuity
movement	stability
stir	quiet
sway	calm
alteration	tranquility

Promoting change, the sages at the same time praised continuity, stability, cessation. The *Yijing* reads: '*Zhen* (震) is the idea of *dong* (动 movement). Things cannot be in movement forever. They are *zhi* (止 stopped), and therefore this is followed by *gen* (艮). *Gen* denotes stop. But things cannot be forever stopped, and so this is followed by *jian* (渐 advance).' Human life, strategic conduct included, is full of transformations and continuities, advances and returns, changes and stops.[65] Without stability, change is meaningless; without continuity, transformation goes nowhere; without stop, change generates no beneficial effects. *Dong* and *jing* define, invite, inhabit one another.

Too philosophical? Can change–stability be attractive companions, not antagonistic opposites? In shareholder capitalism, the answer is no. According to the shareholder model, only continuous change, such as contingent employment and constant downsizing, can ensure adaptability, contain costs and satisfy impatient capital markets. Yet both theoretical exploration and business practice suggest that stable employment is an efficient solution to the hazards of opportunism,[66] benefiting firms via costly-to-imitate resources[67] by supplying 'organisation advantages' such as cognitive routines and social capital.[68] Carrie Leana and Bruce Barry posit: 'stable patterns of behaviour evoke perceptions of interpersonal trust, which, in turn, clears the way for more flexible and adaptive subsequent behaviour.'[69] In short, stability is not the conflicting opposite but the very source of adaptability; stable employment enables adaptive changes. No wonder, amid four consecutive years of economic downturn, the directive from the top of Toyota is 'cut all costs, but don't touch any people'.[70]

Accordingly, if an organisation is to benefit from change, it must, like Mazda, Lenovo and Apple, value continuity and stability, preserve its DNA, its ideals, values, purpose, vision and relationships. The trick is to get the timely balance right. 'That is to say', regarding change and stability, 'nothing is altogether *yin* or *yang* in and of itself, but only in relation to one or more other "things".'[71] Contexts matter. In the mobile phone industry, constant change is the norm; consumers expect Nokia and Samsung to launch new handset models every month if not every week. In the airline industry, however, stability is valued highly; passengers may feel uneasy if airlines change their safety regimes, service standards or flight schedules at such a breathtaking pace. Not middle way or extremes, just getting it right.

Again, we found a striking affinity between Confucian teaching and the experiences of managers. David Hurst of Hugh Russel Inc. may not know the Confucian classics but nevertheless reflects on his front-line experience thus:

> The creative integration of all these activities demands a manager who is sometimes rational and sometimes constrained, often confused, but never powerless ... It demands a feel for the timing of when to act and when to wait, of when to go with the flow and when to oppose it, of when to stay on the beaten track and when to strike out for the distant hills.[72]

Practically wise strategies are based on situated judgements about what, when, where and how to change *and* to stop.[73] Consider the following questions as an indicative starter:

Whether	IBM revived its fortune by selling its loss-making PC division to Lenovo and acquiring the high-value-adding IT consultancy arm from PricewaterhouseCoopers; Coca-Cola's 'New Coke' formula and the Royal Mail's 'Consignia' new brand ended up disasters. *Are changes always a good thing?*
What	Grameen Bank changed the rule of banking, lifting millions of the poorest out of poverty while making a profit; Northern Rock changed banking practice by financing long-term lending with short-term wholesale borrowing, only for the bank to be nationalised. *Are changes justified, for what purpose?*
When	Nokia divested all other operations some 20 years ago and focused on mobile phones; today it is an industry leader. Marconi, once Britain's largest manufacturer, adopted a similar strategy in the mid 1990s, only to bring itself to the brink of bankruptcy. *Similar changes, different outcomes: why?*
How	Carly Fiorina, former CEO of HP, claimed in her book *Hard Choices* that the company's recent good performance was due to her change strategy, which may be true. Nevertheless, she was removed by colleagues, unable to be part of, let alone to lead, the changes. *How to promote changes?*

At root an action-biased tradition promoting 'It is Man who makes *Tao* great, not *Tao* that makes Man great (人能宏道, 非道宏人)' though,[74] Confucianism stresses *wuwei* (无为, non-forced action) and *wuzheng* (无争, non-contentiousness) – the art of making changes 'natural', workable, beneficial.[75] In *Daodejing*, we read: 'Is it not because they strive without contentiousness that no one in the world is able to contend with them (非以其无争与, 故天下莫能与之争)?'[76] In a similar spirit, Confucius proposed: 'There is no contention among exemplary persons (君子无所争).'[77] It is not that they never compete, but that 'even in contesting, they are exemplary persons (其争也君子)'.[78]

This remains true in the twenty-first-century globalising world: competition leads to beneficial efficiency only when it is guided by a long-term vision of realising common goodness, of building harmonious communities, of living in a sustainable bio-ecology. Grameen Bank betters society by creating a new paradigm, not by competing viciously on Wall Street; Yamaha brings happiness to ordinary families by creating a new market, not by replacing grand pianos; Nintendo achieves higher profitability than Goldman Sachs by redefining videogames, not by stealing market share from Microsoft or Sony. They 'win' for a good reason: 'We are building real value in the world, not just taking value from other companies.'[79] Even in contesting, they are exemplary persons, indeed.

And this brings purpose and ethical judgement to the fore. As McKinley and Scherer found in corporate restructuring, changes can be seen as good or bad 'depending on the perspective and interests of the stakeholders making the judgment'.[80] Even from an instrumental perspective, stakeholders' views make a difference. Changes appreciated by stakeholders are easier to make happen – you don't need to force them through – while changes perceived as biased are difficult to implement: one US company union rejected the management's offer of flexible work hours because the workers believed, rightly or wrongly, that they would be asked to work on evenings and weekends.[81] The art of *wuwei* and *wuzheng* is to make changes a beneficial way of life, to be embraced, owned, enjoyed.

Li & Fung: change with continuity

In a 1998 *Harvard Business Review* interview, chairman Victor, with general director William, positioned Li & Fung as 'a Hong Kong-based multinational trading company'.[82] That was apt positioning for the time. Founded by their grandfather in 1906, when China's trade was controlled by foreign powers, Li & Fung was the first Chinese-run export company. As an English teacher who spoke both Chinese and English, the grandfather's added value was in bringing foreign buyers and local suppliers together; for this, Li & Fung charged a 15 per cent commission. The trading-broker business continued into the 1970s when the Fung brothers were called back from the US by their father to breathe new life into the company. Due to changes in technology and international trade, foreign buyers and local suppliers could easily come together, and the margin for Li & Fung's service was squeezed down to 10, 5 and then 3 per cent. Friends warned the brothers that buying agents like Li & Fung would be extinct in ten years: 'Trading is a sunset industry.' Li & Fung had to change, fast.

But change to what, and how? Victor and William decided to stay in the industry; after all, your experience, reputation and connections were rooted there. Perhaps the economics jargon 'path-dependence' influenced the Harvard-trained brothers. Yet they fundamentally changed the way of doing business. They reconfigured the 'business model', as strategy professors might call it. First, the Fung brothers expanded their sourcing base to include the wider region, establishing offices in Taiwan, Korea and Singapore. Li & Fung's added value was now their knowledge of the trade in the region, such as textile quotas. If foreign buyers used up Hong Kong's quota, for example, Li & Fung would source for them from Taiwan. Furthermore, different suppliers and countries were good at different things. Expanding the sourcing base beyond Hong Kong allowed Li & Fung to serve clients with what the brothers call 'assortment packing'. 'Say I sell a tool kit to a major discount chain. I could buy the spanners from one country and the screwdrivers from another and put together a product package. That has some value in it – not great value, but some.'[83] God is in the details; in a low-margin industry, these small things count.

Next, the brothers transformed Li & Fung from a go-between broker into a 'production programme' deliverer. Instead of sourcing ready-made products from suppliers, Li & Fung, with its main business in the apparel sector, would now start with fashion designers' sketches, take their product concepts and develop them in prototypes. Customers could then look at the sample and say, 'No, I don't really like that, I like this. Can you do more of this?' Taking on more and more jobs for their clients, Li & Fung coordinated an entire fashion programme. 'We work with factories to plan and monitor production to ensure quality and on-time delivery.'[84] In doing so, Li & Fung created value in cooperation with fashion retailers, even when the retailers had no clear specifications in mind. In the fashion and apparel sector where consumer preferences changed rapidly and product life cycles were short – with 'six or seven seasons a year instead of two or three' – this generated great value for clients. 'For the first time, retailers are really creating products, not just sitting in their offices with salesman after salesman showing them samples … Instead, retailers are participating in the design process. They are now managing suppliers through us.'[85] Li & Fung saw its customer base expanded and relationships deepened, such as those with Abercrombie & Fitch, Laura Ashley and Levi Strauss.

Then, in the 1990s, Li & Fung undertook further changes. They 'dissected', i.e. breaking up and optimising, the value chain for each customer order, while at the same time expanding their network of suppliers far beyond the Asian region. To produce a European-designed garment for the American market today, for example, Li & Fung may get yarn from Egypt, have it dyed in Thailand, woven in Taiwan, cut in Bangladesh, assembled in Mexico with a zipper from Japan, all planned, financed and quality-controlled in Hong Kong. 'Managing dispersed manufacturing, where not everything is done under one roof, takes a real change of mind-set. But once we figured out how to do it', recalled Victor, 'we began what has turned into a constant search for new and better sources of supply.'[86] By 1998, Li & Fung's network of 35 offices coordinated 7,500 suppliers in 20 countries, of which 2,500 were active at any one time and serving 356 core customers. This moved beyond conventional outsourcing that narrowly focused on bilateral buyer–supplier relationships. 'So to shrink the delivery cycle, I go upstream to organise production', Victor told *Harvard Business Review*.[87] Li & Fung's new model now coordinated capacities and activities across multiple levels of the value chain, far beyond first-tier suppliers. 'Doing it globally' meant competing on everything, anywhere. To Li & Fung, 'supply chain management is about buying the right things and shortening delivery cycles'. 'It's all about flexibility, response time, small production runs, small minimum-order quantities, and the ability to shift direction as trends change.'[88]

Traditionally, global trading companies organised themselves geographically, with country or regional units as profit centres. Li & Fung organises, instead, around customers. The basic Li & Fung operation unit is the 'division', and each division is responsible for a single customer or small group of customers with similar needs. Each division is small, run by a 'lead entrepreneur', responsible for developing a deep understanding of a specific customer's needs and the capabilities of related supply partners. Once a production programme is agreed with the customer, the division makes its own decisions to mobilise the necessary resources across the Li & Fung global network: which supplier to use, whether to stop a shipment or let it go forward at a particular time and so on.[89] Each time, the supply chain is tailored to the specific need of a particular customer. Significantly, the units, and Li & Fung the company, do not micromanage the activities of supplier partners, but macro-coordinate connections between them. Li & Fung regards these customer-centric units as a portfolio that can be created and collapsed quickly as the market changes.[90]

While the benefits to customers are apparent, the question is why are suppliers, or 'partners' as Victor and William call them, keen to join in? For one thing, long-standing relationships with leading fashion designers and apparel retailers enable Li & Fung to deliver substantial, steady business to suppliers. For another, as Li & Fung establishes detailed benchmarks across the supply network, the company is able to give partners valuable insight of their particular strengths and weaknesses. With steady business and in-depth feedback from Li & Fung, partners can focus on more specialised activities, and hence further improve their distinctive capabilities and performances. As understanding and relationships deepen,

Li & Fung needs to exchange with partners only the key bit of information at key moments. The company establishes for itself privileged access to highly specialised, leading-edge capabilities across business functions that allows it to secure the best solution for each customer order. Li & Fung is then able to charge more for such services.[91] If there is win–win strategy, this is it.

Some call the Li & Fung model 'open process network'.[92] This new way of doing business allows Li & Fung to satisfy customer needs both in its original sector, apparel, and in new sectors that involve labour-intensive manufacturing, such as fashion accessories, sports equipment, toys, gifts and electronics. Victor puts it this way: 'If you look at a product market grid, Li & Fung has expertise in sourcing many types of products for many types of retailers.'[93]

This ability to quickly reconfigure to serve customer needs across sectors has proved critical for Li & Fung's survival and growth. After the worldwide textile quota system was lifted in January 2005, no one needed Li & Fung's quota-broker service any more. The company fenced off the threat by expanding into new segments where global supply-chain management was in high demand. Far from shrinking when China's textile products suddenly flooded the world, Li & Fung achieved substantial growth. Today, Li & Fung operates an extensive global sourcing network of 12,000 suppliers, with more than 80 offices in over 40 economies. It offers a comprehensive range of products, with an annual turnover in excess of $14 billion.[94]

On the company's website, Li & Fung no longer positions itself as an apparel supplier or an export trader, but primarily a professional service provider. If your business needs to manage a global supply chain, Li & Fung is readily here to meet your needs. The Li & Fung transformation has captured the attention of seasoned researchers. John Hagel and John Seely Brown comment: 'These initiatives involve fundamentally new businesses at one level, yet at another level they are logical extensions of Li & Fung's specialised process network orchestration business.'[95] Hence we witness remarkable changes in Li & Fung: from a goods broker to a service provider, from an assortment-package supplier under one roof to a process coordinator across customised value chains, from a traditional geographic organisation to a customer-centric structure and from a Hong Kong-based export trader to a leader in global supply management. Li & Fung has transformed itself from a dismal buying agent in a 'sunset industry' into a thriving professional service company in the 'knowledge economy'. Li & Fung reinvents itself as times change.

There is an uninterrupted continuity, however. The company remains, as the Fung brothers repeatedly stress, a 'very narrowly focused company'.[96] The company's key strength is its path-dependent expertise in managing customer–supplier relationships. It is the deep understanding of clients and partners that enables Li & Fung to customise supply chains on a global scale to meet each client's particular needs. At the core of all this is a human touch. In the words of Victor: 'the old relationships, the old values, still matter. I think they matter in our dealings with suppliers, with customers, and with our own staff.'[97] To suppliers, 'it makes a difference when they know that you are dedicated to the business, that you've been honouring your commitments for 90 years [now 100 years]'.[98] To customers, 'In the old days, my father used to read every telex from customers … Today, William and I continue to read faxes from customers … Through close attention to detail, we try to maintain our heritage of customer service'.[99] Then, to Li & Fung's staff:

> As we have transformed a family business into a modern one, we have tried to preserve the best of what my father and grandfather created. There is a family feeling in the company that's difficult to describe. We don't care much for titles and hierarchy. Family life and the company's business spill over into each other. When staff members are in Hong Kong to do business, my mother might have tea with their families. Of course, as we have grown we have had to change. My mother can't know everyone as she once did. But we hold on to our wish to preserve the intimacies that have been at the heart of our most successful relationships.

> If I had to capture it in one phrase, it would be this: Think like a
> big company, act like a small one.[100]

Victor and William are humble men. But they know what they are
doing: the Li & Fung model of 'borderless manufacturing' has become
a new paradigm for twenty-first-century business. *Time* magazine
agrees, honouring the brothers among '60 Years of Asian Heroes',
together with Mahatma Gandhi, Deng Xiaoping, Akio Morita and
Muhammad Yunus.[101]

BALANCING EXPANSION–FOCUS

Now we turn to another pair of companions. Let's begin with the
business front line. When it was just a small-town factory, Honda
had a vision of becoming a global company. The 1956 company credo
reads: 'Expansion of our company is not only meant to contribute
to the happiness of employees and stockholders. The purpose of
our existence is to make customers happy and supply them with
good products, to help our associate companies develop, to raise the
technological level of Japanese industry, and to contribute to the welfare of society.' Yet Honda's expansion had an enduring focus: being
a technology pioneer. Vice president Takeo Fujisawa, when retired,
disapproved of speculating in stocks or property amid Japan's 1980s
bubbles, which put the company, as a result, in a sound financial
position. His lasting influence has helped the company pursue 'the
business that makes us proud'.[102] In contrast, Marconi, once Britain's
largest manufacturer of machinery from fighter jets to vacuum
cleaners, almost bankrupted itself in the mid 1990s by a strategy
exclusively focusing on telecom equipment.[103]

Tata, India's flagship company, generated enviable growth by
expanding from trading tea and salt to making steel and cars to
providing IT and law services. Today, the one-and-a-half-century-
old group has 98 firms across seven key sectors. After acquiring
Corus, an Anglo-Dutch steel-maker, for $12 billion and Jaguar Land
Rover from Ford for $2.3 billion, the Indian conglomerate is now

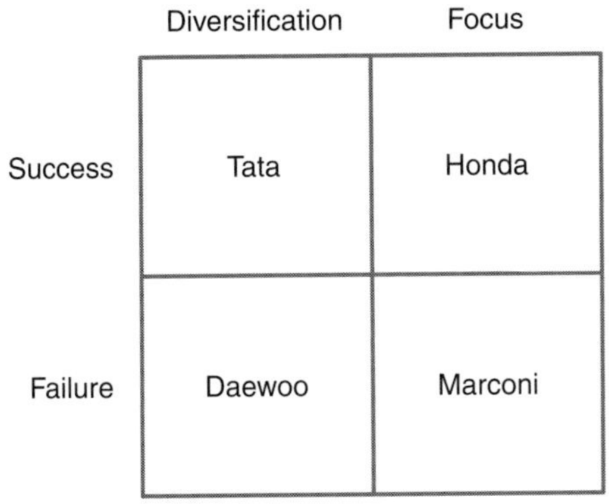

	Diversification	Focus
Success	Tata	Honda
Failure	Daewoo	Marconi

FIGURE 6.4 Diversification vs focus: successes and failures

the largest manufacturer in Britain. The Tata brand is valued at $9.9 billion and the company ranked thirteenth among *BusinessWeek*'s '25 Most Innovative Companies'.[104] Tata's diversified businesses succeed because they fit with circumstances: a fast-growing economy where the capital market is underdeveloped, management talent scarce, consumer activism weak, government regulation and contract enforcement unpredictable.[105] In contrast, Daewoo Group, one of Korea's most powerful conglomerates, collapsed in 1999 with debts of more than $80 billion, turning its founding boss Kim Woochoong into the state's 'most wanted man'. 'My big mistake was being too ambitious', Kim told *Fortune* magazine. 'I tried to do too much too fast.' Indeed, Daewoo's expansion was reckless, 'producing autos, televisions, pianos, aerospace components, grapes for French wine, and practically everything else except significant profits'.[106]

These, to experienced managers, are well-known cases in diversification–focus strategy. The moral is that neither diversification nor focus is good or bad in itself; to perform well, firms must get the balance right, i.e. appropriate, fitting with circumstances. In the corporate world, diversification and focus constitute just one of many pairs to be balanced. Managers face delicate options of merger and divestment, integration and outsourcing, globalisation and localisation, core competence and networked resources and so on. Hence, practically wise strategy demands not only knowing when

Table 6.2 *Expansion–focus companions*

Expansion	Focus
breadth	depth
edge	core
generality	speciality
diversity	coherence
drifting	fixing
amateurish	attentive
dilettante	diligent
flitting	preserving
branching	selecting
loosening	tightening

to change and stop, but also what to do, as well as not to do. That is the virtue of *you wei you buwei* (有为有不为, Do certain things, not all things). Nintendo learned that lesson from its early 'love hotel' and taxi businesses, then focused on videogames and successfully expanding the industry and markets. GE's experience tells a similar story: when Jack Welch was in charge, the strapline was 'Be Number One or Number Two, otherwise ...'; under Jeff Immelt's leadership, the focus is moving back from financial services to industrial businesses, particularly energy technology.[107]

Readers should not be surprised that in Confucian pragmatism expansion and focus are mutually constituting companions (see Table 6.2).

As a human-centred tradition, Confucianism attaches explicit ethical implications to its expansion–focus conception. Let us begin with expansion. The metaphor *chaxü gejü* (差序格局, differential mode of association) is telling here: 'Like the ripples formed from a stone thrown into a lake, each circle spreading out from the center becomes more distant and at the same time more insignificant.'[108]

While we see this happening in Nature, do we humans really live in *chaxü gejü*? Is it a good way to do business? Is the metaphor morally right?

This brings us to a famous debate between Confucianism and its critics. During the fourth and fifth centuries BC, Mozi (墨子), a leading critic of Confucius, promoted 'universal love' (*jianai*, 兼爱): everyone in the world should love everyone else, equally, without discrimination. He supported the doctrine with utilitarian reasoning: if you love other states as your own, there will be no war, hence no suffering. 'Then is it not the case that "mutual all-embracingness" can bring happiness to the world?'[109]

With this, Mencius (孟子), a disciple of Confucius, strongly disagreed. Mencius promoted 'extending love' instead: 'Treat the aged in your family as they should be treated, and extend this treatment to the aged of other people's families. Treat the young in your family as they should be treated, and extend this treatment to the young of other people's families.'[110] While there are degrees and grades of love, the sages extend love one ripple at a time in an ever-extending series, to reach the more distant members of society, until 'everything is here in me'. You must begin with yourself, your family, with what is near-at-hand and then extend outward.[111] Confucius said: 'Correlating one's conduct with those near at hand can be said to be the method of becoming an authoritative person.'[112] Extended love is achievable because, Mencius believed, human nature is originally good: we cannot bear human suffering, for example. By developing our good nature to the full we can extend love across 'four seas'. In Mencius' 'Yes we can!' justification, no utilitarianism is needed.

Whatever the rights and wrongs of Mozi and Mencius in your mind, it is widely acknowledged that *chaxü gejü* pervades business. You begin with what is near, familiar and available at hand, materially, intellectually, socially, inside-out. Meanwhile, managers must respond to environmental emergences in technologies,

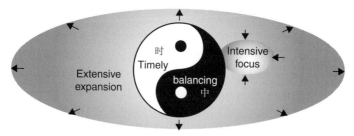

FIGURE 6.5 Balancing expansion–focus

industries, markets, regulations and global trends, outside-in. Business is thus an extensive 'field' of relationships and opportunities, and the manager's job is to expand such 'fields' for creating value. Many leading-edge strategy concepts and practices, such as 'problemistic search', 'community of practice', 'differentiated network', 'dynamic specialisation' and 'power of push-and-pull', appear to be advanced based on the 'expansion' logic.[113] This is the expansion side of the story.

Now turn to the other side: focus. Given limited resources, changing demands, diverse expectations and competition for excellence, business success lies in acting upon purposefully selected, appropriate courses. 'Purposeful action is focused', the late Sumantra Ghoshal told us. Focused action enables us to use limited resources to make a real difference.[114] While expansion generates opportunities, focus supplies commitment, willpower, energy and discipline to get things done that matter. Without focus, expansion leads to 'busy non-action': we may do any, all, an increasing number of things, but achieve nothing.[115] Only with a focused appreciation of the rich opportunities emerging from expanding fields are we able to judge, justify and agree on what to do, here-and-now.[116] Xunzi (荀子), another disciple of Confucius, famously suggested: 'Exemplary persons must be ever circumspect in the uniqueness.'[117] Getting things done demands focus that is timely, appropriate, fitting with uniqueness.

To complete the story: walking in the uncertain world, the art of way-making is timely balancing extensive expansion of fields and intensive focus of efforts (Figure 6.5).

Alibaba and Intel: focused expansion

The growth story of Alibaba is an exemplar of balanced way-making. After creating China's first Internet-based yellow pages, Jack Ma embarked on a ceaseless expansion of the e-commerce business:

1998	Launched the first online bulletin board for businesses to post buy-and-sell trade leads.
1999	Alibaba.com website formally operated for B2B business.
2000	Gold Supplier membership launched to serve B2B business.
2001	International TrustPass launched to serve exporters from China.
2002	China TrustPass launched to serve domestic trade in China.
May 2003	Taobao.com launched for C2C business.
October 2003	AliPay created as an online payment platform.
November 2003	TradeManager available for real-time communication between users.
2004	AliPay linked to Chinese banks.
2006	Alibaba Advertising began promotion service.
2010	Taobao Mall separated from Taobao.com to improve service quality.
2011	Taobao further split into three units: Taobal Mall (B2C), Taobao Marketplace (C2C) and eTao (a shopping-related search engine).

With rapid expansions, in December 2001 Alibaba became the world's first business website to exceed one million registered members. By the end of 2002 the company realised profit. In 2004 it was the biggest B2B online service in the world. In November 2007, Alibaba's Hong Kong listing made it the largest Internet IPO in Asia and second in the world only after Google. At the end of 2010, Alibaba announced a quarterly profit up 55 per cent, with growth in the number of subscribers and the use of the company's value-adding services. By the end of the first half of 2011, the company controlled 80 per cent of China's e-commerce market, with 370 million registered members; Taobao alone accounted for 71.6 per cent of online retail transactions in China.[118]

Back in 2001, Ma explained his focused-expansion strategy: 'when businessmen open up their computers today, they see Windows. Everything is Windows. In the future, what we hope you will see is a full-service window of Alibaba.' Throughout the expansion, Ma's focus was to 'give small-and-medium-size enterprises more opportunities to reach the market place'. This was done by supplying 'an entire infrastructure, including secure payment, delivery logistics, cooperation with banks, and, of course, government regulations'. 'Alibaba will become synonymous with trade.'[119] To Alibaba and Jack Ma, expansion and focus are mutually supportive companions: focus guides expansion while expansion enables focus. 'Middle way' or 'extremes' makes no sense.

Robert Burgelman's story of Intel Corporation, presented in the language of evolution theory, supplies another example.[120] At its best moments, Intel's management had the right attitude, policy and system to tolerate the expansion of autonomous initiatives that extended its capability set, engaged new markets, tested new technologies and reached out to new partners. These autonomous initiatives, or 'internal variation', emerged outside the company's official strategies. Intel technologist Ted Hoff, for example, worked with a Japanese client, Busicom, to launch a general-purpose microprocessor; similarly, another technologist, Les Kohn, worked together with new customers to push Intel into the highly successful RISC business. Both 'unapproved' initiatives eventually revitalised the company's fortunes.[121]

Meanwhile, internal selection processes are needed to ensure that promising initiatives gain sufficient resources. Without focus, company resources could be distributed too thinly across variations, allowing no initiative to survive. 'No firm, no matter how big, can pursue all technological possibilities.'[122] *You wei you buwei* (有为有不为, Do certain things, not all things)! Firms must decide which possibility to pursue and which to abandon. Intel's focusing process is manifested in many ways. The company has a budget mechanism through which, regardless of management plans or awareness, resources are allocated to the most profitable businesses, allowing unofficial but beneficial initiatives to flourish. Top executives also intervene. Once Intel made the decision to exit DRAM, for example, Intel management showed strong determination to implement it. The autonomous, divergent initiative expansion turned into focused, interventionist adjustment. In Andrew Grove's own words, the expansion–focus pendulum swung to the other end. In the face of lingering opposition, Grove himself took charge and made organisational changes. Grove visited those affected by the selected strategy: 'Welcome to the Mainstream Intel.' Those unable to work on the new focus, he let go.[123]

Overall, between expansion and focus, what Intel executives did was neither 'sticking in the middle' nor 'maintaining extremes', but getting the balance just right as situations demanded, patiently allowing autonomous initiatives to work themselves out via purposefully set-up mechanisms, while forcefully exercising managerial discretion to focus the whole company on the new strategy. Against all odds, they saw it through. Acting upon timely balance is a challenging job. Spontaneous local initiatives, though important for strategic success, are no substitute for purposeful judgement, justification or intervention. Burgelman puts it this way:

> Participants differentially situated in the organisation are likely to perceive different strategies as having the best potential for their own and the organisation's advancement. This provides an important source of internal variation [read 'expansion'], as individuals who possess data, ideas, motivation, and resources all strive to undertake specialised initiatives. But unless an organisation is able to establish internal selection mechanisms to maintain a level of coherence [read 'focus'], it seems likely that the strategy eventually will become unrealised.[124]

As products and services become more complicated, design costs soar and risks increase. Companies have learnt to focus on their own capabilities while using extended networks to gain complementary ones. In this area, Intel was again a pioneer.[125] In the microprocessor industry, the challenge was to incorporate dispersed technological changes into volume production of complex products. To cope with this, Intel focused on nurturing a distinctive competence in coordinating hundreds of activities embodying an array of different technologies conducted by other firms. The focus–expansion model allowed Intel to get the balance right: internally combining design and manufacturing processes while externally promoting joint innovations with specialist partners. Again, the vocabulary of 'getting it just right' makes more sense than that of 'the mean' or 'extremes'.[126]

Mayekawa: expanding ba with a sharp focus

To Nonaka, knowledge creation is an ongoing 'flow' in which managers nurture 'an ever-expanding field of relations' that enables problem-solving based on the 'value judgements made according to each particular situation'.[127] The concept and practice of ba illustrate this expansion–focus mindscape well.

Ba, as a shared context in motion, enables participants to transcend formal organisational boundaries, build caring relationships, establish a sense of purpose, open up limited perspectives and embrace the experience of others. Ba is where the heterogeneous contexts of participants intersect to form a larger, richer context from which new knowledge can emerge. The more diverse the participants' original contexts, the more chances new knowledge will be generated through interactions. The task of ba-centred management is thus, to begin with, expansion: the leader's job is to ensure that the organisational ba is connected with those of suppliers, customers, universities, local communities, governments and even competitors. Expanding ba can take various forms: joint ventures, alliances, joint projects, company visits, industry conferences, Internet blogs and messages and socialising in golf clubs and sake bars.[128]

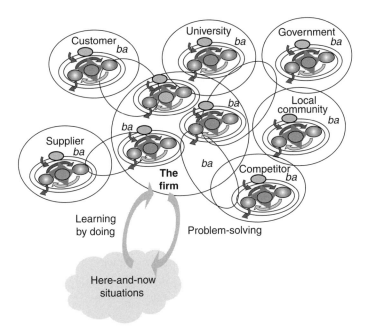

FIGURE 6.6 Expanding multilayered *ba*, focusing on situated problems
Source: Nonaka *et al.* 2008, p. 41; originally published by Palgrave
Macmillan, with modification

Yet knowledge is not a 'thing' to create and keep; it is our ability to act in changing circumstances. Knowledge emerges and produces effects in concrete, situated, specific actions. In this sense,
ba is a process of indwelling in here-and-now situations where
participants share here-and-now concerns, exchange here-and-now
insights, define and solve here-and-now problems.[129] As *ba* expands,
it demands coordination.[130] *Ba*-based management must then nurture a compelling focus for plural *ba* to connect and converge, to balance diversity and coherence, creativity and efficiency. In a world of
limited resources and pressing problems, expanding *ba* with a sharp
focus is not a luxury (see Figure 6.6).

Mayekawa Manufacturing Co. Ltd shows us how to achieve
excellence via balanced *ba*-centred management. Ranked second
in the global industrial refrigeration market, Mayekawa not only
sells refrigerators and compressors, but also designs, installs and

maintains production lines and utilities; it even reaches out to energy consulting business. At the same time, the company focuses sharply on the concept of 'total heat engineering', supplying customers with complete thermal-technology solutions.

To realise its vision of *kyousou* (共創, joint creation, co-creation), Mayekawa innovated a project-based *doppo* organisation, which is a network of small, independent companies. Short for *dokuritsu houjin* (独立法人), *doppo* literally means 'independent legal entity'. Each *doppo* employs from 10 to 15 people and serves a particular market or region. Mayekawa has about 80 *doppos* in Japan and 40 overseas. *Doppos* are autonomous but not isolated from each other. Some share the same office space, while members of different *doppos* spend time together in informal gatherings. Often, several *doppos* work together to form a block to share information and technologies, to supplement each other's projects that are too large for any single *doppo*. Cooperation also takes place between blocks that draw on each other's resources. Small *doppos* are also convenient for members to go out into the field, get close to customers, experience markets. They are well placed to transform technology change and customer needs into new, entrepreneurial businesses (see Figure 6.7). A manager explained:

> Often, customers themselves don't know what they want. Even though they can't articulate it, they are saying something, like they want to change something, cut the cost more, or have better quality. At the beginning, we don't know what to do because we can't understand them. Only after we talk with them many times or dwell in and around their shop floor do we come to understand them.[131]

The company's bread factory *kaizen* project in cooperation with Takaki Bakery is a vivid example of value co-creation. A long-time customer of Mayekawa, Takaki makes European-style bread in Japan. When asked by Takaki to upgrade its bakery system, Mayekawa realised it was no longer enough merely to sell and install equipment; customer needs in the food-processing sector had become

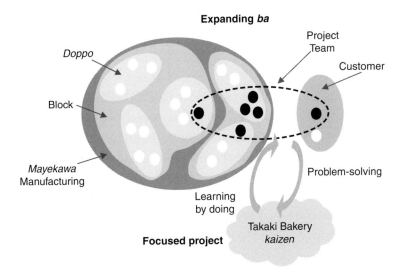

FIGURE 6.7 Mayekawa's 'Total heat solution': an expansion–focus view
Source: Nonaka *et al.* 2008, p. 111; originally published by Palgrave Macmillan, with modification

more complex, requiring novel solutions. To create unique value for Takaki, Mayekawa dispatched its food-product-block engineers to the client's factory, to immerse themselves in the bread-making process.

At the outset, the focus of the project was to improve Takaki's wholesale factory, which produced large volumes of bread for mass-market retailers such as supermarkets and convenience-store chains. Once they were on the ground, block members recognised that *kaizen* improvements wouldn't be enough to match new market trends; they would have to address the root cause of the inefficiencies inhibiting Takaki's long-term competitive advantage. Japanese consumers increasingly valued 'freshness' and 'variety'. Bakers needed to pursue low-volume production and frequent deliveries. This insight led to a fundamental review of Takaki's entire wholesale business. Mayekawa block members engaged Takaki managers in asking the following questions:

- What are the existing and future characteristics of the market?
- Which market is Takaki targeting?

- What kind of relationship does Takaki want to build with consumers?
- What is unique about Takaki?
- What does Takaki value?
- What is Takaki's culture and history?

Through discussions, it became clear that Takaki's problem lay in the discrepancy between its wholesale model that mass-produced American-style bread and its vision of offering high-quality, European-style bread to demanding Japanese consumers. Improvements on the production lines could not overcome this problem. Instead, the company needed to rethink its roles and processes from the viewpoint of retail customers. A new strategic direction gradually took shape: Takaki's business should be redesigned so that it could respond flexibly to fast-moving consumer demands. In the end, the solution was to produce dough in bulk in the Takaki factory and ship it to retail stores to bake, on the spot, a variety of fresh bread.

During the project, Mayekawa established a joint *ba* with Takaki the client so as to co-create knowledge and value. This *ba* expanded to cover not just Mayekawa *doppos* and Takaki departments and factories, but also the customer's customers, up to and including the final consumer. Focusing on *kyousou*, Mayekawa *doppos* were able to draw upon the customers' knowledge to improve production, distribution, technology and consumption. Expanding *ba* allowed Mayekawa *doppos* to see the world through the customers' eyes, focusing on total solution through a new business model that would enable Takaki to satisfy consumers' changing demands. Expansion and focus once again acted as mutually supportive companions, instead of antagonistic extremes.

Toyota recall: the cost of losing balance

For decades, a 'culture of contradictions' was praised as the 'soft innovation' behind Toyota's success. It was showcased in hundreds of books, articles and case studies. The company succeeded, so the story goes, because it deliberately 'created and resolved contradictions'. Toyota was, for example, said to have successfully unleashed 'forces of expansion' and 'forces of integration'. On the one hand, forces of expansion drove the company to experiment and change, resulting in winning strategies. These included: meeting every customer's needs and providing a full line of vehicles in every market, increasing operational complexity and developing new supply chains, standardising auto parts to minimise costs while replacing 'Made in Japan' with 'Made by Toyota' globally. Forces of integration, on the other hand, helped the company to stabilise transformation, preserve value and identity and maintain a unique communication system that allowed the company, with 50 manufacturing facilities outside Japan and selling vehicles in more than 170 countries, to 'function like a small-town company'. Toyota was managed by a handful of Japanese executives at its Japan headquarters in such a way that 'everybody knows everybody else's business'. The implication was provocative: copying any one of these practices would be missing the point; to learn from Toyota, you must masterfully create contradictions and then resolve them. Backed up by Toyota's enviable achievements, particularly when Toyota surpassed General Motors in 2008 to become the world's largest car-maker, the 'culture of contradictions' narrative was, understandably, accepted as one of few enduring truths in an otherwise murky world.

No more. Today, that truth looks neither enduring nor certain. Since November 2009, Toyota has recalled almost 20 million vehicles, including the upmarket Lexus and the flagship Prius hybrid.[132] The massive recall was caused by the accusation that defects in Toyota vehicles were responsible for at least 19 deaths and hundreds of injuries in the US alone.[133] Suspected defects included faulty floor mats, accelerator pedals, braking systems, steering systems and fuel-injection systems.[134] Toyota had to suspend the delivery of thousands of new cars and cut production of affected models.[135] After weeks of silence, Akio Toyoda, president of Toyota Motor Corporation since June 2009 and a grandson of the firm's founder, reluctantly testified to the US Congress and travelled from Brussels to Beijing to offer apologies.[136] In April 2010, the company paid a record $16.4 million to the US government for delaying notification of alleged cases, with a raft of lawsuits still pending.[137] Toyota's market share dropped from 16.4 to 14.8 per cent in the US, from 5.0 to 4.4 in Europe and from 15.2 to 15.0 in Asia.[138] In Britain, Toyota was the fourth-biggest-selling marque in 2009; it slipped to eighth in 2010.[139] Within a month of the first wave of recalls, the company lost more than a fifth of its market value.[140] The value of the Toyota brand had dropped 27 per cent.[141] The decades-long, almost uninterrupted Toyota global growth appeared ready to come to an end.[142]

'Toyota's reputation for peerless quality – its greatest asset – has been lost.'[143] This could be fatal for Toyota: 'People don't buy Toyotas for sexy design or great performance. They are looking for a car that won't let them down. If that reliability is undermined, it takes away one of the main reasons for purchasing a Toyota.'[144] The crisis is regarded as the 'worst-handled auto recall in history'.[145] 'Until very recently, Toyota was the peerless exemplar. For now, at least, it is seen as an awful warning.'[146] 'Toyota must change', an insider said. 'If it doesn't change now, it could become another GM.'[147]

The Toyota recall can be read in many ways. Some look at Toyota's inexperience in crisis management, others blame the US media for exaggerating the quality problem. Still others favour a conspiracy theory: Toyota was a victim rather than the villain – when Toyota was down, GM was up.[148] We choose the 'culture of contradictions' as our point of departure, and investigate how the loss of timely balance drove Toyota into crisis (see Figure 6.8).

Let us begin with Toyota managers' own reflections. In his testimony to Congress, Toyoda acknowledged that Toyota had got the balance wrong. In pursuing growth and profit, the company stretched its lean philosophy to breaking point and became 'confused' about the values that had made it great: the focus on 'putting customer satisfaction first' and the ability to 'stop, think and make improvement'.[149] The misguided strategy warped what he called the 'order of Toyota's traditional priorities' – product safety and quality over sales volume and cost. That order of priorities changed when Toyota

FIGURE 6.8 Toyota's success and setback: an expansion–focus view

started its rapid expansion a decade ago, when increasing market share and cost-cutting became an obsession.[150] 'There was a period when we became too profit oriented'; 'We expanded too fast and did not put the customer first'; '[Our expansion in recent years] attracted much praise from outside the company, and some people just got too big-headed and focused too excessively on profit'. 'Our biggest failing as a company has been a cooling of our passion to make excellent cars', Toyoda said.[151] A top Toyota executive in the US believed 'the root cause of [the] problems is that the company was hijacked, some years ago, by anti-family, financially oriented pirates' who 'didn't have the character to maintain a customer-first focus' but 'sacrificed quality for faster growth and fatter margins'.[152]

Industry observers largely agreed. James Womack, lead author of *The Machine That Changed the World*, dated the origin of the crisis to 2002, when Toyota set a goal of raising its global market share from 11 to 15 per cent, the so-called '2010 Vision'. For that 'vision', the company's production must grow by 600,000 vehicles each year, more than the annual overall volume of Volvo.[153] 'It chased volume at almost any price',[154] while the breakneck expansion was 'totally irrelevant to any customer',[155] Womack said. On the cost-cutting front, to deliver record earnings, *kaizen* (改善) was no longer adequate, a *kakushin* (革新), or revolution, was needed. Hence the CCC21 programme (Construction of Cost Competitiveness for the Twenty-First Century) was launched to reduce the number of car components by half and slash costs by 30 per cent. The ultimate aim of CCC21 was to cut at least $8.5 billion in costs – the equivalent of about $1,000 a vehicle – by 2010, and to keep slashing costs at a similar rate thereafter.[156]

While the disaster was exacerbated by the company's PR incompetence, at its core was bad engineering. Toyota had had many opportunities to sense the coming safety crisis over the years. The company began recalling its T100 pick-up, due to steering-rod problems, in Japan in 2004, and extended the recall to the US in 2005, not long after it set the ambitious '15 per cent' target.[157] In 2006, the Japanese government publicly ordered Toyota to improve quality, after dozens of accidents in which its Hilux Surf cars developed locked steering.[158] The *Wall Street Journal*, among others, delivered a clear warning in 2006:

> Toyota also is coping unevenly with its global expansion. Analysts say its rapid growth is one cause of mushrooming quality-control problems that began a few years ago. Last year in the US, Toyota recalled 2.38 million vehicles, more than the 2.26 million it sold – a sign that indicates Toyota is troubled not only by manufacturing problems but also by design flaws.[159]

In July that year, Toyota's then president Katsuaki Watanabe bowed in public apology and promised to fix things with a 'customer-first' programme.[160] However, once the balance was lost, the trend was difficult to reverse. *The Economist* observed:

> By the middle of the decade recalls of Toyota vehicles were increasing at a sufficiently alarming rate for Mr Toyoda's predecessor, Katsuaki Watanabe, to demand a renewed emphasis on quality control. But nothing was allowed to get in the way of another (albeit undeclared) goal: overtaking General Motors to become the world's biggest carmaker. Even as Toyota swept past GM in 2008, the quality problems and recalls were mounting.[161]

By that time, Toyota's quality problem was for all to see. In a 2007 *Harvard Business Review* interview, Watanabe was pressed repeatedly by the editors on the company's expansion–quality imbalance.

Introducing the interview, the editors wrote: 'In fact, almost every aspect of Toyota is straining to keep pace with the company's rapid expansion ... Toyota's future will depend on its ability to strike the right balance.'[162] The editors posed questions again and again to the Toyota boss: given that the company has recalled more vehicles than ever before, is Toyota poised for long-term growth, or does the company face a crisis? How do you manage the tensions that growth and globalisation have created? Don't you have to fix things as you go along? As you expand faster around the globe, how does Toyota address that risk in strategic terms? Will your long-term strategy to have a full line of products competing in all regions maintain stability? How will Toyota balance demand for its products with the long-term need for human resources? And on and on ...

The questions were explicit, direct and critical; today they appear all the more accurate and pinpointing. In response, the Toyota boss admitted: 'our system may be overstretched', 'we confronted several quality-related problems.' Nevertheless, he insisted: 'The priority of Toyota's top management team is to increase shareholder value steadily over the long term'; 'In Japan we must continue to maintain our market share ... In North America we recently entered the full size pickup truck segment ... In Europe we will expand and strengthen the lineup ... so we will increase our production capacity overseas.' When quality and human resources were mentioned, they were framed in terms of growth, expansion and profit.[163] In philosophy, as in practice, Toyota was losing its way, its value, its purpose, becoming just another mighty car-maker. Who are you? What do you stand for? How could you possibly claim 'putting quality first' when you recalled more vehicles than you sold?

Why did the 'culture of contradictions' not help? Once the balance was lost, that 'culture' turned against the company, in every aspect. The more 'contradictions' you created, the deeper the crisis became.

- To meet the expansion target of satisfying every customer need and providing a full line of vehicles in all the world's markets, Toyota had let its standards slip. Ralph Nader, the consumer advocate, who came to prominence with his 1960s book *Unsafe at Any Speed*, commented: 'They [Toyota] expanded too fast and lost control of their quality control.'[164] Akio Toyoda would fully agree.

- Simplifying and standardising car parts across models had cut Toyota production costs. Yet when there was a defect, it spread to all models and you had to recall an enormous number of cars. The single suspect throttle pedal, for example, affected a dozen Toyota models from the cheapest Aygo and Yaris to Auris, Verso, Avensis, iQ and Corolla to the large Camry, Avalon and RAV4, models produced, sold and then recalled around the world.[165]

- The provincial style of 'a Japanese small-town company' became a damaging 'extreme' not fit for purpose. 'Toyota's expansion across six continents was not matched by a change in management culture.'[166] That culture made Toyota reluctant to yield decision-making to 'outsiders' who were closer to customers. When overseas managers tried to warn the company about safety issues, their concerns were passed on to Toyota City too slowly, and sometimes not at all.[167]

- Toyota's 'unique communication system', too, became a liability. Managers outside headquarters did not know whether or how they should respond to customer concerns. At the congressional hearing, Toyoda apologised for Toyota having 'caused worry for so many people', rather than for building shoddy cars. The problem was framed as drivers' 'feelings' rather than poor engineering. 'Toyota has gone from a family friend to a stranger.'[168] A Toyota executive admitted: 'Communication was a major point that needed improving.'[169]

Amid the crisis, president Akio Toyoda promised a fresh start, a rebalance. 'I want to lead the company in such a way that this sort of thing never happens again.'[170] He is trying to return the company to the values he feels it lost in the relentless expansion, values such as putting the customer first and *genchi genbutsu*. To realise those values, Toyota has put in place various measures:

- setting up a special committee to oversee all operations from R&D to customer service;
- appointing quality officers for each region;
- assigning about 1,000 employees to new quality-related tasks;

- sending 40 engineers from the headquarters to monitor quality at overseas technical centres;
- extending training at the sprawling global operations;
- establishing procedures for quick responses to reported quality problems;
- adding a month to the average four-month testing time for new vehicles;
- promoting non-Japanese managers to run overseas operations;
- reducing the 27 board members to 11 and the number of executives by nearly a quarter;
- seeking foreign as well as female board members;
- creating a new 'regional advisory committee' of foreign academics and experts.[171]

Balancing expansion–focus is an ongoing, delicate challenge for every company. History has shown that Toyota has a remarkable ability to get it right. We have good reason to expect Toyota to get it right again. The unprecedented recall is a valuable lesson for us all. We are all fallible beings; those who learn quickly and honestly from mistakes will prosper.

Together, *wuli–shili–renli* and timely balance represent the Confucian wisdom on 'what to do, how to do it?' To translate this wisdom into fitting conduct, we need pragmatic skill sets. For this, we turn to the next chapter.

7 Orchestrating WSR, orchestrating the firm

Exploring 'what to do, how to do it?' in the last two chapters, we introduced *wuli–shili–renli*, a relational bottom line and timely balance a process mode for doing strategy. In this chapter, we invite readers to look at supporting skill sets which link managers' jobs with firms' existential purposes on the one hand and environmental complexity, ambiguity, uncertainty on the other. This is intended to help managers translate enduring Confucian wisdom into situated conducts. As to researchers, this chapter is directly related to fundamental questions in strategy, such as: what are firms, why are there firms, what are firms for, how do firms differ, how to run firms? Again, we draw from real-world business cases: Nintendo, Google, HP, IBM, Microsoft, Philips, YKK, Rolls-Royce, Huawei, Alibaba, Edison, Honda and more. Let us begin with managerial skill sets that are useful for creating and capturing value in the fuzzy, fast-moving business world.

SENSE IT, SEIZE IT, REALISE IT

Timely balanced strategies demand a broad set of entrepreneurial-managerial skills. For this, we found David Teece's sensing–seizing–reconfiguring explication on dynamic capability useful.[1] In many ways, the Teece framework is highly compatible with Ikujiro Nonaka's 'abilities of *phronesis*'.[2] In the context and terminology of Confucian pragmatism, with a particular focus on timely balancing *wuli–shili–renli* we interpret the pragmatic skill sets as 'sense it, seize it, realise it' (Figure 7.1).

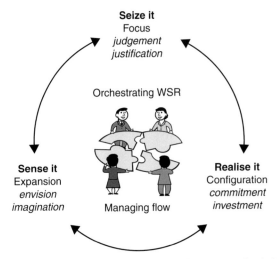

FIGURE 7.1 Skill sets useful for timely balancing *wuli–shili–renli*

Sense it

To begin with, entrepreneur-managers need to nurture skills useful for sensing opportunities. Sensing involves alertness-discovery and imagination-envisioning. Presenting the creative spirit of Confucian pragmatism, in Chapter 2 we distinguish opportunity-discovery vs opportunity-creation. In the long run, *creating* new markets which otherwise would not exist is critical for firms to gain competitive advantages. That said, the ability to *discover* untapped demands ignored by competitors, too, allows firms to exploit profitable opportunities. When managers step back from their daily jobs and reflect on past experiences, the difference between discovering and creating is significant. When making decisions on the spot, amid emergence and confusion, however, the difference becomes blurred. In cases of both discovering and creating, what you need to do is scan, search, explore, imagine, examine and interpret. When Nintendo initiated the Wii project, when Shigeru Miyamoto and his teammates asked the 'moms' what they wanted and turned millions of non-gamers into eager customers, were they *discovering* or *creating* a market? It matters little to the consumer or to the firm. What made the real difference was

Miyamoto's expertise in sensing an opportunity, to design and sell products that customers would love and rivals couldn't touch.

Sensing opportunities involves getting fundamentals right: what potential customers appreciate, what technology will do the job, how our offering differs from those currently in the market, for instance. In the Wii case, the fundamentals are: moms hate violent fantasies; they want collective exercises for their kids; machines must be quick to set up, easy to use and fun to play; technology must enable wireless control via actual body movements not finger manipulations; and so on.

It is here that analytic models have a useful role to play: PLEST, five-forces, experience curve, scenario-building, market segmentation, product–market matrix and an array of market research tools. What counts is the experience and skills of sensing, not the tools themselves. Nintendo's Miyamoto talked to mothers about their kids, not showing them product–market matrices, and Yamaha's Genichi Kawakami envisioned a market for electronic pianos not by accepting but by overriding market research 'findings'.

Beyond scanning and surveying, at the core of sensing is, of course, sense-making, which is about interpretation, imagination, generating meaning, challenging what is taken for granted and expanding what is believed possible. Here, managers' mental models, cognitive styles and ability to think outside the box make the critical difference. While other players busy themselves with upgrading smartphones to accommodate the Internet, Google sees its Android-powered mobile device as 'a small computer that happens to make phone calls'. Android handsets now out-sell Nokia, BlackBerry and Apple's iPhone, with 200,000 new users registered every day.[3] This happens everywhere: Tesco, the UK-based supermarket, sees itself no longer as a jumbo grocery but as a one-stop shopping enterprise, becoming an industry leader by capturing opportunities in clothing and flowers, magazines and DVDs, DIY and electronic goods, insurance and banking, estate agency and mobile phone service. The company diversifies beyond groceries and succeeds because it creates unique value for busy customers.[4] How about automobiles? A car is, after all, a car. Can you see it differently? Well, to BYD (Build Your Dream), the Chinese auto-maker specialising in electric autos, a car is a battery that happens to have four wheels. The founder-CEO, Wang Chuanfu, comfortably drinks, in front of visitors, a glass of the non-toxic, 100-per-cent recyclable electrolyte solution that powers BYD autos. Investors like it and the company has had financial backing from Warren Buffett since 2008.[5]

Due to 'bounded rationality',[6] sensing is usually filtered: what we do not believe, we cannot see, and we tend to interpret what we see in terms of what we already know, which directs us back to red oceans. This is why entrepreneurial opportunities, or blue oceans, which are by definition unconventional, uncertain and unknown, are so difficult to detect and discover, let alone to create. To overcome this difficulty, Nonaka introduces, beside a processual knowledge-creation framework, useful techniques and tools such as metaphors, analogy, brainstorming camps and Zen-enlightening experience.[7]

Seize it

If sensing is about expanding the opportunity horizon, seizing is searching for a focus. Which opportunity should we create or exploit? Why is this one particularly suitable for us? What should the firm choose? What can we do better than other players? As Sumantra Ghoshal posited, to get done things that matter, managers need to focus their efforts and resources. *You wei* (有为, do certain things – things creating value and particularly suitable to you), *you buwei* (有不为, not all things). The most dangerous hazard in strategy is busyness without focus: unable to make hard decisions, unable to let go, attending to each and every conceivable 'opportunity' that appears promising; all demand resources and, in the end, all fail to deliver.[8]

Lessons can be learned from Carly Fiorina's experience at HP, one of America's 20 largest public corporations. Taking on the top job at HP, 'Fiorina wanted to be a leader in all areas of technology'. She pursued 'opportunities' in every sector, hoping to rival Dell in personal computers, IBM in corporate services, Canon in digital cameras and Xerox in copiers. To achieve this, HP needed to be big; to be big, Fiorina reckoned, it needed to buy Compaq. After a highly public, bloody boardroom drama that alienated far too many people, Fiorina got her way, just. Two years after the takeover, however, HP lost its No. 1 position in PCs and saw its market value plunge and several attempts to spin off the profitable printer division. In the end, the HP board demanded Fiorina's resignation. On her departure, shares of the company rose nearly 10 per cent – a verdict on the all-expansion-no-focus strategy. Failing to seize opportunities through which the company could really generate value, Fiorina left HP to 'count the cost of playing the other guy's game', which was not strategy, but busy non-action.[9] As Kenneth Andrews of Harvard Business School posited, whether an opportunity is attractive depends on the firm's unique resources.[10] According to Paul Cook, founder and CEO of Raychem: 'the essence of innovation is discovering what your organisation is uniquely good at'; 'every company has unique strengths. Success comes from leveraging those strengths in the market.'[11]

At the heart of seizing is judgement and justification, or what Teece calls 'informed guesses': which opportunities, why?[12] It involves the cognitive and the political, hard business logic and vested interests. Make no mistake: 'the market' makes no *ex ante* judgement, we managers do. In economics and business, as in other spheres of human life, what is efficient in the short term may not always coincide with what is efficient in the long run. While markets, via price, allow short-term-oriented 'autonomous adaptation' and 'static efficiency', firms are created to achieve 'purposive adaptation' and 'dynamic efficiency' in the long run.[13] The merit of firms over markets lies in 'organisational advantage': cognitive routines, shared values, collective purpose, tacit knowledge, cross-functional *ba* and dynamic capabilities. These help firms reduce the costs of judgement and justification, to seize opportunities inaccessible to the market and opportunities with great value-creating potential that demand long-term investment in complementary assets. Based on the pioneering works of Chester Barnard and Sumantra Ghoshal, Alfred Chandler and Edith Penrose, James March and Herbert Simon, David Teece and Sidney Winter, William Lazonick and Nicolai Foss, we call this 'justification efficiency' of the firm.

There is a downside, however. For one thing, while organisational routines can speed up search activity and problem-solving, they tend to induce groupthink, framing bias, organisational inertia and competence rigidity. They define problems in conventional terms and divert managers' attention away from radical innovations. Recall Polaroid. While digital-image technology in the 1990s opened up many possibilities, the company seized a wrong one, sticking to the razor/blade model. The model, deeply embedded in the firm's routines and systems due to past success, eventually bankrupted Polaroid.

For another, firms are peopled and people have interests. Diverging interests exist in firms, as in markets. In markets, differing interests go their own ways, compete on a level ground and are selected by evolutionary forces that are, at least in theory, objective and fair. In firms, however, differing interests coexist for a much longer time and in a smaller space, competing for limited resources. As a result, power and politics play a more direct, decisive role inside firms in determining which opportunities to seize or abandon.[14] Martin Fransman's study on the 'IBM paradox' is telling. In the contests between the conflicting interests of different divisions inside IBM, the mainframe division usually triumphed. This should not be surprising since many IBM leaders cut their teeth on the tremendous success of Systems 360 and 370. The hegemony of the mainframe division became reactionary, however. Despite data illustrating the obvious, immediate and overwhelming potential of smaller machines, and regardless of its own technology advantage, IBM continued to starve its PC division. It failed to capture due market share, never recovering from this disastrous strategic choice.[15] Teece stresses the difficulties involved in seizing, referring to 'risk aversion', 'excessive optimism', 'bias, delusion, deception and hubris'.[16]

Drawing upon experiences in the cochlear implant and computer software industries, Raghu Garud and colleagues propose a range of social-political-institutional skills, which we consider useful for seizing opportunities. The skills begin with the following:

Problematising: due to inherent ambiguity and uncertainty, the real function and benefit of opportunities are at best 'guessed' in the present. Entrepreneur-managers therefore need to unseat prevailing understanding and uproot inertia, so that 'real' opportunities can be examined and judged in new lights.

Enrolling: to gain support and acceptance for intended focuses, entrepreneur-managers need to mobilise cooperation by taking stakeholders' interests into account, providing them with creditable incentives, psychological ownership, shared meaning and genuine passion.

Institutionalising: this is to ensure that the settled focus can eventually deliver, granting it legitimacy, giving it regulative might and supplying it with necessary resources.

Bricolage: doing all this by inventively deploying the available means at hand so as to reach an agreed focus.[17] Deng Xiaoping, Muhammad Yunus and Liu Chuanzhi are masters of these skills, which enabled them to seize valued opportunities.

Realise it

In 2000, Bill Gates of Microsoft addressed the Consumer Electronic Show in Las Vegas, holding in his hand a new class of computer: the 'tablet'. This new device, claimed Gates, would revolutionise the industry. At the same event in 2010, Microsoft CEO, Steve Ballmer, similarly predicted a world filled with 'slate' machines running on Windows. What happened on the ground during those ten years? It was Apple that made Gates' decade-old vision a reality; between its April launch and the end of 2010, 7.5 million iPads were sold. Microsoft may eventually put its 'slate' into the market (at the time of our writing we are still waiting), but Apple has already released the iPad2 in March 2011, with about 80 competing tablets coming from other players.[18] Microsoft sensed and even seized the opportunity – it was Gates who showcased the world's first tablet prototype. However, despite its financial and technological might, Microsoft failed to make it. This highlights the tremendous strategic importance and challenge of 'realising it'.

According to Teece, the key to realise it is to configure a smart value chain and a competitive business model.[19] While the value-chain concept is useful for analysing the series of value-adding activities that transform raw materials into a specific market offering to final consumers, a business model is a conceptual device that works out, along the value chain, which activities a firm should engage in and how. Supported by value-chain analysis, a business model is a firm's technological, financial and organisational 'architecture'. Business models focus commitment and investment along several dimensions: *market offerings* – products, services, investments; *financial sources* – capital, dept levels, cash flow; *organisational structure* – administrative-operational systems and procedures, including composition and development of the workforce as well as relationships with other firms and stakeholders.

Getting the value chain and business model right are critical to strategic success. Over the years, numerous associated findings, ideas, techniques and tools have been generated based on managers' innovative practices: from scale and scope to enterprise boundary, from value chain to value web, from profit pool to open network, from buy-or-make to value co-creation, from portfolios of products and investments to portfolios of resources and relationships, from managing idiosyncratic resources to renewing complementary capabilities, from handling technical fundamentals to coping with cognitive and incentive challenges; the list goes on. A pragmatic turn is not to abandon or displace this valuable pool of intellectual resources, but to shed new light on how to enrich and use it more creatively, effectively, wisely.

Just consider: should we *buy* from the market, *make* in-house or *co-create* with business partners and customers? There is no one-size-fits-all recipe, which is due to differences in technology requisites, industrial structures, firms' histories, resources, vision and purpose, as well as timing and luck. In light of pragmatism, we found hugely different business models that had enabled firms to create and capture value, which can be taken as useful food for thought when embarking on our own journey:

- In 2006, the Dutch group Philips sold off its volatile semiconductor business, ending its long stretch as a vertically integrated electronics company. Within three months, the company's share was up more than 30 per cent. Who says only big can be beautiful? Less is more; getting the business model right, like Philips, you can do it. Philips' strategy was to get away from battles with Sony, Apple and the like over electronic gadgets, and to reposition itself as a consumer brand that focused on medical, lifestyle and lighting products. With new market offerings you configure new value chains. 'We had overstretched ourselves in the late 1990s', said Gerard Kleisterlee, the then Philips CEO. 'The rules of the game were changing, and the days of vertical integration were over.'[20]

- To some, even the days of 'buy or make' are over. Given globally dispersed resources and the increasing pressure for rapid innovation, more and more companies are adopting 'open innovation', 'open business' and 'open network' practices, acting upon concepts such as 'asset complementary', 'co-specialisation', 'dynamic specialisation' and 'performance fabric'.[21] Renault-Nissan and Daimler 'tie up' to develop smaller, cleaner engines;[22] Google engineers work alongside peers at HTC, Motorola and Samsung on Android-based smartphones.[23] Today, 60 per cent of Procter & Gamble's new products involve at least one outside research partner: other large corporations, government research labs, small and medium-sized firms, even individual entrepreneurs.[24] The 'enterprise-centric' mindset, which underlies the resource-based view of strategy, needs to be updated.[25]

- No so for YKK, the world's leading fastener producer. It is exactly for serving customers with high quality and speedy delivery via relentless innovation and improvement that YKK chooses to develop its technological capabilities exclusively in-house. 'If we are to provide the best product with confidence, we can't leave any part of the process up to any other company', said Tadao Yoshida, the founder. 'We should do it all by ourselves.'[26] Ironically, it is precisely the comprehensive capability accumulated from daily operations throughout the value chain that enables YKK to achieve global success: 118 subsidiaries in 70 countries, a more than 45 per cent global market share, healthy finance and a client base close to 100,000 that includes top brands Louis Vuitton, Ferragamo and Levi Strauss. The firm achieves goals similar to those of Li & Fung, but with a dramatically different business model. YKK's core strength lies in its integrated, in-house technology competence. YKK is not alone. Paul Cook of Raychem puts it this way:

> Companies need a single-minded commitment to their core technologies, a commitment to knowing more about them than anyone else in the world. No partnership or joint venture can substitute for technology leadership.[27]

- Kenneth Andrews' seemingly naive question 'what business are we in?' is a good starting point for (re-)configuring your business model. How you see your business determines how your value chain and business model look like. If Rolls-Royce saw itself as an engine-maker, its business model would end at the product delivery function – putting the engine in the buyer's hands. As the company now considers itself in the business of supplying the power to fly aircraft, it deliberately blurs the line between making engines and offering services. Today, engineers working on computers in the company's operations room in Derby, in the English Midlands, monitor Rolls-Royce engines around the world, in the sky as well as on the ground. They feed real-time analysis to client airlines, and charge a fee for every hour a Rolls-Royce engine runs. 'Make it, sell it, service it' is the new rule of the game, which makes it more difficult for competitors to break in.[28] Rolls-Royce has a complex manufacturing-servicing business model.
- So does Huawei. In merely 20 years, the firm has come from nothing to be the world's second-biggest telecom equipment supplier, serving clients like Vodafone, Telefónica, T-Mobile and BT. This Chinese company has moved deep down the value chain. After a brief period distributing imported PBX, Huawei started to produce its own equipment, supplying low-cost products to telephony network operators. Huawei quickly moved beyond merely selling *products* to improving *processes* that clients could not manage on their own. Huawei then went further, enhancing clients' *performance* with tailored, comprehensive solutions.

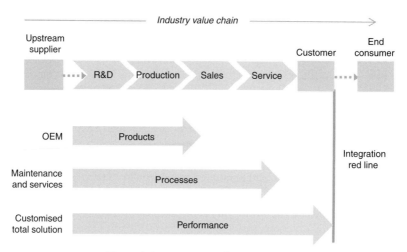

FIGURE 7.2 Huawei: integration with a purpose

As a result, Huawei captures more value from maintenance, upgrading and end-of-life service than merely selling equipment. The company is now a formidable player not merely on low cost, but primarily on innovation and customer service, listed by *BusinessWeek* among 'The World's Most Influential Companies' and ranked by *Fast Company* as the fifth most innovative company in the world.[29] Huawei's 'forward integration' stops only at its self-imposed red line: as a technology leader, the company rules itself out of network operations (Figure 7.2).[30] So far, so unremarkable: Rolls-Royce and the like have already done this.

What is unique about Huawei is 'value co-creation' with customers. While integrating itself 'forward and down', Huawei invites clients to move 'backward and up', involving them in every step of equipment design, software development, network upgrading and project implementation. To achieve this, Huawei supplies clients with a wide range of incentives, from free-of-charge upgrading of whole systems, long-term stationing of Huawei engineers on client sites, to the company's share options for clients. With tremendous commitment and investment, Huawei engages clients at every stage and level of the value-creating process. Through this process, Huawei the vendor gains better understanding of clients' business drivers and supplies them with tailored, complete solutions, while clients gain more value from Huawei's dedicated, specialised, customised services. Both the vendor and the client benefit from the full value of their relationships, 'co-

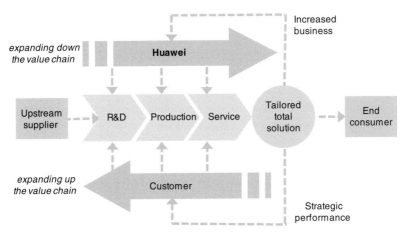

FIGURE 7.3 Huawei's business model: growing into each other with clients

opt' each other's competence, deepen co-specialisation, shape the market together, create value together, prosper together.[31] They 'grow into each other' – an example of *kyosei* (共生) (Figure 7.3). Where customers are few but powerful, as in the telecom sector, value co-creation is a powerful way to increase customer switching costs, lock in clients and raise the barrier to entrance.

- To capture value and achieve profitability, a key component in any business model is the generation of income. Again, here, we observe a huge variety of innovative configurations. Just take the online business sector as an example. Google and Facebook generate income mainly from corporate customer ads; Amazon charges customers for physical goods as well as digital downloads; eBay charges a commission on every transaction conducted on its virtual marketplace; Alibaba allows customers to use its e-commerce site for free while generating revenue from elite membership packages and other value-added services; Shanda, the online game operator, bills gamers based on the minutes they stay on the games. As for Tencent, the all-things-to-all-people-as-long-as-they're-online company, customers use its services for free, apart from those who play Tencent games. In fact, Tencent games are still free, gamers only pay an RMB 10-cent price for each weapon that boys use in cyber warfare and each cloth girls choose to cover their pets. Gamers can choose not to purchase special weapons or clothes, and hence pay nothing. Otherwise, they can pay in the 'currency' issued by the Tencent Bank instead of the official RMB. Which method suits you? What business are you in? What is your offering? Where does your revenue come from? Why should the customer pay you? How would you like them to pay you? Do they agree? Are they happy? Don't forget, in today's open, global, competitive marketplace, consumers can vote with their feet at the speed of light and they know it ... or so we are told.

CONFIGURE FOR THE LONG TERM

'Sense it, seize it, realise it' are the skill sets useful for creating and capturing value via timely balancing *wuli–shili–renli*. You can think of them as components or aspects of strategy formation. To act vigilantly, effectively and profitably, you have to do these things. It is unwise, however, to view them as sequential steps along a well-ordered procedure. We have discussed these skill sets one by one due to the unfortunate linear nature of human language. To compensate for this, in Figure 7.1 we link sensing–seizing–realising with double-arrowhead lines. As Teece posits: while 'the managerial skills needed to sense are quite different from those needed to seize and those needed to reconfigure', 'successful enterprises must build and utilise all three classes of capabilities and employ them, *often simultaneously*.'[32]

Of course, if managers find it helpful in particular situations to apply these skills or arrange their jobs in sequence, please do! Fitting with situated particulars is what pragmatism is about. Just remember, however: in a no-fixed-shape, no-definite-rule world, things usually surprise rational orders. Often, opportunities are seized and even made real well before you sense them. Remember Andrew Grove and Gordon Moore of Intel who 'went through' the 'revolving door' and came back with a new-found 'opportunity' to become a microprocessor company when the opportunity had, in effect, been creating value for years? Hence, rather than putting sensing–seizing–realising into a fixed order, we suggest that managers use those skills holistically, in flow, with ends in view, to achieve the following:

- *Generate a population of strategies.* While against spreading too thin, we should at the same time be mindful of the danger of putting all eggs in one basket. That Marconi, once Britain's largest manufacturer, almost bankrupted itself due to 'focusing', i.e. betting exclusively, on the telecom boom, is a stark warning. To avoid busy-non-action on the one hand and a-single-basket on the other, managers need to generate a population of justified focuses, or what Eric Beinhocker calls 'robust adaptive strategies' and Teece calls 'ecology of strategies'.[33] The aim is to increase a firm's 'adaptive efficiency'. While 'adaptive efficiency' is a phrase borrowed from evolutionary economics, the insight is apt for business. Lacking a God's-eye view and amid huge uncertainty, Nintendo kept its technology strategies open for several years when developing the Wii machine. The development team invented, adopted and tried several options in parallel, including technologies in cellphones, car navigation controls and the company's own touch-panel interface. 'We tested all kinds of technologies', Miyamoto told *BusinessWeek*.[34] In the end, MEMS played itself out, benefiting the firm and the consumer. Football club managers will tell you that their team always goes into the game with a 'population of strategies'. Nature, sport and business could all be thought of as 'complex adaptive systems'.
- *Exercise options.* With an emphasis on timely intervention, a population of strategies can also be seen as 'a portfolio of real options'.[35] In the financial world where the idea was originated, an option is a right, without obligation, to buy an asset within a certain time at a certain price. Options have value because they preserve opportunities to do something ('the right') while permitting flexibility to withdraw commitment ('no obligation'). In other areas, managers are faced with their own 'options': should our R&D go for this new big thing? Should I collaborate with this foreign partner for a joint venture? Should our firm diversify into this industry? All these choices have huge investment implications and, given inherent uncertainty, could end up as 'sunk costs'. By treating strategies as 'options', managers are induced to divide each investment into stages, periodically review progress and make timely decisions on scaling up, scaling down, further commitment or decisive abandonment. Based on stage outcomes, managers can also look for ways to influence the underlying variables so as to increase the value

of options at hand and potential outcomes. It is a process of 'selecting before being selected'.[36]

- *Set up selecting mechanisms.* Exercising 'real options' is just one of many internal mechanisms that firms can use to achieve 'evolution with design'[37] or what we call 'purposeful emergence'.[38] Remember: in Intel it was the internal rule of directing investment towards products that maximised margin-per-manufacturing-activity that changed the company's commitment, seized new markets and benefited from new technologies. At Intel, top managers made a decisive contribution not by cleverly spotting opportunities (at this, they failed), but by creating internal selection mechanisms and allowing them to work. The quintessence of the Confucian-Taoist *wuwei* (无为) is not doing nothing or no-intervention, but doing useful things and intervening wisely so as to allow beneficial outcomes to emerge 'naturally'. Informed by the WSR triple bottom line, managers can purposefully put in place targeting mechanisms, such as: R&D investment rules to cope with *wuli*; Zen sections, idea tournaments and prizes for fast-failure to handle *shili*; corporate governance, promotion and incentive systems to enhance *renli*. Ordinary managers believe their job is to get results; wise managers think their job is to design processes that generate results as a matter of course.[39]

- *Invest in diversity.* In order to select rather than being selected by environmental forces, firms must generate internal variation, or 'requisite variety'.[40] As 3M CEO George Buckley puts it: 'in a creative company, you want to give as much variability as possible.'[41] An effective means to achieve this is to invest in diversity. Based on studies on 'organisational rigidity', Dorothy Leonard-Barton posited that having multiple frameworks is probably the single most powerful attribute for new product development and organisational renewal.[42] While most multinationals invest heavily in demographic diversity in terms of sex, age and national origin, it is useful to note that what calls the shots is diversity in experiences, insights and mindscapes.[43] Recruiting two young computer science graduates, one from MIT in Boston and another from Tsinghua in Beijing, you get only limited diversity. Encourage a Harvard marketing professor and a Bangalore surgeon to work together, the outcome could be eye-opening. Encounters between heterogeneous *ba* make the difference.[44] Not surprisingly, since increasing diversity produces impacts on individual as well as divisional interests, investing

in diversity demands social-political-institutional skills. It is a
challenging job, but that's what managers are paid for.

These are not quick fixes but purposeful configurations for the
long term. Without glamour or catchy headlines, they are useful
for enriching a firm's resource pool so that managers can *bricoleur*
effectively – sense, seize, realise opportunities.

The Tao *of Alibaba*

In April 1995, on an unexpected visit to Seattle, Jack Ma was shown
the Internet. It was a new thing to business: David Filo and Jerry
Yang had just created the Yahoo! Directory in 1994. 'It was my first
time to touch a computer keyboard', Ma recalled. 'I used one finger
to type in the word "beer".' The screen showed Japanese, American,
German and African beer, but no Chinese beer. Ma tried a second
search using the words 'China' and 'beer'; still, 'no data'.[45] While
others might have given up in frustration, Ma became excited and
passionate. From his early experience in founding a translation service enterprise, Ma recognised two important qualities for business
success: 'one is a forward-looking personality that is fairly confident,
not to say courageous. The other is a keen sense of the market.'[46] Ma
determined to put these qualities to full use. He had a sense that the
Internet would change the world and he wanted to be part of it. He
envisioned a new business especially related to the Internet and to
things Chinese.

To seize the opportunity, Ma persuaded an American friend
to set up a homepage for his Hongzhou translation enterprise. The
page was childishly simple, with just an email address and a price-
list for translation services, but it was the first webpage that people
outside China had ever seen for a product from that country. 'At 9:30
we launched the home page, and by 12:30 I had six e-mails. I said,
"Whoa! Interesting!" If I could help Chinese companies promote
themselves on the Internet and help foreigners find their websites,
that might be a good thing.'[47]

In China, a full-function connection to the Internet was launched in 1994 in Beijing; however, there was no regular system for licensing Internet Service Providers (ISPs) until 1998. As an outsider, far from Beijing, Ma had no connections to anyone in Hangzhou who knew about the Internet. There was no path unless Ma beat one. To make his dream real, Ma wasted no time – he is a man 'biased to action'. 'Let's cooperate', Ma told his American friend. 'You'll be responsible for technology in America, and I'll go back to China, promote the service and pull in customers.'[48] Many years later, in MBA classes, professors refer to this as Ma's 'technological' and 'organisational' 'architectures'.

Back in China, Ma managed to collect a starting capital of $2,300 from his own savings and those of his parents and relatives. He called the new company 'Chinapage 中国黄页'. Ma planned to charge $2,380 (¥20,000) for an online page that contained a photo and text up to 3,000 words. Academics, of course years later, call this Ma's 'financial architecture'. Put the 'architectures' together and you have Ma's 'business model'.

Yet promoting the business in China proved a hard sell. Typically, people responded like this: 'Internet? What sort of nonsense? Yellow what?' In the end, Ma got his early clients 'close to hand' – students from his English class who ran businesses and were desperate to find customers. They knew little about e-commerce but had trust in Ma. The first assignment came from the four-star Lakeview Hotel. Ma recalls the exciting (some might say tortuous) experience thus:

> We came to the Lakeview Hotel and asked the staff for printed material of their business. We immediately sent that by courier to America, and the technical people there put it into the Web page ... After the American side finished work, they would courier it back to us in China. Before sending the material to America, we would have had it translated into English ... So we did all this and we took the hard-copy printout of the Web page to the Lakeview Hotel manager and told him his hotel was up

on the Internet. He didn't believe us. We said to him, 'This is an American telephone number on the Web page. You can ask your friends in America to call this number and find out if it's really there or not. If it isn't, come after me. If it is, then you have to pay the fee'.[49]

Shanghai just set up an Internet line with a dial-up number. Ma gathered all his clients in a room, made a long-distance call via a 486 computer, downloaded the Lakeview Hotel webpage from the American site to show that his online service was really working. When the photo of Lakeview finally appeared, Ma burst into tears while the clients cheered. It took three-and-a-half hours for that photo to appear; that was the technology available to Ma at that time.

But time was kind to Ma, too. Just as the Lakeview webpage went live, the United Nations Fourth World Conference on Women was held in Beijing. Many foreign delegates wanted to visit the beautiful city of Hangzhou, perhaps remembering Richard Nixon's praise 'Heaven is up there, Hangzhou is down here'. The only information available to the outside world about accommodation in Hangzhou came from that Lakeview webpage, so after the conference the visitors all came to stay at the Lakeview Hotel. Chinapage is generally recognised as China's first online directory and Internet-based company. By the end of 1997, operating income from the website reached $830,000 (¥7 million), unimaginable at that time.

Despite being computer illiterate, Ma made China's first Internet dream real. In later years, he often debated with Masayoshi Son, the legendary Japanese technology investor, the question 'is it better to have a third-rate idea with first-rate execution, or a first-rate idea with third-rate execution?' Both men agreed that getting jobs done was the key. They are *bricoleurs*. This does not mean they don't bother with strategy or shy away from focus and commitment. Rather, they are skilful in seizing opportunities as well as letting go. They know when to wait and when to strike. Bold in ideal while flexible in action, they are masters of purposeful opportunism. Perhaps most importantly, they never stop learning from experience; it is through experience, on the spot, in flow, that they sense local contexts, refine visions, improvise business models – what to do and how to do it, and fit all this with fast-moving, situated particulars.

Building on his Chinapage experience, Ma launched Alibaba.com in 1999; by 2004 it was considered the world's largest B2B e-commerce website. Then, Taobao was launched in 2003; by 2007, the C2C website had a market share of 83 per cent, leaving eBay, which entered China also in 2003, a 7 per cent share. Behind this breath-taking growth were Ma's profound philosophy, vision, business model and pragmatism.

By now, Ma's guiding mission had taken shape: 'Making it easy to do business anywhere.' He focused particularly on small and medium-sized businesses (SMEs). In his vision, 'Small and medium-sized enterprises are like grains of sand on a beach. The Internet can glue them together. It can make them into an invincible force that is able to go up against the big stones.'[50] To achieve this:

> We aim to create an e-commerce company, and in doing this
> we have three specific goals. First, we want to set up a company
> that lasts for one hundred and two years. Second, we want to
> establish a company that provides e-commerce services to
> China's small and medium-sized enterprises, one that will enter
> the ranks of the top ten names among global Internet sites.[51]

Based at Hangzhou, Zhejiang province, the hotbed of China's private enterprises, Ma had a tremendous advantage over fresh MBAs returning from abroad and working for foreign companies. He had a direct feel for the customers' circumstances. Among China's 42 million SMEs, fewer than one million have any Internet capability. Ma's vision was to create an 'Internet ecosystem' that would offer a full package of value-added services from credit checks and banking facilities to advertising and marketing, allowing SMEs to connect with the global marketplace and grow into global suppliers. For Alibaba, offering a full complement of simple, efficient Internet solutions to

42 million customers was an enormous opportunity. 'We're almost like a real estate developer', said Ma. 'We make sure the space is cleared, the pipes are laid and the utilities work. People can come in and put up their buildings on our site.'[52]

Ma's commitment to SMEs is driven by burning passion as well as cool calculation. 'If you divide enterprises into rich people and poor people, the Internet is a realm for poor people', Ma explained. 'The price of a Web page is basically the same. I want to enable poor people to use this tool to rise in a kind of revolution.'[53] While Marx was aiming to liberate workers of all lands, Ma's mission was to liberate SMEs from the domination of state-owned companies and multinationals. 'In an Internet-based world, we are entering a new business model, where small enterprises can, via the Internet, be independent. A greater diversity of products will be available to a broader range of customers. Humans are going to be organising themselves in wholly new ways; the revolutionary nature of the Internet lies in this structural change.' Or so Ma believes.[54]

By shortening the value chain between ultimate producers and ultimate consumers, the Alibaba 'Internet ecosystem' reduces the number and cost of middlemen, prevents SMEs from being squeezed by large companies, achieves cost-saving on a global scale. Although Samsung, LG, NEC, Motorola, Nokia, Sears, General Motors and the like are all eagerly building their presences on Alibaba, the stars of the show are grass-roots SMEs. 'This gives business back to businessmen. It returns the control of business to those who are actually producing the products.'[55] Watch out, Wal-Mart and middlemen titans.

Over the years since that first day in Seattle, using the Internet to connect Chinese SME suppliers to foreign customers remains the essence of Ma's business model, with revenue coming mainly from Chinese SMEs. The question is how to get it. Here is Ma's answer:

> The most important thing is to help the customer make money. Most enterprises are thinking of how they can take the five

dollars in a customer's pocket out of there and put it into their own pocket. What we want to do is help that customer turn his five dollars into fifty dollars, and then from that fifty take our five.[56]

Western online companies like eBay adhere to a business model that takes a percentage fee for each transaction on their sites. When they entered the China market, they simply plugged in the same model. Chinese consumers weren't impressed: 'The Internet is there for all, why should we fill your pocket?' China's Alibaba agrees: online transactions should be free, at least for now. Registration, listing, transactions and other basic features are all free on Alibaba. With no fear of losing a commission, the company even encourages sellers and buyers to meet each other directly, and allows users put up 'storefront' product ads for free; there are now millions of them. The company's income then comes from the roughly 1 per cent of users who pay for elite membership packages that offer prior search-ranking and other value-adding services such as TrustPass accreditation which increases user trust and the likelihood of successful transactions. Hence, Alibaba and Taobao are free, but users can also pay for value-adding services.[57] So much has been said about putting choices in customers' hands; here it is done in reality. When Yahoo!'s Jerry Yang visited China, he observed this local rule of the global game: 'America doesn't really have this. I myself had not appreciated the usefulness of the Internet as a tool for small and medium-size enterprises to transact business. Our model is generally just revenue from ads.'[58]

A fan of *kongfu* (功夫), bandit stories and Mao's guerrilla warfare, Ma developed a deep sense of 'knowing when to bend and when to fight'. In the early days, Alibaba was in desperate need of capital. Money was so scarce that his CFO told him: 'Ma Yun [Ma's Chinese name], there's no money in our account.' Yet Ma managed to turn away 38 venture capitalists until Goldman Sachs injected $5 million into the company in October 1999. Ma accepted Goldman's investment not simply because the amount was large at that time, but, more importantly, because it provided wonderful publicity for the new-born company.

The day after the Goldman deal, with a pocket full of cash, Ma went to see Softbank's Masayoshi Son, who was visiting China for investment opportunities. Son could only meet for 20 minutes with each of the would-be Internet heavyweights; there were just too many of them. Ma spoke for six minutes, and Son asked how much money he needed. Ma replied that he didn't need any. 'Why did you come to me, then?' 'I was asked to come by others.' Son invited Ma to Japan for several rounds of negotiations; eventually he invested in Alibaba. Today Son holds one-third of Alibaba shares. 'From the very beginning, I said to Jack [Ma], "Jack you are the hero. You make all the decisions and we are just here to support you."' [59] Ma seized the Goldman and Son opportunities at a critical moment. When the high-tech bubble burst in 2000, Alibaba had plenty of grass to eat while others were starving, some died. Decisive foresight? Clever move? Cool calculation? Naturally so? Everyday going-on? Pure luck? That is the debate for bSchool professors in the years to come.

During the last couple of decades, China has become the world's leading supplier of consumer goods. Alibaba has obviously sensed, seized and benefited from this unprecedented opportunity. By bringing tens of millions of Chinese SMEs, accounting for four-fifths of China's business, directly to buyers all over the world, Alibaba has greatly enhanced the width, depth and pace of this great transformation. 'I want to change the history of Chinese e-commerce', Ma let his ambition be known.[60] Like other great companies, Alibaba has, since its birth, been a shaper and mover of history. It has made a tangible, substantial, practical difference.[61] The company and China, with millions of SMEs, have grown together, into each other. Ma and Alibaba have made handsome profits. We wish them to continue doing so; they are generating even greater values for other businesses, the Chinese economy, society and far beyond.

WSR AND THE FIRM

Markets do not correct themselves, industries do not have a purpose, firms do not make decisions. We humans do. It is we who create and implement strategies, run businesses and make the world a better or worse place. The question is how. In the three chapters in this part of the book, we have been investigating this normative question.

Taking process thinking seriously, we do not come up with x-step procedures or y-dimension grids that would guarantee business success. We are not able to find such things in Confucian teaching or front-line business experience. And we do not apologise for this. As Kenichi Ohmae, a strategy consultant at McKinsey & Company, posits, business success has little if anything to do with formulae; it is instead influenced by modes of thinking.[62] What we share with readers is, together with *wuli–shili–renli*, the Confucian timely balance, a pragmatic mode of thinking. Such a mode of thinking is distinctive from the usual Western vocabulary of mean, middle way or extremes. Inquiring how to get business just right, in the last chapter we looked at two generic pairs of companions: change–continuity and expansion–focus. And in this chapter, drawing on Teece and many others, we introduce a broad 'sensing–seizing–realising' skill set that is useful for acting pragmatically.

Together, these three chapters offer managers a pragmatic ideal of '*what to do, how to do it*' in strategy: timely balancing *wuli–shili–renli*. While *wuli–shili–renli* supplies us with a holistic, relational bottom line, timely balance encourages acting on that bottom line in an appropriate, just-right manner (Figure 7.4).

Proposing strategy as timely balancing efficiency–creativity–legitimacy, we pose a great challenge to managers. It is not a comfort zone but a tough call, yet still promising no guarantee for success. But this is what pragmatic strategy is about. It encourages managers to take it as a starting point, adapt it to situated particulars, put it into experimentation and learn from the consequences. Ours is not a Dummies' Guide to Corporate Success. We have had more than

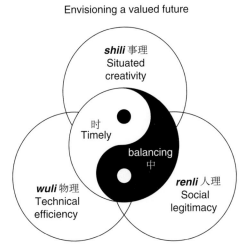

Envisioning a valued future

Getting the fundamentals right   Realising common goodness

FIGURE 7.4 Pragmatic strategy: timely balancing *wuli–shili–renli*

enough dummies' guides over the years, only to suffer bigger collapses, unprecedented failures and deeper cuts, both corporate and societal. It is time for a pragmatic turn. In a no-fixed-shape, no-definite-rule world, pragmatic strategies generated by a relational-processual mode of thinking and supported by a rich pool of sensing–seizing–realising skills would have better chances to succeed. Of this, we have shown plenty of front-line examples; they allow us to be optimistic: looking back, looking around, looking ahead, yes we can!

Most readers of this book work in firms, as founders, owners, managers, workers, or in a combination of roles. So, what are firms? Why do we create and join firms? What makes firms different from markets and each other, and why do some firms do well while others struggle? While these questions lie at the heart of strategy, limited space here allows us only to sketch indicatively a Confucian view of the firm.

Seen through the WSR worldview, the firm is a dynamic constellation of unique *wuli* assets, *shili* capabilities and *renli* relationships

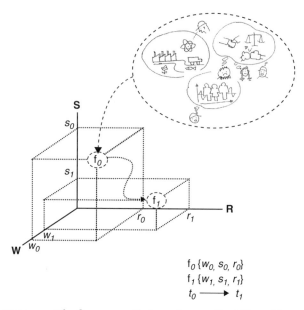

$$f_0 \{w_0,\, s_0,\, r_0\}$$
$$f_1 \{w_1,\, s_1,\, r_1\}$$
$$t_0 \longrightarrow t_1$$

FIGURE 7.5 The firm as a path-dependent *wuli–shili–renli* constellation

evolving in a wider WSR space. At any point in time, each WSR constellation occupies a unique position in the WSR space. Due to path-dependence, there are no duplicated WSR positions, hence no identical firms.[63] As the WSR space consists of an infinite number of possible positions, there is no limit for firms, in fact managers, to innovate, envision and realise valued positions.[64]

A firm does not differ only from other firms; it differs from itself, too. As time passes, say from t_0 to t_1, the 'same' firm transforms from f_0 to f_1. Since the WSR space is in constant flow,[65] the life of firms is an evolutionary one, with or without design.[66] As business becomes more open, interdependent and networked, firms access each other's assets/capabilities/relationships via joint ventures, strategic alliances and other inter-organisational arrangements. In addition, firms are increasingly conscious, active and effective in strategising markets and the wider WSR space.[67] As a result, the boundaries of firms are blurring, which we illustrate with dotted lines in Figure 7.5.

In such an evolutionary perspective, at the heart of the advantages of firms over markets is what we call 'justification efficiency' that enables firms to take on projects which markets would not and could not do, and it is the manager's job to create and capture value by orchestrating the firm's unique *wuli* assets with technical rationality, *shili* capabilities with instrumental rationality and *renli* relationships with ethical rationality.[68]

Assets, capabilities and relationships can be enabling resources for a firm to prosper, to achieve efficiency, creativity and legitimacy. We have illustrated this through case studies, for example, Grameen Bank, Lenovo, Intel, Sony. Alternatively, a firm's assets, capabilities and relationships can be the cause of its undoing. Remember how faulty engineering caused Toyota's recalls just as the firm was becoming the industry leader, Polaroid's razor/blade model once made the company great but eventually bankrupted it, IBM's mainframe success led to its unrecoverable PC market failure and Bernard Madoff's 'social capital' invested in other financial institutions ended up the breeding ground for his fraud?

At stake is hence the 'system effect' of WSR, not a superior position of any single *li*. The bankers showed tremendous capabilities in financial innovation before 2007–2008, only to bring the whole financial system to the brink of collapse. In this disturbing case, creativity was not matched with ethical sensibility. What makes the strategic difference is, hence, managers' willingness and ability to orchestrate in a timely fashion asset complementarity, co-specialisation and capability renewal, to get fundamentals right, envision a valued future and realise common goodness, both inside and between firms. Ordinary managers compete; wise managers orchestrate.[69]

Some Western writers come close to the point, describing strategy as way-finding.[70] To Confucian pragmatism, strategy is way-making: *Tao* is made in the walking of it (道成之于行). As each firm is a unique, dynamic WSR constellation, to perform purposefully, opportunistically, beneficially, managers will do well by orchestrating the firm's assets, capabilities and relationships in a fitting way. For this, timely balancing *wuli–shili–renli* is not *the* way to be discovered, accepted or followed. Rather, it is a walking stick in the hands of managers to embark on their own journey, to make their way in the world. It is managers who make *Tao* great, not *Tao* that makes firms great.[71]

To complete this part of the book, let us examine two more business cases, one from 'the West' – Edison, the icon of innovation genius, the other from 'the East' – Honda, the business legend. Together, they show us how to timely balance *wuli–shili–renli*, how to walk in the world wisely.

Edison, a WSR master[72]

Electric lighting is a complex world of man's making. In ordering this world, Thomas Edison played a significant role of inventor-entrepreneur, skilfully manipulating, with a clear purpose, the rich texture of physical things, scientific laws, economic logic, public imagination and the messy relations between engineers, financiers, politicians and the gas industry. Much of the comfort and convenience we take for granted today is the fruit of the strategic vision, technical competence and political actions of Edison and his associates, thanks to their *wuli–shili–renli* agency par excellence. Against functionalism, we make no suggestion that Edison's system was technically optimal; indeed, his direct-current (DC) design was soon to be replaced by an alternating-current (AC) design, due to the efforts of others, when electric lighting was extended to larger areas. What we are interested in is instead how Edison acted pragmatically in the search for business success via getting fundamentals right, envisioning a bright future and making his central-station model a reality, which, at that historical moment, shaped the world we live in today.

In dealing with *wuli* fundamentals, Edison succeeded where others failed mainly because of his holistic method. Other earlier and contemporary inventors were also working on the components of electric lighting; the British inventor, Joseph Swan, for example, invented the incandescent lamp. However, it was Edison who always did a crucial bit more to configure component inventions into a workable, profitable venture. In his own words:

> It was not only necessary that the lamps should give light and the dynamos generate current, but the lamps must be adapted to the current of the dynamos, and the dynamos must be constructed to give the character of current required by the lamps, and likewise all parts of the system must be constructed with reference to all other parts, since, in one sense, all the parts form one machine, and the connections between the parts being electrical instead of mechanical. Like any other machine the failure of one part to cooperate properly with the other part disorganises the whole and renders it inoperative for the purpose intended ... The problem then that I undertook to solve was stated generally, the production of the multifarious apparatus, methods and devices, each adapted for use with every other, and all forming a comprehensive system.[73]

To get the fundamentals right, Edison hired the best minds. In his Menlo Park laboratory, he worked with superb scientists and craftsmen with a variety of knowledge and skills: mechanics, electricians, chemists, glass-blowers. He supported this community with expensive machinery, chemical apparatus, library resources, scientific instruments and electric equipment. To accomplish this, Edison, through the establishment of the Edison Electric Light Company in 1878, raised substantial funds. He even sold his own shares to finance the project. The Edison laboratory was probably the best electrical laboratory in the world.

For Edison, unlike other inventors, *wuli* fundamentals were not just the scientific-technological, but involved economics as well. 'Edison could not conceive of technology as distinct from economics.'[74] From the start of his lighting project in the autumn of 1878, Edison and his assistants insistently analysed the costs of electricity generation and distribution. His notebooks reveal a constant concern about the cost of the copper needed for wiring, for example:

> In a lighting system the current required to light them in
> great numbers would necessitate such large copper conductors
> for mains, etc., that the investment would be prohibitive and
> absolutely uncommercial. In other words, an apparently remote
> consideration (the amount of copper used for conductors), was
> really the commercial crux of the problem.[75]

From early days, Edison laid down the bottom line that a successful electric lighting system should generate light at a price lower
than gas did. The system must be both technologically workable and
economically viable. According to his own account, Edison began
collecting

> every kind of data about gas; brought all the transactions of
> the gas engineering societies, etc., all the back volumes of gas
> journals. Having obtained all the data and investigated gas-jet
> distribution in New York by actual observations, I made up my
> mind that the problem of the subdivision of the electric current
> could be solved and made commercial.[76]

As observers commented, 'from the economist's viewpoint, the most
significant aspect of Edison's activities in electric lighting was his
concern at every step with economic factors'.[77] Furthermore, focusing on the 'whole system' instead of individual components led
Edison to identify, based on Ohm's law, the critical need for a high-
resistance filament, and to conclude that 'our figures proved that
an electric lamp must have at least 100 ohms resistance to compete
commercially with gas'.[78]

In getting the fundamentals right, Edison worked alongside
engineer-inventors and physical labourers. It is from the long and
tedious on-site experimentations that most fundamentals were got
right and 'eureka' moments emerged:

> In 1882 Edison was in New York supervising construction of
> the Pearl Street system. As chief engineer, he spent long hours,
> week after week, not in an office, but out with the workers

sweating in the hot summer sun as they wrestled with the new and difficult task of laying the underground cables for the Pearl Street station. Edison did not stop at supervision; he worked in the dug-out trenches with the labourers, responding to the most minute problems, many of which arose from the difficulties of maintaining adequate insulation. Often after a frantic day unregulated by the clock, he would sleep for only a few hours on piles of tubes stacked in the station building, his bed place softened only by his overcoat. Invention continued as problems arose during the development and engineering phases of construction. Edison applied for 60 patents in 1880, 89 patents in 1881, and 107 in 1882. Most covered inventions pertaining to the electric lighting system. Only once again in his lifetime, in 1883, a year in which he applied for 64 patents, would the total number of his patents reach the level applied for during the three years he dedicated to electric lighting.[79]

Based on scientific laws and economic calculations, putting natural (coal and water supply) and human (load and demand) geography into consideration, combining inventions in lamps, generators and distribution networks, Edison's ultimate objective was to introduce a central-station, broad-distribution electric lighting system.

A central station would distribute electric light to the public, in contrast to generating plants, or isolated stations, which would be used only by their owners. The steam boilers, steam engines, generators, and auxiliary equipment would be housed in the station building itself; from the central station the distribution system would, in the case of New York City, fan over an area of one square mile. Edison chose 257 Pearl Street, in the financial district, as the location of the New York City station. So located, the central station would supply restaurants and shops that could afford the new light as a way of attracting customers and would illuminate workplaces and offices that could afford it as an unusually effective light without hazardous and noxious

fumes. In the Wall Street district, the station would also catch
the attention of financiers and the investing public, persons who
were needed to fund Edison stations elsewhere.[80]

Beneath these careful calculations along multiple dimensions lies
a question of strategic significance: why did Edison choose the
central-station model? The model was not the only one available, nor,
by many accounts, the most promising. At that time, electric lighting was already in service based on a 'decentralised model'; individual
owners generated their own electricity using small, isolated, in-house
generators. Indeed, Edison himself, with the Edison Company, was
by 1882 successfully manufacturing and selling isolated systems
to hotels, factories and large homes. Furthermore, while decentralised systems required smaller capital investment and provided faster
returns, a central-station model demanded enormous initial investment and would involve a longer return period, due to many factors,
for example the high cost of copper wire. This investment disadvantage immediately introduced tensions between Edison and his financial backers. There were also fears that transmitting electricity via
the mains under crowded districts could accidentally electrify streets
and electrocute workers. So why did Edison choose a design that was
neither technologically superior nor popular with his financiers?

It is exactly this sort of not-quite-optimal choice that made
Edison a successful inventor-entrepreneur, outstanding above mere
technical geeks. Edison was not just good at designing *wuli* technical systems, he was also a master when it came to engineering
shili public imagination. Edison had no doubt about the superiority
of electricity over gas. In promoting the lighting project, he had a
broad, long-term vision: 'the same wire that brings the light to you
will also bring power and heat – with the power you can run an ele-
vator, a sewing machine, or any other mechanical contrivance, and
by means of the heat you may cook your food', and all at 'a fraction
of the cost'.[81] Yet his innovation was to displace gas lighting at a
time when electricity was more expensive than gas while its merits

were not clear, let alone certain, in the public mind. More than half-a-century's domination had made gas, and the central-station model, an entrenched feature of urban people's lives, physically, economically, politically: 'This is the way lighting works.'

To make his system commercially successful, Edison must come up with a robust design that would allow him to locate his innovation within the existing understanding of the old system while at the same time preserving the flexibility to displace it. In short, Edison needed to exploit the public's 'mental model' of how (gas) lighting worked in order to gain acceptance of his (electric) innovation. Of course, people have multiple, overlapping and often contradictory understandings, and this gives designers the opportunity to choose which aspects of the old system to evoke and which of the new to hide. On top of getting the *wuli* fundamentals right, manipulating *shili* imagination skilfully is paramount for innovation to succeed. To mimic gas, Edison chose the central-station, not the decentralised-isolated, model.

To begin with, Edison projected to the public that electricity for lighting was generated centrally and then distributed to surrounding homes and offices, just like gas. He promised that his system would 'utilise the gas burners and chandeliers now in use. In each house I can place a light meter, whence these wires will pass through [existing gas pipes in] the house, tapping small metal contrivances that may be placed over each burner'.[82] In this way, Edison sold to the public a system already familiar to them, while hiding from their view the enormous capital investment needed to install it. To effect the imitation of everything done by gas, Edison made a small light with the same mildness as gas. For this, he did not exploit his technological power to the full, but supplied a light bulb of merely 13 watts, so that 'scarcely anyone would realise rooms were lit by electricity'.[83] As to distribution, Edison buried electric lines underground, like the water and gas mains, instead of using the safer and more economical overhead model of telephone and telegraph. 'Why, you don't lift the water and gas pipes up on stilts',[84] he argued. All this was to reinforce the similarity between electricity and gas, even at the cost of compromising technological advantage. When it came to measuring electricity usage, Edison insisted on using meters to bill customers, like the gas companies, even though the electricity meter had not yet been invented. To clothe electric lighting in the trappings of gas, Edison was willing to pay a price: his company gave customers six months of lighting practically free until the electricity meter was available. The purpose was to manufacture public understanding and acceptance.

At the same time, Edison skilfully promoted the merits of electric lighting that would appeal most to the public: cleaner, simpler, easier to transport and more convenient to use, all you needed to do was turn it on and off. He displayed these advantages in a highly visible way, by lighting the high-profile Wall Street, the headquarters of J.P. Morgan and other landmarks. Edison had the last laugh: his central-station design, despite many technical compromises, gained rapid and widespread public support. By mimicking virtually every aspect of the gas system, he succeeded in displacing it. Academics put it this way:

> Edison succeeded by embodying his innovative ideas in designs
> that were robust enough to exploit the existing institutions of
> a social system without being confined by them. Lampshades,
> burners, gas statutes, and metered billing all presented the public
> with clear signals of how to interpret and interact with Edison's
> new technology, but none precluded the diverse evolution that
> would soon follow.[85]

But the establishment Edison had to handle was not just public understanding. On top of, or you might say underneath, public attitudes ran the powerful interests of the gas monopolies. Andrew Hargadon and Yellowlees Douglas provide an overview picture of the 'stakeholders' who confronted Edison's innovation:

> However bright the future of incandescent lighting appears
> to us now, in 1882 Edison's system still had to tackle a rather

formidable rival. The existing gas industry was not only well established, gas was inextricably woven into the city's physical and institutional environments. New York first lit its streets using gas lamps in 1825; by 1878, gas companies in the US had a capital investment of approximately 1.5 billion dollars. In New York, these companies had integrated themselves deeply within the city's social, economic, political, and physical infrastructure, from their many gas mains buried under the streets to their extensive corps of city-employed lamplighters, to their powerful influence over the aldermen and mayor of New York ... When Edison introduced his competing system of electric lighting, gas lighting was more than an incumbent technology, it was deeply embedded in a web of suppliers, consumers, regulatory agencies, competing firms, and contributory technologies.[86]

These 'vested interests', as sociologists and political scientists call them, blocked Edison's innovation at every step. When Edison first applied for an operating licence, the mayor of New York flatly opposed it. When opposition failed, the city proposed to charge Edison $1,000 per mile for wiring and 3 per cent of the gross receipts, at a time when gas companies were permitted to lay their mains for free and to pay only property tax. To kill off electric lighting, the six New York gas companies drove down the price of gas to levels far below that of electric lighting, then merged into a single company, Consolidated Gas, to take on the fight. To lure customers with technological improvements, the gas companies improved the brightness and steadiness of the flame of gas lamps. They were joined by some strange allies both at home and abroad. In 1878, just months after Edison embarked on his project, a British parliamentary committee of inquiry, after a lengthy consultation with leading British scientists, concluded that the commercial production of incandescent lighting was utterly impossible, and that Edison had demonstrated 'the most airy ignorance of the fundamental principles of both electricity and dynamics'.[87] Even worse, Edison had to deal with financial backers who had invested heavily in the isolated system, asking them, in effect, to switch to his central-station model before their investments in the isolated system were recovered. The *renli* factors Edison had to tackle were formidable.

Edison played the game bravely and skilfully, overcame institutional resistance with a set of new institutions. He forced reluctant investors to support his 'long and expensive wait' for the Pearl Street station, the core of his project. He threatened to abandon electric lighting altogether if he did not get his way. To make his visionary innovation happen, he created a new industrial structure and formed a number of enterprises, which included a company for research and development, another to preside over the operation of the system and still others to manufacture components. He issued territorial franchises to local utility companies far beyond New York City to encourage the use of central-station systems. He cooperated with and relied on many others. Edison was a *renli* master:

> In each case, he allied himself with men whose interests and capabilities complement his own. Persons with legal and financial experience, for instance, compensated for his lack of experience and special aptitude for the complexities of organisation and financing. Despite their presence, however, it was Edison, as inventor-entrepreneur, who pulled most of the strings of the complex system.[88]

Among his allies, a few non-technical associates were crucially important in making the project a success. First was Grosvenor Lowrey. A former lawyer, Lowrey had close contacts with the New York financial and political world. It was Lowrey who, even before the project began, convinced Edison that the money raised through electric-lighting patents would be enough to fulfil his dream. Edison relied on Lowrey in business and legal matters, and as his principal liaison with Wall Street. He wrote to Lowrey: 'Go ahead, I shall agree to nothing, promise nothing and say nothing to any person leaving the whole matter to you. All I want at present is to be provided with funds to push the light rapidly.'[89] In return, to take just one example, Lowrey used his political connections and skills to secure a franchise that allowed Edison to install wire in New York City, a keystone of Edison's commercial success.

Then came Edward Johnson and Samuel Insull. In late 1880 and early 1881, Edison was in desperate need of cash to see his project through. Johnson, who had just returned from Britain, persuaded Edison to hire the 21-year-old Englishman, Insull, as his private secretary. As the story goes:

> When Insull arrived in America, on February 28, 1881, he spent the entire day and night meeting with Johnson and Edison. He offered counsel as to which of Edison's European telephone and telegraph patents and which of his European securities could be sold, for what prices, and to whom. By 4:00 A.M. Insull had become 'Edison's financial factotum,' and at dawn Johnson sailed for Europe to sell the patents and securities. Subsequently Edison used the cash from these sales, along his personal wealth and credit, and funds invested by his intimate associates, to finance the series of manufacturing companies to help fund the creation of EEIC-NY and the Pearl Street Station.[90]

Finally, Henry Villard, a financial entrepreneur who was at that time an agent of the Deutsche Bank buying railroad and utility stocks in the US. He supported Edison's central-station model. In 1889, Villard put together a syndicate of German banks and manufacturing firms, including German General Electric, Siemens and Halske, to purchase several Edison-associated companies, consolidating them into a new entity called Edison General Electric (later renamed GE). This new firm gave Edison's central-station system a solid financial foundation. During Edison's long battle with the powerful financiers who preferred the isolated model, it was Villard who helped him gain access to European investment capital. Villard supported Edison in legal action against the hostile financial might of J. P. Morgan and others, and promoted the Edison model across the

US and Europe. According to business historians, Edison succeeded because he 'happened to be allied to Villard'. 'Central stations owe their predominance at least as much to international financial and political circumstances as to any inherent technical superiority.'[91]

In 1878, Edison began designing an incandescent light bulb. In the same year, he announced a plan to supply electricity to the public from a centrally located generator via underground mains. On 4 September 1882, Edison turned on the Pearl Street system, lighting the Wall Street district. By the early 1890s, central-station lighting was widely adopted to supply electric power to American cities. The age of incandescent lighting had begun; modern public electricity had arrived. We do not know whether Edison dreamed of 'democratising electric lighting', but, to judge by the effect, his central-station system achieved just that. Managing *wuli–shili–renli* willingly and skilfully, Edison made the world a brighter place, for the whole of humanity.

The meaning of Honda

Honda Motor Company is a classic in strategy; the company has been used as a case study in almost all MBA programmes and textbooks around the world. It is also a focal point of persistent controversies among many big names in the strategy industry: Igor Ansoff, Richard Rumelt, Henry Mintzberg, Richard Pascale, James Quinn, Gary Hamel, C.K. Prahalad and renowned consultants, for example, George Stalk and Michael Goold of the Boston Consultant Group. Unfortunately, the studies by the big names, while they generate useful insights, stubbornly reject the analyses of others, only promoting their own views, quite explicitly, as 'the one best way'. This has turned learning from Honda into a partisan, polarised and confusing exercise.[92] Furthermore, the studies have been narrowly confined in terms of learning vs design, industry analysis vs resource-based approaches or core capabilities vs core competence and the like, leaving Honda's purpose, value and vision, which have played a guiding role in the strategy that made the company unique and great, entirely invisible.[93] In the spirit of pragmatism, we intend to take a tentative step to overcome these deficits, to search for a richer understanding of Honda.

Honda the person, Soichiro, was a colourful character with a burning passion for racing and technology. As the legend goes:

> By age 25, Honda was one of the youngest Japanese entrepreneurs around. He became the Hamamatsu [his home town] playboy, not only plying from one geisha house to the next, but piling geishas into his own car for wild drives and drunken revels around the town. In one such escapade his car full of geishas went off a bridge, but landed safely in the mud – no injuries … Honda also loved motors and engines. When the head of Arto Shokai [an auto repair shop in which the young Soichiro worked as the head of its Hamamatsu branch] suggested Honda might build a racer (on his own time), Honda spent months of midnight hours to build a car from spare parts and war surplus aircraft engines. He soon began to drive his products himself, to win races, to make basic changes in racing car designs, and soon to set new speed records. But in the All Japan Speed Rally of 1936, travelling at 120 kph – a record not exceeded for years – another car jumped in front of Honda, demolishing Honda's car and leaving him with lifetime injuries, which redirected his energies from racing toward engineering.[94]

Seeking to understand engineering fundamentals, Honda struggled through painful entrance exams and entered a high school of technology, ten years older than his classmates. He was so problem-solving-oriented and selective that he only attended classes that were of interest to him, listened carefully to what mattered to him and did not even take notes on the rest. He refused to take exams, saying that a diploma was worth less than a movie ticket. The ticket at least allowed you to enter the theatre, but what could you do with a diploma?[95]

Immediately after the Second World War, Honda started to make motorbikes by clipping small, war-surplus gasoline-powered motors to bicycles. They were an instant hit. 'I happened on the idea of fitting an engine to a bicycle simply because I didn't want to ride the incredibly crowded trains and buses myself, and it became impossible for me to drive my car because of the gasoline shortage', Honda later said.[96] Recognising that the simple motorbikes would not last long once the Japanese economy recovered, in 1949 Honda raised $3,800 and designed a motorcycle with a two-stroke, 98-cc, 3-h.p. engine. He named his first motorcycle the 'Type D' – the 'Dream'. Hardly the result of a 1,000-year strategy though; Honda's early products, and many later ones, achieved a perfect fit between his mastery of engineering and situated circumstances. While production and sales did well, Honda faced bankruptcy for failing to collect payments from the small dealers and black marketeers he did business with. This is not surprising: all his life, Soichiro was more interested in products and engineering than in profit.[97] On the one hand, he was known for sweeping factory floors, emptying ash trays and picking up toilet paper from the ground. On the other hand, he refused to attend government meetings to determine incentive policies for Japanese exporters. High-quality products needed no such support and knew no national boundaries, he insisted with 100-per-cent-plus confidence.[98]

Luckily, through the recommendation of friends, Honda had Takeo Fujisawa as the head of finance and marketing, and later vice president, of his young firm. 'Fujisawa's heavy and ponderous style contrasted sharply with Honda's waspish, impatient, even rude directness.'[99] Luckily, again, the two were a pair of complementary companions, not antagonistic adversaries. There was no middle way or synthesis, just mutual appreciation and support. Their friendship extended beyond business, they were lifelong friends. Together, Honda and Fujisawa turned the firm from a small-town enterprise into a global company, and, perhaps more importantly, created the Honda DNA that continues to guide the company making its way in the changing world even when the founders are gone. They called the DNA the company's 'philosophy' and treated it as essential. 'Action without philosophy is a lethal weapon; philosophy without action is meaningless', said Soichiro.[100] The Honda philosophy consists of Three *Gen*s, Three As and Three Joys.

To begin with, at Honda, the proper way of making things is encapsulated in the phrase *Sangenshugi* (三現主義), or the Three *Gen*s. These are: *genba* (現場, go to the actual place), *genbutsu* (現物, know the actual situations) and *genjitsu* (現実, be realistic and disciplined). The founders firmly believed that a company's value is created on the front line where workers have the best knowledge of reality.[101] The Three *Gen*s focus energy and effort, propel Honda people to get fundamentals right, respect theories that work, immerse themselves in unfolding situations and define and solve here-and-now problems. Honda's organisation was, and still is, flat in comparison with other car-makers. Takeo Fukui, ex-Honda chief, told the *Financial Times* not long ago: as a company grows, the tendency is to summon managers to the executive suite, which slows things down; 'Instead, we who make the decisions go directly to their spot on the floor and listen to them.'[102]

With Three *Gen*s, when Honda engineers developed the Fit vehicle for the European market, for example, they first went to Europe to observe, with their own eyes, how consumers used cars in each European region. What the team members sought was not statistical data on 'consumer behaviour', but a direct, on-the-spot appreciation of customers' lifestyles and needs. You must transform yourself into a customer – *wuwo* (无我, losing the self). As one engineer said:

> If all we had wanted was research data, we could have gotten it from our people in Europe. But we experienced for ourselves the weight and bulk of carrying six bottles of wine by hand; we pushed our own shopping carts in the supermarkets, experiencing the hot or cold weather at the time just like the local people. The goods they loaded into their cars varied by country, but we learned that regardless of the country, it was

important that a full shopping cart of items fit into the car. By observing reality at the frontline and thinking with your body, you can dispel the image that you've created in your head.[103]

Next, the Three As promote creativity at Honda by asking questions at three levels of inquiry. The first, Level A, is concerned with operational matters, focusing on product specifications. For example: what specifications does our new car need in order to achieve a particular emission rate? How should we design and build that new model? This pushes Honda to produce highly successful models without peers, such as the Civic, the first car ever to comply with the environmental standards demanded by the Muskie Act in the US.[104] The Civic was followed by other run-away market hits such the Accord and the Fit.

The next level of questioning, A0, focuses on the conceptual. It concerns a fundamental conception of product. This enables Honda to launch products that put people first even before consumers are able to articulate what they want. For example, Honda recently designed its DN-01 motorcycle with a front that evokes the features of a human face, so that other drivers will recognise the motorcycle more quickly, which leads to greater traffic safety. Honda was also the first to adapt airbags for motorcycles to reduce collision injuries.

Finally, the third level of questioning, Level A00, asks existential questions. Why does the company exist? Why should it make a particular product? What is the product for? These A00 questions inspire Honda engineers to envision a valued future not just for the company, but more importantly for society and the environment. Honda has pioneered fuel-cell cars that use no gasoline and emit only water vapour. Apart from advanced research into nanocars too small to be seen by the human eye but with great potential, the company leads in designing robots that can recognise faces, distinguish voices, move to a pointed direction, climb up and down stairs and fulfil many other activities. For the rapidly ageing population within and beyond Japan, such innovations could have huge societal benefits.[105]

With the Three As, Honda has been driven by the power of dreams, generating and overcoming challenges, remaining a company with a 'wholehearted commitment to ideals' and 'fresh, open-minded passion for learning'.[106] In 1954, just six years after he started the company, Soichiro declared that Honda would enter and win the world-famous Isle of Man Tourist Trophy motorbike race. In 1964, shortly after the company started producing automobiles, Soichiro then decided to enter the Formula 1 competition. Many considered the objectives impossible. On both occasions, however, the company not only won trophies but significantly raised technology levels in a very short period, putting the company firmly on the map of auto-engineering pioneers.[107]

Of course, while dreaming and walking in the world, Honda, like any other company, made mistakes.[108] However, the creative spirit embodied in the Three As propelled Honda to learn quickly from mistakes. The company's first passenger car, the H1300, was a market failure despite being equipped with an innovative air-cooling engine. Yet the H1300 experience was a turning point for Honda, enabling its engineers to design the revolutionary and highly successful Civic. Nobuhiko Kawamoto, Honda president from 1986 to 1998, said: 'It's okay to fail. We wanted them [Honda engineers] to feel challenged, like they were climbing a cliff vertically from the start. Then they would pass on this Hondaism to the next generation.'[109]

Then, linking Three *Gen*s and Three As are the Three Joys, which is about company purpose, values and ideals. To Soichiro, 'true joy comes from doing something worthwhile'.[110] The *Honda Philosophy Handbook* reads: 'We believe that sincerely responding to the changing demands of the world through The Three Joys will provide joy to society and make Honda a company that society recognises and wants to exist.'[111] The Three Joys are: 'the joy of buying, the joy of selling and the joy of creating.'

Thoroughly a 'car guy' though, Soichiro injected into Honda a religion-like sense of ethics, or, to use his term, 'philosophy'. 'Philosophy is more important than technologies', he insisted. 'What drives a firm's growth is philosophy ... A true technology is a crystal of philosophy ... Therefore, even in a research lab, the philosophy of the people who work there should take precedence over the technology.' To Soichiro, technology was created to realise common goodness. 'Things like money and technologies are merely the means to serve people',[112] and a company must bring to people joys that 'exceed their expectations'.[113] The people 'near at hand', from a company's point of view, are the customers who buy your product, the engineers and workers who build it and the business partners who contribute their joint efforts. Together with the Three *Gen*s and Three As, the Three Joys define Honda's purpose and compel Honda to improve the well-being of people, society and bio-ecology with leading-edge products.[114]

Soichiro walked his talks. He founded Honda on his 'philosophy' and transformed it into a leading technology company. When Honda engineers rejected his idea of beating the 'Big Three' with the Civic engine, insisting that the engine was for a better future of later generations, Soichiro retired. He felt shame, not because he no longer had the passion or ability to advance technology, but because he considered he himself had failed, at that particular point, to uphold his own ethical standard. Before he retired, Honda made the Civic design widely available, licensing it to Toyota, Ford, Chrysler and Isuzu. Ethics is in everything we do, and Soichiro set a good example. So far, the company appears to be keeping Soichiro's philosophy alive. When asked in 2007 how he felt about being Japan's second-largest car-maker after Toyota, the then president Takeo Fukui said: 'We want to be number one, but not in terms of [market] value – we want to be number one from the customer standpoint.'[115] To Honda, the Three Joys continue to be paramount (Figure 7.6).

The meaning of Honda, in terms of 'process', is best captured by Takeo Fujisawa's 'law of *banbutsu ruten* (万物流転)', meaning 'all things flow'. Remember Confucius' poem about the *wei* river:

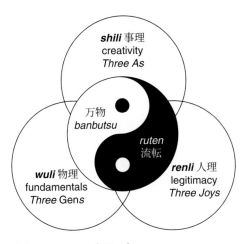

FIGURE 7.6 The meaning of Honda

'Isn't life's passing just like this, never ceasing day or night!'? Like Confucius, Fujisawa was a pragmatist at heart. Acting upon *banbutsu ruten* is not passively accepting whatever happens, but engaging in flows, making real differences, getting fundamentals right with Three *Gen*s, invoking imagination with Three As and bringing Three Joys to people, thus creating value for society. While Takeo was philosophical, Soichiro was playful. True to his character, Soichiro saw strategy as joking: 'Joking is very difficult. You have to grasp the atmosphere of the occasion and the opportunity. It exists only for that particular moment and not anywhere else. The joke is in the timing and it doesn't work at any other moment.'[116] To make a good joke, according to Soichiro, one must 'read' a situation and respond to it quickly, appropriately, creatively.[117] The joke metaphor for strategy emphasises timely fit, being just right and having 'a keen sensitivity to daily change and the ability to see the implications of that change in the bigger picture'.[118] 'Sticking to the middle' or 'keeping both extremes' 'all the time' is destined to fail, to make your jokes confusing, frustrating.

It is *banbutsu ruten* and strategy-as-joking that have guided the company's 'stumble into success'.[119] Honda is most famous for its conquest of the US motorcycle market.[120] Honda was eager and quick to learn, for sure. But its success was made possible, in the first instance, by its founders' distinctive foresight and heroic decisions. It was Fujisawa's top-down, single-handed decision, as record shows, that pushed Honda into the unknown US market. Fujisawa had to fight against his colleagues every inch of the way, overriding their consensual, bottom-up proposal to concentrate on the Asian and European markets.[121] History indicates that Fujisawa's go-for-America strategy was a timely fit, in overall direction if not in every detail. But this is exactly what strategy is about. If Honda had not taken on the American non-market against all odds, all the talk of learning and crafting would have been irrelevant and we would not today have the stimulating 'Honda effect'.[122] In fact, as Japanese researchers have revealed, Fujisawa did intend to use the small Super Cub as a competitive weapon from the outset. This contradicts the textbook claim that selling the Super Cub was merely an accidental adjustment after attempts to sell larger machines failed.[123] In overall strategy and even in some detailed plans, Fujisawa made an excellent 'joke': timely, just right, fitting the 'occasion and opportunity' of 'that particular moment'. Learning and planning are indeed the two legs of strategy.[124] To walk well, the two legs must strive for timely balance amid *banbutsu ruten*.

There is further conscious balancing at Honda. On the one hand, the founders forged a 'Philosophy of Respect for the Individual', encouraging everyone to express opinions and engage in debates, to dream freely and think expansively. The motto was 'All engineers are equal before technology'.[125] 'I am not in a position to give direct orders to the engineers in R&D', says Takeo Fukui.[126] As *Fortune* magazine reported, 'Unlike Toyota, which is stodgy and bureaucratic, Honda's culture is more entrepreneurial, even quirky'.

On the other hand, the company is careful to balance its free-wheeling style. R&D managers, led by the president, meet once or twice a year to review their most promising projects. Each project gets specific timelines that are closely watched; as a project approaches the market, the company imposes more supervision. This is not to clip R&D's wings: 'Within this disciplined framework, though, R&D's expansive charter leads it in directions no other car company would attempt.'[127] The balance mindset crosses departmental boundaries. 'You need a balance of "marketing in" user needs and "product out" to create something that captures the flavor of the times, as well as having absolute value and practical use', said Shinya Iwakura, the team leader who led the development of the first-generation Civic.[128]

Timely balance amid *banbutsu ruten* enables Honda to create and capture value effectively, making many wonderful dreams real: the Asimo robot, the HondaJet aircraft, the nanocar, the thin-film solar-power cells, the motorcycle with the front like a human face, the hydrogen home-refuelling station that takes up no more space than a refrigerator, and on and on.[129]

Balanced strategy demands balanced leadership.[130] 'An accomplished engineer must be not only an excellent engineer but also a preeminent artist', said Soichiro. 'That person should have both the knowledge of a scientist and the feeling of an artist.'[131] As a company, Honda respects people's dreams, emotions, passion and capacity to create. Highly valued are aesthetic experience, corporate culture, philosophy, history, literature and the arts. Remember the Confucian 'six arts' and the 'full character' of exemplary persons? Honda wants its people to be the samurai of our time. So much so that the founder, with his keen interest in almost everything in life, from geisha to racing to engineering, said: 'Honda is not a place to research technology but a place to research human beings.'[132] This, to pragmatism, is the meaning of Honda the people, the dream, the machine, the effect.[133]

PART IV   **Think when we learn**

学而不思则罔，
思而不学则殆。
«论语»

Learning without thinking is labour lost;
thinking without learning is perilous.
– *Analects*

8 Questioning the conventional paradigm

We do strategies not in complete doubt but informed by paradigms.[1] What paradigm was behind the strategies that led to the current crisis and calamity? That question is the focus of this chapter. Our self-examination will be critical, but with a positive purpose: to appreciate the value and urgency of a pragmatic turn. Being critical and positive, we organise our analysis under three headings: 'Closing the practice gap', 'Bringing ethics back in', 'Overcoming specialised deafness'.

CLOSING THE PRACTICE GAP

Harvard University is admired not only for its leading-edge research but also for its wealth – an endowment standing at $37 billion as of 30 June 2008. In past years, the Harvard Management Company (HMC), the university's fund-management arm, made investments in everything from private equity to property to commodities. 'Harvard has become an investment bank with a university attached', said a Harvard employee.[2] Then the 2009 financial year wiped out 30 per cent of the endowment, and the university froze salaries and proposed 275 job cuts. Like the citizens in the main street, the professors at Harvard were unhappy: 'These people have made fortunes losing money for the endowment [HMC managers got paid between $2 million to $6.4 million a year]. Now they want us to foot the bill.'[3] How could this have happened given the numerous *Harvard Business Review* articles and Harvard Business School strategy case studies on everything from industry analysis to risk management to corporate governance?

In February 2010, the UK broadcaster ITV hired as its new head Adam Crozier, with a nearly £16 million five-year pay deal. Six years earlier, Crozier was the chief executive of England's Football Association. 'Having estranged everybody' there, Crozier jumped to the Royal Mail, where he imposed 'one of the worst industrial relations in recent years'. 'The pity of it is that one tends to associate the Royal Mail with bad management.' ITV shareholders were worried, and questioned whether Crozier had the expertise to tackle TV programming and regulatory issues, describing him as 'totally unproven'. Regardless, the hiring went ahead. 'So has he got talent?'[4]

The Harvard and ITV stories raise uncomfortable questions: why do our best strategy theories fail to prevent crisis even in our own backyards? Does domain experience still count? Where does the 'knowing–doing gap' come from?[5] Let us investigate.

Science-based professionalism

Managerial capitalism started during the nineteenth century when the separation between ownership and management created a class of managers in the US. The role of managers then became a social issue, as some questioned the contribution of non-owner managers while others criticised the rift between management and labour. It was a matter of importance for the new managerial class to forge some sort of legitimacy. The strategy was to present management as a profession based on science. At that time, science enjoyed high prestige as being rooted in truth and serving progress. The 'scientific method' was closely associated with notions of reason and efficient causality, bundled with analytical models and quantitative techniques. The identification of management with science underlined both the 'scientific management' movement and the 'human relations' school, with the former applying the scientific method to work efficiency[6] while the latter studied motivation in groups.[7] The manager's job was to uncover the laws of material transformation and principles of human conduct, and to manage accordingly.[8]

After the Second World War, due to the rise of conglomerates in the booming economy, there was an enormous demand for techniques that would enable managers to plan for expansion and exert control over expanding operations. Under these circumstances, the conception of management gradually moved away from the human relations approach towards a more narrow focus on analytical skills. Managers were pushed to become rational decision-makers distanced from the messy front line. If Henry Ford's assembly line separated design from production in the factory, a strategy–operation divide now became the wisdom of the day.[9] The hero was Robert McNamara, CEO of the Ford Company and later the US Secretary of Defense. In a 1973 book, *The Best and the Brightest*, David Halberstam caught the flavour:

> if the body was tense and driven, the mind was mathematical, analytical, bringing order and reason out of chaos. Always reason. And reason supported by facts, by statistics – he could prove his rationality with facts – intimidates others. Once, sitting at CINCPAC for eight hours, watching as hundreds and hundreds of slides flashed across the screen ... he finally said ... 'Stop the projector. This slide number 869 contradicts slide 11.' Slide 11 was flashed back, and he was right. They did contradict each other ... Everyone was in awe.[10]

This 'analytic movement'[11] continued into the 1970s when the US experienced relative productivity decline and lost markets to Germany, Japan and the 'Asian tigers'. In their 1980 article 'Managing our way to economic decline', Robert Hayes and William Abernathy criticised what they called 'the new managerial gospel': when making strategic decisions, managers increasingly favoured analytical detachment and methodological elegance over experience and insights. Hayes and Abernathy were particularly critical of the trend that individuals with no special expertise in any particular industry, with no hands-on knowledge of specific technologies, products, customers or suppliers, nevertheless step in and run any organisation using financial control and portfolio concepts. 'High-level American executives ... seem to come and go and switch around as if playing a game of musical chairs at an Alice in Wonderland party.'[12] Business leaders like Akio Morita and academics such as Alfred Chandler raised similar concerns.[13] Edward Deming, a quality expert, made his criticism more explicit, charging 'interchangeable managers' as the 'footless character of American management'.[14] These criticisms made an impact partly because foreign companies were making further inroads in the 1970s–1980s, shattering conventional values and practices. In the booming 1990s–2000s, however, lessons were quickly forgotten and 'pseudo-professionalism' prevailed, only to be followed by a bigger bust.

Let us be clear: analytic methods and quantitative techniques are not a problem in themselves. The problem is, as Ikujiro Nonaka calls it, the 'scientification of business strategy'.[15] While most serious issues facing managers call upon conviction, commitment, visionary imagination, domain experience and interpersonal skills, the conventional paradigm confined managers to 'scientific' formulas. In the absence of other forms of knowledge, the narrow 'scientific' paradigm is not helpful, but harmful. As Warren Bennis and James O'Toole argue, 'When applied to business – where judgements are made with messy, incomplete data – statistical and methodological wizardry can blind rather than illuminate.'[16]

Practice-absent recipes

> It is also true that much of this rigorous business research is irrelevant to real business managers. In any given issue of a research journal, perhaps only one or two articles actually have the potential to be applied in real organisations. The rest of this work is basic research. It is designed to address theoretical problems, problems that often have limited application potential.[17]

This quotation from an influential strategy textbook lays bare the mindset of our 'discipline'. It is no secret that in business schools there is long-standing dispute about theoretical rigour vs practical relevance.[18] There are also those who argue that the real issue is not rigour vs relevance but good or bad research.[19] Given all this, our question is rather: is research good if it is irrelevant to managers and inapplicable to organisations?

Let us put this into context. When strategy emerged as a field of study in the late 1950s, the Ford and Carnegie Foundations issued devastating reports on the then woeful state of business education and pressed for scientific underpinnings.[20] The reports reinforced the view that management was a science supported by analytical skills that could enable decision-making solely on rational grounds.[21] The goal was to raise the academic status of business schools to a level 'higher than that of physical education'. The foundations backed their demands with cash; the Ford Foundation alone supplied $30 million in 1960.[22]

Driven by money and status, business schools concentrated their efforts on 'scientific rigour'.[23] Since then, the academic standing of bSchools has improved and some of the research is impressive, but it is rarely grounded in actual business practices. 'Findings' have become less and less appealing to managers, and 'strategy management' is increasingly defined as a self-contained 'discipline', rather than a practice of solving business problems.[24] New professors must hold a Ph.D. by default, and yet many have never set foot inside a real enterprise. Instead of entering the real world to see what people actually do, professors set up 'strategy simulations' to play out how people behave, on the Web. Under pressure from biased promotion policies, academics care more about getting articles accepted by learned journals than conducting research useful in real organisations. We have created a 'vast wasteland' of five-star publications while leaving 'applications' to others.[25] The 'others' have turned their backs on us: 62 per cent of CEOs have never heard of any journals other than the *Harvard Business Review*.[26]

This has serious consequences. We produce 150,000 MBA graduates per annum at 1,500 bSchools; the population of MBA-holders exceeds two million. Some 70 per cent of MBA graduates reach senior management positions; they constitute the majority of executives in major companies, particularly financial institutions and consultancies.[27] Nevertheless, we feed them with practice-absent recipes. No wonder 'these kids are just number crunchers' who 'don't want to get their hands dirty'.[28] (A footnote: 'many of the bankers who recently mugged the world's taxpayers were HBS men.'[29]) So much so that in a *Financial Times* article, 'Forget the MBA, give me experience any day', an entrepreneur urges:

> Essays and formulae will not help you here: what you need are common sense, gut instinct, luck and a veteran's wisdom ... At heart I believe in domain knowledge – expertise in a specific sector, gathered in the trenches. To me that hard-won mastery of a subject is more pertinent and productive than a recruit boasting textbook knowledge.[30]

Hollow strategies

For the illusory 'scientific status', strategy paid a high price.[31] The conventional paradigm is found to be as follows.

Detached. We manage to believe that generalised principles work across firms and industries. If someone sells washing powder efficiently, he should be good at managing TV programmes aimed at teenagers. As long as HQ gets the numbers right, strategic formulas should set the firm in motion and expected outcomes will follow. If not, work harder, sort out the numbers. Strategy principles, like laws of nature, cannot be wrong; the problem lies in applications. This belief in 'principles' diverts strategy from what really matters: situated particulars at the front line.[32]

Ideological. Strategies become driven by what Robert Eccles and Nitin Nohria call 'management hype', no longer based on evidence or a firm's unique circumstances.[33] We see it come and go: re-engineering, downsizing, flat organisation, to name just a few. We adopt 'best practices' simply because they are said to work in other firms. Before the 1980s, 'what is good for GM is good for America and what is good for America is good for the world'; after that, it was

'Japan does it better'.[34] With ready-made solutions at hand, we look for problems. The trouble is: to one who holds a hammer, everything looks like a nail.

Narrow. The exclusive emphasis on analytical models concentrates managers' attention on what is measurable, driving out 'fuzzy' issues of purpose, judgement and imagination that make the difference between good and bad strategies.[35] Smart executives occupy themselves with bottom-line tactics: given last quarter's data, shall we put this or that brand of ice cream on the front shelf? We become unable to tackle big questions such as 'what are the consequences of closing down this local factory' or 'should we lobby for "favourable" environmental legislation or innovate greener engines'?

Routine. Analytical techniques are good for modelling certainty.[36] They focus on the average and conventional, glossing over the exceptional and surprising.[37] The tendency is to define problems in terms of what we already know.[38] A manager's job, complained Henry Mintzberg, is no longer to create novel strategies but to select from past ones: under *x*, do *y*.[39] Innovative ideas are difficult to come by.[40] Research tends to be the 'footnote-on-footnote' kind, starting and stopping with hypotheses around accepted theories.[41] Theories not only are trivial but are left behind the front line, 'counting what practising managers have already discovered for themselves'.[42]

The practice gap has produced serious consequences, as the case below illustrates.

The Big Brother *racism row*[43]

Big Brother was a reality TV show on the UK-based Channel 4. It was the broadcaster's most financially successful programme, accounting for around 10 per cent of its total advertising income of £800 million. In the show, a group of strangers from widely different backgrounds were cooped up in a luxury prison with hidden cameras everywhere. The set-up was 'not just likely to create conflicts; it's intended to'.

In an episode of the 'Celebrity' version of the show, aired on 15 January 2007, housemates former Big Brother star Jade Goody, glamour model Danielle Lloyd and former S Club 7 singer Jo O'Meara referred to another housemate, the Indian actress Shilpa Shetty, as a 'dog', 'c***' and, allegedly, 'Paki'. Believing Shilpa had undercooked a chicken, Jo suggested that Indians were thin because they were 'sick all the time' as a result of undercooking their food. Danielle commented that Shilpa used facial hair bleaching cream because 'she wants to be white', adding that the Indian girl 'can't even speak English properly anyway' and should 'f*** off home'. She didn't like Shilpa touching her food, 'you don't know where her hands have been'. Jade referred to the Indian actress as 'Shilpa F***awallah', 'Shilpa Daroopa', 'Shilpa Popadum': 'She makes me feel sick. She makes my skin crawl.' She shouted at Shilpa: 'You're a liar, a f****** fake. You're so far up your a*** you can smell your own s***.' Another housemate chipped in: 'There was a young girl from Bombay. This house was happy, until we got that f****** Paki.' The Indian actress was reduced to tears, but stood her ground, largely silent except for one telling comment: 'This is what today's UK is? Scary.'

Within days, Ofcom the broadcasting watchdog received 44,500 public complaints about the show, while Channel 4 received an additional 3,000 – a record for a television broadcast. The controversy generated over 300 newspaper articles in Britain, 1,200 in English-language newspapers around the world, 3,900 in foreign-language newspapers and 22,000 blog entries. The publicity boosted the show's ratings from 3.9 million to a peak of 8.8 million viewers, the highest figure in the history of the series. After a few days' silence, Channel 4 described the incidents as 'girly rivalry': 'To date there has been no overt racial abuse or racist behaviour directed against Shilpa Shetty.' Channel 4 chief executive Andy Duncan defended the broadcast thus: 'it is good television.'

As public complaints in the UK soared, protesters in India took to the streets and burned effigies of the show's organisers. In a move that threatened to sour relations between the two countries, the Indian Minister of State for External Affairs made a formal complaint to the British Prime Minister, Tony Blair. 'The government will take appropriate measures once it gets to know the full details. Racism has no place in civilised society', an official responded. The Indian Tourism Office invited Jade Goody to visit India and experience its healing culture.

During Prime Minister's Questions in Parliament, Tony Blair declared 'we should oppose racism in all its forms'. Parliament tabled an Early Day Motion to address the row. The Chancellor of the Exchequer, Gordon Brown, on a visit to India, condemned the controversy as 'offensive': 'I want Britain to be seen as a country of fairness and tolerance. Anything detracting from this I condemn.' London's mayor Ken Livingstone criticised the episode as 'completely unacceptable'. The Equality and Human Rights Commission chairman Trevor Phillips complained that Channel 4 was 'failing to deal properly with the crisis'. 'What we are seeing is a noxious brew of old-fashioned class conflict ... and vicious racial bigotry', he said. A former contestant of the show commented: 'It is absolutely disgraceful. I doubt we can trust the honesty of Channel 4 any more.' Under pressure, the police investigated whether or not to classify the harassment as 'racial hatred' under Part III of the Public Order Act 1986, with a view to legal action.

On the financial front, on 18 January Carphone Warehouse suspended its sponsorship of the programme, followed by Beauty-boxes. com, Zamya aromatherapy products, United Biscuits and Cobra Beer. Advertisers including Cow & Gate and MoneySupermarket.com cancelled their contracts with Channel 4. Hertsmere Borough Council, the owner of the *Big Brother* studios in Borehamwood, threatened to refuse permission to film. Perfume Shop the fragrance chain, Boots the chemist and Debenhams the department store all withdrew the Jade Goody brand from their shelves. HarperCollins the publishing house cancelled plans for the paperback version of Jade Goody's autobiography, while LIVINGtv dropped its commercial contract with her. Act Against Bullying, a charity supported by Goody, deleted all mention of her from its website, citing the racism allegations as the cause. Motorcycle insurance company Bennetts followed suit, terminating a six-figure contract with Danielle Lloyd to be its official model.

On 24 May 2007, Ofcom ruled that Channel 4 had breached the broadcasting code of conduct by failing to challenge racist behaviour, offering no justification for its broadcast and attempting to cover up misconduct. Channel 4 was condemned for not knowing or taking responsibility for what contestants said during the show, and was ordered to broadcast an Ofcom-approved apology on three separate occasions. Channel 4 avoided a fine by accepting Ofcom's verdict and agreeing to introduce a strict compliance system. *Big Brother's* producers suspended the show's 2008 series. It returned in 2009 and aired its final series in 2010.

On the human front, Shilpa Shetty said: 'I just want every Indian to be extremely proud that I am here [in the show]. I have zero expectations. The only thing I really hope to keep is my self-respect and my dignity.' Shilpa's UK manager Jaz Barton told the BBC: 'She didn't come into the house to have that sort of harassment. You know, she came in there with the full intention to actually embrace the public at large and to be proud of her culture and her heritage and who she is, and now she's faced with all this sort of harassment.' Carole Malone, an evicted housemate, told the *Asian Network*: 'Shilpa feels that she represents the Indian/Asian community and doesn't want to let them or herself down by retaliating.' Shilpa told the media that she forgave Jade.

Jade Goody eventually visited India and apologised for her behaviour to the Indian people:

> I am sincerely sorry for the pain and hurt I've caused Shilpa's family ... I am wrong and I know that my words and my actions were wrong and I'm not trying to justify that in any way – I am wrong, and the people who have complained are not wrong. They're just insulted by me and I completely take that criticism.

These words came from a girl from a broken family and with little education. After the controversy, Jade received death threats. Just as she was returning to a new TV show to rebuild her life in August 2008, Jade was diagnosed with cervical cancer. She died on 22 March 2009, leaving two young children. She was made famous by *Big Brother*, and destroyed by it.

Andy Duncan, Channel 4's chief executive, who joined the company in 2004, had no previous experience of programme-making; he began his career with Unilever. 'One of the problems these days with people in television is that they have little concept of the wider context of its impact on society', said a Channel 4 board member.

BRINGING ETHICS BACK

Traditionally, strategy was underlined by an emphasis on moral responsibilities, and managers were considered stewards of society's resources to generate value for the well-being of employees, consumers and communities. Chester Barnard's experience, summarised in his 1938 book *The Functions of the Executive*, is a good case in point.[44] During and since the 1970s, a series of events brought this to a halt, turning strategy into a paradigm with 'lopsided brains, icy hearts and shrunken souls'.[45]

Strategy without a head on it

During the 1970s, 'the West' experienced the first oil crisis, followed by recession and social unrest. The relative decline in productivity in the US and Britain led to President Reagan and Prime Minister Thatcher's deregulation regimes in the 1980s. Against this background was the deteriorated performance of conglomerates. Economists and policy-makers called for maximisation of corporate value to discipline management hubris and resource misallocation.[46] But it hadn't worked out like that. Rather, in the name of corporate value, now substituted by shareholder value measured solely by stock prices,[47] corporations, particularly in the US and the UK, went down the road of 'financialisation':[48] resolving all values into financial figures.[49]

Making money became the sole purpose, as exemplified by Friedman that 'few trends could so thoroughly undermine the very foundations of our free society as the acceptance by corporate officials of a social responsibility other than to make as much money for their stockholders as possible'.[50] The consequence is misconceived shareholder primacy, complete profit orientation and systematic exclusion of moral sensibility. Jack Welch of GE, the champion of 'shareholder value', rewarded investors with consistent, higher returns than 'the market'; this was achieved largely by quarter-by-quarter financial manoeuvre supported by earnings from GE Capital.[51] At its peak, the financial arm generated over 40 per cent of the company's profit.[52] Jack became an icon, regarded as the greatest businessman of the second half of the twentieth century. The role of managers was reduced to maximising quick returns for shareholders.[53]

Driven by stock prices, managers benchmarked each other on two strategies. One was cost-cutting. In the name of efficiency, companies focused on cost reduction to achieve short-term gains. We manage to push aside that only long-term investment in technological supremacy can produce superior offerings in the marketplace that enable a company to prosper.[54] Akio Morita, a founding father of Sony, put it this way: 'by saving money instead of investing it in the business you might gain profit on a short-term basis, but in actual fact you would be cashing in the assets that had been built up in the past. To gain profit is important, but you must invest to build up assets that you can cash in the future.'[55] Relying on short-term financial measures also induces risk aversion, which, in turn, kills off innovation. To show profit quickly, corporations moved production offshore, resulting in a 'hollowing out of industry' at home[56] and a decline in national productivity.[57] The strategy was flawed not because it pursues efficiency, but because it ignored the Schumpeterian insight that short-term efficiency does not necessarily lead to long-term efficiency.[58] The question is: do shareholders care?

Another strategy was 'merger mania': boosting stock prices through frantic mergers and acquisitions. 'Some managers have found that they can make more money more easily by trading money rather than goods', Morita commented.[59] In boardrooms, strategy was all about 'which company to buy' or 'which division to sell', and 'restructuring' was meant to fix financial numbers by splitting up and recombining businesses.[60] As an insider remarked, 'the US companies in my industry act like banks'; 'sometimes they act as though they are more interested in buying other companies than they are in selling products to customers'.[61] Eat-or-be-eaten became the 'natural law' of business. We saw this all again when Cadbury was taken over in 2010 by Kraft. 'While the Cadbury managers were good at making deals, they were less skilled at running the business day to day.' The bankers loved this; they charged an approximately $300 million 'service fee' for the Cadbury deal.[62] Under the conventional paradigm, society is run like a business, business like a bank and banks like hedge funds.[63]

Nowadays even the Pope condemns profit-making as the sole purpose of corporations; it is hence not productive to repeat such mantras.[64] Rather, as Sumantra Ghoshal reminded us, 'wishes and hopes are not theory. Sermons and preaching are not theory either'.[65] Accordingly, we should pursue ethical strategy on the basis of evidence: substituting shareholder's private gain for corporation's collective purpose is bad for business. Strategy without ethics brought big booms, but subsequently big busts. The recent financial crisis is just the latest indictment of strategy 'without a head on it'.[66]

When the stock market is worshipped as the ultimate barometer of success, the line is blurred between legal and illegal: Enron cooked its books,[67] Goldman advised its clients to purchase 'products' it was counting on to fall,[68] Tony Blair blocked investigations into the UK defence contractor BAE offering kick-backs to Saudi officials[69] and the Chinese tainted milk sickened 300,000 babies.[70] But ethics is not just about a few bad apples; as long as they are exposed, they will be dumped by the public.[71] Neither is ethics about handing out profits; there is no conclusive evidence that handouts are, in the long run, good for the poor.

Rather, ethics is about why Toyota pursued growth at a speed that outpaced quality assurance, as Akio Toyoda now admits.[72] It is about Facebook converting user profiles into 'publicly available information' without giving users a clear choice; Facebook did this just before the expected initial public offering, with huge advertising profits in the pipeline.[73] It is about whether we should satisfy consumers with a five-blade razor wrapped in luxury packaging, a 'smart product' that demands extra energy to produce and run.[74] It is about whether Channel 4 should broadcast the controversial *Big Brother* episode given its bad language alone, let alone implications of racism.[75] It is about why corporations in Japan today pay 'non-regular workers' half the wages of their 'regular' counterparts for doing the same job.[76] It is about EU farmers receiving 35 per cent of their income from subsidies when competing with African farmers.[77] It is about whether the UK's National Health Service should hire more doctors from the Philippines, India and English-speaking Africa; who is to take care of patients in those countries?[78] The sad irony is that those in question, or most of them, are not bad guys behaving badly; they are decent people and want to do a good job. This makes ethics in strategy all the more critical and urgent.

Ethics is not in abstract principles 'up there' that few will disagree with, but in business conduct 'down here' on the front line. It is not at the moment we open the chequebook to make a donation, but in the core business activities where we generate profits. Ethics is in the products we produce, the services we provide, the relationships we nurture, the buying and selling we do. The lost of moral sensibility only leads to value-destroying strategies. In the end, it hurts everybody. Ethics is a responsibility we should not pass on to others; it is the high ground, and the bottom line, of strategy.

What is business for?

The conventional paradigm is founded on shaky assumptions, and shaky assumptions lead to bad strategies.[79] This is so, as sociologists Robert Merton and Anthony Giddens submit, because social theories, unlike theories in physical sciences, tend to be 'self-fulfilling': they are real in their effects.[80] Sumantra Ghoshal put it this way: 'Whether right or wrong to begin with, the theory can become right as managers – who are both its subjects and the consumers – adapt their behaviours to conform with the doctrine.'[81] According to reports, economics students exposed to the 'prisoner's dilemma' game theory are more likely to betray their partners than students in other subjects. The more you 'know' how criminals behave, the more you behave like them.[82] This is what happens to the prevailing assumptions. Let us have a look at some.

Firms as casino. In the wake of corporate scandals, the management thinker Charles Handy wrote in a 2002 *Harvard Business Review* article: 'We cannot escape the fundamental question, whom and what is a business for?'[83] The answer once seemed clear. In earlier times, business owners such as Henry Ford and Andrew Carnegie saw themselves as the entrepreneurs of a new productive social order. These men were not perfect, and they differed widely: while Ford shattered the going wage with his commitment to pay $5 a day, Carnegie treated workers badly.[84] But they had one thing in common: they loved their businesses and passionately pursued technology investment for long-term prosperity. Between 1880 and 1900, for example, Carnegie increased his company's rate of investment and productivity by a factor of ten.[85]

No more. Under today's stock-market model, businesses are a money-making machine, for shareholders. 'It would, however, be more accurate to call most of them investors, perhaps even gamblers', comments Handy. 'They have none of the pride or responsibility of ownership and are, if truth be told, only there for the money.'[86] Profit, a necessary condition of business, is taken to be the sole purpose. Gamblers do not know, or care, what and how companies are doing.[87] They destroy companies in bad times. Over one October week in 2008, amid the collapse of Lehman, the Royal Bank of Scotland saw its share price plunge by 40 per cent due to panic 'selling' orders. Every night, RBS had to renew about £30 billion in the money market; eventually it was nationalised in everything but name.[88]

Gamblers destroy companies in good times, too. The world's second-biggest retailing group, Carrefour, is a case in point. Thanks to years of hard work, the group's businesses in Brazil since 1975 and in China since 1995 were fast-growing and profitable. Nevertheless, in October 2009, two big shareholders, Colony Capital, an American private equity firm, and the joint holding company Blue Capital (through which the luxury-goods group LVMH invested in Carrefour in 2007) together pressed Carrefour to sell its Asian and Latin American businesses. The sale could bring in as much as €13 billion in cash as a special dividend for shareholders. Colony Capital and Blue Capital's original investments aimed to spin off Carrefour's property portfolio for a one-off gain; that was dashed by the collapsed property market. The proposed sale would restrict Carrefour to low-growth European markets. 'Selling Asia and Latin America would ruin the group's growth prospects, and would not benefit shareholders beyond the one-off cash payment', according to seasoned analysts.[89] But one-off gain is exactly what gamblers are looking for.

Equity as wealth.[90] It is not controversial that strategy is about generating wealth. But what is wealth? In a recent BBC programme, one man said he felt 'wealthier' because his credit-card limit was increased to £5,000. But once he has used the card, is he richer or poorer? Corporations fell for the same logic. While firms frantically purchased other companies with borrowed money, few asked whether the increased price reflected the target's fundamentals or simply because buying and selling businesses had become 'best practice' of the day. Central banks and national governments were not much wiser, as their debt-burdened economies illustrate. We have confused real wealth with equity papers.

Wealth consists of the goods and services we wish to consume, as well as the assets that enable us to produce more goods and services. Financial assets, on the other hand, arise from our desire to postpone consumption so that money can be invested in producing goods and services for future consumption. Financial assets are therefore not 'wealth' but a claim on future wealth. When the price of financial assets increases, say a rise in the stock or housing market, that does not mean the aggregate wealth has increased. 'If a pizza is cut into eight instead of four slices, there is no more food to eat. If everyone sitting at the table is given shares in the pizza and the share prices rises from $1 to $2, the meal won't get any bigger.'[91] Unless we enhance the fundamentals for generating real wealth, the rising price of financial assets does not make us richer. It brings big booms, only to be followed by big busts.[92]

Market as king. In the way the Berlin Wall collapse signified the flaws in the communist doctrine, or rather the distorted practice of it, the recent crisis discredits the 'efficient-market hypothesis'.[93] The hypothesis claims that market prices reflect all the information needed to value assets. Since markets are efficient, interference in markets is by definition counter-productive. We have learned the hard way there are theoretical contradictions inherent in the hypothesis: 'If markets are informationally efficient, why is there so much trade between people who have different views of the same future?'[94]

The hypothesis is popular because it wishes away social, political and cultural influences, allowing us to uphold the illusive *ceteris paribus* ('all other things equal').[95] The hypothesis regards 'the market' as a God-given fixture, and hence releases us from ethical responsibility. Rejecting the view that 'market is always right' does not, we shall submit, necessarily lead to a conclusion that 'market is always wrong'.[96] Markets are just not perfect and sometimes they are inefficient. We know this and take advantage of it. Companies lobby governments, fund politicians, make advertisements and operate loyalty-membership schemes. What for? To manipulate 'the market'. Thus, 'the market' is not God-given, but man-made. We mould 'the market' to suit our purposes. China's newly created stock market and Washington's gigantic bail-outs are evidence at hand.

What happens when the king gets mad? Today, we shape 'the market' in such a way that the financial market, for example, is increasingly run via 'automatic trading'. Software programmes decide, at a speed of 250 microseconds per transaction, when and where to trade financial instruments.[97] On 27 February 2007, 'computer-driven programme trades' plunged leading shares on Wall Street by more than 546 points, or 4.3 per cent.[98] In February 2009, the system in UBS accidentally placed a $31 billion order, 100,000 times larger than intended.[99] The worry is: markets can crash without any sinister plotting. On 6 May 2010, a deluge of automated 'sell' orders caused Procter & Gamble shares to fall by 35 per cent, and Accenture from $40 to just one cent. 'In the minute or so that it takes humans to respond to machine meltdown, billions of dollars of damages can occur.'[100] Indeed, the 6 May 'flash crash' dropped the whole market value by 9.3 per cent, within seconds.[101] What a king!

Despite all this, accepted assumptions die hard, continue to have us take markets as the ideal way to organise all economic activities. In answer to the question 'why do firms exist?', for example, the influential transaction-cost theory refers to firms as an organising form 'of last resort, to be employed when all else fails'. 'Originally, there are markets', we are told. Within firms, activities should be conducted in market terms, as if they were 'a continuation of market relations'.[102] We create firms not for a sense of community or economic well-being but, as the theory goes, to compensate for our bounded rationality and to curb our 'nature' of 'opportunism'. Strategy under the market king is a negative, demoralising, unpleasant undertaking.[103]

Five-forces as enemies. Perhaps no other strategy tool is more effective than Michael Porter's five-forces model in focusing our attention solely on zero-sum value appropriation. Under the model, the essence of strategy is positioning yourself to grab as much as you can, while preventing other guys from eating your lunch.[104] Everyone outside the firm is treated as an enemy: other companies, new comers, suppliers and regulators. Even customers, or 'buyers' as the model calls them, are rivals to be squeezed. 'Customer is king'? No more.[105] The ascent is all about threat, barriers, power and bargaining. Trust, cooperation, collective action and mutual benefit have no place in it. Business is regarded as a kind of well-mannered dog-fight, and success is about being the top dog.[106] It is a game of extracting value from others. You have no choice, because in the model all the five forces are waging the bloody battle against you. The model is a clever, but troubling, combination of industrial organisation economics and social Darwinism.[107]

It is troubling not only because the value-appropriation logic is unpleasant, but also because it is self-defeating. For one thing, positioning in 'attractive' markets and withdrawing from 'unattractive' ones distracts firms from creating new markets. For another, if everyone rushes into 'attractive' industries, the result will be diminishing returns and misallocation of resources. To be top dog, managers must reduce competition by the means of raising entry barriers and the like, with effects of destroying social welfare. And finally, with every round of the dog-fight, companies force each other more and more into the corner, until there is no more value to appropriate, making everyone worse off. Such is the logical conclusion of the zero-sum game.

The real business world is, fortunately, different. More and more managers are questioning the value-appropriation logic. An executive in the UK had this to say:

> We have made a mess of our industry. The short-term power-based relationships have failed us. Many Western companies still believe that it is a superior way to secure competitive advantage. I think they are absolutely wrong ... We must create shared destiny relationships with all our stakeholders: customers, employees, suppliers, governments, and the communities in which we operate. It is not altruism; it is commercial self-interest.[108]

Managers as agent. In the stock-market model, managers are indispensable for bringing profit to shareholders, but cannot be trusted to do the job. Agency theory, perhaps the best-known theory of the firm and strategy, focuses on the conceived 'agency problem' that managers, in pursuit of their own interest under the cover of shareholder value, don't themselves bear the financial consequences of bad decisions. The problem is supposed to be overcome by rewarding managers with shareholdings so that they have the same motivation as shareholders.[109]

We are therefore induced to assume that managers are only interested in using resources and opportunities to pursue their own interests. However, empirical evidence has been highly ambiguous. One proponent, Michael Jensen, admits that business reality has not worked out in quite the way he had hoped.[110] Common sense and research also tell us that 'human nature' can be much richer than mere self-interest. As Amartya Sen, a Nobel Prize-winning economist, notes, 'we should not fall into the trap of presuming that the assumption of pure self-interest is, in any sense, more elementary than assuming other values'.[111] Given all this, why has a reductionist, negative image of managers gained such credence?

According to Ghoshal, the answer lies in a deeper ideology. The ideology holds that ethical problems should be left to individuals and excluded from social theory, and that strategy should focus on the 'negative problem' of preventing bad people from doing harm. These two convictions are associated with a deep-seated belief in 'freedom as the ultimate goal' and 'the individual as the ultimate entity'.[112] It is this belief, fundamental in some cultures, that legitimises the theory about self-centred agents needing to be constantly constrained.

If assumptions have nothing to do with reality, so be it. The problem is that assumptions have normative implications and real consequences. As the self-fulfilling prophecy plays itself out, the managers-as-self-seeking-agents assumption effectively curbs managers' ability to seek a positive role in society, only producing pathologically spiralling behaviours. After Enron, efforts were made to improve corporate governance by increasing the proportion of independent board members, disclosing corporate information, encouraging institutional shareholder activism and other similar prescriptions. Instead of reducing 'opportunism', however, these changes only reinforced it. Acting upon the same old assumption, managers became more skilled in privatising gains and socialising losses. In the recent crisis, when the top dogs of Citigroup, Merrill Lynch and the Royal Bank of Scotland (RBS) were forced to step down because their strategies had wiped out almost the entire shareholder value, each managed to grasp compensation of $100 million-plus.[113] In December 2009, RBS directors threatened to resign if the UK government, which had injected £45.5 billion of taxpayers' money into the bank and owned 83 per cent of its stock, vetoed the £1.5 billion bonus promised to its 'good people', its top bankers.[114]

How can this happen on the brink of total collapse? It happens because the 'reforms' so far have relied on the same shaky paradigm, based on the same disabling assumption and implemented by the same establishments. Should this go on?

Employees as asset. Under the prevailing paradigm, employees are called 'human resources', which is logically confused. Think about it. On the one hand, when shareholders invest in a company, we call their money (not the investors themselves) financial capital. When employees invest in the company, however, we call the employees (not their skill and commitment) human capital. Apparently, the paradigm applies two conflicting logics at the same time, according to which shareholders own the company and the company owns the employees.[115] Thus, like machines, employees are 'assets', to be owned, utilised, replaced, discarded. It should be no surprise that one top-dog executive boasted he was building a company that 'a monkey will be able to run when I'm gone'.[116]

This is a fair deal, as the conventional wisdom goes, because employees are compensated by salaries while the shareholders take risks. But, one should ask, are shareholders not compensated by dividends while employees risk their future? Both are investors, why should we treat one as the owner and the other as a resource? While shareholders often come in and out of a company on a whim to make instant profit, employees usually contribute to the company's well-being every day for a substantial period. If a company goes under, who loses more: the shareholders with their fluid stocks or the employees with their company-specific skills?[117]

Treated as resources, like land and machinery, employees possess only utility, no rights. They can be turned on and off, at the owner's will, in the name of efficiency.[118] Sony's Akio Morita was dismayed:

> Recently, one of these outsiders came into an American company, closed down several factories, laid off thousands of employees – and was hailed by other executives in articles in *The Wall Street Journal* as a great manager. In Japan such a performance would be considered a disgrace. Closing factories and firing employees and changing corporate direction in a business slump may be the expedient and convenient thing to do and may make the balance sheet look better at the end of the next quarter, but it destroys the company spirit. And when the business rebounds, where will the company go to get experienced workers who will produce quality goods and work hard and loyally for the company?[119]

Apparently, Morita lived on another planet; he was an alien to stock-market capitalism. During the current recession, Alcoa, a US-based company, had $1.5 billion in cash at the end of 2009, double what it had on hand at the end of 2008. Terrific performance. How did it achieve this? By cutting 28,000 jobs – 32 per cent of its workforce – and by slashing capital expenditures by 43 per cent.[120] No wonder the relationship between owners and their 'assets' tends to be confrontational. To see this, one does not need to call for Marx. Willie Walsh, the boss of British Airways, openly accused his 'resources' who had gone on strike of 'wanting to destroy BA', while Tony Woodley, joint leader of the union Unite, accused BA of being 'determined to punish loyal and decent employees'.[121] They, the 'owner' and the 'resource', see each other as deadly enemies.

But employees, unlike other resources, do have a right, and the exercise of it can damage everyone. Early 2010, within a couple of months, 15 assembly-line workers committed suicide in a Foxconn factory in the booming city of Shenzhen, southern China. The tragedy shocked society. The factory is owned by Hon Hai Precision Industry, a Taiwan-based company which is the world's largest electronics contract manufacturer, producing gadgets for Apple, Sony, Nintendo, HP, Nokia, Motorola and many other big names. The company is also the largest employer in China, with one million 'human resources' in more than 20 locations. The boss rushed to China, offered a public apology and raised workers' salaries by 30 per cent. This triggered a strike in a Honda factory in Foshan, another southern China city, resulting in a 24 per cent salary rise. Workers in Toyota's parts factory in Tianjin, a northern city near Beijing, followed suit, bringing Toyota's Chinese assembly plants to a standstill. All the strikes took place outside the control of the All-China Federation of Trade Unions, the country's monopoly union organisation.[122] No one knows where the story will end. In Guangdong province, labour disputes rose by nearly 42 per cent in the first quarter of 2009, while in Zhejiang, the annualised increase was almost 160 per cent.[123] China, the model of emerging economies, begins to see the ugly face of stock-market capitalism and taste the bitter consequences of treating employees as assets.[124]

Environment as servant. Concerns for the 'environment' are seldom far from strategy. This is evident in 'outside-in' models of the PEST and five-forces sort. While acknowledging the multidimensionality of the firm's environment, the focus is chiefly on economic, social, legal, political and technological factors, or the 'forces' of rivals, suppliers, buyers, new entrants and substitutions, leaving the natural environment largely outside strategic concerns. As to the 'inside-out' resource-based view, nature is to be exploited for competitive advantages. The eighteenth-century British political economist David Ricardo, an intellectual antecedent of the approach, promoted increasing land utilisation for above-normal rent payments. The 'original, unaugmentable, and indestructible gift of Nature' exists to serve human needs, or so Ricardo taught us.[125] In both outside-in and inside-out approaches, the natural environment is a servant to mankind, with no welfare of its own.

This is true of many influential organisation theories: open-system theory, resource-dependence theory, institutional theory, organisational-ecology theory, to name just a few.[126] According to these theories, well-managed organisations, because they extract resources from the 'environment' for survival and prosperity, should repay shareholders, customers, suppliers, business partners, government agencies and even competitors, anyone but Nature. Insofar as Nature is considered, it is addressed as public policy issues, for example, which social group should take more, or less.[127]

At the core of this prevailing paradigm lies an anthropocentric, anti-naturalistic mentality. Paul Shrivastava posits:

> [Conventional] concepts of the environment presume that nature exists to fulfil human and organisational needs. Human needs unquestioningly received priority over the natural environment. To the extent that firms attempt to fulfil human needs, they are considered to possess legitimate rights over natural resources. This generalisation of human interests serves as a licence to harness and exploit nature ... A fundamental assumption of these views is that the environment is a resource that may be exploited eternally for organisational benefit. Business organisations' sole objective is to exploit the environment to create economic value for its stockholders. No limits to this exploitation are ever acknowledged.[128]

The consequences are for all to see. In the 1950s, when Mao Zedong mobilised the construction of a new China, he proudly declared *ren ding sheng tian* (人定胜天, humankind is sure to overcome Nature), going on to produce a burdensome population and a damaged natural environment. In the 1970s, the American auto industry, led by Lee Iacocca, fought against the Clean Air Act in the US, only to see the Big Three, decades later, losing ground to Japanese and

German greener engines:[129] 'Whenever any new environmental regulation is proposed, Detroit claims that it will damage profitability.'[130] In the summer of 2010, as oil spills burned in the Gulf of Mexico, a section of the British media urged the UK government to 'stand up' to the Obama administration's clean-up payment demands. BP was too important to be allowed to go under; so many UK pension funds relied on it for dividends. In their eyes, there is no doubt which should prevail in the imagined trade-off: Nature's well-being *or* the pensioners' good life.[131]

Knowledge against ethics?

The exclusion of moral sensibility is a logical consequence of the single-minded search for scientific status.[132] Managing by numbers, you have to turn your back on issues of ethics because such issues 'cannot be elegantly modelled – the math does not exist'.[133] Consequently, thinking and acting upon ethics are seen as 'wrongheaded, second class and anti-intellectual'; talking or teaching ethics in strategy makes one seem ideological and 'anti-business'.[134] Being 'scientific' is taken to mean putting efficiency and competitiveness over social value and collective purpose.[135]

The German sociologist Max Weber distinguishes between instrumental and value rationalities. According to Weber, the scientific method, based on instrumental rationality, can determine facts, but facts cannot prove or disapprove value judgements. No matter how many facts are scientifically accumulated, they will be insufficient in themselves to adjudicate between different value standpoints. This is because choices between competing values involve a leap of faith.[136] When the balance between the two rationalities breaks down, trouble prevails. The German-born American sociologist Herbert Marcuse attributes this to technical rationality (associated with Weber's instrumental rationality) that induces us to frame all human questions in technical terms.[137] Friedrich Hayek, a Nobel Prize-winning economist, called it 'the pretence of knowledge' – a propensity to imitate the physical sciences in business, excluding any role for human intentionality and morality.[138]

Under the conventional paradigm, we see and do strategy as a technical activity to achieve ever-increasing efficiency, growth, consumption and profit. Practices and findings other than those contributing directly to efficiency are quickly put aside. We teach strategy as merely a rational means for achieving unquestioned goals, as if it involved no moral commitments.[139] But look at the toxic financial derivatives and tainted milk in 'the market', and the five-blade, battery-powered razor in our hands. We have managed to forget that science is a good servant but a bad master, to Nature, society and ultimately ourselves as human beings.

As a consequence, in all landmark debates in strategy, such as content vs process, planning vs learning, industry-driven vs resources-based or even micro-political approaches,[140] ethics is largely missing. Strategies in boardrooms as well as in classrooms are justified based not on collective purpose but on efficiency grounds. We remember and dare to ask Tolstoy's question 'what shall we do and how shall we live?'[141] only when painful damage has been done on alarming scales, in a cyclical manner: last time, Enron and Tyco; this time, the collapse of Lehman and deaths in Athens; next time …

So far, we have shown how the search for a 'science of strategy' has produced amoral, indeed unethical, strategy. The deeper trouble, however, is that recent popular critiques of positivism have not helped to bring ethics back, but led to more sophisticated exclusion of it. The root of the trouble, as Andrew Wicks and Edward Freeman suggest, lies in circular debates based on entrenched epistemological divisions.[142]

While anti-positivism holds promise to overcome the hostility towards ethics, it unwittingly retains some of the destructive elements of positivism. For example, while positivists seek to be objective truth-finders, anti-positivists present themselves as subjective meaning-interpreters. Though occupying opposite positions, positivism and anti-positivism share the same tendency to exclude moral responsibility. They do it in different ways. Whereas positivism strips away moral responsibility in favour of causal determinism, anti-positivism makes ethical judgements impossible due to deliberate relativism. Anti-positivists claim, for example,

> all theoretical perspectives are infused by the biases inhering in particular world view ... In contrast to the conventional [positivist] model, this paper represents administrative science as a fundamentally subjective enterprise. Because researchers adhere to different worldviews, they generate a variety of alternative perspectives as they impose different meaning and interpretations upon data.[143]

Such a 'fundamentally subjective' alternative is not helpful since its 'all-partial', 'all-biased' position effectively rules out the very possibility of situated, collective judgement which is at the core of ethical strategy. As Wick and Freeman point out:

> If all metaphors are partial truths, given that anti-positivists offer researchers no way outside of a given metaphor to evaluate its 'validity' or superiority, how can one determine which theory or metaphor to use? What counts as a good theory? How does one know when to stop looking for metaphors? Aren't there bad metaphors?[144]

Readers can, in the above quotations, read 'perspective', 'metaphor' and 'theory' as strategy. Obsessed with conventional philosophical distinctions, positivism privileges only scientific *truth*[145] while anti-positivism connects knowledge merely to incompatible *worldviews*.[146] Both are, as the American pragmatist Richard Rorty has argued, many levels of abstraction away from managers' real jobs that are full of ethical dilemmas.[147] Ask yourself: tomorrow I need to decide whether to approve a loan to a small business that is, according to the balance sheet, on the verge of bankruptcy. Should I based my decision on objectivism, subjectivism, functionalism, interpretivism, constructivism, postmodernism or some other '-ism'? Are these neat, fixed 'philosophical engines' helpful for making pressing ethical decisions in the fast-moving business world?[148]

The tragedy is: while most positivists and anti-positivists as persons may not feel hostile to value and purpose, the content and logic of their epistemology nevertheless make ethics a marginalised topic. On the one hand, for example, we have Michael Porter's positivist five-forces model that tells managers to prevent competition by erecting barriers to entry.[149] On the other, we have Robert Chia's anti-positivist 'style-alone' perspective that dismisses strategy content and substance altogether.[150] In both Porter and Chia camps, moral responsibility has no place. They are fully occupied with the question 'what is the world, how do we know it?' and rarely concern themselves with 'how shall we live and what should we do?'

Since Enron, business schools have been busy developing eye-catching courses on corporate social responsibility (CSR),[151] MBA students sign up to an oath of moral conduct,[152] companies are rewriting ethical credos[153] and big multinationals are reaching out to environmental activists.[154] Given these well-meaning efforts, why do we still have bigger scandals, wider collapses and deeper crises? In view of pragmatism, this is because ethics is still far from being woven into the very fabric of strategy. Tokenism such as adding a CSR course or composing ethical statements will not do; we need a fundamental reorientation.[155] Until it is firmly incorporated as an inherent strategy bottom line, ethics will remain remote principles, something tacked on, nice to have, at best a constraining force upon irresponsible behaviours but not an inspiring engine for realising common goodness. Until we take moral sensibility as the heart and soul of strategy, we will continue to have the subprime crisis, the Channel 4 racism incident, the tainted milk in China and BP's explosions and oil spills. Until our strategies are justified in light of Tolstoy's question,[156] we will not be able to prevent greed from becoming good again, and the dream of a 'less selfish capitalism' will remain just that – a wish.[157]

BP: profit over safety?[158]

The rig explosion in the Gulf of Mexico in April 2010, which killed 11 workers and triggered a massive oil spill, was only the latest chapter in BP's safety, or rather un-safety, history. Given BP's recent record and priorities, it was a disaster waiting to happen.

The then chief executive, Tony Hayward, took over BP in 2007, following the unexpected, early departure of Lord Browne. During his 12 years in the top job, Browne had transformed BP from the weakest of the oil giants into one of the 'super majors'. This he achieved by orchestrating two eye-catching acquisitions: the $56 billion purchase of Amoco in 1998 and a $27 billion purchase of Arco in 2000. Inside the company, Browne, 'often viewed as more of a banker than an oil engineer', pursued an aggressive cost-cutting strategy. 'If you look through his statements in recent years they are all about cutting costs, cutting costs and cutting costs', a former oil executive commented. This included phasing out hundreds of skilled engineering jobs and subcontracting out oil-drilling, refinery maintenance, pipeline monitoring and platform construction supervision. The result was stunning. Under Browne's leadership BP's market value and profit rose fivefold to £106 billion and £11.6 billion; its shares outperformed the FTSE 100 share index by about 80 per cent. 'Beyond Petroleum' – BP was no longer 'a boring exploration company but a company of entrepreneurs'. This earned Browne the sobriquet 'the Sun King'; and he was for years regarded by *Fortune* magazine and the like as the most powerful executive outside America.

However, alongside the huge profit were continuous safety disasters. In 2005, BP's Texas City refinery exploded, killing 15 people and injuring 170; the following year, 260,000 gallons of oil gushed out of BP pipelines at the Prudhoe Bay oilfield in Alaska; there were also many other 'minor' accidents. BP's un-safety record was in the spotlight. In 2007, the US Chemical Safety and Hazard Investigation Board concluded that cost-cutting had contributed to the fatal disasters. The Baker Report, based on a 14-month investigation, written by a panel led by James Baker, the former US Secretary of State, found warning signs dating back several years before the disasters. The report criticised BP's 'entrepreneurial' culture that prioritised production targets and financial goals over safety accountabilities.

For years, financial targets and a 'can-do' culture had pushed BP into doing whatever was necessary to keep operations running. A BP technology vice president admitted that 'Texas City's problems were significantly aggravated by the 25 per cent cost reduction' imposed on the site in 1999. BP's director of process safety listed 'incompetence, high tolerance of non-compliance and inadequate maintenance and investments' as the cause of the disasters. Facing orders from Browne to slash costs by 25 per cent, many workers complained that 'managers were not nearly worried enough about the real dangers', adding that 'the top level in London need to understand the consequences of their orders'. BP's internal documents show that the company successfully lobbied against tighter environmental controls in Texas, saving $150 million in monitoring and equipment upgrades prior to the Texas City explosion. For this 'success', the regulatory affairs manager was nominated by BP for a bonus. The upgrade would have, according to the US Chemical Safety Board, prevented or at least mitigated the disaster. 'There is no doubt that cost-cutting and profits have taken precedence over safety and the environment', a former BP engineer in Alaska said. The *Financial Times* sums it up: 'BP's aggressive cost-cutting culture has been driven by the extraordinary pressure that financial markets place on businesses to do anything and everything to boost short-term profitability.'

When Hayward took over the top job in 2007, he noted Browne's legacy: 'We have a management style that has made a virtue of doing more for less.' His priority was 'simple and clear', he declared, 'to implement our strategy by focusing like a laser on safe and reliable operations'. To prevent similar incidents, he took steps to restore the company's core skills in engineering. At the same time, he aggressively pushed BP to the outer limits of deepwater exploration, extracting oil from deeper and more treacherous ocean depths. This was his driving obsession: it was in the Gulf of Mexico and off the coasts of Angola and Egypt that Hayward felt BP could excel and trump its rivals. The state-of-the-art Deepwater Horizon rig that exploded in the Gulf of Mexico was drilled in September 2009 to 10,685 metres below sea level, a world record. The risk was obvious. 'What we do at that depth in the ocean is similar to Nasa's space programme', a production engineering manager at Anadarko, one of BP's drilling partners in the Gulf, said.

Meanwhile, the less-for-more culture lingered on at BP. An executive from another oil company said he was 'shocked' when he saw the low-cost but risky design chosen by BP for its Macondo well. While risk is always present in the oil sector, BP was unprepared for failures of the equipment designed to prevent incidents, nor did a coherent plan exist to deal with the aftermath. In Hayward's words, BP did not have 'the tools you would want in your toolkit'. More chilling is that BP did know in advance the specific danger. In June 2000, the company issued a 'notice of default' regarding the rig to Transocean, the operator of the now-exploded rig; in response, Transocean acknowledged that the equipment did 'not work exactly right'. It is reported that there were arguments between high-ranking officials on the morning before the rig exploded. Another preventable disaster became routine on BP's watch.

BP took efforts to limit the damage. Under the water, submarine robots were deployed to activate a shut-off switch. A 100-tonne steel and concrete containment dome was lowered to cover the well. Both failed. Engineers injected a tube into the broken pipe to siphon off some of the oil into vessels on the water's surface. The last resort was to drill a relief well so as to ease pressure on the leaking well, meanwhile injecting a load of debris into the broken well and using heavy fluids and cement to seal it. At sea, 114 aircraft and more than 4,000 vessels were in action, applying 5.4 million gallons of dispersants to break up the oil.

For a while, Hayward directed the incident command centre at BP's offices in Houston, overseeing the aftermath operation. He pledged 'I will stay here until we have fixed it'. The centre mobilised 500 people from 160 companies across the oil industry. At the same time, the tiny port of Venice on the Mississippi River was turned into a hub for clean-up operations. More than 41,000 federal officials, state coastguards and local workers, plus thousands of trained volunteers, built more than 11,500 km of barriers to protect the coastline. For two months, BP chairman Carl-Henric Svanberg remained almost invisible; the former Ericsson chief had little experience of the oil industry.[159] BP finally killed the well and stemmed the oil gush on 19 September, five months after the explosion.

For the Texas explosion and Alaskan oil leaks, BP paid a $380 million fine. Comparing this with BP's profit, critics dismissed the fine as 'a sick joke'. The clean-up effort following the explosion and spill in the Gulf of Mexico has so far cost $2 billion. 'It was not our accident, but it is our responsibility', said Hayward. Two months after the explosion, BP's share fell by half, its market value dropped from more than £125 billion to less than £63 billion. The company's credit rating was downgraded by Fitch from AA to BBB. According to Goldman Sachs, the costs associated with the spill could reach $70 billion. After a meeting between Obama, Svanberg and Hayward, BP agreed to set aside a $20 billion fund to cover claims related to the spill and another $100 million fund to compensate laid-off oil workers. The company also agreed to suspend dividends for the rest of 2010.[160]

BP has been mocked by the public as Beyond the Pale, Bloated Profit, Broken Pipelines, Bust Petroleum, Big Problem and British Polluter. When Hayward broke his pledge by flying back to London for a board meeting and his birthday party, and was seen on his yacht at the Isle of Wight's Round the Island race ('I'd like my life back'), the oil was still gushing out from the seabed. The company is now under US criminal and civil investigations. If it is found to have acted with 'gross negligence', its executives could face up to 15 years in prison. It is bad, but perhaps not fatal, given BP's 'strong balance sheet' and the spill's 'very, very modest' environmental impact – in the words of Hayward.[161]

Hayward stepped down from the top job in October 2010. He is a human being. He did take steps to change the 'entrepreneurial' culture and (un-)safety regime he inherited from Browne. He was angry that the Gulf of Mexico disaster happened. He was trained in geography, not in law, literature or political science. He does not have Obama's silver tongue. Some of his casual comments during those sleepless nights had annoyed many. At the Congressional hearing, he said what the lawyers told him to say. He did not see his son for three months after the explosion. When he joined his son on the yacht, he did not expect to appear on television at midnight American time. There are many excuses; some are legitimate. The question is: do they help us learn from mistakes and make ethics top on our corporate agendas? The question is not just for Hayward, but for all of us.

OVERCOMING SPECIALISED DEAFNESS

On a visit to the London School of Economics in 2008, Queen Elizabeth II asked the economists, 'Why did no one see the crisis coming?' Apparently no one told her that some did see it coming.[162] Answering this embarrassing question, one of Her Majesty's subjects admitted, 'we all tend to look at just one bit of the clichéd elephant in the room'; another said, 'some of us got the single pieces right, but failed in putting the pieces together'.[163] At last, painfully, we get it.

In strategy, tunnel vision and its painful consequences are not news. In their 1980 paper, Hayes and Abernathy comment:

> US managers want everything to be simple. But sometimes business situations are not simple, and they cannot be divided up or looked at in such a way that they become simple. They are messy, and one must try to understand all the facets. This appears to be alien to the American mentality ... At the strategic level there are not such things as pure production problems, pure financial problems, or pure marketing problems.[164]

It is not just the Americans. The British have their *Big Brother* row,[165] the Chinese their toxic milk,[166] the Japanese the Toyota recall,[167] the Koreans and Indians their corporate bosses in jail[168] and the Arabs plenty of unfinished villas in the desert. It is a question to all of us: why do we behave like the blind men?

Fragmented strategies for an interconnected world?

The field of strategy is characterised by controversies about almost everything with which it concerns itself. Igor Ansoff and Henry Mintzberg, two respected figures, cannot even agree on the existential question 'what is strategy?'[169] The only consensus is perhaps that there is no consensus. As Chris Bilton and Steven Cummings observe, 'not only did strategic management thus become separated from the rest of the organisation, but divided within itself into separate models or approaches'.[170] The fragmentation spreads over many levels.

At the empirical level, despite more than 50 years of investigation, no conclusive answers can be found on pressing strategic questions: diversification or focusing, integration or outsourcing, how much does industry matter, and so on. GE under Jack Welch may appear to support a diversification strategy with its highly unrelated yet profitable businesses. But counter-examples are abundant: the value-destroying effect of the Korean conglomerates exposed during the 1997 financial meltdown, for example. Nokia may serve as an exemplar of focusing strategy, but the same strategy brought Marconi, once the biggest manufacturer in the UK, to its knees.[171] One-size-fits-all 'best practices' turn out to be shaky.[172]

At another level, strategy professors have problems deciding what questions to ask. There are tensions over everything: content vs process, market-oriented vs resources-based, and so forth.[173] Too often, ideas are framed in either/or terms. Once a 'new' insight is proposed, the 'old' must be discredited; 'Learning 1, planning 0', Mintzberg famously claimed.[174] This I-hold-the-key-to-strategy mentality manifests in almost every 'new' agenda. More recently, we've been hearing old arguments on new topics: 'strategy is *not* what the firm has, *but* what people do', 'a dwelling mode is *more basic* than the building mode', and so on.[175] The quest for once-and-forever hierarchy dies hard indeed.

Finally, strategy the applied field is deeply divided by base academic disciplines. Thanks to Porter, economics has since the 1980s gained a firm foothold, although not without its critics.[176] The debate between proponents of organisational economics and structural contingency theory is characteristic,[177] the battle over whether deductive methodology should be pursued above all others is far from over[178] and the controversy about the pedagogical merit of the case-study method is still going on.[179] Alongside economics, cognitive science, political science, sociology and poststructuralist discourse are all ambitious contenders for the 'single best' crown.[180] As to philosophical 'engines', postmodernism has recently been proposed as the 'most suitable' perspective for strategy.[181]

We are where we are: strategy has experienced a prolific development of specialised approaches and has received hugely diverse prescriptions.[182] If diversity is taken as the criterion, strategy is much more advanced than many other management fields – finance, marketing, logistics, for example. However, diversity is not in itself a virtue; it can easily slide into a heap of tunnel visions. Specialisation in a trade, any trade, is valuable only when exchanges take place.[183] Without exchanges, i.e., conversation and mutual learning, the strategy field is deeply confusing. Researchers are frustrated; they describe the field as a 'cacophony of discordant voices',[184] a 'mosaic of fragmented theories'[185] and a 'fragmented adhocracy'.[186]

This has serious impacts on the front line. Managers are bombarded by competing recipes and are left without any help to make sense or use of the diversity. As a Malaysian executive puts it, 'our problem is there are too many solutions'.[187] Managers either 'have come to feel that it has nothing to do with their reality and they no longer pay attention to theoretical development',[188] or, if they take the theoretical heap as guidance, end up with reductionist policies with grave consequences.[189] Companies may increase their stock price at the cost of creating environmental disasters and losing human lives, as the BP case illustrated; broadcasters may boast higher viewer ratings at the expense of racial harmony, as the *Big Brother* saga demonstrated; firms may double their market shares but compromise safety and quality, as the Toyota recalls showed us; they may make a profit from harming hundreds of thousands of babies, as happened in China's tainted-milk scandal.

Boxes syndrome

In 1979, Gibson Burrell and Gareth Morgan published an influential book, titled *Sociological Paradigms and Organisational Analysis*.[190] In that book, the authors classify social theories into four boxes. The boxes are constructed along two dimensions: one polarises under-lying assumptions on ontology, epistemology, human nature and methodology, the other contrasts theories according to their atti-tudes towards social order and change. Bundling this schema with a peculiar interpretation of Kuhn's 'paradigm incommensurability' idea, the book argues for isolated development of theories in order to protect diversity.[191] Since its publication, it has become fashionable to categorise strategies into x-dimension-y-box schemas.

Such schemas, when properly constructed, are useful for inform-ing managers about the multifaceted complexity of strategic issues and the variety of available approaches.[192] Problems arise, however, when it comes to putting the approaches to use. This advice is typical:

> Faced with these oppositions, for every manager the strategy-making process starts with a fundamental strategic choice: which theoretical picture of human activity and environment fits most closely with his or her own view of the world, his or her personal 'theory of action'.

The advice is straightforward: theories informing strategies are antagonistic opposites, managers must make an either/or choice at the outset, and the basis for making that choice is which theory fits with one's taste.

Applied in this way, however, the schemas conflate how theo-rists see their research with how managers ought to solve situated problems.[193] Once we go down the road of polarising-and-choosing, we tend to force strategies into self-sufficient, completed fortresses, closing down the possibility of conversation, mutual learning and complementary synergy. Choosing between fortresses, we lean, perhaps unwillingly, towards fundamentalist 'principles', and turn away from the fuzzy, shifting problems on the front line. The aim is no longer to benefit from each theory in order to enrich our capacity to act, but to seek exclusive conviction or total rejection, regardless of unfolding circumstances. This may be good for theoretical purity, but is it good for coping with strategic challenges that are, in Hayes and Abernathy's words, seldom 'simple and pure'? In the end, what are the dimensions and boxes good for if we must make once-and-forever, either/or choices?

Tunnel vision is a network effect

Why is tunnel vision ingrained so deeply? To begin with, as Porter reminds us in his later work, 'Strategy is ... a field where everything matters. Choices matter, the leader matters, the culture matters, the values matter, random events matter, and so on. Strategy is an inherently integrative subject that has to allow for complexity.'[194] The problem, rooted in a culture of opposites and contradictions, is that the conventional paradigm has turned complexity into fragmentation that precludes coherent strategy.[195]

Furthermore, strategy must satisfy a wide range of practitioners across many sectors (from private businesses to public agencies), in varying industries (from making steel to running football clubs), in diverse markets (from Parisian designer fashion to second-hand cloth trading in Africa), in different institutional contexts (from Wall Street making multi-million-dollar deals to the Grameen Bank lending to millions of the poorest in the vast countryside) and from different professional backgrounds (accountants, lawyers, marketers, engineers and many others). These heterogeneous users have different ideas on what strategic questions are and how they should be answered.[196]

As we mentioned earlier, strategy has a long tradition of appropriating knowledge from base disciplines. Along with valuable insights, these base disciplines offer conflicting assumptions (deterministic vs voluntaristic), contradictory aims (prescriptive vs descriptive), different methodologies (formal modelling vs ethno-graphic), divergent focuses (content, process, context) and layered units of analysis (individual, group, the firm, industry, organisational field, society), as well as difficult-to-share terminologies. The exponents of competing 'world hypotheses' find it difficult talking to each other, let alone to managers.[197]

The problem goes deeper. Humans are interested beings. Along discipline lines, gatekeepers fiercely protect their domains.[198] In a publish-or-perish academic world, there is a 'constant drive for recognition and a place in the scholarly and consultancy marketplace'.[199] In this contest, newness tends to be ranked higher than the enduring, differentiation trumps coherence and assertions speak louder than conversations.[200] As a consequence, 'the over-accentuation of the base disciplines has led to theoretical frameworks that have little to say about the practical problems in strategic management'.[201]

Fragmentation is a network effect between the above factors. The cause is at once material and technical, cognitive and mental, psychological and social, political and institutional. The ambiguity in business logics is real, the differences in disciplinary assumptions are real, the rival knowledge claims of competing worldviews are real, the diverse demands from heterogeneous audiences are real, and the scholars' vested interests and political motives are real. Attributing tunnel vision to a single cause is itself a type of tunnel vision; and achieving coherent strategy demands more than merely sorting out theoretical puzzles or winning epistemological arguments. This brings us to a popular but problematic metaphor: the elephant and the blind men.

Are we all blind men?

Fifty years ago, Kenneth Boulding, a system thinker, expressed his concern about 'specialised deafness':

> Science, that is to say, is what can be talked about profitably
> by scientists in their role as scientists. The crisis of science
> today arises because of the increasing difficulty of such

profitable talk among scientists as a whole. Specialisation
has outrun Trade, communication between the disciples
becomes increasingly difficult, and the Republic of Learning is
breaking up into isolated subcultures with only tenuous lines
of communication between them – a situation which threatens
intellectual civil war.[202]

Today, Boulding's concern has become a reality. Specialised deafness
is no longer considered an illness but a prudent strategy.[203] Tunnel
vision becomes 'skilled incompetence'.[204] Worse, we are not just
unable to see the 'big picture', we become hostile to it. To many,
'big picture' is one and the same thing as central planning, associated with the failed socialist economy, not for the postmodern, post-
collective, cool 'free market'. Our trained incompetence is backed by
the 'end of history' ideology.

The new danger is: while strategy is rapidly expanding its application domain, the conventional paradigm continues to constrain
us with the 'simple and pure' mentality. As system thinkers West
Churchman, Ian Mitroff and Harold Linstone warn us, we may have
included more phenomena in our investigation, but failed to reached
out for multiple perspectives. In other words, we have expanded the
range of things we are to look at, but failed to enrich our way of
seeing things. We 'solve' more 'problems', using the same old single
'solution'.[205]

Is the metaphor of 'the elephant and the blind men' helpful
for overcoming this? Insofar as it encourages us to embrace multiple perspectives, it is useful. As Sony's Morita reminded us, 'seeing
things from many viewpoints is important for businesses'.[206] But the
metaphor can carry us only so far. Relying on this metaphor alone
we will face unintended consequences.

For one thing, the metaphor implies that the elephant is objectively out there and that we fail to comprehend it only because of our
subjective limitations. As long as we are not blind, we will get the
true picture of the real thing. This immediately favours a particular

sort of tunnel vision that accepts only 'one objective reality' and 'one correct representation'. In Rorty's words, the metaphor privileges the illusive 'Mirror of Nature'.[207] In the name of pluralism, the metaphor in fact promotes a single truth. The problem is, many 'things' in strategy are not like the elephant. The market, the firm, customer needs and models of capitalism, just to name a few, are partly the result of our ideals and efforts. They are not given, but made. We do not receive these things from God, we participate in producing and changing them, via our imagination, creativity and moral standing. Strategy is not an elephant and we are not blind men.

Then, the metaphor focuses our attention solely on 'what does the elephant look like, how can I ensure that my knowledge about it is valid?' This is not very helpful because it distracts us from practical purpose. In strategy, getting jobs done is more important than obtaining eternal knowledge, even supposing such knowledge to be obtainable. We seek knowledge in order to solve practical problems. If you want to move logs in the forest, for example, knowledge about the elephant's legs and trunk will be more useful than information about the colour of its skin. In our world of limited resources and plentiful suffering, we need to focus our inquiries. 'The more metaphors the better' instruction is attractive but not helpful in solving here-and-now problems. Mats Alvesson and Hugh Willmott call it the 'supermarket approach'.[208] The challenge lies not in piling up viewpoints but in judging and justifying which viewpoint(s) to use for a specific task, and putting it into action. This is missing in the story of the blind men.

Finally, the elephant and the blind men exclude any sense of ethical accountability. This is a typical case of 'knowledge against ethics'. The metaphor blocks us from considering the ethical question 'what should we do and how shall we live?' with the narrow cognitive question 'what do I know and how do I know what I know is true?' Given that each of the blind men, by definition, only knows part of the elephant, the metaphor is, perhaps unintentionally, powerful in propagating the all-partial, all-biased relativism that denies situated, collective ethical judgements. The bankers in Wall Street will be happy to admit their bad behaviour if everyone else is also considered guilty, and we will have no hope for doing better because next time we are all-partial, all-biased again. Unfortunately, this is the implication of the blind men. They even do not recognise they are blind to ethical responsibility. As we see from the case below, the all-partial, all-biased, all-guilty mentality is bad for strategy. To overcome specialised deafness, we need to move beyond the elephant and the blind men. Strategy should take collective purpose and situated judgement seriously.

Is 'Made in China' safe?[209]

In the summer of 2007, a number of product-safety scandals rocked China and the world, followed by an escalating series of tit-for-tat moves that broke out between China and its trading partners.

Allegedly perilous Chinese goods included pet food, seafood, soy sauce, toothpaste, toys, tyres; the list went on. At least 93 Panamanians and 16 US pets were reported to have died after consuming made-in-China products. Food and safety authorities in the West were alarmed and acted swiftly. The US Food and Drug Administration, for example, blocked shipments of Chinese-made toothpaste and several types of Chinese farm-raised seafood. This was followed by product recalls by Western companies that outsourced production to China. Mattel, the world's biggest toy-maker, for example, recalled 21 million Chinese-made toys, including Barbie dolls and cars, concerned that they were either coated with lead paint or contained small magnets that could be swallowed by children. One child died in 2006 and more than 30 had been injured by the magnets. Mattel was alarmed – of the roughly 800 million toys it produced every year, more than two-thirds were made in China. As the bans and recalls grew, some Western companies began labelling home products 'China-free' in response to consumer concerns. The international media had a field day, and books with titles such as *Poorly Made in China* were on the front shelves of airport bookshops. As the saga went on, the human cost fell not just on Western consumers; after Mattel's first recall, the owner of one of its suppliers in southern China committed suicide.

China's responses were equally swift. A Chinese court sentenced to death Zheng Xiaoyu, the first head of China's State Food and Drug Administration, for approving fake medicines in exchange for bribes. The government banned 750 toy exporters and arrested 774 people within two months as part of a clampdown on substandard products. Wu Yi, the then vice-premier, told reporters that China was engaged in a 'special battle'. At the same time, China suspended imported chicken and drink mixes from the US, pork from Canada, bottled water from France and seafood from Australia, all on safety grounds. At the peak of the 'Made in China' row, in a meeting on 21 September 2007 with Li Changjiang, the chief of China's quality watchdog, Mattel senior executive Thomas Debrowski was seen offering an apology to the Chinese people for the company's unfair accusations against Chinese products. Debrowski admitted that unsafe toys were produced as a result of the company's design, not production flaws in China. The meeting was broadcast in real time via major Chinese TV channels, which was unusual. Only a few hours later, however, Mattel said that Debrowski had not meant to talk to Li in the presence of journalists and that the nature of the meeting had been 'mischaracterised'. To the Chinese, however, such an apology was long overdue. One of the authors of this book was teaching in Hong Kong at the time, and he happened to watch, on a local TV programme, a group of 'famous experts and scholars' enthusiastically condemning the evil attempts of anti-China forces to 'black-wash' Chinese products. One of our Chinese professor friends in Beijing told us that everything in the world was connected with everything else – it was unfair to single out China for blame. Foreign companies had recklessly forced Chinese manufacturers to cut costs, Western consumers relentlessly demanded spiralling lower prices and the US and European governments unfairly used shifting safety standards as trade barriers to protect their uncompetitive industries.

Then, disaster struck. In September 2008, approximately one year after the 'Made in China' row, six babies died and 300,000 fell ill in China after drinking milk powder that was tainted with an industrial chemical. The chemical was known to cause severe kidney damage, but had nevertheless been used for years in water-added milk products to mimic protein in lab tests. Within a few days of this practice being exposed to the public, all Chinese-brand milk powders disappeared from shop shelves despite company bosses eagerly drinking their products in front of TV cameras. No Chinese mother bought Chinese milk for her precious, in most cases only, child any more. The shelves were filled with foreign brands. This time, no foreigners were to blame, although several Asian and African countries immediately banned imports of Chinese milk, ice cream, yoghurt, chocolate, biscuits, sweets, anything that could contain milk from China. Ordinary Chinese citizens were angry. Mothers gathered outside the factories and local government compounds, and academics protested: 'this is the self-destruction of a national industry', 'does a nation deserve a future while it poisons its babies for profit?' Again, heads rolled: four months after the baby deaths, Tian Wenhua, the former chairwoman and general manager of one of the producers, was sentenced to life imprisonment; Geng Jinping, a milk dealer, and Zhang Yujun, a cattle farmer, were executed. Li Changjiang, the chief of China's quality watchdog who had pressed Debrowski for a public apology, was moved to another post.

This is, sadly, only one of many 'normal accidents' in China.[210] In 2004, 50 babies died and another 200 were malnourished after being fed fake baby formula; in 2006, bogus antibiotics killed 6 and made 80 people ill. According to a report by the Asian Development Bank and the World Health Organization, at least 300 million Chinese – roughly the same number as the entire US population – suffer from food-borne diseases annually. A survey released in 2007 by the Chinese authorities showed that, while less than 1 per cent of food for export was substandard or tainted, the figure in domestic markets was 20 per cent. There is a popular joke in China: a young man attempted suicide by drinking DDT but failed; then, just when he changed his mind, he was accidently killed after eating an apple he bought from the fruit market – the DDT was fake while the apple contained chemical fertiliser, pesticide, growth hormone and pigment many times above safety levels.

Instead of maintaining 'everything is connected and everyone is responsible', holistic thinking, used differently, might challenge us to ask uncomfortable but helpful questions, such as: why did it need a push from the New Zealand premier Helen Clark to bring the news to the Chinese public? Why was the public not told until the Beijing Olympics ended, even though authorities had known about the problem months before? Why was only a small portion of media allowed to report the accident? Why were the parents of baby victims prevented from attending the court hearing? Why did these parents have to sue for compensation in Hong Kong, not on the mainland? Why did whistle-blowers who reported in confidence to the authorities end up harassed or murdered? On what grounds was the father of a baby victim sentenced to two years in prison after he talked to reporters in the street? Why were so many people willing to cut corners to make a profit at the cost of human lives? Is the discredited Made-in-China brand a production problem, a standard problem, a management problem, a training problem, a cultural problem, a political problem, a rule-of-law problem, an institutional problem?

No one wants to die with money in one hand and a poisonous apple in the other. We all have a stake in the safety of Made-in-China. After all, the world is indeed connected: China exported 22 billion toys in 2006 alone, 60 per cent of the world's total.

We learn the hard way the problematic of the conventional paradigm. In this chapter we have made a critical examination of it. The paradigm is found to be disabling due to its diminished practical orientation, marginalised ethical sensibility and lack of holistic thinking. It is in order to forge a new strategy paradigm that we call for a pragmatic turn, promoting pragmatism as a timely, workable alternative that is useful for closing the practice gap, bringing ethics back in and overcoming specialised deafness.

Given that people around the world are rooted in diverse cultures, with different histories, heterogeneous experiences and local concerns, can pragmatic strategy be meaningful, doable and workable across these vast differences? What are the similarities and differences between cultural traditions, as far as pragmatism is concerned? How can people around the world learn from each other in the pursuit of practically wise strategy? With these questions, we invite readers to the next, and the final, chapter of this book, 'Pragmatism East and West'.

9   Pragmatism East and West

In previous chapters we drew mainly on Confucianism. As readers may have already noted, we have also been incorporating what we consider useful from the traditions and practices of other people, East and West, South and North. This is inspired by pragmatism: *bricolage* making-do, we need to enlarge our resource pool. Meanwhile, whatever we learn from others, we need to adapt to local circumstances. To achieve this, it is imperative to heighten our sensitivity towards the differences between traditions.

Hence, undertaking a pragmatic turn, it is useful to appreciate what the similarities and differences are, how different pragmatist traditions can learn from each other, and, most importantly, how they can inform strategic actions of today. A thousand-mile journey begins with a small step (千里之行始于足下), as a Confucian proverb goes. Taking such a step in this chapter, we will explore the key intellectual sources that inform current pragmatic thinking and practices in 'the East' and 'the West'.

By 'examining traditions', we do not mean digging up ancient canons on oracles or bamboo slips to discover their 'genuine meaning'.[1] We do not claim such meaning. There can be no 'objective reading' of Confucius, Dewey or Aristotle;[2] there is always a 'distance' between our current concerns and those of past thinkers.[3] Neither do we regard 'authorial' Confucian or Deweyan or Aristotelian teachings as ideal states to be emulated; there is no sense, no hope, no way in returning to the past.[4] Rather, we will analyse contemporary interpretations of Confucian, Deweyan and Aristotelian wisdom. As John Dewey suggested, past doctrines require reconstruction in order to remain useful for solving present problems.[5] Talking about

Marx, Richard Rorty posited: 'the question is not who the real Marx was but which Marx is relevant for today.'[6] We agree.

We shall begin with American pragmatism. We intend to explore converging ideals between Confucian and American pragmatisms, one originated in the ancient 'East', the other developed in the modern 'West'. We will then contrast Confucius the Asian with Aristotle the European, analysing the differences between their practice-oriented teachings and the impacts of these on contemporary strategy. We will finally suggest how strategists in this plural and interconnected world can benefit from appreciating and acting upon similarities and differences.

PRAGMATISM, A SHARED TREASURE

Just as Confucianism is not a homogeneous tradition, American pragmatism is not a single doctrine, but ongoing experiences that raise open questions and accommodate a great deal of diversity.[7] As early as 1908, Arthur Lovejoy entitled his classic article 'The thirteen pragmatisms'.[8] Nevertheless, it is possible, and useful, to discern concerns and ideals that are shared among the great pragmatists: Charles Sanders Peirce, William James, John Dewey, George Herbert Mead, Hilary Putnam and Richard Rorty.[9] In comparing pragmatism in 'the East' and 'the West', we deliberately structure our reading of American pragmatism to parallel the 'six spirits' of Confucianism.[10] We recognise that, in doing so, we are taking the risk of reading our own culture into the 'other'.[11] Nevertheless, as all learning relies on some sort of structure, the best strategy is not to pretend having no structure, but to make the merits and risks of our structure transparent. Fully aware of being selective and fallible, let us embark on the comparison journey.

Practical: action vs truth

What is pragmatism? This is James' ideal:

> [A pragmatist] turns away from abstractions and insufficiency, from verbal solutions, from bad *a priori* reasons, from fixed

principles, closed systems, and pretended absolutes and
origins. He turns towards concreteness and adequacy, towards
facts, towards action and towards power ... The attitude of
looking away from the first things, principles, 'categories',
supposed necessities; and of looking towards last things, fruits,
consequences, facts.[12]

In the same spirit, Peirce equated the meaning of a concept with its
operational consequences. For Dewey, theories are tools for solving
practical problems, a means of meeting human desires. The emphasis
is on the active, the doing. Human inquiries are not about copying
the world but coping with life's demands.[13] Instead of a focus on the
essence of things, the pragmatists' prior concern has always been the
appropriateness of action.[14]

In contrast to 'spectator's theory', pragmatists promote 'par-
ticipant's perspective'. Instead of 'god's-eye view', they value 'agent's
point of view'.[15] To Dewey, knowledge is an instrument for successfully carrying out certain performance.[16] The value of knowledge
lies 'in their ability to facilitate the pursuit of ends'.[17] The purpose
of inquiry is to 'enrich human possibilities and open up new aims or
ends-in-view'. The role of theorising is not to discover eternal truths
but to inspire imagination in the course of solving ordinary problems of ordinary people.[18]

The 'primacy of problem-solving', as writers in 'the West' like
to call it, remains lively today. Edgar Arthur Singer, an assistant of
James, argued that 'philosophy as thinking' had to give way to 'philosophy as doing'.[19] To Rorty, a 'new' pragmatist, knowledge is inseparable from accomplishing what we want to achieve.[20] Theories are
interesting insofar as they feed into ongoing discourses that lead to
practical differences. 'Theory is a servant to practical ends.'[21]

This attitude distances pragmatists from the entrenched
enterprise of truth-seeking. Foucault once said that the search for
truth is '*the* question for the West'.[22] According to our reading, it is
not the question for 'the West' as a whole, surely not for American

pragmatists. 'All pragmatists would rather focus on what is useful rather than what is true.'[23] The pragmatist West is a spiritual ally of the Confucian East.

For Peirce, 'The crux of our knowledge of things does not lie in their descriptive characterization; rather it is a matter of knowing what to do with them'.[24] James maintained that 'truth happens to an idea. It becomes true, is made true by events'.[25] This reminds us nicely of Zhuangzi's (庄子) teaching 'Tao is made in the walking of it (道成之于行)'. Dewey distinguished truth, true and truly thus: 'The adverb "truly" is more fundamental than either the adjective true, or the noun, truth. An adverb expresses a way, a mode of acting.'[26] Using a metaphor 'mirror of Nature', Rorty challenged the belief that some descriptions, by claiming to capture the essence of the outer world, are more privileged than others.[27] Corresponding truth is untenable, truth-seeking is not interesting and theoretical differences that do not make a practical difference are not worthwhile.[28] As to strategy, pragmatists suggest:

> The focus of discussions should be on the concerns of managers, communities, and other key stakeholders, rather than the abstract and often obtuse discourse of philosophers … Starting with metaphysics and theology not only unnecessarily clouds the issues, it seems to violate the spirit of democracy. Thus, in terms of collective efforts, it is best to start by asking what set of goals can be agreed upon, what kinds of agreements people require to create community, and how they can be implemented.[29]

Indeed, what is the point of debating 'the metaphysical outlook' of Nintendo's Wii console or 'the epistemological paradigm' behind Lehman's collapse? Instead of metaphysical essence or corresponding truth, pragmatists base judgement and justification on contexts, purposes and consequences. It is in and through our purposeful coping with life problems that the world becomes structured by us.[30]

When we do problem-solving, we solve specific problems located in specific situations.[31] For Dewey, 'discourse that is not controlled by reference to a situation is not discourse but a meaningless jumble'.[32] 'We are always in the middle of things'[33] and things are usually confusing, engendering doubt, embarking us on inquiries to ease that doubt and to get on in the world.[34]

God is in the details, so is the devil and everything else. Knowledge must be justified in relation to situated particulars, and strategy must be close to reality.[35] 'Go to experience', wrote Dewey, 'and see what it is experienced *as*'.[36] Yes, Toyoda and Honda would wholeheartedly agree: '*genchi genbutsu* (现地现物).' James was concerned with what worked best in a particular situation. David Hall and Roger Ames suggest: 'to say that no position may be held superior to another by appeal to evidence and argument is one thing. To deny that one position may be more effective or useful than another in specific circumstances, or that one might be required to act upon a principle even if that principle is unproven, is quite another.'[37] Human inquiry is purposeful, intentful, goal-directed.[38] Our purpose defines what knowledge is, causes problems to exist and constructs actionable solutions. After all is said and done, strategies are justified by the consequences of acting upon them. Peirce introduced pragmatism famously thus: 'what we can do – and all that we can do – is to act on our beliefs and take note of the result.'[39] The emphasis on consequences provides the starting point for any pragmatic inquiry.[40]

What does all this mean to theory? Pragmatism is not against theory. 'It simply gives it a different, less exalted role.'[41] While theory is an abstraction from experience, posited Dewey, it must ultimately return to inform experience. 'Ideas are useless unless used.'[42] Engaging in abstraction is not the sin; the sin is treating abstract concepts as existing prior to and independently of experience.[43] Hence, we are not to abandon theory or deny that we are using it, but to reflect on it, justify and improve it based on consequences.[44] We are against theories of the 'so what' kind: 'If you are wrong about this, who will notice? Nobody.'[45]

Processual: truth is made in events[46]

American pragmatism has always been hand in hand with 'processism'.[47] Sharing Alfred North Whitehead's 'all things flow' conception, pragmatists take the experienced world as contingent, indeterminate, changeable. There is no necessity, certainty, immovable knowledge or eternal value; truth is an emergent property. Pragmatists are truth-makers, not truth-finders.

A pragmatist's world is real but not fixed.[48] In Peirce's conception, the universe is in a state of 'constant change and development'. The world to James is one of 'flux, spontaneity and creative novelty'.[49] For Dewey, every existence is an event; having come into being, each will pass away.[50] In strategy as in life, one needs above all to maintain flexibility and speed of readjustment to changes in the world.

Dewey is particularly famous for challenging the *quest for certainty*. 'The world is a scene of risk; it is uncertain, unstable, uncannily unstable. Its dangers are irregular, inconstant, not to be counted upon as to their times and seasons.'[51] Nicholas Rescher posits: 'it was precisely because he saw human experience in terms of an emplacement within an environment of unstable flux that Dewey dismissed the prospect of governing life by rules and fixities, and saw the need of a flexible approach geared pragmatically to the changing demands of changing situations.'[52] Confucius could not have agreed more: walking in the no-fixed-shape (无容), no-definite-rule (无则) world, what is timely, appropriate, we shall follow – *shizhong* (时中, timely balance).

Armed with notions such as 'emergent present', the pragmatic view of change does not fit well with the Hegel–Marx doctrine of progressive inevitability.[53] Dewey believed that our world 'has not consistently made up its mind where it is going'.[54] The future is open and indeterminate; it depends, at least partly, on what we choose to do.[55] Strategy matters precisely because we live in a world 'which may be made this way or that as men judge, prize, love, and labour'.[56]

This enabled Dewey to promote 'critical optimism': if we put our heads together and approach difficult situations honestly, we can hopefully generate meaningful actions and 'make the world better and happier'.[57] Putnam interprets: 'Dewey was not someone with a blind faith in progress; he was, rather, a strategic optimist; and strategic optimism is something we badly need at the present time.'[58] After 9/11 in New York, the near-collapse of Wall Street and the March 2011 disaster in Japan, such 'critical optimism' is all the more urgent, fit, inspiring.

To pragmatists, human intelligence is not a mental faculty but a way of interacting with emerging situations.[59] Peirce wrote: 'Our knowledge of objects arises in the practical relationship we have to those objects, and it follows that, as our practical relationship changes so our knowledge changes.'[60] We cannot step outside historical contingency; rationality, beauty and morality are 'situated', 'made'.

> The right, or appropriate, course of action in any situation
> cannot be given in advance but depends on the precise character
> of the deliberating agent and on the situation in which she finds
> herself. Some course of action which is praiseworthy in one set
> of circumstances might not be in some other.[61]

Indeed, one-size-fits-all, timeless 'best practice' is an illusory, misleading idea. As human experience is indeterminate, nothing is ever 'once true, always true'.[62] In Peirce's view, knowledge is fluid and ever-changing. James agreed: 'instead of resting on apodictic bedrock, we submit our knowledge to critical examination and revision.'[63] Why is it so? Because, first of all, knowledge is interested and interests change. Explained Rorty:

> all descriptions of everything are the product of attempts to
> gratify human needs and interests. Those needs and interests
> change, so our sense of what's important will, in many areas,
> keep changing. 'Relativism' doesn't strike me as the right word.
> Maybe 'fallibilist' would be better.[64]

According to Dewey, we are only able to envisage and solve problems using the materials we have to hand.[65] We should not cheat ourselves by generalising what we learn in a particular encounter into universal principles that can be unproblematically applied to other situations.[66] In an evolving world, 'there is no belief so settled as not to be exposed to further inquiry'.[67]

Dewey used the term 'working hypothesis' to emphasise the provisional, fallible characteristics of knowledge. To the pragmatists, if science is to be successful it must be open to criticism.[68] Thomas Powell, a contemporary strategy writer, submits:

> To a pragmatist, a true proposition is one that facilitates fruitful paths of human discovery. So long as a proposition provides a profitable leading, we retain it, deploy it, and improve it. But when it begins to frustrate discovery, and alternative propositions become more attractive, we abandon our original proposition, and call it false.[69]

Crucially, fallibilism does not lead pragmatists to scepticism. That we are fallible does not mean we know nothing about what to do or how to do. We do not come from nowhere; we are always resourced. As reflective beings, we learn from past experiences. Not just beliefs need to be justified, so do doubts. 'Doubting is not as easy as lying', Peirce famously claimed.[70] Putnam explains:

> Indeed, from the earliest of Peirce's Pragmatist writings Pragmatism has been characterised by *antiscepticism*: Pragmatists hold that *doubt* requires justification just as much as belief ...; and by *fallibilism*: Pragmatists hold that there are no metaphysical guarantees to be had that even our most firmly-held beliefs will never need revision. That one can be both fallibilist *and* antisceptical is perhaps the basic insight of American Pragmatism.[71]

Implications for strategy? From a process point of view, pragmatic strategies are not perfect (or true); they are just the best available at the time (anti-sceptical), useful for getting jobs done (instrumental) and open to revision (fallible). With this Deng Xiaoping would have felt very much at home: 'crossing the river by searching for stones.' If you aren't willing to get your feet wet, you'd better stay on the river-side and you won't cross the river, ever.

Creative: enlarging human potentials

One conceptual consequence of process thinking is that, being open, indeterminate and (as yet) unrealised, the 'future always brings new situations to realisation, the present is ever the locus of novelty, innovation, and creativity'.[72]

What is creativity? Hans Joas examines the subject matter through four metaphors: (1) Johann Gottfried Herder's metaphor of *expression*, which circumscribes creativity in relation to the subjective world; (2) Karl Marx's metaphor of *production*, which relates creativity to the objective world; (3) *revolution*, another metaphor from Marx which assumes the human potential for reorganising institutions in the social world; and (4) Arthur Schopenhauer's metaphor of *life*, which emphasises self-freedom. Joas found a problematic tendency in all of these metaphors: they attribute creativity to one type of action at the expense of others.[73]

It is, then, in Peirce, James and Dewey's metaphors of *intelligence* and *reconstruction* that Joas discerns the holistic, engaging idea of creativity related to all dimensions of human action. Peirce sees human action as inhabiting the tension between the non-reflected habitual and acts of creativity. For Dewey, creativity is the liberation of the capacity for new action, the reconstruction of a better and happier world.[74] He 'lauds anticipation and projection as distinctive features of human doings and undertakings ... [and] highlights the future, the forward-looking character of human experience'.[75]

Where does creativity come from? In Mead's conception, it emerges from the tension between the impulsive 'I' and the socialised 'me'. While the 'me' is associated with the way we organise the social attitude of others, the 'I' is our creative response to it, which is unknown to others or the self. While the 'me' tends to call out sacrificing the self for the community, the 'I' tends to reconstruct that communal order. Through the spontaneous response of the 'I' to unfolding situations we gain a distance from the 'me' convention, free ourselves from customs and step into the unconventional.[76]

This converges well with Dewey's account of human 'positive freedom'.[77] For Dewey, on the one hand, 'every individual is social-ised somewhat differently',[78] 'every invention, every improvement ... has its genesis in the observation and ingenuity of a particular innovator'.[79] On the other hand, Dewey submitted, the ability to cre-ate is not an individual possession or innate endowment but a social asset, communal and evolving, derived not just from historical-cul-tural legacies but also through ongoing interactions with others.[80]

In light of pragmatism, creativity is a process both cognitive and democratic. It is cognitive insofar as it expresses the human cap-acity for reflective thinking; it is democratic insofar as every rational person is considered capable of coping intelligently with emerging problems.[81] A person's ability to act differently is not God-given, but hard-earned; it depends on both personal effort and the kind of social experience one is exposed to:[82] 'individual and social creativity are thus just two different phases of the same process by which original and innovative solutions are imagined so as to answer the problems individuals and groups face in everyday life.'[83]

Hence, to pragmatists, creativity has a moral dimension: an ideal society should increase its members' potential for creativity. While Marx worried that workers had lost control of the means of production in the capitalist system, Dewey was concerned that workers in corporate America had lost their creative capabilities and become dissatisfied, unfulfilled, insecure.[84]

Creativity produces consequences. Novel solutions to practical problems become a new 'habit' of action, through which our ability to act increases; hence knowledge creation.[85] Meanwhile, creativity is a risky undertaking. Ours is a complex world in which, even with our best efforts, our chosen course of action may be defeated. Creativity 'begins in uncertainty – and often ends there, too'.[86] Nevertheless, to the extent that our action is truly a manifestation of intelligent choice, we learn something even from failure; we can turn frustration into something useful for further choices.[87] Be creative, yes we can, because we are intentional, reflective, learning beings.

Holistic: enriching the resource pool

As creativity involves 'choosing to act differently', its very possibility lies in the diversities in conceptions, imaginations and courses of action. The richer our resource pool, the more effective our *bricolage*. Not surprisingly, pragmatism is in all its strands inclusive, embracing, accommodating: 'let a thousand flowers bloom.'[88]

To 'classical pragmatism' with a 'scientific' flavour, as represented by Peirce:

> There is, in principle, no theoretical limit to the different lines of consideration available to yield descriptive truths about any real thing whatever. Our knowledge of the real is in principle inexhaustible.[89]

While to the 'new pragmatists' informed by postmodernism, most visibly in Rorty:

> it is no accident that in everyday language we employ many different kinds of discourses, ... no accident because it is an illusion that there could be just one sort of language game which could be sufficient for the description of all of reality.[90]

For pragmatists old and new, 'different people have different things to say about the problematic situation',[91] 'multiplying perspectives on a problem help solve it better',[92] 'having multiple frameworks available ... is probably the single most powerful attribute of self-renewing ... organisations'.[93] Indeed, there is a growing recognition among managers and policy-makers that strategy is too important to leave to any single discipline, paradigm, methodology or school of thought.[94]

Peirce promoted pluralism by using a metaphor of knowledge as a cable that remains strong despite the weakness of any single filament, while James said this about pragmatism: 'at the outset, at least, it stands for no particular results. It has no dogmas, and no doctrines save its methods.'[95] Like Confucius, James would have 'rejected the four devils (子绝四)'.[96] As for Dewey, diversity is indispensable for solving immediate problems as well as for the growth of communities.[97]

On one hand, Dewey posited, every novel conception differing from that authorised by current belief must have its origin in a person.[98] On the other hand, no single piece of prior knowledge can supply the new concepts needed to cope with flowing uncertainties. For this reason, plurality and participation have a better chance of solving problems that would defeat any of us individually.[99] Plurality and participation are hence the key to the survival and success of a community.[100]

In promoting pragmatism, Dewey saw the expert's role not as 'framing and executing policies', but as 'discovering and making known the facts, upon which the former depend'.[101] 'For Dewey, neither scientific knowledge nor commonsense knowledge is privileged. Either or both may be relevant in a given context of inquiry ... All knowledge from all relevant scientific disciplines and from common sense can and should be brought to bear in inquiry.'[102]

In a similar holistic spirit, West Churchman and Russell Ackoff posit that (1) all problems in science are interrelated; (2) all sciences are required in any particular scientific inquiry; (3) science must consider the whole system, including non-scientific viewpoints; (4) the scientific strategy is to be your own enemy: we should formulate the optimal approach from a scientific point of view and then subject it to criticism from other viewpoints, such as politics, morality, aesthetics and religion; and (5) science is judged from an ethical point of view, on what scientists ought to do. In short, each 'inquiry system' reveals insights about the problem that are not obtainable from others. No inquiry system by itself suffices to resolve life problems, but together they supply a richer base for practically wise actions. To limit perspectives would be to limit the chances of success.[103]

This is particularly insightful to strategy the applied field which is expected to generate practical consequences that affect the well-being of people, communities, society and Nature. As Dewey

saw it, 'For making the difficult, value-laden choices among alternatives, there is no expertise, as such; decisions that will affect lives
and livelihoods belong to the democratic and cooperative process of
social inquiry involving all who might be affected.'[104]

Dealing with diverse knowledge, the pragmatic questions are:
do they make sense to us, how useful are they in this particular
situation, what effect would adopting them be likely to have?[105]
Furthermore, while there are many language games in town, some
are more useful than others for specific tasks in hand.[106] The same
applies to metaphors: are there not bad metaphors, such as 'axis of
evil', 'clash of civilisations', 'God's work'?[107] Answering these questions is, in the final analysis, a matter of ethical judgement. James
posited that God's powers are limited so that humankind is free,
and indeed compelled, to develop and exercise moral choices. Since
God did not supply us with a definitive picture of the world, the
decision to select or construct a particular one on which to base our
action is ultimately a heroic, rather than a 'logical', act. The choice
is among the greatest risks we humans ever face,[108] to which we
now turn.　·

Ethical: value is in everything we do

Creativity, and strategy for that matter, is in itself neither good nor
bad. It has to be agreed upon via ethical judgement and justification.[109]
Dewey was disturbed to see 'the subject matter of moral inquiry has
been increasingly pushed out of the range of the concrete problems
of economic and political inquiry'.[110] To Rorty, since the future is not
closed nor given but made by people, 'people cannot escape the responsibility to make the future more just and equal than the past'.[111]

For pragmatists from Peirce and Dewey to Rorty and Putnam,
ethics is concerned with solving 'specific and situated problems as
opposed to abstract, idealised, or theoretical problems'.[112] This is
in accordance with Confucian teaching: 'Tao is not far from Man
(道不远人).' Ethics should not be a small corner of moral theorists
tasked with formulating principles or rules. Rather, it should be

taken as a project of democratic, intelligent inquiry, of problem-solving and experiential work, in everything we reflective human beings engage in every day.

Dewey questioned Weber's fact–value distinction, insisted on 'the thoroughly reciprocal character of means and end in practical judgement'.[113] Interpreting Dewey, Rorty rejected the distinction between morality and prudence. We do not need a big distinction between morality and everything else:

> [Morality is] all a matter of solving the problems that arise in relations between human beings. When these problems become acute we call them moral problems, when they don't become acute we call them prudential problems. It's a matter of importance rather than, as Kant thought, a difference between reason and emotion, or reason and sentiment, or the *a priori* and the *a posteriori*, or the philosophical and the empirical, and so on.[114]

Yes, Confucius would agree, smartness and morality cannot be separated. Ethics is deeply embedded in the part and parcel of human experience, and of strategy. For Dewey, institutions and politics provide more than mere economic efficiency; they 'help develop the ability of the members of a community to live lives that are imbued with a rich aesthetic sense of significance and worth'.[115] We must make space for ethics rather than explaining it away. In strategy, it is paramount to balance technical and instrumental rationality with value rationality by consciously asking questions such as where do we come from, who are we, where do we want to be, what is desirable and good, how to realise it?[116]

Pragmatists recognise that ethical issues are wide-ranging: from abstract ideals such as human rights with which no one appears to disagree, to specific conducts such as genetically modified crops and animal testing which evoke passionate, entrenched tensions. In the face of situated problems, it is not that there can be no 'principles', but that principles should be taken as fallible hypotheses to be worked out. Value and purpose are not injected like a vitamin shot into experience; rather they grow out of experience, they are created through the process of work.[117]

Pragmatism has long been condemned as morally relativistic for promoting situated ethics, particularly when Dewey appeared to endorse 'relativity'.[118] But the Deweyan 'relativity' is explicitly qualified. Dewey embraced only what he called 'historic relativity' and 'application relativity'. The former implies that rationality is historically conditioned, so that judgement and justification cannot step outside history; while the latter highlights the social dimension of context and promotes participative discussion on courses of action.

Because of 'historic relativity', past experience matters. What is logical, sensible and ethical depends on prior actions. It is not sufficient to consider human action as being contingent on situations, it should also be recognised that situations are constitutive of human experiences. We are not just thrown into situations, shaped by industry structures, changing technologies or government regulations. Situations are, at least partly, our own making.[119]

According to 'application relativity', context-dependence is not merely a more complex form of environmental determinism. It means open-ended relationships between contesting interpretations. Each community with a stake in the situation constructs problems and solutions differently, based on the community's unique experiences.[120] In solving situated problems, we must assume and accept diverse, even conflicting propositions, from which ethically wise solutions are to be generated. The whole point of Dewey's 'relativity' is that:

> All universal generalisations are subject to restriction in
> the dimensions of space and time; Dewey extended such
> restrictions into the moral and aesthetic dimensions as well.
> Different communities constitute different moral and aesthetic
> contexts.[121]

Community! With this, let us proceed to explore perhaps the most significant contribution of pragmatism to human experience in general and ethical strategy in particular.

Communal: sociality and history the only foundation

'Communitarian pragmatists', represented by Dewey, believe that democracy is not about political arrangements, but about community: people's attitudes and ways of living together.[122] 'Liberal pragmatists', such as Rorty, promote 'benign ethnocentrism', on the grounds that humans have no choice but to think and act initially from where they are, with a 'we-consciousness'.[123] In every strand of pragmatism, human life is a communal matter. 'Universal laws of nature, scientific principles, or logical categories, do not best serve to define us at the levels of personal, social, and political existence. Our cultural narratives tell us who we are.'[124] It is usually taken that 'Easterners' (for example, the Japanese) have a collective orientation, whereas 'Westerners' (typically Americans) are individualistic 'in nature'.[125] In our view, American pragmatism represents a significant variant that resists such stereotyping. For American pragmatists, community and associated social habits, customs and traditions are the 'funded experiences' from which all knowledge, morality, identity and problem-solving begin.[126] 'We are communal beings from the start.'[127] To quote Dewey: 'Only in social groups does a person have a chance to develop individuality.'[128] To Mead, the self is 'something achieved', an evolving self-in-communal-context.[129] We are who we are because of our interactions with the 'generalised other'. We learn to act in the ways we act because of what others approve of, disapprove of, protest at, encourage or resist.[130]

According to Whitehead, people and community are always part of a reciprocally constituting process. Community has no existence except in the people who constitute it. Those people, in turn, are who they are largely by virtue of participating in the community.[131] Hence, like individuals, communities are not given but constructed, not determined but contingent.[132] Purpose, value and common good, as well as habits of action, are not the procession of a super subject, be that subject a group or a society; they must be made and remade by people interacting with each other. Every generation must build its own community. Thus, community always remains in question, in the making, 'ever not quite'.[133] In a world of uncertainties and open-ended possibilities, an ideal community constantly transforms itself so that its members can adapt to and guide 'the constant flows' around them. As Rorty suggested, community is not to be discovered and joined, but configured and maintained.[134]

What makes a community 'work'? It is the quality of communication.[135] 'Men live in a community by virtue of the things they have in common; communication is the way in which they come to possess things in common.'[136] While 'natural associations are the condition for the existence of a community, a community adds the function of communication in which emotions and ideas are shared as well as joint undertakings engaged'.[137] Engaged communication allows members of a community to negotiate and share the meanings of world events, and permits enough agreement for collective action.[138] It is through communication that communal life is 'emotionally, intellectually, consciously sustained'.[139] Don't we see here the American pragmatist version of the Japanese *ba*?[140]

An ideal community is harmonious.[141] For Dewey, as for Confucius, harmony is not uniformity; it is 'unity of variety'. Similarity and difference are both required; neither is more fundamental than the other. Ideal communication is not we-all-see-things-the-same-way, but an increase in flexible 'meaning-overlaps', or, in Gadamer's words, 'fusion of horizons'.[142] At its core, a community is where 'overlaps' extend and 'fusions' deepen. The art of achieving harmony between differences (和而不同) is hence to embrace diversity, tension and resistance, against ultimate closure, final end or homogeneous identity.[143]

A group becomes a community only when it willingly interacts with other communities, and contributes to the growth of others affected by its action.[144] A mafia or a gang is not a community.[145] Echoing the Confucian ideal of 'extending love',[146] Mead suggested 'the rational solution of the conflicts, however, calls for the reconstruction of both habits and values, and this involves transcending the border of the community'.[147] For Dewey, ethical growth means including the well-being of others in one's ends-in-view.[148] Similarly, Ackoff posits that ethics is about increasing the legitimate options available to others.[149] Ethics is, in this sense, not an outside-in exercise that begins with universal codes, but an inside-out process that starts with a specific community and reaches out to others.

A person associates with more than one community; we construct and live in multiple communities. We are persons-in-communities.[150] In other words, we as persons are constituted by many different relationships and informed by multiple interests and perspectives. The us-versus-them mentality has no place in pragmatism.

This brings us to what Peirce called the 'community of inquirers'. Inquirers are doubters who generate, experiment, test knowledge and moral claims; they can be convinced only by successful application.[151] Peirce stressed 'intersubjectivity', in contrast with objectivity and subjectivity, according to which knowing the truth as well as the right is not a matter of individual perspective or fixed foundations, but of the long-term convergence of opinions emerging from shared experiences.[152] 'The opinion which is fated to be ultimately agreed upon by all who investigate, is what we mean by truth.'[153] As a method of inquiry, Peirce promoted 'abduction', in contrast with deduction and induction:

> Under pragmatism, hypotheses can be justified through the
> inferential method of 'abduction', sometimes called 'inference to
> the best explanation' ... Inference by abduction does not require
> a theory to conform to the ordinary demands of formal logic,
> so long as the theory has been subjected to fair, sustained and
> rigorous competition among plausible rivals.[154]

For Dewey, a community of inquiry consists of three components: problematic situation, scientific attitude and participatory democracy.[155] The first, *problematic situation*, is a catalyst that causes the community to form, and provides a reason to undertake inquiry. Dig deeper: problematic situations are not just there to be discovered and improved. Rather, situations and inquirers are mutually constitutive.[156] Situations come and go, while communities are more enduring. Situations are situated in cultures; 'a situation is often but a window of opportunity for carrying out an ideological project that had been awaiting the right moment to express itself'.[157]

Then, the method of *scientific inquiry* can be extended to ethical judgements, in that 'every new idea and theory has to be submitted to this community for confirmation and tests'.[158] 'What matters in science are the liberal social virtues that encourage participants to conduct critical and tolerant inquiries.'[159] Dewey favoured epistemological and moral fallibility, and submitted that no knowledge claim or moral rule is immune from revision. If there is progress, then it can only be made by the cultivation of intelligent habits that encourage continuous inquiry. Knowledge and morality are the outcome of ongoing, communal activities; they become accepted only when affirmed by the experiences of a community.[160] In the end, 'experience is the final arbiter, for ethical issues as well as for other problems'.[161]

Last but not least, *participatory democracy* in communities of inquiry is a great deal more than one-person-one-vote or giving-everyone-a-say. It is 'a way of communicating' that allows 'mutual respect, mutual toleration, give and take and the pooling of experience' in ongoing service to a common good.[162] 'Democracy is the belief that even when needs and ends or consequences are different for each individual, the habit of amicable cooperation – which may include, as in sport, rivalry and competition – is itself a priceless addition to life.'[163] Yes, put in the Confucius way, 'even in contests, they are exemplary persons (君子无所争，其争也君子)'.

By 'habit of amicable cooperation' Dewey encouraged listening to others: 'The connection of the ear with vital and outgoing thought and emotion are immensely closer and more varied than those of the eye. Vision is a spectator; hearing is a participator.'[164] Good listening is just the first step, however. What matters is mutual 'responsiveness' that avoids passivity on the one hand and partisanship on the other,[165] and that facilitates sweeping-in, appreciating and revising perspectives.[166] Remember the Chinese *kanji* 'sage' (聖) consisting of an ear (耳) and a mouth (口)?

Taking a sufficiently long-term view, like Confucius, Dewey conceived of an aesthetic dimension inherent in ethical judgement.[167] For Dewey, experimentation has aesthetic, moral and contextual dimensions. Deweyan pragmatism assures us that 'moral, as well as aesthetic and cognitive, values are constantly present in the most esoteric of scientific theories, just as they are in the most concrete of everyday practices'.[168] Dewey's reform project – 'education for democracy' – converges remarkably well with the Confucian emphasis on the cultivation of people's whole character through tradition-based education.[169] Commenting on Dewey's project, Hall and Ames posit:

> Education for democracy is practical, aesthetic, growth-oriented, historicist, and communitarian. If we recall that, for Dewey, the self is irreducibly social, then we may say that the central aim of education is self-cultivation. Self-cultivation captures the life-long nature of the educational process, as well as its essentially moral character. Self-cultivation is the cultivation of democratic community.[170]

Aesthetic education, in view of pragmatism, is in the end the most reliable, productive, empowering and enjoyable means for achieving ethical consensus and moral accomplishment, in contrast with quick-fit, hyper-rational, interventionist, procedure-based 'methods'. It does not surprise us that both Confucius and Dewey, the greatest representatives of Eastern and Western pragmatism, were tireless teachers.[171]

Confucian and American pragmatisms, though speaking different languages and being rooted in different histories, together provide front-line managers with an urgently needed context, attitude and mode of thinking to overcome the pressing problems of impracticality, fragmentation and moral insensitivity, to transform strategy into a positive force for getting fundamentals right, envisioning a valued future and realising common goodness.

ARISTOTLE MEETS CONFUCIUS

Let us now bring together Aristotle and Confucius, who, perhaps more than any other thinkers, have nurtured the enduring intellectual traditions which have profoundly affected the lives of people far beyond the two thinkers' birthplaces. Indeed, insofar as practical wisdom is concerned, Aristotle and Confucius have achieved today undisputed iconic status of the two civilisations. A comparison of the two masters is useful for our purpose since it is Aristotle and Confucius' teachings that chiefly inform the recent search for pragmatic strategy.[172] We will focus mainly on current interpretations of Aristotle and Confucius. After an overview, we shall conduct our comparison along five dimensions.

Overview: different paths to practical wisdom?

The current search for practically wise strategy in 'the West' has been largely under the flag of Aristotelian ethics, particularly Aristotle's elaboration on *phronesis*. This should not be surprising since 'Aristotle's *Nichomachean Ethics* is perhaps the text *par excellence* for anyone concerned with what practical knowledge is about'.[173]

According to a current account, Aristotle conceived of three forms of human intellectual virtues that enable an individual to achieve well-being.[174] First, there is *episteme* (scientific knowledge), which is judgement about things that are universal and necessary. It seeks to discover laws, principles and the essence of things. Then there is *techne* (craft knowledge), which examines how to make things and originates in the maker, not in the things made. Finally, there is *phronesis* (practical knowledge), which deals with both universals and particulars; it is about knowing what is good for human beings in general as well as having the ability to apply such knowledge to particular situations.

For Aristotle, both *techne* and *phronesis* are *praktikes* (practical knowledge), in contrast with *episteme* which is *theoretikes* (theoretical knowledge). Aristotle distinguished between *techne* and *phronesis* thus: the former studies things with an eye to production, the latter to action. 'While making [production] has an end other than itself, action cannot; for good action itself is its end.'[175]

Of the three kinds of knowledge, Aristotle considered *phronesis* the most valuable. 'While it includes a general awareness of the highest human good, it also involves the appreciation of particular facts; its function is to put into practice the values that the moral virtues provide.' In other words, 'practical wisdom involves knowing the right values *and* being able to put them into practice in concrete situations'.[176]

In another account, which differs slightly in terminology,[177] Aristotle suggested that *episteme* seeks unchanging natural principles or laws. Distinct from *episteme* is *metis* (cunning knowledge) which seeks not truth but advantage, and concerns itself with the means rather than the end. Aristotle rejected the idea that *episteme* could be applied to the social world because he thought that world was too complex and unpredictable to be known with certainty. At the same time, Aristotle did not believe *metis* alone was capable of promoting 'good life'.

In view of the tension between *episteme* and *metis*, Aristotle defined *phronesis* as the virtuous habit of taking actions that serve the common good. Where the predictive capacity of *episteme* breaks down, *phronesis* addresses normatively what future should occur. Similarly, though *phronesis* may draw on *metis* to realise normative goals, it disciplines *metis* so as to avoid deception and focuses on advantages that may be shared by a community.

Again, in this second account, Aristotle praised *phronesis* and nurtured 'an interest in describing the form of human intelligence that is most relevant for and appropriate to ambiguous or uncertain circumstance in which the limits of scientific knowledge and cunning action are approached or surpassed'. To Aristotle, 'this form of intelligence must be both effective and ethical' and 'cannot be dissociated from the normativity of action'.[178]

Now turn to Confucius. As discussed in previous chapters, our pragmatic turn is informed by Confucian teachings on the *Eight Wires* and pragmatism-upon-time. The *Eight Wires*, or *eight exemplary doings* (八条目), are as follows:

> The ancients who wished to manifest illustrious virtue throughout the world, first ordered well their own states. Wishing to order well their own states, they first regulated their own families. Wishing to regulate their own families, they first cultivated their own selves. Wishing to cultivate their own selves, they first rectified their own minds. Wishing to rectify their own minds, they first sought for absolute sincerity in their thoughts. Wishing for absolute sincerity in their thoughts, they first extended their knowledge. This extension of knowledge consists in the investigation of things.
>
> Things being investigated, only then did their knowledge become extended. Their knowledge being extended, only then did their thought become sincere. Their thought being sincere, only then did their mind become rectified. Their mind being rectified, only then did their selves become cultivated. Their selves being cultivated, only then did their families become regulated. Their families being regulated, only then did their states become rightly governed. Their states being rightly governed, only then could the world be at peace.[179]

The first two steps – investigating things (格物) and extending knowledge (至知) – are directed toward the goal of understanding the world. The next three steps – making sincere one's intentions (诚意), rectifying one's mind (正心) and cultivating or improving one's person (修身) – are directed toward the goal of perfecting oneself within, so that one can be ready for social and political responsibility in order to better others. The last three steps – regulating a family (齐家), governing a State well (治国), and pacifying the world (平天下) – are directed toward extending one's virtues among men so that one can be said to realise one's potentiality in a reality of relationships.[180]

Walking in the world, the sages coped with flows of *wuli* (物理), *shili* (事理) and *renli* (人理). How did they do it? According to Confucius, to act wisely entails balancing the rational, the creative and the normative in accordance with situated particulars. This is the quintessence of *shizhong* (时中, timely balance): be purposefully opportunistic in action. Take a firm moral stand, yet not bent to or against anything. Be comfortable with uncertainty, ambiguity and surprises. Appreciate emerging possibilities, draw on contingent resources and generate workable solutions to realise common goodness.

We hope that the above brief introduction to Aristotle and summary of Confucius may serve as a platform for an exploratory comparison. Overlaps are apparent. Both our call for a pragmatic turn and efforts in 'the West' to achieve practically wise strategy are critical of the detached, reductionist, amoral tendencies in the conventional paradigm. Both aim to bring back practicality, ethics and holistic thinking. Time and again, writers in 'the West' link *phronesis* with pragmatism explicitly, for example: 'Phronesis, an Aristotelian term, refers to a discipline that is pragmatic, variable, context depending, based on practical rationality, leading not to a concern with generating formal covering law-like explanations but to building contextual, case-based knowledge.'[181] Furthermore, the Aristotelian *episteme–techne–phronesis* categorisation seems broadly compatible with the Confucian *wuli–shili–renli* teaching. *Episteme* and *wuli* pertain to the natural and the technical, efficiency and rationality – what it is; *techne* and *shili* concern ways of seeing and making things – how to do; while *phronesis* and *renli* promote the common good and emphasise value, purpose and

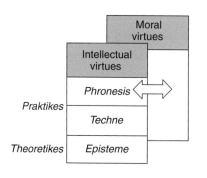 

Aristotelian hierarchical 'what': phronesis as the highest intellectual virtue

Confucian circular 'how': timely balancing *wuli–shili–renli*

FIGURE 9.1 Aristotle meets Confucius: different paths to practical wisdom?

morality – why we do it. The Confucian timely balance appears, too, largely compatible with what Aristotle meant by *phronesis* – taking ethical-prudent actions that serve the common good in here-and-now circumstances.

Meanwhile, differences are substantial and may have significant impacts on how practically wise strategies are conceived and pursued. Figure 9.1 illustrates an overview. Let us have a brief look at the differences along five dimensions.

What is vs how to act

Popular interpretations of Aristotle, represented by the two accounts cited earlier, tend to concentrate on *what is* practical knowledge (*phronesis*) and what differentiates it from other forms of knowledge (*episteme* and *techne*). In contrast, Confucian pragmatism begins with *how to act* wisely – what the sages did, how they did it and why they did it in the ways they did. While Aristotle studied the *whats*, relying mainly on inert nouns: *praktikes, phronesis*, etc., Confucius looked at the *hows*, using active verbs: investigating things, extending knowledge, getting it just right, and so on. On the one hand we receive rigorous Aristotelian categories of knowledge, on the other we witness Confucius' appeal to how sages walk in the world. Is this accidental? Does it matter? How will it impact on contemporary strategy?

Angus Charles Graham heuristically contrasted the Anglo-European and the Asian Confucians respectively as truth-seekers and way-makers who tended to ask different questions:[182]

> The Western 'What' question is usually expressed in something like this manner: 'What kinds of things are there?' 'What is the world made of?' or simply, 'What *is* this?' Such questions have resulted in a catalogue of facts and principles that assist one in taking an inventory of the world around us. The Chinese 'Where' question, on the other hand, led to a search for the right path, the appropriate model of conduct to lead one along the path, the 'way' that life is to be lived, and where to stand.[183]

Truth-seekers and way-makers also tend to ask and answer the *how* question differently. For truth-seekers, the question is 'How might I classify or define this and that?', while for way-makers, the question is 'How may this or that be brought into the service of our purpose?' Lin Yütang, a famous Chinese writer, observed: on encountering a strange animal, whereas the 'Westerner' is concerned with 'how shall I classify this?', the 'Easterner' is interested in 'how may it be cooked?'[184] Ames and Rosemont make a similar point. They suggest that the dominant mode of learning in 'the West', as represented by Aristotle and early Greek thought, has been to acquire knowledge *about* the world, to learn what the world *is* and to search for an underlying ultimate *reality*. In 'the East', Confucius' followers have been more concerned with *how to get on* in this-worldly affairs.[185] Closer to business, Akio Morita of Sony posited: 'Our perhaps peculiarly Japanese reaction when we learn of some new development or come across a phenomenon, is invariably "How can I use this? What can I make with it? How can it be used to produce a useful product?".'[186]

Let us not be confused by surface similarity. Aristotle and Confucius were human beings, as are we. We all ask what, where and how questions, in theorising as in daily activities. Critical are the different mentalities underneath these seemingly common questions. When the Aristotelians ask *how*, their eyes are still on *what* (e.g. what kind of knowledge enables good strategy); when Confucians ask *what*, they are already looking for *how* (e.g. how to act practically wise in a particular context). Zhang Dongsun, a new-Confucian scholar, regarded the attitudes as what- vs how-priorities.[187] Joseph Needham observed the difference, too:

> At any rate, the Chinese thought, always concerned with relations, prefers to avoid the problems and pseudo-problems of substance, and thus persistently eluded all metaphysics. Where Western minds asked '*what essentially is it?*', Chinese minds asked '*how* is it related in its beginnings, functions, and endings with everything else, and *how* ought we to react to it?'[188]

Hence, instead of telling disciples 'what practical wisdom is', Confucian Masters encouraged them to beat their own paths in exploring 'how to act wisely'.[189]

Articulative reasoning vs suggestive exemplars

To bring *phronesis* to the fore, writers in 'the West' work very hard to introduce more, supposedly clarifying, categories, dimensions, boxes. Our question is: with ever-increasing categorisation, sophistication and complexity, are we getting closer to or farther away from the concerns and activities of front-line managers?

Admittedly, we cannot avoid using categories. Confucius used quite a lot (exemplary man and small man, change and stability, for example); in this book we touch upon some. However, there is a difference in attitudes. In East Asian traditions, there has been an 'antipathy toward categorisation'.[190] Laozi (老子) and Zhuangzi (庄子), for example, are famous for their caution against abstract concepts, fixed categories, all-purpose definitions and context-free frameworks. They called these things *dawei* (大伪, great artifice, grand false pretentions).[191] *Dawei* are man-made devices imposed on Nature. Zhuangzi insisted: 'the problem of ... how terms and attributes are to be delimited, leads one in precisely the wrong direction. Classifying or delimiting knowledge fractures greater knowledge.'[192] Laozi, in poetic language, warns us about the harmful effect of obsessive categorisation:

> The five colours cause one's eyes to be blind.
> The five tones cause one's ears to be deaf.
> The five flavours cause one's palate to be spoiled.[193]

The lack of faith in abstract categorisation is associated with a dislike of perpetual logical reasoning and analytic articulation. In contrast to the Aristotelian articulative style, the Confucian style is suggestive. After all, the East Asian tradition is one in which *The Analects* and *Daodejing*, the 'bibles' of life for around two thousand five hundred years, each contains no more than five thousand words. 'The *tao* that can be comprised in words is not the eternal *Tao* (道可道, 非常道)', Laozi famously said. In contrast with Plato and Aristotle, who believed that verbal articulation and symbolic reasoning could lead to truth,[194] Zen Buddhism holds that words are neither necessary nor sufficient for wisdom but are an obstruction of one's path to it.[195] Whereas some in 'the West' see this as 'anti-codification',[196] 'Easterners' themselves regard it as 'methodological simplicity'.[197] If small can be beautiful, so can simplicity. Fung Youlan suggested:

> Articulateness and suggestiveness are, of course, incompatible.
> The more an expression is articulate, the less it is suggestive –
> just as the more an expression is prosaic, the less it is poetic.
> The sayings and writings of the Chinese philosophers are so
> inarticulate that their suggestiveness is almost boundless.[198]

In contrast to Aristotelian abstraction, logic and reasoning, Confucianism appeals to aesthetic traditions that are expressed through language, music, art, play, rites, rituals, legendary sages and cultural heroes. Whenever he was asked for principles or definitions, Confucius supplied 'case studies'. He was alien to *ceteris paribus* ('all other things being equal'). Confucius was unable to codify a context-free, general definition of what authoritative conduct (仁) was, although it was a key concept in his whole teaching. Instead, he always described how the sages (聖人) and exemplary persons (君子) acted authoritatively yet differently in unique situations.

Ignorance of analytic articulation and formal reasoning further discourages rhetorical confrontation. Xunzi (荀子), a third-century-BC Confucian, proposed that argumentation must be a cooperative affair, and that contentiousness should therefore be avoided.[199] Confucius said: 'In hearing litigation, I am like any other person. What is necessary, however, is to cause people to have no litigation.'[200] This spirit seems quite different from Aristotelian participation and politics, according to which 'a collective activity whose object was to arrive at decisions on public matters (*ta koina*) after a process of collective deliberation ... Being part of a community and debating its norms and standards were inextricably linked'.[201] In Confucianism, such an 'inextricable link' is not assumed. Rather, like Dewey, Confucians appealed to a communally shared understanding and moral consensus, achieved chiefly through long-term education, particularly aesthetic-cultural cultivation.

Hierarchical vs circular knowledge

Knowledge for Aristotle is unmistakenly hierarchical: 'In Aristotle's framework, practical wisdom is clearly the highest intellectual virtue'; 'for Aristotle, craft knowledge is ultimately subordinate to *phronesis*.'[202] In one sense, all knowledge is equal; Aristotle did consider *episteme*, *techne* and *phronesis* all necessary for achieving *eudaimonia* (well-being). In contemporary interpretations, however, a particular type, i.e. *phronesis*, is 'clearly the highest' among equals.

In Confucian pragmatism, as in James, Dewey, Singer, Churchman, Putnam and Rorty, such a knowledge hierarchy is thoroughly rejected. No doubt, Confucius was wholeheartedly concerned with morality and ethics; one may rightly say that Confucianism is basically a set of moral teachings about how to engage in this-worldly affairs. But for Confucius, *wuli*, *shili* and *renli* are conceived as a circular flow where no particular *li* is always, across time or space, primary, central, above or more fundamental than others.[203] The relationships between rationality-efficiency, imagination-creativity and morality-legitimacy in Confucian pragmatism are, metaphorically, flat.

There appears to be a linear order if not a hierarchy in the Confucian *eight exemplary doings*: 'those who wish to do that, must first do this', 'when this is done, then they can do that.' Such an 'order' is nevertheless misconceived. What Confucius emphasised is the reciprocities and complementarities among exemplary doings, not a logical or temporal order. To Confucius, in doing as in learning, there is no fixed starting point or 'upward path'. One shall 'begin', according to the *eight exemplary doings*, by investigating things in Nature (格物); meanwhile, in a Confucian school, the first sentence a child learned was 'human nature is originally good (人之初, 性本善)'.[204] Confucians see no contradiction or hierarchy between Nature and humanity, fact and value, instrumentality and morality.

Hence, we have Aristotle's hierarchically ranked knowledge on the one hand, and Confucius' circular, reciprocal knowledge on the other. The differences do not stop here. In Aristotle, the three 'intellectual virtues' are separated from 'moral virtues' (Figure 9.1).[205] As Yushiko Yuasa notes:

> Western philosophy regards the problem of action, namely,
> that of the will, to be an issue for practical ethics, but not
> theoretical epistemology ... This is because modern Western
> philosophy seeks human essence in rational, thinking subject;
> its epistemology excludes the problem of the body. This attitude
> obviously originates in the rationalistic view of the human
> being.[206]

That is, if contemporary accounts are accurate, Aristotle first split intelligence from morality, the two 'types' of virtues, and then took great pains to reconnect them via the sophisticated category of *phronesis*. This prefigures Weber's 'antagonism' between fact-based scientific knowledge and faith-based moral judgement. Conversely, in Confucius, as in the American pragmatists, intelligence and morality are integrated from the outset. As Shih-ying Yang and Robert Sternberg put it, in 'Western tradition', morality is largely separated from intelligence and people can be viewed as immoral or amoral but smart. In Confucian pragmatism, there is a closer link between intelligence and morality in one's 'whole character', which is developed through long-term, holistic, aesthetic learning practice.[207]

The different images of knowledge may reflect deeply ingrained metaphysical outlooks. If Nature and humanity, object and subject, body and mind, are considered not much separated, then intelligence and morality tend to be treated as mutually implying, inviting, penetrating; if transience, instead of certainty, is assumed in life, then hierarchies between 'things' make little sense – suppose you found a hierarchy, it changes or disappears quickly.

Polarising-and-choosing vs associating-and-complementing

Closely linked to categories and hierarchies are the notions in 'the West' of contradiction and dichotomy. As communication scholar Robert Logan pointed out, the Greeks 'became slaves to the linear, either-or orientation of their logic'.[208] In considering strategy, Matt Statler and Johan Roos note Aristotle's 'decisive differentiation' of ethics from physics and metaphysics,[209] while Tsoukas and Cummings draw our attention to the subsequent 'splits' between means and end, facts and value, doing and thinking, *mythos* and *logos*.[210]

On the surface of it, Confucius shared with Aristotle a 'polar sensibility' if by this one means contrasting juxtapositions.[211] As we note above, Confucian pragmatism utilises many correlative terms: *yin* and *yang*, *tian* and *ren*, knowing and doing, emptiness and fullness, and so on. It is critical, however, to note the difference: while Aristotelian polar sensibility usually leads to contradictions and either/or choices, Confucian polar sensibility emphasises interdependence, interpenetration and reciprocity.

In previous chapters, we have shared with readers the Confucian metaphor 'lips and teeth'. With Confucian traditions, we do not 'choose' between lips and teeth, nor do we 'transcend', 'integrate', 'synthesise' or 'resolve' them into a 'higher whole' or 'higher viewpoint' of the Hegelian thesis–antithesis–synthesis sort. Neither do we follow the 'boxing of logic' where 'one winner (i.e., either A or B) emerges after confrontation'.[212] Which should be the winner, lips or teeth, fact or value, science or morality? In Confucianism, this is nonsense. Rather, we shall live comfortably with lips and teeth, *yin* and *yang*, appreciate their complementarities, dynamics and generative power.

When one searches for transcendence, integration, synthesis or resolution, or adopts a polarising-and-choosing strategy, complementarities are gone and one's capacity to act decreases. One ends up with a single hammer at hand, a heavier one perhaps. Instead, pragmatists use polar sensibility intelligently to understand the dynamic relations between differing objects, events, ideas, methods or conducts, to accommodate apparent opposites, embrace clashing viewpoints, make sense of emergent tensions and explore contingent possibilities. Choice, like change, another c-word, is an unquestioned ideology in a particular culture.[213] By contrast, choice, especially the 'principled', 'fundamental', 'either/or' sort, has not been a high priority for most of the world's people.[214] As McDonald's spreads all over the world, so, it seems, does that ideology.

Brain-mind driven vs heart-mind inspired

Where is the mind? How do we think? Are cognition and reason separated from emotion and passion? Should they be? What is the relationship between aesthetic feeling, rational rules and logical procedures in our decisions, conducts and strategies?

In 'the West', since ancient times, it has been widely accepted that we think with the brain. To the Greeks, the human soul consisted of thought, will and desire, which were located respectively in the brain, heart and kidneys. As separate organs, their functions were logically distinctive and should not be confused. Modern medicine since the nineteenth century has seemed to reinforce the imagined relationship between thought–mind–brain.

How about the heart? In colloquial English, by 'heart to heart' or 'learn by heart', we refer merely to emotion or will, not to cognition, reason or intelligence. When we say 'winning people's hearts and minds', we tacitly link passion-feeling to the heart and rationality-thinking to the mind. Let us call this the *brain-mind* tradition of 'the West': we think with brain-mind, which is viewed as the foundation for scientific decisions and good strategies.

No so in Confucianism. 'Easterners' think with their hearts. In *Mencius*, we read: 'Thinking is the function of the heart (心之官則思).'[215] It is a *heart-mind* tradition. Of course, the Confucians were sophisticated enough not to reduce thinking to the heart alone. Heart-mind is a functional notion, not an anatomical one. What it emphasises is the inseparability between heart and mind, emotion and cognition, will and logic, bodily experience and rational reasoning. Tellingly, the Chinese *kanji* 'think (思)' is composed of a brain and a heart (the upper half a 脑 and the bottom half a 心).

Without such a holistic heart-mind conception, it is hard to understand why Confucianism associated almost all human intelligence, cognition and comprehension, as well as emotion, intention and determination, to 'the heart':

思 *si*	think, consider, ponder, contemplate
想 *xiang*	gather, assume, imagine, expect, reckon, suppose, desire
慧 *hui*	wisdom, intelligence
意 *yi*	meaning, conception, idea, sense, understanding, wish, desire, intention, spirit, purpose, will
志 *zhi*	wish, will, ideal, aspiration, ambition, determination

念 *nian*　　think of, bear in mind, thought, idea, intention
性 *xing*　　character, tendency, potency, nature, temperament
情 *qing*　　passion, emotion, feeling, sentiment, affection,
　　　　　　conscience
悟 *wu*　　　realise, awaken, enlighten, understanding,
　　　　　　comprehension

How does this matter? According to Wang Qian, a culture scholar, while a *brain-mind* tradition emphasises logical inference, rational analysis, conceptual categories and the separation of subject and object, a *heart-mind* tradition tends to connect cognition, emotion, intention and contextual initiation. While *brain-mind* prioritises rigour, accuracy and generalities, *heart-mind* values the tacit, aesthetic and holistic. Wang further suggests that this difference in 'thinking styles' explains, in part, the Confucians' achievements in ancient civilisation and backwardness in modern science on the one hand, and the rapid development of Western scientific power with destructive legacies on the other. To Wang, the deep-seated difference in thinking styles underlines other differences between cultures, presumably including those we have been discussing in this section.[216]

Wang is not alone in noting the difference and its significance. Roger Ames and David Hall similarly stress that unless we appreciate 'the heart thinks as well as feels', we cannot make sense of the Confucian civilisation:

> The point, of course, is that in this classical Chinese world view, the mind cannot be divorced from the heart. The cognitive is inseparable from the affective ... [T]here are no rational thoughts devoid of feeling, nor any raw feelings altogether lacking in cognitive content.[217]

What would modern science in the twenty-first century say about this? As reported in 2011, according to research findings by scientists at University College London, the human brain is not only associated with anxiety and emotions, optimism and courage, but

Table 9.1 *Contrasting Aristotelian and Confucian practical teaching*

	Aristotelian practical wisdom	Confucian pragmatism
Underlying question	What is practical knowledge?	How to act practically wisely?
Pattern of knowing	Articulative reasoning	Suggestive exemplars
Image of knowledge	Dualist and hierarchical	Circular and flat
Strategy forward	Polarising and choosing	Associating and complementing
Style of thinking	Brain-mind driven	Heart-mind inspired

also left- and right-wing political views.[218] Alas, it appears that, after all, Confucius got the connectivity thesis largely right two thousand five hundred years ago, although modern science suggests that the connection happens to take place in the brain, rather than the heart. Perhaps it is time for brain-mind and heart-mind to inform, invite, complement, enrich and celebrate one another.

LEARNING FROM DIFFERENCES

Does all this matter to strategy, to the pressing problems of impracticability, fragmentation, moral insensitivity, to managers' everyday activities?

As 'outsiders', we highly value Aristotle's idea of *phronesis*. We consider it a powerful metaphor for directing commitment, effort and resources so as to bring practicality, creativity and morality back to business, to restore strategy as a positive force for serving the common good. However, our 'Eastern' reading of contemporary appropriations of Aristotle exposes us to a deep irony: Aristotle appeared to handle practical wisdom in a highly rational, analytical, reasoned manner. In our view, the 'what' question, articulative style, hierarchical knowledge, polarising-and-choosing tactic and brain-driven conception all contribute to that irony.

When we concentrate on theorising what is and is not *phronesis*, packaging it with fixed nouns, searching for actor-independent attributes, relying on abstract categorisation and articulating logic, we effectively distract managers and researchers from *bricolage*, from shaping and solving problems at the business front line. We intend to close the *phronetic* gap, in effect we are widening it. This is no good for practical strategy.

Once we polarise strategy theories and models, fit them into competing categories, force them into antagonistic dichotomies, rank them into hierarchies, we immediately provoke paradigm wars, invite defensive closures, intensify political struggles, shut down conversations and drive out complementarities. Which discipline, methodology, rationality, knowledge, *praktikes* or *theoretikes*, *phronesis* or *techne* or *episteme*, *mythos* or *logos*, should dominate or be 'the highest'? It is bad for coherent strategy.

This is far from being merely an academic matter. It has vital, and potentially fatal, practical implications. When we advise managers to start 'the strategic process' by making a 'fundamental choice' between 'radically opposed recommendations', *either* a deliberate *or* an emergent approach, for example, are we serious? What practical difference do we want to make?

Strategy writers in 'the West' tend to blame the decline of *phronesis* and the domination of *episteme* over 'the last three hundred years' for bad strategies in our own time. They take great pains to rediscover Aristotle's *phronesis* and introduce it into strategy.[219] While we appreciate our colleagues' good intentions, we consider it useful, and perhaps necessary, to come to terms with Aristotle's ambivalent legacy.

There are two Aristotles: a *phronetic* Aristotle who promotes practical knowledge, and a rational Aristotle who is the exemplar of analytic categorisation, either/or logic and abstract reasoning. Judged by the practical consequence that the analytic tradition has become a significant, some would say a dominant, part of Western cultures,[220] it appears that the rational Aristotle has overshadowed his *phronetic* counterpart. It is unfair, and not helpful, to set up

Descartes as a convenient scapegoat and blame every fault on him. Descartes was himself a product of a deep-rooted tradition; he did not come from nowhere. The analytical bias of Western civilisations did not begin suddenly three hundred years ago in Descartes' hands. The lost of *phronesis* and the dominance of *logos* was, at least in part, of Aristotle's making.[221] Aristotle's tragic legacy has proved that promoting his practical philosophy via his reasoned style amounts to an uphill battle.[222] The question you ask (what vs how), the style you nurture (articulative vs suggestive), the image of knowledge you take (dualist-hierarchical vs circular-flat), the version of polar sensibility you adopt (polarising-and-choosing vs associating-and-complementing), and the source of strategic excellence you assume (brain-driven vs heart-inspired) are not a trivial matter. Particularly for an applied field such as strategy, the reasoned Aristotle can be as much part of the problem as of the solution. Unless we take note of and be frank about Aristotle's double-edged power, appealing uncritically to his theorisation of *phronesis* will likely leave the project for practically wise strategy unfulfilled.

We wholeheartedly welcome the efforts of some other strategy researchers in 'the West' to restore a balanced Aristotle.[223] These writers show us a different Aristotle, less analytic, rationalistic, reasoned, abstract or cold, more pragmatic, humane, humble, friendly and helpful to managers on the front line. Recent efforts such as those in the strategy-as-practice programme, the 'practice turn', clearly signify a critical departure from the overly analytical, articulating paradigm. Inspired mainly by the social theories of practice of Bourdieu, de Certeau and Giddens, such efforts represent a determined search for practically wise strategies.[224] Put into such a cross-cultural context, our call for a pragmatic turn is not a lonely cry, but part of an emerging, growing, wider movement.[225]

Before we conclude, some reflections are in order. We have in this chapter attempted a comparison between Aristotelian and Confucian intellectual sources; we expressed our strong views. We will not be surprised if readers respond differently. Some may find it informative, others may strongly disagree. We may have read too much of our Confucian perspective into 'the other', or interpreted our own traditions 'incorrectly' – 'One does not know the true face of Mountain Lu because of being in it (不识庐山真面目, 只缘身在此山中)', to quote a Tang-Dynasty Chinese poem. Like everyone else, we are fallible and have prejudices.[226] We can only hope that those who see things differently will present their views and challenge our thinking. This is what pragmatic inquiry is about; strategy can only benefit.

Second, we believe the 'Confucian tradition' is not only different from other traditions but heterogeneous within itself as well. Lumping Chinese and Japanese traditions into 'Confucian pragmatism' and contrasting it with 'Western' teachings and practices cannot be other than crude and simplistic. We are aware that there are huge differences between Chinese and Japanese traditions; there are at least two Confucianisms, a Chinese and a Japanese. In addition, there are many other deeply influential traditions at work in the region, such as Taoism and Buddhism, which we have frequently referred to. Furthermore, China and Japan have certainly had their non-pragmatic moments, with serious, lasting consequences. We recognise, too, the huge diversity in 'Western' traditions. We have suggested some differences between 'classical' and 'new' American pragmatisms, and have discerned variations in 'Western' accounts of Aristotle. Similarities and differences are complex, ambiguous, evolving and always surprise settled contrasts.

Hence, in this book we do not wish to perpetuate a supposed, sharp divide between 'the East' and 'the West', let alone 'the West' and 'the Rest'.[227] This book is not just for Chinese and Japanese managers. We believe the pragmatic turn we call for is not merely useful in 'Confucian societies', but equally sensible and actionable in other cultures as well. Remember: pragmatism respects what works and the real world tends to reward what works and punish what doesn't. Pragmatism is a shared intellectual treasure, a common strategic practice of the whole of humankind. People in different cultures can be pragmatic in different ways, true to local traditions, in coping with local concerns. This we must appreciate and learn from. We believe that this pragmatic attitude will enable us to avoid, on the one hand, assuming cultural differences away, and to guard against, on the other, turning cultural differences into 'clashes of civilisations'.

Third, we strive to be holistic and positive. We need to see things through the eyes of our 'enemies',[228] to enlarge our vision horizon and resource pool so as to *bricoler* effectively. Although we are critical of Aristotle's overly rationalistic style, we do not devalue *episteme* and *logos* because, to say the least, strategy cannot turn its back on technical efficiency or the power of scientific rationality. Nature cannot be fooled; we are not free to construct whatever we want. Science, technology, efficiency and the technical rationality behind them are useful insofar as they serve rather than dictate human purpose. We promote value rationality to balance technical and instrumental rationalities, not to displace them. We need simply to remind ourselves of the wiring problem that grounded the A380 jumbo jet, disappointed customers, destroyed the value of the EADS company and escalated political tensions between several EU member states. After all, as Dewey, Rorty, Churchman and Putnam posit, the end and the means are mutually constitutive and co-evolving. Rationality, beauty and morality are inseparable. Newton, Picasso and Confucius are good friends in our search for pragmatic strategy. Nobody wants to fly over the Atlantic on a socially constructed aircraft void of science and technology. We cannot fulfil human potential with inefficiency.

Finally, readers will surely have noted that, in this chapter particularly, we emphasise the affinity between American and Confucian pragmatism while juxtaposing Confucius and Aristotle in contrasting terms. We do this for a purpose. Our purpose is to establish that pragmatism is our best hope for practically wise strategy, and that pragmatism is not the exclusive property of the Chinese and the Japanese. For this, we play up the similarities between Confucius and Dewey while downplaying their differences. On the other hand, we believe that, for comparison purposes, the strongest insights will be gained by juxtaposing the most contrasting *yin*s and *yang*s. In light of this, we consider current accounts of Confucius and Aristotle to offer a useful contrast insofar as practical wisdom is concerned. We are careful to differentiate two Aristotles. By bringing Confucius, Dewey and Aristotle together, we desire to enrich our understanding of what pragmatic strategy is and is not, of how people with different cultural roots can learn from and support each other in the fast-moving, diverse, interconnected world.[229] Perhaps we should change the subtitle of this book from 'Eastern Wisdom, Global Success' into 'Shared Wisdom, Global Success'.

With this book, we question the conventional paradigm, promote pragmatic spirits, call for a pragmatic turn, investigate what pragmatic strategies look like, explore what to do and how to do it, and locate pragmatic strategy in a cross-cultural context. *Tao* is made in the walking of it. It is time to walk the talks. We wish you success in strategising pragmatically. Together let us 'make the world better and happier' (Dewey) and 'realise great harmony' (Confucius).

Notes

I   INTRODUCTION

1 Amazon.com and Google Scholar (accessed 1 June 2010).
2 See: Andrews 1971; Ansoff 1965, 1988; Chandler 1962, 1977, 1990a; Sloan 1963.
3 The phrase 'The world is flat' is borrowed from the title of a book by Thomas L. Friedman 2006.
4 *Daily Telegraph* 16 September 2008, 'Capitalism: it's painful, but it works' by Jeff Randall; 'Wall St suffers worst day for 7 years' by James Quinn and Dominic White; *The Times* 14 October 2008, 'Paulson lays down law as bankers hear details of his $700bn bailout' by Suzy Jagger; *The Times* 10 October 2009, 'We came close to not being able to get money from bank machines' by Katherine Griffiths.
5 *Financial Times* 23 June 2010, 'Daunted by deficits'.
6 *Financial Times* 15 July 2011, 'A nation taken to the limit'.
7 *Sunday Times* 13 March 2011, 'At last, America agrees it can't go on like Greece' by Irwin Stelzer.
8 *Financial Times* 3 August 2011, 'US retreats from brink of debt default' by James Politi; *Sunday Times* 7 August 2011, 'Divided America' by Tony Allen-Mills.
9 *The Economist* 9 April 2011, 'Portugal seeks help: and then there were three'.
10 *Sunday Times* 7 August 2011, 'Europe's dilemma' by Bojan Panceviski.
11 *Financial Times* 3 May 2010, 'Eurozone agrees Greek bail-out' by Kerin Hope, Nikki Tait and Quentin Peel; *Financial Times* 5 May 2010, 'A bail-out for Greece is just the beginning' by Martin Wolf; *Times* 3 May 2010, 'Staring at "collapse or salvation", Greece agrees new austerity plan' by Robert Lindsay and John Carr.
12 *Financial Times* 31 December 2010, 'The year of the unconventional' by Lionel Barber.

13 *Sunday Times* 12 October 2008, 'Is this the end of the American era?' by
Paul Kennedy; *Sunday Times* 12 April 2009, 'Has the bubble finally burst
for capitalism?' by Paul Mason; *The Times* 6 May 2010, 'Bank workers
killed in riots as Greece stares into the abyss' by Phillip Pangalos.

14 Rajan 2010; also see *Financial Times* 21 June 2010, 'We were all to
blame for the crash' by Clive Crook.

15 Reflecting on the role 'the rest of us' played in the crisis, Bethany
McLean, a former Wall Street banker, writes: 'You've got to be a believer
in personal responsibility or our society comes to an end.' See *Sunday
Times* 5 December 2010, 'Guiltiest men in the room' by John Artidge.

16 *Financial Times* 3 December 2008, 'Global imbalances threaten the
survival of liberal trade' by Martin Wolf.

17 *The Economist* 13 September 2008, 'Lehman Brothers: Fuld again'.

18 Nouried Roubini, an economist at New York University, delivered a
speech in the autumn of 2006 to the International Monetary Fund,
warning that the 'United States was likely to face a once-in-a-lifetime
housing bust, an oil shock, sharply declining consumer confidence and
ultimately a deep recession' along with 'homeowners defaulting on
mortgages, trillions of dollars of mortgage-backed securities unravelling
worldwide and the global financial system shuddering to a halt'. At the
World Economic Forum meeting in Davos in January 2007, Roubini
issued the same warning. At that time, he was dismissed as 'slightly
mad'. See *Financial Times* 8–9 May 2010, 'You must come to Cannes
too!' – interview with Nouried Roubini by Gillian Tett; *Sunday Times*
26 October 2008, 'When this man predicted a global financial crisis more
than a year ago, people laughed. Not any more. And now he says ...' by
Dominic Rushe. For the works of those who saw the crisis coming see,
e.g., Roubini and Mihm 2010; Shiller 2000, 2003; Tett 2009.

19 *Financial Times* 7 October 2008, 'Conservatism overshoots its limit'
by Gideon Rachman; *Financial Times* 9 March 2010, 'Seeds of its own
destruction' by Martin Wolf; *Financial Times* 13 March 2009, 'Read the
big four to know capitalism's fate' by Paul Kennedy; *Financial Times* 16
March 2009, 'A quest for other ways' by David Pilling and Ralph Athkins;
Financial Times 20 March 2009, 'Do not let the "cure" destroy capitalism'
by Gary Becker and Kevin Murphy; *The Times* 9 December 2008, 'A crash
as historic as the end of communism' by Robert Peston; *The Times* 19 June
2010, 'It was the end of the world as we knew it: and the dawn of a new
capitalism' by Anatole Kaletsky.

20 *The Economist* 11 October 2008, 'When fortune frowned: a special report on the world economy'.

21 *Financial Times* 15 December 2009, 'World counts true cost of the rescue' by Lionel Barber.

22 *Financial Times* 9 October 2008, 'Financial crisis marks out a new geopolitical order' by Philip Stephens.

23 *The Economist* 17 April 2010, 'The new masters of management'.

24 *Financial Times* 29 October 2008, 'Why Asia stays calm in the storm' by Kishore Mahbubani.

25 *The Economist* 17 April 2010, 'The BRICs: the trillion-dollar club'; 'Schumpeter: an emerging challenge'.

26 *Fianncial Times* 9 October 2008, 'New geopolitical order'.

27 *Financial Times* 2 November 2010, 'The optimistic doomsayer' by Andrew Hill.

28 See *Civilization: The West and the Rest* (Ferguson 2011).

29 *Financial Times* 6 October 2008, 'A global downturn in the power of the West' by Dominique Moisi; *Financial Times* 11 December 2009, 'Money is moving east: and the bankers will follow' by Gillian Tett; *The Times* 29 October 2008, 'West goes cap in hand to the East for help' by Phillip Webster and Gary Duncan.

30 *The Times* 13 October 2006, 'IBM transfers its procurement HQ to southern China' by Tom Bawden.

31 *Financial Times* 26/27 September 2009, 'HSBC chief to be based in Hong Kong' by Patrick Jenkins and Sundeep Tucker; *Financial Times* 5 October 2009, 'Homeward bound' by Patrick Jenkins.

32 *The Economist* 17 April 2010, 'The world turned upside down: a special report on innovation in emerging markets'.

33 *Financial Times* 12 May 2010, 'A change in gear' by Stefan Wagstyl.

34 *Financial Times* 11 May 2010, 'Europe is unprepared for austerity' by Gideon Rachman; *Financial Times* 14 May 2010, 'Europe enters era of belt-tightening' by Victor Mallet.

35 *The Economist* 14 February 2009, 'Burgeoning bourgeoisie: a special report on the new middle classes in emerging markets'; *The Economist* 14 March 2009, 'India and China are creating millions of entrepreneurs'.

36 *Newsweek* 18 October 2010, 'Made for China' by Sonia Kolesnikov-Jessop and Rana Foroohar.

37 *The Economist* 16 December 2010, 'Globalisation: the redistribution of hope'.

38 *Financial Times* 9 August 2007, 'China's prosperity brings income gap' by Richard McGregor; *Sunday Times* 21 October 2007, 'China's rich spark dissent from below' by Michael Sheridan; *Time* 13 December 2010, 'Thank you for sharing' by Sarabjit Singh.

39 *Sunday Times* 8 December 2009, 'History's back from the dead' – interview with Francis Fukuyama by Bryan Appleyard.

40 Serra and Stiglitz 2008.

41 Zhu 2007a.

42 *Sunday Times* 7 December 2008, 'It's bad news when politicians replace markets' by Irwin Stelzer; *Sunday Times* 12 April 2009, 'Survival of fittest gives way to bailout politics' by Irwin Stelzer.

43 *Financial Times* 15 December 2009, 'Cold war victory was a start and an end' by Martin Wolf.

44 *Financial Times* 16 October 2009, 'Bankers, bonuses and the market: plus ca change' by Philip Stephens.

45 Bremmer 2010; Halper 2010; also see: *The Economist* 20 March 2010, 'Middle-income and developing countries: crumbs from the BRICs-man's table'; *The Economist* 8 May 2010, 'The China model: the Beijing consensus is to keep quiet'; *The Economist* 5 June 2010, 'The state and the economy: re-enter the dragon'.

46 See, e.g., Ferguson 2011.

47 *The Times* 7 February 2011, 'Statism is not the way to lasting prosperity' by Sam Fleming.

48 *Financial Times* 31 December 2010, 'The year of the unconventional'.

49 *The Economist* 21 February 2009, 'Globalisation: turning their backs on the world'.

50 *The Economist* 29 September 2001, 'Globalisation and its critics: a survey of globalisation'; *The Economist* 18 May 2002, 'Capitalism and its troubles: a survey of international finance'; *The Times* 19 February 2007, 'Globalisation fails to help the poorest' by Joseph Stiglitz.

51 *Financial Times* 23 July 2007, 'Globalisation generates dark thoughts' by Chris Giles.

52 *Financial Times Weekend Magazine* 19/20 March 2011, 'Manufacturing is all over the place' by Gillian Tett; *The Economist* 21 February 2009, 'Turning their backs'.

53 *The Times* 4 February 2009, 'EU warns of global trade wars over \$800bn "Buy American" rescue plan' by David Charter, Rory Watson and Philip Webster.

54 *The Times* 19 June 2010, 'BP's next great battle is already looming: to restore its battered reputation' by Robin Tagnamenta and Robert Lea.

55 See, e.g., Shrivastava 1994, 1995.

56 *Sunday Times* 20 December 2009, 'Hot air in our time' by Jonathan Leake; *The Times* 19 December 2009, 'Copenhagen cuts corners on climate' by Ben Webster and Sam Coates.

57 *Financial Times* 16 January 2009, 'Airport operator balks at runway's pressing deadline' by Kevin Done.

58 *Sunday Times* 18 January 2009, 'Heathrow rebel alliance is cleared for take-off' by Jon Ungoed-Thomas, Chris Gourlay and Jonathan Oliver; *Times* 17 January 2009, 'Heathrow runway backers got special BA privileges' by Ben Webster.

59 Nair 2011.

60 Kuhn 1970.

61 For 'normal science', see Kuhn 1970.

62 *Financial Times* 15 February 2010, 'Business has not yet found its Copernicus' by Michael Skapinker.

63 See, e.g., Chia and Holt 2009; Stacey 2010; also Editorial, *European Management Review* special issue 2004, 1 (1); Pettigrew *et al.* 2002; Volberda and Elfring 2001; Whittington 2001.

64 Kuhn 1970.

65 Hamel 2009.

66 *Financial Times* 22/23 November 2008, 'It's about getting stuff done' – interview with Tom Peters by Stefan Stern.

67 Eccles and Nohria 1992, p. 7.

68 Hayes and Abernathy 1980; see the 2007 reprint in *Harvard Business Review*.

69 Hayes 2007, in Hayes and Abernathy 2007, p. 141.

70 Collins and Porras 1994, p. 46.

71 See *Financial Times* 1 May 2006, 'Lessons in Darwinism for the western world' by Geoffrey Moore.

72 Zhu 2007a.

73 *Sunday Times* 14 February 2010, 'I'm the guy who saved Wall Street' – interview with Hank Paulson by Iain Dey.

74 Pascale 1984.

75 *The Economist* 26 June 2008, 'The meaning of Bill Gates'.

76 *Forbes Asian* 10 December 2007, 'The second coming' by Christopher Helman.

77 Academics call this 'philosophical pragmatism'.

78 Kaletsky 2010; also see *Financial Times* 23 May 2008, 'Growth challenge: pragmatism is replacing the old "Washington Consensus"'.

79 For a pragmatic turn in philosophy and the social sciences, see Bernstein 2010.

80 For an excellent introduction to Confucian pragmatism, see Ames and Hall 2001; Ames and Rosemont 1998.

81 For the relevance of Aristotelian practical wisdom to strategy, see Nonaka and Toyama 2007; Nonaka *et al.* 2008 on *phronesis*.

82 For the contributions to strategy by these influential writers, see, as an introduction, Andrews 1971; Ansoff 1965; Barnard 1938; Barney 1991; Chandler 1962, 1977, 1990a; Collins and Porras 1994; Hamel and Prahalad 1994; Kim and Mauborgne 2004; Mintzberg 2009; Porter 1980, 1985, 1990; Teece 2009; Walton 1992.

83 Morita 1986; Nonaka and Takeuchi 1995.

84 There is one exception: in recent years there has been a growing number of publications on Indian strategic thinking and business practice, which, we gather, is due to the strong presence of India-born, English-speaking professors in elite business schools.

85 The 6Cs of strategy have their intellectual roots in Nonaka's six abilities that constitute *phronesis* leadership. See Nonaka and Toyama 2007; Nonaka *et al.* 2008.

86 The words 'active non-action' is borrowed from the late India-born, Harvard/INSEAD/London Business School strategy professor Sumantra Ghoshal. See Bruch and Ghoshal 2004.

87 Here we refer to the American pragmatist Charles S. Peirce's famous statement 'We cannot begin with complete doubt'. See Joas 1996, p. 128.

88 The way we use case studies in this book is partly informed by recent critical comments on the popular, conventional but misguided fashion. Among the critical comments, Chris Bones, Ralph Stacey and Russell Ackoff's stand out:

In North America, the MBA is a pre-experience qualification, with the majority of students fresh from their first degree, and it relies on a lot of fabricated case studies and abstracted 'what would you do if you were in charge?' conversations. (*Financial Times* 27 September 2010, 'Letter: Maturity is what counts in learning' by Chris Bones)

The session took the form of a report back by small groups on their discussion of a number of case studies of strategic success and failure in other large companies. The conversation ran entirely in terms of abstract entities. Toyota was said to have decided to enter the Chinese market and an intense discussion followed on why Toyota had done this, what China expected in return and whether it had been the 'right' strategy or not. The whole discussion was purely speculative since none of the discussants, including the presenter, had any involvement with Toyota and few if any had actually been to China. When a particular decision looked puzzling, discussants looked for rational reasons for Toyota having made it and if they could find none they concluded that it had been a mistake. No one ever suggested that we might need to understand the figuration of power relations amongst senior managers and their Chinese counterparts might have had something to do with the decisions. It took only a few minutes discussion at the start of my session for participants to see just how abstract their discussion had been and how totally absent human beings had been. (Stacey 2010, p. 114)

Case studies usually provide examples of uncreative solutions to problems. Learning a business principle from a case may help one practice that principle, but it doesn't show you how to creatively solve problems. (Ackoff 2003, p. 24)

89 This case is excerpted from the *Wall Street Journal* (Eastern edition) 13 July 2007, p. A13, 'Sick propaganda' by Paul Offit; the copyright of the Dow Jones & Company Inc. is acknowledged.

2   SPIRITS OF PRAGMATISM

1 *The Times* 25 March 2011, 'Pragmatism is king in our vague new world' by Anatole Kaletsky.

2 *Financial Times* 23 May 2008, 'Growth challenge: pragmatism is replacing the old "Washington Consensus"'.

3 *The Times* 19 June 2010, 'It was the end of the world as we knew it: and the dawn of a new capitalism' by Anatole Kaletsky.

4 *Sunday Times* 10 April 2009, 'Corporate pragmatism will get us out of this mess' by John Waples.

5 *Financial Times* 19 June 2007, 'Why Rorty's search for what works has lessons for business' by John Kay.

6 See, e.g., Bellah 1957; Benedict 1946; Chan 1963; Fung 1948; Hall and
   Ames 1987; Tsunoda 1958.

7 Hall and Ames 1999.

8 Statler and Roos 2005; Statler *et al.* 2003; Tsoukas and Cummings 1997.

9 Joas 1996.

10 Baert 2005; Flyvbjerg 2001; Gascoigne 2008; Outhwaite 2009;
    Silva 2007.

11 Joas 1996.

12 See 'Praise the sword' – an interview with Masahiko Gujiwara, *Financial
    Times Weekend Magazine* 10/11 March 2007.

13 Hall and Ames 1999.

14 For corner-cutting 'pragmatism' see, e.g., *Wall Street Journal* 13–15
    July 2007, 'Made in China' by Emily Parker; for China's tainted-milk
    scandal, see Chapter 8 'Questioning the conventional paradigm'.

15 See, e.g., Baert 2005; Bernstein 2010; Hildebrand 2005; Joas 1996;
    Ormerod 2006; Powell 2001, 2002, 2003; Rorty 1979, 1982, 1991, 1999;
    Wicks and Freeman 1998.

16 See *Financial Times* 1 May 2006, 'Lessons in Darwinism for the western
    world' by Geoffrey Moore.

17 Bernstein 1983, 1991, 2010; Dewey 1930; Fung 1948; Hall and Ames
    1987, 1999; Joas 1996; Putnam 1995; Rorty 1979, 1982, 1991, 1999; Zhu
    2007a, 2008.

18 For readers who are more deeply interested in pragmatic theorising,
    Chapter 9 'Pragmatism East and West' supplies a more detailed
    introduction.

19 For an excellent explanation of why *Tao* is better translated as 'way-
    making' (a verb), instead of the usual translation as 'the way' (a noun),
    see Ames and Hall 2003.

20 See, e.g., Archer 2000; Bourdieu 1998; Emirbayer 1994; Emirbayer and
    Mische 1998; Johnson *et al.* 2007; Sewell 1992.

21 Fung 1948; Nakamura 1967; Nitobe 1899.

22 *Analects* 15/29.

23 *Zhongyong* 13.

24 *Zuozhuan*; cf.: Fung 1952, p. 32.

25 *Zhuangzi* 4/2/33.

26 Ackoff 1996; Bruch and Ghoshal 2004; Drucker 1994.

27 Hirschmeier and Yui 1975.

28 See Yuasa 1987, p. 68.

29 Ames and Rosemont 1998, p.5.

30 Hall and Ames 1999, p. 209.

31 Tan 2003, p. 95.

32 Hall and Ames 1999, pp. 149–150.

33 Nonaka and Takeuchi 1995, p. 27.

34 Cf.: Nisbett 2003, p. 8.

35 Bruch and Ghoshal 2004.

36 Mintzberg 1987, p. 74.

37 This section is based mainly on: *Banker to the Poor* (Yunus 1998); *Financial Times* 9/10 December 2006, 'Give the man credit' by Jo Johnson; *Financial Times* 1 March 2011 'Bangladesh moves to oust Nobel winner Yunus from microlender' by Amy Kazmin; *Guardian* 16 February 2008, 'What's the big idea?' by Madeleine Bunting; *Time* 13 November 2006, 'Muhammad Yunus: a Nobel laureate banker envisions an end of poverty' by Ishaan Tharoor; *The Times* 14 October 2006, 'Follow me and beat poverty, winner of peace prize tells West' by Nick Meo.

38 Yunus 1998, p. 4.

39 Yunus 1998, p. 9.

40 Yunus 1998, p. 11.

41 Yunus 1998, p. 96.

42 *Wikipedia*: 'Muhammad Yunus' (http://en.wikipedia.org/wiki/Muhammad_Yunus; accessed 29 June 2010).

43 Microcredit is not without its critics and there are concerted efforts by some Bangladeshi politicians to oust Yunus from the bank. The usual charges are its high interest rates, distracting funding from public infrastructure projects, and so on; see, e.g., *Financial Times* 20/21 December 2008, 'Microfinance's "iron law": local economies reduced to poverty' by Milford Bateman; *Financial Times Weekend Magazine* 6/7 December 2008, 'Conflicts of interest' by Tim Harford. Recently, politicians in South Asia took the lead in attacking the Grameen Bank; see, e.g., *Financial Times* 8 December 2010, 'Microfinance backlash grows' by Amy Kazmin; *Financial Times* 1 March 2011, 'Banglalesh moves to oust Nobel winner'. Muhammad Yunus supplies some counter-arguments in his book *Banker to the Poor*. Readers need to be aware of the different viewpoints and make their own judgements. In the debate, we found the *Financial Times* 20 December 2010 Editorial, 'Microfinance and financial inclusion', to be a balanced view:

Microfinance has come under attack in south Asia. Politicians have lined up to attack the industry ... It is not above criticism. But these attacks are unfair and threaten to discredit an industry that is, for all its faults, a global engine of financial inclusion. A crackdown would not help anyone, except perhaps traditional money-lenders and feudal landlords ... Microfinance brings a crucial service to poor people. Rather than being attacked, it should be helped to do an even better job of assisting them to assert their financial autonomy.

44 Takahashi 2000.

45 *Analects* 9/17.

46 See Keene 1967, p. xviii.

47 *Zhongyong* 26.

48 *Huainanzi* 9/1/2.

49 See, e.g., Chia 2002; Chia and MacKay 2007; Chia and Tsoukas 2003; Tsoukas and Chia 2002.

50 For details of China's tainted-milk scandal, see Chapter 8, 'Questioning the conventional paradigm'.

51 For a critique, see John Dewey's *The Quest for Certainty*.

52 See Keene 1967, p. xviii.

53 *Analectic* 4/10.

54 *Analectic* 6/20.

55 *Commentaries on Yijing* 10.

56 Fei 1992 [1947], p. 75.

57 Tan 2003.

58 Ghoshal 2005, p. 81.

59 Mintzberg 1994a, p. 109.

60 Ames and Rosemont 1998, p. 30.

61 Main sources of this section: Best 1990, 2001; Fujimoto 1999; Womack *et al.* 1990; *Wikipedia* on 'Toyota Production System', 'Just-in-Time' and 'Lean manufacturing'.

62 Taylor 1967 [1911], p. 39.

63 Womack *et al.* 1990, p. 31.

64 Womack *et al.* 1990, p. 33.

65 Womack *et al.* 1990, p. 129.

66 Womack *et al.* 1990, p. 63.

67 Best 1990, p. 155.

68 See Best 1990, p. 52.

69 Best 1990, pp. 55–56, 58.

70 Fujimoto 1999.

71 Womack *et al.* 1990, p. 57.

72 Imai *et al.* 1985, p. 353.

73 See Best 2001, pp. 35–40.

74 We give more details on the *kanban* system in Chapter 4, 'Strategy as purposeful emergence'.

75 Womack *et al.* 1990, p. 68.

76 On a related point, Fujimoto insightfully distinguishes universal, regional- and firm-specific capabilities, or routines (1999, p. 27). It is interesting to note that TPS is a Toyota, not a Japanese, production system. There have been considerable differences between Japanese car-makers. While TPS had largely taken shape in Toyota, in other Japanese car-makers the situation varied greatly. In their study of the 'Mazda turnaround', Pascale and Rohlen depict the situation in the then Mazda factory thus:

> The factory had expensive, built-in safeguards against failure. Among the luxuries, Yamasaki [the new Mazda president] ruefully recalls the large parts inventories on the factory floor that ranged from a two-day supply to an entire week's supply ... 'If the level of a river is very high, it is difficult to see the many rocks underneath,' says Yamasaki. In a characteristic Japanese reliance on metaphor, he adds, 'It is necessary to reduce the water level to find the rocks' ... The 'water level' began to fall. Inventory was reduced to a half-day for most parts, and to only a couple of hours for some, the common standard among leading Japanese car manufacturers. To guard against recidivism, Yamasaki established a rule that, in some areas of the plants, there could be no more than two boxes of parts along the assembly line at any one time. (1983, p. 243)

77 See Best 1990, p. 1.

78 Hall and Ames 1999, p. 160.

79 *Zhongyong* 20, 25.

80 Fung 1948, p. 8.

81 *The Economist* 31 May 1997, 'Mr. Knowledge'; Nonaka 1991, 1994; Nonaka and Takeuchi 1995; Nonaka and von Krogh 2009; von Krogh *et al.* 2000.

82 Porter 1980, 1985.

83 Barney and Clark 2007.

84 Also see Lazonick 1991; Schumpeter 1934; Teece 2007a, 2007b, 2009.

85 Morita 1986, pp. 208–209.

86 Hall and Ames 1999, p. 168; also see Law 2004; Maturana and Varela 1980.

87 *Zhongyong* 21.

88 Joas 1996, p. 131.

89 Dell 1999.

90 Kim and Mauborgne 2005.

91 See Alvarez and Barney 2007.

92 Here we refer to Kim and Mauborgne's 2000 *Harvard Business Review* article 'Knowing a winning business idea when you see one'.

93 Main sources of this section: Ohmae 1988; *The Economist* 8 June 2002, 'Obituary: Genichi Kawakami'; 'Memoriam: Genichi Kawakami' (www.yamaha.com/publicatins/acceent/Accent302; accessed 14 March 2007).

94 *The Economist* 8 June 2002, 'Obituary'.

95 Morita 1986, p. 79.

96 Drucker 1994, p. 102.

97 Ohmae 1988, p. 152.

98 Ohmae 1988.

99 Fingarette 1983, p. 217.

100 Takahashi 2000, p. 225.

101 *Analects* 6/30.

102 *Mencius* 7/1/4.

103 In *Liji*; cf.: Jung 1987, p. 232.

104 All cited from *Analects*.

105 Latour 1993, p. 6.

106 Hayes and Abernathy 2007 [1980].

107 Vaughan 1996.

108 Zhu 2008.

109 *Analects* 13/23.

110 *Analects* 2/14.

111 *Analects* 5/4.

112 *Zhuangzi* 33. Such openness towards plurality is evident throughout the Confucian traditions:

[These] different views are single aspects of way-making (道 *Tao*). The essence of way-making is constant and includes all changes. It cannot be grasped by a single corner. Those with perverted knowledge who see only a single aspect of way-making will not be able to comprehend its totality. (*Xunzi* 21; the realist wing of Confucianism)

The reason why I hate that holding to one point is the injury it does to way-making. It takes up one point and disregards a hundred others. (*Mencius* 7/26; the idealist wing of Confucianism)

There are many ways of investigating *li* to the utmost. One way is to read about and discuss truth and principles. Another way is to talk about the people and events of the past as well as the present, and to distinguish which is right and which is wrong. Still another way is to handle affairs and settle them in the proper way. (Cheng Yi *Yishu* 18/5/2; a Song Dynasty Neo-Confucian)

113 Morita 1986, p. 290.

114 *Financial Times* 27 September 2007, 'GLG takes historical perspective' by James Mackintosh.

115 March and Simon 1958; Miles and Snow 1978; Nohria and Berkley 1994.

116 Hirsch *et al.* 1990, p. 88.

117 Feyerabend 2011, p. 130.

118 James 1907, 1909.

119 Rorty 1982.

120 Mintzberg 2001, p. 41.

121 Main sources for this section: Weng 2004; Hisap company website (www.cnpcmall.com; accessed 9 July 2010).

122 Interestingly, Dell has learnt to add the human touch into its business model while competing in China; see *Financial Times* 26 August 2005, 'In China the agent enters the equation' by Mure Dickie and Scott Morrison.

123 Schumpeter 1942.

124 For more on business models, see Chapter 7, 'Orchestrating WSR, orchestrating the firm'.

125 *Analects* 4/16, 12/1, 7/30.

126 *Mencius* 5/2/5.

127 *Analects* 15/9, 18/1, 7/34.

128 Xu 1988, p. 292.

129 Fung 1948, p. 73.

130 Tan (2003) interprets: 'Knowing *tianming* is knowing how one should act, given what one knows of how the world is and how it should be. Insofar as everyone, in acting, has a capacity to be guided by a desire to

become better and to make the world a better place, *tianming* is a call to self-realisation through communal participation.' (p. 144)

131 Bellah 1957; Fujiwara 2007; Fung 1948.

132 Fei 1992 [1947], pp. 43, 78.

133 *Analects* 18/8.

134 *Analects* 4/10.

135 Donaldson and Dunfee 1994.

136 Cummings 2002, p. 187.

137 Whetten *et al.* 2002, p. 393.

138 Hall and Ames 1999.

139 Promoting the communal spirit, Confucius had no faith in politics of the Aristotelian sort in which 'a collective activity whose object was to arrive at decisions on public matters (*ta koina*) after a process of collective deliberation' (Tsoukas and Cummings 1997, p. 670) because public rhetoric combat is no good for harmony (Hall and Ames 1999; Nisbett 2003). Rather, Confucius emphasised the importance of people's 'inside' character. From the Confucian perspective, people's character is the platform of human acts (Nonaka and Takeuchi 1995, p. 29). The exemplary sages act wisely because their cultivated characters embody the virtue of benevolence and enable them to act according to what is right in specific circumstances (Yang and Sternberg 1997).

140 *Analects* 15/13.

141 Nonaka and Takeuchi 1995, p. 29.

142 Sternberg *et al.* 1981.

143 Yang and Sternberg 1997.

144 *Analects* 8/11.

145 *The Economist* 31 July 2010, 'Schumpeter: a post-crisis case study, the new dean of Harvard Business School promises "radical innovation"'.

146 *Liji* 9/35/63/26.

147 *Analects* 15/18.

148 Jung 1987, p. 233.

149 Hall and Ames 1999, p. 182.

150 The phrase 'soft power' was coined by Joseph Nye of Harvard University in a 1991 book *Bound to Lead: The Changing Nature of American Power*. He further develops the concept in a 2004 book *Soft Power: The Means to Success in World Politics*.

151 *Analects* 1/1.

152 *Analects* 19/22. This is compatible with what Dewey called 'the traditions, outlooks, and interests which characterise a community'; see Dewey, *The Later Works*, vol. II, p. 331. It is also closely in line with Nietzsche, Heidegger, Wittgenstein and Foucault's notions of 'sociality' and 'historicality'; see, e.g., Flyvbjerg 2001.

153 Hall and Ames 1999. For more, see Chapter 9, 'Pragmatism East and West'.

154 This section is based mainly on Pascale and Rohlen's (1983) classic study; also 'Manufacturing miracle', video programme; Locke 1996.

155 Even before this crisis, Mazda car sales in America had already dropped by 60 per cent in one year after the US Environmental Protection Agency showed that Mazda's rotary engine got only 10 miles per gallon in city driving in comparison with 20 for Toyota's (Pascale and Rohlen 1983, p. 223).

156 Pascale and Rohlen 1983, p. 220.

157 Pascale and Rohlen 1983, pp. 257–259.

158 Pascale and Rohlen 1983, p. 228.

159 Pascale and Rohlen 1983, pp. 227–228.

160 Pascale and Rohlen 1983, p. 239.

161 Pascale and Rohlen 1983, p. 242.

162 Pascale and Rohlen 1983, p. 238.

163 Hall and Ames 1999, p. 128.

164 Handy 2002, p. 53.

165 de Geus 1996, p. 81.

166 Mintzberg 2007, p. 25.

167 Chen 2000. For a slightly different interpretation, see Ames and Rosemont 1998, p. 62.

168 Ames and Hall 2001, pp. 61–89; Ames and Rosemont 1998, pp. 45–65.

169 Stacey 2010.

170 Morita 1986, p. 146.

171 Tan 2003, p. 32.

172 *Analects* 13/23.

173 Fung 1948, p. 174.

174 North 1990.

175 Fujimoto 1999, p. 264.

176 *Financial Times* 9 April 2010, 'Former Citi chiefs say sorry for losses' by James Politi, Francesco Guerrera and Alan Rappeport.

177 *Analects* 15/22.

178 Tan 2003, p. 68

179 Ackoff 1996, p. 23.

180 Best 1990, p. 80.

181 *Financial Times* 13 May 2010, 'Facebook's open disdain for privacy' by John Gapper; *Financial Times* 18 May 2010, 'Facebook's hunt for value has come at a cost' by Brett Self.

182 *Analects* 13/3.

183 *Mencius* 7/2/14.

184 Fung 1952, p. 113.

185 Main sources of this section: Aoki 2001, chs. 4 and 10; Best 1990, chs. 7 and 8.

186 Best 1990, ch. 7.

187 Best 1990, ch. 7.

188 For more on value chain, see Chapter 7, 'Orchestrating WSR, orchestrating the firm'.

189 Aoki 2001, pp. 253–254.

190 Best 1990, p. 271.

191 Best 1990, pp. 215–216.

192 For 'the tragedy of the commons', see Hardin 1968.

193 Best 1990, p. 209.

194 Aoki 2001, pp. 254–255.

195 Best 1990, pp. 236–238.

196 Nonaka and Takeuchi 1995.

197 Tsoukas and Knudsen 2002.

198 Kay 1997.

199 Foss 1996.

200 Rorty 1991.

201 Stacey 2007.

202 Hayek 1945.

203 Schumpeter 1934.

204 Knight 1921.

205 Barnard 1938; Ghoshal 2005.

206 Clegg *et al.* 2006; Clegg *et al.* 2011; Crozier and Friedberg 1980; Hardy 1995.

207 Jacobson 1992.

208 Porter 1996.

209 Kay 1998.

210 Drucker 1994, p. 100.

3 STRATEGIES IN A PRAGMATIC WORLD

1 Mintzberg 2003, pp. 7–8.
2 Stacey 2007.
3 Tsoukas and Cummings 1997, p. 658.
4 For critiques see, e.g., Mintzberg 2004; Pfeffer and Fong 2002.
5 For 'portfolio planning matrix', see Day 1977; Hedley 1977; for 'balanced scorecard', see Kaplan and Norton 1992.
6 Drucker 1994.
7 Collis and Rukstad 2008, p. 84.
8 Kay 1998.
9 See Barney 2007, p. 8.
10 Bruch and Ghoshal 2004.
11 For the concept of 'situated activity', see Joas 1996, p. 133.
12 Chia and Holt 2009, p. 123.
13 Hafsi and Thomas 2005.
14 'Unintended consequence' has become a concept with significance in sociology. Robert Merton, for example, wrote in his classic book *Social Theory and Social Structure*: 'the distinctive intellectual contributions of the sociologists are found primarily in the study of unintended consequences ... of social practices, as well as in the study of anticipated consequences' (1957, p. 120). On the other side of the Atlantic, Anthony Giddens noted in another sociology classic, *The Constitution of Society*: 'Human history is created by intentional activities but is not an intended project; it persistently eludes efforts to bring it under conscious direction' (1984, p. 27).
15 Ackoff 1981.
16 Mintzberg 2003, p. 8.
17 This section is based on Zhu 2007a.
18 Qian 1999; Raby 2001.
19 Clark 1994, p. 458.
20 Prybyla 1986, pp. 43–44.
21 We shall explore the *wuli–shili–renli* triad in more detail in Chapter 5, 'Dealing with *wuli–shili–renli*'.
22 Qian and Roland 1998.
23 Naughton 1995; Putterman 1997.
24 Lin *et al.* 2003.
25 Berliner 1993; Sachs and Woo 1994.

26 Qin 2002.

27 *Daodejing*, 1, 56.

28 Boisot and Child 1988, pp. 521–522.

29 Interestingly, this is compatible with what some in 'the West' said, e.g. Andrew Grove of Intel: 'You need to be ambiguous in some circumstances' (see Collins and Porras 1994, p. 252); Henry Mintzberg of McGill University: 'Sometimes strategies must be left as broad visions, not precisely articulated, to adapt to a changing environment' (Mintzberg 1994a, p. 112).

30 CRF 2001, p. 413.

31 Chow 1997; Weitzman and Xu 1994.

32 Lindblom 1959, p. 251.

33 Casson 1993, p. 427.

34 Lin 1992, p. 37.

35 Kelliher 1992, p. 57.

36 Fukuyama 1995.

37 Fukuyama 1995, pp. 93–94.

38 McClelland 1961.

39 Jones 2001.

40 Wong 1985.

41 Redding 1990.

42 Ng 2000, p. 201.

43 Fukuyama 1995, p. 94.

44 Nee 1986, p. 186.

45 Boisot 1996, p. 926.

46 Zhu 2007a, p. 1515.

47 This is a critical summary; we quote from Pascale (1984). For a fuller critique, see his full paper.

48 The story is based on Burgelman 1991, 1994.

49 Gordon Moore is another founder and executive of Intel Corporation.

50 *Analects* 2/13.

51 Mintzberg 1987; Pascale 1984.

52 Morita 1986, pp. 83–85.

53 Burgelman 1991, p. 246.

54 Burgelman 1991, p. 244.

55 For 'profit pool', see Gadiesh and Gilbert 1998a, 1998b.

56 Nonaka and Takeuchi 1995.

57 Pascale 1984, p. 70.

58 Mintzberg 1994a, p. 112.

59 Leavitt 2003, p. 100.

60 We borrow this from the concept of 'McUniversities'; see Ritzer 1999, p. 24.

61 Leavitt 2003.

62 Mintzberg 1987, p. 73.

63 Leavitt 2003.

64 Pascale 1984, p. 66.

65 Pfeffer and Salancik 1978.

66 Pascale 1984, p. 70.

67 For theorising about strategy and power, see, e.g., Clegg *et al.* 2006, 2011; Hardy 1995; Perrow 1986; Pettigrew 1985; Pfeffer 1981.

68 O'Reilly and Tushman 2004.

69 Ashby 1956.

70 An early version of this section appeared as a book chapter (Zhu 2006), which is based on Garud and Rappa 1994 and Garud and Ahlstrom 1997.

71 For a good introduction to such technology innovations, see Tushman and Anderson 2004.

72 Garud and Rappa 1994.

73 The 6Cs of strategy has its intellectual roots in Nonaka's six abilities that constitute *phronetic* leadership; see Nonaka and Toyama 2007; Nonaka *et al.* 2008.

74 Mintzberg 1994a, p. 109.

75 Liu and Avery 2009; *Wall Street Journal* 12–14 November 2010, 'Softbank maintains Alibaba stake' by Juro Osawa and Daisuke Wakabayashi.

76 Collins and Porras 1994, 141.

77 *Analectic* 4/10.

78 Joas 1996, p. 133.

79 Collins and Porras 1994, p. 248.

80 Markides 1999, p. 6.

81 Collis and Rukstad 2008, p. 86.

82 Luehrman 1998, p. 76.

83 Cohen and Levinthal 1990; Fujimoto 1999, p. 325.

84 Barnett and Burgelman 1996.

85 Dosi *et al.* 2000; Teece 2007a.

86 Arthur 1989; Nelson and Winter 1982; North 1990.

87 March 1988.

88 Bateson 1972, p. 300.

89 McCulloch 1970, p. 154.

90 Habermas 2003, p. 12.

91 Collins and Porras 1994, p. 140.

92 Collins and Porras 1994, p. 148.

93 Leavitt 2003, p. 102.

94 Watson 2008.

95 Collins and Porras 1994, p. 27.

96 Drucker 1994, p. 101.

97 Drucker 1994, p. 102.

98 Nonaka *et al.* 2008.

99 Stacey 2010, p. 152.

100 Regnér 2005.

101 Burgelman 1991.

102 Kotter 1995, p. 59.

103 Mintzberg 1994a, pp. 111–112.

104 *The Times* 24 November 2008, 'The peasants who left their thumb-prints on history' by Jane Macartney.

105 See Collins and Porras 1994, p. 93.

106 *The Times* 9 February 2009, 'The day Boeing brought the world to everyone's door' by David Robertson.

107 Burgelman 1991, p. 243.

108 Spender 1995, p. 166.

109 Hafsi and Thomas 2005.

110 See Eccles and Nohria 1992, p. 41; also Mahoney 2005, p. 61.

111 Ling 2005.

112 Burgelman 1994.

113 Ansoff 1965; Pascale 1984.

114 Drucker 1994; Leavitt 2003.

115 Kotter 1995, p. 60.

116 The case is based on Collins and Porras 1994, pp. 158–159; Garud and Karnøe 2005, pp. 91–92.

117 See Garud and Karnøe 2005, p. 92.

118 Garud and Karnøe 2005; see Takeuchi and Nonaka 1986.

119 Nonaka and Toyama 2007; Nonaka *et al.* 2008.

120 Cui 2008.

121 *Financial Times* 2 August 2010, 'Thai Airways and Tiger to launch new airline' by Tim Johnston; Liu and Avery 2009; *Wall Street Journal* 8 April 2010, 'Daimler, Nissan, Renault seal pact' by Sebastian Moffett.

122 Arthur 1989, 1994.

123 *Financial Times* 18 March 2010, 'Tencent warns on impact of China texts crackdown' by Kathrin Hille.

124 For a good introduction, see Bijker *et al.* 1987; Fuller 2007.

125 For introduction to actor-network theory (ANT), see Latour 2005; Law 2004; Law and Hassard 1999.

126 Hargadon and Douglas 2001. For more on Edison's electric lighting venture, see Chapter 7, 'Orchestrating WSR, orchestrating the firm'.

127 Barley 1986; Orlikowski 1992, 2000, 2002.

128 Hacking 1999.

129 Giddens 1979, 1984.

130 Von Glasersfeld 1995.

131 Von Glasersfeld 1995, p. 73.

132 Habermas 2003.

133 Volberda 2005.

134 Lévi-Strauss 1966.

135 Garud and Van de Ven 2002.

136 Baker and Nelson 2005; Gabriel 2002.

137 Freeman 2007.

138 Nohria and Berkley 1994, p. 133.

139 Lanzara 1999, p. 347.

140 Dewey 1916, 1939.

141 Yunus 1998, ch. 16.

142 Yunus 1998, pp. 124–125.

143 Yunus 1998, p. 127.

144 Yunus 1998, p. 127.

145 Drucker 1994, p. 100.

4 STRATEGY AS PURPOSEFUL EMERGENCE

1 The debate continues from Mintzberg and Ansoff's 1990s 'Plan 0, Learning 1' controversy to Chia and Holt's 2009 book *Strategy without Design* – just to mention the most eye-catching examples.

2 In Chapter 5, 'Dealing with *wuli–shili–renli*', for analytical and operational purposes, we suggest clustering the wide range of diverse factors into a *wuli–shili–renli* triad.

3 For perspectives compatible with our 'purposeful emergence' view, see, e.g., Augier and Teece 2008; Barnett and Burgelman 1996; Fujimoto 1999; Lovas and Ghoshal 2000.

4 For dynamic capability, see, e.g., Teece 2009.

5 Burgelman 1991; Fujimoto 1999.

6 For a critique of this weakness in conventional evolutionary approaches to strategy, see, e.g., Lovas and Ghoshal 2000, p. 893.

7 See Augier and Teece 2008, p. 1200.

8 Stacey 2007; Zhu 2007b, 2010.

9 Brown and Duguid 2001c, p. 46.

10 See, e.g., Child 1972; Hannan and Freeman 1989; Powell and DiMaggio 1991.

11 Augier and Teece 2008.

12 Lovas and Ghoshal 2000, p. 875.

13 *Zuozhuan*; cf.: Fung 1952, p. 32.

14 The discussion of the Toyota Just-in-Time evolution is based on Fujimoto 1999.

15 Fujimoto 1999, p. 79.

16 Fujimoto 1999, p. 61.

17 Augier and Teece 2008; Collins and Porras 1994; Lovas and Ghoshal 2000.

18 Barnett and Burgelman 1996.

19 Burgelman 1994, p. 50.

20 Burgelman 1991, 1994.

21 Fujimoto 1999.

22 Burgelman 1991; Lovas and Ghoshal 2000.

23 Bower 1970; Chandler 1962; Ouchi 1980.

24 Mintzberg 1987, p. 75.

25 See, e.g., Chandler 1990a, 1990b; Lazonick 1991; Teece 2009.

26 Pitelis and Teece 2009.

27 *Financial Times* 27 July 2007, 'Carmakers in last-ditch stand against fuel economy rules' by Edward Luce and Bernard Simon.

28 Best 1990.

29 *Financial Times* 24 May 2007, 'Euro factor stalls Honda plant' by Chris Giles and Tim Harford.

30 *Financial Times* 26 August 2005, 'EU and China renew talks in bid to end dispute'.

31 *The Times* 14 October 2008, 'Paulson lays down law as bankers hear details of his $700bn bailout' by Suzy Jagger.

32 *Financial Times* 27/28 September 2008, 'A pragmatic dealmaker'.

33 See, e.g., Fligstein and Mara-Drita 1996.

34 *BBC News*, 'Q&A: the Lisbon Treaty' (http://news.bbc.co.uk/1/hi/world/europe/6901353.stm; accessed 17 January 2011).

35 Fujimoto 1999, pp. 275–276.

36 This section is based mainly on Zhu 2008.

37 Naisbitt 1994, p. 244.

38 Kelliher 1992, p. 236.

39 See Zhou 1996, pp. 13–14.

40 Kelliher 1992, p. 133.

41 *People's Daily* 13 June 1987.

42 Perotti *et al.* 1999, p. 159.

43 *Forbes* 23 September 1996, 'Small is beautiful' by Andrew Tanzer.

44 Wang 1992.

45 Zhou 1996, p. 95.

46 *China Daily* 31 March 1995.

47 Wang 1989.

48 For an introduction to Mead's theory with application to organisation and strategy, see, e.g., Stacey 2010; for a more general introduction to Mead, see Silva 2007.

49 *Financial Times* 18 May 2010, 'Letter: claims of historical inevitability are dangerous' by Paul Nabavi.

50 See *Sunday Times* 5 December 2010, 'Enron's nemesis exposes devils of Wall St' by John Arlidge.

51 Mintzberg 1987.

52 De Geus 1988.

53 Schendel 1992, p. 3.

54 Our call for a pragmatic turn is triggered at the first instance by the changed, and changing, business world and the devastating consequences of the conventional paradigm. See Chapter 1, 'Introduction' and Chapter 8, 'Questioning the conventional paradigm'.

55 We appreciate other insightful proposals, such as the European 'practice turn' promoted by Richard Whittington and colleagues (see Johnson *et al.* 2007), and the American 'Management 2.0' suggested by a team of scholars, consultants and executives led by Gary Hamel (see Hamel 2009).

56 Tsoukas and Knudsen 2002, pp. 423–424.

57 Kay 1993, p. 357.

58 Cummings 2002, p. 279.

59 Foucault 1997, p. 450.

60 Foucault 1990, p. 9.

61 Powell and DiMaggio 1991.

62 Tsoukas and Knudsen 2002, p. 428.

63 Drucker 1994, p. 104.

64 Schendel 1992, p. 3.

65 Cave 2007.

66 Ghoshal 2005, p. 77.

67 Victor 2005, p. 238.

68 Elster 1983.

69 Ghoshal 2005; Victor 2005.

70 Ghoshal and Moran 1996, p. 37.

71 Mintzberg 1987, pp. 70–71.

72 Mintzberg 1994a, p. 111.

73 *The Economist* 2 August 2008, 'Apple: Jobs's job'; *Times Magazine* 24 July 2010, 'Computer nerd. Control freak. Genius: inside the secret world of Steve Jobs' by Farhad Manjoo.

74 Ames and Hall 2003, p. 103.

75 For 'the power of pull', see Hagel *et al.* 2010.

76 Ames and Hall 2003.

77 *Analects* 3/7.

78 *Daodejing* 66.

79 Hagel and Brown 2005, p. 11.

80 Rumelt 1987.

81 Best 1990, p. 11.

82 Morita 1986, p. 166.

83 Bilton and Cummings 2010, p. 91.

84 Brown and Duguid 2001a, p. 93.

85 Ames and Hall 2003, p. 182.

86 We are here referring to Chuck Prince, then boss of Citigroup, who famously said, 'as long as the music is playing, you've to get up and dance'.

87 Chia and Holt 2006, p. 643.

88 Tsoukas and Knudsen 2002.

89 The articles can be found in the English version of *Selected Works of Mao Zedong*.

90 Chia and Holt 2009, p. 200.

91 Instead of intentless indirect action, more mindful researchers suggest 'deliberate emergence' (Mintzberg 1987, p. 71) or 'intended emergence' (Jacobs and Statler 2005).

92 Drucker 1994, p. 100.

93 Andrews 1971; Ansoff 1965; Hannan and Freeman 1989; Latour 2005; Lindblom 1959; Mintzberg and Waters 1985; Pettigrew 1977; Porter 1980, 1985; Quinn 1980; Smircich and Stubbart 1985; Weick 1979.

94 Cf.: Spender 2001, p. 30.

5 DEALING WITH *WULI–SHILI–RENLI*

1 Latour 2005, p. 56.

2 Hurst 1995, p. 5.

3 Hurst 1995.

4 Hurst 1995, p. 4.

5 Hurst 1995, p. 55.

6 Hurst 1995, p. 57.

7 Hurst 1995, p. 59.

8 Hurst 1995, p. 68.

9 Hurst 1995, p. 64.

10 Hurst 1995, p. 61.

11 Hurst 1995, pp. 66, 67.

12 Hurst 1995, p. 67.

13 Hurst 1995, p. 10.

14 Hurst attributes the perspectives to Jeffery Pfeffer. See Pfeffer 1982.

15 Hurst 1995, p. 103.

16 Hurst 1995, p. 115.

17 Hurst 1995, p. 6.

18 Hurst 1995, p. 48.

19 Recall 'obtaining legitimacy' as one of strategy's functionalities we discussed in Chapter 3, 'Strategies in a pragmatic world', as well as relevant theories such as open systems and resource dependence.

20 Hurst 1995, p. 127.

21 Recall the evolutionary perspective in Chapter 4, 'Strategy as purposeful emergence'.

22 Recall what we learn from Mead's gesture–response thesis: rules can never cover every contingency, therefore to act effectively actors must

particularise the generalised. 'Rules' work at the moment we take action, which allows imagination, novelty, creativity.

23 Hurst 1995, p. 8.

24 Hurst 1995, pp. 10, 115.

25 Recall Burgelman and Ghoshal's ideas of 'guided', 'purposeful' evolution, and Mintzberg's 'deliberate emergence'; see Chapter 3, 'Strategies in a pragmatic world'.

26 Hurst 1995, p. 7.

27 For more details on the *Eight Wires*, see Chapter 9, 'Pragmatism East and West'.

28 See, e.g., Chan 1963; Chen 1986; Cheng 1972, 1997.

29 Wu 1972.

30 Similarly, in traditional Chinese *kanji*, there was no differentiation between 'I' and 'We'. There was only *wu* (吾), both the singular and the plural. In the spirit of relationality, 吾 in fact graphically means the plural: 五口 (five mouths).

31 Takahashi 2000, p. 217.

32 Roberts 2004.

33 For these cases, see Chapter 8, 'Questioning the conventional paradigm'.

34 Hurst 1995, p. 59.

35 The case is based mainly on Brown and Duguid 2000, 2001b; Kikawada and Holtshouse 2001; Orr 1990.

36 Nisbett 2003.

37 For what-is vs how-to-act, see Chapter 9, 'Pragmatism East and West'.

38 Source: Nonaka *et al.* 2008, ch. 6.

39 Source: *Financial Times* 5 October 2006, 'An insider talks …'; *Financial Times* 15 October 2007, 'Airbus hopes its trouble will finally take flight'; *The Economist* 7 October 2006, 'The airliner that fell to earth'.

40 The A380 was further disturbed by an accident caused by the Rolls-Royce engine on a Qantas Airways aircraft in November 2010. See, e.g., *Financial Times* 5 November 2010, 'Airbus superjumbo under scrutiny after engine failure on Qantas flight' by Peter Smith and Pilita Clark.

41 For Toyota's recall, see a case study in Chapter 6, 'Timely balanced way-making'; for Sony's battery recall, see, e.g., *Time* 13 November 2006, 'Has Sony got game?' by Daren Fonda.

42 *Financial Times* 14 July 2010, 'Apple faces backlash over latest iPhone' by Joseph Menn.

43 *Financial Times* 8 September 2010, 'It's the little things that matter' by Jonathan Moules.

44 The insight of 'wikinomics' refers to the cyber environment where collaboration is getting rapidly cheaper and easier. See *The Economist* 25 September 2010, 'Schumpeter: the wiki way'.

45 *Financial Times* 24 August 2010, 'HP locks horns with Dell over data group' by Helen Thomas and Joseph Menn; *Financial Times* 24 August 2010, 'Big tech hunts for profit in data mountains' by Joseph Menn; *Financial Times* 3 September 2010, 'HP set to acquire 3Par as Dell pulls out' by Joseph Menn; *Times* 3 September 2010, 'HP emerges triumphant in battle over "cloud computing"' by Christine Seib.

46 *Financial Times* 29 December 2009, 'Why Tencent could teach Twitter a few tricks' by Kathrin Hille; *Financial Times* 18 March 2010, 'Tencent warns on impact of China texts crackdown' by Kathrin Hille.

47 For the contribution of the consultant houses, see, e.g., Kiechel 2010.

48 *Wall Street Journal* 29 June 2010, 'European firms increase focus on Asia' by Javier Espinoza.

49 *Financial Times* 16 March 2010, 'Huawei plays long game to win trust and business in US' by Andrew Parker; *Financial Times* 30 July 2010, 'US government divided on how to tackle Huawei' by Stephanie Kirchgaessner and Helen Thomas; *Financial Times* 5 August 2010, 'Why America sees red in corporate China' by David Pilling; *Financial Times* 9 March 2011, 'Huawei targets corporate contracts in direct challenge to western competitors' by Andrew Parker; Zhang 2008.

50 Upon this point, John Authers writes: 'The most important words in economics are also the words that doom it to failure; *ceteris paribus*, or "all other things equal". Assume all else is equal and you can build a decent model. Physicists and chemists do this with controlled experiments. Economists cannot ... Economists can still build models but they are inevitably flawed' (see *Financial Times* 13 March 2011, 'We need new models in an uncertain world' by John Authers).

51 Collis and Montgomery 1995.

52 Ghoshal 2005.

53 Cartwright 1999, p. 31.

54 For more on Marconi, see Chapter 6, 'Timely balanced way-making'.

55 Khanna and Palepu 1997; also see Guillén 1994.

56 Best 1990, ch. 7.

57 *Financial Times* 20 August 2010, 'Needed: a new economic paradigm' by Joseph Stiglitz.

58 Ghoshal 2005, p. 81.

59 *The Economist* 22 September 2007, 'The great Northern run'.

60 *The Times* 18 September 2007, 'Panic infects other mortgage lenders as fears grow about exposure to crisis' by Christine Seib, James Rossiter, Grainne Gilmore and Douglas Sheard.

61 *The Economist* 22 September 2007, 'Briefing – Securitisation: when it goes wrong ...'.

62 *Financial Times* 18 February 2008, 'Fury over Rock nationalisation' by Jane Croft and Chris Giles; *Financial Times* 5 June 2008, 'Tough questions on Rock's viability'; *The Times* 7 February 2008, 'Northern Rock faces 2,400 job cuts under management's plans' by Christine Seib and Siobhan Kennedy.

63 *Financial Times* 15/16 September 2007, 'Impregnable self-belief takes a battering' by Chris Hughes and Chris Tighe; *The Times* 15 September 2007, 'Geordies are aghast as the city's biggest player runs into trouble' by Russell Jenkins.

64 *Financial Times* 16 September 2007, 'The Lex column: Rock bottom'.

65 *Financial Times* 20 September 2007, 'Northern Rock: who dares comes unstuck' by Jonathan Guthrie.

66 *Financial Times* 16 September 2007, 'It is absurd to blame foreigners for Northern Rock's woes' by John Gapper.

67 *Financial Times* 16 September 2007, 'Drama ends after weeks of upheaval' by Peter Thal Larsen and Chris Giles.

68 *The Times* 15 September 2007, 'Northern Rock white knights turn tail at market volatility' by Patrick Hosking and Christine Seib.

69 *The Times* 17 October 2007, 'Northern Rock board offered to fall on sword if investors said "go"' by Christine Seib and Patrick Hosking.

70 *Financial Times* 17 October 2007, 'Blame heaped on Northern Rock chiefs' by Jean Eaglesham and Jane Croft.

71 *Financial Times* 18 September 2007, 'Takeover is now the only way to prop up the Rock' by Andrew Hill.

72 *The Times* 15 September 2007, 'Hopefully institution will become quarry' by Patrick Hosking.

73 *The Economist* 22 September 2007, 'Briefing – Securitisation'.

74 *Financial Times* 21 September 2007, 'The modern-day parable of the run on Northern Rock' by Philip Stephen.

75 *Financial Times* 21 September 2007, 'The modern-day parable'.

76 *The Times* 25 September 2007, 'MPs call on Northern Rock to scrap £60m dividend payout' by Christine Seib and Patrick Hosking.

77 *The Times* 17 June 2010, 'BP bows to Obama and cancels its dividends' by Catherine Philp and Giles Whittell.

78 *Financial Times* 28 May 2010, 'Global 500'; *Asian Banker* 20 March 2009, 'China Merchants Bank's Ma Weihua named Retail Banker of the Year'; *The Economist* 7 June 2008, 'Asian banking: taking wing'.

79 There are recent reports that, after the banking crisis in 'the West', there has suddenly emerged in China a 'virtually unregulated market for securitisation and off-balance sheet bank lending', with Merchants Bank as one of the eager players. See *Financial Times* 11 August 2010, 'Beijing urges banks to strike right balance' by Jamil Anderlini.

80 This CMB case is based mainly on Zhang 2009.

81 This Polaroid story is based on Tripsas and Gavetti 2000.

82 See Tripsas and Gavetti 2000, p. 23.

83 See Tripsas and Gavetti 2000, pp. 24–25.

84 See Tripsas and Gavetti 2000, pp. 23–25.

85 See Tripsas and Gavetti 2000, p. 27.

86 Best 2001, p. 44.

87 This Swatch story is based mainly on Glasmeier 1991; *Financial Times* 11 September 2010, 'Charm, charisma and a sense of humour' by Haig Simonian; *Financial Times* 11 September 2010, 'Tribute to technology that has redefined an industry' by Timothy Barber.

88 *Financial Times* 29 June 2010, 'Swiss watch saviour Hayek dies aged 82' by Haig Simonian.

89 Drucker 1985, p. 100.

90 Schumpeter 1942.

91 For 'groupthink', 'competence trap' and 'core rigidities', see, e.g., Janis 1972; Leonard-Barton 1992; Levitt and March 1988.

92 For an introductionary review, see Porac and Thomas 2002.

93 See, e.g., Nonaka and Takeuchi 1995; Tushman and Anderson 2004.

94 Nonaka *et al.* 2008; Taylor 1990, p. 102.

95 Teece 2007a, 2007b.

96 Glasmeier 1991, p. 51.

97 See Tripsas and Gavetti 2000, p. 28.

98 Tushman and Anderson 2004, p. xi.

99 Schumpeter 1942, p. 84.

100 Drucker 1985, p. 98.

101 Kim and Mauborgne 1999.

102 Stopford 2001, p. 168.

103 Drucker 1985, p. 96.

104 Levitt 1963, pp. 138, 144.

105 See Bruch and Ghoshal 2004; Teece 2007a, 2007b.

106 Morita 1986, p. 55.

107 Cf.: *Wall Street Journal* 29 June 2010, 'European firms increase focus'. With a similar view, John Seely Brown, ex-Xerox research chief, warned the Americans in early 2011 that they must adjust to changed circumstances: 'We really have to get back to building things. We can't just design things' (see *Financial Times* 29/30 January 2011, 'Light dims for Silicon Valley as China shines' by Richard Waters).

108 *Wikipedia*: 'Wii' (http://en.wikipedia.org/wiki/Wii).

109 *Financial Times* 14 June 2010, 'Wii rivals take aim with new products' by Chris Nuttall.

110 *Financial Times* 22 February 2007, 'Wiis are the champions as Xbox and PS3 play catch-up' by Leo Lewis.

111 *Financial Times* 17 September 2007, 'Nintendo Wii success helps component makers score' by Mariko Sanchanta.

112 *Financial Times* 16 September 2008, 'Nintendo makes more profit per employee than Goldman' by Robin Harding.

113 *Fortune* 11 June 2007, 'How Wii won' by Jeffrey M. O'Brien.

114 *The Times* 18 July 2008, 'Toying with the future would be much more than a game' by Rob Fahey.

115 *Financial Times* 16 September 2008, 'Winning Wii seeks to raise its game' by Robin Harding and Michiyo Nakamoto.

116 *Financial Times* 2/3 October 2010, 'The list: five most influential video games' by Tony Mott.

117 *The Economist* 22 June 2002, 'Video games: console wars'.

118 *Sunday Times* 27 April 2008, 'Working out the future with Mr Wii' by John Arlidge.

119 *Fortune* 11 June 2007, 'How Wii won'.

120 *Fortune* 11 June 2007, 'How Wii won'.

121 *The Times* 18 July 2008, 'From joystick to helmet: the next leap forward is all in the mind' by Chris Ayres.

122 *Fortune* 11 June 2007, 'How Wii won'.

123 *Sunday Times* 27 April 2008, 'Working out the future'.

124 *Sunday Times* 27 April 2008, 'Working out the future'.

125 *Businessweek* 16 November 2006, 'The big ideas behind Nintendo's Wii' by Kenji Hall.

126 *Businessweek* 16 November 2006, 'The big ideas'.

127 *Sunday Times* 27 April 2008, 'Working out the future'.

128 *Fortune* 11 June 2007, 'How Wii won'.

129 *Businessweek* 16 November 2006, 'The big ideas'.

130 *Fortune* 11 June 2007, 'How Wii won'.

131 *Forbes* 28 April 2006, 'Iwata's Nintendo lampooned for Wii'.

132 *Forbes* 19 May 2008, 'Wii fit craze!' by Mary Jane Inwin; *The Times* 18 July 2008, 'Toying with the future'.

133 *Financial Times* 27 January 2011, 'The rise, fall and rise again of the gaming company that defined its sector' by Daniel Sloan.

134 *Financial Times* 14 June 2010, 'Wii rivals take aim'; *Financial Times* 27 September 2010, 'Lex column: super-duper Mario'.

135 *Fortune* 11 June 2007, 'How Wii won'.

136 *The Times* 18 July 2008, 'From joystick to helmet'.

137 *Fortune* 11 June 2007, 'How Wii won'.

138 *The Times* 18 July 2008, 'From joystick to helmet'.

139 *Financial Times* 16 September 2008, 'Winning Wii'.

140 Nonaka *et al.* 2008.

141 Kim and Mauborgne 1999, p. 338.

142 Useful contributions from writers in 'the West' can be found from, e.g., Berger and Luckmann 1966; Burt 1992; Coleman 1990; Granovetter 1985; Kramer and Tyler 1996; Pondy and Mitroff 1979; Putnam 1995; Selznick 1957.

143 Uzzi and Dunlap 2005, pp. 53–54.

144 *Financial Times* 17 December 2010, 'Along for the ride?' by Brooke Masters, Megan Murphy and Kara Scannell.

145 Collins and Porras 1994.

146 Best 1990, p. 80.

147 See, e.g., *The Times* 21 November 2009, 'Cadbury family member joins Kraft battle' by Catherine Boyle.

148 See, e.g., *The Economist* 14 August 2010, 'Schumpeter: the curse of HP'.

149 See, e.g., *The Economist* 29 May 2010, 'Suicides at Foxconn: light and death'.

150 Kaku 1997.

151 See, e.g., *Sunday Times* 18 April 2010, 'Is this God's dirty work?' by Iain Dey and Dominic Rushe.

152 *Financial Times Weekend Magazine* 12/13 March 2011, 'In the dock, but not in jail' by Gillian Tett.

153 Bellah *et al.* 1985.

154 For agriculture subsidies and protectionist import tariffs in developed nations, see, e.g., *The Economist* 13 July 2002, 'Europe's farms: will these modest proposals provoke mayhem down on the farm?'; *The Times* 6 December 2010, 'Japan develops new appetite for an economic battle' by Leo Lewis.

155 *The Times* 20 September 2010, 'Business big shot: Indra Nooyi'.

156 Evans and Wurster 1997, p. 82.

157 Achrol and Kotler 1999, p. 161. For latest developments confirming this die-hard practice in Detroit of squeezing suppliers, see, e.g., *Financial Times* 29 November 2010, 'US carmakers revive price cut demand with suppliers' by Bernard Simon.

158 Takeuchi *et al.* 2008.

159 *Financial Times* 24 March 2010, 'Recovery depends on Main Street' by Robert Reich.

160 Ghoshal *et al.* 1999, pp. 16–17.

161 Drucker 1993.

162 Ghoshal *et al.* 1999, p. 14.

163 Hamel and Prahalad 1989.

164 De Wit and Meyer 2004, p. 758.

165 Ghoshal *et al.* 1999.

166 Nonaka *et al.* 2008, p. 91.

167 For the Merck case, see Chapter 1, 'Introduction'.

168 Paul Cook, founder and CEO of Raychem Corporation, told the *Harvard Business Review* interviewer: 'Innovation is an emotional experience. You can train people technically, but you can't teach them curiosity' (cf.: Taylor 1990, p. 99)

169 See Kiechel 2010, p. 120. Kenneth Andrews went on to express his misgiving that his holistic approach had got lost: 'Economists have been harassing my idea of the concept of competitive strategy ever since, in

the sense that the human, and the moral, and the ethical dimensions are largely ignored.'

170 See Kiechel 2010, ch. 15.

171 *Wall Street Journal* 19–21 November 2010, 'Guy Hands reflects on EMI troubles' by Jennifer Bollen.

172 *Financial Times* 24/25 January 2009, 'GE's quarterly profits fall 43%' by Justin Baer and Francesco Guerrera; *Financial Times* 13 March 2009, 'Welch slams the obsession with shareholder value as a "dumb idea"' by Francesco Guerrera; *Financial Times* 17 March 2009, 'Neutron Jack has a change of heart' by Makoto Honjo; *Financial Times* 13 April 2010, 'Replacing the "dumbest idea in the world"' by Michael Skapinker.

173 Kiechel 2010, p. 323.

174 This section is based mainly on *Global Times* 21 September 2009, 'Liu Chuanzhi on Legend's new ownership' (available at: http://business. globaltimes.cn/entrepreneur/2009-09/469714.html); Gold *et al.* 2001; Ling 2005, 2006; Liu 2007.

175 See *Financial Times* 5 July 2010, 'The man who took his chance: Monday interview with Liu Chuangzhi' by Kathrin Hille.

176 See Liu 2007, p. 573.

177 See Gold *et al.* 2001.

178 *Global Times* 21 September 2009, 'Liu Chuanzhi on Legend's new ownership'.

179 Ling 2005, p. 55.

180 Ling 2005, pp. 55–56.

181 Ling 2005, p. 64.

182 Ling 2005, p. 95.

183 Ling 2005, p. 95.

184 Ling 2005, p. 98.

185 Ling 2005, pp. 98–99.

186 Ling 2005, p. 99.

187 Latour 2005.

188 Best 2001.

189 See *Financial Times* 16 August 2010, 'Letter: A philosopher should read the dismal scientists' by Chin-Tai Kim and Yeomin Yoon.

190 Hurst 1995.

191 *Financial Times* 27 September 2010, 'Rational choice model needs help not a coup de grâce' by Tony Jackson.

192 Law 2004, p. 156.

193 Cf.: Scharmer 1996.

194 Putnam 1995, p. 14.

6   TIMELY BALANCED WAY-MAKING

1 *Analects* 9/17.

2 See Keene 1967, p. xviii.

3 *Huainanzi* 9/1/2.

4 *Analects* 4/10.

5 On the loss in translation, Ames and Hall (2001) comment:

> A particularly unfortunate example of inappropriate translation is the common rendering of *Zhongyong* as 'The Doctrine of the Mean.' This rendering was made popular by James Legge in his initial translation of the text. But even Legge himself abandoned this title when he went on to retranslate 'Zhongyong' as a chapter in the *Record of Rites* (*Liji*). In this 1885 publication, he revised the title as 'The State of Equilibrium and Harmony,' a far better indication of its content. (pp. 150–151)

6 Ames and Hall 2001, p. 43.

7 Source: http://en.wikipedia.org/wiki/Golden_mean_%28philosophy%29 (accessed 27 November 2010).

8 Peters and Waterman 1982, p. 318.

9 See, e.g., Bilton and Cummings 2010, pp. 205, 217.

10 Collins and Porras 1994, pp. 43–45.

11 Stacey 2010, p. 100.

12 For an introduction to the Aristotelian formal logic and Hegelian dialectic logic, see, e.g., Ford and Ford 1994.

13 For a critique of 'change as rearrangement of that which is unchanging', see Ames and Hall 2001, p. 11.

14 For questioning the 'just enough this, just enough that' 'dialectic thinking', see Zhu 2007b.

15 Grove 1996, p. 161.

16 *Financial Times* 19 October 2010, 'GE plans return to US-made products' by Jeremy Lemer.

17 *Financial Times* 26 November 2010, 'China rolls out the red carpet for private equity' by Jamil Anderlini.

18 *Financial Times* 19 October 2010, 'GE plans return'; *Financial Times* 7 October 2011, 'Higher labour costs in China begin to push

manufacturing jobs back to US, study finds' and 'Business see value in "made in America" label' by Peter Marsh.

19 This Lego story is based on a case study, 'Rethinking corporate strategy: reduced product range and deliveries', by Carlos Cordon, Ralf Seifert and Edwin Wellian, published in *Financial Times* 25 November 2010.

20 See Fung 1948, p. 173.

21 Fung 1948, p. 173.

22 Fung 1948, p. 391.

23 For elaboration convenience, we attribute timely balance to Confucianism, while we are aware, and acknowledge, that timeliness and timely conduct is an ideal and virtue not just for the Confucians, but for many East Asian traditions. The classics read:

易经 *Yijing* 1123?–100 BC	Looking at the signs of the heaven, one thereby ascertains *timely* changes. 观乎天文, 以察时变.
	Knowing when to move and stop, present and disappear, without losing just-right, only the sage can do this, which is the meaning of *timely* balance. 知进退存亡, 而不失其正者, 其唯圣人乎? 皆时中之义也.
论语 *Analects* 551–479 BC	There are some with whom one can take a firm stand, but with whom one cannot make *emergency* judgements. 可与立, 不可与谋.
	The superior man, in the world, does not set his mind either for anything, or against anything; what is right he will follow. 君子之于天下也, 无适也, 无莫也, 义之与比.
老子 *Laozi* 400? BC	The excellence of any movement is its *timeliness*. 动善时.
孟子 *Mencius* 372?–289? BC	Po I among the Sages was the pure one; Yi Yin was the responsible one; Hui of Liu-hsia was the accommodating one; and Confucius was the *timely* one. 圣之时者也.

庄子 *Zhuangzi* 369?–286? BC	The institutions of the former kings were intended to meet the needs of the *time*. 故先王典礼, 所以适时用也.
国语 *Guoyu* 300? BC	The sage observes the proper time for his actions, which is called keeping the right *timing*. 夫圣人随时而行, 是为守时.
礼记 *Liji* 200? BC	Acting upon *li*, timeliness should be the great consideration. 礼, 时为大也. The *times* of the Five Emperors were different, and therefore they did not each adopt the music of his predecessor. 五帝殊时, 不相沿用.
中庸 *Zhongyong* 200? BC	Exemplary persons exemplify balance and harmony, because they master *timely balance*. 君子之中庸也, 君子而时中. Therefore whatever always pursues is fitting with *time*. 故时措之宜也.

24 *Mencius* 5/2/1.
25 *Zhongyong* 2/1 and 2.
26 *Zhongyong* 1.
27 *Zhongyong* 3.
28 *Zhongyong* 25.
29 Interestingly, some 'middle-way' proponents sometimes suggest 'shift between perspectives'; see, e.g., Bilton and Cummings 2010, p. 176. The puzzle is: at the moment you shift to a particular perspective, and at another moment to another, are you still at 'the middle way'?
30 Fung 1948, pp. 371–372.
31 *Commentary on Zhuangzi* 6/26.
32 Hwa Yol Jung (1987) explains 'logic of correlation' thus: 'Ultimately, in the logic of correlation – unlike the dialectics of Hegel and Marx – the positive (*yang*) and the negative (*yin*) are not resolved categorically or otherwise in terms of a higher synthesis, but preserve the unending flow of their opposition as complementary' (pp. 219–220).

33 Cheng 1997.

34 Fu 1997.

35 Nonaka and Takeuchi 1995, p. 236.

36 For a critique of Western 'default vocabulary', see Ames and Hall 2001, pp. 3–8.

37 Ames and Hall 2001, p. 84.

38 In their 2001 translation of the Confucian classic *Zhongyong*, Ames and Hall emphasise the performative priority and aesthetic feeling over cognition in the Confucian tradition. The fifteenth-century Confucian scholar Wang Yangming posited that to see is to love already; that is, cognition or perception already assumes a degree of emotion and interest (see Ames and Hall 2001, p. 37).

39 For more detailed elaborations, see, e.g., Ghoshal 2005; Ghoshal and Moran 1996; Ghoshal *et al.* 1999.

40 For 'self-fulfilling prophesy', see, e.g., Ghoshal and Moran 1996.

41 Liu 2007, p. 574.

42 *Financial Times* 6 February 2009, 'Lenovo chief replaced in reshuffle' by Kathrin Hille.

43 *The Economist* 15 August 2009, 'Lenovo bets on China: where the heart is'.

44 *Financial Times* 6 February 2009, 'Left behind in the advance of the nimble' by Kathrin Hille.

45 *Financial Times* 6 February 2009, 'Left behind'.

46 *Financial Times*, 26 August 2010, 'China's small towns are big money for PCs' by Kathrin Hille.

47 *Financial Times*, 5 February 2010, 'Lenovo profiting from recovery' by Kathrin Hille.

48 *Financial Times* 6 February 2009, 'Lenovo chief replaced'.

49 *Financial Times* 5 July 2010, 'The man who took his chance' by Kathrin Hille.

50 *Financial Times* 5 July 2010, 'The man who took his chance'.

51 *Financial Times* 29 August 2010, 'Lenovo to take on rivals with console' by Kathrin Hille.

52 *Financial Times* 6–7 November 2010, 'For Obama, "change" may now be note to self' by Anna Fifield.

53 Kotter and Schlesinger 1979, p. 132.

54 Sztompka (1991) comments on the ideology thus: 'Unfortunately from the valid recognition of change, it was only a small step to the invalid

absolutisation of change. The urge for change became the glorification of change. Change was seen as value in itself ... In all cultural forms, change, far from being the tool of modernity for achieving the goal of progress, has become an end in itself' (p. 19).

55 Palmer and Hardy 2000, pp. 192–103.

56 *Financial Times* 28 October 2010, 'The shock of the new name' by Rhymer Rigby.

57 McKinley and Scherer 2000.

58 Eskew 2007, p. 56.

59 Fujimoto 1999, p. 49.

60 *The Economist* 21 February 2009, 'Briefing Chinese business: time to change the act'; *The Economist* 27 November 2010, 'Face value: Softbank's Masayoshi Son – Son also rises'.

61 Mintzberg 1987, p. 78.

62 Teece 2007a, p. 1344; Teece *et al.* 1997, p. 521.

63 Recall Chapter 2, 'Spirits of pragmatism' on the process spirit of Confucian pragmatism.

64 For Thomas Edison's innovation, see Chapter 7, 'Orchestrating WSR, orchestrating the firm'.

65 Again, timely change and continuity is an ideal not just in Confucianism, but many East Asian traditions. This is evident in the classics:

易经 *Yijing* 1123?–100 BC	*Zhen* is the idea of *dong* [movement]. Things cannot be in movement forever. They are stopped, and therefore this is followed by *gen*. *Gen* denotes stopping. But things cannot be forever stopped, and so this is followed by *jian* [advance]. 震者, 动也. 物不可以终动, 止之. 故受之以艮. 艮者, 止也. 物不可以终止, 故受之以渐.
论语 *Analects* 551–479 BC	The Master said, 'The wise enjoy water; those authoritative in their conduct enjoy mountains. The wise are active; the authoritative are still. The wise find enjoyment; the authoritative are long-enduring.' 知者乐水, 仁者乐山. 知者动, 仁者静. 知者乐, 仁者寿.

老子 *Laozi* 400? BC	Attain complete vacuity, maintain steadfast quietude. 致虚极, 守静笃. Constant action overcomes cold; being *jing* [still] overcomes heat. Purity and stillness give rightfulness to all under heaven. 静胜躁, 寒胜热. 清静为天下正. With no desire, at rest and still, all things go right as of their will. 不欲以静, 天下将自正.
庄子 *Zhuangzi* 369?–286? BC	Therefore there cannot but be variety in the way in which conforms to things. 故顺物之迹, 不得不殊.
中庸 *Zhongyong* 200? BC	Confucius said: perfect is the virtue of balance and just-right. 子曰, 中庸其至矣乎. Pursuing balance and harmony, a happy order will prevail throughout heaven and earth, and all things will be nourished and flourish. 致中和, 天地位焉, 万物育焉.

66 Williamson 1985, 1986.

67 Penrose 1959.

68 Barnard 1938; Ghoshal and Moran 1996; Nahapiet and Ghoshal 1998.

69 Leana and Barry 2000, p. 758.

70 Takeuchi *et al.* 2008, p. 102.

71 Ames and Rosemont 1998, p. 25.

72 Hurst 1995, p. 169.

73 Mintzberg appears to agree, as he writes: 'To manage strategy, then, at least in the first instance, is not so much to promote change as to know *when* to do so' (1987, p. 73).

74 The action orientation, or 'bias toward action', is apparent throughout the classics. For example:

论语 *Analects* 551–479 BC	It is Man who makes *Tao* great, not *Tao* that makes Man great. 是人宏道, 非道宏人.
庄子 *Zhuangzi* 369?–286? BC	*Tao* is made in the walking of it. 道行之而成.
左传 *Zuozhuan* 300? BC	The *Tao* of Heaven is distant, while that of Man is near. 天道远, 人道近. This is something pertaining to the *yin* and the *yang*, which are not the producers of good and bad fortunes. It is from men themselves, that good and bad fortunes are produced. 是阴阳之事, 非吉凶所出也, 吉凶由人.
中庸 *Zhongyong* 200? BC	*Tao* is not far from Man. When men try to pursue a course, which is abstracted away from men, this course cannot be considered *Tao*. 道不远人, 人之为道而远人, 不可以为道.

75 *Wuwei wuzheng* (无为, 无争) is a persistent theme in the classics, Confucian as well as Taoist:

论语*Analects* 551–479 BC	May not Shun be instanced as having governed effectively without exertion? 无为而治者其舜也舆?
老子*Laozi* 400? BC	With no desire, at rest and still, all things go right as of their will. 不欲以静, 天下将自正. Governing a big state is like cooking a little fresh fish. 治大国如烹小鲜. *Tao* invariably takes no action, and yet there is nothing left undone. 无为而无不为.
中庸*Zhongyong* 200? BC	Without being seen, makes a display; without any movement, transforms; without any effort, makes complete. 不见而章, 不动而变, 无为而成.

76 *Daodejing* 66.

77 *Analects* 3/7.

78 *Analects* 3/7.

79 This is a line articulated by the founder of Facebook, Mark Zuckerberg. See *The Times* 18 November 2010, 'In a brand new business world, the normal rules simply don't apply' by Alexandra Frean.

80 McKinley and Scherer 2000, p. 747.

81 Kotter and Schlesinger 2008 [1979], p. 133.

82 Magretta 1998, p. 111.

83 Magretta 1998, p. 104.

84 Magretta 1998, pp. 104–105.

85 Magretta 1998, pp. 106–107.

86 Magretta 1998, p. 105.

87 Magretta 1998, p. 108.

88 Magretta 1998, p. 108.

89 Magretta 1998, p. 110.

90 Magretta 1998, p. 110.

91 Hagel 2002, pp. 72–73.

92 Hagel and Brown 2005.

93 Magretta 1998, p. 110.

94 See Li & Fung's company website: www.lifung.com.

95 Hagel and Brown 2005, p. 152.

96 Magretta 1998, p. 114.

97 Magretta 1998, p. 113.

98 Magretta 1998, p. 113.

99 Magretta 1998, p. 113.

100 Magretta 1998, p. 113.

101 *Time* 13 November 2006, '60 years of Asian heroes'.

102 See Nonaka *et al.* 2008.

103 *The Economist* 6 October 2001, 'Communications breakdown: Marconi's share price'.

104 *Financial Times* 6 September 2010, 'Up in the heir' by Joe Leahy; *ReviewAsia* April 2008, 'The high-flying tycoon'; *The Economist* 14 August 2010, 'Tata seeks a chairman: succeeding a success'; *The Times* 10 August 2010, 'Tata Group: contenders line up to sit in the chair' by Rhys Blakely.

105 See Khanna and Palepu 1997.

106 *BBC News* 30 May 2006, 'Daewoo boss gets 10 years in jail'; *Businessweek* 19 February 2001, 'Kim's fall from grace' by Moon

Ihlwan; *Businessweek* 11 February 2003, 'The rise, fall, and spin of Citizen Kim' by Mark Clifford; *Fortune (Asia)* 3 February 2003, 'Wanted' by Louis Kraar.

107 *Financial Times* 22/23 January 2011, 'GE cites improving economy as profits rise' by Jeremy Lemer and Ed Crooks; *Financial Times* 15 February, 'Deal gives GE a crown jewel of the oil industry' by Ed Crooks; *The Economist* 26 October 2002, 'Solving GE's big problem'.

108 See, e.g., Fei 1992 [1947], p. 65.

109 See Fung 1948, p. 55.

110 See Fung 1948, p. 72.

111 For family (家) as the governing metaphor in Confucianism from which the radial locus of human growth expands outward to other human relationships and institutions, see Ames and Hall 2001, pp. 38–40.

112 *Analects* 6/28.

113 See, e.g., Cyert and March 1963; Hagel and Brown 2005; Nohria and Ghoshal 1997.

114 Bruch and Ghoshal 2004.

115 Bruch and Ghoshal 2004.

116 Ames and Hall 2001, pp. 39–40.

117 *Daxue*; cf.: Ames and Hall 2001, p. 46.

118 Sources: *China Daily* 17 June 2011, 'Ma is splitting taobao into three companies' by Chen Limin; Liu and Avery 2009; *Wall Street Journal* 12–14 November 2010, 'Alibaba net rises 55%, but firm stays wary' by Owen Fletcher.

119 See Liu and Avery 2009.

120 Burgelman 1991, 1994.

121 Burgelman 1991, pp. 246–247; 1994, pp. 37–38.

122 Best 2001, p. 75.

123 Burgelman 1991, p. 252. This reminds us of what Tom Curley did when *USAToday* reinvented itself into a thriving multi-media business; see Chapter 3, 'Strategies in a pragmatic world'.

124 Burgelman 1991, p. 244.

125 See Best 2001.

126 The outstanding performances of the Li & Fung global supply chain and the Third Italy specialised clusters can also be seen as evidence of the power of balance between focused competence and expanded resources. See Best 1990; Hagel and Brown 2005.

127 Nonaka *et al.* 2008, pp. 2–3.

128 Nonaka and Konno 1998; Nonaka *et al.* 2008, pp. 33–42.

129 Nonaka *et al.* 2008, p. 40.

130 Nonaka *et al.* 2008, p. 37.

131 See Nonaka *et al.* 2008, p. 113.

132 *Financial Times* 25 November 2010, 'Toyota is still on alert one year after crisis hit' by John Reed; *The Times* 22 October 2010, 'New reverse for Toyota as Lexus models are called back to UK garages' by Robert Lea.

133 *The Times* 4 February 2010, 'Toyota recalls 180,000 British vehicles as safety fears accelerate' by Phillip Pank, Steve Bird, Laura Pitel, Russell Jenkins.

134 *Financial Times* 12 May 2010, 'Toyota reports profit in spite of global recall' by Jonathan Soble; *Times* 30 September 2010, '"We had a big crisis, a terrible time ... we were very worried" says Toyota of 2010' by Robert Lea.

135 *Financial Times* 2 July 2010, 'Engine block: Toyota in further recall'; *The Times* 16 March 2010, 'Prius production is cut after Toyota sales fall by up to 60%' by Robert Lea; *The Times* 4 February 2010, 'UK deliveries halted as car crisis deepens' by Robert Lea and Alexandra Frean.

136 *Financial Times* 6–7 February 2010, 'Toyota chief apologises for recall of 8m vehicles'; *Wall Street Journal* 2 March 2010, 'Toyoda concedes profit focus led to flaws' by Norihiko Shirouzu.

137 *Wall Street Journal* 25–27 June 2010, 'Toyoda apologises to holders' by Yoshio Takahashi.

138 *Financial Times* 25 November 2010, 'Carmaker changes aim to recapture shine' by John Reed, Bernard Simon and Jonathan Soble.

139 *The Times* 30 September 2010, '"We had a big crisis"'.

140 *Financial Times* 6–7 February 2010, 'Toyota's brilliance fades as recall leads to wider concerns' by John Reed and Bernard Simon.

141 *Financial Times* 28 April 2010, 'How to avoid making a drama out of a crisis' by Stefan Stern.

142 *Wall Street Journal* 16 November 2010, 'Toyota, Honda lose US market edge' by Mike Ramsey and Chester Dawson.

143 *Sunday Times* 7 February 2010, 'The fall of mighty Toyota' by Ray Hutton.

144 *Sunday Times* 7 February 2010, 'The fall of mighty Toyota'.

145 *Financial Times* 6–7 February 2010, 'Toyota's stumbling scion' by Jonathan Soble and John Reed.

146 *The Economist* 27 February 2010, 'The machine that ran too hot'.

147 *Financial Times* 25 November 2010, 'Carmaker changes aim'.

148 *Financial Times* 29 April 2010, 'When sorry is the hardest word' by Jonathan Soble; *Financial Times* 1 July 2010, 'It pays to expect the unexpected' by Andrew Edgecliffe-Johnson.

149 See *The Economist* 27 February 2010, 'The machine that ran too hot'.

150 *Wall Street Journal* 2 March 2010, 'Toyoda concedes'.

151 *Sunday Times* 28 March 2010, 'Arrogant? Not us, says Toyota boss'; *Wall Street Journal* 2 March 2010, 'Toyoda concedes'.

152 *Wall Street Journal* 15 April 2010, 'Inside Toyota, senior executives trade blame over the debacle' by Norihiko Shirouzu.

153 *Wall Street Journal* 15 April 2010, 'Inside Toyota'.

154 *The Economist* 12 December 2009, 'Briefing Toyota: losing its shine'.

155 See *The Economist* 27 February 2010, 'The machine that ran too hot'.

156 *Wall Street Journal* 11 December 2010, 'Paranoid tendency: as rivals gain, Toyota CEO spurs efficiency drive' by Nirihiko Shirouzu.

157 *Financial Times* 12 May 2010, 'Toyota reports profit'; *The Times* 12 May 2010, 'Toyota rides out recall storm to return to profit' by Leo Lewis and Robert Lea.

158 *The Times* 10 February 2010, 'Toyota on the hard shoulder'.

159 *Wall Street Journal* 11 December 2006, 'Paranoid tendency'.

160 *The Economist* 12 December 2009, 'Briefing Toyota'.

161 *The Economist* 27 February 2010, 'The machine that ran too hot'.

162 Stewart and Raman 2007, pp. 76–77.

163 See Stewart and Raman 2007.

164 *Sunday Times* 7 February 2010, 'The fall of mighty Toyota'.

165 *Sunday Times* 7 February 2010, 'The fall of mighty Toyota'.

166 *Financial Times* 6–7 February 2010, 'Toyota's brilliance fades'.

167 *Financial Times* 25 June 2010, 'Toyota rejig sees foreign promotions' by Jonathan Soble.

168 *Financial Times* 4 February 2010, 'Damage control efforts misfire' by John Reed; *Financial Times* 29 April 2010, 'When sorry is the hardest word'.

169 *Financial Times* 25 November 2010, 'Carmaker changes aim'.

170 *Financial Times* 12 May 2010, 'Toyota reports profit'.

171 *Financial Times* 25 June 2010, 'Toyota rejig'; *Financial Times* 22 October 2010, 'Toyota dealt further blow with fresh recall in US' by Jonathan Soble; *Financial Times* 25 November 2010, 'Carmaker changes aim'; *Financial Times* 10 March 2011, 'Toyota sets cautious target in shake-up' by Jonathan Soble; *Wall Street Journal* 25–27 June 2010, 'Toyoda apologises'.

7 ORCHESTRATING WSR, ORCHESTRATING THE FIRM

1 To David Teece, sensing–seizing–reconfiguring is part of a wider framework of a dynamic capability theory of the firm and strategy; see Augier and Teece 2008; Pitelis and Teece 2009; Teece 2007a, 2007b, 2009.

2 For 'abilities that constitute *phronesis*' see Nonaka and Toyama 2007; Nonaka *et al.* 2008.

3 *Financial Times* 13 August 2010, 'Google's Android mobiles overtake global iPhone sales' by Tim Bradshaw; *Newsweek* 11 October 2010, 'Attack of the Droids: Google, Apple, and the battle for the future of computing' by Daniel Lyons.

4 See, e.g., *The Times* 7 October 2009, 'Tesco claims market-leading growth as it takes aim at the country's banks' by Marcus Leroux; *The Times* 20 November 2009, 'Tesco strides on to battlefield of broadband and home phones' by Ian King.

5 *Newsweek* 18 October 2010, 'Building a better battery' by Jerry Guo; *Sunday Times* 6 March 2011, 'The car fuelled by Warren Buffett' by John Arlidge.

6 For 'bounded rationality', see Cyert and March 1963; March and Simon 1958.

7 Nonaka 1991; Nonaka and Takeuchi 1995.

8 Bruch and Ghoshal 2004.

9 *Financial Times* 11 February 2005, 'A struggle over strategy: HP counts the cost of "playing the other guy's game"' by Richard Waters and Simon London; *Observer* 13 February 2005, 'Headstrong, pushy … and so farewell to Fiorina' by Edward Helmore.

10 Andrews 1971.

11 See Taylor 1990, p. 106.

12 Teece 2007a, p. 1330.

13 Ghoshal and Moran 1996.

14 Teece 2007a, p. 1333.

15 Fransman 1994.

16 Teece 2007a.

17 See, e.g., Garud and Ahlstrom 1997.

18 *Financial Times* 4 March 2011, 'The iPad 2 is worth the wait' by Chris Nuttall; *The Times* 14 December 2010, 'Microsoft set to unveil its challenge to the iPad' and 'It's all just a touch too late'; *The Times* 8

January 2011, 'Rivals poke their finger in iPad's commanding share of the spoils'; all by Murad Ahmed.

19 Teece 2007a.

20 *Fortune* 22 January 2007, 'Lighting up Philips' by Nelson Schwartz; *Sunday Times* 13 August 2006, 'Philips quits technology race to become a "lifestyle" brand' by Dominic O'Connell.

21 Chesbrough 2007; Hagel and Brown 2005; Nohria and Ghoshal 1997; Teece 2007a.

22 *Financial Times* 6 May 2010, 'Drive to succeed may mean lane sharing' by Daniel Shafer and John Reed; *Wall Street Journal* 8 April 2010, 'Daimler, Nissan, Renault seal pact' by Sebastian Moffett.

23 *Newsweek* 11 October 2010, 'Attack of the Droids'.

24 *Financial Times* 28 December 2010, 'Open innovation powers growth' by Jonathan Birchall.

25 Hagel and Brown 2005; Nohria and Ghoshal 1997.

26 See Nonaka *et al.* 2008, p. 177.

27 See Taylor 1990, p. 102.

28 *The Economist* 10 January 2009, 'Britain's lonely high-flier' and 'Coming in from the cold'.

29 *The Economist* 26 September 2009, 'Up, up and Huawei'.

30 Recall the Huawei case in Chapter 3, 'Strategies in a pragmatic world'.

31 Cui 2008.

32 Teece, 2007a, p. 1347; emphasis ours.

33 Beinhocker 1999; Teece 2007a.

34 *Businessweek* 16 November 2006, 'The big ideas behind Nintendo's Wii' by Kenji Hall.

35 Luehrman 1998.

36 For 'select before being selected', see Chapter 3, 'Strategies in a pragmatic world'.

37 Augier and Teece 2008.

38 See Chapter 3, 'Strategies in a pragmatic world'.

39 Shook 2008.

40 Burgelman 1991; van de Ven 1986; recall Chapter 4, 'Strategy as purposeful emergence'.

41 *Financial Times* 27 February 2011, 'The man who turns Post-it Notes into bank notes' by Hal Weitzman.

42 Leonard-Barton 1992; also see Quinn and Cameron 1988.

43 Beinhocker 1999.

44 See Nonaka *et al.* 2008.

45 See *Fortune* 10 December 2007, 'China's web king' by Clay Chandler.

46 Liu and Avery 2009, p. 18.

47 *Fortune* 10 December 2007, 'China's web king'.

48 Liu and Avery 2009, p. 24.

49 Liu and Avery 2009, p. 27.

50 Liu and Avery 2009, p. 50.

51 Liu and Avery 2009, p. 51.

52 *Fortune* 10 December 2007, 'China's web king'.

53 Liu and Avery 2009, p. 48.

54 Liu and Avery 2009, p. 43.

55 Liu and Avery 2009, p. 77.

56 Liu and Avery 2009, pp. 93–94.

57 *Fortune* 10 December 2007, 'China's web king'.

58 Liu and Avery 2009, p. 76.

59 *Wall Street Journal* 12–14 November 2010, 'Softbank maintains Alibaba stake' by Juro Osawa and Daisuke Wakabayashi.

60 Liu and Avery 2009, p. 186.

61 For examples of SMEs benefiting from Alibaba e-commerce services, see, e.g., *Financial Times* 24 November 2010, 'Web offers a comfortable fit' by Mina Hanbury-Tenison; *Fortune* 10 December 2007, 'China's web king'.

62 Ohmae 1982, p. 2.

63 This is compatible with the resource-based view that 'The RBV sees companies as very different collections of physical and intangible assets and capabilities. No two companies are alike because no two companies have had the same set of experiences, acquired the same assets and skills, or built the same organisational cultures. These assets and capabilities determine how efficiently and effectively a company performs its functional activities' (Collis and Montgomery 1995, p. 119).

64 This is compatible with Schumpeter's idea of continuous innovation as the engine of capitalist economies.

65 Nonaka *et al.* 2008.

66 This is compatible with Nelson and Winter's (1982) evolutionary theory of the firm.

67 This is compatible with David Teece's (2007a, 2007b, 2009) dynamic capability framework of the firm. For 'strategising the market', see Chapter 4, 'Strategy as purposeful emergence'.

68 We adopt the word 'orchestration' from Teece 2007a, 2007b.

69 See Teece 2007a, 2007b.

70 Angwin *et al.* 2007, for example, title their book *The Strategy Pathfinder*; Chia and Holt 2009 also regard strategy as 'wayfinding'.

71 Here we refer to Confucius' teaching: 'It is Man who makes *Tao* great, not *Tao* that makes Man great.'

72 This section is based on Hargadon and Douglas 2001; Hughes 1979, 1983; McGuire *et al.* 1993.

73 See Hughes 1983, p. 22.

74 Hughes 1979, p. 132.

75 See Hughes 1983, p. 33.

76 See Hughes 1983, p. 29.

77 Passer 1953, p. 83.

78 See Hughes 1983, pp. 33–34.

79 See Hughes 1983, p. 42.

80 See Hughes 1983, pp. 41–42.

81 See Hargadon and Douglas 2001, p. 488.

82 See Hargadon and Douglas 2001, p. 489.

83 See Hargadon and Douglas 2001, p. 490.

84 See Hargadon and Douglas 2001, p. 490.

85 Hargadon and Douglas 2001, p. 492.

86 Hargadon and Douglas 2001, p. 484.

87 Hargadon and Douglas 2001, p. 486.

88 Hughes 1983, p. 19.

89 Edison to Lowrey, 2 October 1878; see Hughes 1979, pp. 130–131.

90 McGuire *et al.* 1993, pp. 223–224.

91 McGuire *et al.* 1993, p. 238.

92 For an overview and critique, see Mair 1999.

93 This is a manifestation of what we call 'knowledge against ethics'; see Chapter 8, 'Questioning the conventional paradigm'.

94 See Quinn 2003, p. 200.

95 See Quinn 2003, p. 201.

96 See Quinn 2003, p. 201.

97 See Quinn 2003, p. 201.

98 See Quinn 2003, pp. 202, 206.

99 See Quinn 2003, p. 201.

100 Cf.: Nonaka *et al.* 2008, p. 60.

101 Nonaka *et al.* 2008, pp. 96, 97.

102 *Financial Times* 14 January 2007, 'A speed demon at the corporate wheel' by John Reed and Bernard Simon.

103 See Nonaka *et al.* 2008, pp. 20–21.

104 See Nonaka *et al.* 2008, p. 91.

105 For Honda's Three As levels of inquiry, see Nonaka *et al.* 2008; for Honda's advanced research and products see, e.g., *Fortune* 17 March 2008, 'Inside Honda's brain' by Alex Taylor III.

106 See Nonaka *et al.* 2008, p. 95.

107 See Nonaka *et al.* 2008, pp. 94–95.

108 For an example of Honda's mistakes, see Mair 1999.

109 See Nonaka *et al.* 2008, p. 95.

110 See Nonaka *et al.* 2008, p. 93.

111 See Nonaka *et al.* 2008, p. 92.

112 See Nonaka *et al.* 2008, pp. 56, 89.

113 See Nonaka *et al.* 2008, pp. 90, 91.

114 See Nonaka *et al.* 2008, p. 56.

115 *Financial Times* 14 January 2007, 'A speed demon'.

116 See Nonaka *et al.* 2008, pp. 57–58.

117 Nonaka *et al.* 2008, p. 64.

118 See Nonaka *et al.* 2008, p. 59.

119 Terms borrowed from Mintzberg 1987.

120 For an introduction and summary, see, e.g., Mair 1999.

121 See Mair 1999, p. 37; also Sakiya 1982.

122 Terms borrowed from Pascale's 1996 *California Management Review* article 'The Honda effect'. For the debate around 'The Honda effect', see papers by Mintzberg, Pascale, Goold and Rumelt, among others, in the *California Management Review* 1996 summer issue.

123 See Mair 1999, p. 35; also Sakiya 1982, p. 123.

124 The metaphor of 'two legs of strategy' is borrowed from Mintzberg 1987.

125 Nonaka *et al.* 2008, pp. 98–99.

126 *Fortune* 17 March 2008, 'Inside Honda's Brain'.

127 *Fortune* 17 March 2008, 'Inside Honda's Brain'.

128 See Nonaka *et al.* 2008, p. 98.

129 *Fortune* 17 March 2008, 'Inside Honda's Brain'.

130 For '*phronetic* leadership', see Nonaka and Toyama 2007; Nonaka *et al.* 2008.

131 See Nonaka *et al.* 2008, p. 101.

132 See Nonaka *et al.* 2008, p. 104.

133 Words borrowed from Sakiya's 1982 book *Honda Motor: The Men, the Management, the Machines* and Pascale's 1996 *California Management Review* article 'The Honda effect'.

8 QUESTIONING THE CONVENTIONAL PARADIGM

1 For a formal elaboration of the idea of 'paradigm', see Kuhn 1970.

2 See *Sunday Times* 28 June 2009, 'What they don't teach about cash at Harvard' by Dominic Rushe.

3 *Sunday Times* 28 June 2009, 'What they don't teach'; *The Times* 1 August 2007, 'Harvard suffers as loan crisis hits fund manager it backed' by Tom Bawden.

4 *The Times* 1 February 2010, 'So has he got talent? Investors at ITV ask whether "unproven" Crozier can be worth £16m' by Rebecca O'Connor and Miles Costello; *The Times* 4 June 2010, 'Crozier got £2.5m in final year with Mail' by Alex Spence.

5 The phrase 'knowing–doing gap' is borrowed from Pfeffer and Sutton's 2000 book *The Knowing–Doing Gap*. While we question whether knowing can be separated from doing and hence whether there can be a gap between the two, we consider the phrase useful for a critique of experience-absent strategies.

6 Taylor 1911 [1967].

7 Roethlisberger and Dickson 1939; Mayo 1945.

8 Stacey 2010.

9 Best 1990; Bilton and Cummings 2010, p. 21.

10 Cf: Leavitt 2003, pp. 100–101. Many years later, after he visited Vietnam and met his war-time rivals, McNamara reflected on his Vietnam War strategy thus: my logic was sound, but the Viet-Kung did not act upon it.

11 Leavitt 2003.

12 Hayes and Abernathy 1980.

13 Akio Morita put it this way: 'people who are running a business ought to know their business very well. If the accountant had been in charge of our little company in 1946, our company would be a small operation making parts for the giants.' See Morita 1986, p. 168; also Chandler 1990b.

14 See Best 1990, p. 160.

15 Nonaka and Takeuchi 1995, p. 90.

16 Bennis and O'Toole 2005, p. 99. In a similar vein, Edward Deming criticised the number-obsessing managers: 'They know nothing of the

invisible numbers. Who can put a price on a satisfied customer, and who can figure out the cost of a dissatisfied customer?' (see Best 1990, p. 160).

17 Barney 2007, p. x.

18 See, e.g., Bettis 1991; Bowman 1974; Hafsi and Thomas 2005; Montgomery *et al.* 1989; Mahoney 1993.

19 This is the view held by Kim Clark, the former dean of Harvard Business School. See *Financial Times/Business Education* 10 May 2010, 'Best of two worlds' by Della Bradshaw.

20 Gordon and Howell 1959; Pierson 1959.

21 Stacey 2010, p. 42.

22 Leavitt 1989.

23 See, e.g., Kay 1993; Pettigrew *et al.* 2002; Spender 2001; Tsoukas and Cummings 1997.

24 Bilton and Cummings 2010, p. 31.

25 Bennis and O'Toole 2005.

26 *Financial Times* 25 January 2011, 'Why business still ignores business schools' by Michael Skapinker. See also Astley and Zammuto 1992; Gopinath and Hoffman 1995; Porter and McKibbin 1988.

27 Stacey 2010, p. 23.

28 Leavitt 1989, p. 42.

29 *The Economist* 31 July 2010, 'Schumpeter: a post-crisis case study'; also *Financial Times* 23 December 2008, 'The fallen giants of finance'.

30 *Financial Times* 16 November 2010, 'Forget the MBA, give me experience any day' by Luke Johnson.

31 For critiques see, e.g., Ghoshal 2005; Leavitt 1989; Mahoney 1993; Pettigrew *et al.* 2002; Pfeffer and Fong 2002.

32 Hayes and Abernathy 1980.

33 Eccles and Nohria 1992.

34 Eccles and Nohria 1992, p. 7.

35 Bennis and O'Toole 2005; Leavitt 1989.

36 Bilton and Cummings 2010; Stacey 2010.

37 Leavitt 1989.

38 Bennis and O'Toole 2005, p. 100.

39 Mintzberg 2005, p. 7.

40 Huff 2006.

41 Daft and Lewin 1990, p. 1.

42 Whittington 2002, p. 133.

43 Sources for this section: *BBC News* 16 January 2007, 'Anger over Big Brother "racism"'; *BBC News* 18 January 2007, 'Shetty speaks of Brother "racism"'; *Guardian* 17 January 2007, 'Big Brother "racism" is raised in Commons' by Owen Gibson; *Sunday Times* 21 January 2007, 'Beauty and the bigot' by Richard Woods; *Sunday Times* 27 January 2007, 'After eight years of upsets, Big Brother is to be toned down' by Dan Sabbagh and Adam Sherwin; *The Times* 25 May 2007, 'Big Brother in racism row' by Adam Sherwin; *Wikipedia*: 'Celebrity big brother racism controversy' (accessed 14 May 2010).

44 Barnard 1938.

45 Leavitt 1989.

46 *Financial Times* 13 April 2010, 'Replacing the "dumbest idea in the world"' by Michael Skapinker.

47 Porter 2002, p. 47.

48 *Financial* Times 16 November 2010, 'Forget the MBA'.

49 Hayes and Abernathy 1980.

50 Friedman 2002, p. 133.

51 *Financial Times* 17 March 2009, 'Shareholder value can be illusory and transient' by Matthew Rogers.

52 *The Economist* 26 October 2002, 'Solving GE's big problem'.

53 Handy 2002.

54 For this see, e.g., Hayes and Abernathy 1980.

55 Morita 1986, p. 157.

56 Morita 1986, p. 283.

57 Hayes and Abernathy 1980.

58 For this insight, see Ghoshal and Moran 1996, p. 34.

59 Morita 1986, p. 283.

60 See, e.g., Chandler 1990b; Kay 1998.

61 Hayes and Abernathy 1980.

62 *Financial Times Weekend Magazine* 13/14 March 2010, 'Eat or be eaten: the inside story of how Cadbury fell to a predator from the US' by Jenny Wiggins.

63 *Financial Times* 15 April 2009, 'Cutting back financial capitalism is America's big test' by Martin Wolf.

64 Pope John Paul II supplied a moral code as the foundation for business as follows:

The Church acknowledges that legitimate role of profit as an indication that a business is functioning well. When a firm makes a profit, this means productive forces have been properly employed and corresponding human needs have been duly satisfied. But profitability is not the only indicator of a firm's condition. It is possible for the financial accounts to be in order, and yet for the people – who make up the firm's most valuable asset – to be humiliated and their dignity offended. Besides being morally inadmissible, this will eventually have negative repercussions on the firm's economic efficiency. In fact, the purpose of a business firm is not simply to make a profit, but is to be found in its existence as a community of persons who in various ways are endeavouring to satisfy their basic needs, and who form a particular group at the service of the whole society. Profit is a regulator of the life of a business, but it is not the only one; other human and moral factors must also be considered which, in the long term, are at least equally important for the life of a business. (Cf.: Whetten *et al.* 2002, p. 392)

65 Ghoshal 2005, p. 86.

66 Flyvbjerg 2001, p. 168.

67 *The Economist* 1 December 2001, 'Enron's fall: upended'.

68 *Financial Times* 7 May 2010, 'Goldman to face investor's ire' by Francesco Guerrera and Justin Baer; *Sunday Times* 18 April 2010, 'Is this God's dirty work?' by Iain Dey and Dominic Rushe; *The Times* 17 April 2010, 'Goldman Sachs: $1bn fraud charge' by Christine Seib.

69 *Financial Times* 6/7 February 2010, 'BAE agrees to $400m fine' by Michael Peel and Stephanie Kirchgaessner; *The Times* 11 February 'BAE "gave Saudi official perks worth $5m"', says US government' by David Robertson.

70 *Wall Street Journal* 4 November 2008, 'China milk products were tainted for years' by Gordon Fairclough.

71 *The Economist* 24 January 2009, 'Greed – and fear: a special report on the future of finance'.

72 *Wall Street Journal* 2 March 2010, 'Toyoda concedes profit focus led to flaws' by Norihiko Shirouzu.

73 *Financial Times* 13 May 2010, 'Facebook's open disdain for privacy' by John Gapper; *Financial Times* 18 May 2010, 'Facebook's hunt for value has come at a cost' by Brett Self.

74 *Financial Times* 27 November 2007, 'Cutting edge innovations must avoid costing the earth' by Stefan Stern.

75 *The Times* 25 May 2007, 'Big Brother in racism row'.

76 *The Economist* 1 December 2007 'Going hybrid: a special report on business in Japan'.

77 *The Economist* 13 July 2002, 'Europe's farms: will these modest proposals provoke mayhem down on the farm?'

78 In 2010, for example, almost a quarter (23 per cent) of doctors trained in sub-Saharan Africa worked in developed countries, with Britain one of the most attractive destinations. See *The Times* 25 September 2010, 'Africans afraid of leaving NHS to help their home countries' by Rosemary Bennett.

79 *Financial Times* 28 October 2009, 'How mistaken ideas helped to bring the economy down' by Martin Wolf; *Guardian* 6 October 2008, 'Faith. Belief. Trust. This economic orthodoxy was built on superstition' by Madeleine Bunting.

80 Giddens 1982; Merton 1982.

81 Ghoshal 2005, p. 77.

82 Ghoshal 2005; Wicks and Freeman 1998.

83 Handy 2002.

84 Krass 2003. Also see *The Economist* 1 February 2003, 'Andrew Carnegie: Pittsburgh pirate'.

85 Best 1990, ch. 2.

86 Handy 2002, p. 51.

87 Bartlett and Ghoshal 1994, p. 81; Chandler 1990b, p. 140; Morita 1986, p. 143.

88 *The Times* 10 October 2009, 'We came close to not being able to get money from bank machines' by Katherine Griffiths.

89 *The Economist* 10 October 2009, 'Carrefour in emerging markets: exit the dragon?'

90 This section is based on *The Economist* 10 October 2009, 'Buttonwood: the nature of wealth – The world confused financial assets with real ones'.

91 The rising price of paper wealth can well be due to gamblers' speculations, particularly at times when borrowing is cheap because people far away work harder and save more. It can also be an indication of increasing injustice as the claim of wealth is further transferred from the have-nots to the haves: in the UK, for example, hedge-fund managers pay a lower tax rate than the workers who clean their offices. See *Financial Times* 20 June 2010, 'The issue of capital gains need not be so taxing' by John Kay.

92 *Financial Times* 25 March 2010, 'Bubble, trouble, boom and bust: the economy that Labour built'.

93 *The Times* 9 December 2008, 'A crash as historic as the end of communism' by Robert Peston.

94 *Financial Times* 7 October 2009, 'Markets after the age of efficiency' by John Kay. Also see: *The Economist* 17 April 2010, 'Twin peaks: George Soros has left his mark on many economies. Can he do the same for economics?'; *The Times* 28 October 2009, 'Three cheers for the death of old economics' by Anatole Kaletsky.

95 For critique on *ceteris paribus* in social science, see, e.g., *Financial Times* 13 March 2011, 'We need new models in an uncertain world' by John Authers.

96 *The Times* 29 December 2008, 'Market fundamentalism took us close to disaster in 2008' by Anatole Kaletsky.

97 *Financial Times*, 26 January 2010, 'Computer-driven trading boom raises meltdown fears' by Jeremy Grant.

98 *Times* 28 February 2007, 'Dow plunges 400 points after Chinese rout shakes markets' by Gary Duncan and Jane Macartney.

99 *Financial Times* 18 February 2010, 'Ghost in the machine' by Jeremy Grant and Michael Mackenzie.

100 *Financial Times* 2 June 2010, 'That sinking feeling' by Aline van Duyn, Michael Mackenzie and Jeremy Grant.

101 *Wall Street Journal* 31 May 2010, 'The May 6 "Flash crash"' by Mark Spitznagel.

102 Williamson 1991.

103 For a critique, see Ghoshal 2005; Ghoshal *et al.* 1999.

104 Ghoshal *et al.* 1999.

105 In Ghoshal's words, 'In its constant struggle for appropriating value, the company is pitted against its own employees as well as business rivals and the rest of society'. See Ghoshal *et al.* 1999, p. 12.

106 Chia and Holt 2009, p. 104.

107 It should be acknowledged that Porter has subsequently written on issues such as social responsibility, inner-city regeneration, the ecological environment, and so on; see, e.g., Porter and van der Linde 1995; Porter and Kramer 1999, 2002, 2006. Nevertheless, the Five-forces industrial-analysis model remains his most influential contribution to date.

108 See Ghoshal *et al.* 1999, p. 18.

109 Jensen 1998, 2000. For a critique of this theory against the wider contexts of shareholder capitalism, see Stacey 2010, ch. 2.

110 *The Economist* 16 November 2002, p. 66; see Ghoshal 2005, p. 81.

111 Sen 1998, p. xii.

112 Friedman 2002, p. 6; see Ghoshal 2005, p. 83.

113 *Financial Times* 23 December 2008, 'The fallen giants'; *Fortune* 26 November 2007, 'What were they smoking?'

114 *Financial Times* 5/6 December 2009, 'Risky rewards' by Francesco Guerrera and Mega Murphy; *The Times* 4 December 2009, 'Executives at failed banks ready to gallop off with £1.5bn in bonuses' by Suzy Jagger, Philip Webster and Miles Costello.

115 For a critique of this view, see de Geus 1996.

116 See Ghoshal *et al.* 1999, p. 11.

117 For this argument, see Blair 1995; Monks and Minow 2004; O'Sullivan 2000.

118 Mintzberg 2007; *The Economist* 20 March 2010, 'Productivity growth: slash and earn'.

119 Morita 1986, p. 200.

120 *Financial Times* 24 March 2010, 'Recovery depends on Main Street' by Robert Reich.

121 *Mail Online* 13 May 2010, 'Activists planning to "destroy" BA with 20 days of strikes, says Willie Walsh' by Ray Massey (accessed on 16 June 2010).

122 *Financial Times* 3 June 2010, 'Foxconn raises pay by 30% in China' by Kathrin Hille and Tom Mitchell; *Financial Times* 21 June 2010, 'Push to end strikes in China' by Tom Mitchell and Mure Dickie; *The Economist* 29 May 2010, 'Suicides at Foxconn: light and death'; *Wall Street Journal* 27 May 2010, 'Apple, H-P to investigate supplier over suicides' by Jason Dean and Ting-I Tsai.

123 *The Economist* 8 May 2010, 'China and foreign companies: join the party'; *The Economist* 5 June 2010, 'Unions in China: strike breakers'.

124 Seen from a long-term development perspective, the strikes and wage rise might have positive impacts on fairer distribution of growth benefits, greater spending power of Chinese consumers, rebalancing China's economy towards consumption and away from exports and lessening the trade surpluses that cause tension with the US. See, e.g.,

Financial Times 3 June 2010, 'The Lex column: Mao money'; *Wall Street Journal* 11–13 June 2010, 'The rise of Chinese labour'.

125 Ricardo 1817; cf.: Barney and Clark 2007, p. 8.

126 For introduction to these theories, see, Aldrich and Ruef 2006; Carroll and Hannan 1995; Lawrence and Lorsch 1967; Pfeffer 1981; Powell and DiMaggio 1991; Scott 2003.

127 *Financial Times* 14 June 2010, 'The Lex column: beyond politics'.

128 Shrivastava 1994, pp. 713–714.

129 Porter and van der Linde 1995.

130 *Financial Times* 27 July 2007, 'Carmakers in last-ditch stand against fuel economy rules' by Edward Luce and Bernard Simon.

131 *Financial Times* 12/13 June 2010, 'BP set for dividend retreat' by Ed Crooks, Kate Burgess and Harvey Morris; *Financial Times* 14 June 2010, 'Britain should back down over BP' by Clive Crook; *International Herald Tribune* 12/13 June 2010, 'Failure is now an option' by Timothy Egan; *Sunday Times* 13 June 2010, 'You Brits are gonna' by Tony Allen-Mills; *The Times* 5 June 2010, 'BP sends signal that US oil spill will not stop its dividend flow' by Ian King; *The Times* 12 June 2010, 'BP to start fightback as Obama calls Cameron' by Robin Pagnamenta, Suzy Jagger and Roland Watson.

132 Cummings 2002.

133 Ghoshal 2005, p. 81.

134 Leavitt 1989, p. 41.

135 Levy *et al.* 2003, p. 99; also see Alvesson and Willmott 1996; Shrivastava 1986.

136 Weber 1949, p. 55.

137 Marcuse 1964.

138 Hayek 1989.

139 Alvesson and Willmott 1996; MacIntyre 1981.

140 For critiques see, e.g., Alvesson and Willmott 1996; Ghoshal *et al.* 1999; Scarbrough 1998; Whittington 1992.

141 See Ghoshal 2005.

142 Wicks and Freeman 1998.

143 Astley 1985, p. 497.

144 Wicks and Freeman 1998, p. 128.

145 See, e.g., Flew 1979.

146 See, e.g., Burrell and Morgan 1979.

147 Rorty 1982, p. 168.

148 Rouse 1996.

149 Porter 1980.

150 Chia 2004.

151 Ghoshal 2005.

152 *Financial Times* 7 June 2010, 'A promise of good behaviour' by Della Bradshaw; *The Economist* 6 June 2009, 'Business: a Hippocratic oath for managers – forswearing greed'.

153 Ghoshal 2005.

154 *The Economist* 24 May 2008, 'Companies as activists: strange bedfellows'.

155 Ghoshal 2005, p. 88.

156 *Financial Times* 7 June 2010, 'Time for new kid on the block to lead the way' by Lars-Hendrik Roller.

157 *Financial Times* 12 March 2009, 'Now is the time for a less selfish capitalism' by Richard Layard.

158 Sources: *Financial Times* 19 January 2007, 'Letter: Markets drove BP's cost-cutting culture' by Simon Zadek; *Financial Times* 19 March 2007, 'BP paints grim picture of Texas refinery before blast' by Sheila McNulty; *Financial Times* 21 March 2007, 'Warning signs of disaster for several years' by Sheila McNulty; *Financial Times* 24 March 2007, 'BP fought off Texas safety controls' by Sheila McNulty; *Financial Times* 27/28 October 2007, 'BP to pay $380m to end US probes' by Paul Gregan; *Financial Times* 5 May 2010, 'BP counts high cost of clean-up and blow to brand' by Ed Crooks and Andrew Edgecliffe-Johnson; *Financial Times* 6 May 2010, 'BP is drilling itself into deep water' by John Gapper; *Financial Times* 15/16 May 2010, 'Obama turns BP anger on regulators' by Stephanie Kirchgaessner; *Financial Times* 25 June 2010, 'Oil majors review ties with BP after spill' by Sheila McNulty and Carola Hoyos; *The Economist* 24 March 2007, 'BP: in their own words ...'; *Guardian* 31 May 2010, 'Open heart surgery at 5,000 ft risks making oil gush faster' by Andrew Clark and Graeme Wearden; *Sunday Times* 14 January 2007, 'Browne falls on his sword over BP crises' by Grant Ringshaw; *Sunday Times* 2 May 2010, 'BP warned of rig fault 10 years ago' by Danny Fortson; *Sunday Times* 9 May 2010, 'Boot on BP's throat' by Danny Fortson; *The Times* 17 January 2007, 'Panel hits hard at BP for failure to learn from Grangemouth mistakes' by David Robertson; *The Times* 7 May 2007, 'BP's name is stained by its barrels of hubris' by Robin Pagnamenta; *The Times* 20 May 2010, 'Don't

worry, besieged BP chief tells staff' by Robin Pagnamenta; *The Times* 21 June 2010, 'BP chief sails into storm at White House after day off on his yacht' by Nico Hines; *Wall Street Journal* 3 May 2010, 'BP seeks rivals' help' by Guy Chazan; *Wall Street Journal* 4 May 2010, 'BP starts drilling relief well to halt oil flow' by Jeffrey Ball; *Wall Street Journal* 17 May 2010, 'Crew had argument before rig exploded' by Russel Gold; *Wall Street Journal* 17 May 2010, 'Some success removing oil' by Guy Chazan, Mark Peters and Jeffrey Ball.

159 Figures from *Financial Times* 26 July 2010, 'Oil sleuths struggle to assess spills effect' by Harvey Morris and Fiona Harvey.

160 *The Times* 17 June 2010, 'BP bows to Obama and cancels its dividends' by Catherine Philp and Giles Whittell.

161 *Financial Times* 18 June 2010, 'Hayward responses raise hackles' by Anna Fifield and Edward Luce; *Financial Times* 5/6 June 2010, 'Under pressure' by Ed Crooks; *Financial Times* 24/25 July 2010 'Gloom at the top' by Ed Crooks and Kate Burgess; *Sunday Telegraph* 6 June 2010, 'I'm also angry and frustrated' by Rowena Mason; *The Times* 21 June 2010, 'BP chief sails into storm'; *The Times* 21 July 2010, 'Hayward prepares to quit as BP chief executive' by Robin Pagnamenta and Jacqui Goddard; *The Times* 26 July 2010, 'BP chief to walk away from crisis with £12m' by Robin Pagnamenta.

162 *Financial Times* 15 December 2009, 'How to rebuild a newly shamed subject' by Robert Skidelsky.

163 *Financial Times* 29 December 2008, 'Economists' Forum: an embarrassing admission' by Martin Wolf.

164 Hayes and Abernathy 1980, p. 147.

165 *The Times* 25 May 2007, 'Big Brother in racism row'.

166 *Wall Street Journal* 4 November 2008, 'China milk products'.

167 *Wall Street Journal* 2 March 2010, 'Toyoda concedes'.

168 *Financial Times* 25 March 2010, 'Pardoned Lee back at Samsung' by Song Jung-a; *The Economist* 10 January 2009, 'Corporate governance: India's Enron'.

169 Ansoff 1991; Mintzberg 1990, 1991; also see Tsoukas 1994.

170 Bilton and Cummings 2010, p. 21.

171 *The Economist* 6 October 2001, 'Communications breakdown: Marconi's share price'.

172 Bowman and Helfat 2001; Grant 2002; Markides 1999; McGahan and Porter 1997; Rumelt 1991; Teece 1993; Whittington *et al.* 1999.

173 Chakravarthy and White 2002; Foss 1996.

174 Mintzberg 1991.

175 For the strategy-as-practice movement, see, e.g., Johnson *et al.* 2007; for the partisan arguments, see Chia 2002; Chia and Holt 2006, 2009.

176 Pettigrew *et al.* 2002.

177 Barney 1990; Donaldson 1990a, 1990b.

178 Camerer 1985; Mahoney 1993.

179 Dyer and Wilkins 1991; Eisenhardt 1989.

180 Clegg *et al.* 2006; Knights and Morgan 1991; Pettigrew 1985; Porac and Thomas 2002; Westwood and Clegg 2003.

181 Pettigrew *et al.* 2002.

182 Markides 1999.

183 Boulding 1956; Mahoney 1993.

184 Porter 2002, p. 50.

185 Sanchez and Heene 1997, p. 306.

186 Foss 1996, p. 5. Also see, among many others: Amit and Schoemaker 1993; Bowman and Hurry 1993; Chakravarthy and Doz 1992; Elfring and Volberda 2001; Pettigrew *et al.* 2002; Schoemaker 1993; Spender 2001.

187 Flood 1993.

188 Nonaka *et al.* 2006.

189 Dewey 1910, p. 53.

190 Burrell and Morgan 1979.

191 The practical effects of Burrell and Morgan's polarising-and-isolating strategy have been mixed and controversial; for analysis and critiques see, e.g., Argyris 1999; Deetz 1996.

192 For a beautifully constructed schema, see Whittington 2001.

193 Commenting on paradigmatic boxes, Argyris 1999 posits: 'The Morgan/Smirich paradigmatic model about ontology, human nature, epistemology, metaphors and research methods ... [are] helpful in organising my thoughts about what I observe social scientists do when they conduct their research, ... unhelpful when I attempted to apply the models to creative behaviour' (p. 307).

194 Porter 2002, p. 52.

195 For more details on the culture of opposites and contradictions, see Chapter 9, 'Pragmatism East and West'.

196 Teece 1990; Whittington 2001; Whitley 1984.

197 Pepper 1942; Tsoukas 1994, p. 770.

198 Alvesson 1995, p. 1048.

199 Pettigrew *et al.* 2002, p. 9.

200 Hafsi and Thomas 2005, p. 240.

201 Elfring and Volberda 2001, p. 2; also see Behrman and Levin 1984; Porter and McKibbin 1988; Spender 2001.

202 Boulding 1956, p. 198.

203 See, e.g., Burrell and Morgan 1979.

204 For 'skilled incompetence', see Argyris and Schön 1996, pp. 200–242.

205 Churchman 1971; Mitroff and Linstone 1993.

206 Morita 1986, p. 290.

207 Rorty 1979.

208 Alvesson and Willmott 1996.

209 Sources: *Asia Weekly* 16 July 2007, 'China's fishy exports'; *Financial Times* 17 September 2007, 'China rejects US and Canada port' by Richard McGregor; *Financial Times* 22/23 September 2007, 'Saying sorry: Mattel in public apology to Chinese people'; *Financial Times* 30 October 2007, 'China arrests 774 in drive on food and drug safety' by Geoff Dyer; *Financial Times* 22 December 2007, 'China bans 750 toy exporters in response to west's concern' by Andrew Bounds; *Newsweek* 16 July 2007, 'Unsafe at any speed' by Melinda Liu; *Newsweek* 1 October 2007, 'Recalling Brand China' by William H. Hess; *Straits Times* 22 September 2008, 'Tainted milk scare goes beyond China' by Tessa Wong and Liaw Wy-cin; *Business Times Weekend* 20/21 September 2008, 'Major HK grocers pull top China dairy's milk'; *The Economist* 29 September 2007, 'Plenty of blame to go around'; *The Economist* 20 September 2008, 'China's baby-milk scandal: formula for disaster'; *The Economist* 27 September 2008, 'Food regulation in China: the poison spreads'; *The Economist* 5 June 2010, 'Product liability in China: redress by relocation'; *The Times* 22 September 2007, 'Mattel issues apology to China for design flaws that tarnished industry' by Suzy Jagger; *The Times* 23 January 2009, 'Two are sentenced to death over toxic milk scandal' by Jane Macartney; *Wall Street Journal* 13–15 July 2007, 'Made in China' by Emily Parker; *Wall Street Journal* 16 June 2007, 'Safety supplants quotas as hot-button trade issue' by Andrew Batson; *Wall Street Journal* 4 November 2008, 'China milk products'; *Wall Street Journal* 23–25 January 2009, 'China delivers milk sentences' by Gordon Fairclough.

210 The phrase 'normal accidents' is adopted from Perrow 1984.

9 PRAGMATISM EAST AND WEST

1 For 'intellectual archaeology', see Holliday and Chandler 1986; Takahashi 2000, p. 218.

2 Ames and Rosemont 1998, p. x.

3 Festenstein 1997, p. 11.

4 In this, we concur with Michael Foucault: 'History is history. There is no way, no hope, no positive meaning in turning back on something.' See Flyvbjerg 2001, p. 54.

5 Dewey, *The Middle Works*, vol. XI, p. 18.

6 Cf.: Baert 2005, p. 136.

7 While, among the early pioneers, Peirce's pragmatism can be seen as 'scientifically elitist', James' 'psychologically personalistic' and Dewey's 'democratically populist', there have recently been encounters between 'liberal' and 'communitarian' pragmatist ideals, between Rorty's 'ethnocentric' approach and Putnam's 'direct realism', between Dewey's 'meliorist vision of the person and ethics' and the recent 'preoccupation with clashing values, paradigms, conceptual schemes and forms of life', between 'old' and 'new' pragmatism. See, e.g., Festenstein 1997; Garrison 2000; Miller 2004; Putnam 1995; Shields 2005. While some, including the authors of this book, appreciate the diversity and richness within, others are dismayed by 'The Two Pragmatisms' and concerned by 'Pragmatism at the Crossroads'; see, e.g., Mounce 1997; Rescher 2000, 2005.

8 Lovejoy 1908.

9 Of course, there can be different constructions, with varying emphases alongside overlaps. For Baert (2005), who is concerned with knowledge in and of the social sciences, pragmatism is characterised by a distrust of 'spectator's theory of knowledge', a rejection of atemporal epistemological and ethical foundations, a distaste towards pointless debate upon the 'inner nature of things' or 'first principles' and an objection to corresponding truth. For Festenstein (1997), who is interested in political action that leads to better or worse life in society, pragmatism is about a rejection of foundationally grounded ethical value, a refusal to embrace moral relativism, an emphasis on community and history and promotion of democratic politics. For Bernstein (1991), who is interested in the intelligent encounters between the American and the continental European traditions, 'the pragmatic ethos' is featured by practicality, fallibilism, social characters of inquiry, antifoundationalism, dynamism and engaged

pluralism. For Nohria and Berkley (1994), who talk directly to managers, pragmatism is manifested by sensitivity to context, willingness to make do, focus on outcomes and openness to uncertainty. And so on. Seen from a pragmatist perspective, the diversity is hardly surprising: constructions vary because they are intended to serve different purposes.

10 See Chapter 2, 'Spirits of pragmatism'.

11 Hall and Ames 1999, p. 3.

12 James 1907, pp. 28, 29.

13 Dewey, *The Later Works*, vol. IV, p. 14.

14 Rescher 2003, p. 1.

15 Baert 2005; Habermas 2003; Putnam 1981.

16 See Evans 2000, p. 314; Tan 2003.

17 Ackoff 1996, p. 17; Shields 1996, p. 395.

18 Dewey 1917, p. 95; see Evans 2000, p. 317.

19 Ormerod 2006, p. 904.

20 Baert 2005.

21 Ormerod 2002, p. 349.

22 See Flyvbjerg 2001, p. 125; emphasis original.

23 Miller 2004, pp. 247, 245.

24 See Rescher 2005, p. 356.

25 James 1907, pp. 97, 104; see Thayer 1982, p. 229 and Pihlström 2007, p. 13; emphasis original.

26 Dewey 1920, p. 128; cf.: Ames and Rosemont 1998, p. 46.

27 Rorty 1979.

28 Baert 2005, p. 8.

29 Wicks and Freeman 1998, p. 131.

30 James 1909; Pihlström 2007, p. 4.

31 Miller 2005, p. 364.

32 Dewey 1938a, p. 68; cf.: Webb 2004, p. 488.

33 Webb 1999, p. 26.

34 Evans 2000, pp. 314–315.

35 Flyvbjerg 2001, p. 70; Hafsi and Thomas 2005, p. 245.

36 See Friedman 2006, p. 3; emphasis original.

37 Hall and Ames 1999, p. 5.

38 Bruch and Ghoshal 2004; Churchman 1971.

39 See Rescher 2005, p. 355.

40 Garrison 2000, p. 460.

41 Ormerod 2006, p. 906.

42 Levitt 2002 [1963], p. 141.

43 Webb 2004, p. 487.

44 Baert 2005, p. 143.

45 Flyvbjerg 2001, p. 156.

46 'Truth is made true in events' is James' phrase; see James 1907, p. 97; cf.: Thayer 1982, p. 229.

47 Rescher 1996, p. 18.

48 Evans 2000, p. 316.

49 Rescher 1996, pp. 14, 16.

50 Dewey, *The Later Works*, vol. I, pp. 85, 90, 99.

51 Dewey, *The Later Works*, vol. I, p. 278.

52 Rescher 1996, p. 20.

53 Baert 2005, p. 135.

54 Dewey, *The Later Works*, vol. I, p. 67.

55 Dewey 1917, p. 63.

56 Dewey, *The Middle Works*, vol. XI, p. 50.

57 Dewey 1920, p. 178; cf.: Shields 2003, p. 515.

58 Putnam 2004, p. 11.

59 Dewey, *The Later Works*, vol. XI, p. 47.

60 Benton and Craib 2001, p. 86.

61 Festenstein 1997, p. 107.

62 Rescher 1996, p. 123.

63 See Festenstein 1997, pp. 5, 7.

64 Marchetti 2003, p. 24.

65 Dewey, *The Later Works*, vol. XII, p. 121.

66 Putnam 2004, p. 4; Evans 2000, p. 314.

67 Dewey, *The Later Works*, vol. XII, p. 16.

68 Webb 1999, p. 16.

69 Powell 2001, p. 884.

70 See Putnam 1995, p. 68.

71 Putnam 1995, pp. 20–21; emphasis original.

72 Rescher 1996, p. 74.

73 Joas 1996, ch. 2.

74 Tan 2003.

75 West 1989, p. 90.

76 See Silva 2007.

77 See Festenstein 1997, ch. 3.

78 Dewey, *The Later Works*, vol. II; cf.: Garrison 2000, p. 461.

79 Dewey, *The Later Works*, vol. II, p. 164.
80 Dewey, *The Later Works*, vol. XI, pp. 38–39, 48.
81 Putnam 2004, p. 25.
82 Tan 2003.
83 Silva 2007, p. 121.
84 Evans 2000, p. 311.
85 Joas 1996, p. 129.
86 Freeman 2007, p. 488.
87 Dewey, *The Later Works*, vol. III, p. 105; cf.: Tan 2003, p. 164.
88 Habermas 2003, p. xx.
89 Rescher 1996, p. 130.
90 Putnam 2004, pp. 21–22.
91 Miller 2004, p. 245.
92 Garrison 2000, p. 462.
93 Quinn and Cameron 1988, p. 302.
94 See, e.g., Barney 2002.
95 James 1907, p. 29.
96 The Confucian 'four devils': foregone conclusions, predeterminations, obstinacy, egoism; see Chapter 2, 'Spirits of pragmatism'.
97 Tan 2003.
98 Dewey, *The Middle Works*, vol. IX, p. 305.
99 Tan 2003, pp. 93, 148.
100 Garrison 2000, p. 463.
101 Dewey, *The Later Works*, vol. II, p. 365.
102 Webb 2004, p. 484.
103 Ackoff 1981; Churchman 1971. In this, American pragmatism is not only compatible with the holistic spirit of Confucianism but converges well with some of the greatest thinkers in continental European traditions. Nietzsche, for example, posited that the more eyes, different eyes, we can use to observe one thing, the more complete will be our concept of this thing, and that we need to become a little jaunty and ignorant in the search for creative combination of different logics; Lyotard submitted that diversity is no less important than efficiency, that we need to allow many logics to grate against one another if we are to create and develop; while Gadamer expressed this pluralist spirit via the famous metaphor 'fusion of horizons'. For the link between American pragmatism and these great European thinkers, see, e.g., Bernstein 1991; Cummings 2002; Flyvbjerg 2001.

104 Evans 2000, p. 313.

105 Ormerod 2006, p. 907.

106 The notion 'language game' is adopted from Wittgenstein 1953.

107 In November 2009, Goldman Sachs chairman and chief executive Lloyd Blankfein commented to the *Sunday Times* that Wall Street bankers were 'doing God's work'. See *Financial Times* 20 April 2010, 'Goldman case helps Democrats' quest for Wall Street reform' by Edward Luce; *Sunday Times* 18 April 2010, 'Is this God's dirty work?' by Iain Dey and Dominic Rushe.

108 Mitroff and Linstone 1993, pp. 161–162.

109 Joas 1996, p. 197.

110 Dewey, *The Later Works*, vol. XV, p. 232.

111 See Baert 2005, p. 137.

112 Putnam 2004, p. 28; emphasis original.

113 Dewey, *The Middle Works*, vol. VIII, p. 37; cf.: Garrison 2000, p. 473.

114 See Marchetti 2003, p. 24.

115 Dewey, *The Later Works*, vols. II and XIII; cf.: Alexander 1995, p. 153.

116 Flyvbjerg 2001, p. 167.

117 Stivers 2008, p. 131.

118 See Festenstein 1997, ch. 4.

119 Joas 1996, p. 160; Weick 1995.

120 Flyvbjerg 2001, p. 43.

121 Garrison 2000, p. 468.

122 Evans 2000.

123 Rorty 1991.

124 Hall and Ames 1999, p. 151.

125 See, e.g., Nisbett 2003.

126 Hall and Ames 1999, pp. 156–157.

127 Putnam 2004, p. 102.

128 Dewey, *The Middle Works*, vol. XV, p. 176.

129 Hall and Ames 1999, p. 128.

130 Tan 2003.

131 Cobb 2007.

132 Miller 2005, p. 371.

133 Dewey, *The Later Works*, vol. XI, p. 37.

134 Rorty 1999.

135 Garrison 2000; Tan 2003.

136 Dewey, *The Middle Works*, vol. IX, p. 7.

137 Dewey, *The Later Works*, vol. XIII, p. 176.

138 Evans 2005, p. 252.

139 Dewey 1927, p. 151.

140 See Nonaka and Konno 1998.

141 Tan 2003.

142 Gadamer 1975.

143 Hall and Ames 1999.

144 Dewey, *The Later Works*, vol. II, p. 328.

145 Tan 2003.

146 See Chapter 6, 'Timely balanced way-making'.

147 Mead 1934, p. 146.

148 Tan 2003.

149 Ackoff 1996, p. 23.

150 Cobb 2007.

151 See Rescher 2005, p. 356.

152 Bernstein 1983.

153 See Ormerod 2006, p. 898.

154 Powell 2001, p. 885.

155 Shields 2003.

156 Joas 1996.

157 Miller 2005, p. 364.

158 Dewey, *The Later Works*, vol. V, p. 115.

159 Hoch 2006, p. 391.

160 Dewey, *The Later Works*, vol. XI, p. 142.

161 Webb 2004, p. 488.

162 Dewey, as cited in Shields 2003, p. 522.

163 Dewey 1938b, p. 342.

164 Dewey 1927, pp. 218–219.

165 Stivers 1994, p. 365.

166 Boland and Tenkasi 1995; Churchman 1971.

167 Joas 1996, p. 140.

168 Garrison 2000, p. 468.

169 Tan 2003.

170 Hall and Ames 1999, p. 139.

171 We also note great affinity from continental European thinkers. Nietzsche submitted that our sociality and history is the only foundation we have, the only solid ground under our feet, the best basis for action. Heidegger's idea of 'thrownness' suggested that we

have choices but choices are limited by our being cast in particular directions by our past traditions and connections. Foucault regarded ethics as a contingent process, not neutral or static principles, of developing the self according to personal standards in relation to particular communities, of finding a way of 'carrying oneself' in communities. And to Habermas, truth is experienced, fallible, agreeable, not discovered. For an introduction to the emphasis on history and sociality in human experience, see, e.g., Flyvbjerg 2001.

172 One of the visible efforts in the 'West' in searching for pragmatic strategy is the strategy-as-practice movement, promoted chiefly by Anglo-European scholars. We may call it the 'practice turn'. The practice turn is intended to analyse what people actually do in relation to the development of strategy in organisations so as to reverse the problematic trend of concerning strategy as merely what organisations have. The proponents of the practice turn also regard theirs as a 'pragmatic approach', which makes our comparison more timely and relevant. For an introduction of the practice turn, see, e.g., *European Management Review* 2004, Issue 1; *Journal of Management Studies* 2003, Issue 1; *Human Relations* 2007, Issue 1; for the 'pragmatic' claim, see, e.g., Johnson *et al.* 2007.

173 See, e.g., MacIntyre 1981; Statler and Roos 2005; Tsoukas and Cummings 1997, p. 664.

174 Tsoukas and Cummings 1997.

175 Tsoukas and Cummings 1997, p. 665.

176 Tsoukas and Cummings 1997, pp. 665, 666.

177 Statler and Roos 2005.

178 Statler and Roos 2005, p. 13.

179 *Daxue*, opening section.

180 Cheng 1972, p. 163.

181 Clegg and Ross-Smith 2003, p. 86.

182 Graham 1989. As we indicated earlier in this book, we prefer 'way-making' over 'way-finding' in thinking about strategy.

183 Hall and Ames 1999, p. 103.

184 See Hall and Ames 1999, p. 104.

185 Ames and Rosemont 1998, pp. 32–33.

186 Morita 1986, p. 167.

187 See Wang 2005.

188 Needham 1956, pp. 199–200; emphasis original.

189 Suzuki 1971; Takahashi 2000.

190 See Ames and Rosemont 1998, 'Introduction'.

191 See, e.g., *Daodejing* 18.

192 Cf.: Nisbett 2003, p. 138.

193 *Daodejing* 12.

194 Yang and Sternberg 1997.

195 Takahashi 2000.

196 See, e.g., Boisot and Child 1996.

197 Wu 1972.

198 Fung 1948, p. 12.

199 Hall and Ames 1999, p. 126.

200 *Analects* 12/13.

201 Tsoukas and Cummings 1997, p. 670; for the Aristotelian rhetoric tradition see, e.g., Nisbett 2003; Wang 2005.

202 Tsoukas and Cummings 1997, pp. 665, 666.

203 Linstone and Zhu 2000.

204 Fung 1948, p. 1.

205 Tsoukas and Cummings 1997, p. 664.

206 Yuasa 1987, p. 68.

207 Yang and Sternberg 1997.

208 Nisbett 2003.

209 Statler and Roos 2005.

210 Tsoukas and Cummings 1997.

211 Hall and Ames 1987.

212 Nonaka and Takeuchi 1995, p. 237.

213 March and Olsen 1989.

214 Nisbett 2003, p. 49.

215 Cf.: Wang 2005, p. 3.

216 Wang 2005.

217 Ames and Hall 2001, p. 82.

218 *Sunday Times* 2 January 2011, 'And now we know ...'.

219 See, e.g., Statler and Roos 2005; Tsoukas and Cummings 1997; Wilson and Jarzabkowski 2004.

220 Katz 1950.

221 Labouvie-Vief 1990; Robinson 1990; Takahashi 2000; Yang and Sternberg 1997.

222 We conceive a similarity between our argument here and Chia and Holt's (2008) 'exemplification' style of practice wisdom, albeit they locate their proposal mainly in the context of business education.

223 See, e.g., Bilton and Cummings 2010; Cummings 2002; Flyvbjerg 2001.

224 For the strategy-as-practice agenda, see, e.g., *European Management Review* 2004, Issue 1; *Journal of Management Studies* 2003, Issue 1; *Human Relations* 2007, Issue 1; Jarzabkowski 2005; for the 'pragmatic' claim, see, e.g., Johnson *et al.* 2007.

225 We are grateful to Stephen Cummings who, via personal correspondence, reminds us that 10–15 years ago there was a lot of talk in management studies in the West about *phronesis* but then it died away, and hence that recent events only make our call for a pragmatic turn the more imperative and urgent.

226 Here we refer to Peirce: 'We cannot begin with complete doubt. We must begin with all the prejudices which we actually have when we enter upon the study of philosophy' (cf.: Joas 1996, p. 128).

227 Here we refer to Ferguson's high-profile 2011 book *Civilization: The West and the Rest.*

228 Churchman 1979.

229 For readers interested in more comprehensive comparisons between Confucius, Aristotle and Dewey, these are useful materials: Bernstein 2010; Flyvbjerg 2001; Hall and Ames 1987, 1999; Tan 2003.

References

Achrol, R. S. and Kotler, P. 1999. Marketing in the network economy. *Journal of Marketing* 63 (Special Issue): 146–163

Ackoff, R. L. 1981. *Creating the Corporate Future*. New York: Wiley

Ackoff, R. L. 1996. On learning and the systems that facilitate it. *Reflections* 1: 14–24

Ackoff, R. L. 2003. Russell L. Ackoff: an interview by Robert J. Allio. *Strategy and Leadership* 31 (3): 19–26

Aldrich, H. E. and Ruef, M. 2006. *Organizations Evolving*, 2nd edn. London: Sage

Alexander, T. M. 1995. John Dewey and the roots of democratic imagination. In *Recovering Pragmatism's Voice: The Classical Tradition, Rorty, and the Philosophy of Communication*, L. Langsdorf and A. R. Smith (eds.). Albany: State University of New York Press, pp. 131–154

Alvarez, S. A. and Barney, J. B. 2007. Discovery and creation: alternative theories of entrepreneurial action. *Strategic Entrepreneurship Journal* 1: 11–26

Alvesson, M. 1995. The meaning and meaninglessness of postmodernism: some ironic remarks. *Organization Studies* 16: 1047–1075

Alvesson, M. and Willmott, H. 1996. *Making Sense of Management: A Critical Introduction*. London: Sage

Ames, R. T. and Hall, D. L. 2001. *Focusing the Familiar: A Translation and Philosophical Interpretation of the Zhongyong*. Honolulu, HI: University of Hawaii Press

Ames, R. T. and Hall, D. L. 2003. *Dao De Jing – Making This Life Significant: A Philosophical Translation*. New York: Ballantine Books

Ames, R. T. and Rosemont, H. 1998. *The Analects of Confucius: A Philosophical Translation*. New York: Ballantine Books

Amit, R. and Schoemaker, P. J. H. 1993. Strategic assets and organizational rent. *Strategic Management Journal* 14: 33–46

Andrews, K. R. 1971. *The Concept of Corporate Strategy*. Homewood, IL: Dow Jones-Irwin

Angwin, D., Cummings, S. and Smith, C. 2007. *The Strategy Pathfinder: Core Concepts and Micro-Cases*. Oxford: Blackwell Publishing

Ansoff, H.I. 1965. *Corporate Strategy*. New York: McGraw Hill

Ansoff, H.I. 1988. *The New Corporate Strategy*. New York: Wiley

Ansoff, H.I. 1991. A critique of Henry Mintzberg's design school: reconsidering the basic premise of strategic management. *Strategic Management Journal* 12: 449–461

Aoki, M. 2001. *Toward a Comparative Institutional Analysis*. Cambridge, MA: MIT Press

Archer, M.S. 2000. *Being Human: The Problem of Agency*. Cambridge University Press

Argyris, C. 1999. *On Organizational Learning*. Oxford: Blackwell Publishing

Argyris, C. and Schön, D. 1996. *Organizational Learning II*. Reading, MA: Addison-Wesley

Arthur, W.B. 1989. Competing technologies and lock-in by historical events: the dynamics of allocation under increasing returns. *Economic Journal* 99: 116–131

Arthur, W.B. 1994. *Increasing Returns and Path Dependence in the Economy*. Ann Arbor, MI: University of Michigan Press

Ashby, W.R. 1956. *An Introduction to Cybernetics*. London: Methuen

Astley, G. 1985. Administrative science as socially constructed truth. *Administrative Science Quarterly* 30: 497–513

Astley, G. and Zammuto, R. 1992. Organisation science, managers, and language games. *Organisation Science* 3: 443–513

Augier, M. and Teece, D.J. 2008. Strategy as evolution with design: the foundations of dynamic capabilities and the role of managers in the economic system. *Organization Studies* 29: 1187–1208

Baert, P. 2005. *Philosophy of the Social Sciences: Towards Pragmatism*. Cambridge: Polity

Baker, T. and Nelson, R.E. 2005. Creating something from nothing: resource construction through entrepreneurial *bricolage*. *Administrative Science Quarterly* 50: 329–366

Barley, S.R. 1986. Technology as an occasion for structuring: evidence from observation of CT scanners and the social order of radiology departments. *Administrative Science Quarterly* 31: 78–108

Barnard, C.I. 1938 (reprinted 1968). *The Functions of the Executives*. Cambridge, MA: Harvard University Press

Barnett, W.P. and Burgelman, R.A. 1996. Evolutionary perspectives on strategy. *Strategic Management Journal* 17: 5–19

Barney, J.B. 1990. The debate between traditional management theory and organizational economics: substantive differences or intergroup conflict? *Academy of Management Review* 15: 382–393

Barney, J.B. 1991. Firm resources and sustained competitive advantage. *Journal of Management* 17: 99–120

Barney, J.B. 2002. Strategic management: from informed conversation to academic discipline. *Academy of Management Executive* 16 (2): 53–57

Barney, J.B. 2007. *Gaining and Sustaining Competitive Advantage*, 3rd edn. Upper Saddle River, NJ: Pearson Prentice Hall

Barney, J.B. and Clark, D.N. 2007. *Resource-Based Theory: Creating and Sustaining Competitive Advantage*. Oxford University Press

Bartlett, C.A. and Ghoshal, S. 1994. Changing the role of top management: beyond strategy to purpose. *Harvard Business Review* 72 (November–December): 79–88

Bateson, G. 1972. *Steps to an Ecology of Mind*. New York: Ballantine

Behrman, J.N. and Levin, R.I. 1984. Are business schools doing their job? *Harvard Business Review* 62 (January–February): 140–145

Beinhocker, E.D. 1999. Robust adaptive strategies. *Sloan Management Review* 40 (Spring): 95–106

Bellah, R. 1957. *Tokugawa Religion: The Cultural Roots of Modern Japan*. New York: Free Press

Bellah, R.N., Madsen, R., Sullivan, W.M., Swidler, A. and Tipton, S.M. 1985. *Habits of the Heart: Individualism and Commitment in American Life*. Berkeley, CA: University of California Press

Benedict, R. 1946 (reprinted 2005). *The Chrysanthemum and the Sword: Patterns of Japanese Culture*. Boston, MA: Houghton Mifflin

Bennis, W.G. and O'Toole, J. 2005. How business schools lost their way. *Harvard Business Review* 83 (May): 96–104

Benton, T. and Craib, I. 2001. *Philosophy of Social Science: The Philosophical Foundations of Social Thought*. New York: Palgrave Macmillan

Berger, P.L. and Luckmann, T. 1966. *The Social Construction of Reality*. New York: Doubleday

Berliner, J. 1993. Perestroika and the Chinese model. Mimeo, Brandeis University

Bernstein, R.J. 1983. *Beyond Objectivism and Relativism: Science, Hermeneutics, and Praxis*. Philadelphia, PA: University of Pennsylvania Press

Bernstein, R.J. 1991. *The New Constellation: The Ethical-Political Horizons of Modernity/Postmodernity*. Cambridge: Polity

Bernstein, R.J. 2010. *The Pragmatic Turn*. Cambridge: Polity

Best, M.H. 1990. *The New Competition: Institutions of Industrial Restructuring*. Cambridge: Polity

Best, M.H. 2001. *The New Competitive Advantage: The Renewal of American Industry*. Oxford University Press

Bettis, R.A. 1991. Strategic management and the straitjacket: an editorial essay. *Organisation Science* 2: 315–319

Bijker, W.E., Hughes, T.P. and Pinch, T. 1987. *The Social Construction of Technological Systems.* Cambridge, MA: MIT Press

Bilton, C. and Cummings, S. 2010. *Creative Strategy: Reconnecting Business and Innovation.* Chichester: Wiley

Blair, M.M. 1995. *Ownership and Control: Rethinking Corporate Governance for the Twenty-First Century.* Washington, DC: Brookings Institution

Boisot, M. 1996. Institutionalising the Labour Theory of Value: some obstacles to the reform of state-owned enterprises in China and Vietnam. *Organization Studies* 17: 909–928

Boisot, M. and Child, J. 1988. The iron law of fiefs: bureaucratic failure and the problem of governance in the Chinese economic reforms. *Administrative Science Quarterly* 33: 507–527

Boisot, M. and Child, J. 1996. From fiefs to clans and network capitalism: explaining China's emerging economic order. *Administrative Science Quarterly* 41: 600–628

Boland, R.J. and Tenkasi, R.V. 1995. Perspective making and perspective taking in communities of knowing. *Organisation Science* 6: 350–372

Boulding, K. 1956. General systems theory: the skeleton of science. *Management Science* 2: 197–208

Bourdieu, P. 1998. *Practical Reason: On the Theory of Action.* Cambridge: Polity

Bower, J.L. 1970. *Managing the Resource Allocation Process: A Study of Corporate Planning and Investment.* Boston, MA: Division of Research, Graduate School of Business Administration, Harvard University

Bowman, E.H. 1974. Epistemology, corporate strategy, and academe. *Sloan Management Review* 15 (Winter): 35–50

Bowman, E.H. and Helfat, C.E. 2001. Does corporate strategy matter? *Strategic Management Journal* 22: 1–24

Bowman, E.H. and Hurry, D. 1993. Strategy through the option lens: an integrated view of resource investments and the incremental-choice process. *Academy of Management Review* 18: 760–782

Bremmer, I. 2010. *The End of the Free Market: Who Wins the War Between States and Corporations?* London: Viking

Brown, J.S. and Duguid, P. 2000. Balancing act: how to capture knowledge without killing it. *Harvard Business Review* 78 (May–June): 73–80

Brown, J.S. and Duguid, P. 2001a. Creativity versus structure: a useful tension. *Sloan Management Review* 42 (Summer): 93–94

Brown, J. S. and Duguid, P. 2001b. Knowledge and organisation: a social-practice perspective. *Organisation Science* 12: 198–213

Brown, J. S. and Duguid, P. 2001c. Structure and spontaneity: knowledge and organization. In *Managing Industrial Knowledge*, I. Nonaka and D. Teece (eds.). London: Sage, pp. 44–67

Bruch, H. and Ghoshal, S. 2004. *A Bias for Action*. Boston, MA: Harvard Business School Press

Burgelman, R. A. 1991. Intraorganisational ecology of strategy making and organisational adaptation: theory and field research. *Organisation Science* 2: 239–262

Burgelman, R. A. 1994. Fading memories: a process theory of strategic business exit in dynamic environments. *Administrative Science Quarterly* 39: 24–56

Burrell, G. and Morgan, G. 1979. *Sociological Paradigms and Organisational Analysis*. London: Heinemann

Burt, R. S. 1992. *Structural Holes*. Cambridge, MA: Harvard University Press

Camerer, C. F. 1985. Redirecting research in business policy and strategy. *Strategic Management Journal* 6: 1–15

Carroll, G. R. and Hannan, M. T. (eds.). 1995. *Organizations in Industry: Strategy, Structure and Selection*. Oxford University Press

Cartwright, N. 1999. *The Dappled World: A Study of the Boundaries of Science*. Cambridge University Press

Casson, M. 1993. Cultural determinants of economic performance. *Journal of Comparative Economics* 17: 418–442

Cave, S. 2007. I think therefore I am, I think. *FT Weekend Magazine* 24/25 March

Chakravarthy, B. S. and Doz, Y. 1992. Strategy process research: focusing on corporate self-renewal. *Strategic Management Journal* 13 (Special Issue): 5–14

Chakravarthy, B. S. and White, R. E. 2002. Strategy process: forming, implementing and changing strategies. In *Handbook of Strategy and Management*, A. Pettigrew, H. Thomas and R. Whittington (eds.). London: Sage, pp. 182–205

Chan, W. T. 1963. *A Source Book in Chinese Philosophy*. Princeton University Press

Chandler, A. D. 1962. *Strategy and Structure: Chapters in the History of the American Industrial Enterprise*. Cambridge, MA: Harvard University Press

Chandler, A. D. 1977. *The Visible Hand: The Managerial Revolution in American Business*. Cambridge, MA: Harvard University Press

Chandler, A. D. 1990a. *Scale and Scope: The Dynamics of Industrial Capitalism*. Boston, MA: Harvard Business School Press

Chandler, A. D. 1990b. The enduring logic of industrial success. *Harvard Business Review* 68 (March–April): 130–140

Chen, L. F. 1986. *The Confucian Way: A New and Systematic Study of 'The Four Books'.* London: KPI

Chen, N. 2000. The etymology of *Sheng* (Sage) and its Confucian conception in early China. *Journal of Chinese Philosophy* 27: 409–427

Cheng, C. Y. 1972. Chinese philosophy: a characterisation. In *Invitation to Chinese Philosophy*, A. Naess and A. Hannay (eds.), Scandinavian University Books series. Oslo: Universitetsforlaget, pp. 141–166

Cheng, C. Y. 1997. The origins of Chinese philosophy. In *Companion Encyclopaedia of Asian Philosophy*, B. Carr and I. Mahalingam (eds.). London: Routledge, pp. 493–534

Chesbrough, H. 2007. *Open Business Models: How to Thrive in the New Innovation Landscape.* Boston, MA: Harvard Business School Press

Chia, R. C. H. 2002. Time, duration and simultaneity: rethinking process and change in organisational analysis. *Organization Studies* 23: 863–868

Chia, R. C. H. 2004. Strategy-as-practice: reflections on the research agenda. *European Management Review* 1: 29–34

Chia, R. C. H. and Holt, R. 2006. Strategy as practical coping: a Heideggerian perspective. *Organization Studies* 27: 635–655

Chia, R. C. H. and Holt, R. 2008. The nature of knowledge in business schools. *Academy of Management Learning and Education* 7: 471–486

Chia, R. C. H. and Holt, R. 2009. *Strategy without Design: The Silent Efficacy of Indirect Action.* Cambridge University Press

Chia, R. C. H. and MacKay, R. B. 2007. Post-processual challenges for the emerging strategy-as-practice perspective: discovering strategy in the logic of practice. *Human Relations* 60: 217–242

Chia, R. C. H. and Tsoukas, H. 2003. Everything changes and nothing endures … *Process Studies* 32: 192–224

Child, J. 1972. Organizational structure, environment and performance: the role of strategic choice. *Sociology* 6: 1–22

Chow, G. C. 1997. Challenges of China's economic system for economic theory. *American Economic Review* 87: 321–327

Churchman, C. W. 1971. *The Design of Inquiring Systems.* New York: Basic Books

Churchman, C. W. 1979. *The Systems Approach and Its Enemies.* New York: Basic Books

Clark, P. 1994. Book review: perspectives on the politics of economic reform in China. *The Pacific Review* 7: 457–458

Clegg, S., Carter, C., Kornberger, M. and Schweitzer, J. 2011. *Strategy Theory and Practice.* Los Angeles, CA: Sage

Clegg, S.R. and Ross-Smith, A. 2003. Management education and learning in a postpositivistic world. *Academy of Management Learning and Education* 2: 85–98

Clegg, S.R., Courpasson, D. and Phillips, N. 2006. *Power and Organizations.* London: Sage

Cobb, J.B., Jr. 2007. Person-in-community: Whiteheadian insights into community and institution. *Organization Studies* 28: 567–588

Cohen, W.M. and Levinthal, D.A. 1990. Absorptive capacity: a new perspective on learning and innovation. *Administrative Science Quarterly* 35: 128–152

Coleman, J.S. 1990. *Foundations of Social Theory.* Cambridge, MA: Harvard University Press

Collins, J.C. and Porras, J.I. 1994. *Built to Last: Successful Habits of Visionary Companies.* London: Century Business

Collis, D.J. and Montgomery, C.A. 1995. Competing on resources: strategy in the 1990s. *Harvard Business Review* 73 (July–August): 118–128

Collis, D.J. and Rukstad, M.G. 2008. Can you say what your strategy is? *Harvard Business Review* 86 (April): 82–90

CRF (China Reform Foundation). 2001. 制度的障碍与供给 [*The Obstacle and Supply of Institutions*]. Shanghai: Far East Press (in Chinese)

Crozier, M. and Friedberg, E. 1980. *Actors and Systems: The Politics of Collective Action.* University of Chicago Press

Cui, J.J. 2008. Integrated CRM and VCM to enhance profitability in telecom equipment industry. MBA dissertation, University of Hull Business School

Cummings, S. 2002. *ReCreating Strategy.* London: Sage

Cyert, R.B. and March, J.G. 1963. *A Behavioural Theory of the Firm.* Englewood Cliffs, NJ: Prentice Hall

Daft, R.L. and Lewin, A.Y. 1990. Can organisation studies begin to break out of the normal science straitjacket? An editorial essay. *Organisation Science* 1: 1–9

Day, G.S. 1977. Diagnosing the product portfolio. *Journal of Marketing* 41: 29–38

Deetz, S. 1996. Describing differences in approaches to organisation science: rethinking Burrell and Morgan and their legacy. *Organisation Science* 7: 191–207

de Geus, A. 1988. Planning as learning. *Harvard Business Review* (March–April): 70–74

de Geus, A. 1996. Strategy and learning. *Reflections* 1: 75–81

Dell, M. 1999. *Direct from Dell: Strategies that Revolutionized an Industry.* New York: Harper Business

Dewey, J. 1910 (reprinted 1986). *How We Think*. In *John Dewey: The Later Works*, vol. VIII. Carbondale, IL: Southern Illinois University Press

Dewey, J. 1916. *Democracy and Education: An Introduction to the Philosophy of Education*. New York: Free Press

Dewey, J. 1917 (reprinted 1981). The need for a recovery of philosophy. In *The Philosophy of John Dewey*, J.J. McDermott (ed.). University of Chicago Press, pp. 58–97

Dewey, J. 1920 (reprinted 1948). *Reconstruction in Philosophy*. Boston, MA: Beacon Press

Dewey, J. 1927 (reprinted 1954). *The Public and Its Problem*. Chicago, IL: Swallow Press

Dewey, J. 1930. *The Quest for Certainty: A Study of the Relationship between Knowledge and Action*. London: Allen & Unwin

Dewey, J. 1938a. *Logic: The Theory of Inquiry*. New York: Holt, Rinehart & Winston

Dewey, J. 1938b (reprinted 1998). Creative democracy: the task before us. In *The Essential Dewey: Volume 1 – Pragmatism, Education, Democracy*, L. Hickman and T. Alexander (eds.). Bloomington, IN: Indiana University Press, pp. 340–344

Dewey, J. 1939. *Theory of Valuation*. University of Chicago Press

Dewey, J. 1969–1972. *The Early Works, 1882–1898*, 5 vols., J.A. Boydston (ed.). Carbondale, IL: Southern Illinois University Press

Dewey, J. 1976–1983. *The Middle Works, 1899–1924*, 15 vols., J.A. Boydston (ed.). Carbondale, IL: Southern Illinois University Press

Dewey, J. 1981–1991. *The Later Works, 1925–1953*, 17 vols., J.A. Boydston (ed.). Carbondale, IL: Southern Illinois University Press

de Wit, B. and Meyer, R. 2004. *Strategy: Process, Content, Context*, 3rd edn. London: Thomson Learning

Donaldson, L. 1990a. The ethereal hand: organizational economics and management theory. *Academy of Management Review* 15: 369–381

Donaldson, L. 1990b. A rational basis for criticisms of organizational economics: a reply to Barney. *Academy of Management Review* 15: 394–401

Donaldson, T. and Dunfee, T.W. 1994. Toward a unified conception of business ethics: integrative social contracts theory. *Academy of Management Review* 19: 252–284

Dosi, G., Nelson, R.R. and Winter, S.G. 2000. Introduction. In *The Nature and Dynamics of Organizational Capabilities*, G. Dosi, R.R. Nelson and S.G. Winter (eds.). Oxford University Press, pp. 1–24

Drucker, P.F. 1985 (reprinted 2002). The discipline of innovation. *Harvard Business Review* 80 (August): 95–144

Drucker, P.F. 1993. *Post-Capitalist Society.* New York: Harper Business

Drucker, P.F. 1994. The theory of the business. *Harvard Business Review* 72 (September–October): 95–104

Dyer, W.G. and Wilkins, A.L. 1991. Better stories, not better constructs, to generate better theory: a rejoinder to Eisenhardt. *Academy of Management Review* 16: 613–619

Eccles, R.G. and Nohria, N. 1992. *Beyond the Hype: Rediscovering the Essence of Management.* Boston, MA: Harvard Business School Press

Eisenhardt, K.M. 1989. Building theories from case study research. *Academy of Management Review* 14: 532–551

Elfring, T. and Volberda, H.W. 2001. Schools of thought in strategic management. In *Rethinking Strategy*, H.W. Volberda and T. Elfring (eds.). London: Sage, pp. 1–25

Elster, J. 1983. *Explaining Technical Change.* Cambridge University Press

Emirbayer, M. 1994. Network analysis, culture, and the problem of agency. *American Journal of Sociology* 99: 1411–1454

Emirbayer, M. and Mische, A. 1998. What is agency? *American Journal of Sociology* 103: 962–1023

Eskew, M. 2007. Stick with your vision. *Harvard Business Review* 85 (July–August): 56–57

Evans, K.G. 2000. Reclaiming John Dewey: democracy, inquiry, pragmatism, and public management. *Administration and Society* 32: 308–328

Evans, K.G. 2005. Upgrade or a different animal altogether? Why old pragmatism better informs public management and new pragmatism misses the point. *Administration and Society* 37: 248–255

Evans, P.B. and Wurster, T.S. 1997. Strategy and the new economics of information. *Harvard Business Review* 75 (September–October): 71–82

Fei, X.T. 1947 (1992). *From the Soil: The Foundations of Chinese Society,* G.G. Hamilton and Z. Wang (trans.). Berkeley, CA: University of California Press

Ferguson, N. 2011. *Civilization: The West and the Rest.* London: Allen Lane

Festenstein, M. 1997. *Pragmatism and Political Theory.* Cambridge: Polity

Feyerabend, P. 2011. *The Tyranny of Science.* Cambridge: Polity

Fingarette, H. 1983. The music of humanity in the conversations of Confucius. *Journal of Chinese Philosophy* 10: 331–356

Flew, A. 1979. *A Dictionary of Philosophy,* 2nd edn. New York: St. Martin's Press

Fligstein, N. and Mara-Drita, I. 1996. How to make a market: reflections on the attempts to create a single market in the European Union. *American Journal of Sociology* 102: 1–33

Flood, R. L. 1993. *Beyond TQM*. Chichester: Wiley

Flyvbjerg, B. 2001. *Making Social Science Matter: Why Social Inquiry Fails and How It Can Succeed Again*. Cambridge University Press

Ford, J. D. and Ford, L. W. 1994. Logics of identity, contradiction, and attraction in change. *Academy of Management Review* 19: 756–785

Foss, N. J. 1996. Research in strategy, economics and Michael Porter. *Journal of Management Studies* 33: 1–24

Foss, N. J. 1997. *Resources, Firms and Strategies: A Reader in the Resource-Based Perspectives*. Oxford University Press

Foucault, M. 1990. *The Use of Pleasure: The History of Sexuality*, vol. II. New York: Vintage Books

Foucault, M. 1997. *Essential Works of Foucault 1954–1984*, vol. II. New York: New Press

Fransman, M. 1994. Information, knowledge, vision and theories of the firm. *Industrial and Corporate Change* 3: 713–757

Freeman, R. 2007. Epistemological *bricolage*: how practitioners make sense of learning. *Administration and Society* 39: 476–496

Friedman, M. 2002. *Capitalism and Freedom*, 40th anniversary edn. University of Chicago Press

Friedman, R. L. 2006. Deweyan pragmatism. *William James Studies* 1 (1) (available at http://williamjamesstudies.press.uiuc.edu/1.1/friedman.html)

Friedman, T. L. 2006. *The World Is Flat: The Globalized World in the Twenty-First Century*, 2nd edn. London: Penguin

Fu, C. W. 1997. Daoism in Chinese philosophy. In *Companion Encyclopaedia of Asian Philosophy*, B. Carr and I. Mahalingam (eds.). London: Routledge, pp. 553–574

Fujimoto, T. 1999. *The Evolution of a Manufacturing System at Toyota*. Oxford University Press

Fujiwara, M. 2007. Praise the sword (an interview). *FT Weekend Magazine* 10/11 March 2007

Fukuyama, F. 1995. *Trust: The Social Virtues and the Creation of Prosperity*. London: Hamish Hamilton

Fuller, S. 2007. *New Frontiers in Science and Technology Studies*. Cambridge: Polity

Fung, Y. L. 1948. *A Short History of Chinese Philosophy*. New York: Free Press

Fung, Y.L. 1952. *A History of Chinese Philosophy*, vol. I. Princeton University Press

Fung, Y.L. 1953. *A History of Chinese Philosophy*, vol. II. Princeton University Press

Gabriel, Y. 2002. On paragrammatic uses of organizational theory: a provocation. *Organization Studies* 23: 133–151

Gadamer, H.-G. 1975. *Truth and Method*. London: Sheed & Ward

Gadiesh, O. and Gilbert, J.L. 1998a. Profit pools: a fresh look at strategy. *Harvard Business Review* 76 (May–June): 139–147

Gadiesh, O. and Gilbert, J.L. 1998b. How to map your industry's profit pools. *Harvard Business Review* 76 (May–June): 149–162

Garrison, J. 2000. Pragmatism and public administration. *Administration and Society* 32: 458–477

Garud, R. and Ahlstrom, D. 1997. Researchers' roles in negotiating the institutional fabric of technologies. *The American Behavioural Scientist* 40: 523–538

Garud, R. and Karnøe, P. 2005. Distributed agency and interactive emergence. In *Innovating Strategy Process*, S.W. Floyd, J. Roos, C.D. Jacobs and F.W. Kellermanns (eds.). Oxford: Blackwell Publishing, pp. 88–96

Garud, R. and Rappa, M.A. 1994. A socio-cognitive model of technology evolution: the case of cochlear implants. *Organisation Science* 5: 344–362

Garud, R. and Van de Ven, A.H. 2002. Strategic change process. In *Handbook of Strategy and Management*, A. Pettigrew, H. Thomas and R. Whittington (eds.). London: Sage, pp. 182–205

Gascoigne, N. 2008. *Richard Rorty*. Cambridge: Polity

Ghoshal, S. 2005. Bad management theories are destroying good management practices. *Academy of Management Learning and Education* 4: 75–91

Ghoshal, S. and Moran, P. 1996. Bad for practice: a critique of the transaction cost theory. *Academy of Management Review* 21: 13–47

Ghoshal, S., Bartlett, C.A. and Moran, P. 1999. A new manifesto for management. *Sloan Management Review* 40 (Spring): 9–20

Giddens, A. 1979. *Central Problems in Social Theory: Action, Structure and Contradiction in Social Analysis*. London: Macmillan

Giddens, A. 1982. *Profiles and Critiques in Social Theory*. Berkeley, CA: University of California Press

Giddens, A. 1984. *The Constitution of Society*. Berkeley, CA: University of California Press

Glasmeier, A. 1991. Technological discontinuities and flexible production networks: the case of Switzerland and the world watch industry. *Research Policy* 20: 469–485

Gold, A. R., Leibowitz, G. and Perkins, A. 2001. A computer legend in the making: an interview with Liu Chuanzhi. *The McKinsey Quarterly* 3: 73–83

Gopinath, C. and Hoffman, R. 1995. The relevance of strategy research: practitioner and academic viewpoints. *Journal of Management Studies* 32: 576–594

Gordon, R. and Howell, J. 1959. *Higher Education for Business*. New York: Columbia University Press

Graham, A. C. 1989. *Disputes of the Tao*. La Salle, IL: Open Court

Granovetter, M. 1985. Economic action and social structure: the problem of embeddedness. *American Journal of Sociology* 91: 481–510

Grant, R. M. 2002. Corporate strategy: managing scope and strategy content. In *Handbook of Strategy and Management*, A. Pettigrew, H. Thomas and R. Whittington (eds.). London: Sage, pp. 72–97

Grove, A. S. 1996. *Only the Paranoid Survive: How to Exploit the Crisis Points that Challenge Every Company and Career*. New York: Currency Doubleday

Guillén, M. F. 1994. *Models of Management: Work, Authority, and Organization in a Comparative Perspective*. University of Chicago Press

Habermas, J. 2003. *Truth and Justification*. Cambridge, MA: MIT Press

Hacking, I. 1999. *The Social Construction of What?* Cambridge, MA: Harvard University Press

Hafsi, T. and Thomas, H. 2005. Reflections on the field of strategy. In *Innovating Strategy Process*, S. W. Floyd, J. Roos, C. D. Jacobs and F. W. Kellermanns (eds.). Oxford: Blackwell Publishing, pp. 239–246

Hagel, J. 2002. Leveraged growth: expanding sales without sacrificing profits. *Harvard Business Review* 80 (October): 69–77

Hagel, J. and Brown, J. S. 2005. *The Only Sustainable Edge: Why Business Strategy Depends on Productive Friction and Dynamic Specialization*. Boston, MA: Harvard Business School Press

Hagel, J., Brown, J. S. and Davison, L. 2010. *The Power of Pull: How Small Moves, Smartly Made, Can Set Big Things in Motion*. New York: Basic Books

Hall, D. L. and Ames, R. T. 1987. *Thinking through Confucius*. Albany: State University of New York Press

Hall, D. L. and Ames, R. T. 1999. *The Democracy of the Dead: Dewey, Confucius, and the Hope For Democracy in China*. Chicago, IL: Open Court

Halper, S. 2010. *The Beijing Consensus: How China's Authoritarian Model Will Dominate the Twenty-First Century*. New York: Basic Books

Hamel, G. 2009. Moon shots for management: what great challenges must we tackle to reinvent management and make it more relevant to a volatile world? *Harvard Business Review* (February): 91–98

Hamel, G. and Prahalad, C.K. 1989. Strategic intent. *Harvard Business Review* 67 (May–June): 63–76

Hamel, G. and Prahalad, C.K. 1994. *Competing for the Future*. Boston, MA: Harvard Business School Press

Handy, C. 2002. What's a business for? *Harvard Business Review* 80 (December): 49–55

Hannan, M.T. and Freeman, J.H. 1989. *Organizational Ecology*. Boston, MA: Harvard University Press

Hardin, G. 1968. The tragedy of the commons. *Science* 162: 1243–1248

Hardy, C. 1995. Managing strategic change: power, paralysis and perspective. In *Advances in Strategic Management* vol. 12B, P. Shrivastava and C. Stubbart (eds.). London: JAI Press, pp. 3–30

Hargadon, A.B. and Douglas, Y. 2001. When innovations meet institutions: Edison and the design of the electric light. *Administrative Science Quarterly* 46: 476–501

Hayek, F.A. 1945. The use of knowledge in society. *American Economic Review* 35: 519–530

Hayek, F.A. 1989. The pretence of knowledge. *American Economic Review* 79 (6): 3–7

Hayes, R.H. 2007. 'Managing our way ...': a retrospective. *Harvard Business Review* 85 (July–August): 141

Hayes, R.H. and Abernathy, W.J. 1980 (reprinted 2007). Managing our way to economic decline. *Harvard Business Review* 85 (July–August): 138–149

Hedley, B. 1977. Strategy and the business portfolio. *Long Range Planning* 10 (February): 9–15

Hildebrand, D.L. 2005. Pragmatism, neopragmatism, and public administration. *Administration and Society* 37: 345–359

Hirsch, P.M., Friedman, R. and Mitchell, P.K. 1990. Collaboration or paradigm shift? Caveat emptor: the risk of romance with economic models for strategy and policy research. *Organisation Science* 1: 87–97

Hirschmeier, J. and Yui, T. 1975. *The Development of Japanese Business, 1600–1973*. London: Allen & Unwin

Hoch, C. 2006. What can Rorty teach an old pragmatist doing public administration or planning? *Administration and Society* 38: 389–398

Holliday, S.G. and Chandler, M.J. 1986. *Wisdom: Explorations in Adult Competence*. Basel: Karger

Huff, A.S. 2006. Citigroup's John Reed and Stanford's James March on management research and practice (Academy Addresses edited by Anne Sigismund Huff). *Academy of Management Executive* 14: 52–64

Hughes, T. P. 1979. The electrification of America: the system builder. *Technology and Culture* 20: 124–161

Hughes, T. P. 1983. *Networks of Power: Electrification in Western Society, 1880–1930*. Baltimore, Maryland: Johns Hopkins University Press

Hurst, D. K. 1995. *Crisis and Renewal: Meeting the Challenge of Organizational Change*. Boston, MA: Harvard Business School Press

Imai, K., Nonaka, I. and Takeuchi, H. 1985. Managing the new product development process: how Japanese companies learn and unlearn. In *The Uneasy Alliance: Managing the Productivity-Technology Dilemma*, K. B. Clark, R. H. Hayes and C. Lorenz (eds.). Boston, MA: Harvard Business School Press, pp. 337–381

Jacobs, C. and Statler, M. 2005. Strategy creation as serious play. In *Innovating Strategy Process*, S. W. Floyd, J. Roos, C. D. Jacobs and F. W. Kellermanns (eds.). Oxford: Blackwell Publishing, pp. 47–55

Jacobson, R. 1992. The 'Austrian' School of strategy. *Academy of Management Review* 17: 782–807

James, W. 1907 (reprinted 1975). *Pragmatism: A New Name for Some Old Ways of Thinking*. Cambridge, MA: Harvard University Press

James, W. 1909 (reprinted 1977). *A Pluralist Universe*. Cambridge, MA: Harvard University Press

Janis, I. L. 1972. *Victims of Groupthink*. Boston, MA: Houghton-Mifflin

Jarzabkowski, P. 2005. *Strategy as Practice: An Activity-based Approach*. London: Sage

Jensen, M. C. 1998. *Foundations of Organizational Strategy*. Cambridge, MA: Harvard University Press

Jensen, M. C. 2000. *A Theory of the Firm: Governance, Residual Claims, and Organizational Forms*. Cambridge, MA: Harvard University Press

Joas, H. 1996. *The Creativity of Action*. Cambridge: Polity

Johnson, G., Langley, A., Melin, L. and Whittington, R. 2007. *Strategy as Practice: Research Directions and Resources*. Cambridge University Press

Jones, E. L. 2001. A long-term appraisal of country risk. In *Growth Without Miracles*, R. Garnaut and Y. Huang (eds.). Oxford University Press, pp. 77–87

Jung, H. Y. 1987. Heidegger's way with Sinitic thinking. In *Heidegger and Asian Thought*, P. Graham (ed.). Honolulu, HI: University of Hawaii Press, pp. 217–244

Kaku, R. 1997. The path of *kyosei*. *Harvard Business Review* 75 (July–August): 55–63

Kaletsky, A. 2010. *Capitalism 4.0: The Birth of A New Economy*. London: Bloomsbury

Kaplan, R. S. and Norton, D. P. 1992. The balanced scorecard: measures that drive performance. *Harvard Business Review* 70 (July–August): 172–180

Katz, J. 1950. *The Philosophy of Plotinus.* New York: Appleton-Century-Crofts

Kay, J. 1993. *Foundations of Corporate Success.* Oxford University Press

Kay, J. 1997. The tortoise and the hare: a fable for senior executives. *Financial Times* 5 September

Kay, J. 1998. What is strategy? *Financial Times* 5 August

Keene, D. 1967. *Essays in Idleness: The Tsurezuregusa of Kenko.* New York: Columbia University Press

Kelliher, D. 1992. *Peasant Power in China: The Era of Rural Reform, 1979–1989.* New Haven, CT: Yale University Press

Khanna, T. and Palepu, K. 1997. Why focused strategies may be wrong for emerging markets. *Harvard Business Review* 85 (July–August): 41–50

Kiechel, W. 2010. *The Lords of Strategy: The Secret Intellectual History of the New Corporate World.* Boston, MA: Harvard Business School Press

Kikawada, K. and Holtshouse, D. 2001. The knowledge perspective in the Xerox Group. In *Managing Industrial Knowledge,* I. Nonaka and D. Teece (eds.). London: Sage, pp. 283–314

Kim, W. C. and Mauborgne, R. 1999. Strategy, value innovation, and the knowledge economy. *Sloan Management Review* 40 (Spring): 41–54

Kim, W. C. and Mauborgne, R. 2000. Knowing a winning business idea when you see one. *Harvard Business Review* 78 (September–October): 129–141

Kim, W. C. and Mauborgne, R. 2004. Blue ocean strategy. *Harvard Business Review* 82 (October): 76–84

Kim, W. C. and Mauborgne, R. 2005. *Blue Ocean Strategy: How to Create Uncontested Market Space and Make the Competition Irrelevant.* Boston, MA: Harvard Business School Press

Knight, F. H. 1921 (reprinted 1971). *Risk, Uncertainty and Profit.* University of Chicago Press

Knights, D. and Morgan, G. 1991. Corporate strategy, organizations, and subjectivity: a critique. *Organization Studies* 12: 251–273

Kotter, J. P. 1995. Leading change: why transformation efforts fail. *Harvard Business Review* 73 (March–April): 59–67

Kotter, J. P. and Schlesinger, L. A. 1979 (reprinted 2008). Choosing strategies for change. *Harvard Business Review* 86 (July–August): 130–139

Kramer, R. M. and Tyler, T. R. (eds.) 1996. *Trust in Organizations.* London: Sage

Krass, P. 2003. *Carnegie.* Chichester: John Wiley

Kuhn, T. S. 1970. *The Structure of Scientific Revolution,* 2nd edn. University of Chicago Press

Labouvie-Vief, G. 1990. Wisdom as integrated thought: historical and developmental perspectives. In *Wisdom: Its Nature, Origins, and Development*, R.J. Sternberg (ed.). Cambridge University Press, pp. 52–83

Lanzara, G.F. 1999. Between transient constructs and persistent structures: designing systems in action. *Journal of Strategic Information Systems* 8: 331–349

Latour, B. 1993. *We Have Never Been Modern*. Cambridge, MA: Harvard University Press

Latour, B. 2005. *Reassembling the Social: An Introduction to Actor-Network-Theory*. Oxford University Press

Law, J. 2004. *After Method: Mess in Social Science Research*. London: Routledge

Law, J. and Hassard, J. 1999. *Actor Network Theory and After*. Oxford: Blackwell Publishing

Lawrence, P.R. and Lorsch, J.W. 1967. *Organization and Environment: Managing Differentiation and Integration*. Boston, MA: Graduate School of Business Administration, Harvard University

Lazonick, W. 1991. *Business Organization and the Myth of the Market Economy*. Cambridge University Press

Leana, C.R. and Barry, B. 2000. Stability and change as simultaneous experiences in organizational life. *Academy of Management Review* 25: 753–759

Leavitt, H.J. 1989. Educating our MBAs: on teaching what we haven't taught. *California Management Review* 31 (Spring): 38–50

Leavitt, H.J. 2003. Why hierarchies thrive. *Harvard Business Review* 81 (March): 96–102

Leonard-Barton, D. 1992. Core capabilities and core rigidities: a paradox in managing new product development. *Strategic Management Journal* 13: 111–125

Lévi-Strauss, C. 1966. *The Savage Mind*. Oxford University Press

Levitt, B. and March, J.G. 1988. Organizational learning. *Annual Review of Sociology* 14: 319–340

Levitt, T. 1963 (reprinted 2002). Creativity is not enough. *Harvard Business Review* 80 (August): 137–144

Levy, D., Alvesson, M. and Willmott, H. 2003. Critical approaches to strategic management. In *Studying Management Critically*, M. Alvesson and H. Willmott (eds.). London: Sage, pp. 92–110

Lin, J.Y. 1992. Rural reforms and agricultural growth in China. *American Economic Review* 82: 34–51

Lin, J.Y., Fang, C. and Zhou, L. 2003. *The China Miracle: Development Strategy and Economic Reform*. Hong Kong: Chinese University Press

Lindblom, C.E. 1959. The science of 'muddling through'. *Public Administration Review* 19 (2): 79–88

Ling, Z.J. 2005. 联想风云 [*The Lenovo Affair*]. Beijing: CITIC Publishing House (in Chinese)

Ling, Z.J. 2006. *The Lenovo Affair: The Growth of China's Computer Giant and Its Takeover of IBM-PC*, M. Avery (trans.). Singapore: John Wiley & Sons (Asia) Pte. Ltd

Linstone, H. and Zhu, Z. 2000. Towards synergy in multiperspective management: an American-Chinese case. *Human Systems Management* 19: 25–37

Liu, C.Z. 2007. Lenovo: an example of globalization of Chinese enterprises. *Journal of International Business Studies* 38: 573–577

Liu, S. and Avery, M. 2009. *Alibaba: The Inside Story Behind Jack Ma and the Creation of the World's Biggest Online Marketplace*. New York: Collins Business

Locke, R.R. 1996. *The Collapse of the American Management Mystique*. Oxford University Press

Lovas, B. and Ghoshal, S. 2000. Strategy as guided evolution. *Strategic Management Journal* 21: 875–896

Lovejoy, A.O. 1908. The thirteen pragmatisms. *Journal of Philosophy and Scientific Methods* 5: 5–39

Luehrman, T.A. 1998. Strategy as a portfolio of real options. *Harvard Business Review* 76 (September–October): 89–99

McClelland, D.C. 1961. *The Achieving Society*. New York: Van Nostrand Reinhold

McCulloch, W.S. 1970. *Embodiments of Mind*. Cambridge, MA: MIT Press

McGahan, A.M. and Porter, M.E. 1997. How much does industry matter, really? *Strategic Management Journal* 18 (Summer Special Issue): 15–30

McGuire, P., Granovetter, M. and Schwartz, M. 1993. Thomas Edison and the social construction of the early electricity industry in America. In *Explorations in Economic Sociology*, R. Swedberg (ed.). New York: Russell Sage Foundation, pp. 213–246

MacIntyre, A.E. 1981. *After Virtue: A Study of Moral Theory*. London: Duckworth

McKinley, W. and Scherer, A.G. 2000. Some unanticipated consequences of organizational restructuring. *Academy of Management Review* 25: 735–752

Magretta, J. 1998. Fast, global, and entrepreneurial: supply chain management, Hong Kong style – an interview with Victor Fung. *Harvard Business Review* 76 (September–October): 103–114

Mahoney, J.T. 1993. Strategic management and determinism: sustaining the conversation. *Journal of Management Studies* 30: 173–191

Mahoney, J. T. 2005. *Economic Foundations of Strategy.* Thousand Oaks, CA: Sage

Mair, A. 1999. Learning from Honda. *Journal of Management Studies* 36: 25–44

March, J. G. 1988. *Decisions and Organizations.* Oxford: Basil Blackwell

March, J. G. and Olsen, J. P. 1989. *Rediscovering Institutions: The Organizational Basis of Politics.* New York: Free Press

March, J. G. and Simon, H. A. 1958. *Organizations.* New York: John Wiley and Sons

Marchetti, G. 2003. Interview with Richard Rorty. *Philosophy Now* 43 (October–November): 22–25

Marcuse, H. 1964. *One-Dimensional Man: Studies in the Ideology of Advanced Industrial Society.* Boston, MA: Beacon Press

Markides, C. C. 1999. In search of strategy. *Sloan Management Review* 40 (Spring): 6–7

Maturana, H. R. and Varela, F. J. 1980. *Autopoiesis and Cognition: The Realization of the Living.* London: Reidel

Mayo, E. 1945. *The Social Problems of an Industrial Civilization.* Boston, MA: Graduate School of Business Administration, Harvard University

Mead, G. H. 1934. *Mind, Self and Society.* Chicago University Press

Merton, R. K. 1957. *Social Theory and Social Structure,* 2nd edn. Glencoe, IL: Free Press

Merton, R. K. 1982. *Social Research and the Practicing Professions.* Cambridge, MA: Abc Books

Miles, R. E. and Snow, C. C. 1978. *Organizational Strategy, Structure and Process.* New York: McGraw-Hill

Miller, H. T. 2004. Why old pragmatism needs an upgrade. *Administration and Society* 36: 243–249

Miller, H. T. 2005. Residues of foundationalism in classic pragmatism. *Administration and Society* 37: 360–374

Mintzberg, H. 1987. Crafting strategy. *Harvard Business Review* 63 (July–August): 66–75

Mintzberg, H. 1990. The design school: reconsidering the basic premises of strategic management. *Strategic Management Journal* 11: 171–195

Mintzberg, H. 1991. Learning 1, planning 0: reply to Igor Ansoff. *Strategic Management Journal* 12: 463–466

Mintzberg, H. 1994a. The fall and rise of strategic planning. *Harvard Business Review* 72 (January–February): 107–114

Mintzberg, H. 1994b. *The Rise and Fall of Strategic Planning: Reconceiving Roles for Planning, Plans, and Planners.* New York: Free Press

Mintzberg, H. 2001. Thoughts on schools. In *Rethinking Strategy,* H. W. Volberda and T. Elfring (eds.). London: Sage, pp. 41–42

Mintzberg, H. 2003. Five Ps for strategy. In *The Strategy Process: Concepts, Contexts, Cases*, Global 4th edn., H. Mintzberg, J. Lampel, J.B. Quinn and S. Ghoshal (eds.). Harlow: Pearson Education, pp. 3–9

Mintzberg, H. 2004. *Managers not MBAs*. London: Prentice Hall

Mintzberg, H. 2005. Introduction – strategy for fun. In *Strategy Bites Back*, H. Mintzberg, B. Ahlstrand and J. Lampel (eds.). Harlow: FT Prentice Hall, pp. 1–11

Mintzberg, H. 2007. Opinion: productivity is killing American enterprise. *Harvard Business Review* 85 (July–August): 25

Mintzberg, H. 2009. *Tracking Strategies ... Toward a General Theory*. Oxford University Press

Mintzberg, H. and Waters, J.A. 1985. Of strategies, deliberate and emergent. *Strategic Management Journal* 6: 257–272

Mintzberg, H., Ahlstrand, B. and Lampel, J. 2001. Researching configuration. In *Rethinking Strategy*, H.W. Volberda and T. Elfring (eds.). London: Sage, pp. 198–211

Mitroff, I.I. and Linstone, H.A. 1993. *Unbounded Mind: Breaking the Chains of Traditional Business Thinking*. Oxford University Press

Monks, R.A.G. and Minow, N. 2004. *Corporate Governance*, 3rd edn. Oxford: Blackwell Business

Montgomery, C.A., Wernerfelt, B. and Balakrishnan, S. 1989. Strategy content and the research process: a critique and commentary. *Strategic Management Journal* 10: 189–197

Morita, A. 1986. *Made in Japan*. Glasgow: William Collins

Mosakowski, E. and Earley, P.C. 2000. A selective review of time assumptions in strategy research. *Academy of Management Review* 25: 796–812

Mounce, H.O. 1997. *The Two Pragmatisms*. London: Routledge

Nahapiet, J. and Ghoshal, S. 1998. Social capital, intellectual capital, and the organizational advantage. *Academy of Management Review* 23: 242–266

Nair, C. 2011. *Consumptionomics: Asia's Role in Reshaping Capitalism and Saving the Planet*. Oxford: Infinite Ideas

Naisbitt, J. 1994. *Global Paradox*. New York: Avon

Nakamura, Y. 1967. *Tetsugaku Nyumon* [*Introduction to Philosophy*]. Tokyo: Chuo Koronsha (in Japanese)

Naughton, B. 1995. *Growing Out of the Plan: Chinese Economic Reform 1978–1993*. Cambridge University Press

Nee, V. 1986. Peasant household economy and decollectivization in China. *Journal of Asian and African Studies* 21: 185–203

Nee, V. 1992. Organizational dynamics of market transition: hybrid forms, property rights, and mixed economy in China. *Administrative Science Quarterly* 37: 1–27

Nee, V. 1996. The emergence of a market society: changing mechanisms of stratification in China. *American Journal of Sociology* 101: 908–949

Needham, J. 1956. *Science and Civilisation in China*, vol. 2. Cambridge University Press

Nelson, R.R. and Winter, S.G. 1982. *An Evolutionary Theory of Economic Change*. Cambridge, MA: Harvard University Press

Ng, D. 2000. Succession in the 'bamboo network'. In *Mastering entrepreneurship*, S. Birley and D.F. Muzyka (eds.). London: Prentice Hall, pp. 200–204

Nisbett, R.E. 2003. *The Geography of Thought: How Asians and Westerners Think Differently and Why*. London: Nicholas Brealey Publishing

Nitobe, I. 1899. *Bushido: The Soul of Japan*. Philadelphia, PA: Leeds & Biddle

Nohria, N. and Berkley, J.D. 1994. Whatever happened to the take-charge manager? *Harvard Business Review* 72 (July–August): 128–137

Nohria, N. and Ghoshal, S. 1997. *The Differentiated Network: Organizing Multinational Corporations for Value Creation*. San Francisco, CA: Jossey-Bass Publishers

Nonaka, I. 1991. The knowledge-creating company. *Harvard Business Review* 69 (November–December): 96–104

Nonaka, I. 1994. A dynamic theory of organisational knowledge creation. *Organisation Science* 5: 14–37

Nonaka, I. and Konno, N. 1998. The concept of '*Ba*': building a foundation for knowledge creation. *California Management Review* 40 (Spring): 40–54

Nonaka, I. and Takeuchi, H. 1995. *The Knowledge-Creating Company: How Japanese Companies Create the Dynamics of Innovation*. Oxford University Press

Nonaka, I. and Toyama, R. 2007. Strategic management as distributed practical wisdom (*phronesis*). *Industrial and Corporate Change* 16: 371–394

Nonaka, I. and von Krogh, G. 2009. Tacit knowledge and knowledge conversation: controversy and advancement in organisational knowledge creation theory. *Organisation Science* 20: 635–652

Nonaka, I., Toyama, R. and Hirata, T. 2008. *Managing Flow: A Process Theory of the Knowledge-Based Firm*. New York: Palgrave Macmillan

Nonaka, I., von Krogh, G. and Voelpel, S.C. 2006. Organizational knowledge creation theory: evolutionary paths and future advances. *Organization Studies* 27: 1179–1208

North, D.C. 1990. *Institutions, Institutional Change and Economic Performance: Political Economy of Institutions and Decisions.* Cambridge University Press

Nye, J.S. 1991. *Bound to Lead: The Changing Nature of American Power.* New York: Basic Books

Nye, J.S. 2004. *Soft Power: The Means to Success in World Politics.* New York: Public Affairs

Ohmae, K. 1982. *The Mind of the Strategist: The Art of Japanese Business.* New York: McGraw-Hill

Ohmae, K. 1988. Getting back to strategy. *Harvard Business Review* 66 (November–December): 149–156

Ormerod, R. 2002. Should critical realism really be critical for OR? A comment on Mingers (2000): the contribution of critical realism as an underpinning philosophy for OR/MS and systems. *Journal of the Operational Research Society* 53: 347–351

Ormerod, R. 2006. The history and ideas of pragmatism. *Journal of the Operational Research Society* 57: 892–909

Orlikowski, W.J. 1992. The duality of technology: rethinking the concept of technology in organisations. *Organisation Science* 3: 398–427

Orlikowski, W.J. 2000. Using technology and constituting structures: a practice lens for studying technology in organisations. *Organisation Science* 11: 404–428

Orlikowski, W.J. 2002. Knowing in practice: enacting a collective capability in distributed organising. *Organisation Science* 13: 249–273

Orr, J. 1990. Sharing knowledge, celebrating identity: war stories and community memory in a service culture. In *Collective Remembering: Memory in Society*, D.S. Middleton and D. Edwards (eds.). Beverley Hills, CA: Sage, pp. 169–189

O'Reilly, C.A. and Tushman, M.L. 2004. The ambidextrous organization. *Harvard Business Review* 82 (April): 74–81

O'Sullivan, M.A. 2000. *Contests for Corporate Control: Corporate Governance and Economic Performance in the United States and Germany.* Oxford University Press

Ouchi, W.G. 1980. Markets, bureaucracies and clans. *Administrative Science Quarterly* 25: 129–141

Outhwaite, W. 2009. *Habermas*, 2nd edn. Cambridge: Polity

Palmer, I. and Hardy, C. 2000. *Thinking about Management.* London: Sage

Pascale, R.T. 1984. Perspectives on strategy: the real story behind Honda's success. *California Management Review* 26 (Spring): 47–72

Pascale, R.T. 1996. The Honda effect. *California Management Review* 38 (Summer): 80–91

Pascale, R.T. and Rohlen, T.P. 1983. The Mazda turnaround. *Journal of Japanese Studies* 9: 219–263

Passer, H. 1953. *The Electrical Manufacturers, 1875–1900: A Study of Competition, Entrepreneurship, Technical Change, and Economic Growth.* Cambridge, MA: Harvard University Press

Penrose, E.T. 1959. *The Theory of the Growth of the Firm.* Oxford University Press

Pepper, S. 1942. *World Hypotheses.* Berkeley, CA: University of California Press

Perotti, E.C., Sun, L. and Zou, L. 1999. State-owned versus township and village enterprises in China. *Comparative Economic Studies* 16: 151–179

Perrow, C. 1984. *Normal Accidents: Living with High-Risk Technology.* Princeton University Press

Perrow, C. 1986. *Complex Organizations: A Critical Essay,* 3rd edn. Glenview, IL: Scott, Foresman

Peters, T.J. and Waterman, R.H. 1982. *In Search of Excellence: Lessons from America's Best-Run Companies.* New York: HarperCollins Publishers

Pettigrew, A.M. 1977. Strategy formulation as a political process. *International Studies of Management and Organisation* 7 (2): 78–87

Pettigrew, A.M. 1985. *The Awakening Giant: Continuity and Change in ICI.* Oxford: Blackwell

Pettigrew, A.M., Thomas, H. and Whittington, R. 2002. Strategic management: the strengths and limitations of a field. In *Handbook of Strategy and Management,* A.M. Pettigrew, H. Thomas and R. Whittington (eds.). London: Sage, pp. 3–30

Pfeffer, J. 1981. *Power in Organizations.* Marshfield, MA: Pitman

Pfeffer, J. 1982. *Organizations and Organization Theory.* Marshfield, MA: Pitman

Pfeffer, J. and Fong, C.T. 2002. The end of business school? Less success than meets the eye. *Academy of Management Learning and Education* 1: 78–95

Pfeffer, J. and Salancik, G.R. 1978. *The External Control of Organizations.* New York: Harper & Row

Pfeffer, J. and Sutton, R.I. 2000. *The Knowing-Doing Gap.* Boston, MA: Harvard Business School Press

Pierson, R.C. 1959. *The Education of American Businessmen.* New York: McGraw-Hill

Pihlström, S. 2007. Metaphysics with a human face: William James and the Prospects of pragmatist metaphysics. *William James Studies* 2 (1) (available at http://williamjamesstudies.press.uiuc.edu/2.1/pihlstrom.html)

Pitelis, C.N. and Teece, D.J. 2009. The (new) nature and essence of the firm. *European Management Review* 6: 5–15

Pondy, L.R. and Mitroff, I.I. 1979. Beyond open system models of organisation. In *Research in Organisational Behavior*, vol. I, B.M. Staw (ed.). Greenwich, CT: JAI Press, pp. 3–39

Porac, J.F. and Thomas, H. 2002. Managing cognition and strategy: issues, trends and future directions. In *Handbook of Strategy and Management*, A.M. Pettigrew, H. Thomas and R. Whittington (eds.). London: Sage, pp. 165–181

Porter, L.W. and McKibbin, L.E. 1988. *Management Education and Development: Drift or Thrust into the 21st Century*. New York: McGraw-Hill

Porter, M.E. 1980. *Competitive Strategy: Techniques for Analysing Industries and Competition*. New York: Free Press

Porter, M.E. 1985. *Competitive Advantage: Creating and Sustaining Superior Performance*. New York: Free Press

Porter, M.E. 1990. *The Competitive Advantage of Nations*. New York: Free Press

Porter, M.E. 1996. What is strategy? *Harvard Business Review* 74 (November–December): 61–78

Porter, M.E. 2002. An interview with Michael Porter – by Nicholas Argyres and Anita M. McGahan. *Academy of Management Executive* 15 (2): 43–52

Porter, M.E. and Kramer, M.R. 1999. Philanthropy's new agenda: creating value. *Harvard Business Review* 77 (November–December): 121–130

Porter, M.E. and Kramer, M.R. 2002. The competitive advantage of corporate philanthropy. *Harvard Business Review* 80 (December): 57–68

Porter, M.E. and Kramer, M.R. 2006. Strategy and society. *Harvard Business Review* 84 (December): 78–92

Porter, M.E. and van der Linde, C. 1995. Green and competitive: ending the stalemate. *Harvard Business Review* 73 (September–October): 120–134

Powell, T.C. 2001. Competitive advantage: logical and philosophical considerations. *Strategic Management Journal* 22: 875–888

Powell, T.C. 2002. Research notes and commentaries: the philosophy of strategy. *Strategic Management Journal* 23: 873–880

Powell, T.C. 2003. Research notes and commentaries: strategy without ontology. *Strategic Management Journal* 24: 285–291

Powell, W.W. and DiMaggio, P.J. 1991. *New Institutionalism in Organizational Analysis*. University of Chicago Press

Prybyla, J.S. 1986. Mainland China and Hungary: to market, to market. Paper presented at the Fifteenth Sino-American Conference on Mainland China. Institute of International Relations, National Chengchi University, Taipei, 8–14 June

Putnam, H. 1981. *Reason, Truth and History*. Cambridge University Press

Putnam, H. 1987. *The Many Faces of Realism*. La Salle, IL: Open Court

Putnam, H. 1990. *Realism with a Human Face*, J. Conant (trans.). Cambridge, MA: Harvard University Press

Putnam, H. 1995. *Pragmatism: An Open Question*. Oxford: Blackwell

Putnam, H. 2004. *Ethics without Ontology*. Cambridge, MA: Harvard University Press

Putnam, R.D. 1995. Bowling alone: America's declining social capital. *Journal of Democracy* 6: 65–78

Putterman, L. 1997. On the past and future of China's township and village-owned enterprises. *World Development* 25: 1639–1655

Qian, Y. 1999. The process of China's market transition (1978–98): the evolutionary, historical, and comparative perspectives. Paper presented at the *Journal of Institutional and Theoretical Economics* symposium on 'Big-Bang Transformation of Economic Systems as a Challenge to New Institutional Economics', Wallerfangen/Saar, Germany, 9–11 June

Qian, Y. and Roland, G. 1998. Federalism and the soft budget constraint. *American Economic Review* 98: 1143–1162

Qin, H. 2002. 转型经济的比较研究 [A comparative study on transitional economies]. *Beijing University Business Review*, Issue 50 (in Chinese)

Quinn, J.B. 1980. *Strategies for Change: Logical Incrementalism*. Homewood, IL: Irwin

Quinn, J.B. 2003. Honda Motor Company 1994. In *The Strategy Process: Concepts, Contexts, Cases*, Global 4th edn., H. Mintzberg, J. Lampel, J.B. Quinn and S. Ghoshal (eds.). Harlow: Pearson Education, pp. 200–216 (Case Section)

Quinn, R. and Cameron, K. (eds.) 1988. *Paradox and Transformation: Toward a Theory of Change in Organization and Management*. Cambridge, MA: Ballinger Publishing

Raby, G. 2001. The 'neither this nor that' economy. In *Growth without Miracles*, R. Garnaut and Y. Huang (eds.). Oxford University Press, pp. 19–35

Rajan, R.D. 2010. *Fault Lines: How Hidden Fractures Still Threaten the World Economy*. Princeton University Press

Redding, S. G. 1990. *The Spirit of Chinese Capitalism*. Berlin: de Gruyter

Regnér, P. 2005. The pre-history of strategy process. In *Innovating Strategy Process*, S. W. Floyd, J. Roos, C. D. Jacobs and F. W. Kellermanns (eds.). Oxford: Blackwell Publishing, pp. 23–32

Rescher, N. 1996. *Process Metaphysics*. Albany, NY: State University of New York Press

Rescher, N. 2000. *Realistic Pragmatism: An Introduction to Pragmatic Philosophy*. Albany, NY: State University of New York Press

Rescher, N. 2003. *Epistemology: On the Scope and Limits of Knowledge*. Albany, NY: State University of New York Press

Rescher, N. 2005. Pragmatism at the crossroads. *Transactions of the Charles S. Peirce Society* 16: 355–365

Ricardo, D. 1817 (reprinted 1966). *Principles of Political Economy and Taxation*. London: John Murray

Ritzer, G. 1999. *Enchanting a Disenchanted World: Revolutionizing the Means of Consumption*. Thousand Oaks, CA: Pine Forge Press

Roberts, J. 2004. *The Modern Firm: Organizational Design for Performance and Growth*. Oxford University Press

Robinson, D. N. 1990. Wisdom through the ages. In *Wisdom: Its Nature, Origins, and Development*, R. J. Sternberg (ed.). Cambridge University Press, pp. 13–24

Roethlisberger, F. J. and Dickson, W. J. 1939. *Management and the Worker*. Cambridge, MA: Harvard University Press

Rorty, R. 1979. *Philosophy and the Mirror of Nature*. Princeton University Press

Rorty, R. 1982. *Consequences of Pragmatism*. Minneapolis, MN: University of Minnesota Press

Rorty, R. 1991. *Objectivity, Relativism, and Truth*. Cambridge University Press

Rorty, R. 1999. *Philosophy and Social Hope*. London: Penguin

Roubini, N. and Mihm, S. 2010. *Crisis Economics: A Crash Course in the Future of Finance*. London: Allen Lane

Rouse, J. 1996. *Engaging Science: How to Understand Its Practices Philosophically*. Ithaca, NY: Cornell University Press

Rumelt, R. P. 1987. Theory, strategy, and entrepreneurship. In *The Competitive Challenge*, D. J. Teece (ed.). Cambridge, MA: Ballinger, pp. 137–158

Rumelt, R. P. 1991. How much does industry matter? *Strategic Management Journal* 12: 167–186

Sachs, J. D. and Woo, W. T. 1994. Reform in China and Russia. *Economic Policy* 9:102–145

Sakiya, T. 1982. *Honda Motor: The Men, The Management, The Machines*. Tokyo: Kodanasha

Sanchez, R. and Heene, A. 1997. Reinventing strategic management: new theory and practice for competence-based competition. *European Management Journal* 15: 303–317

Scarbrough, H. 1998. Path(ological) dependency? Core competence from an organizational perspective. *British Journal of Management* 9: 219–232

Scharmer, C. O. 1996. Knowledge has to do with truth, goodness, and beauty: conversation with Professor Ikujiro Nonaka (available at www.dialogonleadership. org)

Schendel, D. 1992. Introduction to the summer 1992 special issue on 'strategy process research'. *Strategic Management Journal* 13 (Summer Special Issue): 1–4

Schoemaker, P. J. H. 1993. Strategic decisions in organizations: rational and behavioural views. *Journal of Management Studies* 30: 107–129

Schumpeter, J. 1934. *The Theory of Economic Development*. Cambridge, MA: Harvard University Press

Schumpeter, J. 1942. *Capitalism, Socialism and Democracy*. New York: Harper and Brothers

Scott, W. R. 2003. *Organizations: Rational, Natural, and Open Systems*, 5th edn. Upper Saddle River, NJ: Prentice Hall

Selznick, P. 1957. *Leadership in Administration*. New York: Harper & Row

Sen, A. 1998. Foreword. In *Economics, Values, and Organization*, A. Ben-Ner and L. G. Putterman (eds.). Cambridge University Press, pp. vii–xiii

Serra, N. and Stiglitz, J. (eds.) 2008. *The Washington Consensus Reconsidered: Toward a New Global Governance*. Oxford University Press

Sewell, W. H. 1992. A theory of structure: duality, agency, and transformation. *American Journal of Sociology* 98: 1–29

Shields, P. M. 1996. Pragmatism: exploring public administration's policy imprint. *Administration and Society* 28: 390–411

Shields, P. M. 2003. The community of inquiry: classical pragmatism and public administration. *Administration and Society* 35: 510–538

Shields, P. M. 2005. Classical pragmatism does not need an upgrade: lessons for public administration. *Administration and Society* 37: 504–518

Shiller, R. 2000. *Irrational Exuberance*. Princeton University Press

Shiller, R. 2003. *The New Financial Order: Risk in the 21st Century*. Princeton University Press

Shook, J. 2008. *Managing to Learn: Using the A3 Management Process to Solve Problems, Gain Agreement, Mentor, and Lead*. London: Lean Enterprise Institute

Shrivastava, P. 1986. Is strategic management ideological? *Journal of Management* 12: 363–377

Shrivastava, P. 1994. Castrated environment: greening organizational studies. *Organization Studies* 15: 705–726

Shrivastava, P. 1995. Ecocentric management for a risk society. *Academy of Management Review* 20: 118–137

Silva, F.C.D. 2007. *G. H. Mead: A Critical Introduction*. Cambridge: Polity

Sloan, A.P. 1963. *My Years with General Motors*. London: Sidgwick & Jackson

Smircich, L. and Stubbart, C. 1985. Strategic management in an enacted world. *Academy of Management Review* 10: 724–736

Spender, J.-C. 1995. Organizations are activity systems, not merely systems of thought. In *Advances in Strategic Management* vol. 12B, P. Shrivastava and C. Stubbart (eds.). London: JAI Press, pp. 153–174

Spender, J.-C. 2001. Business policy and strategy as a professional field. In *Rethinking Strategy*, H.W. Volberda and T. Elfring (eds.). London: Sage, pp. 26–40

Stacey, R.D. 2007. *Strategic Management and Organisational Dynamics: The Challenge of Complexity*, 5th edn. London: FT Prentice Hall

Stacey, R.D. 2010. *Complexity and Organizational Reality: Uncertainty and the Need to Rethink Management after the Collapse of Investment Capitalism*. New York: Routledge

Statler, M. and Roos, J. 2005. Re-framing strategy preparedness: an essay on practical wisdom. Working Paper No. 63. Switzerland: Imagination Lab (available at www.imagilab.org)

Statler, M., Roos, J. and Victor, B. 2003. Illustrating the need for practical wisdom. Working Paper No. 9. Switzerland: Imagination Lab (available at www.imagilab.org)

Sternberg, R.J., Conway, B.E., Ketron, J.L. and Bernstein, M. 1981. People's conceptions of intelligence. *Journal of Personality and Social Psychology* 41: 37–55

Stewart, T.A. and Raman, A.P. 2007. Lessons from Toyota's long drive: interview with Katsuaki Watanabe. *Harvard Business Review* 85 (July–August): 74–83

Stivers, C. 1994. The listening bureaucrat. *Public Administration Review* 54: 364–369

Stivers, C. 2008. *Governance in Dark Times: Practical Philosophy in Public Service*. Washington, DC: Georgetown University Press

Stopford, J. 2001. Should strategy makers become dream weavers? *Harvard Business Review* 79 (January): 165–169

Suzuki, D.T. 1971. *What is Zen?* New York: Harper & Row

Sztompka, P. 1991. *Society in Action: The Theory of Social Becoming*. University of Chicago Press

Takahashi, M. 2000. Toward a culturally inclusive understanding of wisdom: historical roots in the east and west. *International Journal of Aging and Human Development* 51: 217–230

Takeuchi, H. and Nonaka, I. 1986. The new new product development game. *Harvard Business Review* 64 (January–February): 137–146

Takeuchi, H., Osono, E. and Shimizu, N. 2008. The contradictions that drive Toyota's success. *Harvard Business Review* 86 (June): 96–104

Tan, S.H. 2003. *Confucian Democracy: A Deweyan Reconstruction*. Albany, NY: State University of New York Press

Taylor, F.W. 1911 (reprinted 1967). *The Principles of Scientific Management*. New York: Norton

Taylor, W. 1990. The business of innovation: an interview with Paul Cook. *Harvard Business Review* 68 (March–April): 97–106

Teece, D.J. 1990. Contributions and impediments of economic analysis to the study of strategic management. In *Perspectives on Strategic Management*, J.W. Fredrickson (ed.). New York: Harper & Row, pp. 39–80

Teece, D.J. 1993. The dynamics of industrial capitalism: perspectives on Alfred Chandler's scale and scope. *Journal of Economic Literature* 31: 199–225

Teece, D.J. 2007a. Explicating dynamic capabilities: the nature and microfoundations of (sustainable) enterprise performance. *Strategic Management Journal* 28: 1319–1350

Teece, D.J. 2007b. Managers, markets, and dynamic capabilities. In *Dynamic Capabilities: Understanding Strategic Change in Organizations*, C.E. Helfat (ed.). Oxford: Blackwell Publishing, pp. 19–29

Teece, D.J. 2009. *Dynamic Capabilities and Strategic Management*. Oxford University Press

Teece, D.J., Pisano, G. and Shuen, A. 1997. Dynamic capabilities and strategic management. *Strategic Management Journal* 18: 509–533

Tett, G. 2009. *Fool's Gold: How Unrestrained Greed Corrupted a Dream, Shattered Global Markets and Unleashed a Catastrophe*. London: Abacus

Thayer, H.S. 1982. *Pragmatism: The Classic Writings*. Indianapolis, IN: Hackett

Tripsas, M. and Gavetti, G. 2000. Capabilities, cognition, and inertia: evidence from digital imaging. *Strategic Management Journal* 21: 1147–1161

Tsoukas, H. 1994. Refining common sense: types of knowledge in management studies. *Journal of Management Studies* 31:761–780

Tsoukas, H. and Chia, R.C.H. 2002. On organisational becoming: rethinking organisational change. *Organisation Science* 23: 863–868

Tsoukas, H. and Cummings, S. 1997. Marginalization and recovery: the emergence of Aristotelian themes in organization studies. *Organization Studies* 18: 655–683

Tsoukas, H. and Knudsen, C. 2002. The conduct of strategy research. In *Handbook of Strategy and Management*, A. Pettigrew, H. Thomas and R. Whittington (eds.). London: Sage, pp. 411–435

Tsunoda, R. 1958. *Sources of the Japanese Tradition*. New York: Columbia University Press

Tushman, M.L. and Anderson, P. 2004. *Managing Strategic Innovation and Change: A Collection of Readings*, 2nd edn. Oxford University Press

Uzzi, B. and Dunlap, S. 2005. How to build your network. *Harvard Business Review* 83 (December): 53–60

van de Ven, A. 1986. Central problems in the management of innovation. *Management Science* 32: 590–607

Vaughan, D. 1996. *The Challenger Launch Decision: Risky Technology, Culture, and Deviance at NASA*. University of Chicago Press

Victor, B. 2005. On the moral necessity of strategy making. In *Innovating Strategy Process*, S.W. Floyd, J. Roos, C.D. Jacobs and F.W. Kellermanns (eds.). Oxford: Blackwell Publishing, pp. 235–238

Volberda, H.W. 2005. Rethinking the strategy process: a co-evolutionary approach. In *Innovating Strategy Process*, S.W. Floyd, J. Roos, C.D. Jacobs and F.W. Kellermanns (eds.). Oxford: Blackwell Publishing, pp. 81–87

Volberda, H.W. and Elfring, T. (eds.) 2001. *Rethinking Strategy*. London: Sage

von Glasersfeld, E. 1995. *Radical Constructivism: A Way of Knowing and Learning*. London: Routledge Falmer

von Krogh, G., Ichijo, K. and Nonaka, I. 2000. *Enabling Knowledge Creation: How to Unlock the Mystery of Tacit Knowledge and Release the Power of Innovation*. Oxford University Press

Walton, S. 1992. *Made in America: My Story*. New York: Bantam Doubleday Dell

Wang, L. 1989. The years after Mao Zedong. *Kunlun*, 6: 4–53 (trans in *JPRS-CAR* 89–079, July: 1–16)

Wang, Q. 2005. 中西文化比较概论 *[Introduction to Sino-Western Cultural Comparison]*. Beijing: People's University Press (in Chinese)

Wang, S. 1992. 中国改革百科全书 *[China Reform Encyclopaedia]*. Dalian: Dalian Press (in Chinese)

Watson, R. 2008. Celebrate Failure. *Fast Company* 8 July

Webb, J. 1999. Dewey and discourse: some implications for institutionalism and postmodernist. Paper presented at the meeting of the Western Social Science Association, Denver, CO

Webb, J. 2004. Comment on Hugh T. Miller's 'why old pragmatism needs an upgrade'. *Administration and Society* 36: 479–495

Weber, M. 1949. *The Methodology of the Social Sciences*. New York: Free Press

Weick, K.E. 1979. *The Social Psychology of Organizing*. London: Addison-Wesley

Weick, K.E. 1995. *Sensemaking in Organizations*. Thousand Oaks, CA: Sage

Weitzman, M.L. and Xu, C. 1994. Chinese township-village enterprises as vaguely defined cooperatives. *Journal of Comparative Economics* 18: 121–145

Weng, J.Y. 2004. 商业模式的创新 [*Business Model Innovations*]. Beijing: Economics and Management Publishing House (in Chinese)

Wenger, E. 1998. *Communities of Practice: Learning, Meaning and Identity*. Cambridge University Press

West, C. 1989. *The American Evasion of Philosophy: A Genealogy of Pragmatism*. Madison: University of Wisconsin Press

Westwood, R. and Clegg, S. 2003. *Debating Organization: Point-Counterpoint in Organization Studies*. Oxford: Blackwell Publishing

Whetten, D.A., Rands, G. and Godfrey, P. 2002. What are the responsibilities of business to society? In *Handbook of Strategy and Management*, A. Pettigrew, H. Thomas and R. Whittington (eds.). London: Sage, pp. 373–410

Whitley, R. 1984. The fragmented state of management studies: reasons and consequences. *Journal of Management Studies* 21: 331–348

Whittington, R. 1992. Putting Giddens into action: social systems and managerial agency. *Journal of Management Studies* 29: 693–712

Whittington, R. 2001. *What is Strategy – and Does It Matter?* 2nd edn. London: Thomson Learning

Whittington, R. 2002. Corporate structure: from policy to practice. In *Handbook of Strategy and Management*, A. Pettigrew, H. Thomas and R. Whittington (eds.). London: Sage, pp. 113–138

Whittington, R., Pettigrew, A.M., Peck, S., Fenton, E. and Conyon, M. 1999. Change and complementarities in the new competitive landscape. *Organisation Science* 10: 583–600

Wicks, A.C. and Freeman, R.E. 1998. Organisation studies and the new pragmatism: positivism, anti-positivism, and the search for ethics. *Organisation Science* 9: 123–140

Williamson, O.E. 1985. *The Economic Institutions of Capitalism*. New York: Free Press

Williamson, O.E. 1986. *Economic Organization: Firms, Markets and Policy Control*. New York University Press

Williamson, O.E. 1991. Comparative economic organization: the analysis of discrete structural alternatives. *Administrative Science Quarterly* 36: 269–296

Wilson, D.C. and Jarzabkowski, P. 2004. Thinking and acting strategically: new challenges for interrogating strategy. *European Management Review* 1: 14–20

Wittgenstein, L. 1953. *Philosophical Investigations*. Oxford: Basil Blackwell

Womack, J.P., Jones, D.T. and Roos, D. 1990. *The Machine that Changed the World*. New York: Maxwell Macmillan International

Wong, S.L. 1985. The Chinese family firm: a model. *British Journal of Sociology* 36: 58–72

Wu, J.S. 1972. Western philosophy and the search for Chinese wisdom. In *Invitation to Chinese Philosophy*, A. Naess and A. Hannay (eds.), Scandinavian University Books series. Oslo: Universitetsforlaget, pp. 1–18

Xu, F.G. 1988. *Confucian Political Thought and Democracy, Freedom, and Human Rights*. Taipei: Student Press

Yang, S.Y. and Sternberg, R.J. 1997. Conceptions of intelligence in ancient Chinese philosophy. *Journal of Theoretical and Philosophical Psychology* 17: 101–119

Yuasa, Y. 1987. *The Body: Toward an Eastern Mind-Body Theory*, S. Nagatomi and T.P. Kasulis (trans). Albany: State University of New York Press

Yunus, M. 1998. *Banker to the Poor*. Dhaka: University Press Limited

Zhang, L.S. 2008. 军人总裁任正非: 从普通士兵到通信霸主 *[Soldier CEO Ren Zhengfei: From an Average Soldier to the King of Telecommunication]*. Beijing: Central Compilation & Translation Press (in Chinese)

Zhang, L.S. 2009. 中国需要好银行: 蔚华与中国招商银行 *[China Needs Good Banks: Ma Weihuan and China Merchants Bank]*. Beijing: Central Compilation & Translation Press (in Chinese)

Zhou, K.X. 1996. *How the Farmers Changed China: Power of the People*. Oxford: Westview Press

Zhu, Z. 2006. Constructing healthcare knowledge. In *Healthcare Knowledge Management: Issues, Advances, and Successes*, R.K. Bali and A.N. Dwivedi (eds.). New York: Springer, pp. 112–129

Zhu, Z. 2007a. Reform without a theory: why does it work in China? *Organization Studies* 28: 1503–1522

Zhu, Z. 2007b. Complexity science, systems thinking and pragmatic sensibility. *Systems Research and Behavioural Science* 24: 445–464

Zhu, Z. 2008. Who created China's household farms and township-village enterprises: the conscious few or the ignorant many? In *Academy of Management Annual Meeting Best Paper Proceedings* (CDROM), G. T. Solomon (ed.). Washington, DC: George Washington University

Zhu, Z. 2010. Knowledge of the natural and the social: how are they different and what do they have in common? *Knowledge Management Research and Practice* 8: 173–188

Index